# Philosophy Looks at the Arts

# Philosophy Looks at the Arts

## Contemporary Readings in Aesthetics
### Third Edition

Edited by
Joseph Margolis

**Temple University Press**
**Philadelphia**

**Library of Congress Cataloging-in-Publication Data**

Philosophy looks at the arts.

Bibliography: p.
Includes index.
1. Aesthetics.   2. Art—Philosophy.   3. Hermeneutics.
I. Margolis, Joseph Zalman, 1924-
BH39.P48   1986          111'.85          87-6521
ISBN 0-87722-439-0
ISBN 0-87722-440-4 (pbk.)

Temple University Press, Philadelphia, 19122
Copyright © 1987 by Temple University, All rights reserved
Published 1987
Printed in the United States of America

# Contents

# Preface

The invitation to revise *Philosophy Looks at the Arts* for a third edition surprised me only because of the sharply accelerating change in theoretical taste that it implied. The change itself was bound to come. We have for some longish time been passing through, and continue to undergo, radical changes in conceptual orientation—not only with regard to the arts but to the very nature of human culture, the prospects of the sciences, and the formation of a global view of human existence. I should say, risking frontal pronouncements, that, at least since the French Revolution, the major theoretical puzzles of the entire terrestrial community of understanding have been focused on the significance of history, the loss of conviction that the world is cognitively transparent, and the dawning realization that, whatever we make of the human condition, man cannot be assigned an essential nature sufficiently determinate that universally compelling characterizations of knowledge, communication, interpretation, interests, norms, desires, objectives, or the like can be fixed or approximated by easy reference to its aptitudes. This is nowhere more evident than in the world of the arts. But the very acceleration of conceptual change seems to be accelerating.

In the philosophy of art—or aesthetics (I frankly don't much care for the second term or for any of the customary professional phrases associated with it: "aesthetic interests," "aesthetic values" and the like)—I believe I have detected, in the last thirty years or so, three distinct changes in orientation belonging chiefly to the pertinent Anglo-American tradition. They are by no means confined to that tradition. But it is perhaps only in the most recent years that there has developed a definite sense of effectively recovering a comprehensive Western or European-oriented philosophical community that means to overcome the isolationist tendencies of the more narrowly Anglo-American. I confess I should like to believe that the three editions of *Philosophy Looks at the Arts* have both anticipated and to some extent promoted those changes, serially—against establishment reticence. I'm accustomed to that reticence and I expect it. But if, as the themes I've mentioned suggest, there is no timeless philosophy to be drummed into people, then there's nothing for it but to be forever alert to the signs of shifting dissatisfaction with older ways of thinking and of inventive newer strategies that are not altogether ephemeral. If there is any surprise in this, it belongs to the accelerating pace with which large changes are now succeeding one another.

The first edition of this reader (1962) was intended to collect very good, possibly the best, specimens of analytic aesthetics—a general mode of working that departed abruptly but penetratingly from the then-dominant idealist tradition, with its penchant for the global, for erasing middle-sized problems and conceptual distinctions, for baffling every sense of being able to test or call to account grandly Hegelian and Crocean visions. The second edition (1978) was doubled in size and safer; for against the protests of many (how well I remember!), the analytic currents—there are, after all, many different ones—eventually prevailed in the English-speaking world. What that edition sought to do was to offer a broader sample of the characteristic work of the new breed. Inevitably, the collection became more definitely a sampler: impossible to ensure a clear sense of the very best work, impossible to ensure even a varied enough array of specimens of very good work. I reconciled myself to that double limitation by favoring a volume that, first of all, identified what I took to be the salient problems of the interval represented (which still caught up a good deal of the concerns of the first period); secondly, made an honest selection of those papers that helped to provide the best orientation to the issues raised; and third, collectively identified the main thrust of this "middle" period.

In this respect the second edition preserves a sense of the dynamism of the analytic movement. I should say that the local features of the entire interval largely point to the gathering appreciation of the hopeless inadequacy of empiricism—or empiricist-like insistence—within the usual inquiries of the philosophy of art. It would have been easy to confirm this tendency in the Continental literature, but it comes as more of a surprise to see how rapidly it has coalesced in the Anglo-American. One has only to think of the influential contributions, in this period, made by Goodman, Danto, Wollheim, Dickie, and others, to appreciate the fact that the empiricist orientation—which had really dominated analytic aesthetics—has pretty well run its course. It is in fact just this development that exposes what is so misleading about the continued use of expressions incorporating the term "aesthetic." Along congruent lines, the middle period has increasingly favored a return to questions belonging to the ontology of art and human culture, which in various detailed respects have pretty well obliged us to examine the theoretical, largely non-perceptual (non-sensory) background conditions complicating and coloring our involvement with the arts. My own impression has been that the rejection of classical idealisms (and their confidence about the discovery of large universal truths) and the defeat of empiricisms (and their primitive insistence on cognitive certainty, palpable self-evidence, and good sense) had come to signify an increasing drift in the direction of historicizing and relativizing within pertinent theory. Reflections on the "aesthetic" must now come to terms— disastrously, for empiricism—with a most peculiar marriage of interests between whatever (largely ignoring the distinction between art and nature) affects us in narrowly perceptual or sensory ways and whatever (largely unconfined to the merely sensory) pertinently focuses our understanding of those culturally complex achievements we call artworks. That, I admit, follows my own persuasion—but I believe that time is on my side in this regard.

The present edition is another story altogether. The philosophy of art is now impossible to collect or sample in an entirely fair-minded way. No one who gives shape to an anthology (the term "anthology" is rather a pejorative one, I think) can fail to admit in his heart that he has omitted many selections without the inclusion of which his own choices threaten to lose their very purpose and point. One overcomes the seeming insouciance of just taking some of these and some of them and some of those by giving priority to a perceived theme not seen by all. That theme, as I understand matters, lies with the felt need, on the part of both analytic and Continental theorists, to bridge the differences between their respective kinds of work—and to begin to explore the incomparably richer puzzles such work first made possible, and even impossible (thereupon) to avoid or ignore. There is, therefore, a new kind of risk and a new kind of promise the third edition means to introduce. I should add at once that · someone else, favoring the same finding in, say, another five years or so, would probably wish to redirect things in quite a different way—possibly impatiently, bored perhaps with a mild, backward-looking tact (as of this third edition) that prefers the sense and record of an evolving continuum. I have no doubt whatsoever that the themes of history and relativism, of the radical contingency of theorizing in the middle of things without ever being able to fix one's bearings except in terms of that ongoing effort itself, will dominate the philosophy and science of the next generation. But even if they do not dominate—one must have a care after all in speaking of the secret forms of societal power and change—they will nag our assured world more and more mortally. The predictable irony instructs us that those themes will be more openly admitted in the arts than in the philosophy of art.

In any event, in this edition, I have deliberately introduced selections

from a number of the best-known contemporary Continental
theorists—philosophers and men of letters—who have actually influenced the
speculations of the Anglo-American community in a fresh way, along the
lines just noted. But, as with the Anglo-American, it has proved impossible
to include more than a small sample of these. There is, also, a distinct
difference in the gauge of analysis and argument belonging to the two
strands of Western philosophy. I found it necessary to include only those
Continentals whose statements could be treated more or less congruently
with the Anglo-American selections—in the important sense that the mere
juxtaposition of the two proves how smoothly and how naturally such an
altered and enlarged idiom can actually take form and sustain an ongoing
discourse without serious disruption. There's the marvel of the thing. The
Anglo-American and Continental traditions have been moving, somewhat
isolated from one another, along increasingly sympathetic lines. They have
done so through their own rather different philosophical argots. Perhaps
it's the telephone, the airplane, the mails, the rise of English as the lingua
franca of the world, that have encouraged this new convergence. But it is
more convincing to suppose that our perceptions converge as our experience converges, and that the international media largely facilitate the
exchange of a discovery of which they are themselves an important
manifestation. It is certainly true that the Continentals selected include
those who have been among the most active in attempting to reconcile the
"two" traditions as well as those who have been most hospitably received
in the English-speaking world, in person or in print (possibly more in
American parts than in British). There is now, in fact, a distinct sense, in
American professional work, of turning to the themes of Continental
Europe, without abandoning its own; and, to judge from transatlantic
patterns, there is every reason to believe that a common market of
philosophy (more noticeable at the moment than a common market in a
narrowly construed philosophy of art) is erasing the old isolations more
rapidly than political and economic visions have as yet proved capable of
fostering.

This is not the place to attempt to sketch the general movement of
modern Western philosophy. I do believe that, with a bit of care and with
some additional detail, it would be entirely plausible to construe the three
moments of the editions of *Philosophy Looks at the Arts* as pinpointing
the major changes in Western philosophy in general (seen from an Anglo-
American perspective) and even the major changes in the entire intellectual
orientation of the West. But even if there is some distortion in such a
projection, its correction would be much more instructive than any
descriptive account that would not feature these essential themes. As I
have already hinted, one may pretty well take it as a rule of thumb that

the larger shifts in thinking are first recorded and promoted in the arts and in similarly unmonitored channels—well before the theory of the arts coalesces in a coherent way around such themes; and that, belatedly, but also at times adventurously, philosophical reflections on the arts strike out in what appear to be (and are, at least modestly) new lines of theorizing.

Having said this much, I feel bound to offer a penny summary of the principal changes in general philosophy that are likely to become more influential in the present interval of work in the philosophy of art—and that, to some extent, are already noticeable there. There is, first of all, a deep suspicion that we cannot hope to fix any single ontology, any universally adequate or unchanging account of human cognition or human interests or human convictions, although there are reasonably salient features that would need to be seriously addressed in any responsible speculation—changing and diversifying, gaining and losing prominence, in different ways and at different rates from age to age. Secondly, there is the growing conviction that that very condition, the contingent historicizing of human life, largely focused in terms of the tacit practices by which man survives and human societies reproduce themselves, must be made central to philosophical reflection—if it is to have any grounding at all, given that first suspicion. And thirdly, once these are in place, it becomes a foregone conclusion that there cannot then be any canon or principles or reliable table of topics or conceptual priorities in accord with which philosophical theories may be shown to be approaching systematic closure on any question. These summary themes are, of course, peculiarly abstract, although they can be instantiated pointedly enough by anyone familiar with recent Western philosophy—both Anglo-American and Continental—in terms of pragmatism, deconstruction, Marxism, hermeneutics, and late phenomenology at least. The challenge, and the charm of the challenge, of such a spare summary is, quite frankly, to thread through the developments of recent philosophy of art in order to judge to what extent there is any instructive congruity between the one and the other. I am convinced that there is a profound convergence, nowadays, between general philosophy and philosophy of art, and that we are on the edge of much more radical changes in both—possibly in tandem. It is certainly true that that conviction informs this new edition, and has influenced its new selections.

Every age understands itself as a transition: consolidating what is best, against disruptive pressures; absorbing new conceptions, to liberate us from what confines our entrenched habits of thought; doubting the viability of legitimating either commitment, previously endorsed or now admired. Certainly, the movement of the philosophy of art is dialectical in this sense, historicized even before it becomes explicitly historical.

Where it will lead is also a matter of open history. This third edition serves, then, as a provisional resting place within a field of continual change—to which perhaps it may contribute once again a sense of promising new directions well worth pursuing.

I have scandalously picked the brains of a great many of my professional friends, in preparing this collection. And, I must admit, I have largely failed to incorporate their suggestions. If I could have put together a volume of at least two hundred additional pages, I probably would have accommodated their recommendations—and gladly. But it was impossible. I shall, therefore, not mention these friends by name here. There's no reason to encumber them in any way; and they will know—the entire army of them—that I'm most grateful for their having offered their advice on my request. I have also benefited, I may say, from some anonymous advice solicited by the press. The principal gap in the readings which I had hoped to fill (and have tried in part to fill by clever indirection) really requires some of the better, more technically informed papers on the structure of the various arts themselves. I do feel that that need still poses a serious limitation in this third edition. I should very much like to see a companion volume that, in the spirit of this edition, addresses the actual arts in an ample and detailed way.

I must single out for special mention that agreeable kind of encouragement, verging on nudging, that I only slowly came to notice, first sounded by my very good friends at Temple University Press, Jane Cullen and David Bartlett. I know I would not have made the effort but for them.

# Part One
# Aesthetic Interests and Aesthetic Qualities

It is notoriously difficult to define the boundaries of such large and lively interests as the scientific, the moral, and the aesthetic. At least since Immanuel Kant, philosophers have hoped to be able to mark out nice logical distinctions among the kinds of judgments corresponding to such interests. In fact, Kant imposed one of the great obstacles to modern philosophy in this respect: enormous effort has been required to show that the demarcation lines Kant favored—or other similarly construed distinctions—actually falsify or distort the uniformities and differences favored among our conceptual networks. This is not to say that questions that belong to the very heart of empirical science, moral judgment, the appreciation and criticism of fine art are not easily identified. They are, of course. But since Kant, philosophers have been inclined to hope that when they are sorted, such questions will lead to neat categorical differences justifying their having been distinguished in the ways in which they have. Hence, there is a certain embarrassment at stake in failing to discover the required distinctions.

On the other hand, one may very well question the notion of *discovering* the difference between the scientific, the moral, and the aesthetic. What would such a discovery be like? It seems fairly clear that the distinctions would prove to be some philosopher's proposal, not a discovery at all. One need not deny that there are certain hard-core questions that belong unquestionably to each of these domains. But that hardly means that the boundaries of each are open to inspection. Criticism shades into science, and moral considerations into appreciation. In the moral domain, for instance, it is often maintained that moral judgments are inherently action-guiding, that there is no point to a moral judgment if it is not intended to direct another or oneself to act appropriately in a relevant situation. But if that is so, then how are we to understand valid moral judgments in situations in which the required action is impossible ("you ought to, or are obliged to, pay that loan today though you've squandered the money at the racetrack") or in which the action appraised or appreciated is beyond the capacity of normal persons to perform at will ("St. Francis acted as a saint")?

Even after it develops that no simple logical differences exist among scientific, moral, and aesthetic judgments, philosophers may enthusiastically continue their attempt to distinguish the aesthetic domain. Inquiry then turns to another sort of distinction—for instance, the controlling interest of each of these domains. So one may argue that distinctive sets of reasons are regularly put forward to defend those sorts of judgments we call aesthetic, economic, or moral. The judgments themselves need not differ in their logical properties; it may be only that there are clusters or classes of reasons that would be relevant to each. And the question arises whether these are overlapping for the sorts of judgment distinguished, whether they may be sharply defined, or whether they may be exhibited only by way of admissible samples.

Beneath all this lurks the question of the nature of such large category-terms as the aesthetic, the moral, the scientific. It may be asked, for instance, whether philosophers are primarily explicating the meaning of "aesthetic" or whether, by an ellipsis, they are really generalizing about the properties of certain sorts of judgments or remarks that are taken without dispute (though they are not infrequently disputed) to belong within the scope of aesthetic interest. That is, one may ask whether an analysis of the meaning of "aesthetic" will be fruitful independently of the second sort of issue, whether in fact it can even be undertaken. The point is not without some interest (given the professional literature), because it is well known that philosophers have quite regularly disputed among themselves whether this or that is *really* appropriate to the aesthetic point of view. It may then be that statements about the aesthetic point of view are actually elliptical summaries of findings upon this or that set of *favored* data—which some philosophers at least will have thought to be related in an important way to our concern with fine art; other philosophers, appearing to dispute the very meaning of the aesthetic, may either be disputing those findings or providing alternative findings for other sets of data.

J. O. Urmson's contribution, some years ago, to the Aristotelian Society's symposium on "What makes a situation aesthetic?" (1957) threads through this sort of consideration. His method is in accord both with some traditional conceptions of the central features of aesthetic interest and with a certain powerful theme in recent Anglo-American philosophy (associated originally with the name of Wittgenstein): that the use of terms in actual currency in our language need not, and may not be able to, be defined by means of necessary and sufficient conditions. There are, however, certain telltale features of Urmson's account. Urmson adopts the cautious approach of distinguishing between the "simpler cases" and the more difficult cases of aesthetic evaluation. He favors the view—associated with the original sense of the "aesthetic"—that the aesthetic aspects of things are concerned with how objects or phenomena appear to, or are discriminated by, the senses. He saves the thesis by admitting both that non-perceptual properties may be included "by courtesy" and by conceding that the more complex cases of aesthetic concern cannot be satisfactorily reduced to the formula for the simpler cases. He also distinguishes between the merit of things as being good things of a kind and the aesthetic merit of things, that is, their merit judged from a certain point of view. It is, in his view, merely contingent that the criteria for judging the goodness of a thing of a kind may well be the same as the criteria for being aesthetically meritorious (dining room tables, for instance). But the combination of these two concessions forces us to request a more detailed account of what it is, precisely, that makes a situation aesthetic.

Here, the difficulties encountered are of the greatest importance. For one thing, the extension of the terms "aesthetic" and "work of art" are clearly not the same, though it is often supposed that the point of aesthetics is to clarify the nature of our appreciation of fine art: natural phenomena and objects not designated artworks are ordinarily admitted to be aesthetically eligible. But then, the very range of artworks changes in rather surprising ways (see Part Two) and, with that, the range of what might be viewed as aesthetically relevant changes as well. The principal pressure points regarding the meaning of aesthetic interest, however, are all centered in one way or another, on the aesthetic relevance of the imperceptible or the non-perceptual. But the quarrelsome nature of the non-perceivable cannot be denied. For instance, the distinction of forgeries and fakes in art suggests a consideration that cannot normally be restricted to what is perceptually accessible. Sometimes, as in print-making, it may merely be that the intention to produce a print from an authentic plate contrary to the original artist's authorization makes a particular print a forgery. *If* that consideration is aesthetically relevant, then the aesthetic cannot be confined to the perceptible. But the question remains whether *that* consideration is actually relevant aesthetically—rather than in some other way. Commentators disagree. Again, it is extremely difficult to see how the literary arts can be subsumed under the formula for the "simpler cases." Clive Bell had already admitted this in pressing the general thesis that Urmson's view approaches: it occasioned the most acrobatic adjustments imaginable; some theorists were led to hold that reading texts in order to understand the meaning of what was written was simply not essential to (though it was needed to occasion) one's aesthetic appreciation of a poem or novel. A third difficulty concerns the relevance of background information—cultural, biographical, intentional factors (see Part Five). If one must grasp something of the context in which a work of art is produced in order to appreciate *it* aesthetically, then even if one centers one's interest on what is perceivable, non-perceptual factors will and must relevantly inform what is perceivable. For example, to understand a style, a genre, a representation, a symbol, a historical tradition, a personal intention, is to understand what cannot be explicated solely in perceptual terms. Finally, if these difficulties be conceded, then one must concede as well that the appreciation of works of art may entail the exercise of capacities other than perceptual—for instance, imagination or conceptual understanding. The point is that the properties of a work of art may not be such as either to invite perceptual inspection at all or to invite perception primarily or exclusively. So-called conceptual art is often not perceptually accessible at all, though for that reason some will dispute whether conceptual art is not a contradiction in terms. And much art, not only literature but painting and music as well, seems to be appreciated only when certain imagining abilities are called into play. The empathists had pressed the thesis in a certain restricted way, but there seems to be a larger range of abilities at stake. The perception of physiognomic aspects of the lines in a painting, discrimination of the "movement" of a musical line, the appreciation of scenes depicted in novels or of the motivation of characters in a play all suggest our reliance on abilities that may inform sensory perception but that cannot be characterized merely as such.

Monroe Beardsley's comparatively recent effort (1970) to isolate the aesthetic point of view and the nature of aesthetic qualities is cognizant of all these difficulties. Beardsley attempts nevertheless to salvage a thesis, associated with his well-known effort to construe aesthetic appreciation as an objective undertaking, in which aesthetic properties or values are actually possessed by objects, objects that may be examined for them in certain assignably correct ways by normally endowed percipients. He shifts here from earlier formulations, in speaking of the *experiencing* rather than the *perceiving* of artworks (or other suitable objects); and he holds that aesthetic gratification is primarily obtained by attending to the "formal unity" and "regional qualities" of an object or phenomenon. This raises questions about whether such properties can be shown actually to obtain *in* a given object, to be somehow discernible in it, to preclude the tenability of alternative and incompatible ascriptions of such properties (see Part Six); it also imposes on us the problem of specifying how to give "correct" and "complete" instructions about experiencing the actual aesthetic values that an object may be supposed to have. Whatever the difficulties Beardsley's account generates, it constitutes the most forthright and informed effort we have to recover the objectivity of aesthetic discourse as such from the pressures of the sort already adduced.

Timothy Binkley's recent paper (1977) is a witty, iconoclastic piece—one of a number he has written in the same spirit—in which the more received and conventional views about the aesthetic appreciation of works of art are threatened by attention to implications drawn from bolder, more recent, and more extreme efforts in the arts themselves. Here, relying on certain novel developments in so-called conceptual art, Binkley shows effectively that there are actually works of art (if such they may be called) that *cannot* be explicated in perceptual terms. Even if one contests his specimens—though the dubious force of doing so is clear enough—Binkley does oblige us to see that, even in more conventional settings, intentional, contextual, background considerations are all but impossible to eliminate (see Parts Four and Five). So construed, his account challenges not only the more straightforward presumption of Urmson's discussion but also the prospect of sustaining the kind of objective discovery that Beardsley favors.

Perhaps the most important implication of Binkley's account is that it is quite impossible to separate the characterization of the aesthetic from one's sense of the range of what constitutes art. This is not to say that definitions isolate essential properties (see Part Two) but only that the point of defining the aesthetic is to throw into relief the kinds of properties prized in the context of appreciating art. Contemporary linguistic analysis has benefited aesthetics, in a very noticeable way, by subjecting to detailed scrutiny large lists of the familiar terms we use to characterize works of art. The truth is that this examination has never been attempted before in a fully systematic way or with the advantage of a powerful and well-developed philosophical method. The result has been some discoveries of considerable importance.

The pivotal question for all such analysis is, what are the conditions on which we correctly apply a characterizing (aesthetic) term to a given work of art? The finding has been that these vary strikingly with different sets of terms. The question is obviously important, since only by means of the analysis indicated could we hope to describe the logical nature of aesthetic disputes about works of art. Is, for example, this Rembrandt *somber*? Are those colors *garish*? Would you say she has a *regal* manner? Clearly, the issue spreads far beyond the narrow confines of art to the appreciative remarks we make in general conversation.

There is, of course, an extraordinarily large number of respects in which all of our characterizing terms may be classified. Can we state necessary conditions for their use? sufficient conditions? necessary and sufficient conditions? Are there terms for which we can supply neither necessary nor sufficient conditions? If there are, how is their use supported? Are there purely descriptive terms? purely evaluative terms? terms that are mixed in this regard? Are there descriptive and evaluative terms whose proper use depends on affective responses on our part? on dispositions to respond? Are there terms for which one can provide paradigm cases? terms for which one cannot? And if the latter (think of epithets like "He's the Michelangelo of poetry"), can and how can they be supported?

From the vantage of a large perspective, one can see that the sort of analysis indicated is simply the application, to a range of terms having a somewhat local interest for specialists in aesthetics and the arts, of a general method of working. The main force of this strategy has already been marked out very clearly in the philosophical contributions of such authors as Wittgenstein, John Wisdom, and J. L. Austin. But what is fascinating to observe is the correspondence among findings made in the most disparate fields of philosophical analysis.

The point can be made in either of two ways. We have been made to notice that a large number of expressions central to talk in different domains are readily but informally associated with paradigm instances, without, however, permitting us to formulate either necessary or sufficient conditions for their use. Otherwise stated, we have been made to notice that arguments supporting certain sorts of judgment central in different domains cannot be classified as deductive or inductive but depend on some "intermediate" logic in accord with which we may specify only "characteristically" favorable or unfavorable evidence. There are cases, that is, in which we argue more from instance to instance than from principle or rule to application, more analogically than by appealing to formal canons. And this, it turns out, is particularly worth emphasizing in the domain of aesthetics.

Frank Sibley's discussion (1959) of qualities prominent in aesthetic discourse is probably the most thoroughgoing effort made to date to fix the "intermediate" logic of the bulk of the expressions employed there. It has actually provoked an immense number of responses and counter-responses. And in doing so, it has led us to sort out a good number of central distinctions that any comprehensive theory of aesthetic interest, aesthetic perception, aesthetic qualities, would need to consider. Sibley is quite explicit about aesthetic discrimination's being a perceptual ability, but a perceptual ability involving the exercise of taste. He has also pressed as uncompromisingly as possible the thesis that aesthetic qualities are not condition-governed in any way that bears on the confirmation or disconfirmation of relevant aesthetic claims: they are, apparently, emergent qualities of some sort, dependent on nonaesthetic properties, possessed by the objects in question, and discriminable by percipients having the requisite taste. These details of his theory fix the sense in which it would be a mistake to construe his thesis as intuitionistic.

But it has invited a variety of challenges. For one thing, it raises a question about how to decide—as well as what the theoretical ground may be for deciding—between whether a candidate object actually *has* or merely *seems* to have the aesthetic quality assigned. These—*graceful, delicate, dainty, handsome, comely, elegant, garish*, to take one troublesome array of terms that Sibley himself provides—are supposed to enter into valid, objective judgments about matters of fact. But there can be no matters of fact where the *is/seems* contrast is not assigned a critical epistemic function. This thesis is clearly advanced for instance by Isabel Hungerland. For another, it raises a question about whether aesthetic appreciation and perception—in any generous sense of those notions—can be confined to perceptual considerations. Sometimes, it seems that aesthetic appreciation may well be non-perceptual; sometimes, it seems that aesthetic perception itself can only function as such when properly informed by relevant background considerations, as of history, biography, intention (see Parts Four and Five). If so, then aesthetic perception must be an ability that cannot be adequately characterized as a merely *perceptual* ability. This is the theme of the strong objection that Kendall Walton advances (1970). The very categories of art, Walton argues, in terms of which works of art are properly perceived, require that our perception be appropriately oriented in terms of a wide variety of factors bearing on the origin of a given work, factors not normally construed as being of aesthetic relevance. Here, Walton opposes the views of both Sibley and Beardsley. Walton also manages to draw attention to the variety of aesthetically relevant features of works of art that are either not directly considered by Sibley or that would appear to be anomalous from the point of view of either Sibley or Beardsley—in particular, conceptual art and representational art. His reflections, here, tend to confirm the distinctively cultural nature of art (see Parts Two and Three)—hence, of the culturally informed nature of pertinent perceptions.

The enlargement of the range of aesthetically relevant qualities and features suggests both the inescapability of a mixed array of distinctions and the unlikelihood of any thesis like Sibley's holding without exception. The mere mention of representational qualities (see Part Four), for instance, signifies the implausibility of construing certain sorts of discriminations as being not condition-governed in Sibley's sense. Some authors, notably Peter Kivy and Ted Cohen, have persuasively shown that either relevant aesthetic properties (for instance, unity in music) may be taken to be condition-governed or else the putative demarcation between aesthetic and nonaesthetic perception is merely a question-begging version of the original thesis. Cohen (1973) in fact mounts a direct attack—a pragmatic attack, he calls it—on the very distinction between aesthetic and nonaesthetic perception. To the extent that we favor the challenge, emphasizing the intrusion of taste and appreciation in putatively perceptual discrimination, we are inexorably led to consider the possible defensibility of alternative, non-convergent ways of "seeing" a work of art (see Part Six); and, correspondingly, of the need to replace a narrowly perceptual thesis with one that accommodates the relevance (*a*) of background information; (*b*) of non-perceptual discrimination; (*c*) of interpretation; (*d*) of taste and appreciative orientation. Kivy (1973) attempts to show, more directly, that among the very concepts that Sibley had supposed to be not condition-governed we must admit salient predicates that actually are condition-governed. Cohen, therefore, challenges the entire distinction between the aesthetic and the nonaesthetic; Kivy, the logical uniformity of just those distinctions that Sibley regards as involving aesthetic concepts.

Among the more energetic opponents of the very usefulness of aesthetic categories—in particular, of that of the aesthetic "attitude" (allegedly addressed to distinctly aesthetic "qualities")—we must count George Dickie (1964). What Dickie attempts to do is trace the vacuity of the notion of the aesthetic attitude through a large number of influential theorists from Clive Bell and Edward Bullough to Beardsley and more recent authors. The main charge Dickie presses is that a certain receptiveness to a special set of determinate qualities is usually assigned to calling into play the "aesthetic attitude"; but, as he argues, its champions fail to mark off suitably any such operative preparation for pertinently appreciating eligible objects—usually but not necessarily artworks. Unfortunately, Dickie himself does not address with equal force the question of what might be the generic features of the very properties the intended orientation is supposed to render accessible or naturally salient. That question has never been satisfactorily explored: on the one hand, "aesthetic" qualities are specified, the systemic distinction of which is hard to formulate in a way at once theoretically important and defensible; on the other, aesthetic "interest" or "attitude" is specified in great detail, without however demonstrating how it either justifies featuring certain qualities only, or how it sensitizes us to some such selection.

The distinguished Polish aesthetician, Roman Ingarden, represents an entirely different approach to the aesthetic. Ingarden (even more than Maurice Merleau-Ponty) is the influential phenomenologist best known to Anglo-American philosophers of art. Ingarden's account (1964) links the aesthetic not only to appreciation—the appreciation of art—but also, in an essential way, to the very structure of artworks themselves. It is critical to Ingarden's thesis that a work of art is inherently "schematic" or at least "partially" indeterminate. This of course raises serious difficulties about the sense in which artworks are real at all, since the idea that something is both actual *and* indeterminate in structurally important respects (not concerned with issues of vague boundaries or the like) verges on the incoherent or the ontologically monstrous. Nevertheless, in a way that has clearly influenced literary theorists like Wolfgang Iser (1978) and even more recent varieties of reader-response theory, the aesthetic is taken by Ingarden to center on the "co-creative" activity of observers or percipients of art, on the way in which a work is "completed," rendered fully determinate, by responding to the "schematic structure" of the work in question. Here, of course, the notion of the aesthetic threatens to become quite a radical one. In particular, in Ingarden's hands, it can hardly be counted on to support the sense of perceptual objectivity favored by such theorists as Beardsley and Sibley—which is not to say that Ingarden does not insist on pertinent constraints on the exercise of aesthetic sensibility. One sees here, therefore, a certain distant convergence between the problems of phenomenological aesthetics and hermeneutic aesthetics, even though their motivation and inspiration are distinctly different. For both attack the pervasive theme of perceptual objectivity (what is sometimes called "objectivism"—as by Edmund Husserl) so dear to Anglo-American philosophy. The "aesthetic," therefore, proves to be the rather rampantly spreading field within which all pertinent quarrels about the nature and appreciation of art are simply collected—without itself remaining a suitably manageable or explicit focus of particular conceptual quarrel. It marks for that reason a family of terms that threaten to become more and more vestigial.

# 1. The Aesthetic Point of View
## MONROE C. BEARDSLEY

There has been a persistent effort to discover the uniquely aesthetic component, aspect, or ingredient in whatever is or is experienced. Unlike some other philosophical quarries, the object of this chase has not proved as elusive as the snark, the Holy Grail, or Judge Crater—the hunters have returned not empty-handed, but overburdened. For they have found a rich array of candidates for the basically and essentially aesthetic:

|  |  |
|---|---|
| aesthetic experience | aesthetic objects |
| aesthetic value | aesthetic concepts |
| aesthetic enjoyment | aesthetic situations |
| aesthetic satisfaction | |

Confronted with such trophies, we cannot easily doubt that there *is* something peculiarly aesthetic to be found in our world or our experience; yet its exact location and its categorial status remain in question. This is my justification for conducting yet another raid on the ineffable, with the help of a different concept, one in the contemporary philosophical style.

## I

When the conservationist and the attorney for Con Edison argue their conflicting cases before a state commission that is deciding whether a nuclear power plant shall be built beside the Hudson River, we can say they do not merely disagree; they regard that power plant from different points of view. When the head of the Histadrut Publishing House refused

From *Contemporary Philosophic Thought*, Volume 3, edited by Howàrd E. Kiefer and Milton K. Munitz (Albany: State University of New York Press, 1970), pp. 219–237. Reprinted with permission of the State University of New York Press.

to publish the novel *Exodus* in Israel, he said: "If it is to be read as history, it is inaccurate. If it is to be read as literature, it is vulgar."[1] And Maxim Gorky reports a remark that Lenin once made to him:

> 'I know nothing that is greater than [Beethoven's] *Appassionata*. I would like to listen to it every day. A marvelous, superhuman music. I always say with pride—a naive pride perhaps: What miracles human beings can perform!' Then screwing his eyes [Lenin] added, smiling sadly, 'But I can't listen to music too often; it affects your nerves. One wants to say stupid nice things and stroke on the head the people who can create such beauty while living in this vile hell. And now you must not stroke anyone on the head: you'll have your hands beaten off. You have to hit them on the head without mercy, though our ideal is not to use violence against anyone. Hmm, hmm,—an infernally cruel job we have.'[2]

In each of these examples, it seems plausible to say that one of the conflicting points of view is a peculiarly aesthetic one: that of the conservationist troubled by threats to the Hudson's scenic beauty; that of the publisher who refers to reading *Exodus* "as literature"; that of Lenin, who appears to hold that we ought to adopt the political (rather than the aesthetic) point of view toward Beethoven's sonata, because of the unfortunate political consequences of adopting the aesthetic point of view.

If the notion of the aesthetic point of view can be made clear, it should be useful from the philosophical point of view. The first philosophical use is in mediating certain kinds of dispute. To understand a particular point of view, we must envision its alternatives. Unless there can be more than one point of view toward something the concept breaks down. Consider, for example, the case of architecture. The classic criteria of Vitruvius were stated tersely by Sir Henry Wotton in these words: "Well-building hath three conditions: Commodity, Firmness, and Delight." Commodity is function: that it makes a good church or house or school. Firmness is construction: that the building holds itself up. Suppose we were comparing a number of buildings to see how well built they are, according to these "conditions." We would find some that are functionally effective, structurally sound, and visually attractive. We would find others—old wornout buildings or new suburban shacks—that are pretty poor in each of these departments. But also we would find that the characteristics vary independently over a wide range; that some extremely solid old bank buildings have Firmness (they are knocked down at great cost) without much Commodity or Delight, that some highly delightful buildings are functionally hopeless, that some convenient bridges collapse.

Now suppose we are faced with one of these mixed structures, and invited to say whether it is a good building, or how good it is. Someone might say the bank is very well built, because it is strong; another might reply that nevertheless its ugliness and inconvenience make it a very poor building. Someone might say that the bridge couldn't have been much good if it collapsed; but another might reply that it was a most excellent bridge, while it lasted—that encomium cannot be taken from it merely because it did not last long.

Such disputes may well make us wonder—as Geoffrey Scott wonders in his book on *The Architecture of Humanism*[3]—whether these "conditions" belong in the same discussion. Scott says that to lump them together is confusing: it is to "force on architecture an unreal unity of aim," since they are "incommensurable virtues." For clarity in architectual discussion, then, we might separate the three criteria, and say that they arise in connection with three different points of view—the practical, the engineering, and the aesthetic. In this way, the notion of a point of view is introduced to break up a dispute into segments that seem likely to be more manageable. Instead of asking one question—whether this is a good building—we divide it into three. Considering the building from the aesthetic point of view, we ask whether it is a good work of architecture; from the engineering point of view, whether it is a good structure; and from the practical point of view, whether it is a good machine for living.

Thus one way of clarifying the notion of a point of view would be in terms of the notion of being *good of a kind*.[4] We might say that to adopt the aesthetic point of view toward a building is to classify it as belonging to a species of aesthetic objects—namely, works of architecture—and then to take an interest in whether or not it is a *good* work of architecture. Of course, when an object belongs to one obvious and notable kind, and we judge it in relation to that kind, the "point of view" terminology is unnecessary. We wouldn't ordinarily speak of considering music from a musical point of view, because it wouldn't occur to us that someone might regard it from a political point of view. In the same way, it would be natural to speak of considering whiskey from a medical point of view but not of considering penicillin from a medical point of view. This shows that the "point of view" terminology is implicitly rejective: it is a device for setting aside considerations advanced by others (such as that the bridge will fall) in order to focus attention on the set of considerations that *we* wish to emphasize (such as that the sweep and soar of the bridge are a joy to behold).

The "point of view" terminology, however, is more elastic than the "good of its kind" terminology. To consider a bridge or music or sculpture as an aesthetic object is to consider it from the aesthetic point of view, but what about a mountain, a sea shell, or a tiger? These are neither musical compositions, paintings, poems nor sculptures. A sea shell cannot be *good* sculpture if it is not sculpture at all. But evidently we can adopt the aesthetic point of view toward these things. In fact, some aesthetic athletes (or athletic aesthetes) have claimed the ability to adopt the aesthetic point of view toward anything at all—toward *The Story of O* (this is what Elliot Fremont-Smith has called "beyond pornography"), toward a garbage dump, toward the murders of three civil-rights workers in Philadelphia, Mississippi. (This claim has been put to a severe test by some of our more far-out sculptors.) Perhaps even more remarkable is the feat recently performed by those who viewed the solemn installation of an "invisible sculpture" behind the Metropolitan Museum of Art. The installation consisted in digging a grave-size hole and filling it in again. "It is really an underground sculpture," said its conceiver, Claes Oldenburg. "I think of it as the dirt being loosened from the sides in a certain section of Central Park."[5] The city's architectural consultant, Sam Green, commented on the proceedings:

> This is a conceptual work of art and is as much valid as something you can actually see. Everything is art if it is chosen by the artist to be art. You can say it is good art or bad art, but you can't say it isn't art. Just because you can't see a statue doesn't mean that it isn't there.

This, of course, is but one of countless examples of the current tendency to stretch the boundaries of the concept of "art."

The second philosophical use of the notion of the aesthetic point of view is to provide a broad concept of art that might be helpful for certain purposes. We might say:

> A work of art (in the broad sense) is any perceptual or intentional object that is deliberately regarded from the aesthetic point of view.[6]

Here, "regarding" would have to include looking, listening, reading, and similar acts of attention, and also what I call "exhibiting"—picking up an object and placing it where it readily permits such attention, or presenting the object to persons acting as spectators.

## II

What, then, is the aesthetic point of view? I propose the following:

> To adopt the aesthetic point of view with regard to $X$ is to take an interest in whatever aesthetic value $X$ may possess.

I ask myself what I am doing in adopting a particular point of view, and acting toward an object in a way that is appropriate to that point of view;

and, so far as I can see, it consists in searching out a corresponding value in the object, to discover whether any of it is present. Sometimes it is to go farther: to cash in on that value, to realize it, to avail myself of it. All this searching, seeking and, if possible, realizing, I subsume under the general phrase "taking an interest in." To listen to Beethoven's *Appassionata* with pleasure and a sense that it is "marvelous, superhuman music," is to seek—and find—aesthetic value in it. To read the novel *Exodus* "as literature," and be repelled because it is "vulgar," is (I take it) to seek aesthetic value in it, but not find very much of it. And when Geoffrey Scott makes his distinction between different ways of regarding a building, and between that "constructive integrity in fact" which belongs under Firmness, and that "constructive vividness in appearance" which is a source of architectural Delight, he adds that "their value in the building is of a wholly disparate kind"[7]; in short, the two points of view, the engineering and the aesthetic, involve two kinds of value.

This proposed definition of "aesthetic point of view" will not, as it stands, fit all of the ordinary uses of this phrase. There is a further complication. I am thinking of a remark by John Hightower, executive director of the New York State Council on the Arts, about the council's aim to "encourage some sort of aesthetic standards." He said, "There are lots of laws that unconsciously inhibit the arts. Architecture is the most dramatic example. Nobody has looked at the laws from an aesthetic point of view."[8] And I am thinking of a statement in the *Yale Alumni Magazine*[9] that the Yale City Planning Department was undertaking "a pioneering two-year research project to study highway environment from an aesthetic point of view." I suppose the attention in these cases was not on the supposed aesthetic value of the laws or of the present "highway environment," but rather in the aesthetic value that might be achieved by changes in these things. Perhaps that is why these examples speak of "*an* aesthetic point of view," rather than "*the* aesthetic point of view." And we could, if we wish, make use of this verbal distinction in our broadened definition:

> To adopt *an* aesthetic point of view with regard to $X$ is to take an interest in whatever aesthetic value that $X$ may possess *or that is obtainable by means of X.*

I have allowed the phrase "adopting the aesthetic point of view" to cover a variety of activities. One of them is judging:

> To judge $X$ from the aesthetic point of view is to estimate the aesthetic value of $X$.

Those who are familiar with Paul Taylor's treatment of points of view in his book *Normative Discourse* will note how the order I find in these concepts differs from the one he finds. His account applies only to judging, which makes it too narrow to suit me. It also has, I think, another flaw. He holds that:

> Taking a certain point of view is nothing but adopting certain canons of reasoning as the framework within which value judgments are to be justified; the canons of reasoning define the point of view. . . . We have already said that a value judgment is a moral judgment if it is made from the moral point of view.[10]

Thus we could ask of Taylor, What is an aesthetic value judgment? He would reply, It is one made from the aesthetic point of view. And which are those? They are the ones justified by appeal to certain "canons of reasoning," and more particularly the "rules of relevance." But which are the aesthetic rules of relevance? These are the rules "implicitly or explicitly followed by people" in using the aesthetic value-language—that is, in making judgments of aesthetic value. Perhaps I have misunderstood Taylor's line of thought here, but the path it seems to trace is circular. I hope to escape this trap by breaking into the chain at a different point.

I define "aesthetic point of view" in terms of "aesthetic value." And while I think this step is by no means a trivial one, it is not very enlightening unless it is accompanied by some account of aesthetic value. I don't propose to present a detailed theory on this occasion, but I shall extend my chain of definitions to a few more links, and provide some defense against suspected weaknesses. What, then, is aesthetic value?

> The aesthetic value of an object is the value it possesses in virtue of its capacity to provide aesthetic gratification.

There are three points about this definition that require some attention.

First, it will be noted that this is not a definition of "value." It purports to distinguish *aesthetic* value from other kinds of value in terms of a particular capacity. It says that in judging the total value of an object we must include that part of its value which is due to its capacity to provide aesthetic gratification.

The second point concerns "aesthetic gratification." My earliest version of this capacity-definition of "aesthetic value" employed the concept of aesthetic experience.[11] I am still not persuaded that this concept must be abandoned as hopeless, but it needs further elaboration in the face of the criticism coming from George Dickie, whose relentless attack on unnecessarily multiplied entities in aesthetics has led him to skepticism about whether there is such a thing as aesthetic experience.[12] I have tried working with the concept of aesthetic enjoyment instead,[13] and that may be on the right track. For the present occasion, I have chosen a term that I think is somewhat broader in scope, and perhaps therefore slightly less misleading.

Again, however, the term "aesthetic gratification" is not self-explanatory. It seems clear that one kind of gratification can be distinguished from another only in terms of its intentional object: that is, of the properties that the pleasure is taken *in*, or the enjoyment is enjoyment *of*. To discriminate aesthetic gratification—and consequently aesthetic value and the aesthetic point of view—we must specify what it is obtained from. I offer the following:

> Gratification is aesthetic when it is obtained primarily from attention to the formal unity and/or the regional qualities of a complex whole, and when its magnitude is a function of the degree of formal unity and/or the intensity of regional quality.

The defense of such a proposal would have to answer two questions. First, is there such a type of gratification? I think there is, and I think that it can be distinguished from other types of gratification, though it is often commingled with them. Second, what is the justification for calling this type of gratification "aesthetic"? The answer to this question would be more complicated. Essentially, I would argue that there are certain clearcut exemplary cases of works of art—that is, poems, plays, musical compositions, etc.—that must be counted as works of art if anything is. There is a type of gratification characteristically and preeminently provided by such works, and this type of gratification is the type I have distinguished above. Finally, this type of gratification (once distinguished) has a paramount claim to be denominated "aesthetic"—even though there are many other things that works of art can do to you, such as inspire you, startle you, or give you a headache.

If this line of argument can be made convincing, we find ourselves with what might be called primary *marks* of the aesthetic: It is the presence in the object of some notable degree of unity and/or the presence of some notable intensity of regional quality that indicates that the enjoyments or satisfactions it affords are aesthetic—insofar as those enjoyments or satisfactions are afforded by these properties. I shall return to these marks a little later, and show the sort of use I think can be made of them.

### III

But before we come to that, we must consider the third point about the capacity-definition of "aesthetic value"—and this is the most troublesome of them all.

The term "capacity" has been chosen with care. My view is that the aesthetic value of an object is not a function of the actual degree of gratification obtained from it. It is not an average, or the mean degree of gratification obtained from it by various perceivers. It is not a sum, or the total gratification obtained from it in the course of its existence. All these depend in part on external considerations, including the qualifications of those who happen to resort to libraries, museums, and concerts, and the circumstances of their visits. I am thinking in terms of particular exposures to the work—a particular experience of the music, of the poem, of the painting—and of the degree of aesthetic gratification obtained on each occasion. Aesthetic value depends on the highest degree obtainable under optimal circumstances. Thus my last definition should be supplemented by another one:

> The amount of aesthetic value possessed by an object is a function of the degree of aesthetic gratification it is capable of providing in a particular experience of it.

My reason for holding this view is that I want to say that a critical evaluation is a judgment of aesthetic value, and it seems clear to me that estimating capacities is both the least and the most we can ask of the critical evaluator. I take it that when a literary critic, for example, judges the goodness of a poem (from the aesthetic point of view), and is prepared to back up his judgment with reasons, he must be saying something about the relationship of the poem to the experiences of actual or potential readers. The question is, What is this relationship? When a critic says that a poem is good, he is hardly ever in a position to predict the gratification that particular readers or groups of readers will receive from it. Moreover, he is usually not in a position to generalize about tendencies, to say, for instance, that readers of such-and-such propensities, preferences, or preparations will probably be delighted by the poem. If the critic has at his disposal the information required to support such statements, he is of course at liberty to say such things as: "This would have appealed to President Kennedy," or "This is an ideal Christmas gift for your friends who love mountain climbing." But when he simply says, "This is a good poem," we must interpret him as saying something weaker (though still significant) about the capacity of the work to provide a notable degree of aesthetic gratification. For *that* is a judgment he should be able to support, if he understands the poem.

The question, however, is whether the capacity-definition of "aesthetic value" is too weak, as a report of what actually happens in art criticism. I can think of three difficulties that have been or could be raised. They might be called (1) the unrecognized masterpiece problem, (2) the LSD problem, and (3) the Edgar Rice Burroughs problem. Or, to give them more abstract names, they are (1) the problem of falsification, (2) the problem of illusion, and (3) the problem of devaluation.

(1) Some people are troubled by one consequence of the capacity-definition—that objects can possess aesthetic value that never has been and never will be realized, such as the "gems of purest ray serene the dark unfathomed caves of ocean bear." This ought not to trouble us, I think. It is no real paradox that many objects worth looking at can never be looked at. But there is another kind of aesthetic inaccessibility in the highly complicated and obscure work that no critic can find substantial value in, though it may still be there. In Balzac's short story, "Le Chef-d'oeuvre inconnu," the master painter works in solitude for years, striving for the perfection of his greatest work; but in his dedication and delusion he overlays the canvas with so many brush strokes that the work is ruined. When his fellow artists finally see the painting, they are appalled by it. But how can they be sure that the painting doesn't have aesthetic value, merely because they have not found any? The capacity to provide aesthetic gratification of a high order may still be there, though they are not sharp or sensitive enough to take advantage of it.

If my proposed definition entailed that negative judgments of aesthetic value cannot even in principle be justified, then we would naturally mistrust it. But of course this consequence is not necessary. What does follow is that there is a certain asymmetry between negative and affirmative judgments, with respect to their degree of confirmation; but this is so between negative and affirmative existential statements in general. The experienced critic may have good reason in many cases not only for confessing that he finds little value in a painting, but for adding that very probably no one ever will find great value in it.

(2) If aesthetic value involves a capacity, then its presence can no doubt be sufficiently attested by a single realization. What a work *does* provide, it clearly *can* provide. And if my definition simply refers to the capacity, without qualification, then it makes no difference under what conditions that realization occurs. Now take any object you like, no matter how plain or ugly—say a heap of street sweepings awaiting the return of the street cleaner. Certainly we want to say that it is lacking in aesthetic value. But suppose someone whose consciousness is rapidly expanding under the influence of LSD or some other hallucinogenic drug happens to look at this heap and it gives him exquisite aesthetic gratification. Then it has the capacity to do so, and so it has high aesthetic value. But then perhaps every visual object has high aesthetic value, and all to about the same degree—if the reports may be trusted.

I cannot speak authoritatively of the LSD experience, but I gather that when a trip is successful, the object, however humble, may glow with unwonted intensity of color and its shapes assume an unexpected order and harmony. In short, the experience is illusory. This is certainly suggested by the most recent report I have run across.[14] Dr. Lloyd A. Grumbles, a Philadelphia psychiatrist,

> said that while listening to Beethoven's *Eroica*, particularly the third movement, he felt simultaneously "insatiable longing and total gratification." . . . Dr. Grumbles said he also looked at prints of Picasso and Renoir paintings and realized, for the first time, "they were striving for the same goal."

Now you *know* he was under the influence of LSD.

This example suggests a modification of the definition given earlier:

> The aesthetic value of $X$ is the value that $X$ possesses in virtue of its capacity to provide aesthetic gratification when *correctly experienced*.

(3) The problem of devaluation can perhaps be regarded as a generalization of the LSD problem.[15] When I was young I was for a time an avid reader of the Martian novels of Edgar Rice Burroughs. Recently when I bought the Dover paperback edition and looked at them again, I found that I could hardly read them. Their style alone is enough to repel you, if you really pay attention to it.

The problem is this: if on Monday I enjoy a novel very much, and thus know that it has the capacity to provide gratification, then how can I ever reverse the judgment and say the novel lacks that capacity? If the judgment that the novel is a good one is a capacity-judgment, it would seem that downward reevaluations (that is, devaluations) are always false—assuming that the original higher judgment was based on direct experience. There is no problem about upward reevaluations: when I say on Tuesday that the novel is better than I thought on Monday, this means that I have discovered the novel to have a greater capacity than I had realized. But how can we explain the lowering of an aesthetic evaluation and still maintain that these evaluations are capacity-judgments?

Some cases of devaluation can no doubt be taken care of without modifying the definition of "aesthetic value." The devaluation may be due to a shift in our value grades caused by enlargement of our range of experience. I might think that *Gone with the Wind* is a great novel, because it is the best I have read, but later I might take away that encomium and give it to *War and Peace*. Or the devaluation may be due to the belated recognition that my previous satisfaction in the work was a response to extra-aesthetic features. I now realize that my earlier enjoyment of detective stories was probably caused only in small part by their literary qualities, and was much more of a game-type pleasure.

But setting these cases aside, there remain cases where on perfectly sound and legitimate grounds I decide that the work, though it has provided a certain level of aesthetic gratification, is in fact not really that good. I have overestimated it. Evidently the definition of "aesthetic value" must be modified again. One thing we might do is insert a stipulation that the work be a reliable or dependable source of gratification: flukes don't count. We need not change the judgment into a straight tendency-statement. But we might insist that the enjoyment of the novel must at least be a repeatable experience. Something like this notion seems to underlie the frequent claim that our first reactions to a new work of art are not wholly to be trusted, that we should wait awhile and try it again; that we should see whether we can find at least one other person to corroborate our judgment; or that only posterity will be in a position to know whether the work is great.

I grant that all these precautions are helpful—indeed, they enable us to avoid the two sources of error mentioned a moment ago: having an inadequately formulated set of grading terms, and confusing aesthetic with nonaesthetic gratification. But I think it ought to be possible for a person, after a single experience of a work, to have excellent grounds for thinking it good and for commending it to others. And I think he would be justified in pointing out that he has found a potential source of aesthetic gratification that lies ready to be taken advantage of—even though he does not yet know how readily, how easily, how conveniently, or how frequently recourse may be had to it. Thus my escape from the difficulty is to revise the definition of "aesthetic value" again so as to stipulate that it is the value of the whole work that is in question:

> The aesthetic value of $X$ is the value that $X$ possesses in virtue of its capacity to provide aesthetic gratification *when correctly and completely experienced.*

The youth who was carried away by the adventures of Thuvia and the green men of Mars and the other denizens of that strange planet may well have gotten greater aesthetic gratification than the elderly person who returned to them after so many years. For the youth was fairly oblivious to the faults of style, and he filled in the flat characterizations with his own imagination, giving himself up unself-consciously to the dramatic events and exotic scenery. But, though he was lucky in a way, his judgment of the *whole* work was not to be trusted.

*IV*

We saw earlier that the notion of a point of view plays a particular role in focusing or forwarding certain disputes by limiting the range of relevant considerations. We invoke the aesthetic point of view when we want to set aside certain considerations that others have advanced—as that a poem is pornographic, or that a painting is a forgery—or that (as Jacques Maritain remarks) "A splendid house without a door is not a good work of architecture."[16] But the person whose considerations are thus rejected may feel that the decision is arbitrary, and enter an appeal, in the hope that a higher philosophical tribunal will rule that the lower court erred in its exclusions. How do we know whether being pornographic, or being a forgery, or lacking a door, is irrelevant from the aesthetic point of view? I propose this answer:

> A consideration about an object is relevant to the aesthetic point of view if and only if it is a fact about the object that affects the degree to which the marks of aesthetic gratification (formal unity and intensity of regional quality) are present in the object.

Thus: Is the fact that a painting is a forgery relevant to a judgment of it from the aesthetic point of view? No; because it has no bearing on its form or quality. Is the fact that a painting is a seascape relevant? Sometimes. It is when the subject contributes to, or detracts from, its degree of unity or its qualitative intensity. Is the biography of the composer relevant? According to a writer in *The Music Review*:

> It is a well-known fact that knowledge of the circumstances surrounding the composition of a work enhances the audience's appreciation. . . . It is because of this that programme notes, radio comments, and music appreciation courses are in such demand. To secure such knowledge is one of the important tasks of musical research.[17]

Now, I'm not sure that this "well-known fact" is really a fact, but let us assume that it is. Does it follow that information about the circumstances of composition is relevant to consideration of the work from an aesthetic point of view? We can imagine this sort of thing:

> It was a cold rainy day in Vienna, and Schubert was down to his last crust of bread. As he looked about his dingy garret, listening to the rain that beat down, he reflected that he could not even afford to feed his mice. He recalled a sad poem by Goethe, and suddenly a melody sprang into his head. He seized an old piece of paper, and began to write feverishly. Thus was "Death and the Maiden" born.

Now even if everyone, or *nearly* everyone, who reads this program note finds that it increases his appreciation of the song, a condition of appreciation is not necessarily a condition of value. From this information—say, that it was raining—nothing can be inferred about the specifically aesthetic character of the song. (It is relevant, of course, that the words and music match each other in certain ways; however, we know that not by biographical investigation but by listening to the song itself.)

Here is one more example. In a very interesting article "On the Aesthetic Attitude in Romanesque Art," Meyer Schapiro has argued that:

> Contrary to the general belief that in the Middle Ages the work of art was considered mainly as a vehicle of religious teaching or as a piece of craftsmanship serving a useful end, and that beauty of form and color was no object of contemplation in itself, these texts abound in aesthetic judgments and in statements about the qualities and structure of the work. They speak of the fascination of the image, its marvelous likeness to physical reality, and the artist's wonderful skill, often in complete abstraction from the content of the object of art.[18]

Schapiro is inquiring whether medieval people were capable of taking the aesthetic point of view in some independence of the religious and technological points of view. He studies various texts in which aesthetic objects are described and praised, to elicit the grounds on which this admiration is based, and to discover whether these grounds are relevant to the aesthetic point of view. Form and color, for example, are clearly relevant, and so to praise a work for its form or color is to adopt the aesthetic point of view. And I should think the same can be said for "the fascination of the image"—by which Schapiro refers to the extraordinary interest in the grotesque figures freely carved by the stonecutters in Romanesque buildings. These centaurs, chimeras, two-headed animals, creatures with feet and the tail of a serpent, etc., are the images deplored by Saint Bernard with an ambivalence like that in Lenin's remark about Beethoven:

> In the cloister, under the eyes of the brethren who read there, what profit is there in those ridiculous monsters, in that marvelous and deformed beauty, in that beautiful deformity?[19]

But what of Schapiro's other points—the image's "marvelous likeness to physical reality, and the artist's wonderful skill"?

If a person admires skill in depiction, he is certainly not taking a religious point of view—but is he taking the aesthetic point of view? I should think not. No doubt when he notices the accuracy of depiction, reflects on the skill required to achieve it, and thus admires the artist, he may be placed in a more favorable psychological posture toward the work itself. But this contributes to the conditions of the experience; it does not enter into the experience directly, as does the perception of form and color, or the recognition of the represented objects as saints or serpents. So I would say that the fact that the medieval writer admired the skill in depiction is *not* evidence that he took the aesthetic point of view, though it is evidence that he took *an* aesthetic point of view, since skill was involved in the production of the work.


*V*

There is one final problem that may be worth raising and commenting upon briefly—although it is not at all clear to me how the problem should even be formulated. It concerns the justification of adopting the aesthetic point of view, and its potential conflicts with other points of view. On one hand, it is interesting to note that much effort has been spent (especially during recent decades) in getting people to adopt the aesthetic point of view much more firmly and continuously than has been common in our country. The conservationists are trying to arouse us to concern for the preservation of natural beauties, instead of automatically assuming that they have a lower priority than any other interest that happens to come up—such as installing power lines, or slaughtering deer, or advertising beer. And those who are concerned with "education of the eye," or "visual education," are always developing new methods of teaching the theory and practice of good design, the aim being to produce people who are aware of the growing hideousness of our cities and towns, and who are troubled enough to work for changes.

But the effort to broaden the adoption of the aesthetic point of view sometimes takes another form. According to its leading theoretician, the "Camp sensibility" is characterized by the great range of material to which it can respond: "Camp is the consistently aesthetic experience of the world," writes Susan Sontag. "It incarnates a victory of style over content, of aesthetics over morality, of irony over tragedy."[20]

Here is an extreme consequence of trying to increase the amount of aesthetic value of which we can take advantage. But it also gives rise to an interesting problem, which might be called "the dilemma of aesthetic education." The problem is pointed up by a cartoon I saw not long ago (by David Gerard), showing the proprietor of a junkyard named "Sam's Salvage" standing by a huge pile of junked cars, and saying to two other men: "Whattya mean it's an ugly eyesore? If I'd paid Picasso to pile it up, you'd call it a work of art."

The central task of aesthetic education, as traditionally conceived, is the improvement of taste, involving the development of two dispositions: (1) the capacity to obtain aesthetic gratification from increasingly subtle and complex aesthetic objects that are characterized by various forms of unity—in short, the response to beauty in one main sense; and (2) an increasing dependence on objects beautiful in this way (having harmony, order, balance, proportion) as sources of aesthetic satisfaction. It is this impulse that is behind the usual concept of "beautification"—shielding the highways from junkyards and billboards, and providing more trees and flowers and grass. As long as the individual's aesthetic development in this sense is accompanied by increasing access to beautiful sights and sounds, it is all to the good. His taste improves; his aesthetic pleasures are keener; and when he encounters unavoidable ugliness, he may be moved to eliminate it by labor or by law. On the other hand, suppose he finds that his environment grows uglier, as the economy progresses, and that the ugliness becomes harder to escape. Second, suppose he comes to enjoy another kind of aesthetic value, one that derives from intensity of regional quality more than formal fitness. And third, suppose he comes to realize that his aesthetic gratification is affected by the demands he makes upon an object—especially because the intensity of its regional qualities partly depends on its symbolic import. For example, the plain ordinary object may be seen as a kind of symbol, and become expressive (i.e., assume a noteworthy quality) if the individual attends to it in a way that invites these features to emerge. Suddenly, a whole new field of aesthetic gratification opens up. Trivial objects, the accidental, the neglected, the meretricious and vulgar, all take on new excitement. The automobile graveyard and the weed-filled garden are seen to have their own wild and grotesque expressiveness as well as symbolic import. The kewpie doll, the Christmas card, the Tiffany lampshade, can be enjoyed aesthetically, not for their beauty but for their bizarre qualities and their implicit reflection of social attitudes. This is a way of transfiguring reality, and though not everything can be transfigured, perhaps, it turns out that much can.

What I mean by the dilemma of aesthetic education is this: that we are torn between conflicting ways of redirecting taste. One is the way of love of beauty, which is limited in its range of enjoyment, but is reformist by implication, since it seeks a world that conforms to its ideal. The other is the way of aestheticizing everything—of taking the aesthetic point of view wherever possible—and this widens enjoyment, but is defeatist, since instead of eliminating the junkyard and the slum it tries to see them as expressive and symbolic. The conflict here is analogous to that between the social gospel and personal salvation in some of our churches—though no doubt its consequences are not equally momentous. I don't suppose this dilemma is ultimately unresolvable, though I cannot consider it further at the moment. I point it out as one of the implications of the tendency (which I have been briefly exploring) to extend the aesthetic point of view as widely as possible.

But there is another weighty tradition opposed to this expansion. Lenin and Saint Bernard stand witness to the possibility that there may be situations in which it is morally objectionable to adopt the aesthetic point of view. A man who had escaped from Auschwitz commented on Rolf Hochmuth's play: "*The Deputy* should not be considered as a historical work or even as a work of art, but as a moral lesson."[21] Perhaps he only meant that looking for historical truth or artistic merit in *The Deputy* is a waste of time. But he may also have meant that there is something blameworthy about anyone who is capable of contemplating those terrible events from a purely historical or purely aesthetic point of view. Renata Adler, reporting in *The New Yorker*[22] on the New Politics Convention that took place in Chicago on Labor Day weekend, 1967, listed various types of self-styled "revolutionaries" who attended, including "the aes-thetic-analogy revolutionaries, who discussed riots as though they were folk songs or pieces of local theatre, subject to appraisal in literary terms ('authentic,' 'beautiful')." That is carrying the aesthetic point of view pretty far.

This possibility has not gone unnoticed by imaginative writers—notably Henry James and Henrik Ibsen.[23] The tragedy of Mrs. Gereth, in *The Spoils of Poynton*, is that of a woman who could not escape the aesthetic point of view. She had a "passion for the exquisite" that made her prone "to be rendered unhappy by the presence of the dreadful [and] she was condemned to wince wherever she turned." In fact, the things that troubled her most—and she encountered them everywhere, but nowhere in more abundance than the country house known as Waterbath—were just the campy items featured by Miss Sontag: "trumpery ornament and scrapbook art, with strange excrescences and bunchy draperies, with gimcracks that might have been keepsakes for maid-servants [and even] a souvenir from some centennial or other Exhibition." The tragedy of the sculptor, Profes-sor Rubek, in *When We Dead Awaken*, is that he so utterly aestheticized the woman who loved him and who was his model that she was not a person to him. As she says, "The work of art first—then the human being." It may even be—and I say this with the utmost hesitation, since I have no wish to sink in these muddy waters—that this is the theme of Antonioni's film, *Blow-Up*: the emptiness that comes from utter absorption in an aesthetic point of view of a photographer to whom every person and every event seems to represent only the possibility of a new photographic image. In that respect, Antonioni's photographer is certainly worse than Professor Rubek.

The mere confrontation of these two vague and general social philosophies of art will not, of course, take us very far in understanding the possibilities and the limitations of the aesthetic point of view. I leave matters unresolved, with questions hanging in the air. Whatever resolution we ultimately find, however, will surely incorporate two observations that may serve as a pair of conclusions.

First, there are occasions on which it would be wrong to adopt the aesthetic point of view, because there is a conflict of values and the values that are in peril are, in that particular case, clearly higher. Once in a while you see a striking photograph or film sequence in which someone is (for example) lying in the street after an accident, in need of immediate attention. And it is a shock to think suddenly that the photographer must have been on hand. I don't want to argue ethics of news photography, but if someone, out of the highest aesthetic motives, withheld first aid to a bleeding victim in order to record the scene, with careful attention to lighting and camera speed, then it is doubtful that that picture could be so splendid a work of art as to justify neglecting so stringent a moral obligation.

The second conclusion is that there is nothing—no object or event—that is *per se* wrong to consider from the aesthetic point of view. This, I think, is part of the truth in the art-for-art's-sake doctrine. To adopt the aesthetic point of view is simply to seek out a source of value. And it can never be a moral error to realize value—barring conflict with other values. Some people seem to fear that a serious and persistent aesthetic interest will become an enervating hyperaestheticism, a paralysis of will like that reported in advanced cases of psychedelic dependence. But the objects of aesthetic interest—such as harmonious design, good proportions, intense expressiveness—are not drugs, but part of the breath of life. Their cumulative effect is increased sensitization, fuller awareness, a closer touch with the environment and concern for what it is and might be. It seems to me very doubtful that we could have too much of these good things, or that they have inherent defects that prevent them from being an integral part of a good life.

## Notes

1. *New Republic* (Jan. 16, 1961), p. 23. Cf. Brendan Gill, in *The New Yorker* (March 5, 1966): "It is a lot easier to recommend attendance at 'The Gospel According to St. Matthew' as an act of penitential piety during the Lenten season than it is to praise the movie as a movie. Whether or not the life and death of Our Lord is the greatest story ever told, it is so far from being merely a story that we cannot deal with it in literary terms (if we could, I think we would have to

begin by saying that in respect to construction and motivation it leaves much to be desired); our difficulty is enormously increased when we try to pass judgment on the story itself once it has been turned into a screenplay."

2. From Gorky's essay on Lenin, *Collected Works* XVII (Moscow, 1950), 39–40. My colleague Professor Olga Lang called my attention to this passage and translated it for me. Cf. *Days with Lenin* (New York: International Publishers, 1932), p. 52. *Time* (April 30, 1965, p. 50) reported that the Chinese Communists had forbidden the performance of Beethoven's works because they "paralyze one's revolutionary fighting will." A Chinese bacteriologist, in a letter to a Peking newspaper, wrote after listening to Beethoven, "I began to have strange illusions about a world filled with friendly love."

3. New York: Doubleday Anchor Books, 1954, p. 15, where he quotes Wotton.

4. In this discussion, I have been stimulated by an unpublished paper by J. O. Urmson on "Good of a Kind and Good from a Point of View," which I saw in manuscript in 1961. I should also like to thank him for comments on an earlier version of this paper. Cf. his note added to "What Makes a Situation Aesthetic?" in Joseph Margolis, ed., *Philosophy Looks at the Arts* [first edition] (New York: Charles Scribner's Sons, 1962), p. 26. I also note that John Hospers has some interesting remarks on the aesthetic point of view in "The Ideal Aesthetic Observer," *British Journal of Aesthetics* II (1962), 99–111.

5. *The New York Times*, Oct. 2, 1967, p. 55.

6. Cf. my "Comments" on Stanley Cavell's paper, in W. H. Capitan and D. D. Merrill, eds., *Art, Mind, and Religion* (Pittsburgh: University of Pittsburgh Press, 1967), esp. pp. 107–109.

7. *Op. cit.*, p. 89; cf. pp. 90–91, 95. In case it may be thought that architects who have the highest respect for their materials might repudiate my distinction, I quote Pier Luigi Nervi (in his Charles Eliot Norton lectures): "There does not exist, either in the past or in the present, a work of architecture which is accepted and recognized as excellent from the aesthetic point of view which is not also excellent from a technical point of view." From *Aesthetics and Technology in Building* (Cambridge: Harvard University Press, 1965), p. 2. Though arguing that one kind of value is a necessary (but not a sufficient) condition of the other, Nervi clearly assumes that there is a distinguishable aesthetic point of view.

8. *The New York Times*, April 2, 1967, p. 94.

9. Dec. 1966, p. 20.

10. Paul Taylor, *Normative Discourse* (Englewood Cliffs, N.J.: Prentice-Hall, Inc., 1961), p. 109.

11. See *Aesthetics: Problems in the Philosophy of Criticism* (New York: Harcourt, Brace & World, Inc., 1958), ch. 11.

12. See "Beardsley's Phantom Aesthetic Experience," *Journal of Philosophy* LXII (1965), 129–136, and my "Aesthetic Experience Regained," *Journal of Aesthetics and Art Criticism* XXVII (1969), 3–11.

13. "The Discrimination of Aesthetic Enjoyment," *British Journal of Aesthetics* III (1963), 291–300.

14. In the *Delaware County Daily Times* (Chester, Pa.), Feb. 10, 1967.

15. It was discussed briefly in my *Aesthetics* (New York: Harcourt, Brace, &

World, 1958), pp. 534–535, but has since been called to my attention more sharply and forcefully by Professor Thomas Regan.

16. *L'Intuition Créatrice dans l'Art et dans la Poésie* (Paris: Desclée de Brouwer, 1966), p. 53.

17. Hans Tischler, "The Aesthetic Experience," *Music Review* XVII (1956), p. 200.

18. In K. Bharatha Iyer, ed., *Art and Thought* (London: Luzac, 1947), p. 138. I thank my colleague John Williams for calling my attention to this essay.

19. *Ibid.*, p. 133.

20. Susan Sontag, "Notes on Camp," *Partisan Review* XXXI (Fall 1964), p. 526.

21. *The New York Times*, May 4, 1966.

22. Sept. 23, 1967.

23. I set aside the somewhat indelicate verse by W. H. Auden called "The Aesthetic Point of View."

# 2.                          Aesthetic Concepts
## FRANK SIBLEY

The remarks we make about works of art are of many kinds. For the purpose of this paper I wish to indicate two broad groups. I shall do this by examples. We say that a novel has a great number of characters and deals with life in a manufacturing town; that a painting uses pale colors, predominantly blues and greens, and has kneeling figures in the foreground; that the theme in a fugue is inverted at such a point and that there is a stretto at the close; that the action of a play takes place in the span of one day and that there is a reconciliation scene in the fifth act. Such remarks may be made by, and such features pointed out to, anyone with normal eyes, ears, and intelligence. On the other hand, we also say that a poem is tightly knit or deeply moving; that a picture lacks balance, or has a certain serenity and repose, or that the grouping of the figures sets up an exciting tension; that the characters in a novel never really come to life, or that a certain episode strikes a false note. It would be neutral enough to say that the making of such judgments as these requires the exercise of taste, perceptiveness, or sensitivity, of aesthetic discrimination or appreciation; one would not say this of my first group. Accordingly, when a word or expression is such that taste or perceptiveness is required in order to apply it, I shall call it an *aesthetic* term or expression, and I shall, correspondingly, speak of *aesthetic* concepts or *taste* concepts.[1]

Aesthetic terms span a great range of types and could be grouped into various kinds of sub-species. But it is not my present purpose to attempt any such grouping; I am interested in what they all have in common. Their almost endless variety is adequately displayed in the following list: *unified, balanced, integrated, lifeless, serene, somber, dynamic, powerful, vivid, delicate, moving, trite, sentimental, tragic.* The list of course is not limited

From *The Philosophical Review*, LXVII (1959), 421–450. Reprinted with permission of the author and *The Philosophical Review*.

to adjectives; expressions in artistic contexts like *telling contrast, sets up a tension, conveys a sense of,* or *holds it together* are equally good illustrations. It includes terms used by both layman and critic alike, as well as some which are mainly the property of professional critics and specialists.

I have gone for my examples of aesthetic expressions in the first place to critical and evaluative discourse about works of art because it is there particularly that they abound. But now I wish to widen the topic; we employ terms the use of which requires an exercise of taste not only when discussing the arts but quite liberally throughout discourse in everyday life. The examples given above are expressions which, appearing in critical contexts, most usually, if not invariably, have an aesthetic use; outside critical discourse the majority of them more frequently have some other use unconnected with taste. But many expressions do double duty even in everyday discourse, sometimes being used as aesthetic expressions and sometimes not. Other words again, whether in artistic or daily discourse, function only or predominantly as aesthetic terms; of this kind are *graceful, delicate, dainty, handsome, comely, elegant, garish.* Finally, to make the contrast with all the preceding examples, there are many words which are seldom used as aesthetic terms at all: *red, noisy, brackish, clammy, square, docile, curved, evanescent, intelligent, faithful, derelict, tardy, freakish.*

Clearly, when we employ words as aesthetic terms we are often making and using metaphors, pressing into service words which do not primarily function in this manner. Certainly also, many words *have come* to be aesthetic terms by some kind of metaphorical transference. This is so with those like "dynamic," "melancholy," "balanced," "tightly knit" which, except in artistic and critical writings, are not normally aesthetic terms. But the aesthetic vocabulary must not be thought wholly metaphorical. Many words, including the most common (*lovely, pretty, beautiful, dainty, graceful, elegant*), are certainly not being used metaphorically when employed as aesthetic terms, the very good reason being that this is their primary or only use, some of them having no current nonaesthetic use. And though expressions like "dynamic," "balanced," and so forth *have come* by a metaphorical shift to be aesthetic terms, their employment in criticism can scarcely be said to be more than quasi-metaphorical. Having entered the language of art description and criticism as metaphors they are now standard vocabulary in that language.[2]

The expressions I am calling aesthetic terms form no small segment of our discourse. Often, it is true, people with normal intelligence and good eyesight and hearing lack, at least in some measure, the sensitivity required to apply them; a man need not be stupid or have poor eyesight to fail to see that something is graceful. Thus taste or sensitivity is somewhat more rare than certain other human capacities; people who exhibit a sensitivity both wide-ranging and refined are a minority. It is over the application of aesthetic terms too that, notoriously, disputes and differences sometimes go helplessly unsettled. But almost everybody is able to exercise taste to some degree and in some matters. It is surprising therefore that aesthetic terms have been so largely neglected. They have received glancing treatment in the course of other aesthetic discussions; but as a broad category they have not received the direct attention they merit.

The foregoing has marked out the area I wish to discuss. One warning should perhaps be given. When I speak of taste in this paper, I shall not be dealing with questions which center upon expressions like "a matter of taste" (meaning, roughly, a matter of personal preference or liking). It is with an ability to *notice* or *see* or *tell* that things have certain qualities that I am concerned.


*I*

In order to support our application of an aesthetic term, we often refer to features the mention of which involves other aesthetic terms: "it has an extraordinary vitality because of its free and vigorous style of drawing," "graceful in the smooth flow of its lines," "dainty because of the delicacy and harmony of its coloring." It is as normal to do this as it is to justify one mental epithet by other epithets of the same general type, *intelligent* by *ingenious, inventive, acute,* and so on. But often when we apply aesthetic terms, we explain why by referring to features which do *not* depend for their recognition upon an exercise of taste: "delicate because of its pastel shades and curving lines," or "it lacks balance because one group of figures is so far off to the left and is so brightly illuminated." When no explanation of this latter kind is offered, it is legitimate to ask or search for one. Finding a satisfactory answer may sometimes be difficult, but one cannot ordinarily reject the question. When we cannot ourselves quite say what nonaesthetic features make something delicate or unbalanced or powerful or moving, the good critic often puts his finger on something which strikes us as the right explanation. In short, aesthetic terms always ultimately apply because of, and aesthetic qualities always ultimately depend upon, the presence of features which, like curving or angular lines, color contrasts, placing of masses, or speed of movement, are visible, audible, or otherwise discernible without any exercise of taste or sensibility. Whatever kind of dependence this is, and there are various relationships between aesthetic qualities and nonaesthetic features, what I want to make clear in this paper is that there are no nonaesthetic features which service in *any* circumstances as logically *sufficient conditions* for

applying aesthetic terms. Aesthetic or taste concepts are not in *this* respect
condition-governed at all.

There is little temptation to suppose that aesthetic terms resemble words
which, like "square," are applied in accordance with a set of necessary and
sufficient conditions. For whereas each square is square in virtue of the
*same* set of conditions, four equal sides and four right angles, aesthetic
terms apply to widely varied objects; one thing is graceful because of these
features, another because of those, and so on almost endlessly. In recent
times philosophers have broken the spell of the strict necessary-and-sufficient model by showing that many everyday concepts are not of that type.
Instead, they have described various other types of concepts which are
governed only in a much looser way by conditions. However, since these
newer models provide satisfactory accounts of many familiar concepts, it
might plausibly be thought that aesthetic concepts are of some such kind
and that they similarly are governed in some looser way by conditions. I
want to argue that aesthetic concepts differ radically from any of these
other concepts.

Amongst these concepts to which attention has recently been paid are
those for which no *necessary-and-sufficient* conditions can be provided,
but for which there are a number of relevant features, A, B, C, D, E, such
that the presence of some groups or combinations of these features is
*sufficient* for the application of the concept. The list of relevant features
may be an open one; that is, given A, B, C, D, E, we may not wish to
close off the possible relevance of other unlisted features beyond E.
Examples of such concepts might be "dilatory," "discourteous," "posses-
sive," "capricious," "prosperous," "intelligent" (but see below). If we begin
a list of features relevant to "intelligent" with, for example, ability to grasp
and follow various kinds of instructions, ability to master facts and
marshall evidence, ability to solve mathematical or chess problems, we
might go on adding to this list almost indefinitely.

However, with concepts of this sort, although decisions may have to be
made and judgment exercised, it is always possible to extract and state,
from cases which have *already* clearly been decided, the sets of features
or conditions which were regarded as sufficient in those cases. These
relevant features which I am calling conditions are, it should be noted,
features which, though not sufficient *alone* and needing to be combined
with other similar features, nevertheless carry some weight and can count
only in one direction. Being a good chess player can count only *towards*
and not *against* intelligence. Whereas mention of it may enter sensibly
along with other remarks in expressions like "I say he is intelligent
because . . ." or "the reason I call him intelligent is that . . ."; it cannot be
used to complete such negative expressions as "I say he is *un*intelligent

because . . ." But what I want particularly to emphasize about features which function as conditions for a term is that *some* group or set of them *is* sufficient fully to ensure or warrant the application of that term. An individual characterized by some of these features may not yet qualify to be called lazy or intelligent, and so on, beyond all question, but all that is needed is to add some further (indefinite) number of such characterizations and a point is reached where we have enough. There are individuals possessing a number of such features of whom one cannot deny, cannot but admit, that they are intelligent. We have left necessary-and-sufficient conditions behind, but we are still in the realm of sufficient conditions.

But aesthetic concepts are not condition-governed even in this way. There are no sufficient conditions, no nonaesthetic features such that the presence of some set or number of them will beyond question logically justify or warrant the application of an aesthetic term. It is impossible (barring certain limited exceptions, see below) to make any statements corresponding to those we can make for condition-governed words. We are able to say "If it is true he can do this, and that, and the other, then one just cannot deny that he is intelligent," or "if he does A, B, and C, I don't see how it can be denied that he is lazy," but we cannot make *any* general statement of the form "If the vase is pale pink, somewhat curving, lightly mottled, and so forth, it will be delicate, cannot but be delicate." Nor again can one say *any* such things here as "Being tall and thin is not enough *alone* to ensure that a vase is delicate, but if it is, for example, slightly curving and pale colored (and so forth) as well, it cannot be denied that it is." Things may be described to us in nonaesthetic terms as fully as we please but we are not thereby put in the position of having to admit (or being unable to deny) that they are delicate or graceful or garish or exquisitely balanced.[3]

No doubt there are some respects in which aesthetic terms *are* governed by conditions or rules. For instance, it may be impossible that a thing should be garish if all its colors are pale pastels, or flamboyant if all its lines are straight. There may be, that is, descriptions using only nonaesthetic terms which are incompatible with descriptions employing certain aesthetic terms. If I am told that a painting in the next room consists solely of one or two bars of very pale blue and very pale gray set at right angles on a pale fawn ground, I can be sure that it cannot be fiery or garish or gaudy or flamboyant. A description of this sort may make certain aesthetic terms *in*applicable or *in*appropriate; and if from this description I inferred that the picture was, or even might be, fiery or gaudy or flamboyant, this might be taken as showing a failure to understand these words. I do not wish to deny therefore that taste concepts may be governed *negatively* by conditions.[4] What I am emphasizing is that they quite lack governing conditions of a sort many other concepts possess. Though on *seeing* the picture we might say, and rightly, that it is delicate or serene or restful or sickly or insipid, no *description* in nonaesthetic terms permits us to claim that these or any other aesthetic terms must undeniably apply to it.

I have said that if an object is characterized *solely* by certain sorts of features this may count decisively against the possibility of applying to it certain aesthetic terms. But of course the presence of *some* such features need not count decisively; other features may be enough to outweigh those which, on their own, would render the aesthetic term inapplicable. A painting might be garish even though much of its color is pale. These facts call attention to a further feature of taste concepts. One *can* find general features or descriptions which in some sense count in one direction only, only *for* or only *against* the application of certain aesthetic terms. Angularity, fatness, brightness, or intensity of color are typically *not* associated with delicacy or grace. Slimness, lightness, gentle curves, lack of intensity of color are associated with delicacy, but not with flamboyance, majesty, grandeur, splendor or garishness. This is shown by the naturalness of saying, for example, that someone is graceful *because* she's so light, but *in spite of* being quite angular or heavily built; and by the corresponding oddity of saying that something is graceful *because* it is so heavy or angular, or delicate *because* of its bright and intense coloring. This may therefore sound quite similar to what I have said already about conditions in discussing terms like "intelligent." There are nevertheless very significant differences. Although there is this sense in which slimness, lightness, lack of intensity of color, and so on, count only towards not against, delicacy, these features, I shall say, at best count only *typically* or *characteristically* towards delicacy; they do not count towards in the same sense as condition-features count towards laziness or intelligence; that is, no group of them is ever logically sufficient.

One way of reinforcing this is to notice how features which are characteristically associated with one aesthetic term may also be similarly associated with other and rather different aesthetic terms. "Graceful" and "delicate" may be on the one hand sharply contrasted with terms like "violent," "grand," "fiery," "garish," or "massive" which have characteristic nonaesthetic features quite unlike those for "delicate" and "graceful." But on the other hand "graceful" and "delicate" may also be contrasted with aesthetic terms which stand much closer to them, like "flaccid," "weakly," "washed out," "lanky," "anaemic," "wan," "insipid"; and the range of features characteristic of *these* qualities, pale color, slimness, lightness, lack of angularity and sharp contrast, is virtually identical with the range for "delicate" and "graceful." Similarly many of the features typically associated with "joyous," "fiery," "robust," or "dynamic" are identical with those associated with "garish," "strident," "turbulent," "gaudy," or "chaotic." Thus an object which is described very fully, but exclusively in terms of qualities characteristic of delicacy, may turn out on inspection to be not delicate at all, but anaemic or insipid. The failures of novices and the artistically inept prove that quite close similarity in point of line, color, or technique gives no assurance of gracefulness or delicacy. A failure and a success in the manner of Degas may be generally more alike, so far as their nonaesthetic features go, than either is like a successful Fragonard. But it is not necessary to go even this far to make my main point. A painting which has only the kind of features one would associate with vigor and energy but which even so fails to be vigorous and energetic *need* not have some other character, need not be instead, say, strident or chaotic. It may fail to have any particular character whatever. It may employ bright colors, and the like, without being particularly lively and vigorous at all; but one may feel unable to describe it as chaotic or strident or garish either. It is, rather, simply lacking in character (though of course this too is an aesthetic judgment; taste is exercised also in seeing that the painting has no character).

There are of course many features which do not in these ways characteristically count for (or against) particular aesthetic qualities. One poem has strength and power because of the regularity of its meter and rhyme; another is monotonous and lacks drive and strength because of its regular meter and rhyme. We do not feel the need to switch from "because of" to "in spite of." However, I have concentrated upon features which are characteristically associated with aesthetic qualities because, if a case could be made for the view that taste concepts are in any way governed by sufficient conditions, these would seem to be the most promising candidates for governing conditions. But to say that features are associated only *characteristically* with an aesthetic term *is* to say that they can never amount to sufficient conditions; no description however full, even in terms characteristic of gracefulness, puts it beyond question that something is graceful in the way a description may put it beyond question that someone is lazy or intelligent.

It is important to observe, however, that in this paper I am not merely claiming that no sufficient conditions can be stated for taste concepts. For if this were all, taste concepts might not be after all really different from one kind of concept recently discussed. They could be accommodated perhaps with those concepts which Professor H. L. A. Hart has called "defeasible"; it is a characteristic of defeasible concepts that we cannot state sufficient conditions for them because, for any sets we offer, there is always an (open) list of defeating conditions any of which might rule out the application of the concept. The most we can say schematically for a defeasible concept is that, for example, A, B, and C together are sufficient for the concept to apply *unless* some feature is present which overrides or voids them. But, I want to emphasize, the very fact that we *can* say this sort of thing shows that we are still to that extent in the realm of conditions.[5] The features governing defeasible concepts can ordinarily count only one way, *either* for *or* against. To take Hart's example, "offer" and "acceptance" can count only towards the existence of a valid contract, and fraudulent misrepresentation, duress, and lunacy can count only against. And even with defeasible concepts, if we are told that there are no voiding features present, we can know that some set of conditions or features, A, B, C, . . . , is enough, in this absence of voiding features, to ensure, for example, that there is a contract. The very notion of a defeasible concept seems to require that some group of features *would* be sufficient *in certain circumstances*, that is, in the absence of overriding or voiding features. In a certain way defeasible concepts lack sufficient conditions then, but they are still, in the sense described, condition-governed. My claim about taste concepts is stronger; that they are not, except negatively, governed by conditions at all. We could not conclude even in certain circumstances, e.g., if we were told of the absence of all "voiding" or uncharacteristic features (no angularities, and the like), that an object *must* certainly be graceful, no matter how fully it was described to us as possessing features characteristic of gracefulness.

My arguments and illustrations so far have been rather simply schematic. Many concepts, including most of the examples I have used (*intelligent*, and so on, above), are much more thoroughly open and complex than my illustrations suggest. Not only may there be an open list of relevant conditions; it may be impossible to give precise rules telling how many features from the list are needed for a sufficient set or in which combinations; impossible similarly to give precise rules covering the extent or degree to which such features need to be present in those combinations. Indeed, we may have to abandon as futile any attempt to describe or formulate anything like a complete set of precise conditions or rules, and content ourselves with giving only some general account of the concept, making reference to samples or cases or precedents. We cannot fully master or employ these concepts therefore *simply* by being equipped with lists of conditions, readily applicable procedures, or sets of rules, however complex. For to exhibit a mastery of one of these concepts we must be able to go ahead and apply the word correctly to new individual cases, at least to central ones; and each new case may be a uniquely different object, just as each intelligent child or student may differ from others in relevant features and exhibit a unique combination of kinds and degrees of achievement and ability. In dealing with these new cases mechanical rules and procedures would be useless; we have to exercise our judgment, guided by a complex set of examples and precedents. Here then there is a marked *superficial* similarity to aesthetic concepts. For in using aesthetic terms too we learn from samples and examples, not rules, and we have to apply them, likewise, without guidance by rules or readily applicable procedures, to new and unique instances. Neither kind of concept admits of a simply "mechanical" employment.

But this is *only* a superficial similarity. It is at least noteworthy that in applying words like "lazy" or "intelligent" to new and unique instances we say that we are required to exercise *judgment;* it would be indeed odd to say that we are exercising *taste.* In exercising judgment we are called upon to weigh the pros and cons against each other, and perhaps sometimes to decide whether a quite new feature is to be counted as weighing on one side or on the other. But this goes to show that, though we may learn from and rely upon samples and precedents rather than a set of stated conditions, we are not out of the realm of general conditions and guiding principles. These precedents necessarily embody, and are used by us to illustrate, a complex web of governing and relevant conditions which it is impossible to formulate completely. To profit by precedents we have to understand them; and we must argue consistently from case to case. This is the very function of precedents. Thus it is possible, even with these very loosely condition-governed concepts, to take clear or paradigm cases of X and to say "this is X because . . ." and follow it up with an account of features which logically clinch the matter.

Nothing like this is possible with aesthetic terms. Examples undoubtedly play a crucial role in giving us a grasp of these concepts; but we do not and cannot derive from these examples conditions and principles, however complex, which will enable us, if we are consistent, to apply the terms even to some new cases. When, with a clear case of something which is in fact graceful or balanced or tightly knit, someone tells me why it is, what features make it so, it is always possible for me to wonder whether, in spite of these features, it really is graceful, balanced, and so on. No such features logically clinch the matter.

The point I have argued may be reinforced in the following way. A man who failed to realize the nature of aesthetic concepts, or someone who, knowing he lacked sensitivity in aesthetic matters, did not want to reveal this lack might by assiduous application and shrewd observation provide himself with some rules and generalizations; and by inductive procedures and intelligent guessing, he might frequently say the right things. But he could have no great confidence or certainty; a slight change in an object might at any time unpredictably ruin his calculations, and he might as easily have been wrong as right. No matter how careful he has been about working out a set of consistent principles and conditions, he is only in a position to think that the object is very possibly delicate. With concepts like *lazy, intelligent,* or *contract,* someone who intelligently formulated rules that led him aright appreciably often *would* thereby show the beginning of a grasp of those concepts; but the person we are considering is not even beginning to show an awareness of what delicacy is. Though he sometimes says the right thing, he has not seen, but guessed, that the object is delicate. However intelligent he might be, we could easily tell him wrongly that something was delicate and "explain" why without his being able to detect the deception. (I am ignoring complications now about negative conditions.) But if we did the same with, say, "intelligent" he could at least often uncover some incompatibility or other which would need explaining. In a world of beings like himself he would have no use for concepts like delicacy. As it is, these concepts would play a quite different role in his life. He would, for himself, have no more reason to choose tasteful objects, pictures, and so on, than a deaf man would to avoid noisy places. He could not be praised for exercising taste; at best his ingenuity and intelligence might come in for mention. In "appraising" pictures, statuettes, poems, he would be doing something quite different from what other people do when they exercise taste.

At this point I want to notice in passing that there are times when it may look as if an aesthetic word could be applied according to a rule. These cases vary in type; I shall mention only one. One might say, in using "delicate" of glassware perhaps, that the thinner the glass, other things being equal, the more delicate it is. Similarly, with fabrics, furniture, and so on, there are perhaps times when the thinner or more smoothly finished or more highly polished something is, the more certainly some aesthetic term or other applies. On such occasions someone might formulate a rule and follow it in applying the word to a given range of articles. Now it may be that sometimes when this is so, the word being used is not really an aesthetic term at all; "delicate" applied to glass in this way may at times really mean no more than "thin" or "fragile." But this is certainly not always the case; people often *are* exercising taste even when they say that glass is very delicate because it is so thin, and know that it would be less so if thicker and more so if thinner. These instances where there appear to be rules are peripheral cases of the use of aesthetic terms. If someone did merely follow a rule we should not say he was exercising taste, and we should hesitate to admit that he had any real notion of delicacy until he satisfied us that he could discern it in other instances where no rule was available. In any event, these occasions when aesthetic words can be applied by rule are exceptional, not central or typical, and there is still no reason to think we are dealing with a logical entailment.[6]

It must not be thought that the impossibility of stating any conditions (other than negative) for the application of aesthetic terms results from an accidental poverty or lack of precision in language, or that it is simply a question of extreme complexity. It is true that words like "pink," "bluish," "curving," "mottled" do not permit of anything like a specific naming of each and every varied shade, curve, mottling, and blending. But if we were to give special names much more liberally than either we or even the specialists do (and no doubt there are limits beyond which we could not go), or even if, instead of names, we were to use vast numbers of specimens and samples of particular shades, shapes, mottlings, lines, and configurations, it would still be impossible, and for the same reasons, to supply any conditions.

We do indeed, in talking about a work of art, concern ourselves with its individual and specific features. We say that it is delicate not simply because it is in pale colors but because of *those* pale colors, that it is graceful not because its outline curves slightly but because of *that* particular curve. We use expressions like "because of *its* pale coloring," "because of *the* flecks of bright blue," "because of *the* way the lines converge" where it is clear we are referring not to the presence of general features but to very specific and particular ones. But it is obvious that even with the help of precise names, or even samples and illustrations, of particular shades of color, contours and lines, any attempt to state conditions would be futile. After all, the very same feature, say a color or shape or line of a particular sort, which helps make one work may quite spoil another. "It would be quite delicate if it were not for that pale color there" may be said about the very color which is singled out in another picture as being largely responsible for its delicate quality. No doubt one way of putting this is to say that the features which make something delicate or graceful, and so on, are combined in a peculiar and unique way; that the aesthetic quality depends upon exactly this individual or unique combination of just these specific colors and shapes so that even a slight change might make all the difference. Nothing is to be achieved by trying to single out or separate features and generalizing about them.

I have now argued that in certain ways aesthetic concepts are not and cannot be condition- or rule-governed.[7] Not to be so governed is one of their essential characteristics. In arguing this I first claimed in a general way that no nonaesthetic features are possible candidates for conditions, and then considered more particularly both the "characteristic" *general* features associated with aesthetic terms and the individual or *specific* features found in particular objects. I have not attempted to examine what relationship these specific features of a work do bear to its aesthetic qualities. An examination of the locutions we use when we refer to them in the course of explaining or supporting our application of an aesthetic term reinforces with linguistic evidence the fact that we are certainly not offering them as explanatory or justifying *conditions*. When we are asked why we say a certain person is lazy or intelligent or courageous, we are being asked in virtue of what do we *call* him this; we reply with "because of the way he regularly leaves his work unfinished," or "because of the ease with which he handles such and such problems," and so on. But when we are asked to say why, in our opinion, a picture lacks balance or is somber in tone, or why a poem is moving or tightly organized, we are doing a different kind of thing. We may use similar locutions: "his verse has strength and variety *because of the way* he handles the meter and employs the caesura," or "it is nobly austere *because of* the lack of detail and the restricted palette." But we can also express what we want to by using quite other expressions: "it is the handling of meter and caesura which is *responsible for* its strength and variety," "its nobly austere quality is *due to* 'the lack of detail and the use of a restricted palette," "its lack of balance *results from* the highlighting of the figures on the left," "those minor chords *make it* extremely moving," "those converging lines *give it* an extraordinary unity." These are locutions we cannot switch to with "lazy" or "intelligent"; to say what *makes* him lazy, what is *responsible for* his laziness, what it is *due to*, is to broach another question entirely.

One after another, in recent discussions, writers have insisted that aesthetic judgments are not "mechanical": "Critics do not formulate general standards and apply these mechanically to all, or to classes of, works of art." "Technical points can be settled rapidly, by the application of rules," but aesthetic questions "cannot be settled by any mechanical method." Instead, these writers on aesthetics have emphasized that there is no "substitute for individual judgment" with its "spontaneity and speculation" and that "The final standard . . . [is] the judgment of personal taste."[8] What is surprising is that, though such things have been repeated again and again, no one seems to have said what is meant by "taste" or by the word "mechanical." There are many judgments besides those requiring taste which demand "spontaneity" and "individual judgment" and are not "mechanical." Without a detailed comparison we cannot see in what particular way *aesthetic* judgments are not "mechanical," or how they differ from those other judgments, nor can we begin to specify what taste is. This I have attempted. It is a characteristic and essential feature of judgments which employ an aesthetic term that they cannot be made by appealing, in the sense explained, to nonaesthetic conditions.[9] This, I believe, is a logical feature of aesthetic or taste judgments in general, though I have argued it here only as regards the more restricted range of judgments which employ aesthetic terms. It is part of what "taste" means.

*II*

A great deal of work remains to be done on aesthetic concepts. In the remainder of this paper I shall offer some further suggestions which may help towards an understanding of them.

The realization that aesthetic concepts are governed only negatively by conditions is likely to give rise to puzzlement over how we manage to apply the words in our aesthetic vocabulary. If we are not following rules and there are no conditions to appeal to, how are we to know when they are applicable? One very natural way to counter this question is to point out that some other sorts of concepts also are not condition-governed. We do not apply simple color words by following rules or in accordance with principles. We see that the book is red by looking, just as we tell that the tea is sweet by tasting it. So too, it might be said, we just see (or fail to see) that things are delicate, balanced, and the like. This kind of comparison between the exercise of taste and the use of the five senses is indeed familiar; our use of the word "taste" itself shows that the comparison is age-old and very natural. Yet whatever the similarities, there are great dissimilarities too. A careful comparison cannot be attempted here though it would be valuable; but certain differences stand out, and writers who have emphasized that aesthetic judgments are not "mechanical" have sometimes dwelt on and been puzzled by them.

In the first place, while our ability to discern aesthetic features is dependent upon our possession of good eyesight, hearing, and so on, people normally endowed with senses and understanding may nevertheless fail to discern them. "Those who listen to a concert, walk round a gallery, read a poem may have roughly similar sense perceptions, but some get a great deal more than others," Miss Macdonald says; but she adds that she is "puzzled by this feature 'in the object' which can be seen only by a specially qualified observer" and asks, "What is this 'something more'?"[10]

It is this difference between aesthetic and perceptual qualities which in part leads to the view that "works of art are esoteric objects . . . not simple objects of sense perception."[11] But there is no good reason for calling an object esoteric simply because we discern aesthetic qualities in it. The *objects* to which we apply aesthetic words are of the most diverse kinds and by no means esoteric: people and buildings, flowers and gardens, vases and furniture, as well as poems and music. Nor does there seem any good reason for calling the *qualities* themselves esoteric. It is true that someone with perfect eyes or ears might miss them, but we do after all say we *observe* or *notice* them. ("Did you notice how very graceful she was?," "Did you observe the exquisite balance in all his pictures?") In fact, they are very familiar indeed. We learn while quite young to use many aesthetic words, though they are, as one might expect from their dependence upon our ability to see, hear, distinguish colors, and the like, not the earliest words we learn; and our mastery and sophistication in using them develop along with the rest of our vocabulary. They are not rarities; some ranges of them are in regular use in everyday discourse.

The second notable difference between the exercise of taste and the use of the five senses lies in the way we support those judgments in which aesthetic concepts are employed. Although we use these concepts without rules or conditions, we do defend or support our judgments, and convince others of their rightness, by talking; "disputation about art is not futile," as Miss Macdonald says, for critics do "attempt a certain kind of explanation of works of art with the object of establishing correct judgments."[12] Thus even though this disputation does not consist in "deductive or inductive inference" or "reasoning," its occurrence is enough to show how very different these judgments are from those of a simple perceptual sort.

Now the critic's talk, it is clear, frequently consists in mentioning or pointing out the features, including easily discernible nonaesthetic ones, upon which the aesthetic qualities depend. But the puzzling question remains how, by mentioning these features, the critic is thereby justifying or supporting his judgments. To this question a number of recent writers have given an answer. Stuart Hampshire, for example, says that "One engages in aesthetic discussion for the sake of what one might see on the way. . . . If one has been brought to see what there is to be seen in the object, the purpose of discussion is achieved. . . . The point is to bring people to see these features."[13] The critic's talk, that is, often serves to support his judgments in a special way; it helps us to *see* what he has seen, namely, the aesthetic qualities of the object. But even when it is agreed that this is one of the main things that critics do, puzzlement tends to break out again over *how* they do it. How is it that by talking about features of the work (largely nonaesthetic ones) we can manage to bring others to see what they had not seen? "What sort of endowment is this which *talking* can modify? . . . Discussion does not improve eyesight and hearing" (my italics).[14]

Yet of course we do succeed in applying aesthetic terms, and we frequently do succeed by talking (and pointing and gesturing in certain ways) in bringing others to see what we see. One begins to suspect that puzzlement over how we can possibly do this, and puzzlement over the "esoteric" character of aesthetic qualities too, arises from bearing in mind inappropriate philosophical models. When someone is unable to see that the book on the table is brown, we cannot get him to see that it is by talking; consequently it seems puzzling that we might get someone to see that the vase is graceful by talking. If we are to dispel this puzzlement and recognize aesthetic concepts and qualities for what they are, we must abandon unsuitable models and investigate how we actually employ these concepts. With so much interest in and agreement about *what* the critic does, one might expect descriptions of *how* he does it to have been given. But little has been said about this, and what has been said is unsatisfactory.

Miss Macdonald,[15] for example, subscribes to this view of the critic's task as presenting "what is not obvious to casual or uninstructed inspection," and she does ask the question "What sort of considerations are involved, *and how*, to justify a critical verdict?" (my italics). But she does not in fact go on to answer it. She addresses herself instead to the different, though related, question of the interpretation of art works. In complex works different critics claim, often justifiably, to discern different features; hence Miss Macdonald suggests that in critical discourse the critic is bringing us to see what he sees by offering new interpretations. But if the question is "what (the critic) does and how he does it," he cannot be represented either wholly or even mainly as providing new interpretations. His task quite as often is simply to help us appreciate qualities which other critics have regularly found in the works he discusses. To put the stress upon *new* interpretations is to leave untouched the question how, by talking, he can help us to see *either* the newly appreciated aesthetic qualities *or* the old. In any case, besides complex poems or plays which may bear many interpretations, there are also relatively simple ones. There are also vases, buildings, and furniture, not to mention faces, sunsets, and scenery, about which no questions of "interpretation" arise but about which we talk in similar ways and make similar judgments. So the "puzzling" questions remain: how do we support these judgments and how do we bring others to see what we see?

Hampshire,[16] who likewise believes that the critic brings us "to see what there is to be seen in the object," does give some account of how the critic does this. "The greatest service of the critic" is to point out, isolate, and place in a frame of attention the "particular features of the particular object which *make* it ugly or beautiful"; for it is "difficult to see and hear all that there is to see and hear," and simply a prejudice to suppose that while "things really do have colors and shapes . . . there do not exist literally and objectively, concordances of colors and perceived rhythms and balances of shapes." However, these "extraordinary qualities" which the critic "may have seen (in the wider sense of 'see')"[17] are "qualities which are of no direct practical interest." Consequently, to bring us to see them the critic employs "an unnatural use of words in description"; "the common vocabulary, being created for practical purposes, obstructs any disinterested perception of things"; and so these qualities "are normally described metaphorically by some transference of terms from the common vocabulary."

Much of what Hampshire says is right. But there is also something quite wrong in the view that the "common" vocabulary "obstructs" our aesthetic purposes, that it is "unnatural" to take it over and use it metaphorically, and that the critic "is under the necessity of building . . . a vocabulary *in opposition to the main tendency of his language*" (my italics). First, while we do often coin new metaphors in order to describe aesthetic qualities, we are by no means always under the necessity of wresting the "common vocabulary" from its "natural" uses to serve our purposes. There does exist, as I observed earlier, a large and accepted vocabulary of aesthetic terms some of which, whatever their metaphorical origins, are now not metaphors at all, others of which are at most quasi-metaphorical. Second, this view that our use of metaphor and quasi-metaphor for aesthetic purposes is unnatural or a makeshift into which we are forced by a language designed for other purposes misrepresents fundamentally the character of aesthetic qualities and aesthetic language. There is nothing unnatural about using words like "forceful," "dynamic," or "tightly knit" in criticism; they do their work perfectly and are exactly the words needed for the purposes they serve. We do not want or need to replace them by words which lack the metaphorical element. In using them to describe works of art, the very point is that we are noticing aesthetic qualities related to their literal or common meanings. If we possessed a quite different word from "dynamic," one we could use to point out an aesthetic quality unrelated to the common meaning of "dynamic," it could not be used to describe that quality which "dynamic" does serve to point out. Hampshire pictures "a colony of aesthetes, disengaged from practical needs and manipulations" and says that "descriptions of aesthetic qualities, which for us are metaphorical, might seem to them to have an altogether literal and familiar sense"; they might use "a more directly descriptive vocabulary." But if they had a new and "directly descriptive" vocabulary lacking the links with nonaesthetic properties and interests which our vocabulary possesses, they would have to remain silent about many of the aesthetic qualities we can describe; further, if they were more completely "disengaged from practical needs" and other nonaesthetic awarenesses and interests, they would perforce be blind to many aesthetic qualities we can appreciate. The links between aesthetic qualities and nonaesthetic ones are both obvious and vital. Aesthetic concepts, all of them, carry with them attachments and in one way or another are tethered to or parasitic upon nonaesthetic features. The fact that many aesthetic terms are metaphorical or quasi-metaphorical in no way means that common language is an ill-adapted tool with which we have to struggle. When someone writes as Hampshire does, one suspects again that critical language is being judged against other models. To use language which is frequently metaphorical might be strange for some *other* purpose or from the standpoint of doing something else, but for the purpose and from the standpoint of making aesthetic observations it is not. To say it is an unnatural use of language for doing *this* is to imply there is or could be for this purpose some other and "natural" use. But these *are* natural ways of talking about aesthetic matters.

To help understand what the critic does, then, how he supports his judgments and gets his audience to see what he sees, I shall attempt a brief description of the methods we use as critics.[17]

(1) We may simply mention or point out nonaesthetic features: "Notice these flecks of color, that dark mass there, those lines." By merely drawing attention to those easily discernible features which make the painting luminous or warm or dynamic, we often succeed in bringing someone to see these aesthetic qualities. We get him to see B by mentioning something different, A. Sometimes in doing this we are drawing attention to features which may have gone unnoticed by an untrained or insufficiently attentive eye or ear: "Just listen for the repeated figure in the left hand." "Did you notice the figure of Icarus in the Breughel? It is very small." Sometimes they are features which have been seen or heard but of which the significance or purpose has been missed in any of a variety of ways: "Notice how much darker he has made the central figure, how much brighter these colors are than the adjacent ones," "Of course, you've observed the ploughman in the foreground; but had you considered how he, like everyone else in the picture, is going about his business without noticing the fall of Icarus?" In mentioning features which may be discerned by anyone with normal eyes, ears, and intelligence, we are singling out what may serve as a kind of key to grasping or seeing something else (and the key may not be the same for each person).

(2) On the other hand we often simply mention the very qualities we want people to see. We point to a painting and say, "Notice how nervous and delicate the drawing is," or "See what energy and vitality it has." The use of the aesthetic term itself may do the trick; we say what the quality or character is, and people who had not seen it before see it.

(3) Most often, there is a linking of remarks about aesthetic and nonaesthetic features: "Have you noticed this line and that, and the points of bright color here and there . . . don't they give it vitality, energy?"

(4) We do, in addition, often make extensive and helpful use of similes and genuine metaphors: "It's as if there were small points of light burning," "as though he had thrown on the paint violently and in anger," "the light shimmers, the lines dance, everything is air, lightness, and gaiety," "his canvasses are fires, they crackle, burn, and blaze, even at their most subdued always restlessly flickering, but often bursting into flame, great pyrotechnic displays," and so on.

(5) We make use of contrasts, comparisons, and reminiscences: "Suppose he had made that a lighter yellow, moved it to the right, how flat it would have been." "Don't you think it has something of the quality of a Rembrandt?" "Hasn't it the same serenity, peace, and quality of light of those summer evenings in Norfolk?" We use what keys we have to the known sensitivity, susceptibilities, and experience of our audience.

Critics and commentators may range, in their methods, from one extreme to the other, from painstaking concentration on points of detail, line and color, vowels and rhymes, to more or less flowery and luxuriant metaphor. Even the enthusiastic biographical sketch decorated with suitable epithet and metaphor may serve. What is best depends on both the audience and the work under discussion. But this would not be a complete sketch unless certain other notes were added.

(6) Repetition and reiteration often play an important role. When we are in front of a canvas we may come back time and again to the same points, drawing attention to the same lines and shapes, repeating the same words, "swirling," "balance," "luminosity," or the same similes and metaphors, as if time and familiarity, looking harder, listening more carefully, paying closer attention, may help. So again with variation; it often helps to talk round what we have said, to build up, supplement with more talk *of the same kind.* When someone misses the swirling quality, when one epithet or one metaphor does not work, we throw in related ones; we speak of its wild movement, how it twists and turns, writhes and whirls, as though, failing to score a direct hit, we may succeed with a barrage of near-synonyms.

(7) Finally, besides our verbal performances, the rest of our behavior is important. We accompany our talk with appropriate tones of voice, expression, nods, looks, and gestures. A critic may sometimes do more with a sweep of the arm than by talking. An appropriate gesture may make us see the violence in a painting or the character of a melodic line.

These ways of acting and talking are not significantly different whether we are dealing with a particular work, paragraph, or line, or speaking of an artist's work as a whole, or even drawing attention to a sunset or scenery. But even with the speaker doing all this, we may fail to see what he sees. There may be a point, though there need be no limit except that imposed by time and patience, at which he gives up and sets us (or himself) down as lacking in some way, defective in sensitivity. He may tell us to look or read again, or to read or look at other things and then come back again to this; he may suspect there are experiences in life we have missed. But these are the things he does. This is what succeeds if anything does; indeed it is all that can be done.

By realizing clearly that, whether we are dealing with art or scenery or people or natural objects, this is how we operate with aesthetic concepts, we may recognize this sphere of human activity for what it is. We operate with different kinds of concepts in different ways. If we want someone to agree that a color is red we may take it into a good light and ask him to look; if it is viridian we may fetch a color chart and make him compare; if we want him to agree that a figure is fourteen-sided we get him to count; and to bring him to agree that something is dilapidated or that someone is intelligent or lazy we may do other things, citing features, reasoning and arguing about them, weighing and balancing. These are the methods appropriate to these various concepts. But the ways we get someone to see aesthetic qualities are different; they are of the kind I have described. With each kind of concept we can describe what we do and how we do it. But the methods suited to these other concepts will not do for aesthetic ones, or vice versa. We cannot prove by argument or by assembling a sufficiency of conditions that something is graceful; but this is no more puzzling than our inability to prove, by using the methods, metaphors, and gestures of the art critic, that it will be mate in ten moves. The questions raised admit of no answer beyond the sort of description I have given. To go on to ask, with puzzlement, how it is that *when* we do these things people come to see, is like asking how is it that, when we take the book into a good light, our companion agrees with us that it is red. There is no place for this kind of question or puzzlement. Aesthetic concepts are as natural, as little esoteric, as any others. It is against the background of different and philosophically more familiar models that they seem queer or puzzling.

I have described how people justify aesthetic judgments and bring others to see aesthetic qualities in things. I shall end by showing that the methods I have outlined are the ones natural for and characteristic of taste concepts from the start. When someone tries to make me see that a painting is delicate or balanced, I have some understanding of these terms already and know in a sense what I am looking for. But if there is puzzlement over how, by talking, he can bring me to see these qualities in this picture, there should be a corresponding puzzlement over how I learned to use aesthetic terms and discern aesthetic qualities in the first place. We may ask, therefore, how we learn to do these things; and this is to inquire (1) what natural potentialities and tendencies people have and (2) how we develop and take advantage of these capacities in training and teaching. Now for the second of these, there is no doubt that our ability to notice and respond to aesthetic qualities is cultivated and developed by our contacts with parents and teachers from quite an early age. What is interesting for my present purpose is that, while we are being taught in the presence of examples what grace, delicacy, and so on are, the methods used, the language and behavior, are of a piece with those of the critic as I have already described them.

To pursue these two questions, consider first those words like "dynamic," "melancholy," "balanced," "taut," or "gay" the aesthetic use of which is quasi-metaphorical. It has already been emphasized that we could not use them thus without some experience of situations where they are used literally. The present inquiry is how we shift from literal to aesthetic uses of them. For this it is required that there be certain abilities and tendencies to link experiences, to regard certain things as similar, and to see, explore, and be interested in these similarities. It is a feature of human intelligence and sensitivity that we do spontaneously do these things and that the tendency can be encouraged and developed. It is no more baffling that we should employ aesthetic terms of this sort than that we should make metaphors at all. Easy and smooth transitions by which we shift to the use of these aesthetic terms are not hard to find. We suggest to children that simple pieces of music are hurrying or running or skipping or dawdling, from there we move to lively, gay, jolly, happy, smiling, or sad, and, as their experiences and vocabulary broaden, to solemn, dynamic, or melancholy. But the child also discovers for himself many of these parallels and takes interest or delight in them. He is likely on his own to skip, march, clap, or laugh with the music, and without this natural tendency our training would get nowhere. Insofar, however, as we do take advantage of this tendency and help him by training, *we do just what the critic does.* We may merely need to persuade the child to pay attention, to look or listen; or we may simply *call* the music jolly. But we are also likely to use, as the critic does, reiteration, synonyms, parallels, contrasts, similes, metaphors, gestures, and other expressive behavior.

Of course the recognition of similarities and simple metaphorical extensions are not the only transitions to the aesthetic use of language. Others are made in different ways; for instance, by the kind of peripheral cases I mentioned earlier. When our admiration is for something as simple as the thinness of a glass or the smoothness of a fabric, it is not difficult to call attention to such things, evoke a similar delight, and introduce suitable aesthetic terms. These transitions are only the beginnings; it may often be questionable whether a term is yet being used aesthetically or not. Many of the terms I have mentioned may be used in ways which are not straightforwardly literal but of which we should hesitate to say that they demanded much yet by way of aesthetic sensitivity. We speak of warm and cool colors, and we may say of a brightly colored picture that at least it is gay and lively. When we have brought someone to make this sort of metaphorical extension of terms, he has made one of the transitional steps from which he may move on to uses which more obviously deserve to be called aesthetic and demand more aesthetic appreciation. When I said at the outset that aesthetic sensitivity was rarer than some other natural endowments, I was not denying that it varies in degree from the rudimentary to the refined. Most people learn easily to make the kinds of remarks I am now considering. But when someone can call bright canvasses gay and lively without being able to spot the one which is really vibrant, or can recognize the obvious outward vigor and energy of a student composition played *con fuoco* while failing to see that it lacks inner fire and drive, we do not regard his aesthetic sensitivity in these areas as particularly developed. However, once these transitions from common to aesthetic uses are begun in the more obvious cases, the domain of aesthetic concepts may broaden out, and they may become more subtle and even partly autonomous. The initial steps, however varied the metaphorical shifts and however varied the experiences upon which they are parasitic, are natural and easy.

Much the same is true when we turn to those words which have no standard nonaesthetic use, "lovely," "pretty," "dainty," "graceful," "elegant." We cannot say that these are learned by a metaphorical shift. But they still are linked to nonaesthetic features in many ways and the learning of them also is made possible by certain kinds of natural response, reaction, and ability. We learn them not so much by noticing similarities, but by our attention being caught and focused in other ways. Certain phenomena which are outstanding or remarkable or unusual catch the eye or ear, seize our attention and interest, and move us to surprise, admiration, delight, fear, or distaste. Children begin by reacting in these ways to spectacular sunsets, woods in autumn, roses, dandelions, and other striking and colorful objects, and it is in these circumstances that we find ourselves introducing general aesthetic words to them, like "lovely," "pretty," and "ugly." It is not an accident that the first lessons in aesthetic appreciation consist in drawing the child's attention to roses rather than to grass; nor is it surprising that we remark to him on the autumn colors rather than on the subdued tints of winter. We all of us, not only children, pay aesthetic attention more readily and easily to such outstanding and easily noticeable things. We notice with pleasure early spring grass or the first snow, hills of notably marked and varied contours, scenery flecked with a great variety of color or dappled variously with sun and shadow. We are struck and impressed by great size or mass, as with mountains or cathedrals. We are similarly responsive to unusual precision or minuteness or remarkable feats of skill, as with complex and elaborate filigree, or intricate wood carving and fan vaulting. It is at these times, taking advantage of these natural interests and admirations, that we first teach the simpler aesthetic words. People of moderate aesthetic sensitivity and sophistication continue to exhibit aesthetic interest mainly on such occasions and to use only the more general words ("pretty," "lovely," and the like). But these situations may serve as a beginning from which we extend our aesthetic interests to wider and less obvious fields, mastering as we go the more subtle and specific vocabulary of taste. The principles do not change; the basis for learning more specific terms like "graceful," "delicate," and "elegant" is also our interest in and admiration for various nonaesthetic natural properties ("She seems to move *effortlessly*, as if floating," "So very *thin* and *fragile*, as if a breeze might destroy it," "So *small* and yet so *intricate*," "So *economical* and *perfectly adapted*").[18] And even with these aesthetic terms which are not metaphorical themselves ("graceful," "delicate," "elegant"), we rely in the same way upon the critic's methods, including comparison, illustration, and metaphor, to teach or make clear what they mean.

I have wished to emphasize in the latter part of this paper the natural basis of responses of various kinds without which aesthetic terms could not be learned. I have also outlined what some of the features are to which we naturally respond: similarities of various sorts, notable colors, shapes, scents, size, intricacy, and much else besides. Even the non-metaphorical aesthetic terms have significant links with all kinds of natural features by which our interest, wonder, admiration, delight, or distaste is aroused. But in particular I have wanted to urge that it should not strike us as puzzling that the critic supports his judgments and brings us to see aesthetic qualities by pointing out key features and talking about them in the way he does. It is by the very same methods that people helped us develop our aesthetic sense and master its vocabulary from the beginning. If we responded to those methods then, it is not surprising that we respond to the critic's discourse now. It would be surprising if, by using this language and behavior, people could *not* sometimes bring us to see the aesthetic qualities of things; for this would prove us lacking in one characteristically human kind of awareness and activity.

*Notes*

1. I shall speak loosely of an "aesthetic term," even when, because the word sometimes has other uses, it would be more correct to speak of its *use* as an aesthetic term. I shall also speak of "nonaesthetic" words, concepts, features, and so on. None of the terms other writers use, "natural," "observable," "perceptual,"

"physical," "objective" (qualities), "neutral," "descriptive" (language), when they approach the distinction I am making, is really apt for my purpose.

2. A contrast will reinforce this. If a critic were to describe a passage of music as chattering, carbonated, or gritty, a painter's coloring as vitreous, farinaceous, or effervescent, or a writer's style as glutinous, or abrasive, he *would* be using live metaphors rather than drawing on the more normal language of criticism. Words like "athletic," "vertiginous," "silken" may fall somewhere between.

3. In a paper reprinted in *Aesthetics and Language*, ed. W. Elton (Oxford, 1954), pp. 131–146, Arnold Isenberg discusses certain problems about aesthetic concepts and qualities. Like others who approach these problems, he does not isolate them, as I do, from questions about verdicts on the *merits* of works of art, or from questions about *likings* and *preferences*. He says something parallel to my remarks above: "There is not in all the world's criticism a single purely descriptive statement concerning which one is prepared to say beforehand, 'if it is true, I shall *like* that work so much the better'" (p. 139, my italics). I should think *this* is highly questionable.

4. Isenberg (*op. cit.*, p. 132) makes a somewhat similar but mistaken point: "If we had been told that the colors of a certain painting are garish, it would be *astonishing* to find that they are *all* very pale and unsaturated" (my italics). But if we say "all" rather than "predominantly," then "astonishing" is the wrong word. The word that goes with "all" is "impossible"; "astonishing" might go with "predominantly."

5. H. L. A. Hart, "The Ascription of Responsibility and Rights" in *Logic and Language*, 1st ser., ed. A. G. N. Flew (Oxford, 1951). Hart indeed speaks of "conditions" throughout, see p. 148.

6. I cannot in the compass of this paper discuss the other types of apparent exceptions to my thesis. Cases where a man *lacking* in sensitivity might learn and follow a rule, as above, ought to be distinguished from cases where someone who *possesses* sensitivity might know, from a nonaesthetic description, that an aesthetic term applies. I have stated my thesis as though this latter kind of case never occurs because I have had my eye on the logical features of *typical* aesthetic judgments and have preferred to over- rather than understate my view. But with certain aesthetic terms, especially negative ones, there may perhaps be some rare genuine exceptions when a description enables us to visualize very fully, and when what is described belongs to certain restricted classes of things, say human faces or animal forms. Perhaps a description like "One eye red and rheumy, the other missing, a wart-covered nose, a twisted mouth, a greenish pallor" may justify in a strong sense ("must be," "cannot but be,") the judgments "ugly" or "hideous." If so, such cases are marginal, form a very small minority, and are uncharacteristic or atypical of aesthetic judgments in general. Usually when, on hearing a description, we say "it *must* be very beautiful (graceful, or the like)," we mean no more than "it surely must be, it's only remotely possible that it isn't." Different again are situations, and these are very numerous, where we can move quite simply from "bright colors" to "gay," or from "reds and yellows" to "warm," but where we are as yet only on the borderline of anything that could be called an expression of taste or aesthetic sensibility. I have stressed the importance of this transitional and border area between nonaesthetic and obviously aesthetic judgments in Section II.

7. Helen Knight says (Elton, *op. cit.,* p. 152) that "piquant" (one of my "aesthetic" terms) "depends on" various features (a *retroussé* nose, a pointed chin, and the like), and that these features are *criteria* for it; this second claim is what I am denying. She also maintains that "good," when applied to works of art, depends on *criteria* like balance, solidity, depth, profundity (my aesthetic terms again; I should place piquancy in this list). I would deny this too, though I regard it as a different question and do not consider it in this paper. The two questions need separating: the relation of nonaesthetic features (*retroussé*, pointed) to aesthetic qualities, and the relation of aesthetic qualities to "aesthetically good" (verdicts). Most writings which touch on the nature of aesthetic concepts have this other (verdict) question mainly in mind. Mrs. Knight blurs this difference when she says, for example, "'piquant' is the same kind of word as 'good.'"

8. See articles by Margaret Macdonald and J. A. Passmore in Elton, *op. cit.,* pp. 118, 41, 40, 119.

9. As I indicated, above, I have dealt only with the relation of *nonaesthetic* to aesthetic features. Perhaps a description in *aesthetic* terms may occasionally suffice for applying another aesthetic term. Johnson's Dictionary gives "handsome" as "beautiful with dignity"; Shorter O. E. D. gives "pretty" as "beautiful in a slight, dainty, or diminutive way."

10. Macdonald in Elton, *op. cit.,* pp. 114, 119. See also pp. 120, 122.

11. Macdonald, *ibid.,* pp. 114, 120–123. She speaks of nonaesthetic properties here as "physical" or "observable" qualities, and distinguishes between "physical object" and "work of art."

12. *Ibid.,* 115–116; cf. also John Holloway, *Proceedings of the Aristotelian Society,* supp. vol. 23 (1949), pp. 175–176.

13. Stuart Hampshire in Elton, *op. cit.,* p. 165. Cf. also remarks in Elton by Isenberg (pp. 142, 145), by Passmore (p. 38), in *Philosophy and Psychoanalysis* by John Wisdom (Oxford, 1953), pp. 223–224, and in Holloway, *op. cit.,* p. 175.

14. Macdonald, *op. cit.,* pp. 119–120.

15. *Ibid.,* see pp. 127, 122, 125, 115. Other writers also place the stress on interpretation, cf. Holloway, *op. cit.,* p. 173 ff.

16. *Op. cit.,* pp. 165–168.

17. Holloway, *op. cit.,* pp. 173–174, lists some of these very briefly.

18. It is worth noticing that most of the words which in current usage are primarily or exclusively aesthetic terms had earlier nonaesthetic uses and gained their present use by some kind of metaphorical shift. Without reposing too great weight on these etymological facts, it can be seen that their history reflects connections with the responses, interests, and natural features I have mentioned as underlying the learning and use of aesthetic terms. These transitions suggest both the dependence of aesthetic upon other interests, and what some of these interests are. Connected with liking, delight, affection, regard, estimation, or choice—*beautiful, graceful, delicate, lovely, exquisite, elegant, dainty*: with fear or repulsion—*ugly*; with what notably catches the eye or attention—*garish, splendid, gaudy*: with what attracts by notable rarity, precision, skill, ingenuity, elaboration—*dainty, nice, pretty, exquisite*; with adaptation to function, suitability to ease of handling—*handsome*.

# 3.　　　　　　　　　　　　　　Categories of Art
## KENDALL L. WALTON

*I Introduction*

> False judgments enter art history if we judge from the impression
> which pictures of different epochs, placed side by side, make on
> us. . . . They speak a different language.[1]

Paintings and sculptures are to be looked at; sonatas and songs are to be
heard. What is important about these works of art, as works of art, is
what can be seen or heard in them.[2] Inspired partly by apparent commonplaces such as these, many recent aesthetic theorists have attempted
to purge from criticism of works of art supposedly extraneous excursions
into matters not (or not "directly") available to inspection of the works,
and to focus attention on the works themselves. Circumstances connected
with a work's origin, in particular, are frequently held to have no essential
bearing on an assessment of its aesthetic nature—for example, who created
the work, how, and when; the artist's intentions and expectations concerning it, his philosophical views, psychological state, and love life; the artistic
traditions and intellectual atmosphere of his society. Once produced (it is
argued) the work must stand or fall on its own; it must be judged for what
it is, regardless of how it came to be as it is.

Arguments for the irrelevance of such historical circumstances to aesthetic judgments about works of art may, but need not, involve the claim
that these circumstances are not of "aesthetic" interest or importance,
though obviously they are often important in biographical, historical,
psychological, or sociological researches. One might consider an artist's
action in producing a work to be aesthetically interesting, an "aesthetic

From *The Philosophical Review*, LXXIX (1970), 334–367. Reprinted with permission of the
author and *The Philosophical Review*.

object" in its own right, while vehemently maintaining its irrelevance to an aesthetic investigation of the work. Robert Rauschenberg once carefully obliterated a drawing by de Kooning, titled the bare canvas "Erased De Kooning Drawing," framed it, and exhibited it.[3] His doing this might be taken as symbolic or expressive (of an attitude toward art, or toward life in general, or whatever) in an "aesthetically" significant manner, perhaps somewhat as an action of a character in a play might be, and yet thought to have no bearing whatever on the aesthetic nature of the finished product. The issue I am here concerned with is how far critical questions about works of art can be *separated* from questions about their histories.[4]

One who wants to make this separation quite sharp may regard the basic facts of art along the following lines. Works of art are simply objects with various properties, of which we are primarily interested in perceptual ones—visual properties of paintings, audible properties of music, and so forth.[5] A work's perceptual properties include "'aesthetic" as well as "nonaesthetic" ones—the sense of mystery and tension of a painting as well as its dark coloring and diagonal composition; the energy, exuberance, and coherence of a sonata, as well as its meters, rhythms, pitches, timbres, and so forth; the balance and serenity of a Gothic cathedral as well as its dimensions, lines, and symmetries.[6] Aesthetic properties are features or characteristics of works of art just as much as nonaesthetic ones are.[7] They are *in* the works, to be seen, heard, or otherwise perceived there. Seeing a painting's sense of mystery or hearing a sonata's coherence might require looking or listening longer or harder than does perceiving colors and shapes, rhythms and pitches; it may even require special training or a special kind of sensitivity. But these qualities must be discoverable simply by examining the works themselves if they are discoverable at all. It is never even partly *in virtue* of the circumstances of a work's origin that it has a sense of mystery or is coherent or serene. Such circumstances sometimes provide hints concerning what to look for in a work, what we might reasonably expect to find by examining it. But these hints are always theoretically dispensable; a work's aesthetic properties must "in principle" be ascertainable without their help. Surely (it seems) a Rembrandt portrait does not have (or lack) a sense of mystery in virtue of the fact that Rembrandt intended it to have (or to lack) that quality, any more than a contractor's intention to make a roof leakproof makes it so; nor is the portrait mysterious in virtue of any other facts about what Rembrandt thought or how he went about painting the portrait or what his society happened to be like. Such circumstances are important to the result only insofar as they had an effect on the pattern of paint splotches that became attached to the canvas, and the canvas can be examined without in any way considering how the splotches got there. It would not matter in the least to the aesthetic properties of the portrait if the paint had been applied to the canvas not by Rembrandt at all, but by a chimpanzee or a cyclone in a paint shop.

The view sketched above can easily seem very persuasive. But the tendency of critics to discuss the histories of works of art in the course of justifying aesthetic judgments about them has been remarkably persistent. This is partly because hints derived from facts about a work's history, however dispensable they may be "in principle," are often crucially important in practice. (One might simply not think to listen for a recurring series of intervals in a piece of music, until he learns that the composer meant the work to be structured around it.) No doubt it is partly due also to genuine confusions on the part of critics. But I will argue that (some) facts about the origins of works of art have an *essential* role in criticism, that aesthetic judgments rest on them in an absolutely fundamental way. For this reason, and for another as well, the view that works of art should be judged simply by what can be perceived in them is seriously misleading, though there is something right in the idea that what matters aesthetically about a painting or a sonata is just how it looks or sounds.

## II Standard, Variable, and Contra-Standard Properties

I will continue to call tension, mystery, energy, coherence, balance, serenity, sentimentality, pallidness, disunity, grotesqueness, and so forth, as well as colors and shapes, pitches and timbres *properties* of works of art, though "property" is to be construed broadly enough not to beg any important questions. I will also, following Sibley, call properties of the former sort "aesthetic" properties, but purely for reasons of convenience I will include in this category "representational" and "resemblance" properties, which Sibley excludes—for example, the property of representing or being a picture of Napoleon, that of depicting an old man (as) stooping over a fire, that of resembling, or merely suggesting, a human face, claws (the petals of Van Gogh's sunflowers), or (in music) footsteps or conversation. It is not essential for my purposes to delimit with any exactness the class of aesthetic properties (if indeed any such delimitation is possible), for I am more interested in discussing particular examples of such properties than in making generalizations about the class as a whole. It will be obvious, however, that what I say about the examples I deal with is also applicable to a great many other properties we would want to call aesthetic.

Sibley points out that a work's aesthetic properties depend on its nonaesthetic properties; the former are "emergent" or "*Gestalt*" properties based on the latter.[8] I take this to be true of all the examples of aesthetic properties we will be dealing with, including representational and resemblance ones. It is because of the configuration of colors and shapes on a painting, perhaps in particular its dark colors and diagonal composition, that it has a sense of mystery and tension, if it does. The colors and shapes of a portrait are responsible for its resembling an old man and (perhaps with its title) its depicting an old man. The coherence or unity of a piece of music (for example, Beethoven's *Fifth Symphony*) may be largely due to the frequent recurrence of a rhythmic motive, and the regular meter of a song plus the absence of harmonic modulation and of large intervals in the voice part may make it serene or peaceful.

Moreover, a work *seems* or *appears* to us to have certain aesthetic properties because we observe in it, or it appears to us to have, certain nonaesthetic features (though it may not be necessary to notice consciously all the relevant nonaesthetic features). A painting depicting an old man may not look like an old man to someone who is color-blind, or when it is seen from an extreme angle or in bad lighting conditions so that its colors or shapes are distorted or obscured. Beethoven's *Fifth Symphony* performed in such a sloppy manner that many occurrences of the four-note rhythmic motive do not sound similar may seem incoherent or disunified.

I will argue, however, that a work's aesthetic properties depend not only on its nonaesthetic ones, but also on which of its nonaesthetic properties are "standard," which "variable," and which "contra-standard," in senses to be explained. I will approach this thesis by way of the psychological point that what aesthetic properties a work seems to us to have depends not only on what nonaesthetic features we perceive in it, but also on which of them are standard, which variable, and which contra-standard *for us* (in a sense also to be explained).

It is necessary to introduce first a distinction between standard, variable, and contra-standard properties relative to perceptually distinguishable categories of works of art. Such categories include media, genre, styles, forms, and so forth—for example, the categories of paintings, cubist paintings, Gothic architecture, classical sonatas, paintings in the style of Cézanne, and music in the style of late Beethoven—if they are interpreted in such a way that membership is determined solely by features that can be perceived in a work when it is experienced in the normal manner. Thus whether or not a piece of music was written in the eighteenth century is irrelevant to whether it belongs to the category of classical sonatas (interpreted in this way), and whether a work was produced by Cézanne or Beethoven has nothing essential to do with whether it is in the style of Cézanne or late Beethoven. The category of etchings as normally construed is not perceptually distinguishable in the requisite sense, for to be an etching is, I take it, simply to have been produced in a particular manner. But the category of *apparent* etchings, works which *look* like etchings from the quality of their lines, whether they are etchings or not, is perceptually distinguishable. A category will not count as "perceptually distinguishable" in my sense if in order to determine perceptually whether something belongs to it, it is necessary (in some or all cases) to determine which categories it is correctly perceived in partly or wholly on the basis of nonperceptual considerations. (See Section IV below.) This prevents, for example, the category of serene things from being perceptually distinguishable in this sense.

A feature of a work of art is *standard* with respect to a (perceptually distinguishable) category just in case it is among those in virtue of which works in that category belong to that category—that is, just in case the lack of that feature would disqualify, or tend to disqualify, a work from that category. A feature is *variable* with respect to a category just in case it has nothing to do with works' belonging to that category; the possession or lack of the feature is irrelevant to whether a work qualifies for the category. Finally, a *contra-standard* feature with respect to a category is the absence of a standard feature with respect to that category—that is, a feature whose presence tends to *disqualify* works as members of the category. Needless to say, it will not be clear in *all* cases whether a feature of a work is standard, variable, or contra-standard relative to a given category, since the criteria for classifying works of art are far from precise. But clear examples are abundant. The flatness of a painting and the motionlessness of its markings are standard, and its particular shapes and colors are variable, relative to the category of painting. A protruding three-dimensional object or an electrically driven twitching of the canvas would be contra-standard relative to this category. The straight lines in stick-figure drawings and squarish shapes in cubist paintings are standard with respect to those categories respectively, though they are variable with respect to the categories of drawing and painting. The exposition-development-recapitulation form of a classical sonata is standard, and its thematic material is variable, relative to the category of sonatas.

In order to explain what I mean by features being standard, variable, or contra-standard *for a person on a particular occasion,* I must introduce the notion of perceiving a work in, or as belonging to, a certain (perceptually distinguishable) category.[9] To perceive a work in a certain category is to perceive the "*Gestalt*" of that category in the work. This needs some explanation. People familiar with Brahmsian music—that is, music in the style of Brahms (notably, works of Johannes Brahms)—or impressionist paintings can frequently recognize members of these categories by recognizing the Brahmsian or impressionist *Gestalt* qualities. Such recognition is dependent on perception of particular features that are standard relative to these categories, but it is not a matter of *inferring* from the presence of such features that a work is Brahmsian or impressionist. One may not notice many of the relevant features, and he may be very vague about which ones are relevant. If I recognize a work as Brahmsian by first noting its lush textures, its basically traditional harmonic and formal structure, its superimposition and alternation of duple and triple meters, and so forth, and recalling that these characteristics are typical of Brahmsian works, I have not recognized it by hearing the Brahmsian *Gestalt*. To do that is simply to recognize it by its Brahmsian *sound*, without necessarily paying attention to the features ("cues") responsible for it. Similarly, recognizing an impressionist painting by its impressionist *Gestalt*, is recognizing the impressionist *look* about it, which we are familiar with from other impressionist paintings; not applying a rule we have learned for recognizing it from its features.

To *perceive* a *Gestalt* quality in a work—that is, to perceive it in a certain category—is not, or not merely, to *recognize* that *Gestalt* quality. Recognition is a momentary occurrence, whereas perceiving a quality is a continuous state which may last for a short or long time. (For the same reason, seeing the ambiguous duck-rabbit figure as a duck is not, or not merely, recognizing a property of it.) We perceive the Brahmsian or impressionist *Gestalt* in a work when, and as long as, it *sounds* (*looks*) Brahmsian or impressionist to us. This involves perceiving (not necessarily being aware of) features standard relative to that category. But it is not *just* this, nor this plus the intellectual realization that these features make the work Brahmsian, or impressionist. These features are perceived combined into a single *Gestalt* quality.

We can of course perceive a work in several or many different categories at once. A Brahms sonata might be heard simultaneously as a piece of music, a sonata, a romantic work, and a Brahmsian work. Some pairs of categories, however, seem to be such that one cannot perceive a work as belonging to both at once, much as one cannot see the duck-rabbit both as a duck and as a rabbit simultaneously. One cannot see a photographic image simultaneously as a still photograph and as (part of) a film, nor can one see something both in the category of paintings and at the same time in the category (to be explained shortly) of *guernicas*.

It will be useful to point out some of the *causes* of our perceiving works in certain categories. (*a*) In which categories we perceive a work depends in part, of course, on what other works we are familiar with. The more works of a certain sort we have experienced, the more likely it is that we will perceive a particular work in that category. (*b*) What we have heard critics and others say about works we have experienced, how they have categorized them, and what resemblances they have pointed out to us is also important. If no one has ever explained to me what is distinctive about Schubert's style (as opposed to the styles of, say, Schumann, Mendelssohn, Beethoven, Brahms, Hugo Wolf), or even pointed out that there is such a distinctive style, I may never have learned to hear the Schubertian *Gestalt* quality, even if I have heard many of Schubert's works, and so I may not hear his works as Schubertian. (*c*) How we are introduced to the particular work in question may be involved. If a Cézanne painting is exhibited in a collection of French Impressionist works, or if before seeing it we are told that it is French Impressionist, we are more likely to see it as French Impressionist than if it is exhibited in a random collection and we are not told anything about it beforehand.

I will say that a feature of a work is standard for a particular person on a particular occasion when, and only when, it is standard relative to some category in which he perceives it, and is not contra-standard relative to any category in which he perceives it. A feature is variable for a person on an occasion just when it is variable relative to *all* the categories in which he perceives it. And a feature is contra-standard for a person on an occasion just when it is contra-standard relative to *any* of the categories in which he perceives it.[10]

## III A Point About Perception

I turn now to my psychological thesis that what aesthetic properties a work seems to have, what aesthetic effect it has on us, how it strikes us aesthetically often depends (in part) on which of its features are standard, which variable, and which contra-standard for us. I offer a series of examples in support of this thesis.

(*a*) Representational and resemblance properties provide perhaps the most obvious illustration of this thesis. Many works of art look like or resemble other objects—people, buildings, mountains, bowls of fruit, and so forth. Rembrandt's "Titus Reading" looks like a boy, and in particular like Rembrandt's son; Picasso's "Les Demoiselles d'Avignon" looks like five women, four standing and one sitting (though not *especially* like any particular women). A portrait may even be said to be a *perfect* likeness of the sitter, or to capture his image *exactly*.

An important consideration in determining whether a work *depicts* or *represents* a particular object, or an object of a certain sort (for example, Rembrandt's son, or simply *a* boy), in the sense of being a picture, sculpture, or whatever of it[11] is whether the work resembles that object, or objects of that kind. A significant degree of resemblance is, I suggest, a necessary condition in most contexts for such representation or depiction,[12] though the resemblance need not be obvious at first glance. If we are unable to see a similarity between a painting purportedly of a woman and women, I think we would have to suppose either that there is such a similarity which we have not yet discovered (as one might fail to see a face in a maze of lines), or that it simply is not a picture of a woman. Resemblance is of course not a *sufficient* condition for representation, since a portrait (containing only one figure) might resemble both the sitter and his twin brother equally but is not a portrait of both of them. (The title might determine which of them it depicts.)[13]

It takes only a touch of perversity, however, to find much of our talk about resemblances between works of art and other things preposterous. Paintings and people are *very* different sorts of things. Paintings are pieces of canvas supporting splotches of paint, while people are live, three-dimensional, flesh-and-blood animals. Moreover, except rarely and under special conditions of observation (probably including bad lighting) paintings and people *look* very different. Paintings look like pieces of canvas (or anyway flat surfaces) covered with paint and people look like flesh-and-blood animals. There is practically no danger of confusing them. How, then, can anyone seriously hold that a portrait resembles the sitter to any significant extent, let alone that it is a perfect likeness of him? Yet it remains true that many paintings strike us as resembling people, sometimes very much or even exactly—despite the fact that they look so very different!

To resolve this paradox we must recognize that the resemblances we perceive between, for example, portraits and people, those that are relevant in determining what works of art depict or represent, are resemblances of a somewhat special sort, tied up with the categories in which we perceive such works. The properties of a work which are standard for us are ordinarily irrelevant to what we take it to look like or resemble in the relevant sense, and hence to what we take it to depict or represent. The properties of a portrait which make it *so* different from, so easily distinguishable from, a person—such as its flatness and its *painted* look—are standard for us. Hence these properties just do not count with regard to what (or whom) it looks like. It is only the properties which are variable for us, the colors and shapes on the work's surface, that make it look to us like what it does. And these are the ones which are taken as relevant in determining what (if anything) the work represents.[14]

Other examples will reinforce this point. A marble bust of a Roman emperor seems to us to resemble a man with, say, an aquiline nose, a wrinkled brow, and an expression of grim determination, and we take it to represent a man with, or as having, those characteristics. But why don't we say that it resembles and represents a perpetually motionless man, of uniform (marble) color, who is severed at the chest? It is similar to such a man, it seems, and much more so than to a normally colored, mobile, and whole man. But we are not struck by the former similarity when we see the bust, obvious though it is on reflection. The bust's uniform color, motionlessness, and abrupt ending at the chest are standard properties relative to the category of busts, and since we see it as a bust they are standard for us. Similarly, black-and-white drawings do not look to us like colorless scenes and we do not take them to depict things as being colorless, nor do we regard stick-figure drawings as resembling and depicting only very thin people. A cubist work might look like a person with a cubical head to someone not familiar with the cubist style. But the standardness of such cubical shapes for people who see it as a cubist work prevents them from making that comparison.

The shapes of a painting or a still photograph of a high jumper in action are motionless, but these pictures do not look to us like a high jumper frozen in mid-air. Indeed, depending on features of the pictures which are variable for us (for example, the exact positions of the figures, swirling brush strokes in the painting, slight blurrings of the photographic image) the athlete may seem in a frenzy of activity; the pictures may convey a vivid sense of movement. But if static images exactly like those of the two pictures occur in a motion picture, and we see it as a motion picture, they probably would strike us as resembling a static athlete. This is because the immobility of the images is standard relative to the category of still pictures and variable relative to that of motion pictures. (Since we are so familiar with still pictures it might be difficult to see the static images as motion pictures for very long, rather than as [filmed] still pictures. But we could not help seeing them that way if we had no acquaintance at all with the medium of still pictures.) My point here is brought out by the tremendous aesthetic difference we are likely to experience between a film of a dancer moving *very* slowly and a still picture of him, even if "objectively" the two images are very nearly identical. We might well find the former studied, calm, deliberate, laborious, and the latter dynamic, energetic, flowing, or frenzied.

In general, then, what we regard a work as resembling, and as representing, depends on the properties of the work which are variable, and not on those which are standard for us.[15] The latter properties serve to determine what *kind* of a representation the work is, rather than what it represents or resembles. We take them for granted, as it were, in representations of that kind. This principle helps to explain also how clouds can look like elephants, how diatonic orchestral music can suggest a conversation or a person crying or laughing, and how a twelve-year-old boy can look like his middle-aged father.

We can now see how a portrait can be an *exact* likeness of the sitter, despite the huge differences between the two. The differences, insofar as they involve properties standard for us, simply do not count against likeness, and hence not against exact likeness. Similarly, a boy not only can resemble his father but can be his "spitting image," despite the boy's relative youthfulness. It is clear that the notions of resemblance and exact resemblance that we are concerned with are not even cousins of the notion of perceptual indistinguishability.

(*b*) The importance of the distinction between standard and variable properties is by no means limited to cases involving representation or resemblance. Imagine a society which does not have an established medium of painting, but does produce a kind of work of art called *guernicas*. *Guernicas* are like versions of Picasso's "Guernica" done in various bas-relief dimensions. All of them are surfaces with the colors and shapes of Picasso's "Guernica," but the surfaces are molded to protrude from the wall like relief maps of different kinds of terrain. Some *guernicas* have rolling surfaces, others are sharp and jagged, still others contain several relatively flat planes at various angles to each other, and so forth. Picasso's "Guernica" would be counted as a *guernica* in this society—a perfectly flat one—rather than as a painting. Its flatness is variable and the figures on its surface are standard relative to the category of *guernicas*. Thus the flatness, which is standard for us, would be variable for members of the other society (if they should come across "Guernica") and the figures on the surface, which are variable for us, would be standard for them. This would make for a profound difference between our aesthetic reaction to "Guernica" and theirs. It seems violent, dynamic, vital, disturbing to us. But I imagine it would strike them as cold, stark, lifeless, or serene and restful, or perhaps bland, dull, boring—but in any case *not* violent, dynamic, and vital. We do not pay attention to or take note of "Guernica"'s flatness; this is a feature we take for granted in paintings, as it were. But for the other society this is "Guernica"'s most striking and noteworthy characteristic—what is *expressive* about it. Conversely, "Guernica"'s color patches, which we find noteworthy and expressive, are insignificant to them.

It is important to notice that this difference in aesthetic response is not due *solely* to the fact that we are much more familiar with flat works of art than they are, and they are more familiar with "Guernica"'s colors and shapes. Someone equally familiar with paintings and *guernicas* might, I think, see Picasso's "Guernica" as a painting on some occasions, and as a *guernica* on others. On the former occasion it will probably look dynamic, violent, and so forth to him, and on the latter cold, serene, bland, or lifeless. Whether he sees the work in a museum of paintings or a museum of *guernicas*, or whether he has been told that it is a painting or a *guernica*, may influence how he sees it. But I think he might be able to shift at will from one way of seeing it to the other, somewhat as one shifts between seeing the duck-rabbit as a duck and seeing it as a rabbit.

This example and the previous ones might give the impression that in general only features of a work that are variable for us are aesthetically important—that these are the expressive, aesthetically active properties, as far as we are concerned, whereas features standard for us are aesthetically inert. But this notion is quite mistaken, as the following examples will demonstrate. Properties standard for us are not aesthetically lifeless, though the life that they have, the aesthetic effect they have on us, is typically very different from what it would be if they were variable for us.

(c) Because of the very fact that features standard for us do not seem striking or noteworthy, that they are somehow expected or taken for granted, they can contribute to a work a sense of order, inevitability, stability, correctness. This is perhaps most notably true of large-scale structural properties in the time arts. The exposition-development-recapitulation form (including the typical key and thematic relationships) of the first movements of classical sonatas, symphonies, and string quartets is standard with respect to the category of works in sonata-allegro form, and standard for listeners, including most of us, who hear them as belonging to that category. So proceeding along the lines of sonata-allegro form seems *right* to us; to our ears that is how sonatas are *supposed* to behave. We feel that we know where we are and where we are going throughout the work—more so, I suggest, than we would if we were not familiar with sonata-allegro form, if following the strictures of that form were variable rather than standard for us.[16] Properties standard for us do not always have this sort of unifying effect, however. The fact that a piano sonata contains only piano sounds, or uses the Western system of harmony throughout, does not make it seem unified to us. The reason, I think, is that these properties are *too* standard for us in a sense that needs explicating (see note 10). Nevertheless, sonata form is unifying partly because it is standard rather than variable for us.

(d) That a work (or part of it) has a certain determinate characteristic (for example, of size, speed, length, volume) is often variable relative to a particular category, when it is nevertheless standard for that category that the variable characteristic falls within a certain range. In such cases the aesthetic effect of the determinate variable property may be colored by the standard limits of the range. Hence these limits function as an aesthetic catalyst, even if not as an active ingredient.

Piano music is frequently marked *sostenuto, cantabile, legato*, or *lyrical.* But how can the pianist possibly carry out such instructions? Piano tones diminish in volume drastically immediately after the key is struck, becoming inaudible relatively promptly, and there is no way the player can prevent this. If a singer or violinist should produce sounds even approaching a piano's in suddenness of demise, they would be nerve-wrackingly sharp and percussive—anything but *cantabile* or lyrical! Yet piano music *can* be *cantabile, legato,* or lyrical nevertheless; sometimes it is extraordinarily so (for example, a good performance of the *Adagio Cantabile* movement of Beethoven's *Pathetique* sonata). What makes this possible is the very fact that the drastic diminution of piano tones cannot be prevented, and hence never is. It is a standard feature for piano music. A pianist can, however, by a variety of devices, control a tone's rate of diminution and length within the limits dictated by the nature of the instrument.[17] Piano tones may thus be *more or less* sustained within these limits, and *how* sustained they are, how quickly or slowly they diminish and how long they last, within the range of possibilities, is variable for piano music. A piano passage that sounds lyrical or *cantabile* to us is one in which the individual tones are *relatively* sustained, given the capabilities of the instrument. Such a passage sounds lyrical only because piano music is limited as it is, and we hear it as piano music; that is, the limitations are standard properties for us. The character of the passage is determined not merely by the "absolute" nature of the sounds, but by that in relation to the standard property of what piano tones can be like.[18]

This principle helps to explain the lack of energy and brilliance that we sometimes find even in very fast passages of electronic music. The energy and brilliance of a fast violin or piano passage derives not merely from the absolute speed of the music (together with accents, rhythmic characteristics, and so forth), but from the fact that it is fast *for that particular medium*. In electronic music different pitches can succeed one another at any frequency up to and including that at which they are no longer separately distinguishable. Because of this it is difficult to make electronic music *sound* fast (energetic, violent). For when we have heard enough electronic music to be aware of the possibilities we do not feel that the speed of a passage approaches a limit, no matter how fast it is.[19]

There are also visual correlates of these musical examples. A small elephant, one which is smaller than most elephants with which we are familiar, might impress us as charming, cute, delicate, or puny. This is not simply because of its (absolute) size, but because it is small *for an elephant*. To people who are familiar not with our elephants but with a race of mini-elephants, the same animal may look massive, strong, dominant, threatening, lumbering, if it is large for a mini-elephant. The size of elephants is variable relative to the class of elephants, but it varies only within a certain (not precisely specifiable) range. It is a standard property of elephants that they do fall within this range. How an elephant's size affects us aesthetically depends, since we see it as an elephant, on whether it falls in the upper, middle, or lower part of the range.

(*e*) Properties standard for a certain category which do not derive from physical limitations of the medium can be regarded as results of more or less conventional "rules" for producing works in the given category (for example, the "rules" of sixteenth-century counterpoint, or those for twelve-tone music). These rules may combine to create a dilemma for the artist which, if he is talented, he may resolve ingeniously and gracefully. The result may be a work with an aesthetic character very different from what it would have had if it had not been for those rules. Suppose that the first movement of a sonata in G major modulates to C-sharp major by the end of the development section. A rule of sonata form decrees that it must return to G for the recapitulation. But the keys of G and C-sharp are as unrelated as any two keys can be; it is difficult to modulate smoothly and quickly from one to the other. Suppose also that while the sonata is in C-sharp there are signs that, given other rules of sonata form, indicate that the recapitulation is imminent (for example, motivic hints of the return, an emotional climax, or a cadenza). Listeners who hear it as a work in sonata form are likely to have a distinct feeling of unease, tension, uncertainty, as the time for the recapitulation approaches. If the composer with a stroke of ingenuity accomplishes the necessary modulation quickly, efficiently, and naturally, this will give them a feeling of relief—one might say of deliverance. The movement to C-sharp (which may have seemed alien and brashly adventurous) will have proven to be quite appropriate, and the entire sequence will in retrospect have a sense of correctness and perfection about it. Our impression of it is likely, I think, to be very much like our impression of a "beautiful" or "elegant" proof in mathematics. (Indeed the composer's task in this example is not unlike that of producing such a proof.)

But suppose that the rule for sonatas were that the recapitulation must be *either* in the original key *or* in the key one half-step below it. Thus in the example above the recapitulation could have been in F-sharp major rather than G major. This possibility removes the sense of tension from the occurrence of C-sharp major in the development section, for a modulation from C-sharp to F-sharp is as easy as any modulation is (since C-sharp is the dominant of F-sharp). Of course, there would also be no special *release* of tension when the modulation to G is effected, there being no tension to be released. In fact, that modulation probably would be rather surprising, since the permissible modulation to F-sharp would be much more natural.

Thus the effect that the sonata has on us depends on which of its properties are dictated by "rules," which ones are standard relative to the category of sonatas and hence standard for us.

(*f*) I turn now to features which are contra-standard for us—that is, ones which have a tendency to disqualify a work from a category in which we nevertheless perceive it. We are likely to find such features shocking, or disconcerting, or startling, or upsetting, just because they are contra-standard for us. Their presence may be so obtrusive that they obscure the work's variable properties. Three-dimensional objects protruding from a canvas and movement in a sculpture are contra-standard relative to the categories of painting and (traditional) sculpture respectively. These features are contra-standard for us, and probably shocking, if despite them we perceive the works possessing them in the mentioned categories. The monochromatic paintings of Yves Klein are disturbing to us (at least at first) for this reason: we see them as paintings, though they contain the feature contra-standard for paintings of being one solid color. Notice that we find other similarly monochromatic surfaces—for example, walls of living rooms—not in the least disturbing, and indeed quite unnoteworthy.

If we are exposed frequently to works containing a certain kind of feature which is contra-standard for us, we ordinarily adjust our categories to accommodate it, making it contra-standard for us no longer. The first painting with a three-dimensional object glued to it was no doubt shocking. But now that the technique has become commonplace we are not shocked. This is because we no longer see these works as *paintings*, but rather as members of either (*a*) a new category—*collages*—in which case the offending feature has become standard rather than contra-standard for us, or (*b*) an expanded category which includes paintings both with and without attached objects, in which case that feature is variable for us.

But it is not just the rarity, unusualness, or unexpectedness of a feature that makes it shocking. If a work differs *too* significantly from the norms of a certain category we do not perceive it in that category and hence the difference is not contra-standard for us, even if we have not previously experienced works differing from that category in that way. A sculpture which is constantly and vigorously in motion would be so obviously and radically different from traditional sculptures that we probably would not perceive it as one even if it is the first moving sculpture we have come across. We would either perceive it as a *kinetic* sculpture, or simply remain confused. In contrast, a sculptured bust which is traditional in every respect except that one ear twitches slightly every thirty seconds would be perceived as an ordinary sculpture. So the twitching ear would be contra-standard for us and would be considerably more unsettling than the much greater movement of the other kinetic sculpture. Similarly, a very small colored area of an otherwise entirely black-and-white drawing would be very disconcerting. But if enough additional color is added to it we will see it as a colored rather than a black-and-white drawing, and the shock will vanish.

This point helps to explain a difference between the harmonic aberrations of Wagner's *Tristan and Isolde* on the one hand and on the other Debussy's *Pelleas et Melisande* and *Feux* and Schoenberg's *Pierrot Lunaire* as well as his later twelve-tone works. The latter are not merely *more* aberrant, *less* tonal, than *Tristan*. They differ from traditional tonal music in such respects and to such an extent that they are not heard as tonal at all. *Tristan*, however, retains enough of the apparatus of tonality, despite its deviations, to be heard as a tonal work. For this reason its lesser deviations are often the more shocking.[20] *Tristan* plays on harmonic traditions by selectively following and flaunting them, while *Pierrot Lunaire* and the others simply ignore them.

Shock then arises from features that are not just rare or unique, but ones that are contra-standard relative to categories in which objects possessing them are perceived. But it must be emphasized that to be contra-standard relative to a certain category is not merely to be rare or unique *among things of that category*. The melodic line of Schubert's song, "*Im Walde*," is probably unique; it probably does not occur in any other songs, or other works of any sort. But it is not contra-standard relative to the category of songs, because it does not tend to disqualify the work from that category. Nor is it contra-standard relative to any other category to which we hear the work as belonging. And clearly we do not find this melodic line at all upsetting. What is important is not the rarity of a feature, but its connection with the classification of the work. Features contra-standard for us are perceived as being misfits in a category which the work strikes us as belonging to, as doing *violence* to such a category, and being rare in a category is not the same thing as being a misfit in it.

It should be clear from the above examples that how a work affects us aesthetically—what aesthetic properties it seems to us to have and what ones we are inclined to attribute to it—depends in a variety of important ways on which of its features are standard, which variable, and which contra-standard for us. Moreover, this is obviously not an isolated or exceptional phenomenon, but a pervasive characteristic of aesthetic perception. I should emphasize that my purpose has not been to establish general principles about how each of the three sorts of properties affects us. How any particular feature affects us depends also on many variables I have not discussed. The important point is that in many cases whether a feature is standard, variable, or contra-standard for us has a great deal to do with what effect it has on us. We must now begin to assess the theoretical consequence of this.

## IV Truth and Falsity

The fact that what aesthetic properties a thing seems to have may depend on what categories it is perceived in raises a question about how to determine what aesthetic properties it really does have. If "Guernica" appears dynamic when seen as a painting, and not dynamic when seen as a *guernica*, is it dynamic or not? Can one way of seeing it be ruled correct, and the other incorrect? One way of approaching this problem is to deny that the apparently conflicting aesthetic judgments of people who perceive a work in different categories actually do conflict.[21]

Judgments that works of art have certain aesthetic properties, it might be suggested, implicitly involve reference to some particular set of categories. Thus our claim that "Guernica" is dynamic really amounts to the claim that it is (as we might say) dynamic *as a painting*, or for people who see it as a painting. The judgment that it is not dynamic made by people who see it as a *guernica* amounts simply to the judgment that it is not dynamic *as a guernica*. Interpreted in these ways, the two judgments are of course quite compatible. Terms like "large" and "small" provide a convenient model for this interpretation. An elephant might be both small as an elephant and large as a mini-elephant, and hence it might be called truly either "large" or "small," depending on which category is implicitly referred to.

I think that aesthetic judgments are in *some* contexts amenable to such category-relative interpretations, especially aesthetic judgments about natural objects (clouds, mountains, sunsets) rather than works of art. (It will be evident that the alternative account suggested below is not readily applicable to most judgments about natural objects.) But most of our aesthetic judgments can be forced into this mold only at the cost of distorting them beyond recognition.

My main objection is that category-relative interpretations do not allow aesthetic judgments to be mistaken often enough. It would certainly be natural to consider a person who calls "Guernica" stark, cold, or dull, because he sees it as a *guernica*, to be *mistaken*: he misunderstands the work because he is looking at it in the wrong way. Similarly, one who asserts that a good performance of the *Adagio Cantabile* of Beethoven's *Pathétique* is percussive, or that a Roman bust looks like a unicolored, immobile man severed at the chest and depicts him as such, is simply wrong, even if his judgment is a result of his perceiving the work in different categories from those in which we perceive it. Moreover, we do not accord a status any more privileged to our own aesthetic judgments. We are likely to regard, for example, cubist paintings, serial music, or Chinese music as formless, incoherent, or disturbing on our first contact with these forms largely because, I suggest, we would not be perceiving the works as cubist paintings, serial music, or Chinese music. But after becoming familiar with these kinds of art we would probably *retract* our previous judgments, admit that they were mistaken. It would be quite inappropriate to protest that what we meant previously was merely that the works were formless or disturbing for the categories in which we then perceived them, while admitting that they are not for the categories of cubist paintings, or serial, or Chinese music. The conflict between apparently incompatible aesthetic judgments made while perceiving a work in different categories does not simply evaporate when the difference of categories is pointed out, as does the conflict between the claims that an animal is large and that it is small, when it is made clear that the person making the first claim regarded it as a mini-elephant and the one making the second regarded it as an elephant. The latter judgments do not (necessarily) reflect a real disagreement about the size of the animal, but the former do reflect a real disagreement about the aesthetic nature of the work.

Thus it seems that, at least in some cases, it is *correct* to perceive a work in certain categories, and *incorrect* to perceive it in certain others; that is, our judgments of it when we perceive it in the former are likely to be true, and those we make when perceiving it in the latter, false. This provides us with absolute senses of "standard," "variable," and "contra-standard": features of a work are standard, variable, or contra-standard absolutely just in case they are standard, variable, or contra-standard (respectively) for people who perceive the work correctly. (Thus an absolutely standard feature is standard relative to some category in which the work is correctly perceived and contra-standard relative to none, an absolutely variable feature is variable relative to all such categories, and an absolutely contra-standard feature is contra-standard relative to at least one such category.)

How is it to be determined in which categories a work is correctly perceived? There is certainly no very precise or well-defined procedure to be followed. Different criteria are emphasized by different people and in different situations. But there are several fairly definite considerations which typically figure in critical discussions and fit our intuitions reasonably well. I suggest that the following circumstances count toward its being correct to perceive a work, $W$, in a given category, $C$:

(*i*) The presence in $W$ of a relatively large number of features standard with respect to $C$. The correct way of perceiving a work is likely to be that in which it has a minimum of contra-standard features for us. I take the relevance of this consideration to be obvious. It cannot be correct to perceive Rembrandt's "Titus Reading" as a kinetic sculpture, if this is possible, just because that work has too few of the features which make kinetic sculptures kinetic sculptures. But of course this does not get us very far, for "Guernica," for example, qualifies equally well on this count for being perceived as a painting and as a *guernica*.

(*ii*) The fact, if it is one, that $W$ is better, or more interesting or pleasing aesthetically, or more worth experiencing when perceived in $C$ than it is when perceived in alternative ways. The correct way of perceiving a work is likely to be the way in which it comes off best.

(*iii*) The fact, if it is one, that the artist who produced *W* intended or expected it to be perceived in *C*, or thought of it as a *C*.

(*iv*) The fact, if it is one, that *C* is well established in and recognized by the society in which *W* was produced. A category is well established in and recognized by a society if the members of the society are familiar with works in that category, consider a work's membership in it a fact worth mentioning, exhibit works of that category together, and so forth—that is, roughly if that category figures importantly in their way of classifying works of art. The categories of impressionist painting and Brahmsian music are well established and recognized in our society; those of *guernicas*, paintings with diagonal composition containing green crosses, and pieces of music containing between four and eight F-sharps and at least seventeen quarter notes every eight bars are not. The categories in which a work is correctly perceived, according to this condition, are generally the ones in which the artist's contemporaries did perceive or would have perceived it.

In certain cases I think the mechanical process by which a work was produced, or (for example, in architecture) the non-perceptible physical characteristics or internal structure of a work, is relevant. A work is probably correctly perceived as an apparent etching[22] rather than, say, an apparent woodcut or line drawing, if it was produced by the etching process. The strength of materials in a building, or the presence of steel girders inside wooden or plaster columns counts toward (not necessarily conclusively) the correctness of perceiving it in the category of buildings with visual characteristics typical of buildings constructed in that manner. Because of their limited applicability I will not discuss these considerations further here.

What can be said in support of the relevance of conditions (*ii*), (*iii*), and (*iv*)? In the examples mentioned above, the categories in which we consider a work correctly perceived seem to meet (to the best of our knowledge) each of these three conditions. I would suppose that "Guernica" is better seen as a painting than it would be seen as a *guernica* (though this would be hard to prove). In any case, Picasso certainly intended it to be seen as a painting rather than a *guernica*, and the category of paintings is, and that of *guernicas* is not, well established in his (that is, our) society. But this of course does not show that (*ii*), (*iii*), and (*iv*) *each* is relevant. It tends to indicate only that one or other of them, or some combination, is relevant. The difficulty of assessing each of the three conditions individually is complicated by the fact that by and large they can be expected to coincide, to yield identical conclusions. Since an artist usually intends his works for his contemporaries he is likely to intend them to be perceived in categories established in and recognized by his society. Moreover, it is reasonable to expect works to come off better when perceived in the intended categories than when perceived in others. An artist tries to produce works which are well worth experiencing when perceived in the intended way and, unless we have reason to think he is totally incompetent, there is some presumption that he succeeded at least to some extent. But it is more or less a matter of chance whether the work comes off well when perceived in some unintended way. The convergence of the three conditions, however, at the same time diminishes the *practical* importance of justifying them individually, since in most cases we can decide how to judge particular works of art without doing so. But the theoretical question remains.

I will begin with (*ii*). If we are faced with a choice between two ways of perceiving a work, and the work is very much better perceived in one way than it is perceived in the other, I think that, at least in the absence of contrary considerations, we would be strongly inclined to settle on the former way of perceiving it as the *correct* way. The process of trying to determine what is in a work consists partly in casting around among otherwise plausible ways of perceiving it for one in which the work is good. We feel we are coming to a correct understanding of a work when we begin to like or enjoy it; we are finding what is really there when it seems to be worth experiencing.

But if (*ii*) is relevant, it is quite clearly not the *only* relevant consideration. Take any work of art we can agree is of fourth- or fifth- or tenth-rate quality. It is quite possible that if this work were perceived in some farfetched set of categories that someone might dream up, it would appear to be first-rate, a masterpiece. Finding such *ad hoc* categories obviously would require talent and ingenuity on the order of that necessary to produce a masterpiece in the first place. But we can sketch how one might begin searching for them. (*a*) If the mediocre work suffers from some disturbingly prominent feature that distracts from whatever merits the work has, this feature might be toned down by choosing categories with respect to which it is standard, rather than variable or contra-standard. When the work is perceived in the new way the offending feature may be no more distracting than the flatness of a painting is to us. (*b*) If the work suffers from an overabundance of clichés it might be livened up by choosing categories with respect to which the clichés are variable or contra-standard rather than standard. (*c*) If it needs ingenuity we might devise a set of rules in terms of which the work finds itself in a dilemma and then ingeniously escapes from it, and build these rules into a set of categories. Surely, however, if there are categories waiting to be discovered which would transform a mediocre work into a masterpiece, it does not follow that the work really is a hitherto unrecognized masterpiece. The fact that when perceived in such categories it would appear exciting, ingenious, and so forth, rather than grating, cliché-ridden, pedestrian, does not make it so. It *cannot* be correct, I suggest, to perceive a work in categories which are totally foreign to the artist and his society, even if it comes across as a masterpiece in them.[23]

This brings us to the historical conditions (*iii*) and (*iv*). I see no way of avoiding the conclusion that one or the other of them at least is relevant in determining in what categories a work is correctly perceived. I consider both relevant, but will not argue here for the independent relevance of (*iv*). (*iii*) merits special attention in light of the recent prevalence of disputes about the importance of artists' intentions. To test the relevance of (*iii*) we must consider a case in which (*iii*) and (*iv*) diverge. One such instance occurred during the early days of the twelve-tone movement in music. Schoenberg no doubt intended even his earliest twelve-tone works to be heard as such. But this category was certainly not then well established or recognized in his society: virtually none of his contemporaries (except close associates such as Berg and Webern), even musically sophisticated ones, would have (or could have) heard these works in that category. But it seems to me that even the very first twelve-tone compositions are correctly heard as such, that the judgments one who hears them otherwise would make of them (for example, that they are chaotic, formless) are mistaken. I think this would be so even if Schoenberg had been working entirely alone, if *none* of his contemporaries had any inkling of the twelve-tone system. No doubt the first twelve-tone compositions are much better when heard in the category of twelve-tone works than when they are heard in any other way people might be likely to hear them. But as we have seen this cannot *by itself* account for the correctness of hearing them in the former way. The only other feature of the situation which could be relevant, so far as I can see, is Schoenberg's intention.

The above example is unusual in that Schoenberg was extraordinarily self-conscious about what he was doing, having explicitly formulated rules—that is, specified standard properties—for twelve-tone composition. Artists are of course not often so self-conscious, even when producing revolutionary works of art. Their intentions as to which categories their works are to be perceived in are not nearly as clear as Schoenberg's were, and often they change their minds considerably during the process of creation. In such cases (as well as ones in which the artists' intentions are unknown) the question of what categories a work is correctly perceived in is, I think, left by default to condition (*iv*), together with (*i*) and (*ii*). But it seems to me that in almost all cases at least one of the historical conditions, (*iii*) and (*iv*), is of crucial importance.

My account of the rules governing decisions about what categories works are correctly perceived in leaves a lot undone. There are bound to be a large number of undecidable cases on my criteria. Artists' intentions are frequently unclear, variable, or undiscoverable. Many works belong to categories which are borderline cases of being well established in the artists' societies (perhaps, for example, the categories of rococo music—for instance, C. P. E. Bach—of music in the style of early Mozart, and of very thin metal sculptured figures of the kind that Giacometti made). Many works fall between well-established categories (for example, between impressionist and cubist paintings), possessing *some* of the standard features relative to each, and so neither clearly qualify nor clearly fail to qualify on the basis of condition (*i*) to be perceived in either. There is, in addition, the question of what relative weights to accord the various conditions when they conflict.

It would be a mistake, however, to try to tighten up much further the rules for deciding how works are correctly perceived. To do so would be simply to legislate gratuitously, since the intuitions and precedents we have to go on are highly variable and often confused. But it is important to notice just where these intuitions and precedents are inconclusive, for doing so will expose the sources of many critical disputes. One such dispute might well arise concerning Giacometti's thin metal sculptures. To a critic who sees them simply as sculptures, or sculptures of people, they look frail, emaciated, wispy, or wiry. But that is not how they would strike a critic who sees them in the category of thin metal sculptures of that sort (just as stick figures do not strike us as wispy or emaciated). He would be impressed not by the thinness of the sculptures, but by the expressive nature of the positions of their limbs, and so forth, and so no doubt would attribute very different aesthetic properties to them. Which of the two ways of seeing these works is correct is, I suspect, undecidable. It is not clear whether enough such works have been made and have been regarded sufficiently often as constituting a category for that category to be deemed well established in Giacometti's society. And I doubt whether any of the other conditions settle the issue conclusively. So perhaps the dispute between the two critics is essentially unresolvable. The most that we can do is to point out just what sort of a difference of perception underlies the dispute, and why it is unresolvable.

The occurrence of such impasses is by no means something to be regretted. Works may be fascinating precisely because of shifts between equally permissible ways of perceiving them. And the enormous richness of some works is due in part to the variety of permissible, and worthwhile, ways of perceiving them. But it should be emphasized that even when my criteria do not clearly specify a *single* set of categories in which a work is correctly perceived, there are bound to be possible ways of perceiving it (which we may or may not have thought of) that they definitely rule out.

The question posed at the outset of this section was how to determine what aesthetic properties a work has, given that which ones it seems to have depend on what categories it is perceived in, on which of its properties are standard, which variable, and which contra-standard for us. I have sketched in rough outline rules for deciding in what categories a work is *correctly* perceived (and hence which of its features are absolutely standard, variable, and contra-standard). The aesthetic properties it actually possesses are those that are to be found in it when it is perceived correctly.[24]

### V Conclusion

I return now to the issues raised in Section I. (I will adopt for the remainder of this paper the simplifying assumption that there is only one correct way of perceiving any work. Nothing important depends on this.) If a work's aesthetic properties are those that are to be found in it when it is perceived correctly, and the correct way to perceive it is determined partly by historical facts about the artist's intention and/or his society, no examination of the work itself, however thorough, will by itself reveal those properties.[25] If we are confronted by a work about whose origins we know absolutely nothing (for example, one lifted from the dust at an as yet unexcavated archaeological site on Mars), we would simply not be in a position to judge it aesthetically. We could not possibly tell by staring at it, no matter how intently and intelligently, whether it is coherent, or serene, or dynamic, for by staring we cannot tell whether it is to be seen as a sculpture, a *guernica*, or some other exotic or mundane kind of work of art. (We could attribute aesthetic properties to it in the way we do to natural objects, which of course does not involve consideration of historical facts about artists or their societies. [Cf. Section IV.] But to do this would not be to treat the object as a *work* of art.)

It should be emphasized that the relevant historical facts are not merely useful aids to aesthetic judgment; they do not simply provide hints concerning what might be found in the work. Rather they help to *determine* what aesthetic properties a work has; they, together with the work's nonaesthetic features, *make* it a coherent, serene, or whatever. If the origin of a work which is coherent and serene had been different in crucial respects, the work would not have had these qualities; we would not merely have lacked a means for *discovering* them. And of two works which differ *only* in respect of their origins—that is, which are perceptually indistinguishable—one might be coherent or serene, and the other not.

Thus, since artists' intentions are among the relevant historical considerations, the "intentional fallacy" is not a fallacy at all. I have of course made no claims about the relevance of artists' intentions as to the aesthetic properties that their works should have, and these intentions are among those most discussed in writings on aesthetics. I am willing to agree that whether an artist intended his work to be coherent or serene has nothing essential to do with whether it is coherent or serene. But this must not be allowed to seduce us into thinking that *no* intentions are relevant.

Aesthetic properties, then, are not to be found in works themselves in the straightforward way that colors and shapes or pitches and rhythms are. But I do not mean to deny that we perceive aesthetic properties in works of art. I see the serenity of a painting, and hear the coherence of a sonata, despite the fact that the presence of these qualities in the works depends partly on circumstances of their origin, which I cannot (now) perceive. Jones's marital status is part of what makes him a bachelor, if he is one, and we cannot tell his marital status just by looking at him, though we can thus ascertain his sex. Hence, I suppose, his bachelorhood is not a property we can be said to perceive in him. But the aesthetic properties of a work do not depend on historical facts about it in anything like the way Jones's bachelorhood depends on his marital status. The point is not that the historical facts (or in what categories the work is correctly perceived, or which of its properties are absolutely standard, variable, and contra-standard) function as *grounds* in any ordinary sense for aesthetic judgments. By themselves they do not, in general, count either for or against the presence of any particular aesthetic property. And they are not part of a larger body of information (also including data about the work derived from an examination of it) from which conclusions about the work's aesthetic properties are to be deduced or inferred. We must learn to *perceive* the work in the correct categories, as determined in part by the historical facts, and judge it by what we then perceive in it. The historical facts help to determine whether a painting is, for example, serene *only* (as far as my arguments go) by affecting what way of perceiving the painting must reveal this quality if it is truly attributable to the work.

We must not, however, expect to judge a work simply by setting ourselves to perceive it correctly, once it is determined what the correct way of perceiving it is. For one cannot, in general, perceive a work in a given set of categories simply by setting himself to do it. I could not possibly, merely by an act of will, see "Guernica" as a *guernica* rather than a painting, or hear a succession of street sounds in any arbitrary category one might dream up, even if the category has been explained to me in detail. (Nor can I imagine except in a rather vague way what it would be like, for example, to see "Guernica" as a *guernica*.) One cannot merely decide to respond appropriately to a work—to be shocked or unnerved or surprised by its (absolutely) contra-standard features, to find its standard features familiar or mundane, and to react to its variable features in other ways—once he knows the correct categories. Perceiving a work in a certain category or set of categories is a skill that must be acquired by training, and exposure to a great many other works of the category or categories in question is ordinarily, I believe, an essential part of this training. (But an effort of will may facilitate the training, and once the skill is acquired one may be able to decide at will whether or not to perceive it in that or those categories.) This has important consequences concerning how best to approach works of art of kinds that are new to us—contemporary works in new idioms, works from foreign cultures, or newly resurrected works from the ancient past. It is no use just immersing ourselves in a particular work, even with the knowledge of what categories it is correctly perceived in, for that alone will not enable us to perceive it in those categories. We must become familiar with a considerable variety of works of similar sorts.

When dealing with works of more familiar kinds it is not generally necessary to undertake deliberately the task of training ourselves to be able to perceive them in the correct categories (except perhaps when those categories include relatively subtle ones). But this is almost always, I think, only because we have been trained unwittingly. Even the ability to see paintings as paintings had to be acquired, it seems to me, by repeated exposure to a great many paintings. The critic must thus go beyond the work before him in order to judge it aesthetically, not only to discover what the correct categories are, but also to be able to perceive it in them. The latter does not require consideration of historical facts, or consideration of facts at all, but it requires directing one's attention nonetheless to things other than the work in question.

Probably no one would deny that *some* sort of perceptual training is necessary, in many if not all instances, for apprehending a work's serenity or coherence, or other aesthetic properties. And of course it is not only *aesthetic* properties whose apprehension by the senses requires training. But the kind of training required in the aesthetic cases (and perhaps some others as well) has not been properly appreciated. In order to learn how to recognize gulls of various kinds, or the sex of chicks, or a certain person's handwriting, one must usually have gulls of those kinds, or chicks of the two sexes, or examples of that person's handwriting pointed out to him, practice recognizing them himself, and be corrected when he makes mistakes. But the training important for discovering the serenity or coherence of a work of art that I have been discussing is not of this sort (though this sort of training might be important as well). Acquiring the ability to perceive a serene or coherent work in the correct categories is not a matter of having had serene or coherent things pointed out to one, or having practiced recognizing them. What is important is not (or not merely) experience with other serene and coherent things, but experience with other things of the appropriate categories.

Much of the argument in this paper has been directed against the seemingly common-sense notion that aesthetic judgments about works of art are to be based solely on what can be perceived in them, how they look or sound. That notion is seriously misleading, I claim, on two quite different counts. I do not deny that paintings and sonatas are to be judged solely on what can be seen or heard in them—when they are perceived correctly. But examining a work with the senses can by itself reveal neither how it is correct to perceive it, nor how to perceive it that way.

## Notes

1. Heinrich Wölfflin, *Principles of Art History*, trans. M. D. Hottinger (7th ed.; New York, 1929), p. 228.

2. [W]e should all agree, I think, . . . that any quality that cannot even in principle be heard in it [a musical composition] does not belong to it as music." Monroe Beardsley, *Aesthetics: Problems in the Philosophy of Criticism* (New York, 1958), pp. 31–32.

3. Cf. Calvin Tompkins, *The Bride and the Bachelors* (New York, 1965), pp. 210–211.

4. Monroe Beardsley argues for a relatively strict separation (*op. cit.,* pp. 17–34). Some of the strongest recent attempts to enforce this separation are to be found in discussions of the so-called "intentional fallacy," beginning with William Wimsatt and Beardsley, "The Intentional Fallacy," *Sewanee Review*, vol. 54 (1946), which has been widely cited and reprinted. Despite the name of the "fallacy" these discussions are not limited to consideration of the relevance of artists' *intentions*.

5. The aesthetic properties of works of literature are not happily called "perceptual." For reasons connected with this it is sometimes awkward to treat literature together with the visual arts and music. (The notion of perceiving a work in a category, to be introduced shortly, is not straightforwardly applicable to literary works.) Hence in this paper I will concentrate on visual and musical works, though I believe that the central points I make concerning them hold, with suitable modifications, for novels, plays, and poems as well.

6. Frank Sibley distinguishes between "aesthetic" and "nonaesthetic" terms and concepts in "Aesthetic Concepts," *Philosophical Review*, vol. 68 (1959).

7. Cf. Paul Ziff, "Art and the 'Object of Art,'" in Ziff, *Philosophic Turnings* (Ithaca, N.Y., 1966), pp. 12–16 (originally published in *Mind*, n. s. vol. 60 [1951]).

8. "Aesthetic and Nonaesthetic," *Philosophical Review*, vol. 72 (1965).

9. This is a very difficult notion to make precise, and I do not claim to have succeeded entirely. But the following comments seem to me to go in the right direction, and, together with the examples in the next section, they should clarify it sufficiently for my present purposes.

10. In order to avoid excessive complexity and length, I am ignoring some considerations that might be important at a later stage of investigation. In particular, I think it would be important at some point to distinguish between different *degrees* or *levels* of standardness, variableness, and contra-standardness for a person; to speak, e.g., of features being *more* or *less* standard for him. At least two distinct sorts of grounds for such differences of degree should be recognized. (*a*) Distinctions between perceiving a work in a certain category to a greater and lesser extent should be allowed for, with corresponding differences of degree in the standardness for the perceiver of properties relative to that category. (*b*) A feature which is standard relative to more, and/or more specific, categories in which a person perceives the work should thereby count as more standard for him. Thus, if we see something as a painting and also as a French Impressionist painting, features standard relative to both categories are more standard for us than features standard relative only to the latter.

11. This excludes, e.g., the sense of "represent" in which a picture might represent justice or courage, and probably other senses as well.

12. This does not hold for the special case of photography. A photograph is a photograph of a woman no matter what it looks like, I take it, if a woman was in front of the lens when it was produced.

13. Nelson Goodman denies that resemblance is necessary for representation—and obviously not merely because of isolated or marginal examples of non-resembling representations (p. 5). I cannot treat his arguments here, but rather than reject *en masse* the common-sense beliefs that pictures do resemble significantly what they depict and that they depict what they do partly because of such resemblances, if Goodman advocates rejecting them, I prefer to recognize a sense of "resemblance" in which these beliefs are true. My disagreement with him is perhaps less sharp than it appears since, as will be evident, I am quite willing to grant that the relevant resemblances are "conventional." Cf. Goodman, *Languages of Art* (Indianapolis, 1968), p. 39, n. 31.

14. The connection between features variable for us and what the work looks like is by no means a straightforward or simple one, however. It may involve "rules" which are more or less "conventional" (e.g., the "laws" of perspective). Cf. E. H. Gombrich, *Art and Illusion* (New York, 1960), and Nelson Goodman, *op. cit.*

15. There is at least one group of exceptions to this. Obviously features of a work which are standard for us because they are standard relative to some *representational* category which we see it in—e.g., the category of nudes, still lifes, or landscapes—do help determine what the work looks like to us and what we take it to depict.

16. The presence of clichés in a work sometimes allows it to contain drastically disorderly elements without becoming chaotic or incoherent. Cf. Anton Ehrenzweig, *The Hidden Order of Art* (London, 1967), pp. 114–116.

17. The timing of the release of the key affects the tone's length. Use of the sustaining pedal can lessen slightly a tone's diminuendo by reinforcing its overtones with sympathetic vibrations from other strings. The rate of diminuendo is affected somewhat more drastically by the force with which the key is struck. The more forcefully it is struck the greater is the tone's relative diminuendo. (Obviously the rate of diminuendo cannot be controlled in this way independently of the tone's

initial volume.) The successive tones of a melody can be made to overlap so that each one's sharp attack is partially obscured by the lingering end of the preceding tone. A melodic tone may also be reinforced after it begins by sympathetic vibrations from harmonically related accompanying figures, contributed by the composer.

18. "[T]he musical media we know thus far derive their whole character and their usefulness as musical media precisely from their limitations." Roger Sessions, "Problems and Issues Facing the Composer Today," in Paul Henry Lang, *Problems of Modern Music* (New York, 1960), p. 31.

19. One way to make electronic music sound fast would be to make it sound like some traditional instrument, thereby trading on the limitations of that instrument.

20. Cf. William W. Austin, *Music in the 20th Century* (New York, 1966), pp. 205-206; and Eric Salzman, *Twentieth-Century Music: An Introduction* (Englewood Cliffs, N.J., 1967), pp. 5, 8, 19.

21. I am ruling out the view that the notions of truth and falsity are not applicable to aesthetic judgments, on the ground that it would force us to reject so much of our normal discourse and common-sense intuitions about art that theoretical aesthetics, conceived as attempting to understand the institution of art, would hardly have left a recognizable subject matter to investigate. (Cf. the quotation from Wölfflin, above.)

22. Cf. p. 339.

23. To say that it is incorrect (in my sense) to perceive a work in certain categories is not necessarily to claim that one *ought not* to perceive it that way. I heartily recommend perceiving mediocre works in categories that make perceiving them worthwhile whenever possible. The point is that one is not likely to *judge* the work correctly when he perceives it incorrectly.

24. This is a considerable oversimplification. If there are two equally correct ways of perceiving a work, and it appears to have a certain aesthetic property perceived in one but not the other of them, does it actually possess this property or not? There is no easy general answer. Probably in some such cases the question is undecidable. But I think we would sometimes be willing to say that a work is, e.g., touching or serene if it seems so when perceived in one correct way (or, more hesitantly, that there is "something very touching, or serene, about it"), while allowing that it does not seem so when perceived in another way which we do not want to rule incorrect. In some cases works have aesthetic properties (e.g., intriguing, subtle, alive, interesting, deep) which are not apparent on perceiving it in any single acceptable way, but which depend on the multiplicity of acceptable ways of perceiving it and relations between them. None of these complications relieves the critic of the responsibility for determining in what way or ways it is correct to perceive a work.

25. But this, plus a general knowledge of what sorts of works were produced when and by whom, might.

[Ed.—Walton wishes to add the following note: "Since the original publication of this paper I have changed my views concerning resemblance in representational art. Cf. my 'Pictures and Make-Believe,' *Philosophical Reivew*, vol. 82 (1973)."]

# 4.          Piece: Contra Aesthetics
### *TIMOTHY BINKLEY*

## *I What Is This Piece?*

1. The term "aesthetics" has a general meaning in which it refers to the philosophy of art. In this sense, any theoretical writing about art falls within the realm of aesthetics. There is also a more specific and more important sense of the term in which it refers to a particular type of theoretical inquiry which emerged in the eighteenth century when the "Faculty of Taste" was invented. In this latter sense, "aesthetics" is the study of a specific human activity involving the perception of aesthetic qualities such as beauty, repose, expressiveness, unity, liveliness. Although frequently purporting to be a (or even *the*) philosophy of art, aesthetics so understood is not exclusively about art: it investigates a type of human experience (aesthetic experience) which is elicited by artworks, but also by nature and by nonartistic artifacts. The discrepancy is generally thought to be unimportant and is brushed aside with the assumption that if aesthetics is not exclusively about art, at least art is primarily about the aesthetic. This assumption, however, also proves to be false, and it is the purpose of this piece to show why. Falling within the subject matter of aesthetics (in the second sense) is neither a necessary nor a sufficient condition for being art.

2. Robert Rauschenberg erases a DeKooning drawing and exhibits it as his own work, "Erased DeKooning Drawing." The aesthetic properties of the original work are wiped away, and the result is not a nonwork, but another work. No important information about Rauschenberg's piece is presented in the way it *looks*, except perhaps *this* fact, that looking at it is artistically inconsequential. It would be a mistake to search for aestheti-

From *The Journal of Aesthetics and Art Criticism*, XXXV (1977), 265–277. Reprinted with the permission of the author and *The Journal of Aesthetics and Art Criticism*.

cally interesting smudges on the paper. The object may be bought and sold like an aesthetically lush Rubens, but unlike the Rubens it is only a souvenir or relic of its artistic meaning. The owner of the Rauschenberg has no privileged access to its artistic content in the way the owner of the Rubens does who hides the painting away in a private study. Yet the Rauschenberg piece is a work of art. Art in the twentieth century has emerged as a strongly self-critical discipline. It has freed itself of aesthetic parameters and sometimes creates directly with ideas unmediated by aesthetic qualities. An artwork is a piece: and a piece need not be an aesthetic object, or even an object at all.

3. This piece is occasioned by two works of art by Marcel Duchamp, *L.H.O.O.Q.* and *L.H.O.O.Q. Shaved.* How do I know they are works of art? For one thing, they are listed in catalogues. So I assume they are works of art. If you deny that they are, it is up to you to explain why the listings in a Renoir catalogue are artworks, but the listings in a Duchamp catalogue are not. And why the Renoir show is an exhibition of artworks, while the Duchamp show is not, and so forth. Anyway, whether the Duchamp pieces are works of art is ultimately inconsequential, as we shall see.

This piece is also, shall we say, about the philosophical significance of Duchamp's art. This piece is primarily about the concept "piece" in art; and its purpose is to reformulate our understanding of what a "work of art" is.

## II  What Is L.H.O.O.Q.?

These are Duchamp's words:

> This Mona Lisa with a moustache and a goatee is a combination readymade and iconoclastic Dadaism. The original, I mean the original readymade is a cheap chromo 8x5 on which I inscribed at the bottom four letters which pronounced like initials in French, made a very risqué joke on the Gioconda.[1]

Imagine a similar description of the *Mona Lisa* itself. Leonardo took a canvas and some paint and put the paint on the canvas in such-and-such a way so that—presto—we have the renowned face and its environs. There is a big difference between this description and Duchamp's description. The difference is marked by the unspecified "such-and-such" left hanging in the description of Leonardo's painting. I could, of course, go on indefinitely describing the look of the *Mona Lisa,* and the fidelity with which your imagination reproduced this look would depend upon such things as how good my description is, how good your imagination is, and chance. Yet regardless of how precise and vivid my description is, one thing it will never do is acquaint you with the painting. You cannot claim to know that work of art on the basis of reading the most exquisite description of it, even though you may learn many interesting things *about* it. The way you come to know the *Mona Lisa* is by looking at it or by looking at a decent reproduction of it. The reason reproductions count is not that they faithfully reproduce the work of art, but rather because what the work of art is depends fundamentally upon how it looks. And reproductions can do a more or less acceptable job of duplicating (or replicating) the salient features of the appearance of a painting. This does not mean that a person is entitled to limit his or her aesthetic judgments to reproductions. What it means is that you can't say much about a painting until you know how it looks.

Now reconsider the description of Duchamp's piece: *L.H.O.O.Q.* is a reproduction of the Mona Lisa with a moustache, goatee, and letters added. There is no amorphous "such-and-such" standing for the most important thing. The description tells you what the work of art is; you now know the piece without actually having seen it (or a reproduction of it). When you do see the artwork there are no surprises: Yes, there is the reproduction of the *Mona Lisa*; there is the moustache, the goatee; there are the five letters. When you look at the artwork you learn nothing of artistic consequence which you don't already know from the description Duchamp gives, and for this reason it would be pointless to spend time attending to the piece as a connoisseur would savor a Rembrandt. Just the opposite is true of the *Mona Lisa*. If I tell you it is a painting of a woman with an enigmatic smile, I have told you little about the work of art since the important thing is how it *looks*; and that I can only *show* you, I cannot tell you.

This difference can be elucidated by contrasting ideas and appearances. Some art (a great deal of what is considered traditional art) creates primarily with appearances. To know the art is to know the look of it; and to know that is to *experience* the look, to perceive the appearance. On the other hand, some art creates primarily with ideas.[2] To know the art is to know the idea; and to know an idea is not necessarily to experience a particular sensation, or even to have some particular experience. This is why you can know *L.H.O.O.Q.* either by looking at it or by having it described to you. (In fact, the piece might be better or more easily known by description than by perception.) The critical analysis of appearance, which is so useful in helping you come to know the *Mona Lisa*, bears little value in explaining *L.H.O.O.Q.* Excursions into the beauty with which the moustache was drawn or the delicacy with which the goatee was made to fit the contours of the face are fatuous attempts to say something meaningful about the work of art. If we do look at the piece, what is important to notice is *that* there is a reproduction of the *Mona Lisa*, *that* a moustache has been added, etc. It hardly matters exactly *how* this was done, how it looks. One views the *Mona Lisa* to see what it looks like, but one approaches Duchamp's piece to obtain information, to gain access to the thought being expressed.

### III What is L.H.O.O.Q. Shaved?

Duchamp sent out invitations to preview the show called "Not Seen and/or Less Seen of/by Marcel Duchamp/Rrose Selavy 1904–64: Mary Sisler Collection." On the front of the invitation he pasted a playing card which bears a reproduction of the *Mona Lisa*. Below the card is inscribed, in French, "L.H.O.O.Q. Shaved." This piece looks like the *Mona Lisa* and the *Mona Lisa* looks like it: since one is a reproduction of the other, their aesthetic qualities are basically identical.[3] Differences in how they look have little, if any, artistic relevance. We do not establish the identity of one by pointing out where it looks different from the other. This is due to the fact that Duchamp's piece does not articulate its artistic statement in the language of aesthetic qualities. Hence, its aesthetic properties are as much a part of *L.H.O.O.Q. Shaved* as a picture of a mathematician in an algebra book is part of the mathematics.

Appearances are insufficient for establishing the identity of a work of art if the point is not in the appearance. And if the point is in the appearance, how do we establish that? What is to keep a Duchamp from stealing the look for ulterior purposes? Here occurs the limit of the ability of aesthetics to cope with art, since aesthetics seeks out appearances. To see why and how, we need to examine the nature of aesthetics.

### IV What Is Aesthetics?

1. *The Word.* The term "aesthetics" has come to denote that branch of philosophy which deals with art. The word originated in the eighteenth century when Alexander Gottlieb Baumgarten adopted a Greek word for perception to name what he defined to be "the science of perception."[4] Relying upon a distinction familiar to "the Greek philosophers and the Church fathers," he contrasted things perceived (aesthetic entities) with things known (noetic entities), delegating to "aesthetics" the investigation of the former. Baumgarten then gathered the study of the arts under the aegis of aesthetics. The two were quickly identified and "aesthetics" became "the philosophy of art" in much the way "ethics" is the philosophy of morality.

2. *Aesthetics and Perception.* From the outset aesthetics has been devoted to the study of "things perceived," whether reasoning from the "aesthetic attitude" which defines a unique way of perceiving, or from the "aesthetic object" of perception. The commitment to perceptual experience was deepened with the invention of the Faculty of Taste by eighteenth-century philosophers anxious to account for the human response to Beauty and to other aesthetic qualities. The Faculty of Taste exercises powers of discrimination in aesthetic experiences. A refined person with highly developed taste is enabled to perceive and recognize sophisticated and subtle artistic expressions which are closed to the uncultured person with poorly developed taste. This new faculty was characterized by its operation in the context of a special "disinterested" perception, a perception severed from self-interest and dissociated from so-called "practical concerns." The development of the concept of disinterestedness reinforced the perceptual focus of aesthetics, since removing "interest" from experience divests it of utility and invests its value in immediate awareness. An aesthetic experience is something pursued "for its own sake." Eventually aesthetics came to treat the object of aesthetic perception as a kind of illusion since its "reality"—i.e., the reality of disinterested perception—stands disconnected from the reality of practical interest. The two realities are incommensurable: The cows in Turner's paintings can be seen, but not milked or heard.

It is important to note that aesthetics is an outgrowth of the ancient tradition of the philosophy of the Beautiful. Beauty is a property found in both art and nature. A man is beautiful; so is his house and the tapestries hung inside. Aesthetics has continued the tradition of investigating a type of experience which can be had in the presence of both natural and created objects. As a result, aesthetics has never been strictly a study of artistic phenomena. The scope of its inquiry is broader than art since aesthetic experience is not an experience unique to art. This fact has not always been sufficiently emphasized, and as a result aesthetics frequently appears in the guise of philosophy-of-art-in-general.

As aesthetics and the philosophy of art have become more closely identified, a much more serious confusion has arisen. The work of art has come to be construed as an aesthetic object, an object of perception. Hence the meaning and essence of all art is thought to inhere in appearances, in the looks and sounds of direct (though not necessarily unreflective) awareness. The first principle of philosophy of art has become: all art possesses aesthetic qualities, and the core of a work is its nest of aesthetic qualities. This is why "aesthetics" has become just another name for the philosophy of art. Although it is sometimes recognized that aesthetics is not identical to the philosophy of art, but rather a complementary study, it is still commonly assumed that all art is aesthetic in the sense that falling within the subject matter of aesthetics is at least a necessary (if not a sufficient) condition for being art.[5] Yet as we shall see, being aesthetic is neither a necessary nor a sufficient condition for being art.

Devotees of modern aesthetics may believe that Baumgarten's "science of perception" is a moribund enterprise befitting only pre-Modern aesthetics rapt in pursuit of ideal Beauty. Yet a survey of contemporary aesthetic theory will prove that this part of philosophy still accepts its *raison d'être* to be a perceptual entity—an appearance—and fails to recognize sufficiently the distinction between "aesthetics" in the narrow sense and the philosophy of art. In his essay "Aesthetic and Non-Aesthetic," Frank Sibley has articulated this commitment to perception:

> It is of importance to note first that, broadly speaking, aesthetics deals with a kind of perception. People have to *see* the grace of unity of a work, *hear* the plaintiveness or frenzy in a music, *notice* the gaudiness of a color scheme, *feel* the power of a novel, its mood, or its uncertainty of tone. . . . The crucial thing is to see, hear, or feel. To suppose indeed that one can make aesthetic judgments without aesthetic perception . . . is to misunderstand aesthetic judgement.[6]

Despite the many new directions taken by the philosophy of art in the twentieth century, it is still practised under the guidance of aesthetic inquiry, which assumes that the work of art is a thing perceived.

The reason aesthetic qualities must be perceived in order to be judged is that they inhere in what Monroe Beardsley has called the "perceptual object": "A perceptual object is an object some of whose qualities, at least, are open to direct sensory awareness."[7] This he contrasts with the "physical basis" of aesthetic qualities, which "consists of things and events describable in the vocabulary of physics."[8] Hence the work of art turns out to be an entity possessed of two radically different aspects, one aesthetic and the other physical:

> When a critic . . . says that Titian's later paintings have a strong atmospheric quality and vividness of color, he is talking about aesthetic objects. But when he says that Titian used a dark reddish underpainting over the whole canvas, and added transparent glazes to the painting after he laid down the pigment, he is talking about physical objects.[9]

This "aesthetic object" is taken by the philosophy of art to be its subject of study. Appearances are paramount, from expressionist theories which construe the artwork as an "imaginary object" through which the artist has articulated his or her "intuition," to formalist theories which venerate perceptual form.[10] Clive Bell's "significant form" is clearly a perceptual form since it must be perceived and arouse the "aesthetic emotion" before it functions artistically.[11] Susanne Langer has christened aesthetic appearances "semblances," and has undertaken what is probably the most extensive investigation of artistic semblance in her book *Feeling and Form.* Aesthetics perceives all the arts to be engaged in the creation of some kind of semblance or artistic "illusion" which presents itself to us for the sake of its appearance.

It has been difficult, however, to maintain a strictly perceptual interpretation of the aesthetic "appearance." Literature is the one major art form which does not easily accommodate the perceptual model of arthood. Although we perceive the printed words in a book, we do not actually perceive the literary *work* which is composed with intangible linguistic elements. Yet as Sibley points out, the reader will "feel the power of a novel, its mood, or its uncertainty of tone," so that its aesthetic qualities are at least *experienced* through reading if not actually perceived by one of the senses. There are various things we experience without perceiving them. Like an emotion, the power of a novel is "felt" without its being touched or heard or seen. Thus, although it will not be quite correct to say that one cannot know the aesthetic qualities of a novel without "direct perceptual access," it is true that one cannot know them without directly experiencing the novel by reading it. This rules out the possibility of coming to know a literary work by having it described to you (as one may very well come to know *L.H.O.O.Q.*). Just as you must look at the particular object constituting a painting, you must read the particular words comprising a novel in order to judge it aesthetically. Hence, although perception is the paradigm of aesthetic experience, an accurate aesthetic theory will locate aesthetic qualities more generally in a particular type of *experience* (aesthetic experience) so that literature can be included.

3. *The Theory of Media.* What does it mean to have the requisite "direct experience" of an aesthetic object? How do you specify *what* it is that one must experience in order to know a particular artwork? Here we encounter a problem. Aesthetic qualities cannot be communicated except through direct experience of them. So there is no way of saying just what the aesthetic qualities of a work are independently of experiencing them. As Isabel Hungerland puts it, there are no intersubjective criteria for testing the presence of aesthetic qualities.[12] This is why one cannot communicate the *Mona Lisa* by describing it. It is impossible to establish criteria for identifying artworks which are based on their aesthetic qualities. And this is the point where aesthetics needs the concept of a

medium. Media are the basic categories of art for aesthetics, and each work is identified through its medium. Let's see how this is done.

In recent aesthetics, the problem of the relationship between the aesthetic and the nonaesthetic properties of an object has been much discussed. Whatever the particular analysis given, it is generally conceded that aesthetic qualities *depend* in some way upon nonaesthetic qualities.[13] There is no guarantee that a slight change in color or shape will leave the aesthetic qualities of a painting unaffected, and this is why reproductions often have aesthetic qualities different from those of the original.[14] Changing what Beardsley calls the "physical" properties, however slightly can alter those features of a work of art which are experienced in the "aesthetic experience" of the object. Aesthetic objects are vulnerable and fragile, and this is another reason why it is important to have identity criteria for them.

Since aesthetic qualities depend on nonaesthetic qualities, the identity of an aesthetic artwork can be located through conventions governing its nonaesthetic qualities. These conventions determine the nonaesthetic parameters which must remain invariant in identifying particular works. A medium is not simply a physical material, but rather a network of such conventions which delimits a realm over which physical materials and aesthetic qualities are mediated. For example, in the medium of painting there is a convention which says that the paint, but not the canvas, stretcher, or frame, must remain invariant in order to preserve the identity of the artwork. On the other hand, paint is not a conventional invariant in the art of architecture but is applied to buildings (at least on the inside) according to another art, interior decorating. The same architectural work could have white walls or pink walls, but a painting could not have its white clouds changed to pink and still remain the same painting. Similarly, the medium of painting is invariant through modifications of the frame holding a painting, while a building is not invariant through modifications in, say, the woodwork. Moving a Rubens from an elaborate Baroque frame into a modern Bauhaus frame will not change the work of art, but making a similar change in the woodwork of a building will change, however slightly, the architectural work.

In its network of conventions, each artistic medium establishes a nonaesthetic criteria for identifying works of art. By being told which medium a work is in, we are given the parameters within which to search for and experience its aesthetic qualities. As we watch a dance, we heed how the dancers move their bodies. As we watch a play on the same stage, we concentrate instead on what is being acted out. Treating a piece of writing as a poem will make us focus on different nonaesthetic features than if we approach it as a short story: when the type is set for a poem the individual lines are preserved, as they are not in a short story. Thus Susanne Langer's characterization of media in terms of the particular type of semblance they create is pointed in the wrong direction. She holds that painting creates the illusion of space, music the illusion of the passage of time, etc. Yet it is not the "content" of an aesthetic illusion which determines the medium. Before we can tell whether something presents a semblance of space, we have to know where to look for the semblance; and this we know by understanding the conventions, i.e., the medium, within which the thing is proffered for aesthetic experience. Anything that can be seen can be seen aesthetically, i.e., it can be viewed for the sake of discerning its aesthetic qualities. The reason we know to look at the aesthetic qualities on the front of a painting is not because the back lacks aesthetic qualities, but rather because the conventions of painting tell us to look there. Even if the back of a painting looks more interesting than the front, the museum director is nevertheless required to hang the painting in the conventional way with the front out. The medium tells you what to experience in order to know the aesthetic artwork.

In the twentieth century we have witnessed a proliferation of new media. A medium seems to emerge when new conventions are instituted for isolating aesthetic qualities differently on the basis of new materials or machines. Film became an artistic medium when its unique physical structure was utilized to identify aesthetic qualities in a new way. The filmmaker became an artist when he or she stopped recording the creation of the playwright and discovered that film has resources for creation which theater lacks. The aesthetic qualities that can be presented by a film photographed from the orchestra and obedient to the temporal structure of the play are, basically, the aesthetic properties of the play itself. But when the camera photographs two different actions in two different places at two different times, and the images end up being seen at the same time and place, aesthetic properties can be realized which are inaccessible to theater. A new convention for specifying aesthetic properties has emerged. We say "See this film" instead of "See this play." In each case, what you look for is determined by the conventions of the medium.

The aesthetic theory of media has given rise to an analogy which seems to be gaining acceptance: a work of art is like a person. The dependence of aesthetic qualities on nonaesthetic ones is similar to the dependence of character traits on the bodily dispositions of persons. As Joseph Margolis has put it, works of art are *embodied* in a physical object (or physical event) in much the way a person is embodied in a human body:

> To say that a work of art is embodied in a physical object is to say that its identity is necessarily linked to the identity of the physical

object in which it is embodied, though to identify the one is not to identify the other; it is also to say that, *qua* embodied, a work of art must possess properties other than those ascribed to the physical object in which it is embodied, though it may be said to possess (where relevant) the properties of that physical object as well. Also, *if* in being embodied, works of art are, specifically, *emergent entities*, then the properties that a work of art possesses will include properties *of a kind* that cannot appropriately be ascribed to the object in which it is embodied.[15]

The "emergent" entities of aesthetic art are aesthetic qualities which are accessible only through direct experience. The aesthetic and physical properties of the artwork fuse into a person-like whole, the former constituting the "mind," the latter the "body" of the work. When we want to locate a person we look for his or her body—likewise, when we want to locate an artwork we look for its "body," namely the physical material in which it is embodied, as delimited by the conventions of media.

Although not universally accepted, this person analogy appears frequently in aesthetic theory because it provides a suitable model for understanding the artwork as a single entity appealing to two markedly different types of interest. It explains, for example, the basis of the connection between Beauty and Money.

The analogy has recently been carried to the extent of claiming that works of art, like persons, have rights.[16] To deface a canvas by Picasso or a sculpture by Michelangelo is not only to violate the rights of its owner, but also to violate certain rights of the work itself. The work is a person; to mar the canvas or marble is to harm this person. So we see that aesthetic works of art are also mortal. Like people, they age and are vulnerable to physical deterioration.

4. *Art and Works.* Aesthetics has used the conventions of media to classify and identify artworks, but its vision of the nature of art does not adequately recognize the thoroughly conventional structure within which artworks appear. This is because aesthetics tends to view a medium as a kind of substance (paint, wood, stone, sound, etc.) instead of as a network of conventions.

Its preoccupation with perceptual entities leads aesthetics to extol and examine the "work of art," while averting its attention almost entirely from the myriad other aspects of that complex cultural activity we call "art." In other words, art for aesthetics is fundamentally a class of things called works of art which are the sources of aesthetic experience. To talk about art is to talk about a set of objects. To define art is to explain membership in this class. Thus we frequently find aesthetic discussions of the question "What is art?" immediately turning to the question "What is a work of art?" as though the two questions are unquestionably identical. Yet they are not the same.

What counts as a work of art must be discovered by examining the practice of art. Art, like philosophy, is a cultural phenomenon, and any particular work of art must rely heavily upon its artistic and cultural context in communicating its meaning. *L.H.O.O.Q. Shaved* looks as much like the *Mona Lisa* as any reproduction of it does, but their artistic meanings could hardly be more different. Just as I cannot tell you what the word "rot" means unless you say whether it is English or German, I cannot explain the meaning of a painting without viewing it immersed in an artistic milieu. The shock value of Manet's *Olympia*, for example, is largely lost on modern audiences, although it can be recovered by studying the society in which the painting emerged. Even so simple a question as what a painting represents cannot be answered without some reference to the conventions of depiction which have been adopted. Whether a smaller patch of paint on the canvas is a smaller person or a person farther away—or something else—is determined by conventions of representation. The moribund prejudice against much of the "unrealistic" art of the past comes from misjudging it according to standards which are part of the alien culture of the present.

Thus trying to define "art" by defining "work of art" is a bit like trying to define philosophy by saying what constitutes a philosophy book. A work of art cannot stand alone as a member of a set. Set membership is not the structure of that human activity called art. To suppose we can examine the problem of defining art by trying to explain membership in a class of entities is simply a prejudice of aesthetics, which underplays the cultural structure of art for the sake of pursuing perceptual objects. Yet even as paradigmatic an aesthetic work as the *Mona Lisa* is a thoroughly cultural entity whose artistic and aesthetic meanings adhere to the painting by cultural forces, not by the chemical forces which keep the paint intact for a period of time.

As media proliferated, the aesthetic imperatives implied in their conventions weakened. Art has become increasingly nonaesthetic in the twentieth century, straining the conventions of media to the point where lines between them blur. Some works of art are presented in "multimedia," others (such as Duchamp's) cannot be placed within a medium at all. The concept of a medium was invented by aesthetics in order to explain the identity of artworks which articulate with aesthetic qualities. As art questions the dictates of aesthetics, it abandons the conventions of media. Let us see why.

*V Art Outside Aesthetics*

Art need not be aesthetic. *L.H.O.O.Q. Shaved* makes the point graphic by duplicating the appearance of the *Mona Lisa* while depriving it of its aesthetic import. The two works look exactly the same but are completely different. As the risqué joke is compounded by *L.H.O.O.Q. Shaved*, the *Mona Lisa* is humiliated. Though restored to its original appearance, it is not restored to its original state. Duchamp added only the moustache and goatee, but when he removed them the sacred aura of aesthetic qualities vanished as well—it had been a conventional artistic covering which adhered to the moustache and goatee when they were removed, like paint stuck to tape. The original image is intact but literalized; its function in Duchamp's piece is just to denote the *Mona Lisa*. *L.H.O.O.Q.* looked naughty, graffiti on a masterpiece. It relies upon our seeing both the aesthetic aura and its impudent violation. But as its successor reinstates the appearance, the masterpiece is ironically ridiculed a second time with the disappearance of the dignity which made *L.H.O.O.Q.* a transgression. The first piece makes fun of the Gioconda, the second piece destroys it in the process of "restoring" it. *L.H.O.O.Q. Shaved* re-indexes Leonardo's artwork as a derivative of *L.H.O.O.Q.*, reversing the temporal sequence while literalizing the image, i.e., discharging its aesthetic delights. Seen as "*L.H.O.O.Q.* shaved," the image is sapped of its artistic/aesthetic strength—it seems almost vulgar as it tours the world defiled. This is because it is placed in a context where its aesthetic properties have no meaning and its artistic "person" is reduced to just another piece of painted canvas.

It has already been pointed out that one can know the work *L.H.O.O.Q.* without having any direct experience of it, and instead by having it described. This it shares with a great deal of recent art which eschews media. When Mel Bochner puts lines on a gallery wall to measure off the degrees of an arc, their purpose is to convey information, not to proffer aesthetic delights. The same is true of On Kawara's "I GOT UP" postcards, which simply note his time of rising each day.[17] What you need to see, to experience, in order to know this art is subject to intersubjective tests—unlike aesthetic art—and this is why description will sometimes be adequate in communicating the artwork.

When Duchamp wrote "*L.H.O.O.Q.*" beneath the image of the *Mona Lisa*, he was not demonstrating his penmanship. The beauty of a script depends upon aesthetic properties of its line. The meaning of a sentence written in the script, however, is a function of how the lines fit into the structure of an alphabet. Aesthetics assumes that artistic meaning must be construed according to the first type of relation between meaning and line, but not the second. It mistakes the experience of aesthetic qualities for the substance of art. Yet the remarkable thing about even aesthetic art is not its beauty (or any other of its aesthetic qualities), but the fact that it is human-created beauty *articulated* in a medium.

The flaw in aesthetics is this: how something looks is partly a function of what we bring to it, and art is too culturally dependent to survive in the mere look of things. The importance of Duchamp's titles is that they call attention to the cultural environment which can either sustain or suffocate the aesthetic demeanor of an object. Duchamp's titles do not name objects; they put handles on things. They call attention to the artistic framework within which works of art are indexed by their titles and by other means. The culture infects the work.

A great deal of art has chosen to articulate in the medium of an aesthetic space, but there is no *a priori* reason why art must confine itself to the creation of aesthetic objects. It might opt for articulation in a semantic space instead of an aesthetic one so that artistic meaning is not embodied in a physical object or event according to the conventions of a medium. Duchamp has proven this by creating nonaesthetic art, i.e., art whose meaning is not borne by the appearance of an object. In particular, the role of line in *L.H.O.O.Q.* is more like its role in a sentence than in a drawing or painting.[18] This is why the appearance of the moustache and goatee are insignificant to the art. The first version of *L.H.O.O.Q.* was executed not by Duchamp, but by Picabia on Duchamp's instructions, and the goatee was left off. It would be an idle curiosity to speculate about whose version is better or more interesting on the basis of how each looks. The point of the artwork cannot be ascertained by scrutinizing its appearance. It is not a person-like union of physical and perceptual qualities. Its salient artistic features do not *depend* upon nonaesthetic qualities in the sense of being embodied in them. The aesthetic qualities of *L.H.O.O.Q.*, like the aesthetic qualities of Rauschenberg's erased DeKooning, are not offered up by the artist for aesthetic delectation, but rather are incidental features of the work, like its weight or its age. Line is perceived in Duchamp's piece just as it is in a sentence in a book, and in both cases we can descry the presence of aesthetic qualities. But the point of neither can be read off its physiognomy. The lines are used to convey information, not to conjure up appearances; consequently the relationship of meaning to material is similar to what it is in a drawing of a triangle in a geometry book.

If an artwork is a person, Duchamp has stripped her bare of aesthetic aura. *L.H.O.O.Q.* treats a person as an object by means of the joke produced by reading the letters in French. It also treats an artwork as a "mere thing." The presence of the moustache violates the *Mona Lisa*'s aesthetic rights and hence violates the artwork "person." In making fun of these persons, Duchamp's piece denies its own personhood.

Aesthetics is limited by reading the artwork on the model of a person. Some person-like entities are works of art, but not all artworks are persons. If not a person, what is an artwork?

### VI What Is an Artwork?

An artwork is a piece. The concept "work of art" does not isolate a class of peculiar aesthetic personages. The concept marks an indexical function in the artworld. To be a piece of art, an item need only be indexed as an artwork by an artist. Simply recategorizing an unsuspecting entity will suffice. Thus "Is it art?" is a question of little interest. The question is "So what if it is?" Art is an epiphenomenon over the class of its works.[19]

The conventions of titling works of art and publishing catalogues facilitate the practice of indexing art. However, it is important to distinguish between the artist's act of indexing by creating and the curator's act of indexing by publishing the catalogue. It is the former act which makes art; the latter act usually indexes what is already art under more specific headings, such as works by a certain artist, works in a particular show, works owned by a person or a museum, etc. To make art is, basically, to isolate something (an object, an idea, . . . ) and say of it, "This is a work of art," thereby cataloguing it under "Artworks." This may seem to devolve responsibility for arthood upon the official creators of art called artists, and the question of determining arthood turns into a question of determining who the artists are. But this wrongly places emphasis upon entities again, overshadowing the practice of art. Anyone can be an artist. To be an artist is to utilize (or perhaps invent) artistic conventions to index a piece. These might be the conventions of a medium which provide for the indexing of an aesthetic piece by means of nonaesthetic materials. But even the aesthetic artist has to stand back from the painting or play at a certain point and say "That's it. It's done." This is the point where the artist relies upon the basic indexing conventions of art. The fundamental art-making (piece-making) act is the specification of a piece: "The piece is———." Putting paint on canvas—or making any kind of product—is just one way of specifying what the work of art is. When Duchamp wrote "L.H.O.O.Q." below the reproduction, or when Rauschenberg erased the DeKooning, it was not the work (the labor) they did which made the art. A work of art is not necessarily something worked on; it is basically something conceived. To be an artist is not always to make something, but rather to engage in a cultural enterprise in which artistic pieces are proffered for consideration. Robert Barry once had an exhibition in which nothing was exhibited:

My exhibition at the Art & Project Gallery in Amsterdam in December, '69, will last two weeks. I asked them to lock the door and nail my announcement to it, reading: "For the exhibition the gallery will be closed."[20]

The fact that someone could be an artist by just christening his or her radio or anxiety to be an artwork may seem preposterous. However, the case of the Sunday Painter who rarely shows his or her paintings to anyone is not substantially different. We need to beware of confusing issues about arthood with issues about good or recognized arthood. The amateur indexer may index trivially, and the effortlessness of the task will only seem to compound the artistic inconsequence. But things are not so different when the Sunday Painter produces a few terrible watercolors which are artistically uninteresting. Despite their artistic failures, both the casual indexer and the casual painter are still artists, and the pieces they produce are works of art, just as the economics student's term paper is a piece of economics, however naive or poorly done. Simply by making a piece, a person makes an artistic "statement"; good art is distinguished by the interest or significance of what it says. Of course, interesting art, like interesting economics, is usually produced by people who, in some sense, are considered "professionals." Thus there are senses of "artist" and "economist" which refer to people who pursue their disciplines with special dedication. But what these "professionals" do is no different from what the amateurs do; it is just a difference in whether the activity is selected as a vocation. This shows that the question "Is that person an artist?" like the question "Is that thing an artwork?" is not a question with great artistic import.

A useful analogy is suggested. Art is a practised discipline of thought and action, like mathematics, economics, philosophy, or history. The major difference between art and the others is that doing art is simply employing indexing conventions defined by the practice. The reason for this is that the general focus of art is creation and conception for the sake of creation and conception, and consequently the discipline of art has devised a piece-making convention which places no limits on the content of what is created. In other words, art, unlike economics, has no general subject matter. The artworld develops and evolves through a complex network of interrelated interests, so it does have the general structure of a "discipline." But part of the recent history of art includes the loosening of conventions on what can be art until they are purely "formal." The wider use of the term "piece" instead of "work" reflects this liberalization, as does the decreasing importance of media. "Work of art" suggests an object. "Piece" suggests an item indexed within a practice. There are many kinds of "pieces," differing according to the practices they are indexed within. A "piece" could be a piece of mathematics or economics or art; and some pieces may be addressed to several disciplines. An artwork is just a piece (of art), an entity specified by conventions of the practice of art.

This view of art has one very important point of difference with aesthetics. Media are set up to identify works extensionally. Joseph Margolis relies on this idea when he argues that the identity of an artwork depends upon the identity of the physical object in which it is embodied:

> So works of art are said to be the particular objects they are, *in intensional contexts*, although they may be identified, by the linkage of embodiment, through the identity of what may be identified *in extensional contexts*. That is, works of art are identified extensionally, in the sense that their identity (whatever they are) is controlled by the identity of what they are embodied in.[21]

Some difficulties for this view are already suggested by Duchamp's "double painting." a single stretcher with *Paradise* painted on one side and *The King and Queen Surrounded by Swift Nudes* on the other. The decisive cases, however, are found among artworks which are produced merely by indexing, such as Duchamp's readymades. Indexes index their items intensionally: from the fact that "the morning star" occurs in an index, one cannot infer that "the evening star" occurs there also, even though the two expressions denote the same object. *L.H.O.O.Q. Shaved* could, for the sake of argument, be construed as residing in the same physical object as the *Mona Lisa* itself. Then there is one extensionally specified object, but two intensionally specified artworks. Rauschenberg has suggested this possibility since the only things of substance he changed by erasing the DeKooning drawing were aesthetic qualities. To complete the cycle in the way Duchamp did, Rauschenberg should buy a DeKooning painting and exhibit it in his next show: "Unerased DeKooning." The point is that artworks are identified intensionally, not extensionally. The reason *L.H.O.O.Q. Shaved* and the *Mona Lisa* are different artworks is not that they are different objects, but rather that they are different ideas. They are specified as different pieces in the art practice.

That an artwork is a piece and not a person was established by the Readymade. Duchamp selected several common objects and converted them into art simply by indexing them as artworks. Sometimes this was accomplished in conjunction with explicit indexing ceremonies, such as signing and dating a work, giving it a title, entering it in a show. But always what separates the readymade artwork from the "readymade" object it was ready-made from is a simple act of indexing. Duchamp says,

"A point I want very much to establish is that the choice of these Readymades was never dictated by aesthetic delectation. The choice was based on a reaction of *visual indifference* with a total absence of good or bad taste."[22] The Readymade demonstrates the indexical nature of the concept "work of art" by showing that whether something is an artwork is not determined by its appearance but by how it is regarded in the artworld. The same shovel can be a mere hardware item at one time and an artwork at another depending upon how the artworld stands in relation to it. Even an old work of art can be converted into a new one without changing the appearance of the old work, but only "creating a new idea for it," as Duchamp has said of the urinal readymade called *Fountain*. The significance of the title of this piece has not been fully appreciated. A urinal is a fountain; that is, it is an object designed for discharging a stream of water. The reason most urinals are *not* fountains, despite their designs, is that their locations and use differ from similar devices we do consider fountains. The objects are structurally similar, but their cultural roles are very different. Putting a urinal in a gallery makes it visible as a "fountain" and as a work of art because the context has been changed. Cultural contexts endow objects with special meanings; and they determine arthood.[23]

It has been pointed out that *Fountain* was accepted as a work of art only because Duchamp had already established his status as an artist by producing works in traditional forms. This is probably true: not just anyone could have carried it off. You cannot revolutionize the accepted conventions for indexing unless you have some recognition in the artworld already. However, this does not mean that Duchamp's piece is only marginal art and that anyone desiring to follow his act of indexing has to become a painter first. When Duchamp made his first nonaesthetic work, the conventions for indexing artworks were more or less the media of aesthetics: to make an artwork was to articulate in a medium. Duchamp did not simply make an exception to these conventions, he instituted a new convention, the indexing convention which countenances nonaesthetic art, though perhaps it should be said rather that Duchamp *uncovered* the convention, since it lies behind even the use of media, which are specialized ways of indexing aesthetic qualities. In any event, once the new convention is instituted anyone can follow it as easily as he or she can follow the indexing conventions of aesthetics. The Sunday Indexer can have just as good a time as the Sunday Painter.

### VII Duchamp's Legacy

Because of Duchamp's wit and humor, it was easy at first to dismiss his art, or maybe just to be confused by it. Yet it is not trivial because it is funny. With the art of Duchamp, art emerged openly as a practice. His *Large Glass*, whose meaning is inaccessible to anyone who merely examines the physical object, stands as the first monument to an art of the mind.

This kind of art developed historically; it is not an anomaly. Probably it originates in what Clement Greenberg calls "Modernism," whose characteristic feature is self-criticism. Like philosophy, art developed to the point where a critical act about the discipline (or part of it) could be part of the discipline itself. Once embarked on self-scrutiny, art came to realize that its scope could include much more than making aesthetic objects. It is a practice, which is why jokes about art can be art in the way jokes about philosophy can be philosophy. Art is a practice which can be characterized about as well and as usefully as philosophy can be. Defining art is not likely to be a very interesting pursuit. An artwork is a piece indexed within conventions of this practice, and its being an artwork is determined not by its properties, but by its location in the artworld. Its properties are used to say *what* the particular work is.

If art must be aesthetic, the tools of the art indexer must be media, whether mixed or pure. To make a work of art is to use a medium to join together literal physical qualities and created aesthetic qualities. An aesthetic person is born in the intercourse.

Aesthetics treats aesthetic experience, not art. Anything, from music to mathematics, can be seen aesthetically. This is the basis for the traditional preoccupation of aesthetics with Beauty, a quality found in both art and nature. Aesthetics deals with art and other things under the heading of aesthetic experience. Conversely, not all art is aesthetic. Seeing its marriage to aesthetics as a forced union, art reaches out to find meaning beyond skin-deep looks. The indexers create with ideas. The tools of indexing are the languages of ideas, even when the ideas are aesthetic.

.

*Notes*

1. Quoted from *Marcel Duchamp*, catalogue for the show organized by the Museum of Modern Art and the Philadelphia Museum of Art, edited by Anne d'Harnoncourt and Kynaston McShine (New York: Museum of Modern Art; Philadelphia, Philadelphia Museum of Art, 1973), p. 289. When pronounced in French, the letters produce a sentence meaning "She has a hot ass."

2. For numerous examples see Lucy Lippard, *Six Years: The Dematerialization of the Art Object from 1966 to 1972* (New York, 1973). There is no sharp dichotomy between idea art and appearance art. Most traditional art is concerned with ideas, even though they may be expressed visually.

3. One might even consider the *Mona Lisa* an instance of *L.H.O.O.Q. Shaved.*

Duchamp refers to the earlier piece *L.H.O.O.Q.* as *"this Mona Lisa* with a moustache and goatee."

4. See Alexander Gottlieb Baumgarten, *Reflections on Poetry*, trans. Karl Aschenbrenner and William B. Holther (Berkeley, 1954), p. 78. The translators translate *scientia cognitionis sensitivae* as "the science of perception." Monroe Beardsley gives a somewhat more precise translation: "the science of sensory cognition." See his *Aesthetics from Classical Greece to the Present* (New York, 1966), p. 157. For useful discussions of the emergence of "aesthetics" in eighteeneth-century philosophy, see Beardsley's history and also George Dickie, *Aesthetics: An Introduction* (New York, 1971).

5. George Dickie expresses what is occasionally realized: "The concept of art is certainly related in important ways to the concept of the aesthetic, but the aesthetic cannot completely absorb art." (See *Aesthetics: An Introduction*, p. 2.) However, it turns out that one way art is related to aesthetics is that both the philosophy of art and the philosophy of criticism, like aesthetics itself, are grounded in what Dickie calls "aesthetic experience." (See the diagram on p. 45 of *Aesthetics*.) It seems that for Dickie, what differentiates aesthetics from the other two is simply the manner in which each studies aesthetic experience. See also his *Art and the Aesthetic* (Ithaca, 1974). Dickie takes a very important first step in distinguishing the concepts "art" and "aesthetics," but his search for a definition of "work of art" seems to me to follow an aesthetic development based upon the notion of "appreciation." Dickie's views are discussed at greater length in my essay "Deciding about Art: A Polemic against Aesthetics," in *Culture and Art*, ed. Lars Aagaard-Mogensen (Atlantic Highlands, N.J., 1976).

6. Frank Sibley, "Aesthetic and Non-Aesthetic," pp. 135–159, *The Philosophical Review* LXXIV (1965), reprinted in Matthew Lipman, ed., *Contemporary Aesthetics* (Boston, 1973), p. 434. See also Sibley's "Aesthetic Concepts," *The Philosophical Review* LXVIII (1959), 421–450.

7. Monroe Beardsley, *Aesthetics: Problems in the Philosophy of Criticism* (New York, 1958), p. 31.

8. *Ibid.*, p. 31.

9. *Ibid.*, p. 33. George Dickie presents arguments against Beardsley's notion of the aesthetic object, but I do not find them very persuasive. See Dickie's *Art and the Aesthetic*, pp. 148 ff.

10. See Benedetto Croce, *Aesthetic* (New York, 1929), and R. G. Collingwood, *The Principles of Art* (New York, 1938). In the expression theory developed by Croce and Collingwood, it is not the concept of expression itself which is aesthetic, but rather the concept of intuition.

11. See Clive Bell, *Art* (New York, 1959). Formalist criticism has maintained its commitment to aesthetics. See for example, Clement Greenberg, *Art and Culture* (Boston, 1961), and "Modernist Painting," *Art and Literature*, vol 9 (1965).

12. See Isabel Creed Hungerland, "The Logic of Aesthetic Concepts," *The Proceedings and Addresses of the American Philosophical Association,* vol. 40 (1963), and "Once Again, Aesthetic and Non-Aesthetic," *The Journal of Aesthetics and Art Criticism* XXVI (1968), 285–295.

13. See Sibley, "Aesthetic and Non-Aesthetic," for a discussion of the dependency of aesthetic qualities on nonaesthetic qualities.

14. E. H. Gombrich, in *Art and Illusion* (New York, 1960), demonstrates how a simple change in contrast in a photograph can change its aesthetic properties.

15. Joseph Margolis, "Works of Art as Physically Embodied and Culturally Emergent Entities," *The British Journal of Aesthetics* XV (1975), 189.

16. See Alan Tormey, "Aesthetic Rights," *The Journal of Aesthetics and Art Criticism* XXXII (1973), 163–170.

17. See Ursula Meyer, *Conceptual Art* (New York, 1972).

18. It is interesting that Duchamp says there are *four* letters in the title *L.H.O.O.Q.*" There are five letter tokens, each with its own particular appearance. But there are only four letter types, and a letter type does not have any particular appearance.

19. George Dickie develops a related notion in his "Institutional Theory of Art." See especially *Art and the Aesthetic*. His basic idea is that something is art which has been christened art. One difficulty with this view is that it does not provide for the intensional specification of a work of art. This point is discussed later on. The notion of indexing introduced here is discussed further in "Deciding about Art" (see note 5).

20. In Meyer, *Conceptual Art*, p. 41.

21. Margolis, "Works of Art as Physically Embodied and Culturally Emergent Entities," p. 191. An extensional context is one in which expressions denoting the same entity can replace one another without altering the truth of what is said.

George Dickie holds that making art involves a kind of status-conferral. This theory has insights to offer, but it does have the shortcoming that status-conferral is basically extensional. If it is true that Cicero has had the status of statesman conferred on him, the same is true of Tully, since the two names belong to the same person.

22. *Marcel Duchamp*, p. 89.

23. Cf. Arthur Danto, "The Artworld," *The Journal of Philosophy*, vol. 61 (1964), where a similar point is made, pp. 571–584.

I am grateful to Lars Aagaard-Mogensen, Linda Ashley, and Monroe Beardsley for their helpful comments on earlier drafts of this paper.

# 5.    The Myth of the Aesthetic Attitude
## GEORGE DICKIE

Some recent articles[1] have suggested the unsatisfactoriness of the notion of the aesthetic attitude and it is now time for a fresh look at that encrusted article of faith. This conception has been valuable to aesthetics and criticism in helping wean them from a sole concern with beauty and related notions.[2] However, I shall argue that the aesthetic attitude is a myth and while, as G. Ryle has said, "Myths often do a lot of theoretical good while they are still new,"[3] this particular one is no longer useful and in fact misleads aesthetic theory.

There is a range of theories which differ according to how strongly the aesthetic attitude is characterized. This variation is reflected in the language the theories employ. The strongest variety is Edward Bullough's theory of psychical distance, recently defended by Sheila Dawson.[4] The central technical term of this theory is "distance" used as a verb to denote an action which either constitutes or is necessary for the aesthetic attitude. These theorists use such sentences as "He distanced (or failed to distance) the play." The second variety is widely held but has been defended most vigorously in recent years by Jerome Stolnitz and Eliseo Vivas. The *central* technical term of this variety is "disinterested"[5] used either as an adverb or as an adjective. This weaker theory speaks not of a special kind of action (distancing) but of an ordinary kind of action (attending) done in a certain way (disinterestedly). These first two versions are perhaps not so different as my classification suggests. Hoever, the language of the two is different enough to justify separate discussions. My discussion of this second variety will for the most part make use of Jerome Stolnitz's book[6] which is a thorough, consistent, and large-scale version of the attitude theory. The weakest version of the attitude theory can be found in Vincent

From *American Philosophical Quarterly*, I (1964), 55–65. Reprinted with permission of the author and *American Philosophical Quarterly*.

Tomas's statement "If looking at a picture and attending closely to how it looks is not really to be in the aesthetic attitude, then what on earth is?"[7] In the following I shall be concerned with the notion of *aesthetic* attitude and this notion may have little or no connection with the ordinary notion of an *attitude*.

## *I*

Psychical distance, according to Bullough, is a psychological process by virtue of which a person *puts* some object (be it a painting, a play, or a dangerous fog at sea) "out of gear" with the practical interests of the self. Miss Dawson maintains that it is "the beauty of the phenomenon, which captures our attention, puts us out of gear with practical life, and forces us, if we are receptive, to view it on the level of aesthetic consciousness."[8]

Later she maintains that some persons (critics, actors, members of an orchestra, and the like) "distance deliberately."[9] Miss Dawson, following Bullough, discusses cases in which people are unable to bring off an act of distancing or are incapable of being induced into a state of being distanced. She uses Bullough's example of the jealous ("under-distanced") husband at a performance of *Othello* who is unable to keep his attention on the play because he keeps thinking of his own wife's suspicious behavior. On the other hand, if "we are mainly concerned with the technical details of its [the play's] presentation, then we are said to be over-distanced."[10] There is, then, a species of action—distancing—which may be deliberately done and which initiates a state of consciousness—being distanced.

The question is: Are there actions denoted by "to distance" or states of consciousness denoted by "being distanced"? When the curtain goes up, when we walk up to a painting, or when we look at a sunset are we ever induced into a state of being distanced either by being struck by the beauty of the object or by pulling off an act of distancing? I do not recall committing any such special actions or of being induced into any special state, and I have no reason to suspect that I am atypical in this respect. The distance-theorist may perhaps ask, "But are you not usually oblivious to noises and sights other than those of the play or to the marks on the wall around the painting?" The answer is of course—"Yes." But if "to distance" and "being distanced" simply mean that one's attention is focused, what is the point of introducing new technical terms and speaking as if these terms refer to special kinds of acts and states of consciousness? The distance-theorist might argue further, "But surely you put the play (painting, sunset) 'out of gear' with your practical interests?" This question seems to me to be a very odd way of asking (by employing the technical metaphor "out of gear") if I attended to the play rather than thought about my wife or wondered how they managed to move the scenery about. Why not ask me straight out if I paid attention? Thus, when Miss Dawson says that the jealous husband under-distanced *Othello* and that the person with a consuming interest in techniques of stagecraft over-distanced the play, these are just technical and misleading ways of describing two different cases of inattention. In both cases something is being attended to, but in neither case is it the action of the play. To introduce the technical terms "distance," "under-distance," and "over-distance" does nothing but send us chasing after phantom acts and states of consciousness.

Miss Dawson's commitment to the theory of distance (as a kind of mental insulation material necessary for a work of art if it is to be enjoyed aesthetically) leads her to draw a conclusion so curious as to throw suspicion on the theory.

> One remembers the horrible loss of distance in *Peter Pan*—the moment when Peter says "Do you believe in fairies? . . . If you believe, clap your hands!" the moment when most children would like to slink out of the theatre and not a few cry—not because Tinkerbell may die, but because the magic is gone. What, after all, should we feel like if Lear were to leave Cordelia, come to the front of the stage and say, "All the grown-ups who think that she loves me, shout 'Yes'."[11]

It is hard to believe that the responses of any children could be as theory-bound as those Miss Dawson describes. In fact, Peter Pan's request for applause is a dramatic high point to which children respond enthusiastically. The playwright gives the children a momentary chance to become actors in the play. The children do not at that moment lose or snap out of a state of being distanced because they never had or were in any such thing to begin with. The comparison of Peter Pan's appeal to the hypothetical one by Lear is pointless. *Peter Pan* is a magical play in which almost anything can happen, but *King Lear* is a play of a different kind. There are, by the way, many plays in which an actor directly addresses the audience (*Our Town, The Marriage Broker. A Taste of Honey*, for example) without causing the play to be less valuable. Such plays are unusual, but what is unusual is not necessarily bad; there is no point in trying to lay down rules to which every play must conform independently of the kind of play it is.

It is perhaps worth noting that Susanne Langer reports the reaction she had as a child to this scene in *Peter Pan*.[12] As she remembers it, Peter Pan's appeal shattered the illusion and caused her acute misery. However, she reports that all the other children clapped and laughed and enjoyed themselves.

## II

The second way of conceiving of the aesthetic attitude—as the ordinary action of attending done in a certain way (disinterestedly)—is illustrated by the work of Jerome Stolnitz and Eliseo Vivas. Stolnitz defines "aesthetic attitude" as "disinterested and sympathetic attention to and contemplation of any object of awareness whatever, for its own sake alone."[13] Stolnitz defines the main terms of his definition: "disinterested" means "no concern for any ulterior purpose.";[14] "sympathetic" means "accept the object on its own terms to appreciate it";[15] and "contemplation" means "perception directed toward the object in its own right and the spectator is not concerned to analyze it or ask questions about it."[16]

The notion of disinterestedness, which Stolnitz has elsewhere shown[17] to be seminal for modern aesthetic theory, is the key term here. Thus, it is necessary to be clear about the nature of disinterested attention to the various arts. It can make sense to speak, for example, of listening disinterestedly to music only if it makes sense to speak of listening interestedly to music. It would make no sense to speak of walking *fast* unless walking could be done *slowly*. Using Stolnitz's definition of "disinterestedness," the two situations would have to be described as "listening with no ulterior purpose" (disinterestedly) and "listening with an ulterior purpose" (interestedly). Note that what initially appears to be a perceptual distinction—listening in a certain way (interestedly or disinterestedly)—turns out to be a motivational or an intentional distinction—listening for or with a certain purpose. Suppose Jones listens to a piece of music for the purpose of being able to analyze and describe it on an examination the next day and Smith listens to the same music with no such ulterior purpose. There is certainly a difference between the motives and intentions of the two men: Jones has an ulterior purpose and Smith does not, but this does not mean Jones's *listening* differs from Smith's. It is possible that both men enjoy the music or that both be bored. The attention of either or both may flag and so on. It is important to note that a person's motive or intention is different from his action (Jones's listening to the music, for example). There is only one way to *listen* to (to attend to) music, although the listening may be more or less attentive and there may be a variety of motives, intentions, and reasons for doing so and a variety of ways of being distracted from the music.

In order to avoid a common mistake of aestheticians—drawing a conclusion about one kind of art and assuming it holds for all the arts—the question of disinterested attention must be considered for arts other than music. How would one look at a painting disinterestedly or interestedly? An example of alleged interested viewing might be the case in which a painting reminds Jones of his grandfather and Jones proceeds to muse about or to regale a companion with tales of his grandfather's pioneer exploits. Such incidents would be characterized by attitude-theorists as examples of using a work of art as a vehicle for associations and so on, i.e., cases of interested attention. But Jones is not looking at (attending to) the painting at all, although he may be facing it with his eyes open. Jones is now musing or attending to the story he is telling, although he had to look at the painting at first to notice that it resembled his grandfather. Jones is not now looking at the painting interestedly, since he is not now looking at (attending to) the painting. Jones's thinking or telling a story about his grandfather is no more a part of the painting than his speculating about the artist's intentions is and, hence, his musing, telling, speculating, and so on cannot properly be described as attending to the painting interestedly. What attitude-aestheticians are calling attention to is the occurrence of irrelevant associations which distract the viewer from the painting or whatever. But distraction is not a special kind of attention, it is a kind of inattention.

Consider now disinterestedness and plays. I shall make use of some interesting examples offered by J. O. Urmson,[18] but I am not claiming that Urmson is an attitude-theorist. Urmson never speaks in his article of aesthetic attitude but rather of aesthetic satisfaction. In addition to aesthetic satisfaction, Urmson mentions economic, moral, personal, and intellectual satisfactions. I think the attitude-theorist would consider these last four kinds of satisfaction as "ulterior purposes" and, hence, cases of interested attention. Urmson considers the case of a man in the audience of a play who is delighted.[19] It is discovered that his delight is *solely* the result of the fact that there is a full house—the man is the impresario of the production. Urmson is right in calling *this* impresario's satisfaction economic rather than aesthetic, although there is a certain oddness about the example as it finds the impresario sitting *in the audience*. However, my concern is not with Urmson's examples as such but with the attitude theory. This impresario is certainly an interested party in the fullest sense of the word, but is his behavior an instance of interested attention as distinct from the supposed disinterested attention of the average citizen who sits beside him? In the situation as described by Urmson it would not make any sense to say that the impresario is attending to the play at all, since his *sole* concern at the moment is the till. If he can be said to be attending to anything (rather than just thinking about it) it is the size of the house. I do not mean to suggest that an impresario could not attend to his play if he found himself taking up a seat in a full house; I am challenging the sense of disinterested attention. As an example of personal satisfaction Urmson mentions the spectator whose daughter is in the play.

Intellectual satisfaction involves the solution of technical problems of plays and moral satisfaction the consideration of the effects of the play on the viewer's conduct. All three of these candidates which the attitude-theorist would propose as cases of interested attention turn out to be just different ways of being distracted from the play and, hence, not cases of interested attention to the play. Of course, there is no reason to think that in any of these cases the distraction or inattention must be total, although it could be. In fact, such inattentions often occur but are so fleeting that nothing of the play, music, or whatever is missed or lost.

The example of a playwright watching a rehearsal or an out-of-town performance with a view to rewriting the script has been suggested to me as a case in which a spectator is certainly attending to the play (unlike our impresario) and attending in an interested manner. This case is unlike those just discussed but is similar to the earlier case of Jones (not Smith) listening to a particular piece of music. Our playwright—like Jones, who was to be examined on the music—has ulterior motives. Furthermore, the playwright, unlike an ordinary spectator, can change the script after the performance or during a rehearsal. But how is our playwright's *attention* (as distinguished from his motives and intentions) different from that of an ordinary viewer? The playwright might enjoy or be bored by the performance as any spectator might be. The playwright's attention might even flag. In short, the kinds of things which may happen to the playwright's attention are no different from those that may happen to an ordinary spectator, although the two may have quite different motives and intentions.

For the discussion of disinterested-interested reading of literature it is appropriate to turn to the arguments of Eliseo Vivas whose work is largely concerned with literature. Vivas remarks that "By approaching a poem in a nonaesthetic mode it may function as history, as social criticism, as diagnostic evidence of the author's neuroses, and in an indefinite number of other ways."[20] Vivas further notes that according to Plato "the Greeks used Homer as an authority on war and almost anything under the sun," and that a certain poem "can be read as erotic poetry or as an account of a mystical experience."[21] The difference between reading a poem *as* history or whatever (reading it nonaesthetically) and reading it aesthetically depends on how *we* approach or read it. A poem "does not come self-labelled,"[22] but presumably is a poem only when it is read in a certain way—when it is an object of aesthetic experience. For Vivas, being an aesthetic object means being the object of the aesthetic attitude. He defines the aesthetic experience as "an experience of rapt attention which involves the intransitive apprehension of an object's immanent meanings and values in their full presentational immediacy."[23] Vivas maintains that his definition "helps me understand better what I can and what I cannot do when I read *The Brothers* [*Karamazov*]" and his definition "forces us to acknowledge that *The Brothers Karamazov* can hardly be read as art."[24] This acknowledgment means that we probably cannot intransitively apprehend *The Brothers* because of its size and complexity.

"Intransitive" is the key term here and Vivas's meaning must be made clear. A number of passages reveal his meaning but perhaps the following is the best. "Heaving once seen a hockey game in slow motion, I am prepared to testify that it was an object of pure intransitive experience [attention]—for I was not *interested* in which team won the game and no external factors mingled with my interest in the beautiful rhythmic flow of the slow-moving men."[25] It appears that Vivas's "intransitive attention" has the same meaning as Stolnitz's "disinterested attention," namely, "attending with no ulterior purpose."[26] Thus, the question to ask is "How does one attend to (read) a poem or any literary work transitively?" One can certainly attend to (read) a poem for a variety of different purposes and because of a variety of different reasons, but can one attend to a poem transitively? I do not think so, but let us consider the examples Vivas offers. He mentions "a type of reader" who uses a poem or parts of a poem as a springboard for "loose, uncontrolled, relaxed day-dreaming, wool-gathering rambles, free from the contextual control" of the poem.[27] But surely it would be wrong to say such musing is a case of transitively attending to a poem, since it is clearly a case of not attending to a poem. Another supposed way of attending to a poem transitively is by approaching it "as diagnostic evidence of the author's neuroses." Vivas is right if he means that there is no critical point in doing this since it does not throw light on the poem. But this is a case of *using* information gleaned from a poem to make inferences about its author rather than attending to a poem. If anything can be said to be attended to here it is the author's neuroses (at least they are being thought about). This kind of case is perhaps best thought of as a rather special way of getting distracted from a poem. Of course, such "biographical" distractions might be insignificant and momentary enough so as scarcely to distract attention from the poem (a flash of insight or understanding about the poet). On the other hand, such distractions may turn into dissertations and whole careers. Such an interest may lead a reader to concentrate his attention (when he does read a poem) on certain "informational" aspects of a poem and to ignore the remaining aspects. As deplorable as such a sustained practice may be, it is at best a case of attending to certain features of a poem and ignoring others.

Another way that poetry may allegedly be read transitively is by reading it as history. This case is different from the two preceding ones since poetry often *contains* history (makes historical statements or at least references) but does not (usually) contain statements about the author's neuroses and so on nor does it contain statements about what a reader's free associations are about (otherwise we would not call them "*free* associations"). Reading a poem as history suggests that we are attending to (thinking about) historical events by way of attending to a poem—the poem is a time-telescope. Consider the following two sets of lines:

> In fourteen hundred and ninety-two
> Columbus sailed the ocean blue.

> Or like stout Cortez when with eagle eyes
> He star'd at the Pacific—and all his men
> Look'd at each other with a wild surmise—
> Silent, upon a peak in Darien.

Someone might read both of these raptly and not know that they make historical references (inaccurately in one case)—might this be a case of intransitive attention? How would the above reading differ—so far as attention is concerned—from the case of a reader who recognized the historical content of the poetic lines? The two readings do not differ as far as attention is concerned. History is a part of these sets of poetic lines and the two readings differ in that the first fails to take account of an aspect of the poetic lines (its historical content) and the second does not fail to do so. Perhaps by "reading as history" Vivas means "reading *simply* as history." But even this meaning does not mark out a special kind of attention but rather means that only a single aspect of a poem is being noticed and that its rhyme, meter, and so on are ignored. Reading a poem as social criticism can be analyzed in a fashion similar to reading as history. Some poems simply are or contain social criticism, and a complete reading must not fail to notice this fact.

The above cases of alleged interested attending can be sorted out in the following way. Jones listening to the music and our playwright watching the rehearsal are both attending with ulterior motives to a work of art, but there is no reason to suppose that the attention of either is different in kind from that of an ordinary spectator. The reader who reads a poem as history is simply attending to an aspect of a poem. On the other hand, the remaining cases—Jones beside the painting telling of his grandfather, the gloating impresario, daydreaming while "reading" a poem, and so on—are simply cases of not attending to the work of art.

In general, I conclude that "disinterestedness" or "intransitiveness" cannot properly be used to refer to a special kind of attention. "Disinterestedness" is a term which is used to make clear that an action has certain kinds of motives. Hence, we speak of disinterested findings (of boards of inquiry), disinterested verdicts (of judges and juries), and so on. Attending to an object, of course, has its motives but the attending itself is not interested or disinterested according to whether its motives are of the kind which motivate interested or disinterested action (as findings and verdicts might), although the attending may be more or less close.

I have argued that the second way of conceiving the aesthetic attitude is also a myth, or at least that its main content—disinterested attention—is; but I must now try to establish that the view misleads aesthetic theory. I shall argue that the attitude-theorist is incorrect about (1) the way in which he wishes to set the limits of aesthetic relevance; (2) the relation of the critic to a work of art; and (3) the relation of morality to aesthetic value.

Since I shall make use of the treatment of aesthetic relevance in Jerome Stolnitz's book, let me make clear that I am not necessarily denying the relevance of the specific items he cites but disagreeing with his criterion of relevance. His criterion of relevance is derived from his definition of "aesthetic attitude" and is set forth at the very beginning of his book. This procedure leads Monroe Beardsley in his review of the book to remark that Stolnitz's discussion is premature.[28] Beardsley suggests "that relevance cannot be satisfactorily discussed until after a careful treatment of the several arts, their dimensions and capacities."[29]

First, what is meant by "aesthetic relevance"? Stolnitz defines the problem by asking the question: "Is it ever 'relevant' to the aesthetic experience to have thoughts or images or bits of knowledge which are not present within the object itself?"[30] Stolnitz begins by summarizing Bullough's experiment and discussion of single colors and associations.[31] Some associations absorb the spectator's attention and distract him from the color and some associations "fuse" with the color. Associations of the latter kind are aesthetic and the former are not. Stolnitz draws the following conclusion about associations:

> If the aesthetic experience is as we have described it, then whether an association is aesthetic depends on whether it is compatible with the attitude of "disinterested attention." If the association re-enforces the focusing of attention upon the object, by "fusing" with the object and thereby giving it added "life and significance," it is genuinely aesthetic. If, however, it arrogates attention to itself and away from the object, it undermines the aesthetic attitude.[32]

It is not clear how something could *fuse* with a single color, but "fusion" is one of those words in aesthetics which is rarely defined. Stolnitz then makes use of a more fruitful example, one from I. A. Richards's *Practical Criticism*.[33] He cites the responses of students to the poem which begins:

> Between the erect and solemn trees
> I will go down upon my knees;
> I shall not find this day
> So meet a place to pray.

The image of a rugby forward running arose in the mind of one student-reader on reading the third verse of this poem. A cathedral was suggested to a second reader of the poem. The cathedral image "is congruous with both the verbal meaning of the poem and the emotions and mood which it expresses. It does not divert attention away from the poem."[34] The rugby image is presumably incongruous and diverts attention from the poem.

It is a confusion to take compatibility with disinterested attention as a criterion of relevance. If, as I have tried to show, *disinterested attention* is a confused notion, then it will not do as a satisfactory criterion. Also, when Stolnitz comes to show why the cathedral image is, and the rugby image is not relevant, the criterion he actually uses is *congruousness with the meaning of the poem*, which is quite independent of the notion of disinterestedness. The problem is perhaps best described as the problem of relevance to a poem, or more generally, to a work of art, rather than aesthetic relevance.

A second way in which the attitude theory misleads aesthetics is its contention that a critic's relationship to a work of art is different in kind from the relationship of other persons to the work. H. S. Langfeld in an early statement of this view wrote that we may "slip from the attitude of aesthetic enjoyment to the attitude of the critic." He characterizes the critical attitude as "intellectually occupied in coldly estimating . . . merits" and the aesthetic attitude as responding "emotionally to" a work of art.[35] At the beginning of his book in the discussion of the aesthetic attitude, Stolnitz declares that if a percipient of a work of art "has the purpose of passing judgment upon it, his attitude is not aesthetic."[36] He develops this line at a later stage of his book, arguing that appreciation (perceiving with the aesthetic attitude) and criticism (seeking for reasons to support an evaluation of a work) are (1) distinct and (2) "psychologically opposed to each other."[37] The critical attitude is questioning, analytical, probing for strengths and weakness, and so on. The aesthetic attitude is just the opposite: "It commits our allegiance to the object freely and unquestion-ingly"; "the spectator 'surrenders' himself to the work of art."[38] "Just because the two attitudes are inimical, whenever criticism obtrudes, it reduces aesthetic interest."[39] Stolnitz does not, of course, argue that criticism is unimportant for appreciation. He maintains criticism plays an important and necessary role in preparing a person to appreciate the nuances, detail, form, and so on of works of art. We are quite right, he says, thus to read and listen perceptively and acutely, but he questions, "Does this mean that we must analyze, measure in terms of value-criteria, etc., *during* the supposedly aesthetic experience?"[40] His answer is "No" and he maintains that criticism must occur "*prior* to the aesthetic encounter,"[41] or it will interfere with appreciation.

How does Stolnitz know that criticism will always interfere with appreciation? His conclusion sounds like one based upon the observations of actual cases, but I do not think it is. I believe it is a logical consequence of his definition of aesthetic attitude in terms of disinterested attention (no ulterior purpose). According to his view, to appreciate an object aesthetically one has to perceive it with no ulterior purpose. But the critic has an ulterior purpose—to analyze and evaluate the object he perceives—hence, insofar as a person functions as a critic he cannot function as an appreciator. But here, as previously, Stolnitz confuses a perceptual distinction with a motivational one. If it were possible to *attend* disinterestedly or interestedly, then perhaps the critic (as percipient) would differ from other percipients. But if my earlier argument about attending is correct, the critic differs from other percipients only in his motives and intentions and not in the way in which he attends to a work of art.

Of course, it might just be a fact that the search for reasons is incompatible with the appreciation of art, but I do not think it is. Several years ago I participated in a series of panel discussions of films. During the showing of each film we were to discuss, I had to take note of various aspects of the film (actor's performance, dramatic development, organization of the screen-plane and screen-space at given moments, and so on) in order later to discuss the films. I believe that this practice not only helped educate me to appreciate subsequent films but that it enhanced the appreciation of the films I was analyzing. I noticed and was able to appreciate things about the films I was watching which ordinarily out of laziness I would not have noticed. I see no reason why the same should not be the case with the professional critic or any critical percipient. If many professional critics seem to appreciate so few works, it is not because they are critics, but perhaps because the percentage of good works of art is fairly small and they suffer from a kind of combat fatigue.

I am unable to see any significant difference between "perceptively and acutely" attending to a work of art (which Stolnitz holds enhances appreciation) and searching for reasons, so far as the experience of a work of art is concerned. If I attend perceptively and acutely, I will have certain standards and/or paradigms in mind (not necessarily consciously) and will be keenly aware of the elements and relations in the work and will evaluate them to some degree. Stolnitz writes as if criticism takes place and then is over and done with, but the search for and finding of reasons (noticing this fits in with that, and so on) is continuous in practiced appreciators. A practiced viewer does not even have to be looking for a reason, he may just notice a line or an area in a painting, for example, and the line or area becomes a reason why he thinks the painting better or worse. A person may be a critic (not necessarily a good one) without meaning to be or without even realizing it.

There is one final line worth pursuing. Stolnitz's remarks suggest that one reason he thinks criticism and appreciation incompatible is that they compete with one another for time (this would be especially bad in the cases of performed works). But seeking and finding reasons (criticism) does not compete for time with appreciation. First, to seek for a reason means to be ready and able to notice something and to be thus ready and able as one attends does not compete for time with the attending. In fact, I should suppose that seeking for reasons would tend to focus attention more securely on the work of art. Second, finding a reason is an achievement, like winning a race. (It takes time to run a race but not to win it.) Consider the finding of the following reasons. How much time does it take to "see" that a note is off key (or on key)? How long does it take to notice that an actor mispronounces a word (or does it right)? How much time does it take to realize that a character's action does not fit his already established personality? (One is struck by it.) How long does it take to apprehend that a happy ending is out of place? It does not take time to find any of these reasons or reasons in general. Finding a reason is like coming to understand—it is done in a flash. I do not mean to suggest that one cannot be mistaken in finding a reason. What may appear to be a fault or a merit (a found reason) in the middle of a performance (or during one look at a painting and so forth) may turn out to be just the opposite when seen from the perspective of the whole performance (or other looks at the painting).

A third way in which the attitude theory misleads aesthetic theory is its contention that aesthetic value is always independent of morality. This view is perhaps not peculiar to the attitude theory, but it is a logical consequence of the attitude approach. Two quotations from attitude-theorists will establish the drift of their view of morality and aesthetic value.

We are either concerned with the beauty of the object or with some other value of the same. Just as soon, for example, as ethical considerations occur to our mind, our attitude shifts.[42]

> Any of us might reject a novel because it seems to conflict with our
> moral beliefs. ... When we do so ... we have *not* read the book
> aesthetically, for we have interposed moral ... responses of our own
> which are alien to it. This disrupts the aesthetic attitude. We cannot
> then say that the novel is *aesthetically* bad, for we have not permitted
> ourselves to consider it aesthetically. To maintain the aesthetic at-
> titude, we must follow the lead of the object and respond in concert
> with it.[43]

This conception of the aesthetic attitude functions to hold the moral
aspects and the *aesthetic* aspects of the work of art firmly apart. Presumably,
although it is difficult to see one's way clearly here, the moral aspects of
a work of art cannot be an object of aesthetic attention because aesthetic
attention is by definition disinterested and the moral aspects are somehow
practical (interested). I suspect that there are a number of confusions
involved in the assumption of the incompatibility of aesthetic attention
and the moral aspects of art, but I shall not attempt to make these clear,
since the root of the assumption—disinterested attention—is a confused
notion. Some way other than in terms of the aesthetic attitude, then, is
needed to discuss the relation of morality and aesthetic value.

David Pole in a recent article[44] has argued that the moral vision which
a work of art may embody is *aesthetically* significant. It should perhaps
be remarked at this point that not all works of art embody a moral vision
and perhaps some kinds of art (music, for example) cannot embody a
moral vision, but certainly some novels, some poems, and some films and
plays do. I assume it is unnecessary to show how novels and so on have
this moral aspect. Pole notes the curious fact that while so many critics
approach works of art in "overtly moralistic terms," it is a "philosophical
commonplace ... that the ethical and the aesthetic modes ... form different
categories."[45] I suspect that many philosophers would simply say that these
critics are confused about their roles. But Pole assumes that philosophical
theory "should take notice of practice"[46] and surely he is right. In agreeing
with Pole's assumption I should like to reserve the right to argue in specific
cases that a critic may be misguided. This right is especially necessary in
a field such as aesthetics because the language and practice of critics is so
often burdened with ancient theory. Perhaps *all* moralistic criticism is
wrong, but philosophers should not rule it out of order at the very
beginning by use of a definition.

Pole thinks that the moral vision presented by a particular work of art
will be either true or false (perhaps a mixture of true and false might
occur). If a work has a false moral vision, then something "is lacking
within the work itself. But to say that is to say that the [work] is internally

incoherent; some particular aspect must jar with what—on the strength of the rest—we claim a right to demand. And here the moral fault that we have found will count as an aesthetic fault too."[47] Pole is trying to show that the assessment of the moral vision of a work of art is just a special case of coherence or incoherence, and since everyone would agree that coherence is an aesthetic category, the assessment of the moral vision is an aesthetic assessment.

I think Pole's conclusion is correct but take exception to some of his arguments. First, I am uncertain whether it is proper to speak of a moral vision being true or false, and would want to make a more modest claim—that a moral vision can be judged to be acceptable or unacceptable. (I am not claiming Pole is wrong and my claim is not inconsistent with his.) Second, I do not see that a false (or unacceptable) moral vision makes a work incoherent. I should suppose that to say a work is coherent or incoherent is to speak about how its parts fit together and this involves no reference to something outside the work as the work's truth or falsity does.

In any event, it seems to me that a faulty moral vision can be shown to be an aesthetic fault independently of Pole's consideration of truth and coherence. As Pole's argument implies, a work's moral vision is a *part* of the work. Thus, any statement—descriptive or evaluative—about the work's moral vision is a statement about the *work*; and any statement about a *work* is a critical statement and, hence, falls within the aesthetic domain. To judge a moral vision to be morally unacceptable is to judge it defective and this amounts to saying that the work of art has a defective part. (Of course, a judgment of the acceptability of a moral vision may be wrong, as a judgment of an action sometimes is, but this fallibility does not make any difference.) Thus, a work's moral vision may be an aesthetic merit or defect just as a work's degree of unity is a merit or defect. But what justifies saying that a moral vision is a part of a work of art? Perhaps "part" is not quite the right word but it serves to make the point clear enough. A novel's moral vision is an essential part of the novel and if it were removed (I am not sure how such surgery could be carried out) the novel would be greatly changed. Anyway, a novel's moral vision is not like its covers or binding. However, someone might still argue that even though a work's moral vision is defective and the moral vision is part of the work, that this defect is not an *aesthetic* defect. How is "aesthetic" being used here? It is being used to segregate certain aspects or parts of works of art such as formal and stylistic aspects from such aspects as a work's moral vision. But it seems to me that the separation is only nominal. "Aesthetic" has been selected as a name for a certain subset of characteristics of works of art. I certainly cannot object to such a stipulation, since an underlying aim of this essay is to suggest the vacuousness of the term "aesthetic." My concern at this point is simply to insist that a work's moral vision is a part of the work and that, therefore, a critic can legitimately describe and evaluate it. I would *call* any defect or merit which a critic can legitimately point out an aesthetic defect or merit, but what we call it does not matter.

It would, of course, be a mistake to judge a work solely on the basis of its moral vision (it is only one part). The fact that some critics have judged works of art in this way is perhaps as much responsible as the theory of aesthetic attitude for the attempts to separate morality from the aesthetic. In fact, such criticism is no doubt at least partly responsible for the rise of the notion of the aesthetic attitude.

If the foregoing arguments are correct, the second way of conceiving the aesthetic attitude misleads aesthetic theory in at least three ways.

*III*

In answer to a hypothetical question about what is seen in viewing a portrait with the aesthetic attitude, Tomas in part responds "If looking at a picture and attending closely to how it looks is not really to be in the aesthetic attitude, then what on earth is?"[48] I shall take this sentence as formulating the weakest version of the aesthetic attitude. (I am ignoring Tomas's distinction between appearance and reality. See footnote 7. My remarks, thus, are not a critique of Tomas's argument; I am simply using one of his sentences.) First, this sentence speaks only of "looking at a picture," but "listening to a piece of music," "watching and listening to a play," and so on could be added easily enough. After thus expanding the sentence, it can be contracted into the general form: "Being in the aesthetic attitude is attending closely to a work of art (or a natural object)."

But the aesthetic attitude ("the hallmark of modern aesthetics") in this formulation is a great letdown—it no longer seems to say anything significant. Nevertheless, this does seem to be all that is left after the aesthetic attitude has been purged of *distancing* and *disinterestedness*. The only thing which prevents the aesthetic attitude from collapsing into simple attention is the qualification *closely*. One may, I suppose, attend to a work of art more or less closely, but this fact does not seem to signify anything very important. When "being in the aesthetic attitude" is equated with "attending (closely)," the equation neither involves any mythical element nor could it possibly mislead aesthetic theory. But if the definition has no vices, it seems to have no virtues either. When the aesthetic attitude finally turns out to be simply attending (closely), the final version should perhaps not be called "the weakest" but rather "the vacuous version" of the aesthetic attitude.

Stolnitz is no doubt historically correct that the notion of the aesthetic attitude has played an important role in the freeing of aesthetic theory from an overweening concern with beauty. It is easy to see how the slogan, "Anything can become an object of the aesthetic attitude," could help accomplish this liberation. It is worth noting, however, that the same goal could have been (and perhaps to some extent was) realized by simply noting that works of art are often ugly or contain ugliness, or have features which are difficult to include within beauty. No doubt, in more recent times people have been encouraged *to take an aesthetic attitude toward a painting* as a way of lowering their prejudices, say, against abstract and nonobjective art. So if the notion of aesthetic attitude has turned out to have no theoretical value for aesthetics, it has had practical value for the appreciation of art in a way similar to that of Clive Bell's suspect notion of significant form.

*Notes*

1. See Marshall Cohen, "Appearance and the Aesthetic Attitude," *Journal of Philosophy*, vol. 56 (1959), p. 926; and Joseph Margolis, "Aesthetic Perception," *Journal of Aesthetics and Art Criticism*, vol. 19 (1960), p. 211. Margolis gives an argument, but it is so compact as to be at best only suggestive.
2. Jerome Stolnitz, "Some Questions Concerning Aesthetic Perception," *Philosophy and Phenomenological Research*, vol. 22 (1961), p. 69.
3. *The Concept of Mind* (London, 1949), p. 23.
4. "'Distancing' as an Aesthetic Principle," *Australasian Journal of Philosophy*, vol. 39 (1961), pp. 155–174.
5. "Disinterested" is Stolnitz's term. Vivas uses "intransitive."
6. *Aesthetics and Philosophy of Art Criticism* (Boston, 1960), p. 510.
7. "Aesthetic Vision," *The Philosophical Review*, vol. 68 (1959), p. 63. I shall ignore Tomas's attempt to distinguish between appearance and reality since it seems to confuse rather than clarify aesthetic theory. See F. Sibley, "Aesthetics and the Looks of Things," *Journal of Philosophy*, vol. 56 (1959), pp. 905–915; M. Cohen, *op. cit.*, pp. 915–926; and J. Stolnitz, "Some Questions Concerning Aesthetic Perception," *op. cit.*, pp. 69–87. Tomas discusses only visual art and the aesthetic attitude, but his remarks could be generalized into a comprehensive theory.
8. Dawson, *op. cit.*, p. 158.
9. *Ibid.*, pp. 159–160.
10. *Ibid.*, p. 159.
11. *Ibid.*, p. 168.
12. *Feeling and Form* (New York, 1953), p. 318.
13. *Aesthetics and Philosophy of Art Criticism*, pp. 34–35.
14. *Ibid.*, p. 35.

15. *Ibid.*, p. 36.
16. *Ibid.*, p. 38.
17. "On the Origins of 'Aesthetic Disinterestedness'," *The Journal of Aesthetics and Art Criticism*, vol. 20 (1961), pp. 131–143.
18. "What Makes a Situation Aesthetic?" in *Philosophy Looks at the Arts*, Joseph Margolis (ed.), (New York, 1962). Reprinted from *Proceedings of the Aristotelian Society*, Supplementary Volume 31 (1957), pp. 75–92.
19. *Ibid.*, p. 15.
20. "Contextualism Reconsidered," *The Journal of Aesthetics and Art Criticism*, vol. 18 (1959), pp. 224–225.
21. *Ibid.*, p. 225.
22. *Loc. cit.*
23. *Ibid.*, p. 227.
24. *Ibid.*, p. 237.
25. *Ibid.*, p. 228. (Italics mine.)
26. Vivas's remark about the improbability of being able to read *The Brothers Karamazov* as art suggests that "intransitive attention" may sometimes mean for him "that which can be attended to at one time" or "that which can be held before the mind at one time." However, this second possible meaning is not one which is relevant here.
27. Vivas, *op. cit.*, p. 231.
28. *The Journal of Philosophy*, vol. 57 (1960), p. 624.
29. *Loc cit.*
30. *Op. cit.*, p. 53.
31. *Ibid.*, p. 54.
32. *Ibid.*, pp. 54–55.
33. *Ibid.*, pp. 55–56.
34. *Ibid.*, p. 56.
35. *The Aesthetic Attitude* (New York, 1920), p. 79.
36. *Op. cit.*, p. 35.
37. *Ibid.*, p. 377.
38. *Ibid.*, pp. 377–378.
39. *Ibid.*, p. 379.
40. *Ibid.*, p. 380.
41. *Loc. cit.*
42. H. S. Langfeld, *op. cit.*, p. 73.
43. J. Stolnitz, *op. cit.*, p. 36.
44. "Morality and the Assessment of Literature," *Philosophy*, vol. 37 (1962), pp. 193–207.
45. *Ibid.*, p. 193.
46. *Loc. cit.*
47. *Ibid.*, p. 206.
48. Tomas, *op. cit.*, p. 63.

# 6.    Artistic and Aesthetic Values
### *ROMAN INGARDEN*

In this lecture I shall be concerned mainly with the differentiation of artistic and aesthetic values. With this in view it will be necessary for me to make various other distinctions: first that between the work of art and the aesthetic object, and also a distinction between an aesthetically valuable quality on the one hand and value and its further determinations on the other. These distinctions have been elaborated in my various writings on aesthetics and theory of art, beginning with the book *Das literarische Kunstwerke* (1931), but I shall here try to take further than before the differentiation between artistic and aesthetic values.

In contrasting the work of art and the aesthetic object I shall omit for the sake of brevity discussion of the manner in which the work of art exists, whether as a real object or in some other way. But I will mention shortly the question whether a work of art is a physical object having a specific form or whether it is rather something which is constructed on the basis of a physical object as an entirely new creation brought into being by the creative activity of the artist. The essence of this activity consists of specific acts of consciousness in an artist, but these invariably manifest themselves in certain physical operations directed by the artist's creative will which bring into being or transform a certain physical object—the material—bestowing upon it that form whereby it becomes the existential substrate of the work of art itself, for example a work of literature or music, a picture, a piece of architecture, etc., and at the same time assuring to it relative durability and accessibility to a multiplicity of observers. Nevertheless in its structure and properties a work of art always extends beyond its material substrate, the real 'thing' which ontologically supports it, although the properties of the substrate are not irrelevant to

From *British Journal of Aesthethics*, IV (1964), 198-213. Reprinted with permission of the British Society of Aesthetics.

the properties of the work of art which depends upon it. The work of art is the true object to the formation of which the creative acts of the artist are directed, while the fashioning of its existential substrate is a subsidiary operation ancillary to the work of art itself which is to be brought into being by the artist.

Every work of art of whatever kind has the distinguishing feature that it is not the sort of thing which is completely determined in every respect by the primary level varieties of its qualities; in other words, it contains within itself characteristic lacunae in definition, areas of indeterminateness: it is a schematic creation. Furthermore, not all its determinants, components, or qualities are in a state of actuality, but some of them are potential only. In consequence of this a work of art requires an agent existing outside itself, that is an observer, in order—as I express it—to render it *concrete*. Through his co-creative activity in appreciation the observer sets himself as is commonly said to 'interpret' the work or, as I prefer to say, to reconstruct it in its effective characteristics, and in doing this as it were under the influence of suggestions coming from the work itself he fills out its schematic structure, plenishing at least in part the areas of indeterminacy and actualizing various elements which are as yet only in a state of potentiality. In this way there comes about what I have called a 'concretion' of the work of art. The work of art then, is the product of the intentional activities of an artist; the *concretion* of the work is not only the reconstruction thanks to the activity of an observer of what was effectively present in the work, but also a completion of the work and the actualization of its moments of potentiality. It is thus in a way the common product of artist and observer. In the nature of things a concretion goes beyond the schematic structure of a work of art, but at the same time it is—or at any rate it can be—that for the emergence of which the work serves or rather that in which the work achieves its full and complete image—or at any rate a more complete image than in any likeness which is at variance with the work itself. Empirically a work is always manifested to an observer in some concretion. But this does not prevent the observer's trying to apprehend the work in its pure schematic structure together with all its characteristic potentialities. But this mode of apprehending a work of art demands a special attitude and exertions in the observer if he is to withhold himself from all arbitrary completion of qualitative indeterminacies while at the same time taking full account of the special character of its every moment of potentiality. Such apprehension of a work of art is rather rare and is not realized in the everyday 'consumer's' attitude in his commerce with works of art.

As the joint product of artist and observer a concretion will differ to a greater or less extent from one instance to another, but the nature and extent of the variations depend both on the character of the work (particularly the type of art to which it belongs) and on the competence of the observer as also on the empirical nature of his observation and the particular conditions in which it takes place. There are two possible ways in which a work of art may be perceived. The act of perception may occur within the context of the aesthetic attitude in the pursuit of aesthetic experience or it may be performed in the service of some extra-aesthetic preoccupation such as that of scientific research or a simple consumer's concern, either with the object of obtaining the maximum of pleasure from commerce with the work or—as frequently happens in the reading of literature—with the object of informing oneself about the vicissitudes of the characters depicted in the work or some other matter of extra-literary fact about which a reader can obtain information on the basis of the work of art (as, for example, by reading Homer, classical scholars seek to inform themselves about the life of the ancient Greeks, their customs, dress, etc.).

Within the context of both attitudes either of two perceptive aims may predominate. Either the observer will seek in commerce with the work to realize the concretion most authentic to it or this will not be a matter of particular concern or he may even seek to give free rein to phantasy and up to a point to concretize the work in accordance with personal whim (for example, a stage manager). If a concretion occurs within the aesthetic attitude, there emerges what I call an aesthetic object. This object will resemble or be congenial to what was present to the mind of the artist when creating the work if the concretion is carried through with the endeavor to conform to the effective characteristics of the work and to respect the indications it gives as to the limits of permitted fulfilment. But even if he tries to remain true to the work itself, the aesthetic object actually produced by the observer often differs in many details of articulation from what is permitted or—if one may use the term—demanded by the work itself. Because of this the basic character of the whole is changed or at the least a mass of details will conflict in different reconstructions of the same work of art—which is one source of quarrels and controversy. To every work of art there pertains a limited number of *possible* aesthetic objects—possible in various senses: In the broad sense we are concerned with concretions which are achieved genuinely within the context of an aesthetic attitude taken up by the observer but without consideration whether the effective reconstruction is faithful to the work of art or whether the plenishing and actualization of its moments of potentiality accord with its effective aspects, or to some extent deviate from it. In the narrower sense we speak of possible aesthetic objects only where both the concretions of a given work involve faithful reconstructions of it and also the plenishing of the work and the actualization of its moments of potentiality lie within the boundaries indicated by its effective qualities. These concretions may still differ among themselves in various respects because a work of art always admits of diverse ways in which its areas of indeterminacy may be filled out and completed: some of these plenishings harmonize better and some worse with the fully articulated moments of the work and with the rest of the implementations of its indeterminacies.

The effective emergence of the 'possible' concretions of a work of art—in either of the above senses of the word—obviously depends not only on the work itself but also on the presence of competent observers and on its being apprehended by them in one way rather than another. This in turn depends on various historical conditions. Hence any work of art (and this operates differently for the different arts) passes through various periods of brilliance, that is, periods in which it attracts frequent and correct aesthetic concretions, and other periods when its attractiveness is weakened or even disappears if it is no longer 'legible' to its public. Or again it may meet with observers who have a completely different manner of emotional reaction, who have become insensitive to certain values of the work or frankly hostile to them, and who therefore are unqualified to produce the sort of concretion in which these values shine forth and act upon the observer. When this happens a work of art is not only unreadable but, as it were, dumb.

The alternate periods of brilliance and obscurity and the variations in the number of potential observers which are bound up with them—the fact that at different times one and the same work of art appears in differently moded concretions and that it changes as it were its features and lineaments, loses its power of acting upon observers and is able only imperfectly to display its potential values—all this explains why the theory of the. relativity and subjectivity of aesthetic and artistic values is so popular and seems so plausible. The sense of the words 'subjective' and 'relative' in this context depends on the nature of the philosophic background against which they are intended to be understood. I cannot go more closely into this matter here but in connection with the question whether or in what sense the theory may be entertained I would like to suggest certain preliminary considerations. The first step is the distinction between a work of art and an aesthetic object and the next is the differentiation of artistically valuable from aesthetically valuable qualities. Without these distinctions it is impossible to reach agreement about the subjectivity or relativity of aesthetic (or artistic) values.

There exists, however, a sense of 'subjective'—usually not formulated precisely—in which the theory of the subjectivity of aesthetic (or artistic) values ought to be rejected outright, despite its popularity. This is the view that the value of a work of art (or an aesthetic object, which is usually confused with it) is nothing else but pleasure (or, in the case of negative value, disagreeableness) understood as a specific psychical state or experience, lived through by an observer in contact with a given work of art. The greater the pleasure he obtains the greater the value the observer attributes to the work of art. In truth, however, on this theory the work of art possesses no value. The observer indeed announces his pleasure by 'valuing' the work of art, but strictly speaking he is valuing his own pleasure: his pleasure is valuable to him and this he uncritically transfers to the work of art which arouses his pleasure. But the same work evokes different pleasures in different subjects or perhaps none at all and even in one and the same subject it may evoke different pleasure at different times. Hence the so-called value of the work of art would be not merely subjective but relative to the observer and his states. The relativity of the value of a work of art so understood is a simple consequence of its subjectivity in the foregoing sense.

He who would embrace the theory so elucidated has in his support the obvious fact that some works of art cause us pleasure, a pleasure which may vary with the circumstances, and others either do not evoke pleasure or may even cause displeasure of one sort or another. This fact, banal as it is, admits of no doubt—as also the other fact that in general people prize their pleasures and shun what is disagreeable. Acknowledging this fact we would only complain at the failure to recognize the *kind* of pleasure which is imparted to us by works of art and how its varieties are related to the varieties of value inherent in the work of art. By recognizing that these pleasures have a special character of their own and exist in a different manner from the pleasures deriving from a good meal or fresh air or a good bath we should carry our affair a little forward although it would contribute nothing to the question whether or how values inhere in works of art themselves. For it seems certain that these pleasures, being either actual states of mind or qualities of mental states and experiences, are not included in the work of art or tied to it. But if these pleasures constituted the sole value which is manifested in our commerce with works of art, it would not be possible to attribute value to the work itself. For the pleasure remains entirely outside the work of art. The work is something which transcends the sphere of our experiences and their contents, it is something completely transcendent in relation to ourselves. And the same can be said of the aesthetic objects constructed on its basis. It is precisely in the sphere of the work of art and its concretions, a sphere beyond that of our experiences and their content, that we must look to see whether it is or is not possible to find something which can be recognized as specifically and truly valuable.

Neither can this value be found in the work of art itself (or in its aesthetic concretion) so long as it is conceived as a kind of reflection of the instrumental value attributed to the work on account of the several pleasures which we experience in contact with it, or if the work of art is treated as a tool for evoking this or that sensation of delight. The experiencing of such pleasures is of course often the occasion for their appearing to the experient as a delusive mirage of value in the work of art. It is especially with naive people who, lacking education in the arts, are particularly susceptible to their emotional influences that this kind of delusion arises and for this reason those of little experience are inclined to be carried away by enthusiasm for works of art which lack genuine value. The emergence of such mirages of value is not identical with genuine worth whether artistic or aesthetic and cannot provide an argument that value depends solely on this type of reflected pleasures and is therefore subjective or relative. The value of a work of art is not to be sought in such qualities but can be expected to be found only in some self-subsistent characteristic.

As regards the instrumental values of works of art as tools for arousing pleasures and delights in those who observe them, this kind of value can be attributed but only in a derivative sense as a consequence of the fact that states of pleasure are themselves valuable for the subject, not in the sense that the work of art is itself endowed with some attribute and strictly speaking without regard to the attributes it has. This derivative type of value is usually ascribed to tools in almost complete disregard for the nature and structure of the object they are used to produce. If the consumer is subjected to an emotionally pleasant influence from a certain work, this is enough for him to attribute to the source of his delight the instrumental value of a tool causing that delight. This instrumental value is obviously relational: by virtue of its determination as a value-type such value is related on the one hand to the object which serves as tool and on the other hand to the effect for which the tool serves. The stamp or seal of this value lies wholly in its relation to the quite different, non-relational value ascribed to the delight or pleasure. Moreover, the value of an instrument is relative in another sense too: it is in its very occurrence dependent and mutable, changing its qualitative determination according to the nature and the value of whatever the tool serves to produce. And finally it is dependent on the observer and the state in which he happens to be at a given moment. When an observer ceases to react emotionally to it or is no longer sensitive to it as a work of art, so far as it is treated as an instrument of enjoyment, it is not valued by him either positively or negatively but becomes an object of indifference. But the work of art itself undergoes no change in its properties during these modifications of subjective mood and response. It remains something finished, complete for itself, through the changing forms of contact, unaffected by the multiform appreciations of different observers. Yet those values or value qualities which I am here searching for are able to manifest themselves to the observer only at the moment when the latter achieves some apprehension of the work itself, even though a partial and as yet imperfect one, when his commerce with the work achieves an unveiling of the intrinsic features of the work (features which seldom obtrude themselves at first contact), and when an apprehension of its structure and properties enables him to descry its essential values, those which are peculiar to any work, which give witness and in fact are the evidence for its claim to be a work of artistic value. The observer must of course succeed in achieving this apprehension and appreciative commerce: if his skill in perceiving or responding to the work is fallacious, neither its properties nor its values will reveal themselves to him. But this does not mean that the work is then deprived of value, only that the observer is in one way or another inefficient—either through a general lack of artistic culture or because he is unequipped or at that particular moment unable to appreciate the particular work.

This is to say, if we are seeking what I want to call the 'artistic value' of a work of art, it must conform to the following requirements:

(1)  It is neither a part nor an aspect of any of our empirical experiences or mental states during commerce with a work of art and therefore does not belong to the category of pleasure or enjoyment.

(2)  It is not something attributed to the work in virtue of being regarded as an instrument for arousing this or that form of pleasure.

(3)  It reveals itself as a specific characteristic of the work itself.

(4)  It exists if and only if the necessary conditions for its existence are present in the qualities of the work itself.

(5)  It is such a thing that its presence causes the work of art to partake of an entirely special form of being distinct from all other cultural products.

In other words, if any object lacks this thing which I here call artistic value, it ceases in consequence to be a work of art. If on the other hand it appears in its negative form—as an imperfection rather than a merit—then the work is to some degree abortive, i.e., it can only be counted as a work of art at all if some positive values (that is, values in the narrower, and strictly correct, sense of the word) are manifested in addition to negative ones.

It behooves now to indicate some examples of this kind of value. But first I must distinguish between qualities (i.e., determinants of value) which are valuable in the artistic or aesthetic or moral sense and a value which appears in an object as a necessary consequence of its possessing a particular aggregate of valuable qualities in a given category. In other words, value emerges on the foundation of a specific aggregate of valuable qualities and it is dependent *inter alia* on this aggregation both for the degree of its value and for its type. Values differ from one another only in virtue of having their specific determinants and qualifying properties. Some of these qualities determine the general type of value (*i.e.*, whether it is aesthetic or moral or economic or utilitarian), while others determine the specific variety within the general type, as for example 'beauty,' 'prettiness' or 'ugliness' within the general range of aesthetic values. And to these variants within a general type belongs what I have called the 'degree' or 'elevation' of any value. As will be seen, we are confronted with many different distinctions and it is only by analyzing them and elaborating them in detail that it is possible to make any progress in the little studied field of general theory of value. The examples to follow will enable readers to grasp what I intend when I speak for instance of qualities as opposed to values themselves and their closer determinations (or qualities of value).

For the moment we will simply state. *Artistic value*—if we are to acknowledge its existence at all—is something which arises in the work of art itself and has its existential ground in that. *Aesthetic value* is something which manifests itself only in the aesthetic object and as a particular moment which determines the character of the whole. The ground of aesthetic value consists of a certain aggregation of aesthetically valuable qualities, and they in turn rest upon the basis of a certain aggregate of properties which render possible their emergence in an object. Both the one and the other kind of value assumed the existence of a complete work of art (or aesthetic object). It is not important here how the constitution of both types of object has been arrived at. What is indubitable is the fact that for the constitution of an aesthetic object the co-creative activity of an observer is necessary and therefore several aesthetic objects may emerge on the basis of one and the same work of art and that these may differ among themselves in their aesthetic value. But, as has been said, this is not an argument in support of the subjectivity of that value. This genetic way of considering the whole matter cannot be repudiated or disparaged and yet it is not this which is decisive as to the existential character of aesthetic values themselves.

Irrespective of what its origin may be and the part taken by the observer in constituting it, the aesthetic object in the moment of being constituted is something with which the observer is in direct contact however he may apprehend it or respond to it. And for all that this object is something standing in relation to the observer and his experiences, it is at the same time transcendent (a separate self-subsistent whole) just as much as is the work of art or any other existentially independent natural object which exists of its own right. This transcendence extends not only to those properties of a work of art or aesthetic object which are neutral in point of value but also to its valuable qualities and to the values which are constituted on their basis.

We will now return to the work of art. We distinguish two aspects, aspects which are neutral as regards value and those which are axiologically potent, using the latter term to cover both valuable qualities and the values themselves and their particular determinations.

To the first category belong primarily those attributes which determine the type of art with which we have to do, whether it is a work of literature, painting, music, etc. So, for example, a work of literature is a construct of multiple strata and has a quasi-temporal structure, since its parts follow one another in temporal sequence, and this enables it to present events in the time of its presented world. A painting is not quasi-temporal in this sense, *i.e.*, its parts do not follow each other in sequence, and therefore if a painting is representational it can present only a single incident at a particular moment of occurrence. On the other hand, unlike a literary work, a painting is characterized by two or three dimensional extension in visual space. A literary work is first and foremost a linguistic construct. Its basic structure comprises a twofold linguistic stratification: on the one hand the layer of phonemes and linguistic sound-phenomena; on the other hand the meanings of the words and sentences, in virtue of which the higher-level units of meaning emerge and from them the representational content of the work and the aspects in which the subject matter is presented. Although a painting lacks the dual stratification of language, it has its own proper means of presenting aspects of objects and through the objects presented and the manner of their representation may be constructed higher-level elements such as situation or narrative. All the features which belong in a painting to the representation of the actual world are absent to non-figurative painting; and still another situation with regard to the axiologically indifferent features of a work of art arises in connection with music or architecture.

Besides these axiologically neutral features which determine the basic type of a work of art, there occur in all types of art other axiologically neutral features which together combine to constitute an artistic 'individual' in its absolute uniqueness. Thus in a literary work there are completely determinate sentences arranged in a definite order possessing an established sense and precise syntactical formation. These are composed of words which possess a fixed sound and which belong to a given language and are chosen out of the vocabulary of that language in such a way as to create an individual linguistic style peculiar to the author or even to the particular work. There are many other axiologically neutral properties, all of which together with the general features which determine its type form what I shall call the axiologically neutral skeleton of the work, without which the work would not exist as just this unique work of art and no other. It is clear, however, that this skeleton does not constitute the whole work of art irrespective of whether we are concerned with it in its purely schematic form or with one of its concretions. Despite their axiological neutrality the features which belong to the skeleton of a work are not without bearing for a whole range of axiologically significant features. On the contrary, so long as the skeleton is appropriately endowed, its properties lead to the emergence of entirely new features which belong just as intimately to the work of art but differ in that they are axiologically significant, artistically valuable qualities which emerge in this or that aggregation and endow the work with various artistic values. They are basically of two kinds: there are those which are allied to the excellences or defects of 'artistic craftsmanship'—that is, virtues of artistic technique—and next there are various sorts of competence possessed by a work of art in virtue of its having certain properties and components and not others. We will first give examples.

In literary work the individual sentences may be simple or complex, their structure may be paratactic or hypotactic. Such features are in themselves axiologically neutral and belong to the axiologically neutral skeleton of the work. Similarly when we find in one work a preponderance of nouns and in another of verbs, or a preponderance of general, abstract names in one while another is so constructed that even intricate concepts are expressed through names of particular things. We do not attach value to such features in themselves. But if we say of a sentence (irrespective of whether it is simple or compound) that it is clear and transparent in structure while another is intricate in a sense which precludes clarity, or if we say that it is obscure or incomprehensible, we are in such case indicating characteristic features of the sentences which are not artistically indifferent. They are, or at any rate they may be, valuable and particularly so if their occurrence is no longer sporadic or if a casual occurrence is not justified by the manner in which the sentence is used or the situation in which it occurs. When obscure sentences become a mass phenomenon which cannot be explained by the necessity of using such sentences in order to express certain objective situations or to evoke a certain artistic effect (by which we mean something not indifferent as regards aesthetic value), then we are alleging, whether for the work as a whole or for certain parts of it, characteristics which carry positive or negative significance for its artistic value. There may, of course, be various sources for the obscurity of particular sentences or of a text, but with the exception of one case which will be mentioned later unclarity, obscurity, unintelligibility, are a defect in a given sentence or work while lucidity, clarity of expression, and precision of construction are a virtue. These properties of linguistic components then become value qualities characterizing the literary work itself. (It might be objected that this is not a matter of artistic value but simply a value of a general natural kind which appears when the work is not purely an artistic creation but, for example, has a scientific aim as well. But all we are concerned with at the moment is the fact that it is an emergent feature of the work positively or negatively significant in regard to value.) In the field of literary art this lucidity (or its opposite), occurring along with other similar value qualities, may acquire a special character, a special role in the structured organic whole which is the work of art, and harmonizing with other artistic value qualities it may induce the emergence of new features of value either in the work of art or in its concretions. Indeed, the above-mentioned features of sentences or of the language generally may entail some properties of the presented world in a given work. If the language is unclear, ambiguous, difficult to understand, then the presented objects take on a characteristic imprecision. Both particular details and the relations between them become blurred in their outlines; one might say that their constitution becomes incompletely articulated, disorganized, and does not give a clear impression of the thing presented.

Obscurity, imprecision, partial or complete unintelligibility, and the like, are not only blemishes in themselves but are signs of bad workmanship, defects of literary technique, betraying inadequate mastery of language or ineptitude in its employment. Such shortcomings in the creative powers of an author bring in their train blemishes in the work which is the fruit of his activity and these blemishes in their turn constitute a negative value in the work of art.

Of course the above negative value-characteristics of sentences or whole sentence-aggregates may on occasion be introduced into a literary work of set purpose by the author. But when this is done the purpose must be apparent from the work itself. Vagueness in the meaning of a sentence may be utilized for some artistic effect; or the feature of a badly constructed and defective sentence may form part of the presented material of the work, being spoken or written by one of the characters in it. In this way an author could represent the incompetence of an inexperienced writer whose vicissitudes form the theme of his book. In these circumstances obscurity is not a defect of the work itself but a feature of one of the objects represented in the work, a feature which is directly shown instead of being indirectly described. Obscurity in a sentence or some larger section of a work may be intentional, lastly, for the sake of contrast in order that the contrary virtues of the remainder may be enhanced to greater prominence the more vaguely, clumsily, or otherwise defectively those parts are constructed which function merely to serve as contrast. In such case defectiveness is merely a means of reinforcing merits which otherwise might not strike us. Intentional faultiness which fulfils a special function within the work as a whole is not evidence of any lack of literary skill in a writer and is not a technical fault in the work itself. On the contrary, it is a sign of technical skill; it is as it were a simulation of unskillfulness whose purpose is the better to display technical proficiency and craftsmanship in the art product.

By analogy certain regional features of composition of a work, whether literature, music, or painting, are in themselves axiologically neutral properties of the organic structural whole and can be indicated by a purely objective analysis of the work. For example, such and such a disposition of the parts whether serially or in spatial order, a particular way of arranging the elements of one part of a whole so as to contrast with the freer or looser dissemination of elements in other parts of the same work—are structural features in themselves neutral as regards value. One may affirm their presence in a work quite objectively without any implied judgment of value. But these structural properties again, in themselves neutral in respect of value, may entail other properties which do have a positive or negative value significance. For example a too harmonious arrangement of details or parts may reveal itself as an excess of pedantry, overmuch solicitude for creating the impression of orderliness which becomes obtrusive in its uniformity, a certain affectation in ascribing a predominant role to compositional qualities as if correctness of composition were sufficient of itself to determine the final value of a work of art. A certain type of perfection in composition when it goes along with perceptible defects of another kind, that is of content, becomes a source of monotony, tediousness and so on. Compositional irregularity which serves no obviously intended artistic purpose in the work is a plain defect, upsetting the balance of forces within the whole. Again it may be evidence of inexperience in the author, a technical shortcoming in the work, which has negative value as such irrespective of what negative value qualities it entails. On the other hand it may happen that in a particular work disorder in the composition may be seen on the basis of the other qualities of the work to be intentional and to fulfil definite functions within the whole. It does not cease thereby to be disorder but its role as a factor of disvalue may nevertheless ultimately conduce to the emergence of a moment of positive value in the organic whole. It may, but it need not. For the fact that a certain irregularity of composition was intended does not of itself guarantee that the intention was correct or that it was successfully realized so that in the final outcome it gave rise to some positive value in the structure of the whole. For example, the narration of the fortunes of the characters in a novel may not accord with the temporal sequence of the events—a well-known and frequently used technique of novelists. One may doubt, however, whether this device as used for example by Aldous Huxley really conduces to the intended artistically valuable effect. In this connection, in order to discover whether a certain aspect of a work has positive or negative value it is not enough to examine the value characteristics of that aspect in isolation; it is necessary to extend one's survey to the whole work, since various qualities of this kind may, and sometimes must, exercise a mutual influence on each other in regard to their value characteristics, and it is only in the whole organic unity of the work (where both its neutral and its value-significant features are taken into account) that their final form is revealed. This is in agreement with the earlier statement that the real function of artistically valuable moments is revealed only on the basis of an appreciation of the work, which is not possible so long as we confine ourselves to the enjoyment of these or the other empirical pleasures mediated by it.

To give one more example of an artistic value quality I will refer to features of certain of Rodin's sculptures in marble. What strikes us in them is the extraordinary precision and at the same time the softness in the working of the surfaces, reproducing the softness of a woman's body represented by the statue. This method of working the surface of the marble plays here an essential role in the function of representing an object—a woman's body—different in character from the material from which the sculpture is formed in such a way that the observer is to some extent put under the impression that he is in visual contact not with marble but with human flesh. This is an artistic function, and its virtue consists in the skillful representation of an object whose qualities are basically unlike the material of the sculpture. But this skill is not the only merit here, not the only artistic value in the work. The perfection which consists in technical mastery displayed in the shaping of the surface of the stone may also contribute something of artistic value to a work, something detectable in the work itself and not to be identified with any subjective experience or psychological state of admiration or pleasure. Indeed, admiration presupposes that we have successfully apprehended the feature of which I am speaking in the work itself and is something separate superadded to what is visibly present in the work.

One could multiply examples of artistic values and disvalues at will. One might speak for instance of the unsuitably chosen material of some works of art—*e.g.*, the neo-Gothic university buildings at Chicago made of concrete instead of stone—or we might contrast 'noble' baroque with one which is cheap and tawdry, overloaded with ornament. But I believe that the examples I have already given will be sufficient to indicate what I have in mind when I speak of artistically valuable qualities in a work of art, though it would be less easy to convey a correct notion of qualities of this kind or that of the artistic value quality whose notion emerges on their basis as their final resultant. I will therefore now proceed to give in contrast some examples of *aesthetic* value qualities, positive and negative, leading on to the exemplification and determination of aesthetic value and its potential varieties.

A very great variety of aesthetically valuable qualities is exhibited in constituted aesthetic objects. All of them are characterized by being something given directly to perception, or if one prefers the expression they are directly presented phenomena not something indirectly deducible from other data or something whose existence can only be inferred on the basis of the apprehension of the whole work. They are concretely present to experience. In order that aesthetically valuable qualities may be constituted, an aesthetic experience must be achieved since it is only in this kind of experience that these qualities come to realization. (The difficulty of distinguishing them from artistically valuable qualities may lie partly in the fact that it does not seem impossible that some of the properties which we have treated as artistically valuable qualities may also enter into experience—as valuable—within the context of a given aesthetic object. In such cases do we have to do with artistically valuable or aesthetically valuable qualities? But to avoid complicating the matter in advance I will proceed to give a certain number of examples.)

There first come to mind various emotional qualities such as those suggested by the expressions 'sad,' 'threatening,' 'serene,' 'festive,' 'sublime,' 'pathetic,' 'dramatic,' 'tragic,' etc. But there also, such qualities as in contrast with the foregoing, one might call intellectual, as for example 'witty,' 'clever,' 'acute,' 'interesting,' 'profound,' 'boring,' 'dull,' 'trite,' 'pedestrian,' and so on. There are also aspects of a formal character, such as uniformity and variety, harmony and disharmony, awkwardness, compactness, coherence, expressiveness, dynamism, and so on. Another class are 'artificial,' 'affected,' 'natural,' 'simple and unaffected,' 'exaggerated,' 'genuine,' 'false,' 'insincere,' 'lacking in integrity,' and so on.

We may distinguish these qualities into two main types: (1) those which are aesthetically valuable in a positive or negative sense both in themselves (when they emerge in an aesthetic object) and also when they are associated with other qualities of this class; (2) qualities which are in themselves neutral as regards aesthetic value but which acquire an aesthetic value when they are exhibited in association with other aesthetically valuable qualities. We call the first type unconditionally valuable and the second conditionally valuable (aesthetically), although even the former are not entirely independent of the context in which they are manifested. To the class of conditional aesthetic values belong at least some of the emotional qualities. If someone is sad in everyday life on account of some grievous loss, this sadness which imposes itself on his ordinary life-experience is aesthetically neutral. But the character of sadness which arises for example in the music of Chopin, a sadness be it noted which is uniquely produced by musical means, is in a given work (that is in a particular performance and audition, *i.e.*, an aesthetic concretion) indubitably a feature relevant to aesthetic value, an element in the complete set of determinant qualities of a given work (*e.g., Étude* Op. 25, No. 7). Similarly the dramatic tension of some quotidian human conflict may be entirely devoid of aesthetic value, but in the *Revolutionary Study* (Op. 10, No. 12) such dramatic tension is an aesthetically valuable feature. On the other hand the qualities which we name by such words as 'solemn,' 'profound,' 'tedious,' or 'banal' belong to the category of unconditionally aesthetically valuable qualities. Why it is that approximately the same emotional quality at one time has an aesthetic value and another time has none, constitutes a vast theme in itself connected on the one hand with the unique function of the aesthetic experience by which the aesthetic object is brought into being and on the other hand with a peculiar modification which characterizes the mode of existence of the content of an aesthetic object—matters which I have tried to elucidate elsewhere[1] but which are too complex to deal with here.

The question [of] which aesthetically valuable qualities can co-exist in a single aesthetic object in such a way as not to diminish but strengthen their own valuableness while leading to other higher-level qualities which are themselves aesthetic value determinants; which qualities are mutually exclusive or bring about a diminution or conflict of qualities; which finally exert a mutual attenuation in respect of aesthetic value—these are matters whose theoretical analysis has barely been begun. Their investigation must begin with analysis designed to clarify this or that particular aesthetically valuable quality by bringing about their intuitive elucidation, more particularly as the names we generally use to refer to them are for the most part ambiguous and too vague. This kind of research is likely to succeed only when we make constant use of concrete examples of works of art, or their corresponding aesthetic objects, where we have reached agreement that a specific quality is manifested in them and are at the same time in a position to point to some allied qualities which are exhibited in combination with different sets of associated qualities so that we can directly grasp the way in which particular qualities are modified in accordance with their context. There is no doubt that the practical study of possible (and necessary) relations among aesthetically valuable qualities has existed for a very long time in art. Every truly creative artist, musician, poet, painter, etc., in creating new works carries out certain experiments in this field. In composing his work the artist as it were sees ahead by creative intuition into possible complexes of aesthetically valuable qualities and how they will conduce to the emergence of an overall aesthetic value in the work as a whole. At the same time, he tries to find the technical means to realize a particular complex by his choice of those aesthetically neutral qualities (colors, sounds, shapes, etc.) which by forming the skeleton of a work create the objective conditions (*i.e.*, those on the side of the work of art) necessary for the realization of the subjective conditions: that is, the existence of a suitable observer and the achievement of an aesthetic experience, without which neither these neutral qualities could be exhibited, nor [could] the aesthetically valuable qualities which together cause the emergence of a particular complex of qualities and the constitution of a corresponding aesthetic value determined by this whole complex substrate.

It will be apparent from what has been said that aesthetic value, made concrete on the basis of a given work of art, is nothing else but a particular quality determination marked by a selection of interacting aesthetically valuable qualities which manifest themselves on the basis of the neutral skeleton of a work of art reconstructed by a competent observer.

*Note*

1. Cp. *Das literarische Kunstwerk*, § 25 and O *poznawaniu dziala literackiego* (Concerning the cognition of a literary work), § 24: also in English 'Aesthetic Experience and Aesthetic Object,' *Journal of Philosophical and Phenomenological Research*, vol. 21, no. 3, 1961.

# Bibliography to Part One

A comparatively recent summary of the historical development of aesthetics is provided in:
Ruth Saw and Harold Osborne, "Aesthetics as a Branch of Philosophy," *British Journal of Aesthetics* I (1960), 8–20.
A fuller survey is provided in:
Monroe C. Beardsley, *Aesthetics from Classical Greece to the Present* (New York, 1966);
and a sense of the changing status of the fine arts is conveyed in:
Paul O. Kristeller, "The Modern System of the Arts," *Journal of the History of Ideas* XII (1951), 469–527; and XIII (1952), 17–46.

General doubts about the fruitfulness of aesthetics may be found in:
William E. Kennick, "Does Traditional Aesthetics Rest on a Mistake?" *Mind* XVII (1958), 317–334;
J. A. Passmore, "The Dreariness of Aesthetics," reprinted in William Elton (ed.), *Aesthetics and Language* (Oxford, 1954).
One of the early symposia of an analytic sort, with contributions by J. O. Urmson and David Pole, appears in:
"What Makes a Situation Aesthetic?" *Proceedings of the Aristotelian Society*, supplementary vol. 31 (1957), 75–106.
Various other attempts to explicate aspects of the aesthetic point of view are to be found in:
Henry Aiken, "The Aesthetic Relevance of Belief," *Journal of Aesthetics and Art Criticism* IX (1951), 301–315;
Virgil Aldrich, "Picture Space," *Philosophical Review* LXVII (1958), 342–352;
Monroe C. Beardsley, *Aesthetics* (New York, 1958), ch. 1;
George Dickie, *Art and the Aesthetic* (Ithaca, 1974);
W. B. Gallie, "The Function of Philosophical Aesthetics," reprinted in William Elton (ed.), *Aesthetics and Language* (Oxford, 1954);
Joseph Margolis, *Art and Philosophy* (New York, 1978), chs. 2–3;
I. A. Richards, *Principles of Literary Criticism* (London, 1925), ch. 2;

Jerome Stolnitz, *Aesthetics and Philosophy of Art Criticism* (Boston, 1960);
Vincent Tomas, "Aesthetic Vision," *Philosophical Review* LXVIII (1959), 52–67;
Eliseo Vivas, "A Definition of the Esthetic Experience," reprinted in his *Creation and Discovery* (New York, 1955).

An important exchange on the meaning of the aesthetic appears in:
George Dickie, "The Myth of the Aesthetic Attitude," *American Philosophical Quarterly* I (1964), 56–66;
George Dickie, "Beardsley's Phantom Aesthetic Experience," *Journal of Philosophy* LXII (1965), 129–136;
Monroe C. Beardsley, "Aesthetic Experience Regained," *Journal of Aesthetics and Art Criticism* XXVIII (1969), 3–11.

Beardsley's more recent discussions of the nature of aesthetic categories may be found in:
Monroe C. Beardsley, *The Aesthetic Point of View*, ed. Michael J. Wreen and Donald M. Callen (Ithaca, 1982);
Monroe C. Beardsley, "In Defense of Aesthetic Value," *Proceedings and Addresses of The American Philosophical Association*, vol. 52 (1979), 723–749.
His contributions are examined in:
John Fisher (ed.), *Essays on Aesthetics; Perspectives on the Work of Monroe C. Beardsley* (Philadelphia, 1983).

Frank Sibley's essay has generated a rather large industry. Among his own related papers may be mentioned:
Aesthetic and Non-Aesthetic," *Philosophical Review* LXXIV (1965), 135–159;
"Aesthetic Concepts: A Rejoinder," *Philosophical Review* LXXII (1963), 79–83;
"Objectivity and Aesthetics," *Proceedings of the Aristotelian Society*, suppl. vol. 42 (1968), 31–54.

Reviews by various hands of the principal issues may be found in:
Ted Cohen, "Aesthetic/Non-aesthetic and the Concept of Taste: A Critique of Sibley's Position," *Theoria* XXXIX (1973), 113–152;
Isabel Hungerland, "Once Again, Aesthetic and Non-Aesthetic," *Journal of Aesthetics and Art Criticism* XXVI (1968), 285–295;
Peter Kivy, *Speaking of Art* (The Hague, 1973);
H.R.G. Schwyzer, "Sibley's 'Aesthetic Concepts'," *Philosophical Review* LXXII (1963), 72–78;
Gary Stahl, "Sibley's 'Aesthetic Concepts': An Ontological Mistake," *Journal of Aesthetics and Art Criticism* XXIX (1971), 385–389.

The relevance of forgery, intentional considerations, and imagination is aired in:
Virgil C. Aldrich, *Philosophy of Art* (Englewood Cliffs, 1963);
Timothy Binkley, "Deciding about Art," in Lars Aagaard-Mogensen (ed.), *Culture and Art* (Nyborg and Atlantic Highlands, 1976);

Arthur C. Danto, "Artworks and Real Things," *Theoria* XXXIX (1973), 1–17;
Nelson Goodman, *Languages of Art* (Indianapolis, 1969);
Nelson Goodman, "The Status of Style," *Critical Inquiry* I (1974), 799–811;
Alfred Lessing, "What Is Wrong with a Forgery?" *Journal of Aesthetics and Art Criticism* XXIII (1965), 464–471;
Leonard B. Meyer, "Forgery and the Anthropology of Art," in Lars Aagaard-Mogensen (ed.), *Culture and Art* (Nyborg and Atlantic Highlands, 1976);
Melvin Rader, "The Imaginative Mode of Awareness," *Journal of Aesthetics and Art Criticism* XXXIII (1974), 411–429;
Richard Rudner, "On Seeing What We Shall See," in Richard Rudner and Israel Scheffler (eds.), *Logic & Art* (Indianapolis, 1972);
Mark Sagoff, "The Aesthetic Status of Forgeries," *Journal of Aesthetics and Art Criticism* XXXV (1976), 169–180.

On forgery, see further, Part Three and its Bibliography.
For Ingarden's views, see further, the Bibliography for Part Three; but also, for a sense of the complications of the phenomenological use of "aesthetic" due to Ingarden:

Wolfgang Iser, *The Act of Reading* (Baltimore, 1978).

Background views against which to fix the distinction of Sibley's thesis may be found in:

P. H. Nowell-Smith, *Ethics* (London, 1954), chapters 5–6;
John Wisdom, "Gods," reprinted in his *Philosophy and Psycho-Analysis* (Oxford, 1953);
Ludwig Wittgenstein, *The Blue and Brown Books* (Oxford, 1958).
None of these is narrowly concerned with aesthetics.

# Part Two
# The Definition of Art

Aestheticians are perennially trying to define what a work of art is. The variety of answers advanced is itself worth noting, because it suggests that the question may be irregular in some way. Still, there is perhaps no quicker introduction to classical discussions of art than to summarize the master definitions that have been provided, say, from Plato to Clive Bell.

It should be noticed that "work of art" is used in two entirely different ways, at the very least. For one, it is a value-laden term applied to things in virtue of certain alleged excellences. And for a second, it is one of the most basic category-terms in aesthetics, designating the principal objects that are to be examined from a certain point of view—objects possibly, though not necessarily, entitled to be characterized as "works of art" on the first use of the phrase. This distinction is often overlooked, though it would appear to affect decisively the nature of any effort to define "work of art."

The trouble with any effort to fix the basic category-term, "work of art," is that it will depend on what counts as an aesthetic point of view. But what counts as an aesthetic point of view cannot itself be decided by some simple inspection of actual usage. Philosophers seem to decide, more than to find, what the boundaries of aesthetic interest are (see Part One). And the definition of "work of art" may vary according to the varying boundaries assigned to the aesthetic. This means that at least some apparent incompatibilities in definition may reflect the shifting decisions of philosophers regarding the definition of the aesthetic. Furthermore, as already remarked, the "aesthetic" tends to ignore the distinction of art as such—whatever we may choose to feature in speaking of art: even its history as a specialized term has only an uncertain linkage, systematically, with the nature and appreciation of art. To make the definition of "art" depend on how we specify the meaning of "aesthetic," then, is inevitably to invite a measure of conceptual disorder.

Comparatively recently, the question had been raised whether (following the lead of Wittgenstein) it is at all possible to isolate the essential and distinctive properties of works of art. It has been argued, for instance, that works of art exhibit only "family resemblances" or "strands of similarities" but not essential and distinctive properties common to all admitted instances. The question is a vexed one, because it is not entirely clear what sort of initial restrictions may properly be placed on the collection of things for which this claim, or the counterclaim, could be confirmed. Hence, if no restriction is allowed, it would seem trivially true that no definition of the required sort could be put forward, since an expression like "work of art" is probably used in a great variety of somewhat unrelated ways. (Is a sunset a work of art, for instance? Is life a work of art? Is driftwood art?) And if an initial restriction is allowed, will it be a logical or an empirical matter that a definition of the required sort cannot be found? The question at stake is not, specifically, *the* definition of art but the eligibility of the effort to define art. Though if "art" be definable, we surely would want to know what the best formulation is.

Still, if "work of art" is a basic category-term, its importance probably is to be located elsewhere than in the presumed effort to discover its essential conditions (which may, nevertheless, remain legitimate). Because to identify such essential conditions is to summarize the findings of other primary investigations—for instance, the nature and orientation of criticism upon the fine arts. That is, the definition probably serves to indicate the focus of a systematic account of other questions of aesthetics more directly concerned with the professional and amateur examination of works of art themselves.

Morris Weitz's Matchette Prize essay (1955) has undoubtedly been responsible for a lively reconsideration of what are perhaps the best-known theories in aesthetics, which have regularly been advanced in the form of definitions of art. It represents a turning point in aesthetic theory precisely by raising a "meta-aesthetic" question. But as with so many parallel efforts in other fields, it proves to be extremely difficult to separate sharply "object"-level questions and "meta"-level questions, that is, questions about the status of "object"-level questions—in particular, the question, What is art? In effect an entire industry has developed canvassing the force of Weitz's challenge.

Intuitively, it seems preposterous to deny that it is possible to say, and worth saying, what fine art is. The nature of Weitz's demurrer is rather less obvious than may at first appear. Weitz seems to press the point that if it is to be provided, a definition of art should identify what is really essential to it, what its necessary and sufficient conditions are. Apparently, a definition can be provided "for a special purpose," but this, Weitz believes, is not the same thing.

We are bound to raise several questions here. Are there any definitions that do not serve a special purpose? Do definitions, if they serve a special purpose—for instance, facilitating reference and focus for a set of competing theories about art—fail for that reason to capture the essence of art? And is it the case that serviceable definitions must, and must be supposed to, capture the real essence of what they characterize? It is in fact a feature of the more recent, changed reception of definitional requests (for instance, in the account provided by Hilary Putnam) that we may characterize the distinctive traits or conditions of art without pretending to fix its essence or without insisting that empirical definitions be addressed to real essences.

One of the most notable recent discussions of the peculiar nature of works of art is Arthur Danto's paper "The Artworld" (1964). In effect, Danto does not disqualify definitions but rather shows why it is that, particularly with regard to art, the inventive possibilities oblige us to keep adjusting our antecedently stabilized characterizations. In doing so, Danto clearly links the treatment of the definition of art with the deeper question of the metaphysical status of a work of art. He hints at a difference between physical nature and human culture and he introduces, without development, what he calls the "'is' of artistic identification." What we may suggest, here, without pursuing that issue (see Part Three) is that definitions may serve only to fix the properties of what, in accord with the prevailing current of competing theories, are thought to be the normal or central instances. In this sense, as we say, definitions fix only the nominal, not the real, essences of things; that is, definitions are practical and alterable instruments servicing developing theories that cover at least certain undeniable specimens. It is entirely possible, therefore, that works of art that are somewhat deviant relative to the standard cases can be admitted as works of art and can be admitted to have properties quite different from those focused by our definition, without contradiction at all. It is only when such discrepancies begin to take on a systematic importance that earlier serviceable definitions will have to give way: then, the meaning of "art" will have to change, whereas it need not have changed in accommodating our changing beliefs about what a work of art could be like. This explains in a sense the tolerance that is possible in speaking of driftwood, readymades, *l'art trouvé*, machine art, the art of chimpanzees, and so-called conceptual or idea art. It also suggests the sense in which we may proceed by genus and difference, by necessary and sufficient conditions, or by characteristic conditions, without in the least violating any logical constraints on the formulation of empirical definitions. The definitions of empirical terms in the sciences are intended to facilitate discourse that is primarily explanatory (in the causal sense) and predictive. Where art is concerned, no such constraints obtain, though there is a clear sense in which definitions must be brought into fair agreement with the general sorts of theories and activities that characterize our aesthetic concern with the arts themselves. The concession, it may be admitted, points as well to the possible vacuity of definitional disputes. But, more important, it signifies a refinement in the theory of definition and a sense of the function and validity of particular definitions of art.

Danto has, more recently, pursued (1981) some of the intentional complexities of art, characteristically ignored in aesthetic theory—particularly of the Anglo-American sort. It would not be amiss to say that, as with the "Artworld" paper, he is benignly influenced, here, by a reading of Jean-Paul Sartre's phenomenologically oriented account of imagination (1984). Nevertheless, he does not return to clarify the "is" of artistic identification.

Sartre himself, of course, has—in a deliberately paradoxical but also conceptually troublesome way—raised art to a higher status than the "merely" real by dubbing it "unreal." (This use of "mere" is itself not merely accidental in Danto's papers on art.) Sartre's intention, here, is to dramatize the intentional, imaginative complexity of what is said to be represented in painting and the other arts. But his account obliges us, admitting his generic thesis about art, to consider what we may usefully say about the definition of art. And Danto, in a lively and even more recent paper, "The End of Art" (1984), has usefully collected the historically unfolding record of the art tradition in a way that confirms the conceptual puzzle of what we take ourselves to be doing in defining art—both with respect to his claim that art has "become transmuted into philosophy" and that the boundaries between the various arts have "become radically unstable." Still, what we should understand by the definitional question remains for others to examine (for instance, Robert Matthews, 1979), particularly if there is no final or essential theoretical discovery about the nature of art (see for instance Francis Sparshott, 1982).

Nelson Goodman (1977) has, for reasons rather different from Danto's, eschewed the definition of art. In speaking of the "symptoms" of art as opposed to its "defining properties," however, he does actually consider a set of disjunctively necessary and conjunctively sufficient conditions that tempt us—against his demurrer—to view his thesis as definitional. These are linked to symbolic functioning; to features of symbols, to features symbolized, and to functioning at least by way of exemplification. One may perhaps say that, effectively, Goodman favors a functional essentialism with regard to art rather than a substantive essentialism—which is both subtler than the latter and also not entirely congruent with his own more recent commitment to a proliferation of "made" worlds. But if he were to concede that much, artworks might be shown not to exhibit the salient symbolic functions he favors and yet remain significant artworks for all that, Goodman might well be obliged to curb considerably his semiotic orientation, both in general and in detail. The theory that works of art are symbols or symbolic forms is perennially of interest, of course. Goodman introduces a particularly subtle version of it, by means of which he is able to expose certain anomalies in formalist theories of art. But in doing so, he obliges us to consider once again how minimal the basis may be on which to construe an object as functioning symbolically—hence, the vulnerability of the theory that art exhibits in some strong sense a symbolic function. The key to Goodman's entire theory of art rests with the concept of exemplification. Granted that to exemplify is to symbolize; the question remains whether in possessing whatever properties it does possess (non-symbolic properties), a work of art must be said to refer to or symbolize any or all such properties. Goodman's account, therefore, suggests a possible asymmetry between validating and invalidating definitions of art or, more informally, characterizations of what serves as strong (or even decisive) evidence of the presence of art. It also suggests the variety of strategies by which we may recover some of the purposes of definition without conceding that the specification of "salient," "characteristic," "symptomatic," and similar traits are to count as actually definitional in nature.

Jack Glickman (1976) adopts another strategy. Instead of challenging what is normally thought to be a defining property of art, namely, being an artifact, Glickman attempts to show that being an artifact does not entail having been made by anyone. He explores, in passing, the notion of creativity and centers on the kind of art that is thought to be creative in nature. By this strategy, Glickman shows the possibility of dispute even about what is entailed by admittedly defining properties. And his claim that "particulars are made, types created" draws us on to the profound ontological problem of how a work of art can be a particular and combine concrete and abstract properties (see Part Three).

Perhaps the so-called "institutional" theory of art advanced by George Dickie (1969) is the most recently debated of standard attempts at defining art. Ted Cohen's criticism of it (1973) both introduces the thesis in a convenient and fair-minded way and musters the principal objections to it. There is no question that *some* sense of the institutional or societal complexities of art is essential to our theorizing. But Dickie's thesis has puzzled his readers primarily because, as Cohen very clearly shows, we cannot sort out satisfactorily whether the prior achievements of some putative artwork are marked as such by a knowledgeable clientele or whether some (somehow) authorized public body fixes the pertinent properties of a would-be artwork by selecting some artifact for artwork status. Questions both about how to legitimate those who legitimate the art status of artifacts and about the dubious (and parasitic) function of status-fixing itself have been raised against Dickie's view (for instance, by Beardsley, 1982; and by Wartofsky, 1980). Cohen's own emphasis rests chiefly with the performative feature of Dickie's defining conditions: both with respect to "conferring" (in Dickie's account) a status that must already obtain before the would-be enabling act itself and with respect to the difficulty of supposing that relevant conferring moves need be (or can be) directly linked with what Dickie has in mind in speaking of appreciation. But all these challenges pale somewhat in the face of the fact that we generally lack a sustained account of the institutional, societal, and historical nature of art itself.

# 7.    The Role of Theory in Aesthetics
## *MORRIS WEITZ*

Theory has been central in aesthetics and is still the preoccupation of the philosophy of art. Its main avowed concern remains the determination of the nature of art which can be formulated into a definition of it. It construes definition as the statement of the necessary and sufficient properties of what is being defined, where the statement purports to be a true or false claim about the essence of art, what characterizes and distinguishes it from everything else. Each of the great theories of art—Formalism, Voluntarism, Emotionalism, Intellectualism, Intuitionism, Organicism—converges on the attempt to state the defining properties of art. Each claims that it is the true theory because it has formulated correctly into a real definition the nature of art; and that the others are false because they have left out some necessary or sufficient property. Many theorists contend that their enterprise is no mere intellectual exercise but an absolute necessity for any understanding of art and our proper evaluation of it. Unless we know what art is, they say, what are its necessary and sufficient properties, we cannot begin to respond to it adequately or to say why one work is good or better than another. Aesthetic theory, thus, is important not only in itself but for the foundations of both appreciation and criticism. Philosophers, critics, and even artists who have written on art agree that what is primary in aesthetics is a theory about the nature of art.

Is aesthetic theory, in the sense of a true definition or set of necessary and sufficient properties of art, possible? If nothing else does, the history of aesthetics itself should give one enormous pause here. For, in spite of the many theories, we seem no nearer our goal today than we were in Plato's time. Each age, each art-movement, each philosophy of art, tries

From *The Journal of Aesthetics and Art Criticism*, XV (1956), 27–35. Reprinted with permission of the author and the editor of *The Journal of Aesthetics and Art Criticism*.

over and over again to establish the stated ideal only to be succeeded by a new or revised theory, rooted, at least in part, in the repudiation of preceding ones. Even today, almost everyone interested in aesthetic matters is still deeply wedded to the hope that the correct theory of art is forthcoming. We need only examine the numerous new books on art in which new definitions are proffered; or, in our own country especially, the basic textbooks and anthologies to recognize how strong the priority of a theory of art is.

In this essay I want to plead for the rejection of this problem. I want to show that theory—in the requisite classical sense—is *never* forthcoming in aesthetics, and that we would do much better as philosophers to supplant the question, "What is the nature of art?" by other questions, the answers to which will provide us with all the understanding of the arts there can be. I want to show that the inadequacies of the theories are not primarily occasioned by any legitimate difficulty such as, e.g., the vast complexity of art, which might be corrected by further probing and research. Their basic inadequacies reside instead in a fundamental misconception of art. Aesthetic theory—all of it—is wrong in principle in thinking that a correct theory is possible because it radically misconstrues the logic of the concept of art. Its main contention that "art" is amenable to real or any kind of true definition is false. Its attempt to discover the necessary and sufficient properties of art is logically misbegotten for the very simple reason that such a set and, consequently, such a formula about it, is never forthcoming. Art, as the logic of the concept shows, has no set of necessary and sufficient properties; hence a theory of it is logically impossible and not merely factually difficult. Aesthetic theory tries to define what cannot be defined in its requisite sense. But in recommending the repudiation of aesthetic theory I shall not argue from this, as too many others have done, that its logical confusions render it meaningless or worthless. On the contrary, I wish to reassess its role and its contribution primarily in order to show that it is of the greatest importance to our understanding of the arts.

Let us now survey briefly some of the more famous extant aesthetic theories in order to see if they do incorporate correct and adequate statements about the nature of art. In each of these there is the assumption that it is the true enumeration of the defining properties of art, with the implication that previous theories have stressed wrong definitions. Thus, to begin with, consider a famous version of Formalist theory, that propounded by Bell and Fry. It is true that they speak mostly of painting in their writings but both assert that what they find in that art can be generalized for what is "art" in the others as well. The essence of painting, they maintain, is the plastic elements in relation. Its defining property is significant form, i.e., certain combinations of lines, colors, shapes, volumes—everything on the canvas except the representational elements—which evoke a unique response to such combinations. Painting is definable as plastic organization. The nature of art, what it *really* is, so their theory goes, is a unique combination of certain elements (the specifiable plastic ones) in their relations. Anything which is art is an instance of significant form; and anything which is not art has no such form.

To this the Emotionalist replies that the truly essential property of art has been left out. Tolstoy, Ducasse, or any of the advocates of this theory, find that the requisite defining property is not significant form but rather the expression of emotion in some sensuous public medium. Without projection of emotion into some piece of stone or words or sounds, etc., there can be no art. Art is really such embodiment. It is this that uniquely characterizes art, and any true, real definition of it contained in some adequate theory of art, must so state it.

The Intuitionist disclaims both emotion and form as defining properties. In Croce's version, for example, art is identified not with some physical, public object but with a specific creative, cognitive, and spiritual art. Art is really a first stage of knowledge in which certain human beings (artists) bring their images and intuitions into lyrical clarification or expression. As such, it is an awareness, non-conceptual in character, of the unique individuality of things; and since it exists below the level of conceptualization or action, it is without scientific or moral content. Croce singles out as the defining essence of art this first stage of spiritual life and advances its identification with art as a philosophically true theory or definition.

The Organicist says to all of this that art is really a class of organic wholes consisting of distinguishable, albeit inseparable, elements in their causally efficacious relations which are presented in some sensuous medium. In A. C. Bradley, in piecemeal versions of it in literary criticism, or in my own generalized adaptation of it in my *Philosophy of the Arts*, what is claimed is that anything which is a work of art is in its nature a unique complex of interrelated parts—in painting, for example, lines, colors, volumes, subjects, etc., all interacting upon one another on a paint surface of some sort. Certainly, at one time at least it seemed to me that this organic theory constituted the one true and real definition of art.

My final example is the most interesting of all, logically speaking. This is the Voluntarist theory of Parker. In his writings on art, Parker persistently calls into question the traditional simpleminded definitions of aesthetics. "The assumption underlying every philosophy of art is the existence of some common nature present in all the arts."[1] "All the so popular brief definitions of art—'significant form,' 'expression,' 'intuition,' 'objectified pleasure'—all fallacious, either because, while true of art, they are also true of much that is not art, and hence fail to differentiate art from other things; or else because they neglect some essential aspect of art."[2]

But instead of inveighing against the attempt at definition of art itself, Parker insists that what is needed is a complex definition rather than a simple one. "The definition of art must therefore be in terms of a complex of characteristics. Failure to recognize this has been the fault of all the well-known definitions."[3] His own version of Voluntarism is the theory that art is essentially three things: embodiment of wishes and desires imaginatively satisfied, language, which characterizes the public medium of art, and harmony, which unifies the language with the layers of imaginative projections. Thus, for Parker, it is a true definition to say of art that it is "the provision of satisfaction through the imagination, social significance, and harmony. I am claiming that nothing except works of art possesses all three of these marks."[4]

Now, all these sample theories are inadequate in many different ways. Each purports to be in a complete statement about the defining features of all works of art and yet each of them leaves out something which the others take to be central. Some are circular, e.g., the Bell-Fry theory of art as significant form which is defined in part in terms of our response to significant form. Some of them, in their search for necessary and sufficient properties, emphasize too few properties, like (again) the Bell-Fry definition, which leaves out subject-representation in painting, or the Croce theory, which omits inclusion of the very important feature of the public, physical character, say, of architecture. Others are too general and cover objects that are not art as well as works of art. Organicism is surely such a view since it can be applied to *any* causal unity in the natural world as well as to art.[5] Still others rest on dubious principles, e.g., Parker's claim that art embodies imaginative satisfactions, rather than real ones; or Croce's assertion that there is nonconceptual knowledge. Consequently, even if art has one set of necessary and sufficient properties, none of the theories we have noted or, for that matter, no aesthetic theory yet proposed has enumerated that set to the satisfaction of all concerned.

Then there is a different sort of difficulty. As real definitions, these theories are supposed to be factual reports on art. If they are, may we not ask, Are they empirical and open to verification or falsification? For example, what would confirm or disconfirm the theory that art is significant form or embodiment of emotion or creative synthesis of images? There does not even seem to be a hint of the kind of evidence which might be forthcoming to test these theories; and indeed one wonders if they are perhaps honorific definitions of "art," that is, proposed redefinitions in terms of some *chosen* conditions for applying the concept of art, and not true or false reports on the essential properties of art at all.

But all these criticisms of traditional aesthetic theories—that they are circular, incomplete, untestable, pseudo-factual, disguised proposals to change the meaning of concepts—have been made before. My intention is to go beyond these to make a much more fundamental criticism, namely, that aesthetic theory is a logically vain attempt to define what cannot be defined, to state the necessary and sufficient properties of that which has no necessary and sufficient properties, to conceive the concept of art as closed when its very use reveals and demands its openness.

The problem with which we must begin is not "What is art?" but "What sort of concept is 'art'?" Indeed, the root problem of philosophy itself is to explain the relation between the employment of certain kinds of concepts and the conditions under which they can be correctly applied. If I may paraphrase Wittgenstein, we must not ask, What is the nature of any philosophical x? or even, according to the semanticist, What does "x" mean?, a transformation that leads to the disastrous interpretation of "art" as a name for some specifiable class of objects; but rather, What is the use or employment of "x"? What does "x" do in the language? This, I take it, is the initial question, the begin-all if not the end-all of any philosophical problem and solution. Thus, in aesthetics, our first problem is the elucidation of the actual employment of the concept of art, to give a logical description of the actual functioning of the concept, including a description of the conditions under which we correctly use it or its correlates.

My model in this type of logical description or philosophy derives from Wittgenstein. It is also he who, in his refutation of philosophical theorizing in the sense of constructing definitions of philosophical entities, has furnished contemporary aesthetics with a starting point for any future progress. In his new work, *Philosophical Investigations*,[6] Wittgenstein raises as an illustrative question, What is a game? The traditional philosophical, theoretical answer would be in terms of some exhaustive set of properties common to all games. To this Wittgenstein says, let us consider what we call "games": "I mean board-games, card-games, ball-games, Olympic games, and so on. What is common to them all?—Don't say: 'there *must* be something common, or they would not be called "games"' but *look and see* whether there is anything common to all. For if you look at them you will not see something that is common to *all,* but similarities, relationships, and a whole series of them at that. . . ."

Card games are like board games in some respects but not in others. Not all games are amusing, nor is there always winning or losing or competition. Some games resemble others in some respects—that is all. What we find is no necessary and sufficient properties, only "a complicated network of similarities overlapping and crisscrossing," such that we can say of games that they form a family with family resemblances and no common trait. If one asks what a game is, we pick out sample games, describe these, and add, "This and *similar things* are called 'games.'" This is all we need to say and indeed all any of us knows about games. Knowing what a game is is not knowing some real definition or theory but being able to recognize and explain games and to decide which among imaginary and new examples would or would not be called "games."

The problem of the nature of art is like that of the nature of games, at least in these respects: If we actually look and see what it is that we call "art," we will also find no common properties—only strands of similarities. Knowing what art is is not apprehending some manifest or latent essence but being able to recognize, describe, and explain those things we call "art" in virtue of these similarities.

But the basic resemblance between these concepts is their open texture. In elucidating them, certain (paradigm) cases can be given, about which there can be no question as to their being correctly described as "art" or "game," but no exhaustive set of cases can be given. I can list some cases and some conditions under which I can apply correctly the concept of art but I cannot list all of them, for the all-important reason that unforeseeable or novel conditions are always forthcoming or envisageable.

A concept is open if its conditions of application are emendable and corrigible; i.e., if a situation or case can be imagined or secured which would call for some sort of *decision* on our part to extend the use of the concept to cover this, or to close the concept and invent a new one to deal with the new case and its new property. If necessary and sufficient conditions for the application of a concept can be stated, the concept is a closed one. But this can happen only in logic or mathematics where concepts are constructed and completely defined. It cannot occur with empirically descriptive and normative concepts unless we arbitrarily close them by stipulating the ranges of their uses.

I can illustrate this open character of "art" best by examples drawn from its sub-concepts. Consider questions like "Is Dos Passos' *U.S.A.* a novel?" "Is V. Woolf's *To the Lighthouse* a novel?" "Is Joyce's *Finnegans Wake* a novel?" On the traditional view, these are construed as factual problems to be answered yes or no in accordance with the presence or absence of defining properties. But certainly this is not how any of these questions is answered. Once it arises, as it has many times in the development of the novel from Richardson to Joyce (e.g., "Is Gide's *The School for Wives* a novel or a diary?"), what is at stake is no factual analysis concerning necessary and sufficient properties but a decision as to whether the work under examination is similar in certain respects to other works, already called "novels," and consequently warrants the extension of the concept to cover the new case. The new work is narrative, fictional, contains character delineation and dialogue but (say) it has no regular time-sequence in the plot or is interspersed with actual newspaper reports. It is like recognized novels, A, B, C . . . , in some respects but not like them in others. But then neither were B and C like A in some respects when it was decided to extend the concept applied to A to B and C. Because work N + 1 (the brand new work) is like A, B, C, . . . N in certain respects—has strands of similarity to them—the concept is extended and a new phase of the novel engendered. "Is N + 1 a novel?," then, is no factual, but rather a decision problem, where the verdict turns on whether or not we enlarge our set of conditions for applying the concept.

What is true of the novel is, I think, true of every sub-concept of art: "tragedy," "comedy," "painting," "opera," etc., of "art" itself. No "Is X a novel, painting, opera, work of art, etc.?" question allows of a definitive answer in the sense of a factual yes or no report. "Is this *collage* a painting or not?" does not rest on any set of necessary and sufficient properties of painting but on whether we decide—as we did!—to extend "painting" to cover this case.

"Art," itself, is an open concept. New conditions (cases) have constantly arisen and will undoubtedly constantly arise; new art forms, new movements will emerge, which will demand decisions on the part of those interested, usually professional critics, as to whether the concept should be extended or not. Aestheticians may lay down similarity conditions but never necessary and sufficient ones for the correct application of the concept. With "art" its conditions of application can never be exhaustively enumerated since new cases can always be envisaged or created by artists, or even nature, which would call for a decision on someone's part to extend or to close the old or to invent a new concept. (E.g., "It's not a sculpture, it's a mobile.")

What I am arguing, then, is that the very expansive, adventurous character of art, its ever-present changes and novel creations, make it logically impossible to ensure any set of defining properties. We can, of course, choose to close the concept. But to do this with "art" or "tragedy" or "portraiture," etc., is ludicrous since it forecloses on the very conditions of creativity in the arts.

Of course there are legitimate and serviceable closed concepts in art. But these are always those whose boundaries of conditions have been drawn for a *special* purpose. Consider the difference, for example, between "tragedy" and "(extant) Greek tragedy." The first is open and must remain so to allow for the possibility of new conditions, e.g., a play in which the hero is not noble or fallen or in which there is no hero but other elements that are like those of plays we already call "tragedy." The second is closed. The plays it can be applied to, the conditions under which it can be correctly used are all in, once the boundary, "Greek," is drawn. Here the critic can work out a theory or real definition in which he lists the common properties at least of the extant Greek tragedies. Artistotle's definition, false as it is as a theory of all the plays of Aeschylus, Sophocles, and Euripides, since it does not cover some of them,[7] properly called "tragedies," can be interpreted as a real (albeit incorrect) definition of this closed concept; although it can also be, as it unfortunately has been, conceived as a purported real definition of "tragedy," in which case it suffers from the logical mistake of trying to define what cannot be defined—of trying to squeeze what is an open concept into an honorific formula for a closed concept.

What is supremely important, if the critic is not to become muddled, is to get absolutely clear about the way in which he conceives his concepts; otherwise he goes from the problem of trying to define "tragedy," etc., to an arbitrary closing of the concept in terms of certain preferred conditions or characteristics which he sums up in some linguistic recommendation that he mistakenly thinks is a real definition of the open concept. Thus, many critics and aestheticians ask, "What is tragedy?," choose a class of samples for which they may give a true account of its common properties, and then go on to construe this account of the chosen closed class as a true definition or theory of the whole open class of tragedy. This, I think, is the logical mechanism of most of the so-called theories of the sub-concepts of art: "tragedy," "comedy," "novel," etc. In effect, this whole procedure, subtly deceptive as it is, amounts to a transformation of correct criteria for *recognizing* members of certain legitimately closed classes of works of art into recommended criteria for *evaluating* any putative member of the class.

The primary task of aesthetics is not to seek a theory but to elucidate the concept of art. Specifically, it is to describe the conditions under which we employ the concept correctly. Definition, reconstruction, patterns of analysis are out of place here since they distort and add nothing to our understanding of art. What, then, is the logic of "X is a work of art"?

As we actually use the concept, "Art" is both descriptive (like "chair") and evaluative (like "good"); i.e., we sometimes say, "This is a work of art," to describe something and we sometimes say it to evaluate something. Neither use surprises anyone.

What, first, is the logic of "X is a work of art," when it is a descriptive utterance? What are the conditions under which we would be making such an utterance correctly? There are no necessary and sufficient conditions but there are the strands of similarity conditions, i.e., bundles of properties, none of which need be present but most of which are, when we describe things as works of art. I shall call these the "criteria of recognition" of works of art. All these have served as the defining criteria of the individual traditional theories of art; so we are already familiar with them. Thus, mostly, when we describe something as a work of art, we do so under the conditions of there being present some sort of artifact, made by human skill, ingenuity, and imagination, which embodies in its sensuous, public medium—stone, wood, sounds, words, etc.—certain distinguishable elements and relations. Special theorists would add conditions like satisfaction of wishes, objectification or expression of emotion, some act of empathy, and so on; but these latter conditions seem to be quite adventitious, present to some but not to other spectators when things are described as works of art. "X is a work of art and contains *no* emotion, expression, act of empathy, satisfaction, etc.," is perfectly good sense and may frequently be true. "X is a work of art and . . . was made by no one," or ". . . exists only in the mind and not in any publicly observable thing," or ". . . was made by accident when he spilled the paint on the canvas," in each case of which a normal condition is denied, are also sensible and capable of being true in certain circumstances. None of the criteria of recognition is a defining one, either necessary or sufficient, because we can sometimes assert of something that it is a work of art and go on to deny any one of these conditions, even the one which has traditionally been taken to be basic, namely, that of being an artifact: Consider, "This piece of driftwood is a lovely piece of sculpture." Thus, to say of anything that it is a work of art is to commit oneself to the presence of *some* of these conditions. One would scarcely describe X as a work of art if X were not an artifact, or a collection of elements sensuously presented in a medium, or a product of human skill, and so on. If none of the conditions was present, if there were no criteria present for recognizing something as a work of art, we would not describe it as one. But, even so, no one of these or any collection of them is either necessary or sufficient.

The elucidation of the descriptive use of "Art" creates little difficulty. But the elucidation of the evaluative use does. For many, especially theorists, "This is a work of art" does more than describe; it also praises. Its conditions of utterance, therefore, include certain preferred properties or characteristics of art. I shall call these "criteria of evaluation." Consider a typical example of this evaluative use, the view according to which to say of something that it is a work of art is to imply that it is a *successful* harmonization of elements. Many of the honorific definitions of art and its sub-concepts are of this form. What is at stake here is that "Art" is construed as an evaluative term which is either identified with its criterion or justified in terms of it. "Art" is defined in terms of its evaluative property, e.g., successful harmonization. On such a view, to say "X is a work of art" is (1) to say something which is taken *to mean* "X is a successful harmonization" (e.g., "Art *is* significant form") or (2) to say something praiseworthy *on the basis* of its successful harmonization.

Theorists are never clear whether it is (1) or (2) which is being put forward. Most of them, concerned as they are with this evaluative use, formulate (2), i.e., that feature of art that *makes* it art in the praise-sense, and then go on to state (1), i.e., the definition of "Art" in terms of its art-making feature. And this is clearly to confuse the conditions under which we say something evaluatively with the meaning of what we say. "This is a work of art," said evaluatively, cannot mean "This is a successful harmonization of elements"—except by stipulation—but at most is said in virtue of the art-making property, which is taken as a (the) criterion of "Art," when "Art" is employed to assess. "This is a work of art," used evaluatively, serves to praise and not to affirm the reason that it is said.

The evaluative use of "Art," although distinct from the conditions of its use, relates in a very intimate way to these conditions. For, in every instance of "This is a work of art" (used to praise), what happens is that the criterion of evaluation (e.g., successful harmonization) for the employment of the concept of art is converted into a criterion of recognition. This is why, on its evaluative use, "This is a work of art" implies "This has P," where "P" is some chosen art-making property. Thus, if one chooses to employ "Art" evaluatively, as many do, so that "This is a work of art and not (aesthetically) good" makes no sense, he uses "Art" in such a way that he refuses to *call* anything a work of art unless it embodies his criterion of excellence.

There is nothing wrong with the evaluative use; in fact, there is good reason for using "Art" to praise. But what cannot be maintained is that theories of the evaluative use of "Art" are true and real definitions of the necessary and sufficient properties of art. Instead they are honorific definitions, pure and simple, in which "Art" has been redefined in terms of chosen criteria.

But what makes them—these honorific definitions—so supremely valuable is not their disguised linguistic recommendations; rather it is the *debates* over the reasons for changing the criteria of the concept of art which are built into the definitions. In each of the great theories of art, whether correctly understood as honorific definitions or incorrectly accepted as real definitions, what is of the utmost importance is the reasons proffered in the argument for the respective theory, that is, the reasons given for the chosen or preferred criterion of excellence and evaluation. It is this perennial debate over these criteria of evaluation which makes the history of aesthetic theory the important study it is. The value of each of the theories resides in its attempt to state and to justify certain criteria which are either neglected or distorted by previous theories. Look at the Bell-Fry theory again. Of course, "Art is significant form" cannot be accepted as a true, real definition of art; and most certainly it actually functions in their aesthetics as a redefinition of art in terms of the chosen condition of significant form. But what gives it its aesthetic importance is what lies behind the formula: In an age in which literary and representational elements have become paramount in painting, *return* to the plastic ones since these are indigenous to painting. Thus, the role of theory is not to define anything but to use the definitional form, almost epigrammatically, to pinpoint a crucial recommendation to turn our attention once again to the plastic elements in painting.

Once we, as philosophers, understand this distinction between the formula and what lies behind it, it behooves us to deal generously with the traditional theories of art; because incorporated in every one of them is a debate over and argument for emphasizing or centering upon some particular feature of art which has been neglected or perverted. If we take the aesthetic theories literally, as we have seen, they all fail; but if we reconstrue them, in terms of their function and point, as serious and argued-for recommendations to concentrate on certain criteria of excellence in art, we shall see that aesthetic theory is far from worthless. Indeed, it becomes as central as anything in aesthetics, in our understanding of art, for it teaches us what to look for and how to look at it in art. What is central and must be articulated in all the theories are their debates over the reasons for excellence in art—debates over emotional depth, profound truths, natural beauty, exactitude, freshness of treatment, and so on, as criteria of evaluation—the whole of which converges on the perennial problem of what makes a work of art good. To understand the role of aesthetic theory is not to conceive it as definition, logically doomed to failure, but to read it as summaries of seriously made recommendations to attend in certain ways to certain features of art.

### Notes

1. D. Parker, "The Nature of Art," reprinted in E. Vivas and M. Krieger, *The Problems of Aesthetics* (New York, 1953), p. 90.

2. *Ibid.,* pp. 93–94.

3. *Ibid.,* p. 94.

4. *Ibid.,* p. 104.

5. See M. Macdonald's review of my *Philosophy of the Arts, Mind,* October 1951, pp. 561–564, for a brilliant discussion of this objection to the Organic theory.

6. L. Wittgenstein, *Philosophical Investigations,* tr. E. Anscombe (Oxford, 1953); see especially part 1, sec. 65–75. All quotations are from these sections.

7. See H.D.F. Kitto, *Greek Tragedy* (London, 1939), on this point.

# 8.

# The Artworld
## ARTHUR DANTO

> Hamlet:
> Do you see nothing there?
> The Queen:
> Nothing at all; yet all that is I see.
> *Shakespeare: Hamlet, Act 3, Scene 4*

Hamlet and Socrates, though in praise and depreciation respectively, spoke of art as a mirror held up to nature. As with many disagreements in attitude, this one has a factual basis. Socrates saw mirrors as but reflecting what we can already see; so art, insofar as mirrorlike, yields idle accurate duplications of the appearances of things, and is of no cognitive benefit whatever. Hamlet, more acutely, recognized a remarkable feature of reflecting surfaces, namely that they show us what we could not otherwise perceive—our own face and form—and so art, insofar as it is mirrorlike, reveals us to ourselves, and is, even by Socratic criteria, of some cognitive utility after all. As a philosopher, however, I find Socrates' discussion defective on other, perhaps less profound grounds than these. If a mirror image of *o* is indeed an imitation of *o*, then, if art is imitation, mirror images are art. But in fact mirroring objects no more is art than returning weapons to a madman is justice; and reference to mirrorings would be just the sly sort of counterinstance we would expect Socrates to bring forward in rebuttal of the theory he instead uses them to illustrate. If that theory requires us to class *these* as art, it thereby shows its inadequacy: "is an imitation" will not do as a sufficient condition for "is art." Yet, perhaps because artists *were* engaged in imitation, in Socrates' time and after, the insufficiency of the theory was not noticed until the invention of photog-

From *The Journal of Philosophy*, LXI (1964), 571–584. Reprinted with permission of the author and *The Journal of Philosophy*.

raphy. Once rejected as a sufficient condition, mimesis was quickly discarded as even a necessary one; and since the achievement of Kandinsky, mimetic features have been relegated to the periphery of critical concern, so much so that some works survive in spite of possessing those virtues, excellence in which was once celebrated as the essence of art, narrowly escaping demotion to mere illustrations.

It is, of course, indispensable in Socratic discussion that all participants be masters of the concept up for analysis, since the aim is to match a real defining expression to a term in active use, and the test for adequacy presumably consists in showing that the former analyzes and applies to all and only those things of which the latter is true. The popular disclaimer notwithstanding, then, Socrates' auditors purportedly knew what art was as well as what they liked; and a theory of art, regarded here as a real definition of 'Art', is accordingly not to be of great use in helping men to recognize instances of its application. Their antecedent ability to do this is precisely what the adequacy of the theory is to be tested against, the problem being only to make explicit what they already know. It is *our* use of the term that the theory allegedly means to capture, but we are supposed able, in the words of a recent writer, "to separate those objects which are works of art from those which are not, because . . . we know how correctly to use the word 'art' and to apply the phrase 'work of art'." Theories, on this account, are somewhat like mirror images on Socrates' account, showing forth what we already know, wordy reflections of the actual linguistic practice we are masters in.

But telling artworks from other things is not so simple a matter, even for native speakers, and these days one might not be aware he was on artistic terrain without an artistic theory to tell him so. And part of the reason for this lies in the fact that terrain is constituted artistic in virtue of artistic theories, so that one use of theories, in addition to helping us discriminate art from the rest, consists in making art possible. Glaucon and the others could hardly have known what was art and what not: otherwise they would never have been taken in by mirror images.

*I*

Suppose one thinks of the discovery of a whole new class of artworks as something analogous to the discovery of a whole new class of facts anywhere, viz., as something for theoreticians to explain. In science, as elsewhere, we often accommodate new facts to old theories via auxiliary hypotheses, a pardonable enough conservatism when the theory in question is deemed too valuable to be jettisoned all at once. Now the Imitation Theory of Art (IT) is, if one but thinks it through, an exceedingly powerful theory, explaining a great many phenomena connected with the causation and evaluation of artworks, bringing a surprising unity into a complex domain. Moreover, it is a simple matter to shore it up against many purported counterinstances by such auxiliary hypotheses as that the artist who deviates from mimeticity is perverse, inept, or mad. Ineptitude, chicanery, or folly are, in fact, testable predications. Suppose, then, tests reveal that these hypotheses fail to hold, that the theory, now beyond repair, must be replaced. And a new theory is worked out, capturing what it can of the old theory's competence, together with the heretofore recalcitrant facts. One might, thinking along these lines, represent certain episodes in the history of art as not dissimilar to certain episodes in the history of science, where a conceptual revolution is being effected and where refusal to countenance certain facts, while in part due to prejudice, inertia, and self-interest, is due also to the fact that a well-established, or at least widely credited theory is being threatened in such a way that all coherence goes.

Some such episode transpired with the advent of Postimpressionist paintings. In terms of the prevailing artistic theory (IT), it was impossible to accept these as art unless inept art: otherwise they could be discounted as hoaxes, self-advertisements, or the visual counterparts of madmen's ravings. So to get them accepted *as* art, on a footing with the *Transfiguration* (not to speak of a Landseer stag), required not so much a revolution in taste as a theoretical revision of rather considerable proportions, involving not only the artistic enfranchisement of these objects, but an emphasis upon newly significant features of accepted artworks, so that quite different accounts of their status as artworks would now have to be given. As a result of the new theory's acceptance, not only were Postimpressionist paintings taken up as art, but numbers of objects (masks, weapons, etc.) were transferred from anthropoligical museums (and heterogeneous other places) to *musées des beaux arts*, though, as we would expect from the fact that a criterion for the acceptance of a new theory is that it account for whatever the older one did, nothing had to be transferred out of the *musée des beaux arts*—even if there were internal rearrangements as between storage rooms and exhibition space. Countless native speakers hung upon suburban mantelpieces innumerable replicas of paradigm cases for teaching the expression 'work of art' that would have sent their Edwardian forebears into linguistic apoplexy.

To be sure, I distort by speaking of a theory: historically, there were several, all, interestingly enough, more or less defined in terms of the IT. Art-historical complexities must yield before the exigencies of logical exposition, and I shall speak as though there were one replacing theory, partially compensating for historical falsity by choosing one which was actually enunciated. According to it, the artists in question were to be understood not as unsuccessfully imitating real forms but as successfully creating new ones, quite as real as the forms which the older art had been thought, in its best examples, to be creditably imitating. Art, after all, had long since been thought of as creative (Vasari says that God was the first artist), and the Postimpressionists were to be explained as genuinely creative, aiming, in Roger Fry's words, "not at illusion but reality." This theory (RT) furnished a whole new mode of looking at painting, old and new. Indeed, one might almost interpret the crude drawing in Van Gogh and Cézanne, the dislocation of form from contour in Rouault and Dufy, the arbitrary use of color planes in Gauguin and the Fauves, as so many ways of drawing attention to the fact that these were *non-imitations*, specifically intended not to deceive. Logically, this would be roughly like printing "Not Legal Tender" across a brilliantly counterfeited dollar bill, the resulting object (counterfeit *cum* inscription) rendered incapable of deceiving anyone. It is not an illusory dollar bill, but then, just because it is non-illusory it does not automatically become a real dollar bill either. It rather occupies a freshly opened area between real objects and real facsimiles of real objects: it is a non-facsimile, if one requires a word, and a new contribution to the world. Thus, Van Gogh's *Potato Eaters*, as a consequence of certain unmistakable distortions, turns out to be a non-facsimile of real-life potato eaters; and inasmuch as these are not facsimiles of potato eaters, Van Gogh's picture, as a non-imitation, had as much right to be called a real object as did its putative subjects. By means of this theory (RT), artworks reentered the thick of things from which Socratic theory (IT) had sought to evict them: if no *more* real than what carpenters wrought, they were at least no *less* real. The Post-Impressionist won a victory in ontology.

It is in terms of RT that we must understand the artworks around us today. Thus Roy Lichtenstein paints comic-strip panels, though ten or twelve feet high. These are reasonably faithful projections onto a gigantesque scale of the homely frames from the daily tabloid, but it is precisely the scale that counts. A skilled engraver might incise *The Virgin and the Chancellor Rollin* on a pinhead, and it would be recognizable as such to the keen of sight, but an engraving of a Barnett Newman on a similar scale would be a blob, disappearing in the reduction. A *photograph* of a Lichtenstein is indiscernible from a photograph of a counterpart panel from *Steve Canyon*; but the photograph fails to capture the scale, and hence is as inaccurate a reproduction as a black-and-white engraving of Botticelli, scale being essential here as color there. Lichtensteins, then, are not imitations but *new entities*, as giant whelks would be. Jasper Johns, by contrast, paints objects with respect to which questions of scale are irrelevant. Yet his objects cannot be imitations, for they have the remarkable property that any intended copy of a member of this class of objects is automatically a member of the class itself, so that these objects are logically inimitable. Thus, a copy of a numeral just *is* that numeral: a painting of 3 is a 3 made of paint. Johns, in addition, paints targets, flags, and maps. Finally, in what I hope are not unwitting footnotes to Plato, two of our pioneers—Robert Rauschenberg and Claes Oldenburg—have made genuine beds.

Rauschenberg's bed hangs on a wall, and is streaked with some desultory housepaint. Oldenburg's bed is a rhomboid, narrower at one end than the other, with what one might speak of as a built-in perspective: ideal for small bedrooms. As beds, these sell at singularly inflated prices, but one *could* sleep in either of them: Rauschenberg has expressed the fear that someone might just climb into his bed and fall asleep. Imagine, now, a certain Testadura—a plain speaker and noted philistine—who is not aware that these are art, and who takes them to be reality simple and pure. He attributes the paint streaks on Rauschenberg's bed to the slovenliness of the owner, and the bias in the Oldenburg bed to the ineptitude of the builder or the whimsy, perhaps, of whoever had it "custom-made." These would be mistakes, but mistakes of rather an odd kind, and not terribly different from that made by the stunned birds who pecked the sham grapes of Zeuxis. They mistook art for reality, and so has Testadura. But it was meant to *be* reality, according to RT. Can one have mistaken reality for reality? How shall we describe Testadura's error? What, after all, prevents Oldenburg's creation from being a misshapen bed? This is equivalent to asking what makes it art, and with this query we enter a domain of conceptual inquiry where native speakers are poor guides: *they* are lost themselves.

## II

To mistake an artwork for a real object is no great feat when an artwork is the real object one mistakes it for. The problem is how to avoid such errors, or to remove them once they are made. The artwork is a bed, and not a bed-illusion; so there is nothing like the traumatic encounter against a flat surface that brought it home to the birds of Zeuxis that they had been duped. Except for the guard cautioning Testadura not to sleep on the artworks, he might never have discovered that this was an artwork and not a bed; and since, after all, one cannot discover that a bed is not a bed, how is Testadura to realize that he has made an error? A certain sort of explanation is required, for the error here is a curiously philosophical one, rather like, if we may assume as correct some well-known views of P. F. Strawson, mistaking a person for a material body when the truth is that a person *is* a material body in the sense that a whole class of predicates, sensibly applicable to material bodies, are sensibly, and by appeal to no different criteria, applicable to persons. So you cannot *discover* that a person is not a material body.

We begin by explaining, perhaps, that the paint streaks are not to be explained away, that they are *part* of the object, so the object is not a mere bed with—as it happens—streaks of paint spilled over it, but a complex object fabricated out of a bed and some paint streaks: a paint-bed. Similarly, a person is not a material body with—as it happens—some thoughts superadded, but is a complex entity made up of a body and some conscious states: a conscious-body. Persons, like artworks, must then be taken as irreducible to *parts* of themselves, and are in that sense primitive. Or, more accurately, the paint streaks are not part of the real object—the bed—which happens to be part of the artwork, but are, *like* the bed, part of the artwork as such. And this might be generalized into a rough characterization of artworks that happen to contain real objects as parts of themselves: not every part of an artwork $A$ is part of a real object $R$ when $R$ is part of $A$ and can, moreover, be detached from $A$ and seen *merely* as $R$. The mistake thus far will have been to mistake $A$ for *part* of itself, namely $R$, even though it would not be incorrect to say that $A$ is $R$, that the artwork is a bed. It is the 'is' which requires clarification here.

There is an *is* that figures prominently in statements concerning artworks which is not the *is* of either identity or predication; nor is it the *is* of existence, of identification, or some special *is* made up to serve a philosophic end. Nevertheless, it is in common usage, and is readily mastered by children. It is the sense of *is* in accordance with which a child, shown a circle and a triangle and asked which is him and which his sister, will point to the triangle saying "That is me"; or, in response to my question, the person next to me points to the man in purple and says "That one is Lear"; or in the gallery I point, for my companion's benefit, to a spot in the painting before us and say "That white dab is Icarus." We do not mean, in these instances, that whatever is pointed to stands for, or represents, what it is said to be, for the *word* 'Icarus' stands for or represents Icarus: yet I would not in the same sense of *is* point to the word and say "That is Icarus." The sentence "That $a$ is $b$" is perfectly compatible with "That $a$ is not $b$" when the first employs this sense of *is* and the second employs some other, though $a$ and $b$ are used nonambiguously throughout. Often, indeed, the truth of the first *requires* the truth of the second. The first, in fact, is incompatible with "That $a$ is not $b$" only when the *is* is used nonambiguously throughout. For want of a word I shall designate this the *is of artistic identification*; in each case in which it is used, the $a$ stands for some specific physical property of, or physical part of, an object; and, finally, it is a necessary condition for something to be an artwork that some part or property of it be designable by the subject of a sentence that employs this special *is*. It is an *is*, incidentally, which has near relatives in marginal and mythical pronouncements. (Thus, one *is* Quetzalcoatl; those *are* the Pillars of Hercules.)

Let me illustrate. Two painters are asked to decorate the east and west walls of a science library with frescoes to be respectively called *Newton's First Law* and *Newton's Third Law*. These paintings, when finally unveiled, look, scale apart, as follows:

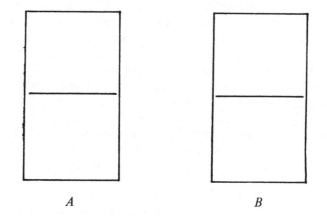

A                          B

As objects I shall suppose the works to be indiscernible: a black, horizontal line on a white ground, equally large in each dimension and element. *B* explains his work as follows: a mass, pressing downward, is met by a mass pressing upward: the lower mass reacts equally and oppositely to the upper one. *A* explains his work as follows: the line through the space is the path of an isolated particle. The path goes from edge to edge, to give the sense of its *going beyond*. If it ended or began within the space, the line would be curved: and it is parallel to the top and bottom edges, for if it were closer to one than to another, there would have to be a force accounting for it, and this is inconsistent with its being the path of an *isolated* particle.

Much follows from these artistic identifications. To regard the middle line as an edge (mass meeting mass) imposes the need to identify the top and bottom half of the picture as rectangles, and as two distinct parts (not necessarily as two masses, for the line could be the edge of *one* mass jutting up—or down—into empty space). If it is an edge, we cannot thus take the entire area of the painting as a single space: it is rather composed of two forms, or one form and a non-form. We could take the entire area as a single space only by taking the middle horizontal as a *line* which is not an edge. But this almost requires a three-dimensional identification of the whole picture: the area can be a flat surface which the line is *above* (*Jet-flight*), or *below* (*Submarine-path*), or *on* (*Line*), or *in* (*Fissure*), or *through* (*Newton's First Law*)—though in this last case the area is not a flat surface but a transparent cross section of absolute space. We could make all these prepositional qualifications clear by imagining perpendicular cross sections to the picture plane. Then, depending upon the applicable prepositional clause, the area is (artistically) interrupted or not by the horizontal element. If we take the line as *through* space, the edges of the picture are not really the edges of the space: the space goes beyond the picture if the line itself does; and we are in the same space as the line is. As *B*, the edges of the picture can be *part* of the picture in case the masses go right to the edges, so that the edges of the picture are *their* edges. In that case, the vertices of the picture would be the vertices of the masses, except that the masses have four vertices more than the picture itself does: here four vertices would be part of the artwork which were not part of the real object. Again, the faces of the masses could be the face of the picture, and in looking at the picture, we are looking at these faces: but *space* has no face, and on the reading of *A* the work has to be read as faceless, and the face of the physical object would not be part of the artwork. Notice here how one artistic identification engenders another artistic identification, and how, consistently with a given identification, we are *required* to give others and *precluded* from still others: indeed, a given identification determines how many elements the work is to contain. These different identifications are incompatible with one another, or generally so, and each might be said to make a different artwork, even though each artwork contains the identical real object as part of itself—or at least parts of the identical real object as parts of itself. There are, of course, senseless identifications: no one could, I think, sensibly read the middle horizontal as *Love's Labour's Lost* or *The Ascendency of St. Erasmus*. Finally, notice how acceptance of one identification rather than another is in effect to exchange one *world* for another. We could, indeed, enter a quiet poetic world by identifying the upper area with a clear and cloudless sky, reflected in the still surface of the water below, whiteness kept from whiteness only by the unreal boundary of the horizon.

And now Testadura, having hovered in the wings throughout this discussion, protests that *all he sees is paint*: a white painted oblong with a black line painted across it. And how right he really is: that is all he sees or that anybody can, we aesthetes included. So, if he asks us to show him what there is further to see, to demonstrate through pointing that this is an artwork (*Sea and Sky*), we cannot comply, for he has overlooked nothing (and it would be absurd to suppose he had, that there was something tiny we could point to and he, peering closely, say "So it is! A work of art after all!"). We cannot help him until he has mastered the *is of artistic identification* and so *constitutes* it a work of art. If he cannot achieve this, he will never look upon artworks: he will be like a child who sees sticks as sticks.

But what about pure abstractions, say something that looks just like *A* but is entitled No. 7? The 10th Street abstractionist blankly insists that there is nothing here but white paint and black, and none of our literary identifications need apply. What then distinguishes him from Testadura, whose philistine utterances are indiscernible from his? And how can it be an artwork for him and not for Testadura, when they agree that there is nothing that does not meet the eye? The answer, unpopular as it is likely to be to purists of every variety, lies in the fact that this artist has returned to the physicality of paint through an atmosphere compounded of artistic theories and the history of recent and remote painting, elements of which he is trying to refine out of his own work; and as a consequence of this his work belongs in this atmosphere and is part of this history. He has achieved abstraction through rejection of artistic identifications, returning to the real world from which such identifications remove us (he thinks), somewhat in the mode of Ch'ing Yuan, who wrote:

> Before I had studied Zen for thirty years, I saw mountains as mountains and waters as waters. When I arrived at a more intimate knowledge, I came to the point where I saw that mountains are not mountains, and waters are not waters. But now that I have got the very substance I am at rest. For it is just that I see mountains once again as mountains, and waters once again as waters.

His identification of what he has made is logically dependent upon the theories and history he rejects. The difference between his utterance and Testadura's "This is black paint and white paint and nothing more" lies in the fact that he is still using the *is* of artistic identification, so that his use of "That black paint is black paint" is not a tautology. Testadura is not at that stage. To see something as art requires something the eye cannot decry—an atmosphere of artistic theory, a knowledge of the history of art: an artworld.

## *III*

Mr. Andy Warhol, the Pop artist, displays facsimiles of Brillo cartons, piled high, in neat stacks, as in the stockroom of the supermarket. They happen to be of wood, painted to look like cardboard, and why not? To paraphrase the critic of the *Times*, if one may make the facsimile of a

human being out of bronze, why not the facsimile of a Brillo carton out
of plywood? The cost of these boxes happens to be $2 \times 10^3$ that of their
homely counterparts in real life—a differential hardly ascribable to their
advantage in durability. In fact the Brillo people might, at some slight
increase in cost, make their boxes out of plywood without these becoming
artworks, and Warhol might make *his* out of cardboard without their
ceasing to be art. So we may forget questions of intrinsic value, and ask
why the Brillo people cannot manufacture art and why Warhol cannot *but*
make artworks. Well, his are made by hand, to be sure. Which is like an
insane reversal of Picasso's strategy in pasting the label from a bottle of
Suze onto a drawing, saying as it were that the academic artist, concerned
with exact imitation, must always fall short of the real thing: so why not
just *use* the real thing? The Pop artist laboriously reproduces machine-
made objects by hand, e.g., painting the labels on coffee cans (one can hear
the familiar commendation "Entirely made by hand" falling painfully out
of the guide's vocabulary when confronted by these objects). But the difference cannot consist in craft: a man who carved pebbles out of stones and
carefully constructed a work called *Gravel Pile* might invoke the labor
theory of value to account for the price he demands; but the question is,
What makes it art? And why need Warhol *make* these things anyway? Why
not just scrawl his signature across one? Or crush one up and display it as
*Crushed Brillo Box* ("A protest against mechanization . . .") or simply display a Brillo carton as *Uncrushed Brillo Box* ("A bold affirmation of the
plastic authenticity of industrial . . .")? Is this man a kind of Midas, turning
whatever he touches into the gold of pure art? And the whole world consisting of latent artworks waiting, like the bread and wine of reality, to be
transfigured, through some dark mystery, into the indiscernible flesh and
blood of the sacrament? Never mind that the Brillo box may not be good,
much less great art. The impressive thing is that it is art at all. But if it is,
why are not the indiscernible Brillo boxes that are in the stockroom? Or
*has* the whole distinction between art and reality broken down?

Suppose a man collects objects (readymades), including a Brillo carton;
we praise the exhibit for variety, ingenuity, what you will. Next he exhibits
nothing but Brillo cartons, and we criticize it as dull, repetitive, self-
plagiarizing—or (more profoundly) claim that he is obsessed by regularity
and repetition, as in *Marienbad*. Or he piles them high, leaving a narrow
path; we tread our way through the smooth opaque stacks and find it an
unsettling experience, and write it up as the closing in of consumer products, confining us as prisoners: or we say he is a modern pyramid builder.
True, we don't say these things about the stockboy. But then a stockroom
is not an art gallery, and we cannot readily separate the Brillo cartons from
the gallery they are in, any more than we can separate the Rauschenberg

bed from the paint upon it. Outside the gallery, they are pasteboard cartons. But then, scoured clean of paint, Rauschenberg's bed is a bed, just what it was before it was transformed into art. But then if we think this matter through, we discover that the artist has failed, really and of necessity, to produce a mere real object. He has produced an artwork, his use of real Brillo cartons being but an expansion of the resources available to artists, a contribution to *artists' materials*, as oil paint was, or *tuche*.

What in the end makes the difference between a Brillo box and a work of art consisting of a Brillo Box is a certain theory of art. It is the theory that takes it up into the world of art, and keeps it from collapsing into the real object which it is (in a sense of *is* other than that of artistic identification). Of course, without the theory, one is unlikely to see it as art, and in order to see it as part of the artworld, one must have mastered a good deal of artistic theory as well as a considerable amount of the history of recent New York painting. It could not have been art fifty years ago. But then there could not have been, everything being equal, flight insurance in the Middle Ages, or Etruscan typewriter erasers. The world has to be ready for certain things, the artworld no less than the real one. It is the role of artistic theories, these days as always, to make the artworld, and art, possible. It would, I should think, never have occurred to the painters of Lascaux that they were producing *art* on those walls. Not unless there were neolithic aestheticians.

## IV

The artworld stands to the real world in something like the relationship in which the City of God stands to the Earthly City. Certain objects, like certain individuals, enjoy a double citizenship, but there remains, the RT notwithstanding, a fundamental contrast between artworks and real objects. Perhaps this was already dimly sensed by the early framers of the IT who, inchoately realizing the nonreality of art, were perhaps limited only in supposing that the sole way objects had of being other than real is to be sham, so that artworks necessarily had to be imitations of real objects. This was too narrow. So Yeats saw in writing "Once out of nature I shall never take / My bodily form from any natural thing." It is but a matter of choice: and the Brillo box of the artworld may be just the Brillo box of the real one, separated and united by the *is* of artistic identification. But I should like to say some final words about the theories that make artworks possible, and their relationship to one another. In so doing, I shall beg some of the hardest philosophical questions I know.

I shall now think of pairs of predicates related to each other as "opposites," conceding straight off the vagueness of this *demodé* term.

Contradictory predicates are not opposites, since one of each of them must apply to every object in the universe, and neither of a pair of opposites need apply to some objects in the universe. An object must first be of a certain kind before either of a pair of opposites applies to it, and then at most and at least one of the opposites must apply to it. So opposites are not contraries, for contraries may both be false of some objects in the universe, but opposites cannot both be false; for of some objects, neither of a pair of opposites *sensibly* applies, unless the object is of the right sort. Then, if the object is of the required kind, the opposites behave as contradictories. If $F$ and non-$F$ are opposites, an object $o$ must be of a certain kind $K$ before either of these sensibly applies; but if $o$ is a member of $K$, then $o$ either is $F$ or non-$F$, to the exclusion of the other. The class of pairs of opposites that sensibly apply to the ($\hat{o}$) $Ko$ I shall designate as the class of *K-relevant predicates*. And a necessary condition for an object to be of a kind $K$ is that at least one pair of $K$-relevant opposites be sensibly applicable to it. But, in fact, if an object is of kind $K$, at least and at most one of each $K$-relevant pair of opposites applies to it.

I am now interested in the $K$-relevant predicates for the class $K$ of artworks. And let $F$ and non-$F$ be an opposite pair of such predicates. Now it might happen that, throughout an entire period of time, every artwork is non-$F$. But since nothing thus far is both an artwork and $F$, it might never occur to anyone that non-$F$ is an artistically relevant predicate. The non-$F$-ness of artworks goes unmarked. By contrast, all works up to a given time might be $G$, it never occurring to anyone until that time that something might be both an artwork and non-$G$; indeed, it might have been thought that $G$ was a *defining trait* of artworks when in fact something might first have to be an artwork before $G$ is sensibly predicable of it—in which case non-$G$ might also be predicable of artworks, and $G$ itself then could not have been a defining trait of this class.

Let $G$ be 'is representational' and let $F$ be 'is expressionist'. At a given time, these and their opposites are perhaps the only art-relevant predicates in critical use. Now letting '+' stand for a given predicate P and '−' for its opposite non-P, we may construct a style matrix more or less as follows:

| F | G |
|---|---|
| + | + |
| + | − |
| − | + |
| − | − |

The rows determine available styles, given the active critical vocabulary: representational expressionistic (e.g., Fauvism); representational nonexpressionistic (Ingres); nonrepresentational expressionistic (Abstract Expressionism); nonrepresentational nonexpressionist (hard-edge abstraction). Plainly, as we add art-relevant predicates, we increase the number of available styles at the rate of $2^n$. It is, of course, not easy to see in advance which predicates are going to be added or replaced by their opposites, but suppose an artist determines that $H$ shall henceforth be artistically relevant for his paintings. Then, in fact, both $H$ and non-$H$ become artistically relevant for *all* painting, and if his is the first and only painting that is $H$, every other painting in existence becomes non-$H$, and the entire community of paintings is enriched, together with a doubling of the available style opportunities. It is this retroactive enrichment of the entities in the artworld that makes it possible to discuss Raphael and De Kooning together, or Lichtenstein and Michelangelo. The greater the variety of artistically relevant predicates, the more complex the individual members of the artworld become; and the more one knows of the entire population of the artworld, the richer one's experience with any of its members.

In this regard, notice that, if there are $m$ artistically relevant predicates, there is always a bottom row with $m$ minuses. This row is apt to be occupied by purists. Having scoured their canvases clear of what they regard as inessential, they credit themselves with having distilled out the essence of art. But this is just their fallacy: exactly as many artistically relevant predicates stand true of their square monochromes as stand true of any member of the Artworld, and they can *exist* as artworks only insofar as "impure" paintings exist. Strictly speaking, a black square by Reinhardt is artistically as rich as Titian's *Sacred and Profane Love*. This explains how less is more.

Fashion, as it happens, favors certain rows of the style matrix: museums, connoisseurs, and others are makeweights in the Artworld. To insist, or seek to, that all artists become representational, perhaps to gain entry into a specially prestigious exhibition, cuts the available style matrix in half: there are then $2^n / 2$ ways of satisfying the requirement, and museums then can exhibit all these "approaches" to the topic they have set. But this is a matter of almost purely sociological interest: one row in the matrix is as legitimate as another. An artistic breakthrough consists, I suppose, in adding the possibility of a column to the matrix. Artists then, with greater or less alacrity, occupy the positions thus opened up: this is a remarkable feature of contemporary art, and for those unfamiliar with the matrix, it is hard, and perhaps impossible, to recognize certain positions as occupied by artworks. Nor would these things be artworks without the theories and the histories of the Artworld.

Brillo boxes enter the artworld with that same tonic incongruity the *commedia dell'arte* characters bring into *Ariadne auf Naxos*. Whatever is the artistically relevant predicate in virtue of which they gain their entry, the rest of the Artworld becomes that much the richer in having the opposite predicate available and applicable to its members. And, to return to the views of Hamlet with which we began this discussion, Brillo boxes may reveal us to ourselves as well as anything might: as a mirror held up to nature, they might serve to catch the conscience of our kings.

# 9. Creativity in the Arts

## JACK GLICKMAN

*I*

What is it to be creative?[1] The answer usually given is that there is a "creative process," and most writers on creativity have taken their task to be a description of the kind of activity that takes place when one is acting creatively. In the first part of this paper I will argue that that is the wrong way to go about characterizing creativity, that one must attend to the artistic product rather than to the process. In Part II, I argue that their failure to properly distinguish creating from making has led some to suppose, erroneously, that some recent trends in art have celebrated the end of artistic creation.

Douglas Morgan, in reviewing a large number of writers on creativity, provides a convenient account of what I'll call the Creative-Process Theory. He finds that

> the "classic" theory of the creative process breaks it down into various stages. From two to five stages are usually thought necessary to describe the process, but the various descriptions bear a revealing community, and I think we may take the "four-step" interpretation as reflecting the consensus:
>
> 1. A period of "preparation" during which the creator becomes aware of a problem or difficulty, goes through trial-and- error random movement in unsuccessful attempts to resolve a felt conflict . . .
>
> 2. A period of "incubation," renunciation, or recession, during which the difficulty drops out of consciousness. The attention is totally redirected . . .

From *Culture and Art*, copyright © 1976 by Lars Aagaard-Mogensen. Reprinted with permission of the author and of Eclipse Books.

3. A period or event of "inspiration" or "insight". . . the "aha!" phenomenon, characterized by a flood of vivid imagery, an emotional release, a feeling of exultation, adequacy, finality . . .

4. A period of "elaboration" or "verification" during which the "idea" is worked out in detail, fully developed.[2]

According to Morgan, not only is it "complacently assumed by nearly all investigators that there is such a thing as the creative process—or a class of processes sharing important sets of characteristics, [it is assumed also] that creative processes in art and in science are identical or very nearly so."[3]

The theory has serious inadequacies. It excludes many instances of creative activity—improvizations in the performing arts, for example, and other instances in which the creating has taken place in a single unreflective burst of energy, as when poets have had a poem come to them all at once. The most objectionable inadequacy of the Creative-Process theory, though, is that what it describes is not at all limited to creative activity. The pattern described fits equally well many instances of genuine creativity and many instances of inept, bungling attempts at creativity. It also fits activities that are not even attempts at creativity: Suppose someone mentions a name that sounds familiar, and I try to recall the person mentioned. Someone asks me, "Do you remember George Spelvin?" "George Spelvin, George Spelvin," I repeat, mulling over the name (step 1—aware of a problem). I can't remember, so I put the problem aside, no longer consciously concerned with it (step 2—incubation). After a while it suddenly comes to me, "Sure, I remember George Spelvin; he's an actor!" (step 3—the "aha"! phenomenon). Then I begin to remember more, "I saw him as the Chorus in *Romeo and Juliet*" (step 4—filling in details). Recalling who a person is, given his name, hardly seems an instance of creative activity; yet it fits the description of the creative process.

In criticizing the Creative-Process theory, I might be accused of flogging a dead horse. Most psychologists seem to have abandoned this sort of account of creativity, as have many philosophers. Yet, as I will argue, in many subsequent accounts of creativity the same crucial error persists—the assumption that creativity consists in some distinctive pattern of thought and/or activity. It persists, for example, in Vincent Tomas's theory of creativity in the arts.

Tomas puts the problem this way: when one asks what's meant in saying that an artist is creative or that something is a work of creative art, "one is asking for a clarification or analysis of the concept of creativity as applied to art. One wants to know explicitly the nature of artistic creation—to be given a description of the conditions an activity must satisfy if it is to be an instance of artistic creation rather than of something else."[4]

This last sentence quoted makes it clear that he wants a set of conditions that are not only necessary but also sufficient for an instance of artistic activity to be creative activity.

Tomas begins with the example of a rifleman aiming and firing at a target: the rifleman knows what he wants to do—hit the bull's-eye—and he knows that if a hole appears in the bull's-eye after he fires, he has succeeded. The rifleman knows what he should do to hit the bull's-eye—what position to assume and how to hold the rifle, get the correct sight picture, and squeeze off the shot. If the rifleman fails, Tomas says, he has not obeyed all the rules, and if he succeeds and is congratulated, he is congratulated for being able to learn and obey all the rules.

But when we congratulate an artist for being creative, Tomas says, it is not because he was able to obey rules and thereby do what had been done before. "We congratulate him because he embodied in colors or in language something the like of which did not exist before."[5] Unlike the rifleman, "the creative artist does not initially know what his target is. . . . Creative activity in art . . .is not . . . activity engaged in and consciously controlled so as to produce a desired result."[6]

Yet, Tomas says,

> the creative artist has a sense that his activity is directed—that it is heading somewhere. . . . Despite the fact that he cannot say precisely where he is going . . . he *can* say that certain directions are not right. After writing a couplet or drawing a line, he will erase it because it is "wrong" and try again. . . .
>
> Creative activity in art, then, is activity subject to critical control by the artist, although not by virtue of the fact that he foresees the final result of the activity. That this way of construing creativity reflects part of what we have in mind when we speak of creative art can be shown if we contrast what results from creative activity so construed with what results from other activities that we do not call creative.
>
> Thus we do not judge a painting, poem, or other work to be a work of creative art unless we believe it to be original. If it strikes us as being a repetition of other paintings or poems, if it seems to be the result of a mechanical application of a borrowed technique or style to novel subject matter, to the degree that we apprehend it as such, to the same degree we deny that it is creative.[7]

It is fairly clear, then, how Tomas relates the following three questions: (1) What characterizes an artist as a creative artist? (2) What characterizes a poem, painting, or other work as a creative work of art? (3) What characterizes an activity as artistic creation? Tomas would answer the first two of these questions in terms of his answer to the third: artists, when they work in the manner described, are engaged in artistic creation; a creative artist is one who is able to achieve artistic creation, and a creative work of art is one that results from artistic creation. Tomas claims that although we judge a poem or painting to be a creative work on the basis of qualities of the work itself, such a judgment is possible because the work reveals features of the activity that produced it.

So far, then, Tomas has set forth two conditions an activity must satisfy to be artistic creation: (1) the artist does not envisage the final result of his work, but (2) the artist exercises "critical control." The first condition, I think, contains a conceptual truth—that if someone knows just what the product of his labors will be, then that product is, in a sense, already created. I'll have more to say about this later. For the present, though, I want to point out only that this first condition does not distinguish the artist who is creative from the one who is not. Tomas allows that a sculptor might know exactly what his sculpture will look like before he begins to work his material, and might even hire someone else to execute his plan. Tomas says that in such a case the creative act is finished: it is the production of the idea, and all that remains is to "objectify the idea" in some material—a matter of skill or work. But for any artist at work, either he does *not* envisage the result, in which case his activity fulfills one of the conditions of artistic creation, or else he *does* envisage the result, in which case he may be objectifying an idea that is the product of a creative act, and so in this case too he may have been creative.

Tomas's second condition raises difficulties, for artists at times produce a work in a single unreflective outpouring of energy. Tomas considers what is supposedly such a case—Nietzsche's writing of *Thus Spake Zarathustra*.

> Even if Nietzsche didn't deliberately change a thing, even if all came out just right from the very first line, was there not a relatively cool hour when Nietzsche (and the same goes for Coleridge and *Kubla Khan*) read what he had written and judged it to be an adequate expression of his thought? . . . If there was such a cool hour and such a critical judgment in Nietzsche's case, this is all that is needed to have made him create *Zarathustra* on the view of creation presented above.[8]

Undoubtedly there was a cool moment when Nietzsche and Coleridge looked over their work, but that was after the work was created. According to Tomas, had either Nietzsche or Coleridge not looked over his work after it was finished it would not be a creative work, but since he did look it over it is a creative work. This is paradoxical: the work is the same in either case. And think of a jazz musician improvizing a performance; whether he later happens to judge it adequate after listening to a recording seems totally irrelevant to whether his performance was creative. At any rate, if critical control can amount to no more than looking over the work, it is certainly an easy condition for any artist, creative or not, to fulfill, but it hardly seems necessary.

Tomas sees one other essential factor in artistic creation—*inspiration.*

> In the creative process, two moments may be distinguished, the moment of inspiration, when the new suggestion appears in consciousness, and the moment of development or elaboration. The moment of inspiration is sometimes accompanied by exalted feelings.[9]

Inspiration seems to be the sort of thing Morgan called the "aha!" phenomenon; in fact, it becomes quite clear at this point that Tomas's theory is simply a more elaborate version of the Creative-Process theory. Tomas introduces the notion of inspiration to explain the "critical control" in creative activity.

> Whenever the artist goes wrong, he feels himself being kicked, and tries another way which, he surmises, trusts, or hopes, will not be followed by a kick. What is kicking him is "inspiration," which is already there. What he makes must be adequate to his inspiration. If it isn't, he feels a kick.[10]

Tomas comments: "admittedly, the concept of inspiration we have been making use of is in need of clarification."[11] I agree. Ordinarily there is no distinction between a good inspiration and a poor one: to say an idea is an inspiration is to say it is a good idea or the right idea; if the idea is a poor one, it is not called an inspiration. But then there can be no characterization of inspiration in terms of the agent's feelings, for on that basis alone one cannot differentiate having an inspiration and having what *seems* to be an inspiration. It is likely that an artist might think he is being creative when he is not. Tomas says that "whenever the artist goes wrong, he feels himself being kicked." Maybe some artists feel such a kick when they *think* they have gone wrong, but surely there have been a lot of kickless goings wrong in the history of artistic activity. Each of two artists may work in the way Tomas describes, each having feelings of inspiration, each critically controlling his work according to the "kicks" he feels, yet one artist may be creative and the other not be creative at all.

The three conditions of artistic creation that Tomas lays down—not envisaging the result, exercising critical control, and undergoing feelings of inspiration—do not help to distinguish the creative artist from the uncreative one. In what follows, I will try to show that the Creative-Process theory rests on a fundamental misconception about creating.

Tomas realizes that "in discourse about art, we use 'creative' in an honorific sense, in a sense in which creative activity always issues in something that is different in an interesting, important, fruitful, or other *valuable* way."[12] This I think is correct and crucially important. It is precisely because we do not call an activity creative unless its product is new and valuable that no characterization of creating simply in terms of the artist's actions, thoughts, and feelings can be adequate, for such a characterization cannot distinguish activity that results in a valuably new product from that which does not. Let's take a closer look, then, at what it is that one "does" when one is creative.

In the arts one might create by composing music, writing, painting—i.e., we might say that someone was not only painting but also creating, or not only writing but also creating. It is not that he is doing two things at the same time. If we say that someone is doing two things at the same time—riding a bicycle and viewing the countryside, for example, or reading and drinking coffee—we can imagine our subject doing one of these things without the other. Creating, however, is not an isolable activity. The creator cannot be just creating; he has to be doing something we could describe as writing, painting, composing, or whatever. One does not always create when one paints, writes, or composes; these are means by which one might create. A number of activities sometimes, qualify as "creating."

To know whether someone has created, we have to see (or be told about) the results of his work. And the creator himself knows he has created only by seeing what he has done. It is unusual to say "I am creating"; "create" is seldom used in the continuous present tense. I suppose we can imagine a painter, say, who after a bit of especially satisfying work explains "I am creating!" but in such a case the creating is not something he is doing at the moment, it is something he has done. If we ask "How do you know you're creating?" he might answer "Just look at what I've painted." Notice that it makes sense to ask "How do you know you're creating?" whereas it would be silly to ask "How do you know you're painting?" Similarly one might be surprised that he has created, but not surprised that he has painted. We say an activity such as painting, writing, or composing is creating if it achieves new and valuable results; no specific isolable activity *creating* corresponds to the verb "create" as painting corresponds to the verb "paint."

These considerations suggest that "create" is one of that class of verbs Gilbert Ryle has labeled "achievement verbs." The verb "win," for example, signifies not an activity but an achievement. Winning a race requires some sort of activity, such as running, but winning is itself not an activity.

One big difference between the logical force of a task verb and that of a corresponding achievement verb is that in applying an achieve-

ment verb we are asserting that some state of affairs obtains over and
above that which consists in the performance, if any, of the subser-
vient task activity. For a runner to win, not only must he run but
also his rivals must be at the tape later than he; for a doctor to effect
a cure, his patient must both be treated and be well again. . . . An
autobiographical account of the agent's exertions and feelings does
not by itself tell whether he has brought off what he was trying to
bring off.[13]

For a painter, conposer, or writer to create, not only must he paint,
compose, or write, he also must achieve new and valuable results; therefore, no description of just the artist's "exertions and feelings" will tell us
whether he has created.

If creating were a specific process or activity we would expect that one
could decide to create. But artists often try unsuccessfully to create. Given
the technical knowledge, one can decide to write, paint, or compose, but
not create.

If creating were a specific process or activity we would expect the
possibility of error. It is easy to *make* something *wrong*. But one cannot
create something wrong; either one creates or one does not. But just as
winning is not an infallible kind of running, creating is not an infallible
kind of making; it is an achievement.

To say that someone created $x$ is often to say that $x$ was, upon being
produced, absolutely new—i.e., new to everyone. To say that someone has
been creative, though, is to say that the product is new to the agent.
Someone may be creative in solving a math problem, for example, if he
devises a solution more elegant and ingenious than the standard way of
solving such a problem, even though others may have devised the same
solution before. I do not think, though, that ordinary usage supports a
hard and fast distinction between *creating*, implying the product is new to
everyone, and *being creative*, implying the product is new to the agent.
One might say, "Horticulturist $A$ thought he had created a new hybrid,
but $B$ had developed the same hybrid years before." But one might as well
say, "$A$ and $B$, independently, both created the same hybrid." In neither
case, though, is there any implication that $A$ was less creative than $B$. To
say, then, that someone created $x$, or that in producing $x$ someone was
being creative, is to imply that $x$ was *new to the agent*. As Kennick points
out, if a contemporary of Cézanne working in Siberia and wholly unac-
quainted with what was going on elsewhere in the art world, produced
canvases just like the late canvases of Cézanne, we would have no reason
not to describe his work as creative.

Judgments of creativity are implicitly comparative, like saying that a man is tall or short. But the comparison is not unrestricted. A work of art is creative only in comparison with works with which it is properly comparable, i.e., with what the artist might reasonably be expected to have been acquainted with.[14]

Although whether we ascribe the verb "create" depends on the product, not on the activity that produced it, it does not follow that the praise conferred by "create" and "creative" applies only to the product; but in saying that the agent is creative, one is praising him for what he has accomplished, not for having gone through some special process in accomplishing it. This brings us to a crucial difference between the consequences of my view and those of a theory such as Tomas's for answering the following three questions: (1) What characterizes an artist as creative? (2) What characterizes a poem, painting or other work as a creative work? and (3) What characterizes an activity as artistic creation? For Tomas, the third question is primary, and the first two are answered in terms of its answer. On my view the answer to all three depends on the product; it is the product that determines whether we call the activity creating, and also whether we call the agent and the work creative.

The Creative-Process theory has been the dominant theory of creativity during the last half century, and it is hardly surprising that it has been the dominant theory of *artistic* creation, since as such it is a variation on a main theme in the expression theory of art, which because of the influence of Croce, Collingwood, Dewey, and others, has been the dominant theory of art. As the expression theory is usually formulated, good art, or "art proper," comes about only as the result of a certain sort of process—"artistic expression." But as critics of the expression theory have emphasized, an examination of the process is irrelevant to an evaluation of the product.[15] This, essentially, has been my criticism of the Creative-Process theory. "Creative" is a term of praise, but there is no specific sort of activity necessary or sufficient for producing things of value.

Tomas argued that we judge a work of art to be creative on the basis of properties of the work itself, but only because we take those properties as evidence that the creator went through a certain sort of process. I think Kennick is correct, though, in insisting that we do nothing of the kind. Rather,

we determine whether a work of art is creative by looking at the work and by comparing it with previously produced works of art in the same or in the nearest comparable medium or genre. . . .

Anyone can tell at a glance whether two paintings or two poems are different, but not just anyone can tell at a glance which of two paintings or poems is the more creative. To tell this, one must be acquainted with properly comparable works of art and be able to appreciate the aesthetic significance of any artistic innovation, see how it enlarges the range of viable artistic alternatives and thereby "places" what has already been done by putting it, so to speak, in a new light.[16]

It might be objected that Kennick's view, which I am endorsing, confuses *evidence* of creativity with what it *means* to say that someone is creative. But the answer to this objection is clear, I think, when we realize that "create" is an achievement verb and so applies only when something besides the performance of some action is the case. Although a patient's recovering his health is evidence that the doctor cured him, it is also the criterion for ascribing the verb "cure" to what the doctor did. To cure someone *means* to make him well as a result of treatment. I suppose that in some sense a valuably new artwork is "evidence" of creativity, but more than that, we apply the verb "create" only when the results are new and valuable, since creating *means* producing what is valuably new.

Tomas considers the possibility that being creative is simply producing what is valuably new, but he dismisses that possibility with the following argument.

Do we want to mean by creation in art *merely* the production of a work that not only is different but is different in a valuable way? In that case, it would follow that a computer would be no less creative than Beethoven was, if it produced a symphony as original and as great as one of his, or that a monkey could conceivably paint pictures which were no less works of creative art than Picasso's. . . . So conceived, artistic creation is not necessarily an action, in the sense of this word that involves intention and critical control, and the traditional distinction between action and mere movement is obliterated.[17]

Concerning Tomas's claim that if monkeys and machines create works of art, then "[1] artistic creation is not necessarily in action . . . and [2] the traditional distinction between action and mere movement is obliterated," the first conjunct of the conclusion seems to follow from the premise, but the second one does not. If machines can create artworks then it seems true that artistic creation is not necessarily an action, but it does not follow that there is no distinction between action and mere movement.

But more to the point, to say that someone is creative is to say that he is creative in some specific way. There are creative painters, creative teachers, creative businessmen, creative mathematicians. We might say of someone creative in a number of ways that he is a creative person, or creative in general, but we can in such instances enumerate the various ways in which he is creative.

Now can a monkey be as creative as Picasso? The proper reply is "As creative a *what* as Picasso?" As creative an *artist*? Only if it is allowed that a monkey can be an artist. Similarly, if we are to make any sense of the question "Is a monkey at a typewriter who produces a sonnet identical with one of Shakespeare's as creative as Shakespeare?" it must mean "Is the monkey as creative a *poet* as Shakespeare?" and the answer is clearly No unless it is allowed that a monkey can be a poet. I would think that being a poet at least encompasses (1) knowing a language, and (2) producing and/or selecting an arrangement of "sentences" of that language as meant to be taken in a certain way: hence a monkey cannot be a poet.[18] I am not concerned to argue this point here, however. I am concerned only to make clear that on the view I am advancing, *if* one allows that a monkey can be an artist or poet, then it is in principle possible for a monkey to be as creative an artist as Picasso or as creative a poet as Shakespeare. If monkeys cannot be artists or poets, then neither can they be creative artists or creative poets, no matter what they produce. The same argument applies *mutatis mutandis* to machine behavior.

I think the problem that Tomas raises here is not so much a problem about creativity as about art—whether what is produced by monkey or machine can properly be called art. If it can, then no doubt some such artworks and "artists" are more creative than others. Even if monkeys are not creative *artists*, however, it doesn't follow that it would never make sense to say that a monkey was creative. After all, ascriptions of creativity implicitly compare what's been created to other things of similar kind and provenance. To say that little Johnny is creative is perhaps to say that *for a five-year-old* he is creative, and it is not to compare him with Picasso. Similarly one might want to say that Bonzo is more creative than the other chimps if he does paintings with a far greater variety of colors and configurations. But to say this would be only to say that he is a more creative *chimp*; it is not to put him in a class with Picasso, or even with little Johnny.

## II

To construe creating, as many have, as a kind of making, is to overlook crucial differences between the concepts *making* and *creating*. Consider the following examples of "make" and "create" in sentences with the same direct object.

> The chef made a new soup today.
> The chef created a new soup today.
>
> The seamstress made a new dress.
> The fashion designer created a new dress.

Although the same noun occurs as direct object in both sentences of each pair, with "make" the noun designates a particular thing, but with "create" the noun is generic. If the chef created a new soup, he created a new kind of soup, a new recipe; he may not have made the soup. But if we say "He made a new soup today," "soup" refers to some particular pot of soup he prepared. The seamstress made some particular dress, but the fashion designer created a new design.[19] Particulars are made, types created.

Suppose a potter makes a vase and creates a new design on the surface. It may seem that the design is a particular thing, but what was created is a particular design only in that it is a particular *type* of design. If I say he created a new design, I do not mean that what he created are just those lines he put on the surface of the vase. Suppose I make a thousand copies of that vase; I could then show the potter any of the copies and ask, "Did you create the design on this vase?" The answer in all cases would be Yes. The answer would be No if I asked, "Did you make the design on this vase?" With "make," "design" refers to an individual; with "create," "design" refers to a type. The use of "create" or "make"—one word rather than the other—does not indicate a different sort of process, but a different sort of product (individual or type). Someone might in the *same* process both make a design (individual) and also thereby create a design (type). When we talk about what is created we are not primarily concerned with some particular individual object and its fabrication, rather we are concerned primarily with the idea, conception, or design that that individual object embodies. If I serve you a dish and say it was created by Brillat-Savarin, I do not mean that he has been resurrected and put to work in my kitchen; he developed the recipe.

At this point it might be objected that the choice between "create" and "make" does not always indicate a different sort of object: we do not distinguish the kind of "product" (individual or type) when, for example, we say, "He created a disturbance" rather than, "He made a disturbance." True, but I am concerned only with creating that is *creative*. One can create all sorts of things; before lighting a fire in the fireplace, we heat the chimney to create a draft; we can create a disturbance, or create a nuisance; we create difficulties, impressions, opinion. If someone creates a certain impression, it is no reason to call him creative; he may create the impression of himself that he is uncreative. If someone creates a draft, or a menace, or difficulties, or a stir, it is usually no reason to call him creative. But if a chef creates a new dish, a businessman creates a new way of merchandising, or a painter creates a work of art, these often are reasons to call that person creative. My remarks about the verb "create" which, like "creative," is honorific. The object of "create" when the creating is noncreative is some specific state of affairs rather than some new conception.

I said earlier that there is a conceptual truth contained in Tomas's claim that in creative activity the artist does not envisage the final result of his work. I have argued similarly that creating is producing what is new to the agent. Also when we consider that what is of primary importance in talk of creativity is not the fabrication of some particular object but rather the idea or conception it embodies, this explains Tomas's example of the sculptor. It is now commonplace for sculptors to send the plans for their sculptures to foundries to be executed; in such a case, the sculptor is clearly the creator of the artwork though the foundry makes the work. In the analogous case of an artist who is executing his work himself from a finished plan, the creative part of the work is done, as Tomas says, and what remains is to objectify the idea. (But of course it is not *only* in being creative that one does not foresee the product of one's efforts.)

An issue that's been debated recently is whether natural objects, such as pieces of driftwood, can be works of art. If they can, a curious question arises: who is the creator of such artworks? When Morris Weitz argued in an oft-quoted passage that a piece of driftwood could be a sculpture, and Joseph Margolis vigorously denied this, they put the issue this way: is being an artifact a necessary condition of something's being a work of art?[20] But what really seems at issue in their dispute is whether a work of art must have been made by someone, and that is another matter. I will now argue that although (1) being an artifact *is* a necessary condition of something's being a work of art, (2) there is no conclusive reason to insist that a work of art must have been made by someone, and so (3) an artist may create a work of art that no one has made.

Most often the term "artifact" is used to refer to an object of archeological or historical interest, such as an ornament, weapon, or utensil; obviously something need not be an artifact in this sense, a relic of some defunct culture, before it can be considered a work of art. But "artifact" is used also to refer to contemporary objects; without stretching the term one can speak of automobile hubcaps and plastic dishes as artifacts of our present-day culture. Practically any sort of alteration of the material environment might count as an artifact—a pile of rocks serving as a marker, for example, or a circle of trees planted to demarcate a certain area. Also a single natural object can be an artifact if it has been invested with some important function. Suppose that a stick—one that has not been materially altered, has not been carved or smoothed by any one—takes on magical significance in some culture. The stick, let's suppose, is believed by everyone in the culture to have certain magical properties; it may be handled only by the high priest, and by him only in accordance with certain rituals. Surely such a stick would count as an artifact of that culture; one can easily imagine it, if its use were known, on display centuries later along with the bowls, spears, and jewelry of that culture.

Now let's take a hypothetical case. Suppose an artist exhibits pieces of driftwood; perhaps the gallery announces a new conception, *Beach Art*. The pieces of driftwood are materially unaltered—i.e., they have not been sanded, smoothed, carved, or reshaped by anyone. Suppose further that this exhibit is warmly accepted by the artworld, and so the pieces of driftwood acquire the status of artworks. The very fact that the pieces of driftwood would have acquired the status of artworks in our culture would qualify them as artifacts of our culture; i.e., any object accepted as a work of art in our culture would thereby automatically qualify as an artifact of our culture. And since being a work of art of a culture is a *sufficient* condition of something's being an artifact of that culture, it follows that being an artifact is a *necessary* condition of something's being a work of art, a *logically* necessary condition though. Just as the stick's being a magic wand would qualify it as an artifact of its culture, the driftwood's being an artwork would qualify it as an artifact of its culture. The argument so far, then, is that being an artifact is a *logically* necessary condition of something's being a work of art. The question that remains is: can a piece of driftwood (or some other natural object) qualify as an artwork?

As was mentioned earlier, an artist need not *make* the work of art he creates. A sculptor might send the plans for a steel sculpture to a foundry there to be fabricated, and in various other ways an artist may have other craftsmen execute the work of art he creates. What is central to the notion of creating something is the new design, idea, or conception, not fabrication; most often one creates a work of art in the process of executing it, but this is not necessary.

But the artist need not even design the art object. Duchamp displayed as art a urinal and entitled it *Fountain*: he did not make the object nor did he design it, yet he created the artwork *Fountain*. Among Duchamp's other "readymades" was a bottlerack, which became an artwork appropriately entitled *Bottlerack*; it is acknowledged by many as an artwork, and as one *created* by Duchamp. So in many cases the creator of a work of art has not fabricated the art object, and in other cases the artist has not only not made the art object, he has not designed it either. And if the artist need not have made and need not even have designed the art object, then I see no conclusive conceptual block to allowing that the artwork be a natural object.

As far as I know, neither pieces of driftwood nor other natural objects are now universally accepted as artworks. So besides separating the question of artifactuality from that of whether an artwork need have been made, what I have been arguing is that there is no conceptual absurdity in the idea of a work of art created by someone but made by no one. There are not sufficient grounds for ruling *a priori* that pieces of driftwood or other natural objects cannot be works of art, and if they are accepted as such, they would not be that much different from objects already widely accepted as artworks. Already we have artworks that were neither made nor designed by the artist who created them.

The direction of the present argument has been influenced by Arthur Danto's paper "The Artworld." Also influenced by Danto's argument that "to see something as art requires something the eye cannot decry—an atmosphere of artistic theory, a knowledge of the history of art: an artworld,"[21] George Dickie has argued that art's institutional setting makes possible a definition of art in terms of necessary and sufficient conditions. Dickie argues that a work of art can be defined as "1) an artifact 2) upon which some person or persons acting on behalf of a certain social institution (the artworld) has conferred the status of candidate for appreciation."[22] This is not the place to discuss Dickie's theory in detail, but in order to raise some pertinent issues I'll briefly register some doubts about it.

First, for the reasons given above, the condition of artifactuality seems to me superfluous. Also, it is doubtful that the definition sets forth conditions sufficient for something's being a work of art. Consider the tools, tableware, textiles, office equipment, and other functional objects in the Museum of Modern Art's Design Collection. Arthur Drexler, director of the department, says that "an object is chosen for its quality because it is thought to achieve, or to have originated, those formal ideals of beauty which have become the major stylistic concepts of our time. . . . It applies to objects not necessarily works of art but which, nevertheless, have contributed importantly to the development of design."[23] Here we have objects—*not necessarily works of art*—upon which someone acting in behalf of the artworld has conferred the status of candidate for appreciation. And granting what Danto says, that to see something as a work of art—or, at least, that to see some things as works of art—required an atmosphere of artistic theory, it doesn't follow, given such an atmosphere, that even in the artworld everyone will see it as art. The artworld is not monolithic. Some painters and sculptors still balk at calling pieces of driftwood works of art. Their hesitation to call such objects works of art does not stem from a reluctance to value such objects: no matter how exquisite such objects may be, they would say, they are no more works of art than is a magnificent sunset. They know, moreover, the intent with which such objects have been proffered as art, they understand fully the theory of *objets trouvés*; their reluctance to call such objects works of art is their reluctance to *accept* that theory. For them the theory does not establish a sufficiently strong link between found natural objects and the body of acknowledged works of art so that they are willing to classify the natural objects as artworks. I do not wish to discuss the question how widely accepted as art an object must be before it can be said unequivocally to be art. I am not even sure that that is the right question to raise. I want only to register a doubt about Dickie's claim that anything proffered as art is to be classified unequivocally as art no matter the extent of its acceptance. Nowadays it would be simply false to claim that a Jackson Pollock painting is not a work of art; similarly, I think, with Duchamp's ready-mades. And perhaps not even pieces of driftwood are a borderline case, although I think they are. In any case, the driftwood dispute is illuminating because it shows that although on Danto's view anything might become a work of art, that doesn't mean *anything goes*: rational argument has a place in formulating and assessing the theory that would extend the concept of art to some new kind of object.

In mentioning Duchamp's ready-mades I claimed that although Duchamp did not make or design the bottlerack, he *created* the artwork *Bottlerack*. He brought into existence a new work of art (although he did not make a new object). It might be objected that if an art museum director decides to put on display a collection of, say, bottles, or doorknobs or shipping bags, objects not generally considered works of art, and they come to be generally considered artworks, it is not the museum director who is credited as the artist who created them, rather it is the person who designed the objects. And if, in general, the person responsible for bringing about acceptance of *x* as an artwork is not considered the artist who created *x*, why should we say it is Duchamp, and not the person who designed the bottlerack, who created *Bottlerack*? But there is a difference between the two cases: Duchamp is creating art and the museum director is only displaying it. Presumably when the museum director decides to put on display doorknobs, shopping bags, or whatever, his gesture is one of calling attention to objects he considers to be already works of art, but ones that have gone unrecognized. But Duchamp and subsequent artists who have transformed mere objects into artworks by signing their names to them have not supposed that there were all these objects, already artworks, lying around unnoticed; they have created those objects artworks. (I purposely choose this locution to parallel the locution "The Monarch created him an Earl.") (I am not, by the way, assuming that all such creatings are creative.)

The Duchamp case I think supports Danto's contention that "it is the role of artistic theories, these days as always, to make the artworld, and art, possible."[24] It is not the case, as I take Dickie to be saying, that it is simply the right institutional setting that confers the status "work of art," but rather it is, as Danto emphasizes, the artistic theory which relates the new object to the existing body of acknowledged artworks. And, I would think, it is because of the specific theory in the context of which Duchamp's ready-mades appeared that they are artworks.

In writing about the Museum of Modern Art's mammoth Duchamp retrospective, Harold Rosenberg points out that "since their first public appearance, [Duchamp's] creations have possessed an inherent capacity to stir up conflict. Sixty years ago, he entered the art world by splitting it, and he still stands in the cleft."[25] "[H]e remains the primary target to those critics and artists whose interest lies in restoring art to a 'normal' continuity with the masterpieces of the past."[26] Rosenberg then sketches the case against Duchamp, one argument of which is the following.

> In adopting the ready-made, Duchamp has introduced the deadly rival of artistic creation—an object fabricated by machine and available everywhere, an object chosen, as he put it, on the basis of pure "visual indifference," in order to "reduce the idea of aesthetic consideration to the choice of the mind, not the ability of cleverness of the hand." In the world of the ready-made, anything can become a work of art through being signed by an artist. . . . The title "artist," no longer conferred in recognition of skill in conception and execution, is achieved by means of publicity.[27]

To repeat a point I've already belabored, skill in execution cannot be considered necessary for artistic creation since works of art are so often not executed by their creators. To exclude readymades on that account would entail excluding too much else. And ingenuity, wit, and insight of conception are not necessarily excluded either. Just as some artworks of great technical skill embody the most banal conceptions and others, brilliant conceptions, is there not a range of conceptual skill exhibited in ready-mades, *objets trovés*, and works of conceptual art? Such art does exclude "ability or cleverness of the hand," but it does not on that account preclude artistic creation.

*Notes*

1. A shorter version of this paper was read at the 8th National Conference of the British Society of Aesthetics, Sept. 22, 1973. The present essay contains

portions of my "Art and Artifactuality," *Proceedings* of the VIIth International Congress of Aesthetics; it also contains portions of "On Creating,"—some comments on W. E. Kennick's "Creative Acts," that were both printed in Kiefer & Munitz, eds., *Perspectives in Education, Religion, and the Arts* (Albany 1970). The argument of the present essay parallels to some extent the argument of D. Henze's "Logic, Creativity and Arts," *Australasian Journal of Philosophy*, vol. 40 (1962). See also D. Brook and M. Wright, "Henze on Logic, Creativity and Art," *Australasian Journal of Philosophy*, vol. 41 (1963), and Henze's rejoinder in that journal, vol. 42 (1964). So many people have given me helpful criticisms and advice on successive drafts on this paper that I cannot hope to list them all. I am very grateful for their help; I hope they will forgive my not trying to name them all here.

2. D. N. Morgan, "Creativity Today," *Journal of Aesthetics and Art Criticism*, vol. 12 (1953), 14.

3. *Ibid.,* p. 12.

4. In his Introduction to V. Tomas, ed., *Creativity in the Arts* (Englewood Cliffs, N.J., 1964), p. 2.

5. V. Tomas, "Creativity in Art," ibid., p. 98.

6. *Ibid.,* p. 98.

7. *Ibid.,* p. 99f.

8. *Ibid.,* p. 106.

9. *Ibid.,* p. 104.

10. *Ibid.,* p. 108.

11. *Ibid.* The sort of thing that Tomas is talking about is clarified by Beardsley in his development of Tomas's theory. See M. C. Beardsley, "On the Creation of Art," *Journal of Aesthetics and Art Criticism* (1965).

12. Tomas, "Creativity in Art," p. 100.

13. G. Ryle, *The Concept of Mind* (New York, 1950), p. 150.

14. In W. E. Kennick, ed., *Art and Philosophy* (New York, 1964), p. 376.

15. See, e.g., J. Hospers "The Croce-Collingwood Theory of Art," *Philosophy*, vol. 31 (1956).

16. W. E. Kennick, "Creative Acts," *op. cit.*, p. 225.

17. Tomas, Introduction, p. 3.

18. Whether a monkey can do these things is of course an empirical question. Current experiments in teaching language to chimps may, for all we know, result in some chimp poetry.

19. This distinction is nicely observed in a recent television commercial for sewing machines. The camera takes us to the workroom of a fashion designer who tells us: "I depend on my machines to make the things I create."

20. "None of the criteria of recognition is a defining one, either necessary or sufficient, because we can sometimes assert of something that it is a work of art and go on to deny one of these conditions, even the one which has traditionally been taken to be basic, namely that of being an artifact: Consider, 'This piece of driftwood is a lovely piece of sculpture.'" [M. Weitz, "The Role of Theory in Aesthetics," repr. in J. Margolis, *Philosophy Looks at the Arts* (New York, 1962), p. 57]. 'What he says is surely *false*. If anyone were pressed to explain the remark, he would of course say that the driftwood looks very much like a sculpture, that

it is as if nature were a sculpture, that we could imagine the driftwood actually fashioned by a human sculptor. In making such a remark, we hardly wish to deny what *is* a necessary condition for an object's being a work of art, in any sense that is seriously relevant, 'namely, that of being an artifact.'" J. Margolis, *The Language of Art and Art Criticism* (Detroit, 1965), p. 40.

21. A. Danto, "The Artworld." [Ed.—"The Artworld" originally appeared in *The Journal of Philosophy* LXI (1964), 571–584.]

22. G. Dickie, *Aesthetics* (Pegasus, 1971), p. 101.

23. Quoted by A. L. Huxtable in "*Moma*'s Immortal Pots and Pans," *New York Times Magazine*, Oct. 6, 1974, p. 74.

24. Danto, *loc. cit.*

25. H. Rosenberg, "The Art World," *The New Yorker*, Feb. 18, 1974, p. 86.

26. *Ibid.,* p. 88.

27. *Ibid.*

# 10.

# The Possibility of Art:
# Remarks on a Proposal by Dickie

*TED COHEN*

Among recent efforts to say what art is, one of the most salubrious is George Dickie's "Defining Art."[1] Like much of Dickie's best work, this essay is brief, direct, and convincing in the way it uncomplicates what philosophers have made murky. This time, however, I think he has tried to make things more simple and ingenuous than they can be. The definition Dickie presents and argues for is this:

> *A work of art in the descriptive sense is (1) an artifact (2) upon which some society or some sub-group of a society has conferred the status of candidate for appreciation* [p. 254b].

This definition is introduced early in Dickie's essay, and the rest of the essay is given to elucidating and defending it. Instead of summarizing here all Dickie has to say, I will quote relevant passages in the course of my criticism. At the beginning, however, it may be helpful to note three special features of Dickie's thesis.

(1) The somewhat checkered history of attempts to define art is usually seen as a series of specifications of art-making properties. These properties, though subtle and sometimes relational, have been understood to be properties the eye can descry. The definitions which require these properties of artworks are widely thought to have been discredited, if not by earlier examples, by the onslaught of problematic cases and counterexamples supplied by twentieth-century art. Each definition (for example, "Art is imitation, or expression, or significant form, or symbolic feeling") seems either to founder straightway, since many obvious artworks do not display the allegedly necessary property, or to retreat into insignificance, since the property it cites cannot be seen and is presumed to be

From *Philosophical Review*, LXXXII (1973), 69–82. Reprinted with permission of the author and *Philosophical Review*.

present only because the objects are artworks. Dickie aims from the outset to specify a property which cannot be found merely by inspecting a putative artwork. He says:

> What the eye cannot descry is a complicated non-exhibited characteristic of the artifacts in question [p. 254a].

The idea is that the property required by the second condition of the definition is to be, as Dickie calls it, a social property, a non-exhibited status obtained within an institution.

(2) Since the eighteenth century there have been a number of definitions of art in terms of something like appreciation. Conceptions of appreciation have varied and so has the strategy of the definition. Usually some minimal requirement is given—for instance, that a thing be an artifact—and then it is held that appreciation of the thing is a necessary or sufficient condition of its being an artwork. The principal refinements have consisted in making the condition more subtle—requiring that a thing be likely to be appreciated, or that it be intended to be appreciated, or that it should be appreciated. Dickie's second condition is subtle enough to transform the character of this kind of definition. All questions of actual appreciation are waived. What is required is that a thing be a candidate for appreciation, and actually being appreciated is neither necessary nor sufficient for that.

(3) Dickie agrees with Morris Weitz in distinguishing two senses—or uses, as he sometimes says—of the term 'work of art,' an evaluative sense and a descriptive sense. Thus the initial qualification in the definition. Dickie is interested in the expression 'work of art' only in its descriptive sense, and he has little to say about its evaluative sense. He does invoke the evaluative sense as an explanation of the propriety of remarks like "This driftwood is a work of art" which precludes their being counterexamples to the requirement that works of art be artifacts. Dickie holds that the descriptive and evaluative senses are distinct at least to this extent, that both artifacts and nonartifacts can be works of art in the evaluative sense, while only artifacts can be works of art in the descriptive sense. Furthermore, works of art in the descriptive sense need not be works of art in the evaluative sense. So being a work of art in one sense is neither necessary nor sufficient for being so in the other sense.

The third feature of the definition is less novel than the others. I mention it because I will claim, toward the end of my criticism, that Dickie's determination to keep out of the definition everything he takes to be a matter of merit has left his conception of art too spare.

The definition falls short, so to speak, both formally and materially, and it is the second condition which is defective. Despite the careful reference to candidacy for appreciation, and not to appreciation itself, we must be told something about appreciation—enough at least to give content to the notion of candidacy. Materially, what Dickie says about appreciation is too strong, even though very general; formally, it lacks a dimension without which it is not acute enough to discriminate art from other things.

*What Appreciation Is*

Dickie first says:

> The kind of appreciation I have in mind is simply the kind characteristic of our experiences of paintings, novels, and the like [p. 255a].

One may wonder whether there is such a kind of appreciation, and I believe there is not. It seems to me it is already too much to suppose that there is a kind of appreciation characteristic of our experiences of, say, Rembrandt, Cézanne, Pollock, Olitski, "and the like." But Dickie thinks this can be overcome.

> Indeed, if we mean by "appreciation" something like "in experiencing the qualities of a thing one finds them worthy or valuable," then there is no problem about the similarity of the various appreciations [p. 255a].

This suggestion fails to meet the one case Dickie speaks much about, that of Duchamp. Dickie calls Duchamp's "Fountain" a work of art with no hesitation, and I think he believes it a substantial achievement of his definition that it easily accommodates things like the works of Dada. But does it? I agree that whatever Dada's practitioners thought, their accomplishment was not simply the creation of Un-art. It was, however, the creation of something *different*. In understanding this I am inclined to follow Michael Fried, who has said this:

> the situation has been complicated still further by the calling into question, first by Dada and within the past decade by Neo-Dada figures such as Cage, Johns and Rauschenberg, of the already somewhat dubious concept of a "work of art." . . . It would, however, be mistaken to think of Dada—the most precious of movements—as opposed to art. Rather, Dada stands opposed to the notion of *value* or *quality* in art, and in that sense represents a reaction against the unprecedented demands modernist painting makes of its practitioners. (It is, I think, significant that Duchamp was a failed modernist—more

exactly, a failed Cubist—before he turned his hand to the amusing inventions by which he is best known.) But there is a superficial similarity between modernist painting and Dada in one important respect: namely, that just as modernist painting has enabled one to see a blank canvas, a sequence of random spatters or a length of colored fabric as a picture, Dada and Neo-Dada have equipped one to treat virtually any object as a work of art—though it is far from clear exactly what this means.[2]

Whether or not one agrees with Fried, it seems clear that the "appreciation" of Dada was and is novel. If Fried is right, then to speak of Dada in terms of experiencing qualities one finds worthy or valuable is exactly wrong. Even if Fried is wrong, surely the one obvious point about Dada is that it is not the occasion for appreciation of the "kind characteristic of our experiences of paintings, novels, and the like." Of course Dickie has not said that Dada is, or is to be, appreciated in this way, but that it has acquired the status of being a candidate for such appreciation. But Dada in general, and certainly Duchamp's urinal, is virtually accompanied by an announcement that traditional appreciation (if there is such a thing) cannot occur. This suggests two things: (1) that being a candidate for appreciation in any but the emptiest sense of 'appreciation' (where it signifies any kind of apprehension appropriate to anything which is an artwork) is not part of what it is to be an artwork, at least not for some works, and (2) that possibilities concerning what *can* be appreciated have some bearing on what can be made a candidate for appreciation. The second point is not considered by Dickie, and this is responsible for what I think of as a formal gap in his definition.

## What Can Be a Work of Art

The second condition Dickie calls a "social property" of art (p. 253b). This idea, that part of what makes a thing a work of art is, so to speak, an institutionalized property, is the genuinely novel feature of Dickie's definition. The idea is present in recent works by Danto and Wollheim,[3] but I find it clearest in Dickie's essay and I shall confine myself to his definition. There are two broad areas for questions about how a thing acquires the social property which makes it art: in what circumstances and by whom can this property be bestowed, and what qualifies a thing to receive this bestowal. In the first area I have some more or less standard questions which are not altogether rhetorical for I, at least, do not see how to answer them on the basis of Dickie's remarks. The second area is more important since there I think Dickie does not see any questions to be answered.

If part of what makes a thing a work of art issues from an "institution" or "social practice," then we need to be told something of the details of the institution. There is merit enough in articulating the claim that art-ness is partly an institutional property—if that is true, and I do not mean to badger Dickie about the details. As he says,

> lines of authority in the politico-legal world are by and large explicitly defined and incorporated into law, while lines of authority (or something like authority) in the artworld are nowhere codified. The artworld carries on its business at the level of customary practice [p. 255a].

What Dickie says about this customary practice, however, leaves things more confusing than they might have been if he had simply referred to such a practice and left it at that. Dickie sees a difference between a plumbing equipment salesman displaying his wares and Duchamp exhibiting his urinal, which he elucidates in this way:

> The difference is analogous to the difference between my uttering "I declare this man to be a candidate for alderman" and the head of the election board uttering the same sentence while acting in his official capacity [p. 255a].

But there is an ambiguity here: whose enfranchisement are we concerned with, some museum director's or Duchamp's? That Dickie means the former, or at least that he does not mean Duchamp, is suggested by this—

> The point is that Duchamp's act took place within a certain institutional setting and that makes all the difference. Our salesman of plumbing supplies could do what Duchamp did [p. 255b]—

and by his remark concerning a different case, "It all depends on the institutional setting" (p. 256a).

If Dickie is read this way, then his analogy is strikingly inept, for it is precisely not the case that our Dickie could do what the head of the election board did (make someone an aldermanic candidate). What the analogy suggests is that to make something art, one first must be an artmaker. I suspect that the analogy appeals to Dickie because it sets making-a-candidate-for-election beside making-a-candidate-for-appreciation. But it is clear that one needs status to bestow status in the political case. What about the case of art? What about the interchangeability of Duchamp and the plumbing supplier? What if a urinal merchant or a junk collector had attempted to carry out Duchamp's act, say with the very object Duchamp used, and had been turned away by the organizers of the show? Is that all there is to it: the urinal did not become art because it did not receive the requisite social property, though it received it later when Duchamp brought it around; and the only way in which Duchamp's being Duchamp figures is contingently (since the organizers knew him, they accepted his urinal)? Well, then what if Duchamp had been rejected as well? If he had then just sulked, that might be an end to it. But what if he displayed the rejected urinal in his own flat, set it out on a roped-off rug in the living room? Does that turn the trick? Then could the merchant do the same?

These are bewildering questions, and they become more annoying if we switch Duchamp and the salesman in the other direction. Suppose it is Duchamp who comes to your home, where perhaps you are in need of plumbing fixtures, and sets before you a number of objects, including the urinal. Now what? Dickie's account of appreciation does not help. Dickie notes (p. 255a) that the ordinary salesman is presenting his wares for appreciation, but insists that he is not conferring on them the status of candidate for appreciation. But he *could* be doing both things, couldn't he? Couldn't Duchamp? Suppose that Picasso came to your house hawking his paintings, and didn't care what you did with them. Or better, since you may believe that Picasso's paintings were already art before he got to your house, suppose that he came and was commissioned by you to do a sketch directly on the wall in order to disguise some cracks in the plaster. That would be art, wouldn't it? And if it is when Picasso does it, why not when the neighborhood painter and plasterer do it? And if Duchamp's urinal is art just as readily for having been brought to your house as for having gotten into the show, why not the salesman's?

Before his discussion of Duchamp and the salesman, Dickie offers an adroit remark to help in accepting the notion of a "conferral of status" when it is clear that for much art this cannot be said to occur overtly (some artists never exhibit).

> What I want to suggest is that, just as two persons can acquire the status of common-law marriage within a legal system, an artifact can acquire the status of a candidate for appreciation within the system which Danto has called "the artworld" [p. 254b].

Then how is it that Picasso's merest scribble and, perhaps, Duchamp's urinal have a status not possessed by just anyone's mere scribble or spare urinal? Perhaps it is like this: one of the ways the "artworld" breeds Art is by way of enfranchising Artmakers. Anyone who did "Nude Descending a Staircase" and the rest would be an Artmaker (however good), but only an Artmaker could make that urinal Art (if it is art). It is because he did "Nude" that Duchamp is an artist; it is because he is Duchamp that "Fountain" is not just a misplaced urinal.[4]

This idea suggests that art and its institutions are inbred and self-justifying in ways that are hard to untangle, and I think that is plausible though I will not argue for it. It seems clear that Dickie does not agree with this. He says, after all, that the salesman could do what Duchamp did, and there is no suggestion that to do this the salesman must first acquire a power Duchamp already has. And, as noted, on this count the creation of an aldermanic candidate is a poor analogue (even Mayor Daley cannot make a man a candidate for alderman: he must make the election board make the man a candidate). The creation of a political candidate, like the act of christening, which Dickie refers to and which I will discuss later, seems an apt analogue of artmaking only so long as only one aspect is considered. In both artmaking and candidate-making there exist constraints in terms of the objects. The head of the election board cannot make just anyone a candidate. Typically there will be a minimum age, a residence requirement, a stipulation that there be no criminal record, a requirement that there be nominating petitions signed by some number of registered voters, and so on. Perhaps Dickie supposes his account of artmaking supplies an analogue for all this in the first condition, that the object be an artifact. But something is missing. There is nothing to match the connection between the qualifications imposed on a would-be alderman and the point in making someone a candidate for alderman. The qualifications, which the election board is bound to impose, derive from considerations of what aldermen do or are supposed to do. There is no doubt a blending together of considerations of what aldermen do and what they do well, but that need not be gone into. What connection of any kind is there between being an artifact and being appreciated? Why is it that only artifacts can be made candidates for appreciation, and, more important, why suppose that every artifact can be made such a candidate? This problem, and the failure of analogy in Dickie's failure to say anything about constraints in terms of the artmaker (about who can make something art as only a deputized official can make someone a political candidate), lead me to abandon Dickie's own analogy. If we are to get to the subtleties implicit in Dickie's suggestion, we need a different analogue for the act of making something art, one in which a distinction appears, not between having a power and not having it (as the head of the election board has a power not possessed by others), but between exercising a power we all have and not exercising it (like Duchamp's act which Dickie thinks anyone could have carried out). I believe that Dickie thinks we are all, or nearly all, in the artworld and that in the artworld everyone is empowered to make art. A suitable analogue may illuminate what limits the exercise of this power.

I take the act of conferring the status of candidate for appreciation to be (or to be like) what Austin called an illocution, or what he earlier might have called a performative.[5] The analogue chosen by Dickie, declaring someone a candidate in the uttering of certain words, is an illocution. To improve on it, we need a different illocution. I will use the act of promising, though it too is an imprecise analogue in some respects. There are a number of obscurities in our understanding of the mechanics of promising, but that is a help here, for it exposes the complexities that arise when we move from formalized rituals and ceremonial acts like christening and political licensing to less canonical ones like promising and, as Dickie thinks, making things art. Before getting back to the definition of art, I need to use promising to illustrate a point about illocutions which is not reflected in Dickie's conception of what is required to make art.

The act of promising accomplished in the saying of "I promise . . ." in appropriate circumstances is an illocution. Characteristically, this illocution precipitates various effects and consequences Austin calls perlocutions. Among possible perlocutions are, for instance, the recipient's feeling gratified in some way, his attributing to the speaker an intention to do what is promised, his acting in ways commensurate with or dependent on the speaker's doing what is promised. Though it oversimplies things, I ask you to think of all these consequences or effects as one perlocution, a kind of generic response I will call "accepting" a promise. Promising is an illocution; having a promise accepted is a perlocution. In the case of promising and securing acceptance, the illocution and the perlocution are associated, I think, on two levels: as a relation between promising and acceptance in general, and as a constraint on promising in particular instances.

In general, the perlocution is something like the rationale, or part of the rationale, for the illocution. It constitutes a general reason, a reason *überhaupt*, for performing the illocution—it gives the act a point. As Kant noted, if there is no acceptance of promises, then the act of promising becomes not merely a vain effort, but it ceases to be that kind of act—it ceases to be promising. This is not to say that there must be acceptance in every case, that there is no such thing as an unaccepted promise. The perlocution is detachable from the illocution in particular cases. But something does follow with regard to individual cases.

In any particular case it must be possible, or at least appear to those concerned to be possible, that the perlocution transpire. It is, so to speak, in the nature of the illocution to effect the perlocution, and if it is obvious to those involved that this effect cannot occur, then the illocution is in some way and to some degree abortive. That is why I cannot promise you something we both know, and know one another knows that I cannot deliver. There may be *some* point in my giving my word knowing you know that I cannot keep it, but it cannot be a point usual in cases of giving one's word, and so I am not simply "giving my word—period."[6]

Sometimes I cannot do an illocution because the illocutionary act is not open to do. I cannot christen a ship I have already christened nor marry you if you are already my wife. The illocution has been preempted. The preempting need not have been done by me: I cannot hire you if my partner has already signed you on, or arrest you if the sheriff has just booked you. But sometimes the illocution is no longer open because the associated perlocution has already been effected, whether or not by means of an illocution. For instance, I cannot argue the point with you if you are already persuaded, or warn you of a danger to which you are already alerted, or point out something you already see. Whether I can do these things is, perhaps, problematic if I am ignorant of what has already happened, but it seems clear that I cannot do them if I know that you are already persuaded, alert, or aware.

I take it as a kind of rule of thumb that the availability of at least some illocutions requires the openness of their associated perlocutions. The perlocution must be neither known to be already effected nor known to be clearly out of the question.

Let me import these points about perlocutions into Dickie's definition. I construe the act of conferring the status of a candidate for appreciation to be like an illocution, and I take the actual appreciation of a thing with this status to be like an associated perlocution. Being appreciated is neither a necessary nor a sufficient condition for something's being a candidate for appreciation, just as having what I say (about what I will do) accepted is neither necessary nor sufficient for its being a promise. But if what I say is a promise, then it must seem possible that it be accepted. And (supposing Dickie's definition correct), if I am to succeed in conferring the status of art on an object, it must seem possible that it be appreciated. My utterance is not a promise just because I say so, just because it has the form 'I promise. . . .' (I cannot promise that I was on time yesterday, or that it will rain tomorrow.) And neither, I think, is $x$ a work of art just because I say so. There are substantive constraints on what I can promise (however difficult it may be to formulate them), and there must be constraints on what I can make art. But what are they? Dickie names one—$x$ must be an artifact.[7] But this is not enough. What of an artifact which clearly cannot be appreciated (in Dickie's sense)? I say that there are such things—for instance, ordinary thumbtacks, cheap white envelopes, the plastic forks given at some drive-in restaurants—and that if Dickie's definition were correct then these things could not be artworks because they could not receive the requisite status. Duchamp's urinal is like that. Things like that cannot acquire the status required by Dickie's second condition because it would be pointless or bizarre to give it to them.

Dickie's concrete mistake has been to suppose that Duchamp's "Fountain" has anything whatever to do with what Dickie calls appreciation. If such eccentric works are art, then if that requires that they have something in common with traditional art, it is not a candidacy for what they were designed to forestall and disdain. This material error is a symptom of a more formal, conceptual gap—namely, supposing that making something a candidate for appreciation can be altogether unilateral, so that anything whatever could become a candidate upon someone's say-so. In fact, the untoward consequence of Dickie's suggestion is that it will rule out the very items Dickie is eager to accommodate. But then what about "Fountain"? Is Duchamp's "Fountain" a work of art, and Dickie's definition wrong because it misses this work, or is Dickie right and so "Fountain" not art? Neither of these choices is a healthy one. I am not clear about whether "Fountain" is a work of art, just like that. I am not as confident as either Dickie or Fried about this. If Fried is right, in the aftermath of Dada we are able to count nearly anything a work of art—but, he says, this leaves unclear what it means to count something as a work of art. What is wrong with Dickie's definition, I think, is that as Dickie takes it, it is clear and it clearly applies to "Fountain." No definition should fit "Fountain" so comfortably. Why not takes some explaining.

To say that an illocution must be "pointless" if its associated perlocution is not open is not quite right. There can be a *point* in saying "I promise to love you forever" or "I promise never to feel anger again." Indeed, saying these things can be splendid ways, perhaps the only ways, of saying and doing some things. But that does not make these sayings promises (I think they cannot be promises because these things cannot be promised). Similarly, there can be a point, I suppose, in invoking a formula for bestowing the status of candidate for appreciation on a thing which cannot be an object of appreciation. But that will not give these things that status. In both kinds of cases, as with "pointless" illocutions in general, the effect is to draw attention from the thing said (or the putative object of appreciation) to the act of saying it (or the act of exhibiting it). If Austin is right, we cannot entirely separate the saying and the said without distortion, but we can identify, so to speak, the locus of significance and import: if the situation is normal and altogether unproblematic, the thing uttered (or the object of appreciation) engages us; if the situation is in certain ways remarkable, then however canonical the thing uttered seems, we will pass behind it to its genesis. What significance we can find in "Fountain" we find not in the urinal but in Duchamp's gesture. It is not that "Fountain" is simply a candidate for appreciation which cannot be appreciated (nor is "I promise to love you forever" simply a promise which cannot be accepted); its transparent resistance to appreciation is the sign that it is not simply a candidate for appreciation (as the fact that love cannot be promised is the sign that this utterance is not simply a promise).

It is not only the questionable conception of appreciation which undermines Dickie's definition. Let us ignore that for a while. At the end of his essay Dickie says:

> Now what I have been saying may sound like saying, "a work of art is an object of which someone has said, 'I christen this object a work of art.'" And I think it is rather like that. So one *can* make a work of art out of a sow's ear, but of course that does not mean that it is a silk purse [p. 256*b*].

What I have been arguing is that it cannot be this simple: even if in the end it is successful christening which makes an object art, not every effort at christening is successful. There are bound to be conditions to be met both by the namer and the thing to be named, and if they are completely unsatisfied, then saying "I christen . . ." will not be to christen. If making a thing art is like an ordinary illocution, then there are prior constraints.[8] Austin's characteristic way of describing a kind of act or thing was to catalogue the dimensions in which it can be irregular. Thus a promise might be untoward, gauche, imprudent, impractical, ineffective, or unaccepted. As we move through various departures from the normal, pedestrian cases, passing through all the gross irregularities Austin called "infelicities," we come eventually to cases which are no longer promises. The boundary between non-promises and more or less failed promises is hard to locate, but (1) it exists, and (2) it is not identical with the boundary between utterances of the form "I promise . . ." and those without it, for this form is neither necessary nor sufficient. If artmaking is like an illocution, then a similar catalogue is in order, an account of the ways in which artmaking can be irregular. I do not blame Dickie for not yet supplying such a catalogue. I do complain that he has not noted the importance of such a catalogue, for if artmaking is simply a matter of informal illocutions, then the catalogue may be the only substantial definition we can get or need. There must be a boundary, however hard to chart, between making art, and trying but failing to make art. Dickie cannot account for this, because the difference is not simply the difference between objects which have been called art (or candidates for appreciation) and those which have not.

Duchamp's "Fountain" is a difficult case. It is difficult in the adjustment it demands of us, but neither of the two adjustments likely to be suggested is in order. One is to give up defining art, pointing to "Fountain" as an illustration of the inevitable failure of any definition. The other is to formulate a definition which covers "Fountain" as neatly as "Nude." Perhaps the most helpful part of Dickie's view is the implicit suggestion of a way to avoid this choice. Instead of either of these responses, I think we must give up the compulsion to *decide* about "Fountain," to rule it in or out; and I think we can do this by taking seriously the suggestion that whether "Fountain" is art depends upon whether and how a certain kind of act was performed.

Succeeding in getting "Fountain" under, or out from under, the term "art" is a delusive achievement: for the sake of a kind of ontological tidiness, most of what is interesting and instructive about "Fountain" is ignored. What we need to discuss are the ways in which "Fountain" is very much like normal art and the ways in which it is altogether unlike normal art, and then how this bears on the character of Duchamp's act of putting it forward and having it called art. When that discussion is done, nothing may be left to do. So it is with promising. Some cases are clearly promises, some clearly are not. Some are unclear. The unclear cases illuminate the clear ones as they bring out parts of the conception according to which the clear cases are clear. "I promise to wring your neck." Not a promise: I cannot promise what you do not want, knowing you do not want it. "I promise to keep all cigarettes out of your reach." This is not clear. Can I promise you something we agree you need even if we both know you do not want it? The hard thing to do is to hold onto the conviction that we know what art and promises are while refusing to suppose that we always can decide or need to decide.

Dickie and others have criticized earlier theories for having lost the good art/bad art distinction, often, as with Collingwood, willfully absorbing it into the very distinction between art and non-art. Ironically, Dickie has effectively reversed this: he has provided for room on the bad art side of the good art/bad art distinction for much of what is normally taken to be non-art. He says:

Please remember that when I say "Fountain" is a work of art, I am not saying it is a good one. And in making this last remark I am not insinuating that it is a bad one either [p. 255b].

This is the view Dickie proposes to take of any object whatever. From this view the real difficulty, the philosophical anguish, will arise after the question of art has been settled, and that question is never more than a nominal problem encountered occasionally because "lines of authority (or something like authority) in the artworld are nowhere codified" (p. 255*a*) and so it may be hard to discover whether the thing has been christened. This view obscures too much. The works of the painters Fried discusses (Stella, Noland, Olitski) are clearly works of art, and the serious questions about them concern what kinds of paintings they are, and whether and why they are good. But there are very few such questions about "Fountain," most Dada works, and many contemporary works. The questions about them concern exactly whether and why they are art, and how they became anything like art. To make these questions easy is both to mistake the nature of these objects and to refuse to take seriously the question of the possibility of the creation of art.

### Notes

1. George Dickie, "Defining Art," *American Philosophical Quarterly* 6 (1969), 253–256. All references to Dickie are to this essay and I will give page numbers parenthetically in the body of the text, using '*a*' and '*b*' to refer to the left and right columns of the pages.

2. Michael Fried, the catalogue essay for *Three American Painters*, an exhibition of Noland, Olitski, and Stella, Fogg Art Museum, Harvard University, 1965, p. 47.

3. Arthur Danto, "The Artworld," *Journal of Philosophy* 61 (1964), 571–584; Richard Wollheim, *Art and Its Objects* (New York, 1968), especially sec. 46, and "Minimal Art," *Arts Magazine* 39 (1965), 26–32. Dickie cites Danto's paper as a stimulus to his own view.

4. This suggestion, I suspect, would be much more agreeable to Danto than to Dickie. I say this only on the basis of some remembered remarks of Danto's made during discussions at the University of Illinois at Chicago Circle Aesthetics Institute, May 1971. Despite Dickie's accurate recognition in Danto of a view broadly similar to his own in the matter of saying what art is, there are acute differences.

5. The outlines of Austin's conceptions of illocutions and perlocutions are, I hope, familiar enough not to need rehearsing here, and it is only a general account that I am concerned with. For Austin's detailed account see his William James Lectures, published as *How to Do Things with Words* (Cambridge, Mass., 1962), especially pp. 98 ff.

6. I leave some principal questions concerning the relations between illocutions and perlocutions untreated here, trusting that I have said enough to clarify the point I will make about Dickie's definition. These questions—for instance, why we

ought not simply to separate promises from non-promises, warnings from non-warnings, etc., without reference to perlocutions, whether every illocution is associated with some perlocution in the way promising is associated with securing acceptance, whether Austin was sufficiently acute in distinguishing illocutions from perlocutions by declaring only the former to be "conventional"—are taken up in my "Illocutions and Perlocutions," forthcoming in *Foundations of Language*.

7. I have completely recast Dickie's formulation, so that it calls for an illocution to be done and imposes one constraint on the circumstances appropriate to that kind of illocution. I should point out that Dickie has a different model in mind. He takes himself to be giving a definition by genus (artifactuality) and differentia (candidacy for appreciation).

8. In Danto's "The Artworld" (*op. cit.*) I find a suggestion of a way to treat artmaking as an extraordinary illocution, one whose constraints are always emendable. In the last section of the essay, Danto ventures some remarks which, in rough summary, are to this effect: there is a set of pairs of artwork-relevant predicates. Each pair consists of two "opposite" predicates (e.g., "representational"/"nonrepresentational," "expressionist"/"nonexpressionist"). Opposites, unlike contradictories as usually construed, do not sensibly apply to all objects; but with regard to any artwork they behave as contradictories. (It is not true that anything is either representational or nonrepresentational; it is true that any artwork is either representational or nonrepresentational.) A necessary condition for an object to be an artwork is that at least one pair of artwork-relevant predicates be sensibly applicable to it. Danto remarks that an artistic breakthrough may consist in adding a pair of artwork-relevant predicates.

Then we might try to think of artmaking in this way: the constraints on what can be christened art are given by the condition that some artwork-relevant predicate pair be sensibly applicable to the object. But it is possible to make art of an unqualified object not by altering the object but by adding to the set of predicate pairs a pair already sensibly applicable to the object.

In order to work out the details of this suggestion, one will have to say something about how a predicate pair can be made a member of the set. The project is complicated by Danto's ingenious observation that once an object is an artwork all artwork-relevant predicate pairs apply. This means that after the fact, the new pair will be as definitive as the older ones of earlier artworks, and the older pairs will sensibly apply to the new work.

I should make clear that Danto's remarks are made in an altogether different context, and their adaptability to a discussion of the illocutionary act of making art is my own tentative suggestion. In any case, the suggestion is of no use to Dickie, who seems to conceive the act as an ordinary illocution. Indeed, whereas Danto's idea might at last give content to Morris Weitz's somewhat dogmatic claim that the conditions for a thing to be art are indefinitely corrigible ("The Role of Theory in Aesthetics," *Journal of Aesthetics and Art Criticism* 15 [1956], 27-35), Dickie's essay is offered as an explicit refutation of Weitz.

# Bibliography to Part Two

Some relatively early discussions of the definition of a work of art include:
Monroe C. Beardsley, "The Definition of the Arts," *Journal of Aesthetics and Art Criticism* XX (1961), 175–187;

Margaret Macdonald, "Art and Imagination," *Proceedings of the Aristotelian Society* LIII (1952–1953);

Joseph Margolis, "Mr. Weitz and the Definition of Art," *Philosophical Studies* IX (1958), 88–94;

Douglas N. Morgan, "Art Pure and Simple," *Journal of Aesthetics and Art Criticism* XX (1961), 187–195;

Mary Mothersill, "Critical Comments," *Journal of Aesthetics and Art Criticism* XX (1961), 195–198; comments on Beardsley and Morgan (above) in a joint symposium;

C. L. Stevenson, "On 'What is a Poem?'" *Philosophical Review* LXVI (1957), 329–362;

Paul Ziff, "The Task of Defining a Work of Art," *Philosophical Review* LXIII (1953), 68–78.

Some more recent discussions of the definition of a work of art moving along rather different lines, include:
Monroe C. Beardsley, "Is Art Essentially Institutional?" in Lars Aagaard-Mogensen (ed.), *Culture and Art* (Nyborg and Atlantic Highlands, 1976);

James D. Carney, "Defining Art," *British Journal of Aesthetics* XV (1975), 191–207;

Ted Cohen, "The Possibility of Art: Remarks on a Proposal by Dickie," *Philosophical Review* LXXXII (1973), 69–82;

George Dickie, "Defining Art II," in Matthew Lipman (ed.), *Contemporary Aesthetics* (Boston, 1973);

George Dickie, *Art and the Aesthetic; An Institutional Analysis* (Ithaca: 1974);

Gary Iseminger, "Appreciation, the Artworld, and the Aesthetic," in Lars Aagaard-Mogensen (ed.), *Culture and Art* (Nyborg and Atlantic Highlands, 1976);

Colin Lyas, "Danto and Dickie on Art," in Lars Aagaard-Mogensen (ed.), *Culture and Art* (Nyborg and Atlantic Highlands, 1976);
M. H. Mitias, "Art as a Social Institution," *Personalist* LVI (1975), 330–335;
Richard J. Sclafani, "Art as a Social Institution: Dickie's New Definition," *Journal of Aesthetics and Art Criticism* XXXII (1973), 111–114;
Richard J. Sclafani, "The Logical Primitiveness of the Concept of a Work of Art," *British Journal of Aesthetics* XV (1975), 14–28;
Jeanne Wacker, "Particular Works of Art," *Mind* LIX (1960), 223–233;
Morris Weitz, "Can 'Art' Be Defined?" in Morris Weitz (ed.), *Problems In Aesthetics* (New York, 1970).
Paul Ziff, "Art and the 'Object of Art,'" reprinted in William Elton (ed.), *Aesthetics and Language* (Oxford, 1954).
Some of these papers bear more on characterizing art institutionally than on definition in the narrow sense.

Reference may also be made, for the general philosophical setting for all these papers (including Weitz's), to:
Ludwig Wittgenstein, *Philosophical Investigations*, trans. by G.E.M. Anscombe (New York, 1953), I, pars. 65–67.

Morris Weitz has himself pursued the issue of definition and open concepts in:
Morris Weitz, *The Opening Mind* (Chicago, 1967), which quite clearly shows that Weitz never relented from his view that definition must be essentialist—and therefore impossible.

A much-discussed account of Wittgenstein's thesis may be found in:
Maurice Mandelbaum, "Family Resemblances and Generalization Concerning the Arts," *American Philosophical Quarterly* II (1965), 219–228.

Other related discussions include:
Haig Khatchadourian, "Family Resemblances and the Classification of Works of Art," *Journal of Aesthetics and Art Criticism* XXVIII (1969), 79–90;
Haig Khatchadourian, *The Concept of Art* (New York, 1971);
Anthony R. Manser, "Games and Family Resemblances," *Philosophy* XLII (1967), 210–225;
Richard Sclafani, "'Art,' Wittgenstein, and Open-textured Concepts," *Journal of Aesthetics and Art Criticism* XXIX (1970), 333–341.

An entirely different but increasingly influential account of definition, applicable to art but not focused on it, is provided in:
Hilary Putnam, *Collected Papers*, vol. 2 (Cambridge, 1975), particularly. "Is Semantics Possible?" and "The Meaning of 'Meaning.'"

On the bearing of Putnam's account, see further:
Joseph Margolis, *Art and Philosophy* (Atlantic Highlands, 1978), ch. 5;
Robert J. Matthews, "Traditional Aesthetics Defended," *Journal of Aesthetics and Art Criticism* XXXVIII (1979), 39–50.

Related papers, concerned with the individuation of works of art, include:
    Monroe C. Beardsley, *Aesthetics* (New York, 1958), ch. 1;
    Donald Henze, "Is the Work of Art a Construct?" *Journal of Philosophy* LII
        (1955), 433–439;
    Margaret Macdonald, "Some Distinctive Features of Arguments Used in
        Criticism of the Arts," reprinted (revised) in William Elton (ed.), *Aesthetics and
        Language* (Oxford, 1954);
    Joseph Margolis, "The Identity of a Work of Art," *Mind* LXVII (1959), 34–50;
    Stephen Pepper, "Further Considerations on the Aesthetic Work of Art,"
        *Journal of Philosophy* XLIX (1952), 274–279.

On issues particularly concerned with Nelson Goodman's views about the identity
and the individuation of works of art, see:
    Adina Armelagos and Mary Sirridge, "Personal Style and Performance Preroga-
        tives," in Maxine Sheets-Johnstone, *Illuminating Dance: Philosophical Ex-
        plorations* (London, 1984);
    Joseph Margolis, "The Autographic Nature of the Dance," in Maxine Sheets-
        Johnstone, (ed.), *Illuminating Dance*;
    Joseph Margolis, "Art as Language," *The Monist* LVIII (1974), 175–186;
    Alan Tormey, "Interdeterminacy and Identity in Art," *The Monist* LVIII (1974),
        203–213;
    William E. Webster, "Music is Not a 'Notational System'," *Journal of Aesthetics
        and Art Criticism* XXIX (1970), 489–497.

Clearly, the issue of the definition and individuation of art cannot be easily
separated from the ontology of art. The bibliography and selections for Part Three,
therefore, are particularly pertinent. Pertinent more narrowly, however, to what, in
a somewhat overly homogenized way, have come to be treated as the problems of
an "institutional" definition of art, one should include:
    Arthur C. Danto, *The Transfiguration of the Commonplace* (Cambridge, 1981);
    Arthur C. Danto, "The End of Art," in Lang, *The Death of Art* (New York,
        1984);
    George Dickie, *The Art Circle* (New York, 1984).
    Berel Lang (ed.), *The Death of Art* (New York, 1984);
It should also be said, however, that Danto's and Dickie's theories have, despite
appearances, hardly anything in common. There is, of course, an important sense in
which the issue, in one respect definitional, is, in another, concerned with ideological
legitimation. On this score, the Frankfurt Critical tradition is particularly relevant.
See for example:
    Ernst Bloch, Georg Lukács, Bertolt Brecht, Walter Benjamin, and Theodor
        Adorno, *Aesthetics and Politics* (trans. ed. Ronald Taylor) (London, 1977);
    Herbert Marcuse, *The Aesthetic Dimension; Toward a Critique of Marxist
        Aesthetics* (Boston, 1978).

# Part Three

# The Ontology of Art

Theorizing about what kind of entity a work of art is cannot but be initially baffling. If, on the one hand, we insist that it is some sort of self-contained entity that exists independently of being appreciated, we have difficulty accommodating literature at least. If, on the other, we insist that a work of art exists only insofar as an aesthetic percipient interacts with some other object—an object less than the work of art that emerges from the putative interaction—we have difficulty fixing a work of art as a public object that may attract critical exchange capable of a measure of objectivity (see Part One). Some works of art, notably in the plastic arts, either are or are quite closely linked to physical objects—or so it seems; and other art works—notably where notations are readily accessible, as in music, literature, drama—seem hardly to be physical objects at all. In some of the arts, we are inclined to think that particular works are uniquely manifested, paintings for instance, or medieval cathedrals—though the qualification suggests a mere contingency. In other of the arts, etchings and music for instance, we are quite prepared to speak of particular printings of the same etching and particular performances of the same sonata. Hence, we are tempted to think that some works of art are particular objects and that some are not particulars of any sort at all. Finally, in this regard, there is good reason to think that the metaphysical peculiarities of art are bound to be matched by every other kind of entity that can be distinguished in the context of human culture—persons, for instance, or words and sentences, even actions of an institutionalized sort. So the ontology of art promises to be a peculiarily strategic inquiry, in terms of which, briefly, the relationship between human culture and physical nature may be perspicuously sketched.

Broadly speaking, the central issues tend to cluster around the question of how to identify and reidentify a particular work of art and around the question of how to specify the nature of the entity thus identified. These questions are not entirely separable, of course, because a favored answer to one will affect the eligibility of answers to the other. And the answers to either are bound to reflect larger strategies concerning a comprehensive philosophy. Thus, for example, an adherence to materialism is likely to encourage the view that works of art are physical objects or at least intimately "associated" in some way with physical objects. The difficulty of maintaining that thesis may incline one toward a form of idealism or at least to an idealistically skewed account; and with that may come support for the claim that works of art are actually not particulars at all, but universals.

There is no tightly linear history of the theory of art. Nevertheless, one can excerpt the views of a number of leading contemporary discussants about the ontology of art that yield a strong sense of continuity and of the pointed and deliberate refinement of the central questions. In this regard, though he cannot rightly be said to have written in the analytic style favored by the Anglo-American tradition, Roman Ingarden (Part One) has, perhaps uniquely, provided a clear picture of the phenomenological aspects of our aesthetic interest in art and of the inescapable ontological complexities that that engenders. Ingarden appreciated the dependence of aesthetically relevant remarks on the public identification of a work of art, but he also wished to accommodate the variety of sensitive discriminations that different percipients differently placed might defensibly be led to make, on the basis (he supposed) of the somewhat schematic structure of actual art works. Ingarden was led, therefore, to think of a work of art as, somehow, the developing construction of a historically changing community of sensitive respondents. In order to fix the identity of particular works, he was attracted to the view that, although a work of art was made up of a number of "levels" of elements, some were more fundamental than others (relative to identity) and perhaps also less amenable to the variable flowering of interpretive and appreciative responses. There is a sense in which Ingarden fixes the field to be analyzed without providing an entirely explicit and coherent analysis of the entities of the field. For we are left with the problem of the precise conditions under which works of art are actually identified and of the precise sense in which a work of art is an object of some particular kind. What one wants to know is, how can the variety of properties attributed to works of art actually be the properties of some particular thing? Ingarden indicates well enough the range of such properties that must be accounted for; but he does not tell us how to collect them in the ontologically relevant sense.

The papers included in Part Three attempt to sort the different kinds of art—given the rather different properties that poems, paintings, sonatas, etchings, and the like exhibit—in a way that will permit us to say whether there is some general rubric that could cover all the arts and, if so, what it might be. Richard Wollheim (1968), for example, is inclined to contrast those arts that either involve performance or depend on notation (the two being quite closely linked, as in music, or, more ambiguously, as in literature) with those arts (chiefly, the plastic arts) that directly involve composition with physical materials. His conclusions are somewhat tentative. He cannot altogether reject a physicalist account of certain of the arts, since on his view, expressive and representational properties may be ascribed to physical objects (see Parts Four and Five); but, on the other hand, he cannot fit such a view to other of the arts and is therefore attracted to the possibility that (some) works of art are universals. What Wollheim makes clear is that the type/token distinction, explored earlier in the literature, is absolutely central to the clarification of the ontology of art. In this regard he attempts to sort out the differences between the class/member distinction, the kind/instance distinction and the type/token distinction. Ironically, it is his adherence to the phenomenological aspects of aesthetic appreciation that complicates his ontology, for it is his attention to the complexities of performance and interpretation that lead him to theorize about art works as universals. We are, however, bound to raise questions about how particular (token) works could conceivably share properties with abstract entities (types) thought somehow to be *the* works of art. For example, *if* music uses sound, then how is it that an abstract entity, a sonata, could possibly have temporal or spatial or sensory properties? And if the entities favored fail to exhibit such properties, then how can they be the works we attend to in the usual way?

Nicholas Wolterstorff (1975), in effect, presses these difficulties against Wollheim, preserving the latter's distinction between "objects" and "performances." Wolterstorff rejects the view that types and tokens can share properties, opting instead for the ingenious view that they share predicates. He therefore finds no difficulty in viewing works of art as universals, in conformity with a more general defense of his, favoring the reality of universals (in *On Universals* [1970]). But Wolterstorff's solution raises difficulties of its own: first of all because it is not clear how types and tokens can "share" predicates or what that entails; secondly because the special difficulties confronting Wollheim's view confront Wolterstorff's as well. In particular, Wolterstorff must face the problem of explaining how it is that works of art can be created and destroyed—even if that involves destroying a notation—as well as the problem of explaining how an abstract entity can be said to have sensory or physical properties of any sort. The puzzle persists, therefore, that, say, a sonata can be heard but heard in different performances in different places at different or the same times.

How to interpret the type/token relationship still presents difficulties. And of course, more fundamentally, Wolterstorff's thesis rests entirely on the plausibility of a Platonist picture of reality. For example, it is not clear in what sense, following Wolterstorff, we may suppose that the "world" of Gogol's *Dead Souls* may be said to be real prior to the historical events of Gogol's Russia. It does look as if Wolterstorff's account could not survive the defeat of Platonism or the denial of or agnostic response to the claim that the whole of nature falls within God's providential order.

Joseph Margolis (1977) has attempted to link the problems of numerical identity and of metaphysical nature together. By insisting on the ontological distinction of culturally emergent entities—in particular, works of art—he interprets tokens as tokens-of-types and construes what is thus individuated as an "embodied" entity of a certain complex sort. There are, therefore, no types distinct from tokens that could be compared or that could be said to share either properties or predicates. Tokens simply are tokens-of-types; and reference to types is heuristically introduced solely for the purpose of facilitating the individuation of particular objects as tokens of one and the same type. Correspondingly, the notion of an embodied entity is intended to facilitate the collection of the entire range of relevant properties—both physical and intentional—that Ingarden and others have insisted may be ascribed to works of art. The solution offered is characterized as a form of nonreductive materialism and suggests something of the ontological oddity of works of art in particular and of cultural entities in general. That solution, however, does not countenance a dualism of substances, only a nonreducible plurality of kinds of properties. Art works, embodied entities in general, are complex (emergent)—not compound or additive—entities, exhibiting properties that obtain only in the indissolubly embodied form in which they exist in the world of human culture.

Nelson Goodman (1976) has focused in a useful way the general problem between what he calls autographic and allographic arts, which the question of art fakes and forgeries dramatizes. For, on Goodman's view, forgeries of musical works, for example, are impossible—in general, forgeries of allographic works. Goodman's account has started a considerable industry (see Dutton, ed., 1983). Because of his nominalism, however, Goodman would be entirely unwilling to construe the autographic/allographic distinction in terms of the strong reading of the type/token distinction favored by Wollheim and Wolterstorff, as opposed, say, to that favored by Margolis. Nevertheless, it may be argued both that so-called allographic works may be forgeries, without boarding the realism/nominalism issue, and (more importantly) that there is no principled distinction to be had between autographic and allographic arts—that all art works are identified and characterized in terms of their history of production and that any art work can, reasonably, in accord with the contingencies of technology and social tolerance, be authentically duplicated or rendered in plural instances. Furthermore, notations or scores *for* art works must themselves be suitably read in autographically relevant terms (see Margolis, 1984).

All these papers, however, force us to consider whether an adequate ontology can be formulated that declines to take into consideration the special products of human culture. In this respect, the philosophy of art serves strategically as an introduction to the largest conceptual issue that confronts us all, namely, that of the relationship between physical nature and human culture. What, we want to know, must be added to our account of nature in order to accommodate the existence of persons, of works of art, of language itself?

# 11.  Art and Its Objects
## *RICHARD WOLLHEIM*

.  .  .

*4*

Let us begin with the hypothesis that works of art are physical objects. I shall call this for the sake of brevity the "physical-object hypothesis." Such a hypothesis is a natural starting point: if only for the reason that it is plausible to assume that things are physical objects unless they very obviously aren't. Certain things very obviously aren't physical objects. Now though it may not be obvious that works of art are physical objects, they don't seem to belong among these other things. They don't, that is, immediately group themselves along with thoughts, or periods of history, or numbers, or mirages. Furthermore, and more substantively, this hypothesis accords with many traditional conceptions of Art and its objects and what they are.

*5*

Nevertheless the hypothesis that all works of art are physical objects can be challenged. For our purposes it will be useful, and instructive, to divide this challenge into two parts: the division conveniently corresponding to a division within the arts themselves. For in the case of certain arts the argument is that there is no physical object that can with any plausibility be identified as the work of art: there is no object existing in space and time (as physical objects must) that can be picked out and thought of as a piece of music or a novel. In the case of other arts—most notably painting and sculpture—the argument is that, though there are physical objects of a

From Richard Wollheim, *Art and Its Objects* (New York: Harper and Row, 1968), sections 4–10, 15–16, 18–20, 35–38. Reprinted with permission of the author and Harper and Row.

standard and acceptable kind that could be, indeed generally are, identified as works of art, such identifications are wrong.

The first part of this challenge is, as we shall see, by far the harder to meet. However it is, fortunately, not it, but the second part of the challenge, that potentially raises such difficulties for aesthetics.

6

That there is a physical object that can be identified as *Ulysses* or *Der Rosenkavalier* is not a view that can long survive the demand that we should pick out or point to that object. There is, of course, the copy of *Ulysses* that is on my table before me now, there is the performance of *Der Rosenkavalier* that I will go to tonight, and both these two things may (with some latitude, it is true, in the case of the performance) be regarded as physical objects. Furthermore, a common way of referring to these objects is by saying things like "*Ulysses* is on my table," "I shall see *Rosenkavalier* tonight": from which it would be tempting (but erroneous) to conclude that *Ulysses* just is my copy of it, *Rosenkavalier* just is tonight's performance.

Tempting, but erroneous; and there are a number of very succinct ways of bringing out the error involved. For instance, it would follow that if I lost my copy of *Ulysses, Ulysses* would become a lost work. Again, it would follow that if the critics disliked tonight's performance of *Rosenkavalier,* then they dislike *Rosenkavalier.* Clearly neither of these inferences is acceptable.

We have here two locutions or ways of describing the facts: one in terms of works of art, the other in terms of copies, performances, etc., of works of art. Just because there are contexts in which these two locutions are interchangeable, this does not mean that there are no contexts, moreover no contexts of a substantive kind, in which they are not interchangeable. There very evidently are such contexts, and the physical-object hypothesis would seem to overlook them to its utter detriment.

7

But, it might not be maintained, of course it is absurd to identify *Ulysses* with my copy of it or *Der Rosenkavalier* with tonight's performance, but nothing follows from this of a general character about the wrongness of identifying works of art with physical objects. For what was wrong in these two cases was the actual physical object that was picked out and with which the identification was then made. The validity of the physical-object hypothesis, like that of any other hypothesis, is quite unaffected by the consequences of misapplying it.

For instance, it is obviously wrong to say that *Ulysses* is my copy of it.

Nevertheless, there is a physical object, of precisely the same order of being as my copy, though significantly not called a "copy" with which such an identification would be quite correct. This object is the author's manuscript: that, in other words, which Joyce wrote when he wrote *Ulysses*.

On the intimate connection, which undoubtedly does exist, between a novel or a poem on the one hand and the author's manuscript on the other, I shall have something to add later. But the connection does not justify us in asserting that one just is the other. Indeed, to do so seems open to objections not all that dissimilar from those we have just been considering. The critic, for instance, who admires *Ulysses* does not necessarily admire the manuscript. Nor is the critic who has seen or handled the manuscript in a privileged position as such when it comes to judgment on the novel. And—here we have come to an objection directly parallel to that which seemed fatal to identifying *Ulysses* with my copy of it—it would be possible for the manuscript to be lost and *Ulysses* to survive. None of this can be admitted by the person who thinks that *Ulysses* and the manuscript are one and the same thing.

To this last objection someone might retort that there are cases (e.g., *Love's Labour Won,* Kleist's *Robert Guiscard*) where the manuscript is lost and the work is lost, and moreover the work is lost because the manuscript is lost. Of course there is no real argument here, since nothing more is claimed than that there are *some* cases like this. Nevertheless the retort is worth pursuing, for the significance of such cases is precisely the opposite of that intended. Instead of reinforcing, they actually diminish, the status of the manuscript. For if we now ask, When is the work lost when the manuscript is lost? the answer is, When and only when the manuscript is unique: but then this would be true for any copy of the work were it unique.

Moreover, it is significant that in the case of *Rosenkavalier* it is not even possible to construct an argument corresponding to the one about *Ulysses*. To identify an opera or any other piece of music with the composer's holograph, which looks the corresponding thing to do, is implausible because (for instance), whereas an opera can be heard, a holograph cannot be. In consequence it is common at that stage of the argument, when music is considered, to introduce a new notion, that of the ideal performance, and then to identify the piece of music with this. There are many difficulties here: in the present context it is enough to point out that this step could not conceivably satisfy the purpose for which it was intended; that is, that of saving the physical-object hypothesis. For an ideal performance cannot be, even in the attenuated sense in which we have extended the term to ordinary performances, a physical object.

*8*

A final and desperate expedient to save the physical-object hypothesis is to suggest that all those works of art which cannot plausibly be identified with physical objects are identical with classes of such objects. A novel, of which there are copies, is not my or your copy but is the class of all its copies. An opera, of which there are performances, is not tonight's or last night's performance, nor even the ideal performance, but is the class of all its performances. (Of course, strictly speaking, this suggestion doesn't save the hypothesis at all: since a class of physical objects isn't necessarily, indeed is most unlikely to be, a physical object itself. But it saves something like the spirit of the hypothesis.)

However, it is not difficult to think of objections to this suggestion. Ordinarily we conceive of a novelist as writing a novel, or a composer as finishing an opera. But both these ideas imply some moment in time at which the work is complete. Now suppose (which is not unlikely) that the copies of a novel or the performances of an opera go on being produced for an indefinite period: then, on the present suggestion, there is no such moment, let alone one in their creator's lifetime. So we cannot say that *Ulysses* was written by Joyce, or that Strauss composed *Der Rosenkavalier*. Or, again, there is the problem of the unperformed symphony, or the poem of which there is not even a manuscript: in what sense can we now say that these things even *exist?*

But perhaps a more serious, certainly a more interesting, objection is that in this suggestion what is totally unexplained is why the various copies of *Ulysses* are all said to be copies of *Ulysses* and nothing else, why all the performances of *Der Rosenkavalier* are reckoned performances of that one opera. For the ordinary explanation of how we come to group copies or performances as being of this book or of that opera is by reference to something else, something other than themselves, to which they stand in some special relation. (Exactly what this other thing is, or what is the special relation in which they stand to it is, of course, something we are as yet totally unable to say.) But the effect, indeed precisely the point, of the present suggestion is to eliminate the possibility of any such reference: if a novel or opera just is its copies or its performances, then we cannot, for purposes of identification, refer from the latter to the former.

The possibility that remains is that the various particular objects, the copies or performances, are grouped as they are, not by reference to some other thing to which they are related, but in virtue of some relation that holds between them: more specifically, in virtue of resemblance.

But, in the first place, all copies of *Ulysses,* and certainly all performances of *Der Rosenkavalier,* are not perfect matches. And if it is now said that the differences do not matter, either because the various copies or performance resemble each other in all relevant respects, or because they resemble each other more than they resemble the copies or performances of any other novel or opera, neither answer is adequate. The first answer begs the issue, in that to talk of relevant respects presupposes that we know how, say, copies of *Ulysses* are grouped together: the second answer evades the issue, in that thought it may tell us why we do not, say, reckon any of the performances of *Der Rosenkavalier* as performances of *Arabella,* it gives us no indication why we do not set some of them up separately, as performances of some third opera.

Secondly, it seems strange to refer to the resemblance between the copies of *Ulysses* or the performances of *Rosenkavalier* as though this were a brute fact: a fact, moreover, which could be used to explain why they were copies or performances of what they are. It would be more natural to think of this so-called "fact" as something that itself stood in need of explanation: and, moreover, as finding its explanation in just that which it is here invoked to explain. In other words, to say that certain copies or performances are of *Ulysses* or *Rosenkavalier* because they resemble one another seems precisely to reverse the natural order of thought: the resemblance, we would think, follows from, or is to be understood in terms of, the fact that they are of the same novel or opera.

## 9

However, those who are ready to concede that some kinds of works of art are not physical objects will yet insist that others are. *Ulysses* and *Der Rosenkavalier* may not be physical objects, but the *Donna Velata* and Donatello's *Saint George* most certainly are.

I have already suggested (Section 5) that the challenge to the physical-object hypothesis can be divided into two parts. It will be clear that I am now about to embark on the second part of the challenge: namely, that which allows that there are (some) physical objects that could conceivably be identified as works of art, but insists that it would be quite erroneous to make the identification.

(To some, such a course of action may seem superfluous. For enough has been said to disprove the physical-object hypothesis. That is true; but the argument that is to come has its intrinsic interest, and for that reason is worth developing. Those for whom the interest of all philosophical argument is essentially polemical, and who have been convinced by the preceding argument, may choose to think of that which is to follow as bearing upon a revised or weakened version of the physical-object hypothesis: namely, that some works of art are physical objects.)

## 10

In the Pitti there is a canvas (No. 245) 85 cm × 64 cm: in the Museo Nazionale, Florence, there is a piece of marble 209 cm high. It is with these physical objects that those who claim that the *Donna Velata* and the *Saint George* are physical objects would naturally identify them.

This identification can be disputed in (roughly) one or other of two ways. It can be argued that the work of art has properties which are incompatible with certain properties that the physical object has, alternatively it can be argued that the work of art has properties which no physical object could have: in neither case could the work of art be the physical object.

An argument of the first kind would run: We say of the *St. George* that it moves with life (Vasari). Yet the block of marble is inanimate. Therefore the *St. George* cannot be that block of marble. An argument of the second kind would run: We say of the *Donna Velata* that it is exalted and dignified (Wölfflin). Yet a piece of canvas in the Pitti cannot conceivably have these qualities. Therefore the *Donna Velata* cannot be that piece of canvas.

These two arguments, I suggest, are not merely instances of these two ways of arguing, they are characteristic instances. For the argument that there is an incompatibility of property between works of art and physical objects characteristically concentrates on the representational properties of works of art. The argument that works of art have properties that physical objects could not have characteristically concentrates on the expressive properties of works of art. The terms "representational" and "expressive" are used here in a very wide fashion, which, it is hoped, will become clear as the discussion proceeds.

.     .     .

## 15

We might begin by considering two false views of how works of art acquire their expressiveness: not simply so as to put them behind us, but because each is in its way a pointer to the truth. Neither view requires us to suppose that works of art are anything other than physical objects.

The first view is that works of art are expressive because they have been produced in a certain state of mind or feeling on the part of the artist: and to this the rider is often attached, that it is this mental or emotional condition that they express. But if we take the view first of all with the rider attached, its falsehood is apparent. For it is a common happening that a painter or sculptor modifies or even rejects a work of his because he finds that it fails to correspond to what he experienced at the time. If, however, we drop the rider, the view now seems arbitrary or perhaps incomplete. For there seems to be no reason why a work should be expressive simply because it was produced in some heightened condition if it is also admitted that the work and the condition need not have the same character. (It would be like trying to explain why a man who has measles is ill by citing the fact that he was in contact with someone else who was also ill when that other person was not ill with measles or anything related to measles.) It must be understood that I am not criticising the view because it allows an artist to express in his work a condition other than that which he was in at the time: my case is rather that the view does wrong both to allow this fact and to insist that the expressiveness of the work can be accounted for exclusively in terms of the artist's condition.

However, what is probably the more fundamental objection to this view, and is the point that has been emphasized by many recent philosophers, is that the work's expressiveness now becomes a purely external feature of it. It is no longer something that we can or might observe, it is something that we infer from what we observe: it has been detached from the object as it manifests itself to us, and placed in its history, so that it now belongs more to the biography of the artist than to criticism of the work. And this seems wrong. For the qualities of gravity, sweetness, fear, that we invoke in describing works of art seem essential to our understanding of them; and if they are, they cannot be extrinsic to the works themselves. They cannot be, that is, mere attributes of the experiences or activities of Masaccio, of Raphael, of Grünewald—they inhere rather in the Brancacci frescoes, in the Granduca Madonna, in the Isenheim Altarpiece.

The second view is that works of art are expressive because they produce or are able to produce a certain state of mind or feeling in the spectator: moreover (and in the case of this view it is difficult to imagine the rider ever detached), it is this mental or emotional condition that they express. This view is open to objections that closely parallel those we have just considered.

For, in the first place, it seems clearly false. Before works even of the most extreme emotional intensity, like Bernini's St. Teresa or the black paintings of Goya, it is possible to remain more or less unexcited to the emotion that it would be agreed they express. Indeed, there are many theories that make it a distinguishing or defining feature of art that it should be viewed with detachment, that there should be a distancing on the part of the spectator between what the work expresses and what he experiences: although it is worth noting, in passing, that those theorists who have been most certain that works of art do not arouse emotion have also been uncertain, in some cases confused, as to how this comes about:

sometimes attributing it to the artist, sometimes to the spectator; sometimes, that is, saying that the artist refrains from giving the work the necessary causal power, sometimes saying that the spectator holds himself back from reacting to this power.

However, the main objection to this view, as to the previous one, is that it removes what we ordinarily think of as one of the essential characteristics of the work of art from among its manifest properties, locating it this time not in its past but in its hidden or dispositional endowment. And if it is now argued that this is a very pertinent difference, in that the latter is, in principle at least, susceptible to our personal verification in a way in which the former never could be, this misses the point. Certainly we can actualize the disposition, by bringing it about that the work produces in us the condition it is supposed to express: and there is clearly no corresponding way in which we can actualize the past. But though this is so, this still does not make the disposition itself—and it is with this, after all, that the work's expressiveness is equated—any the more a property that we can observe.

## 16

And yet there seems to be something to both these views: as an examination of some hypothetical cases might bring out.

For let us imagine that we are presented with a physical object—we shall not for the moment assume that it either is or is supposed to be a work of art—and the claim is made on its behalf, in a way that commands our serious attention, that it is expressive of a certain emotion: say, grief. We then learn that it had been produced quite casually, as a diversion or as part of a game: and we must further suppose that it arouses neither in us nor in anyone else anything more than mild pleasure. Can we, in the light of these facts, accept the claim? It is conceivable that we might; having certain special reasons.

But now let us imagine that the claim is made on behalf not of a single or isolated object, but of a whole class of objects of which our original example would be a fair specimen, and it turns out that what was true of it is true of all of them both as to how they were produced and as to what they produce in us. Surely it is impossible to imagine any circumstances in which we would allow *this* claim.

But what are we to conclude from this? Are we to say that the two views are true in a general way, and that error arises only when we think of them as applying in each and every case? The argument appears to point in this direction, but at the same time it seems an unsatisfactory state in which to leave the matter. (Certain contemporary moral philosophers, it is true, seem to find a parallel situation in their own area perfectly congenial, when they say that an individual action can be right even though it does not satisfy the utilitarian criterion, provided that that sort of action, or that that action in general, satisfies the criterion: the utilitarian criterion, in other words, applies on the whole, though not in each and every case.)

The difficulty here is this: Suppose we relax the necessary condition in the particular case because it is satisfied in general, with what right do we continue to regard the condition that is satisfied in general as necessary? Ordinarily the argument for regarding a condition as necessary is that there could not be, or at any rate is not, anything of the requisite kind that does not satisfy it. But this argument is not open to us here. Accordingly, at the lowest, we must be prepared to give some account of how the exceptions arise: or, alternatively, why we are so insistent on the condition in general. To return to the example: it seems unacceptable to say that a single object can express grief though it was not produced in, nor is it productive of, that emotion, but that a class of objects cannot express grief unless most of them, or some of them, or a fair sample of them, satisfy these conditions—unless we can explain why we discriminate in this way.

At this point what we might do is to turn back and look at the special reasons, as I called them, which we might have for allowing an individual object to be expressive of grief though it did not satisfy the conditions that hold generally. There seem to be roughly two lines of thought which if followed might allow us to concede expressiveness. We might think, "Though the person who made this object didn't feel grief when he made it, yet this is the sort of thing I would make if I felt grief. . . ." Alternatively we might think, "Though I don't feel grief when I look at this here and now, yet I am sure that in other circumstances I would. . . ." Now, if I am right in thinking that these are the relevant considerations, we can begin to see some reason for our discrimination between the particular and the general case. For there is an evident difficulty in seeing how these considerations could apply to a whole class of objects: given, that is, that the class is reasonably large. For our confidence that a certain kind of object was what we would produce if we experienced grief would be shaken by the fact that not one (or very few) had actually been produced in grief: equally, our confidence that in other circumstances we should feel grief in looking at them could hardly survive the fact that no one (or scarcely anyone) ever had. The special reasons no longer operating, the necessary conditions reassert themselves.

.    .    .

*18*

The question, however, might now be raised, Suppose the two criteria, which hitherto have been taken so closely together, should diverge: for they might: how could we settle the issue? And the difficulty here is not just that there is no simple answer to the question, but that it looks as though any answer given to it would be arbitrary. Does this, therefore, mean that the two criteria are quite independent, and that the whole concept of expression, if, that is, it is constituted as I have suggested, is a contingent conjunction of two elements, which could as easily fall apart as together?

I shall argue that the concept of expression, at any rate as this applies to the arts, is indeed complex, in that it lies at the intersection of two constituent notions of expression. We can gain some guidance as to these notions from the two views of expression we have been considering, for they are both reflected in, though also distorted by, these views. But, whereas the two views seem quite contingently connected, and have no clear point of union, once we understand what these notions are we can see how and why they interact. Through them we can gain a better insight into the concept of expression as a whole.

In the first place, and perhaps most primitively, we think of a work of art as expressive: that is to say, we conceive of it as coming so directly and immediately out of some particular emotional or mental state that it bears unmistakable marks of that state upon it. In this sense the word remains very close to its etymology: *ex-primere,* to squeeze out or press out. An expression is a secretion of an inner state. I shall refer to this as "natural expression." Alongside this notion is another, which we apply when we think of an object as expressive of a certain condition because, when we are in that condition, it seems to us to match, or correspond with, what we experience inwardly: and perhaps when the condition passes, the object is also good for reminding us of it in some special poignant way, or for reviving it for us. For an object to be expressive in this sense, there is no requirement that it should originate in the condition that it expresses, nor indeed is there any stipulation about is genesis: for these purposes it is simply a piece of the environment which we appropriate on account of the way it seems to reiterate something in us. Expression in this sense I shall (following a famous nineteenth-century usage) call "correspondence."

We may now link this with the preceding discussion by saying that the preoccupation with what the artist felt, or might have felt, reflects a concern with the work of art as a piece of natural expression: whereas the preoccupation with what the spectator feels, or might feel, reflects a concern with the work of art as an example of correspondence.

But though these two notions are logically distinct, in practice they are bound to interact: indeed, it is arguable that it goes beyond the limit of legitimate abstraction to imagine one without the other. We can see this by considering the notion of appropriateness, or fittingness, conceived as a relation holding between expression and expressed. We might think that such a relation has a place only in connection with correspondences. For in the case of natural expression, the link between inner and outer is surely too powerful or too intimate to allow its mediation. It is not because tears seem like grief that we regard them as an expression of grief: nor does a man when he resorts to tears do so because they match his condition. So we might think. But in reality, at any level above the most primitive, natural expression will always be colored or influenced by some sense of what is appropriate; there will be a feedback from judgment, however inchoate or unconscious this may be, to gesture or exclamation. Again, when we turn to correspondence, it might seem that here we are guided entirely by appropriateness or the fit: that is to say, we appeal uniquely to the appearances or characteristics of objects, which hold for us, in some quite unanalyzed way, an emotional significance. We do not (we might think) check these reactions against observed correlations. But once again this is a simplification. Apart from a few primitive cases, no physiognomic perception will be independent of what is for us the supreme example of the relationship between inner and outer: that is, the human body as the expression of the psyche. When we endow a natural object or an artifact with expressive meaning, we tend to see it corporeally: that is, we tend to credit it with a particular look which bears a marked analogy to some look that the human body wears and that is constantly conjoined with an inner state.

## *19*

To the question, Can a work of art be a physical object if it is also expressive? it now looks as though we can, on the basis of the preceding account of expression, give an affirmative answer. For that account was elaborated with specifically in mind those arts where it is most plausible to think of a work of art as a physical object. But it may seem that with both the two notions of expression that I have tried to formulate, there remains an unexamined or problematic residue. And in the two cases the problem is much the same.

It may be stated like this: Granted that in each case the process I have described is perfectly comprehensible, how do we come at the end of it to attribute a human emotion to an object? In both cases the object has certain characteristics. In one case these characteristics mirror, in the other case they are caused by, certain inner states of ours. Why, on the basis of this, do the names of the inner states get transposed to the objects?

The difficulty with this objection might be put by saying that it treats a philosophical reconstruction of a part of our language as though it were a historical account. For it is not at all clear that, in the cases where we attribute emotions to objects in the ways that I have tried to describe, we have any other way of talking about the objects themselves. There is not necessarily a prior description in nonemotive terms, on which we superimpose the emotive description. Or, to put the same point in nonlinguistic terms, it is not always the case that things that we see as expressive, we can or could see in any other way. In such cases what we need is not a justification, but an explanation, of our language. That I hope to have given.

## 20

We have now completed our discussion of the physical-object hypothesis, and this would be a good moment at which to pause and review the situation.

The hypothesis, taken literally, has been clearly shown to be false: in that there are arts where it is impossible to find physical objects that are even candidates for being identified with works of art (Sections 6-8). However, as far as those other arts are concerned where such physical objects can be found, the arguments against the identification—namely, those based on the fact that works of art have properties not predicable of physical objects—seemed less cogent (Sections 9-19). I have now to justify the assertion that I made at the very beginning of the discussion (Section 5), that it was only insofar as it related to these latter arts that the challenge to this hypothesis had any fundamental significance for aesthetics.

The general issue raised, whether works of art are physical objects, seems to compress two questions: the difference between which can be brought out by accenting first one, then the other, constituent word in the operative phrase. Are works of art *physical* objects? Are works of art physical *objects*? The first question would be a question about the stuff or constitution of works of art, what in the broadest sense they are made of: more specifically, are they mental? or physical? are they constructs of the mind? The second question would be a question about the category to which works of art belong, about the criteria of identity and individuation applicable to them: more specifically, are they universals, of which there are instances? or classes, of which there are members? are they particulars? Roughly speaking, the first question might be regarded as metaphysical, the second as logical. And, confusingly enough, both can be put in the form of a question about what kind of thing a work of art is.

Applying this distinction to the preceding discussion, we can now see that the method of falsifying the hypothesis that all works of art are physical objects has been to establish that there are some works of art that are not objects (or particulars) at all: whereas the further part of the case, which depends upon establishing that those works of art which are objects are nevertheless not physical, has not been made good. If my original assertion is to be vindicated, I am now required to show that what is of moment in aesthetics is the physicality of works of art rather than their particularity.

.     .     .

## 35

... [I want to] go back and take up an undischarged commitment: which is that of considering the consequences of rejecting the hypothesis that works of art are physical objects, insofar as those arts are concerned where there is no physical object with which the work of art could be plausibly identified. This will, of course, be in pursuance of my general aim—which has also directed the preceding discussion—of establishing that the rejection of the hypothesis has serious consequences for the philosophy of art only insofar as those arts are concerned where there *is* such an object.

I have already stated (sections 5, 20) that, once it is conceded that certain works of art are not physical *objects,* the subsequent problem that arises, which can be put by asking, What sort of thing are they? is essentially a logical problem. It is that of determining the criteria of identity and individuation appropriate to, say, a piece of music or a novel. I shall characterize the status of such things by saying that they are (to employ a term introduced by Peirce) *types.* Correlative to the term "type" is the term "token." Those physical objects which (as we have seen) can out of desperation be thought to be works of art in cases where there are no physical objects that can plausibly be thought of in this way, are *tokens.* In other words, *Ulysses* and *Der Rosenkavalier* are types; my copy of *Ulysses* and tonight's performance of *Rosenkavalier* are tokens of those types. The question now arises, What is a type?

The question is very difficult, and, unfortunately, to treat it with the care and attention to detail that it deserves is beyond the scope of this essay.

We might begin by contrasting a type with other sorts of thing that it is not. Most obviously we could contrast a type with a *particular:* this I shall take as done. Then we could contrast it with other various kinds of non-particulars: with a *class* (of which we say that it has *members*), and a *universal* (of which we say that it has *instances*). An example of a class would be the class of red things: an example of a universal would be redness: and examples of a type would be the word "red" and the Red Flag—where this latter phrase is taken to mean not this or that piece of material, kept in a chest or taken out and flown at a masthead, but the flag of revolution, raised for the first time in 1830 and that which many would willingly follow to their death.

Let us introduce as a blanket expression for types, classes, universals, the term *generic entity,* and, as a blanket expression for those things which fall under them, the term *element.* Now we can say that the various generic entities can be distinguished according to the different ways or relationships in which they stand to their elements. These relationships can be arranged on a scale of intimacy or intrinsicality. At one end of the scale we find classes, where the relationship is at its most external or extrinsic: for a class is merely made of, or constituted by, its members which are extensionally conjoined to form it. The class of red things is simply a construct out of all those things which are (timelessly) red. In the case of universals the relation is more intimate: in that a universal is present in all its instances. Redness is in all red things. With types we find the relationship between the generic entity and its elements at its most intimate: for not merely is the type present in all its tokens like the universal in all its instances, but for much of the time we think and talk of the type as though it were itself a kind of token, though a peculiarly important or preeminent one. In many ways we treat the Red Flag as though it were a red flag (cf. "We'll keep the Red Flag flying high").

These varying relations in which the different generic entities stand to their elements are also reflected (if, that is, this is *another* fact) in the degree to which both the generic entities and their elements can satisfy the same predicates. Here we need to make a distinction between sharing properties and properties being transmitted. I shall say that when A and B are both $f$, $f$ is shared by A and B. I shall further say that when A is $f$ because B is $f$, or B is $f$ because A is $f$, $f$ is transmitted between A and B. (I shall ignore the sense or direction of the transmission, i.e., I shall not trouble, even where it is possible, to discriminate between the two sorts of situation I have mentioned as instances of transmission.)

First, we must obviously exclude from consideration properties that can pertain only to tokens (e.g., properties of location in space and time) and equally those which pertain only to types (e.g., "was invented by"). When we have done this, the situation looks roughly as follows: Classes can share properties with their members (e.g., the class of big things is big), but this is very rare: moreover, where it occurs it will be a purely contingent or fortuitous affair, i.e., there will be no transmitted properties. In the cases of both universals and types, there will be shared properties. Red things may be said to be exhilarating, and so also redness. Every red flag is rectangular, and so is the Red Flag itself. Moreover, many, if not all, the shared properties will be transmitted.

Let us now confine our attention to transmitted properties because it is only they which are relevant to the difference in relationship between, on the one hand, universals and types and, on the other hand, their elements. Now there would seem to be two differences in respect of transmitted properties which distinguish universals from types. In the first place, there is likely to be a far larger range of transmitted properties in the case of types than there is with universals. The second difference is this: that in the case of universals no property that an instance of a certain universal has necessarily, i.e., that it has in virtue of being an instance of that universal, can be transmitted to the universal. In the case of types, on the other hand, all and only those properties that a token of a certain type has necessarily, i.e., that it has in virtue of being a token of that type, will be transmitted to the type. Examples would be: Redness, as we have seen, may be exhilarating, and, if it is, it is so for the same reason that its instances are, i.e., the property is transmitted. But redness cannot be red or colored, which its instances are necessarily. On the other hand, the Union Jack is colored and rectangular, properties which all its tokens have necessarily: but even if all its tokens happened to be made of linen, this would not mean that the Union Jack itself was made of linen.

To this somewhat negative account of a type—concentrated largely on what a type is not—we now need to append something of a more positive kind, which would say what it is for various particulars to be gathered together as tokens of the same type. For it will be appreciated that there corresponds to every universal and to every type a class: to redness the class of red things, to the Red Flag the class of red flags. But the converse is not true. The question therefore arises, What are the characteristic circumstances in which we postulate a type? The question, we must appreciate, is entirely conceptual: it is a question about the structure of our language.

A very important set of circumstances in which we postulate types—perhaps a central set, in the sense that it may be possible to explain the remaining circumstances by reference to them—is where we can correlate a class of particulars with a human invention: these particulars may then be regarded as tokens of a certain type. This characterization is vague, and deliberately so: for it is intended to comprehend a considerable spectrum of cases. At one end we have the case where a particular is produced, and is then copied: at the other end, we have the case where a set of instructions is drawn up which, if followed, give rise to an indefinite number of particulars. An example of the former would be the Brigitte Bardot looks: an example of the latter would be the Minuet. Intervening cases are constituted by the production of a particular which was made in order to be copied, e.g., the Boeing 707, or the construction of a mold or matrix which generates further particulars, e.g., the Penny Black. There are many ways of arranging the cases—according, say, to the degree of human intention that enters into the proliferation of the type, or according to the degree of match that exists between the original piece of invention and the tokens that flow from it. But there are certain resemblances between all the cases: and with ingenuity one can see a natural extension of the original characterization to cover cases where the invention is more classificatory than constructive in nature, e.g., the Red Admiral.

*36*

It will be clear that the preceding characterization of a type and its tokens offers us a framework within which we can (at any rate roughly) understand the logical status of things like operas, ballets, poems, etchings, etc.: that is to say, account for their principles of identity and individuation. To show exactly where these various kinds of things lie within this framework would involve a great deal of detailed analysis, more than can be attempted here, and probably of little intrinsic interest. I shall touch very briefly upon two general sets of problems, both of which concern the feasibility of the project. In this section I shall deal with the question of how the type is identified or (what is much the same thing) how the tokens of a given type are generated. In the next section I shall deal with the question of what properties we are entitled to ascribe to a type. These two sets of questions are not entirely distinct: as we can see from the fact that there is a third set of questions intermediate between the other two, concerning how we determine whether two particulars are or are not tokens of the same type. These latter questions, which arise for instance sharply in connection with translation, I shall pass over. I mention them solely to place those which I shall deal with in perspective.

First, then, as to how the type is identified. In the case of any work of art that it is plausible to think of as a type, there is what I have called a piece of human invention: and these pieces of invention fall along the whole spectrum of cases as I characterized it. At one end of the scale, there is the case of a poem, which comes into being when certain words are set down on paper or perhaps, earlier still, when they are said over in the poet's head (cf. the Croce-Collingwood theory). At the other end of the scale is an opera which comes into being when a certain set of instructions, i.e., the score, is written down, in accordance with which performances can be produced. As an intervening case we might note a film, of which different copies are made: or an etching or engraving, where different sheets are pulled from the same matrix, i.e., the plate.

There is little difficulty in all this, so long as we bear in mind from the beginning the variety of ways in which the different types can be identified, or (to put it another way) in which the tokens can be generated from the initial piece of invention. It is if we begin with too limited a range of examples that distortions can occur. For instance, it might be argued that, if the tokens of a certain poem are the many different inscriptions that occur in books reproducing the word order of the poet's manuscript, then "strictly speaking" the tokens of an opera must be the various pieces of sheet music or printed scores that reproduce the marks on the composer's holograph. Alternatively, if we insist that it is the performances of the opera that are the tokens, then, it is argued, it must be the many readings or "voicings" of the poem that are *its* tokens.

Such arguments might seem to be unduly barren or pedantic, if it were not that they revealed something about the divergent media of art: moreover, if they did not bear upon the issues to be discussed in the next section.

## 37

It is, we have seen, a feature of types and their tokens, not merely that they may share properties, but that when they do, these properties may be transmitted. The question we have now to ask is whether a limit can be set upon the properties that may be transmitted: more specifically, since it is the type that is the work of art and therefore that with which we are expressly concerned, whether there are any properties—always of course excluding those properties which can be predicated only of particulars—that belong to tokens and cannot be said *ipso facto* to belong to their types.

It might be thought that we have an answer, or at least a partial answer, to this question in the suggestion already made, that the properties transmitted between token and type are only those which the tokens possess necessarily. But a moment's reflection will show that any answer along these lines is bound to be trivial. For there is no way of determining the properties that a token of a given type has necessarily, independently of determining the properties of that type: accordingly, we cannot use the former in order to ascertain the latter. We cannot hope to discover what the properties of the Red Flag are by finding out what properties the various red flags have necessarily: for how can we come to know that, e.g., this red flag is necessarily red, prior to knowing that the Red Flag itself is red?

There are, however, three observations that can be made here on the basis of our most general intuitions. The first is that there are no properties or sets of properties that cannot pass from token to type. With the usual reservations, there is nothing that can be predicated of a performance of a piece of music that could not also be predicated of that piece of music itself. This point is vital. For it is this that ensures what I have called the harmlessness of denying the physical-object hypothesis in the domain of those arts where the denial consists in saying that works of art are not physical *objects*. For though they may not be objects but types, this does not prevent them from having physical properties. There is nothing that prevents us from saying that Donne's *Satires* are harsh on the ear, or that Dürer's engraving of Saint Anthony has a very differentiated texture, or that the conclusion of "Celeste Aida" is pianissimo.

The second observation is that, though any single property may be transmitted from token to type, it does not follow that all will be: or to put it another way, a token will have some of its properties necessarily, but it need not have all of them necessarily. The full significance of this point will emerge later.

Thirdly, in the case of *some* arts it is necessary that not all properties should be transmitted from token to type: though it remains true that for any single property it might be transmitted. The reference here is, of course, to the performing arts—to operas, plays, symphonies, ballet. It follows from what was said above that anything that can be predicated of a performance of a piece of music can also be predicated of the piece of music itself: to this we must now add that not every property that can be predicated of the former *ipso facto* belongs to the latter. This point is generally covered by saying that in such cases there is essentially an element of *interpretation,* where for these purposes interpretation may be regarded as the production of a token that has properties in excess of those of the type.

"Essentially" is a word that needs to be taken very seriously here. For, in the first place, there are certain factors that might disguise from us the fact that every performance of a work of art involves, or is, an interpretation. One such factor would be antiquarianism. We could—certainly if the evidence were available—imagine a *Richard III* produced just as Burbage played it, or *Das Klagende Lied* performed just as Mahler conducted it. But though it would be possible to bring about in this way a replica of Burbage's playing or Mahler's conducting, we should none the less have interpretations of *Richard III* and *Das Klagende Lied,* for this is what Burbage's playing and Mahler's conducting were, though admittedly the first. Secondly, it would be wrong to think of the element of interpretation—assuming that this is now conceded to be present in the case of all performances—as showing something defective. Suzanne Langer, for instance, has characterized the situation in the performing arts by saying that, e.g., the piece of music the composer writes is "an incomplete work": "the performance," she says, "is the completion of a musical work." But this suggests that the point to which the composer carries the work is one which he could, or even should, have gone beyond. To see how radical a reconstruction this involves of the ways in which we conceive the performing arts, we need to envisage what would be involved if it were to be even possible to eliminate interpretation. For instance, one requirement would be that we should have for each performing art what might be called, in some very strong sense, a universal notation: such that we could designate in it every characteristic that now originates at the point of performance. Can we imagine across the full range of the arts what such a notation would be like? With such a notation there would no longer be any executant arts: the whole of the execution would have been anticipated in the notation. What assurance can we have that the reduction of these arts to mere mechanical skills would not in turn have crucial repercussions upon the way in which we regard or assess the performing arts?

## 38

However, if we no longer regard it as a defect in certain arts that they require interpretation, it might still seem unsatisfactory that there should be this discrepancy within the arts: that, for instance, the composer or the dramatist should be denied the kind of control over his work that the poet or the painter enjoys.

In part, there just *is* a discrepancy within the arts. And this discrepancy is grounded in very simple facts of very high generality, which anyhow lie outside art: such as that words are different from pigments; or that it is human beings we employ to act and human beings are not all exactly alike. If this is the source of dissatisfaction, the only remedy would be to limit art very strictly to a set of processes or stuffs that were absolutely homogeneous in kind.

In part, however, the dissatisfaction comes from exaggerating the discrepancy, and from overlooking the fact that in the nonperforming arts there is a range of ways in which the spectator or audience can take the work of art. It is, I suggest, no coincidence that *this* activity, of taking the poem or painting or novel in one way rather than another, is also called "interpretation." For the effect in the two cases is the same, in that the control of the artist over his work is relaxed.

Against this parallelism between the two kinds of interpretation, two objections can be raised. The first is that the two kinds of interpretations differ in order or level. For whereas performative interpretation occurs only within certain arts, critical interpretation pertains to all: more specifically, a critical interpretation can be placed upon any given performative interpretation—so the point of the parallelism vanishes, in that the performing arts still remain in a peculiar or discrepant situation. Now I do not want to deny that any performance of a piece of music or a play can give rise to a critical interpretation: the question, however, is, When this happens, is this on the same level as a performative interpretation? I want to maintain that we can fruitfully regard it as being so. For insofar as we remain concerned with the play or the piece of music, what we are doing is in the nature of suggesting or arguing for alternative performances, which would have presented the original work differently: we are not suggesting or arguing for alternative ways in which the actual performance might be taken. Our interpretation is on the occasion of a performance, not about it. The situation is, of course, complicated to a degree that cannot be unraveled here by the fact that acting and playing music are also arts, and in criticizing individual performances we are sometimes conversant about those arts: which is why I qualified my remark by saying "insofar as we remain concerned with the play or piece of music."

The second and more serious objection to the parallelism between the two kinds of interpretation is that they differ as to necessity. For whereas a tragedy or a string quartet has to be interpreted, a poem or a painting need not be. At any given moment it may be necessary to interpret them, but that will be only because of the historical incompleteness of our comprehension of the work. Once we have really grasped it, further interpretation will no longer be called for. In other words, critical interpretation ultimately eliminates itself: whereas a piece of music or a play cannot be performed once and for all.

On this last argument I wish to make two preliminary observations: First, the argument must not draw any support (as the formulation here would seem to) from the indubitable but irrelevant fact that a performance is a transient, not an enduring, phenomenon. The relevant fact is not that a piece of music or a play must always be performed anew but that it can always be performed afresh, i.e., that every new performance can involve a new interpretation. The question then is, Is there not in the case of the nonperforming arts the same permanent possibility of new interpretations? Secondly, the argument seems to be ambiguous between two formulations, which are not clearly, though in fact they may be, equivalent: the ostensibly stronger one, that in the case of a poem or painting all interpretations can ultimately be eliminated; and the ostensibly weaker one, that in these cases all interpretations save one can ultimately be eliminated.

Against the eliminability of interpretation, the only decisive argument is one drawn from our actual experience of art. There are, however, supplementary considerations, the full force of which can be assessed only as this essay progresses, which relate to the value of art. Allusions to both can be found in a brilliant and suggestive work, Valéry's "Réflexions sur l'Art."

In the first place the value of art, as has been traditionally recognized, does not exist exclusively, or even primarily, for the artist. It is shared equally between the artist and his audience. One view of how this sharing is effected, which is prevalent but implausible, is that the artist makes something of value, which he then hands on to the audience, which is thereby enriched. Another view is that in art there is a characteristic ambiguity, or perhaps better plasticity, introduced into the roles of activity and passivity: the artist is active, but so also is the spectator, and the spectator's activity consists in interpretation. "A creator," Valéry puts it, "is one who makes others create."

Secondly—and this point too has received some recognition—the value of art is not exhausted by what the artist, or even by what the artist and the spectator, gain from it: it is not contained by the transaction between them. The work of art itself has a residual value. In certain "subjectivist" views—as, e.g., in the critical theory of I. A. Richards—the value of art is made to seem contingent: contingent, that is, upon there being found no better or more effective way in which certain experiences assessed to be valuable can be aroused in, or transmitted between, the minds of the artist and his audience. Now it is difficult to see how such a conclusion can be avoided if the work of art is held to be inherently exhaustible in interpretation. [Earlier] the view was considered that works of art are translucent; the view we are now asked to consider would seem to suggest that they are transparent, and as such ultimately expendable or "throwaway." It is against such a view that Valéry argued that we should regard works of art as constituting "a new and impenetrable element" which is interposed between the artist and the spectator. The ineliminability of interpretation he characterizes, provocatively, as "the creative misunderstanding."

.        .        .

# 12.     Toward an Ontology of Artworks
## NICHOLAS WOLTERSTORFF

What sort of entity is a symphony? A drama? A dance? A graphic art print? A sculpture? A poem? A film? A painting?

Are works of art all fundamentally alike in their ontological status?

These are the questions to be discussed in this paper.

### I A Phenomenology of the Distinctions Among Works of Art

In several of the arts there is application for the distinction between a performance of something and that which is performed. In music, for example, one can distinguish between a performance of *Verklaerte Nacht* and that which is thereby performed, namely, Arnold Schoenberg's work *Verklaerte Nacht*. Similarly, in dance one can distinguish between a performance of *Swan Lake* and that which is thereby performed, namely, the ballet *Swan Lake*.

Some people will be skeptical as to whether, in the cases cited and others of the same sort, we really do have two distinct entities—a performance and that which is performed. But assuming it to be true that the concept of a performance of something and the concept of something performed both have application to the arts, there are two sorts of considerations which force one to the conclusion that that which is performed on a given occasion is distinct from the performance of it.

In the first place, a thing performed and a performance thereof will always diverge in certain of their properties. For example, *having been composed by Schoenberg* is a property of *Verklaerte Nacht* but not of any performance of *Verklaerte Nacht*. On the other hand, *taking place at a certain time and place* is a property of every performance of *Verklaerte Nacht* but not of *Verklaerte Nacht* itself. It is worth noting that a work performed may diverge from performances thereof not only in 'ontological'

From NOUS, IX (1975), 115-142. Reprinted with permission of the author and of the editor.

properties but also in 'aesthetic' properties. For example, it may be that *having the voice part begin on A natural* is not a property of any performance of Schoenberg's *Pierrot Lunaire,* though it is a property of the work itself, indeed, an *essential* one.

A second sort of consideration, one which is actually a specific application of the first, also leads to the conclusion that in certain of the arts one must distinguish between those entities which are performances and those entities which are works performed. This second sort of consideration hinges on applications of the concepts of identity and diversity. That which is performed on one occasion may be identical with that which is performed on another; George Szell, for example, may twice over have conducted a performance of *Verklaerte Nacht.* Thus, there may be two distinct performances of one single musical work. But two distinct things cannot each be identical with some one thing. Thus, the two distinct performances cannot both be identical with the work performed. But if one of them, call it *A,* was identified with the work performed, then the other, call it *B,* would, by virtue of being a performance of the work performed, be a performance of performance *A.* Not only that, but performance *A* would be capable of being performed on many other occasions as well. Both of these consequences, however, seem impossible.

Let us henceforth call a work of art which can be performed, a *performance-work.* Most if not all performance-works are universals, in that they can be multiply performed.

It would seem that performances in the arts are as correctly called "works of art" as are performance-works. The ontological status of performances is relatively clear, however, while that of performance-works is immensely perplexing. Performances are occurrences or events. They take place at a certain time and place, begin at a certain time and end at a certain time, last for a certain stretch of time, and have temporal parts in the sense that each performance is half over at a certain time, three-quarters over at a certain time, one-eighth over at a certain time, etc. But what sort of entity is a performance-work? That is something which we shall have to discuss in considerable detail. What should already be clear, though, is that performance-works are not occurrences (events). Thus, already we can answer one of our opening questions. Works of art are not all alike in their ontological status.

In certain of the nonperforming arts distinctions similar to the performance/performance-work distinction have application. Consider, for example, graphic-art prints. Here, a commonly applied distinction is that between a particular impression and the work of which it is an impression; between, for example, the tenth impression of *Obedient unto Death* and the print of which it is an impression, namely, George Rouault's *Obedient unto Death.* And consider those cases in which sculpture is produced from a mold. Here, a commonly applied distinction is that between a particular casting of, say, *The Thinker* and the sculptural work of which it is a casting, namely, Rodin's *The Thinker.* And consider thirdly those cases in the field of architecture in which many different buildings are produced according to one set of specifications. Here, a commonly applied distinction is that between a given example of, say, the Tech-Bilt House No. 1 and that of which it is an example, namely, the Tech-Bilt House No. 1.

It may be noticed that an impression of a work of graphic art, a casting of a work of sculptural art, and an example of a work of architectural art are all enduring physical objects. This is why we have grouped these particular arts together. In order to have a convenient terminology, let us call the entities of which there can be impressions, castings, or examples, *object-works.* And let us say that impressions, castings, and examples are *objects of* object-works. Thus, as a counterpart to the performance-performance-work distinction, we have the distinction between impressions, castings, and examples on the one hand and object-works on the other.

The considerations which impel us to distinguish between an object-work and those entities which are objects thereof are parallel to those which impel us to distinguish between an entity which is a performance-work and those entities which are performances thereof. One consideration is again that of divergence in properties. For example, *having a thumbprint in the lower left corner* may be a property of a given impression of Rouault's print *Obedient unto Death,* or even of all impressions thereof, though it is not a property of the print *Obedient unto Death.* A second consideration is again to be derived from applications of the concepts of identity and diversity. For example, there can be two different castings of the same sculptural work; and neither both of these castings together nor either one singly can be identified with the work. In the case of object-works there is yet a third sort of consideration which may be adduced, one hinging on applications of the concepts of existence and nonexistence. Any one of the several objects of an object-work can be destroyed without the object-work thereby being destroyed. I could, for example, perform the horrifying operation of burning my impression of Rouault's *Obedient unto Death,* but I would not thereby put the print itself out of existence. Nor could I put the print out of existence by destroying any one of the other impressions, nor even by destroying the original etched plate.

It would seem that both object-works and the objects thereof are entitled to being called "works of art." Further, the ontological status of the latter is relatively unproblematic: They are physical objects. Of course, plenty of things about the nature of physical objects remains unclear. Yet we know what they are, and it is clear that impressions, castings, and examples are to be numbered among them. But what is an object-work? What is *its* ontological status? That is something which we shall have to discuss in detail.

There remain literary works, films, and paintings to consider. A literary work can be both written down and 'sounded out'. There can be both copies of it and utterances of it. Now, a copy is a physical object, whereas an uttering of something is a certain sort of event. Further, the *copy of* relation seems closely similar to the *example of, the impression of,* and the *casting of* relations. Accordingly, I shall say that a copy of a literary work is an object of it; and I shall add literary works to the group of entities to be called object-works. Furthermore, an utterance of a literary work is an event, very much like a performance. Accordingly, in the class of things to be called performance-works I shall include also literary works. Literary works, then, are both performance-works and object-works.

Saying this, however, makes one want to look back to see whether we do not have good ground for saying that works of music and drama are also both performance-works and object-works. In the case of dramatic works I think it is clear that we must say "No." A dramatic performance is a pattern of actions. The actions will in all but the most unusual cases include speech actions. But in all but the most unusual cases they will include other sorts of actions as well. More importantly, that pattern of actions which is a dramatic performance will always include actions of *role-playing.* For these reasons, a reading aloud or a recitation of the script of a drama is not yet a performance of the drama. A copy of the script for a drama is not a copy of the drama but instructions for proper performances thereof. The script may of course be a literary work in its own right. And that work can have both readings aloud and copies. But the drama is not the script. And a copy of the script is not a copy of the drama. The drama has no copies. All it has is performances. Dramas are only performance-works.

Music presents a somewhat less clear situation. The crucial question is this: Does a copy of the score stand to a work of music in a relationship similar enough to that in which a copy stands to a work of literature to justify us in calling the score-copy an object of the work? It seems to me not decisively clear one way or the other. What does seem clear is that a word can be both written down and uttered aloud, whereas a sound cannot be written down but only sounded out. The marks in a copy of a score are not instances of sounds but rather instructions for producing sounds. Of course, an instance of some sequence of words can also be treated as instructions for the utterance of that sequence; yet at the same time it is genuinely an instance of those worlds. Some words, especially those in primitive cultures, are never written down; some, especially those in technical languages, are never sounded out. Yet most words have a dual manifestation. The same is not true of sounds. But suppose someone suggests that music should be thought of as being composed of *notes* rather than sounds, and then goes on to argue that notes, like words, can be both sounded out and written down. Obviously, this is a suggestion worthy of further investigation. Whether it is true or false is not at once clear. But nothing that is said hereafter will depend essentially on whether or not it is true. So I shall continue to suppose that music consists of sounds.

The film seems to have a dual status similar to that of words. One and the same film may have many copies, a copy being a physical object; and it may also have many showings, a showing being an occurrence (event). Thus, a film, like a literary work, has claim to being regarded as both an object-work and a performance-work. There is this difference worth noting, though: A showing of a film will always occur by way of the showing of a certain copy of the film, whereas the utterance of a literary work need not occur by way of the reading of some copy of the work. One can recite it from memory.

As for paintings, it seems that neither the object/object-work distinction nor the performance/performance-work distinction has application, nor does it seem that any close counterpart to these distinctions has application. There is, of course, the distinction between the work and reproductions of the work. But this is a quite different distinction, as can be seen from the fact that one can also have reproductions of each of the various impressions of a print. What is lacking in painting is any counterpart to the print/impression distinction. All one has is a counterpart to the impression/reproduction distinction. The point may be put by saying that all the impressions of a print are originals, none is a reproduction. The conclusion must be that a painting is a physical object. But more will be said on this matter later in our discussion.

To say this is not, of course, to deny that reproductions of paintings along with reproductions of sculpture are, in some cases at least, entitled to being called "works of art" in their own right. So too are films, though they are for the most part 'reproductive' of performances and of visible events and objects. And so too are recordings, though most recordings are 'reproductive' of sounds and of audible performances. It is interesting to note, however, that in the case of visual-art reproductions and sculpture reproductions one again often has application for the print/impression or the work/casting distinction, and that in the case of recordings (records) one can distinguish between the recording on the one hand and the various discs of the recording on the other and, in turn, between a given disc on the one hand and various playings of the disc on the other.

Though I have called what we have done thus far *phenomenology,* what I have said is of course not free from ontological commitment. In saying that the distinction between performances and that which is performed can be applied to the arts, I said something which entails that there are performance-works. And I said that of most if not all of these it is true that they can be multiply performed. A thorough nominalist would deny that there are any multiply performable entities. Similarly, he would deny the existence of 'multiply-objectible' entities. I think it would be worthwhile to consider how the nominalist conviction that there are no such entities might most plausibly be developed; and I also think it would be worthwhile to consider whether any decisive arguments against such nominalism can be offered. But I shall not on this occasion attempt either of these. Rather, the question which I wish to discuss in detail is this: What is the ontological status of performance-works and object-works?

To simplify our terminology, I shall henceforth in this paper call only performance-works and object-works *art works.* And both performances of art works and objects of art works will be called examples of art works. I shall continue to use "work of art" to cover both art works and their examples, along with such things as paintings which are neither. Perhaps here is also a good place to remark that the fact that the performance/performance-work distinction or the object/object-work distinction applies to a certain art does not imply that it applies *throughout* that art. There may be works of that art which are neither. Those works of music, for example, which are *total* improvisations (as distinguished from those which are improvisations on a theme) are neither performances nor performance-works.[1]

## II The Sharing of Predicates and Properties Between Art Works and Examples

We cannot here discuss all competitors to the theory proposed in the following pages. But for an understanding of the theory, it will be useful briefly to consider and put behind us the view that performance-works and object-works are *sets* of their examples. The untenability of this suggestion can be seen by noticing that whatever members a set has it has necessarily, whereas a performance-work or object-work might always have had different and more or fewer performances or objects than it does have; and by noticing that if set $\alpha$ has no members and set $\beta$ has no members, then $\alpha$ is identical with $\beta$, whereas it is not the case that if art work $\gamma$ has no instances and art work $\delta$ has no instances, then $\gamma$ is identical with $\delta$.

That there is but one null set is clear enough. But that a set cannot have had a different membership from what it does have is a fact apt to be confused with related but different facts. The property, *having been a disciple of Saint Francis,* is a property shared in common by all and only the members of a certain set, that one, namely, whose members are all and only the disciples of Saint Francis. Let us for convenience name this set *D.* Now, whoever has the property of *having been a disciple of Saint Francis* has it only contingently. Accordingly, that set which is *D* might have been such that some of its members lacked this property; indeed, all might have lacked it. Alternatively, persons who are not members of *D* might have had this property. Thus, some other set than *D* might have been such that all and only its members have the property of *having been a disciple of Saint Francis.* But all these facts pertaining to what might have been in place of what is, are thoroughly compatible with the fact that *D* has its membership essentially.

To begin, consider some logical predicate which in normal usage can be predicated of two different things in such a way as to assert something true in both cases. Let us say that in such a case those two things *share that predicate.* One striking feature of the relationship between an art work and its examples is the pervasive sharing of predicates between the art work on the one hand and its examples on the other. "Is in the key of C minor" can be predicated truly of Beethoven's *Opus 111* and also of most if not all performances of Beethoven's *Opus 111.* "Has the figure slightly off-center to the right" can be predicated truly of Rouault's *Obedient unto Death* and likewise of most if not all impressions of *Obedient unto Death.* And so on, and on.

Of course, not every predicate which can be predicated truly of an art work or which can be predicated truly of examples of some art work, is shared by the work and its examples. "Is a performance" and "is an occurrence" are never shared, nor are "can be repeatedly performed" and "can repeatedly occur." Nor is "composed by Hindemith" ever shared. "Is thought about by me" is in some cases shared between a certain art work and all its examples, in other cases it is shared between a certain artwork and only some of its examples, while in yet other cases it is not shared between an art work and any of its examples. And "has 'no' as its third word" is unshared between the poem *Sailing to Byzantium* and my particular copy of it, whereas it is shared between the poem and *most* copies of it.

One naturally wonders, at this point, whether when a predicate is shared between an art work and some one or more of its examples, there is normally also a sharing of some property for which the predicate stands. If so, then the predicate is used *univocally.* On the other hand, if the predicate stands for two different properties but if there is some systematic relation between these, then the predicate is used *analogically*. If not even this is true, the predicate is used *equivocally*. Shortly, we shall discuss this issue pertaining to properties. Meanwhile, without yet committing ourselves on it, let us see whether we can find some pattern in this pervasive sharing of predicates. (See also Wolterstorff [9]: 250–254.)

From the start, one feels that there is some connection between a predicate's being true of the examples of an art work and its being true of the work. Can this feeling be substantiated? The example we have already used provides us with evidence for concluding that the following formula will not do: A predicate *P* is true of some art work *W* if *P* is true of every example of *W*. For "is a performance" is true of all the examples of performance-works but cannot be true, in its normal sense, of any of those art works themselves.

So suppose that from here on we discard from consideration those predicates which are true of one or more of the examples of some art work but which, in their normal meaning, *cannot* be true of the work itself. (When a predicate *P* used with normal meaning cannot be true of *W, P* will be said to be *excluded by W*. Likewise, when a property *P* cannot be possessed by *W, P* will be said to be *excluded by W*.) What then about the formula: For any predicate *P* which is not excluded by *W, P* is true of *W* if *P* is true of every example of *W*? One objection to this formula is that it is far more constricted in its application than what we were looking for. For we saw that "has a G sharp in its seventh measure" may be true of Bartok's *First Quartet* even though of many of its performances it is not true. Indeed, it may be true of none of the performances.

A clue to a better formula can be gotten by looking more closely at this example. Is it not the case that "has a G sharp in its seventh measure" is true of Bartok's *First Quartet* in case it is *impossible* that something should be a *correct* performance of Bartok's *First* and lack the property of having a G sharp in its seventh measure? Is it not the case that "has 'no' as its third word" is true of *Sailing to Byzantium* in case it is *impossible* that something should be a *correct* copy of *Sailing to Byzantium* and lack the property of having "no" as its third word?

These examples naturally suggest to us the following formula: For any predicate *P* which is not excluded by *W*, if there is some property *being P* which *P* expresses in normal usage and is such that it is impossible that something should be a correctly formed example of *W* and lack *being P*, then *P* is true of *W*.

But to this general formula as well, there are counterexamples. Consider for instance the predicate "is a performance or was highly thought of by Beethoven." There will be many works such that this predicate used in its normal sense will not be excluded by the work. Likewise, it is impossible that something should be a correctly formed example of some such work and lack the property of *being either a performance or highly thought of by Beethoven;* for it is impossible that that thing should lack the property of being a performance. Yet the predicate in question may very well not be true of the work. For the work cannot be a performance, and it may not have been highly thought of by Beethoven. And in general, take a predicate of the form "is either $A$ or anti-$W$," where "is anti-$W$" represents a predicate such that (i) it is excluded by $W$ and (ii) when predicated of examples of $W$ it stands for a property such that necessarily if something is an example of $W$, then it has that property, and where "is $A$" represents any predicate whatsoever which is not excluded by $W$. Then the 'disjunctive predicate' represented by "is either $A$ or anti-$W$" is itself not excluded by $W$ and is itself such that when predicated of some example of $W$, it stands for a property such that it is impossible that something should be a correct example of $W$ and lack it. Yet obviously the predicate may very well not be true of $W$.

The essence of the difficulty here would seem to be that some predicates stand for properties such that it is impossible that something should be an example of $W$ at all, correct or incorrect, and lack the property. Such properties might be said to be *necessary to* examples of $W$. If we could eliminate from consideration predicates standing for such properties, then counterexamples of the sort suggested will be forestalled. So let us say that a predicate $P$ is *acceptable with respect to $W$* if and only if $P$ is neither excluded by $W$ nor is such that any property for which it stands when truly predicated of examples of $W$ is one which is necessary to examples of $W$. Then our proposed formula becomes this: For any predicate $P$ which is acceptable with respect to $W$, if there is some property *being P* which $P$ expresses in normal usage and is such that it is impossible that something should be a correctly formed example of $W$ and lack *being P,* then $P$ is true of $W$. (It should be noticed that the claim here is not *if and only if,* but just *if.*)

The core feature of this proposal is the suggestion that what is true of correctly formed examples of an art work plays a decisive role in determining what can be predicated truly of the work. Or, to put it yet more indefinitely, the core feature is the suggestion that the concept of an art work is intimately connected with the concept of a correctly formed example of the work.

Perhaps if we considered the matter in detail, we could find still more pattern to the sharing of predicates between artworks and examples than what we have thus far uncovered. But enough has been uncovered for our subsequent purposes. So let us now move from the level of language to the level of ontology and consider whether, when predicates are shared according to the general pattern uncovered, there is also a sharing of properties designated by those predicates.

One is naturally inclined to think that there is. Our dictionaries do not, after all, tell us that a certain word standardly means one thing when truly predicated of an art work and something else when truly predicated of an example of the work. Yet I think that we must in fact come to the conclusion that predicates shared between art works and their examples do not function univocally when the sharing follows the general pattern we have uncovered. For what one means, in truthfully predicating "has 'no' as its third word" of some copy of *Sailing to Byzantium* is that the third word-*occurrence* is "no." But when one truthfully predicates "has 'no' as its third word" of *Sailing to Byzantium* itself, one cannot mean this. For the poem does not consist of word-occurrences. Similarly, what one means in truthfully predicating "has a G sharp in its seventh measure" of some performance of Bartok's *Fifth* is that in its seventh measure there was an *occurrence* of the G-sharp pitch. But the *Quartet* itself does not consist of sound-occurrences. So I think it must be admitted that we have not discovered a systematic identity but only a systematic relation between the property designated by some predicate when it is truthfully predicated of some art examples and the property designated by that same predicate when truthfully predicated of the art work. Our conclusion must be that the sharing of predicates between art works and their examples pervasively exhibits *analogical* predication.

The situation is as follows. Suppose that *P* is a predicate which can be shared between an art work *W* and its examples, and suppose further that a property for which *P* stands when truthfully predicated of examples of *W* is *being P*. Then for those cases in which the sharing of *P* fits the general pattern which we formulated, *P* when truthfully predicated of *W* stands for the property of *being such that something cannot be a correct example of it without having the property of being P*.

### III Art Works Are Kinds

We have seen some of the fundamental relations which hold between an art work and its examples. But we have not yet gained much insight into the ontological status of art works. We are left so far without any satisfying answer to our question: What *is* an art work? We must take a next step.

The proposal I wish to make is that performance-works and object-works are *kinds (types, sorts)*—kinds whose examples are the performances or objects of those works. A performance-work is a certain kind of performance; an object-work is a certain kind of object.

A phenomenon which tends at once to confirm us in the suggestion that art works are kinds whose examples are the examples of those works is the fact that kinds which are not art works are like art works in just the ways that (as we saw earlier) sets of their examples are unlike art works. Just as an art work might have had different and more or fewer performances and objects than it does have, so too the kind Man, for example, might have had different and more or fewer examples than it does have. If Napoleon had not existed, it would not then have been the case that Man did not exist. Rather, Man would then have lacked one of the examples which in fact it had. And secondly, just as there may be two distinct unperformed symphonies, so too may there be two distinct unexampled kinds—e.g., the Unicorn and the Hippogriff.

Not only does it seem that art works are *kinds*. What is even more striking is their many close similarities to those special kinds of kinds familiarly known as *natural* kinds.

It has long been noticed by philosophers that in the case of natural kinds there is a pervasive sharing of predicates and/or properties between kinds and their examples. Let us look at the pattern of such sharing, beginning with a proposal made by Richard Wollheim. Having excluded from consideration those properties which cannot be shared between kinds, and examples, his suggestion is that the following is necessarily true: The K shares a certain property with all Ks if and only if it is impossible that something should be an example of the K and lack the property ([8]:64–65).

What must be clearly perceived about this formula is that it speaks of *properties,* not of predicates. And in many if not most cases, a sharing of a predicate does not have, underlying it, a sharing of a property for which the predicate stands. That property which a grizzly possesses, of *being something that growls,* is not a property which the Grizzly could possess. Once one sees this, it becomes clear that the formula has an extremely limited application. Cases of shared predicates are common. Cases in which those predicates stand for properties which can be shared are relatively uncommon. Thus, the formula gives very little insight into the relation between kinds and their examples. Perhaps it's true that all grizzlies growl. And certainly it is true that the Grizzly growls (though at the same time it's true that something can be an example of the Grizzly while being mute). Yet this is not a counterexample to the formula; because what the Grizzly's growling consists of cannot be identical with what a grizzly's growling consists of. The tenability of the formula with respect to such cases is bought at the price of giving us no illumination with respect to them.

Even so, however, there are rather obvious counterexamples of other sorts to the formula. It could happen that a certain kind would share with all its examples the property of *having been referred to by someone or other.* Yet most kinds are such that something *could* be an example of them and still lack this property.

But now consider once again the sentence "The Grizzly growls." Is it not the case that "growls" is true of the Grizzly if it is impossible that something should be a *properly* formed grizzly and not growl? A grizzly muted is a malformed grizzly, and so also is grizzly born without a growl. What makes "growls" true of the Grizzly is that something cannot be a properly formed grizzly unless it growls. In botanical and zoological taxonomy books, one is not told about the features shared by all examples of a certain kind, nor about the essential features shared by all examples of a certain kind, but about the features which a thing cannot lack if it is to be a properly formed example of the kind. So already we have for natural kinds the same pattern which we earlier uncovered for art works: For any predicate *P* which is acceptable with respect to the *K,* if there is some property *being P* which *P* expresses in normal usage and which is such that it is impossible that something should be a properly formed example of the *K* and lack *being P,* then *P* is true of the *K.*

As in the case of art works, we must raise the question whether when we have a sharing of some predicate between a kind and its examples, we also have a sharing of some property for which that predicate stands. With respect to those cases which fit our general formula, I think the answer must be, "No, we do not." Predications in such cases are not univocal. But neither are they equivocal. They are analogical. When grizzlies growl, they emit from their throats certain characteristic sound-patterns which we English-speaking people call "growling." But the kind, Grizzly, does not do that. Its sound-emission cannot be caught on some record. Yet—the Grizzly growls. "Growls," when truly predicated of the Grizzly, would seem to stand for the property of *being such that something cannot be a properly formed example of its unless it growls.* Thus, there is a systematic non-univocality about "growls." The predicate "growls" stands naturally for two quite different properties, one holding of the Grizzly and one holding of at least every properly formed example thereof. In general, for those cases in which the sharing of predicates between a kind and its examples follows the general pattern which we have formulated, the predicates are used analogically in exactly the way in which they were seen to be used analogically in the corresponding cases for art works.

In concluding this section of our discussion, let us articulate an important assumption which we have been making throughout. Consider the kind: Red Thing. This does seem to be a genuine kind; it differs from the class of all red things in that it might have had different and more or fewer members than it does have. But now notice that there cannot be a distinction, among examples of this kind, between improperly formed examples and properly formed examples of the kind. For it is not possible that some of the examples of the Red Thing should be improperly formed examples of this kind (i.e., things improperly red), nor is it possible that some should be properly formed examples of the kind (i.e., things properly red). Or consider the two kinds: Properly Formed Orchid and Malformed Orchid. There seems no reason to doubt that there are such kinds as these. But neither of these can have properly formed examples, nor can either have improperly formed examples.

When a kind, the *K,* is such that it is possible that it should have properly formed examples and also possible that it should have improperly formed examples, let us say that the *K* is a *norm-kind.* We have assumed throughout our discussion that art works and natural kinds are both norm-kinds.

## IV What Kind of Kinds Are Art Works?

Having suggested that art works are kinds, we must now take the next step of considering which kind a given art work is to be identified with. For the sake of convenience, I shall conduct the discussion by referring exclusively to music. But I shall have an eye throughout on the application to artworks generally.

In performing a musical work, one produces an occurrence of a certain sound-sequence, the sound-sequence itself being capable of multiple occurrences. Accordingly, that particular kind which is some musical work has as its examples various occurrences of sound-sequences. It is a kind whose examples are sound-sequence-occurrences.

But now more specifically, with which of those many kinds whose examples are sound-sequence-occurrences is a given musical work to be identified? An answer which comes immediately to mind is this:

(1) A musical work *W* is identical with that kind whose examples are occurrences of that sound-sequence which correct performances of *W* are occurrences.[2]

About this it must be said, however, that for most if not all musical works there is no such sound-sequence. This is so, for one reason, because standards of correctness by no means wholly determine which sound-sequence must occur if *W* is to be performed correctly. Performances of a given work can all be correct in every detail—yet differ significantly. The musical works which come closest to permitting no divergence among their correct performances are those 'totally serialized' works of the last quarter century. Yet even these permit some divergence.

So (1) must be discarded. And the revised suggestion we should consider is this:

> (2) A musical work $W$ is identical with that kind whose examples are occurrences of members of that set of sound-sequences which correct performances of $W$ are occurrences of.

But this suggestion, though it is better than (1), is also not satisfactory. On this view, an incorrect performance of some work $W$ would not be an example thereof. Yet an incorrect performance of some work is, in spite of its incorrectness, a performance thereof. And is it not on that account an example of the work? Are not all performances of $W$ to be counted among the examples of the kind with which $W$ is identical?

So (2) must be revised by dropping the reference to *correct* performance, this:

> (3) A musical work $W$ is identical with that kind whose examples are occurrences of members of that set of sound-sequences which performances of $W$ are occurrences of.[3]

But now we must in turn raise a question concerning the satisfactoriness of (3), a question which plunges us into a whole nest of subtle matters. In performing a musical work one produces an occurrence of a certain sound-sequence. It is clear, however, that that very same sound-sequence can in principle occur in other ways than by way of someone performing that work—or indeed, *any* work. It can be made to occur, for example, by the blowing of the wind, or by someone's doodling on a piano, or by an electronic organ's going berserk. Performing is one way of producing occurrences of sound-sequences. But the very same sound-sequence which can be produced by the activity of performing can be produced in other ways as well. So a performance is not merely an occurrence of a certain sound-sequence. It is an occurrence produced by the activity of performing.

The question to consider now is whether a musical work is just a certain kind of sound-sequence-occurrence, no matter how produced, or whether a musical work is a certain kind of performance. Is (3) the formula we want, or the following:

> (4) A musical work $W$ is identical with that kind whose examples are performances of $W$ (or, more simply stated, with the kind: Performance of $W$)?

To answer this question we shall have to look a bit into the nature of performing.

Performing is clearly an intentional act. But what is the nature of the intention involved? When someone performs Beethoven's *Opus 111,* what is it that he intends? Does he perhaps intend to follow the directions of the score in producing a sound-sequence-occurrence? Well, often he does indeed have this intent. But even success in this intent is seldom a sufficient condition for having performed the work. For though scores do, among their other functions, provide specifications for producing examples of the work, seldom are all the matters pertaining to correct performance specified in a score. Naturally, many are simply presupposed by the composer as part of the style and tradition in which he is working, and others are suggested without ever being specified. If the performer limits himself to following the specifications in the score, not even attempting in other respects to produce a correct example of the work, it is at the very least doubtful that he has performed the work.

An even more decisive objection is that one can perform some work without at all intending to follow the specifications of the score for the work. For there may be no score. If Beethoven had composed his *Opus 111* before scoring it, it would have been possible for him to perform the work without being guided by the score for that or any other work. That is, it would have been possible for him not merely to produce an occurrence of a sound-sequence which could also occur as a performance of *Opus 111,* but actually to perform the work. In fact, of course, there now is a score for *Opus 111.* But the vast bulk of indigenous folk music remains unscored. So in that case performers are never guided by the scores for the works. Yet those works can be performed.

It is true that specifications can be laid down to performers by means other than scores. The folk-music performer can be told verbally how some passage is to be performed. Or the rhythm can be stomped out for him by foot. But quite clearly it is no significant improvement over our first thought to say that the intention involved in performing a work is the intention to follow the specifications for producing examples of that work. For of most works it is true that even when we include *all* specifications, whether expressed in score notation or otherwise, these specifications are woefully insufficient for determining correct examples. Bartok, in his early career, set about scoring various Hungarian folk songs. His work did not consist of taking specifications which were expressed in something other than the Western scoring system and expressing them in score notation. On the contrary, his work consisted of providing those works, for the first time in their careers, with specifications for performance. And by and large our Western scores contain all the specifications we have for our musical works. But these are not enough. Correct performance requires knowledge of more matters than these.[4]

What emerges from all this is that to perform a work one must have knowledge of what is required for a correct example of the work; and one must then try to act on such knowledge in producing an occurrence of a sound-sequence. It is the producer's acting on his knowledge of the requirements that makes of some sound-sequence-occurrences a performance of the work, instead of merely an occurrence of a sound-sequence that *might also* have occurred in a performance of the work. Such knowledge may be gained in many ways—for example, from scores or other specifications. But seldom will it be gained wholly from specifications which have been expressed. And sometimes it may not be gained from these at all.

It is not necessary, though, if one is to perform a work, that one *succeed* in one's attempt to act on one's knowledge of what is required of a sound-sequence-occurrence if it is to be a correct example of the work. Even if one makes mistakes and so does not actually produce a correct example, still one may have performed the work. Of course there are limits, albeit rather indefinite ones, on how seriously one can fail and still have performed the work.

So my suggestion concerning the nature of performing is this: To perform a musical work $W$ is to aim to produce a sound-sequence-occurrence in accord with one's knowledge of what is required of something if it is to be a correct example of $W$, and to succeed at least to the extent of producing an eample of $W$.[5]

An implication of this understanding of the nature of performing is that when a performer deliberately departs from the requirements for a correct performance of some work $W$, he is then not performing $W$. Sometimes such departures are motivated by the performer's inability to negotiate some passage. In other cases they are motivated by the performer's belief that he can thereby produce an aesthetically better performance. But whatever the motive, if Anthony Newman, say, deliberately departs from what is necessary for a correct example of Bach's *Prelude and Fugue in D minor,* then (strictly speaking) he is not performing that work. He is probably instead performing Newman's variation on Bach's *Prelude and Fugue in D minor.*

We have been discussing at some length the concept of *performing.* It is time now to return to the question which led us into this discussion, namely, which is the correct view as to the nature of the musical work, (3) or (4)? Is a musical work just a certain kind of sound-sequence-occurrence, or is it a certain kind of performance?

What is worth noticing first is that on both (3) and (4), art works can be viewed as norm-kinds. That is evident in (4), but probably not so on (3). For on (3), $W$ is just a kind whose examples are the occurrences of a certain set of sound-sequences. And sound-sequence-occurrences just are or are not occurrences of that sequence of which they are occurrences. It makes no sense to speak of some as correct occurrences thereof and some as incorrect occurrences. However, there seems to be nothing against thinking of certain of the 'member' sound-sequences as correct ones, and the rest as incorrect ones. Then correct examples of the work will be those which are occurrences of the former; incorrect examples will be those which are occurrences of the latter. Thus, the fact that art works are norm-kinds is as compatible with (3) as with (4).

What is also worth noting is that on both (3) and (4) those properties which a work has by virtue of what counts as correctness in examples belong to it essentially. A work which has a G natural in its seventh measure cannot fail to have had a G natural there, on pain of not being that work.

But in addition to the similarities, there are significant differences between the kinds which (3) proposes to identify with art works and those which (4) proposes to identify with them. So let us contrast some of the implications of each of these views. If (3) were true, then one would have to distinguish between examples and performances of works. As a matter of contingent fact, it might be that only performances of $W$ were examples of $W$. But there would be no necessity in this. And as a corollary, on (3) one could hear Bartok's *Second Sonata* without anyone performing it. For, presumably, by hearing an example of the work one can hear the work; and on (3) a work can have nonperformance examples. Also, on (3) one could hear a work $W$ without hearing a performance of $W$, by hearing a performance (correct or incorrect) of a distinct work $W'$. Further, one could hear several different musical works by listening to a performance of just one work. On (4), however, none of these results obtain.

Furthermore, if (3) were true, it would be possible for $W$ to have among its examples sound-occurrences which are also examples of $W'$. For a sound-sequence which could occur as a correct (or indeed incorrect) performance of $W$ might also occur as an incorrect performance of $W'$. One's first inclination is to say that on this point too, (3) and (4) differ. On (4), it would seem, distinct works cannot share any examples. But in fact this is false. On either view, musical works $W$ and $W'$ are identical if and only if whatever is necessary for something to be a correct example of $W$ is also necessary for something to be a correct example of $W'$, and vice versa. And on either view, something is a performance of a work $W$ only if its production is guided by $W$'s requirements for correct examples. But it seems clear that a given performance can be a performance of two distinct works;

and so also it seems clear that the production of a given performance can be guided by the requirements for correct examples of two works at once. This can happen in two sorts of ways. If works $W$ and $W'$ are related in such a way that whatever $W$ requires for correct performance $W'$ also does, but not vice versa (there being matters which $W$ settles in terms of correctness but which $W'$ leaves optional), then, though $W$ and $W'$ are distinct works, whatever is a performance of $W$ will also be one of $W'$. But even when works do not 'overlap' in this way, a group of performers, or even a single performer, can perform two works at once. This indeed is required by some of the works of Charles Ives. To perform them, hymns, folk songs, and patriotic songs must all be performed concurrently. Thus, on (4) as well as on (3), distinct works can share some, and even all, examples. However, on (4) the only cases of shared examples between two works $W$ and $W'$ will be those in which a performance is guided both by the criteria for correct examples of $W$ and by those for correct examples of $W'$. And this limitation does not hold on (3).

But though there are a number of significant differences between the conception of a musical work offered us by (3) and that offered us by (4), none of the differences thus far pointed out seem to provide a solid reason for preferring either of (3) or (4) to the other. On some issues, (3) may give us a more 'natural' understanding; on others, (4). But on none of these issues does either seem to give us a clearly mistaken understanding. And though the implications of the two views diverge on more issues than we have cited. I do not think that these other divergent implications yield any more decisive reason for preferring one view to the other. Though the kinds with which each view proposes to identify a given musical work both exist and are definitely distinct from each other, yet it is simply not clear which of these different kinds is identical with the work. The situation seems to be that when we refer to and speak of what we regard as art works, we, in all likelihood, do not with definiteness mean to pick out entities of either sort as opposed to those of the other. For on most matters entities of these two sorts do not differ. And the matters where they do differ are so far off on the edge of our normal concern in the arts that we have never had to make up our minds as to which of these sorts of entities we intend to be dealing with.

It is possible, of course, that future developments in the arts will force us to make up our minds. And perhaps those developments are already upon us. For example, John Cage's work *4 feet 33 inches* requires no particular sorts of sounds, or sound-sequences whatsoever. There are requirements for a correct performance of the work; namely that the pianist keep his hands poised above a piano keyboard for 4 minutes and 33 seconds. And there are sounds to be listened to, namely, the sounds produced by the audience as they gradually realize what is being perpetrated. But the requirements include no specifications concerning sounds whatsoever. Thus, it is obvious that (3) simply lacks application to this case. (4), though, is still relevant. And if works such as this are eventually regarded as works of music, a decisive shift away from (3) toward (4) will have occurred.[6]

### V What Is It to Compose?

On either of the two views we have been considering, a composer of a musical work can be thought of as one who determines what constitutes correctness of performances of the work. And such determination of correctness has in turn two phases. The composer must think of, or consider, the correctness-conditions in question. And in addition, since in the course of composing a work he normally considers a great many more such than he actually settles on, he must certify these as those he wants. This much is essential to being a composer.

But normally a composer does more than determine what constitutes correctness of performance. Normally he also produces a score. Now, as we remarked earlier, a typical function of a score is to provide specifications for producing (correct) examples of the work associated with the score. Yet it does seem possible for a composer to determine a set of correctness-conditions which he knows to be impossible of being followed by any present performers on any extant or anticipated instruments. And it does seem possible for the composer to score such a work. Of course, he would not expect to hear it, and neither would he think of his score as providing specifications for performances. The score would just be the composer's *record* of his determination. It seems in fact that this is what every score is. Most scores function and are meant to function to guide performances. But what is true of every score is that it is a record of the artist's determination of correctness-conditions. If the record is in addition publicly legible, then it can also serve to communicate to others a knowledge of the conditions, and thus of the work. Musical afficionados can then become acquainted with the work by reading the score, and some may even thereby get some enjoyment from it.

Typically, then, there are at least these two activities involved in composing a work of music: The artist determines what constitutes correctness of performance, and he makes a record of his determination. Normally, of course, these two activities do not take place in neat separation. But sometimes they do. Mozart said that he imagined whole symphonies in his head. Housman said that he imagined poems while shaving. And concerning such cases, a question to consider is whether thereby an art work has been composed. Can one compose "in one's head"? Well, one can determine correctness-conditions in one's head, but one cannot in one's head *record* the determination. Thus, depending on whether one regards recording one's determination as necessary for composing a musical or literary work, different answers will be given.

A consequence of what we have been saying is that two people can compose the same work. For surely it is possible for two people to determine and record the same correctness-conditions. Thus, Beethoven's *Opus 111* is not necessarily just an opus of Beethoven. Indeed, it is not necessarily an opus of Beethoven at all. So also, the same musical work can in principle be known and performed in two different and independent cultures.

Does the artist, by composing his musical work, thereby also *create* it? That is, does he bring it into existence? If (4) is the correct theory as to the nature of the musical work, so that a musical work is a performance-kind, then it certainly seems plausible to hold that he does, at least if composing is understood as consisting just in the determination of correctness-conditions. For on (4) there can be no examples of a work which are not performances thereof. And to perform the work, one must know what is required of something if it is to be a correct example. But no one can know what these correctness-conditions are until they have been determined by someone or other. And for someone to determine the correctness-conditions is just to compose the work. On the other hand, composing the work would seem sufficient for bringing it into existence. Certainly it does not seem necessary that it also be performed. For there seems nothing contradictory in the notion of unperformed musical works.

But if (3) is the correct theory as to the nature of a musical work, it is not plausible to hold that in composing one creates. For on (3) a work may have examples which are not performances. And so there is nothing to prevent its having examples before performances have been made possible by the determination of correctness-conditions. But, surely, if there are examples of a work at a given time, then the work exists at that time. Thus, if (3) is correct, composing a work cannot in general be viewed as bringing it into existence.

But what, then, on (3), are the existence criteria for musical works? One possible view is that there exists such a work as $W$ at time $t$ if and only if $W$ is being exemplified at $t$. But this view has the implausible consequence that musical works not only come into existence and go out, but that most of them exist intermittently. For on this view, the work exists when and only when it is being exemplified. And rare is the musical work which has no pair of exemplifications such that there is some time, between the occurrence of members of the pair, when the work is not being exemplified.

An alternative view would be that there exists such a work as *W* if and only if *W* is being exemplified or has been exemplified. But this view has the consequence that there cannot be a musical work which has not been exemplified. In fact, however, the contemporary literature concerning music is filled with the laments of composers whose works go unexemplified.

So perhaps the best view is that a musical work *W* exists just in case it is *possible* that there be an exemplification of *W*. For this view has none of the untoward consequences of the other views. On this view, it would not be possible for a work to be composed but not exist; on this view, a work would not cease to exist when all exemplifications ceased; and on this view, there could be unexemplified works.

It should be noticed, though, that on this view musical works exist everlastingly. For if it is ever possible that there be something which is an example of *Opus 111,* then it is always possible. Neither by composing nor by any other activity on his part does a composer bring his work into existence. Rather, if (3) is correct, the composer should be thought of as a selector rather than as a creator. To compose would be to select a certain kind of sound-occurrence. The only thing a composer would normally bring into existence would be a token (copy) of his score. Creation would be confined to token creation. Furthermore, since the selection of the work occurs in the process of determining its correctness-conditions, such determination would have to be viewed as consisting in *discovering* the conditions. By contrast, on the view that the artist brings his work into existence by composing it, determination of the conditions for correctness can best be thought of as consisting in *devising* the conditions.

It must be admitted that there is something odd in thinking of musical works as existing everlastingly, waiting to be selected and recorded. But perhaps the correct view is that though the entity which is a musical work *exists* everlastingly, it is not a *musical work* until some composer does something to it. If so, then in answer to the question, "What must be done to a kind in order to make it a musical work?" one can take one's stand at at least two different points. One can hold that it is not a musical work until someone has determined its correctness-conditions, or one can hold that it is not a musical work until its correctness-conditions have been recorded as well as determined.

## VI How to Tell Correctness

Our discussion concerning the ontological status of art works has concentrated on music. The detailed application to the other arts of the points we have made can be left to the reader. But two final matters must be considered. One is this: Why can paintings and sculptures not be viewed as single-exampled kinds rather than as physical objects, thereby giving us a "unified theory" of art works? P. F. Strawson, after saying that "in a certain sense, paintings and works of sculpture" are types, adds this footnote:

> The mention of paintings and works of sculpture may seem absurd. Are they not particulars? But this is a superficial point. The things the dealers buy and sell are particulars. But it is only because of the empirical deficiencies of reproductive techniques that we identify these with the works of art. Were it not for these deficiencies, the original of a painting would have only the interest which belongs to the original manuscript of a poem. Different people could look at exactly the same painting in different places at the same time, just as different people can listen to exactly the same quartet at different times in the same place ([6]:231.)

The situation is not quite as Strawson represents it, however. Of course there is nothing impossible in a certain object-work's having but one object. But object-works are norm-kinds, and being such they have associated with them certain requirements for something's being a correct example of the work. What is different in the case of paintings is that there are no such associated requirements. There simply are no requirements for something's being a correct example of some kind of which *The Odalesque* is the premier example. Of course, one can pick out things which to a certain close degree *resemble* this painting. There is a kind corresponding to them, and the painting is an example of it. But this is not a norm-kind, and none of our names of paintings are names of such entities.

Secondly, a question which has been pressing for a long time is this: How do we tell what constitutes a correct example of some art work? By now, however, the question has almost answered itself. In the case of works produced by some artist, the answer is that we try to discover the relevant features of that artifact which the artist produced (or which he arranged to have produced) as a record of his selection and as a guide or production-item for the making of examples. Of course, we will often discover that we cannot find out with any surety what the relevant features of that artifact were (are). We may no longer have the poet's original copy of the poem nor any very reliable evidence as to what it was like in crucial respects. Or we may have several copies from the poet's hand and not know which he authenticated. Or we may have an original authenticated copy but it may contain mistakes made by the poet, and we may find it impossible to determine which of various possibilities he had in mind. Or we may have an original, authenticated, and correct copy, but we may no longer know how to interpret all the symbols. In all such cases and many others we simply have to acknowledge that we are to some extent uncertain as to what constitutes a correct example. To that extent, we are also uncertain as to the character of the work. Yet it is clear what we must look for: the features of that original artifact.

In the case of those art works sustained in the memory of a culture and for which there is no artifact functioning as guide or production-item, we simply have to find out what the culture would regard as a correct and what it would regard as an incorrect example of the work—which is the same as finding out what the culture takes the art work to be like in those respects.[7]

## References

[1] Collingwood, R. G., *The Principles of Art* (Oxford: Oxford University Press, 1938).

[2] Harrison, Andrew, "Works of Art and Other Cultural Objects," *Proceedings of the Aristotelian Society* XVIII (1967–1968), 105–128.

[3] MacDonald, Margaret, "Art and Imagination," *Proceedings of the Aristotelian Society* LIII (1952–1953), 205–226.

[4] Margolis, Joseph, *The Language of Art and Art Criticism* (Detroit: Wayne State University Press, 1965).

[5] Stevenson, C. L., "On 'What Is a Poem?'" *Philosophical Review* LXVI (1957): 329–362.

[6] Strawson, P. F., *Individuals* (London: Methuen, 1959).

[7] Wellek, R., and A. Warren, *Theory of Literature* (New York: Harcourt, Brace and World, 1956).

[8] Wollheim, Richard, *Art and Its Objects* (New York: Harper and Row, 1968).

[9] Wolterstorff, Nicholas, *On Universals* (Chicago: University of Chicago Press, 1970).

## Notes

1. The general drift of the distinctions made above has been acquiring something of a consensus in recent years among those who have concerned themselves with the nature of works of art. See Harrison [2], MacDonald [3], Margolis [4], Stevenson [5], Wellek and Warren [7], and Wollheim [8].

2. The circular reference to $W$, in (1) and all that follows, is harmless. For we are not discussing how to identify (pick out) art works. Instead, assuming that we are acquainted with art works and that we can identify them, we are discussing their ontological status. Also, this formula and the following ones are not meant to be restricted to works which *actually have* examples. Strictly, it should read "whose examples are or would be occurrences," and "are or would be occurrences of."

3. A question to consider is whether or not this kind is identical with the set of those sound-sequences. Of course the *kind* in question here, a kind whose examples are certain sound-sequence-occurrences, is not identical with the *set* of those same sound-sequence-occurrences—for reasons already rehearsed. But that is not what we are considering. Rather, the question is this: Might a certain set of sound-sequences be identical with the kind whose examples are the occurrences of the members of that set?

A view concerning the nature of a work of music which has a great deal of initial plausibility is that it is a certain sound-sequence. When one notices, however, that among correct performances there is often wide variation in the sound-sequences instantiated, then it is clear that this initial view must be modified. The least modification would seem to be that a work of music is a *set* of sound-sequences, namely, that set whose members can occur as a correct performance. Now this line of thought concerning the nature of the work of music is different from the line pursued in the paper. There, the line pursued is that a work of music is a certain *kind* of sound-sequence-occurrence, rather than a certain sound-sequence or set of sound-sequences. The question posed, however, is whether these two lines of thought are incompatible.

I see no reason for thinking that they are. So far as I can see, a set of sound-sequences is identical with the kind whose examples are occurrences of the members of the set. If this is correct, then the proposal made by (3) is identical with this:

(3a)   *W* is identical with the set of those sound-sequences which performances of *W* are occurrences of.

4. Throughout, in speaking of specifications I have been thinking of specifications for *correct* performances. Possibly some of the specifications to be found in scores are not such but are instead specifications for *excellent* performances. This may be true, for example, for the registrations suggested in the scores for certain organ works. I suspect that in the case of works of folk art for which no scores exist, it is often difficult or even impossible to distinguish between what is *correct* and what is *excellent*.

5. It should be remarked that what is required of something if it is to be a correct performance of some work of music is often not just that the performance *sound* a certain way. It may be required, for example, that the sounds be produced by certain specific instruments, whether or not other instruments could make the same sounds. Is this the case for electronic music? For a correct performance of some work for magnetic tape, must the sounds be produced by playing a tape (a tape, furthermore, which is either the original or genetically derived therefrom)?

6. More than just such a shift would be involved in such a change of concept. In addition, the claim that we made in beginning this discussion, 'In performing a musical work one produces an occurrence of a certain sound-sequence', would then have become false.

7. In thinking through the issues discussed in this paper, I have received a great deal of assistance from my colleagues in the Philosophy Department at Calvin College. I have also received valuable advice from the editor of *Noûs,* from a reader for *Noûs,* and from Kendall Walton.

# 13. The Ontological Peculiarity of Works of Art

## JOSEPH MARGOLIS

In the context of discussing the nature of artistic creativity, Jack Glickman offers the intriguing comment, "Particulars are made, types created."[1] The remark is a strategic one, but it is either false or misleading; and its recovery illuminates in a most economical way some of the complexities of the creative process and of the ontology of art. Glickman offers as an instance of the distinction he has in mind, the following: "If the chef created a new soup, he created a new kind of soup, a new recipe; he may not have made the soup [that is, some particular pot of soup]."[2] *If,* by 'kind,' Glickman means to signify a universal of some sort, then, since universals are not created (or destroyed), it could not be the case that the chef "created" a new soup, a new kind of soup.[3] It must be the case that the chef, in making a particular (new) soup, created (to use Glickman's idiom) a kind of soup; otherwise, of course, that the chef created a new (kind of) soup may be evidenced by his having formulated a relevant recipe (which locution, in its own turn, shows the same ambiguity between type and token).

What is important, here, may not meet the eye at once. But if he can be said to create (to invent) a (new kind of) soup and if universals cannot be created or destroyed, then, in creating a kind of soup, a chef must be creating something other than a universal. The odd thing is that a kind of soup thus created is thought to be individuated among related creations; hence, it appears to be a particular of some sort. But it also seems to be an abstract entity if it is a particular at all. Hence, although it may be possible to admit abstract particulars in principle,[4] it is difficult to concede that what the chef created is an abstract particular *if* one may be said to have *tasted* what the chef created. The analogy with art is plain. If Picasso

From *The Journal of Aesthetics and Art Criticism,* XXXVI (1977), 45–50. Reprinted with permission of the author and *The Journal of Aesthetics and Art Criticism.*

created a new kind of painting, in painting *Les Demoiselles d'Avignon,* it would appear that he could not have done so *by using oils.*

There is only one solution *if* we mean to speak in this way. It must be possible to instantiate particulars (of a certain kind or of certain kinds) as well as to instantiate universals or properties. I suggest that the term 'type'—in all contexts in which the type/token ambiguity arises—signifies abstract particulars of a kind that can be instantiated. Let me offer a specimen instance. Printings properly pulled from Dürer's etching plate for *Melancholia I* are instances of *that* etching; but bona fide instances of *Melancholia I* need not have all their relevant properties in common, since later printings and printings that follow a touching up of the plate or printings that are themselves touched up may be genuine instances of *Melancholia I* and still differ markedly from one another—at least to the sensitive eye. Nothing, however, can instantiate a property without actually instantiating that property.[5] So to think of types as particulars (of a distinctive kind) accommodates the fact that we individuate works of art in unusual ways—performances of the same music, printings of the same etching, copies of the same novel—and that works of art may be created and destroyed. If, further, we grant that, in creating a new soup, a chef stirred the ingredients in his pot and that, in creating a new kind of painting, in painting *Les Demoiselles,* Picasso applied paint to canvas, we see that it is at least normally the case that one does not create a new kind of soup or a new kind of painting without (in Glickman's words) making a particular soup or a particular painting.

A great many questions intrude at this point. But we may bring this much at least to bear on an ingenious thesis of Glickman's. Glickman wishes to say that, though driftwood may be construed as a creation of "beach art," it remains true that driftwood was *made* by no one, is in fact a natural object, and hence that "the condition of artifactuality" so often claimed to be a necessary condition of being a work of art, is simply "superfluous."[6] "I see no conclusive conceptual block," says Glickman, "to allowing that the artwork [may] be a natural object."[7] Correspondingly, Duchamp's "ready-mades" are created out of artifacts, but the artist who created them did not actually make them. Glickman's thesis depends on the tenability of his distinction between making and creating; and as we have just seen, one does not, in the normal case at least, create a new kind of art (type) without making a particular work of that kind (that is, an instance of that particular, the type, not merely an instance of that kind, the universal). In other words, when an artist *creates* (allowing Glickman's terms) "beach art," a new kind of art, the artist *makes* a particular instance (or token) of a particular type—much as with wood sculpture, *this unique token of this driftwood composition.* He cannot create the universals that are newly instantiated since universals cannot be created. He can create a new type-particular, a particular of the kind "beach art" but he can do so only by making a token-particular of that type. What this shows is that we were unnecessarily tentative about the relation between types and tokens. We may credit an artist with having created a new type of art; but there are no types of art that are not instantiated by some token-instances or for which we lack a notation by reference to which (as in the performing arts) admissible token-instances of the particular type-work may be generated.

The reason for this strengthened conclusion has already been given. When an artist creates his work using the materials of his craft, the work he produces must have some perceptible physical properties at least; but it could not have such properties if the work were merely an abstract particular (or, of course, a universal). Hence, wherever an artist produces his work directly, even a new kind of work, he cannot be producing an abstract particular. Alternatively put, to credit an artist with having created a new *type* of art—a particular art-type—we must (normally) be thus crediting him in virtue of the particular (token) work he has made. In wood sculpture, the particular piece an artist makes is normally the unique instance of his work; in bronzes, it is more usually true that, as in Rodin's peculiarly industrious way, there are several or numerous tokens of the very same (type) sculpture. But though we may credit the artist with having created the type, the type does not exist except instantiated in its proper tokens. We may, by a kind of courtesy, say that an artist who has produced the cast for a set of bronzes has created an artwork-type; but the fact is: (i) he has *made* a particular cast, and (ii) the cast he's made is not the work *created*. Similar considerations apply to an artist's preparing a musical notation for the sonata he has created: (i) the artist makes a token instance of a type notation; and (ii) all admissible instances of his sonata are so identified by reference to the notations. The result is that, insofar as he creates a type, an artist must make a token. A chef's assistant may actually make the first pot of soup—of the soup the chef has created, but the actual soup exists only when the pot is made. Credit to the chef in virtue of his recipe is partly an assurance that his authorship is to be acknowledged in each and every pot of soup that is properly an instance of his creation, whether he makes it or not; and it is partly a device for individuating proper token instances of particular type objects. But only the token instances *of* a type actually exist and aesthetic interest in the type is given point only in virtue of one's aesthetic interest in actual or possible tokens—as in actual or contemplated performances of a particular sonata.

But if these distinctions be granted, then, normally, an artist makes a token of the type he has created. He could not create the type unless he made a proper token or, by the courtesy intended in notations and the like, he provided a schema *for* making proper tokens of a particular type. Hence, what is normally made, in the relevant sense, is a token of a type. It must be the case, then, that when Duchamp created his *Bottlerack,* although he did not make a bottlerack—that is, although he did not manufacture a bottlerack, although he did not first bring it about that an object instantiate being a bottlerack—nevertheless, *he did make a token of the Bottlerack.* Similarly, although driftwood is not a manufactured thing, when an artist creates (if an artist can create) a piece of "beach art," *he makes a token of that piece of "beach art."* He need not have made the driftwood. But that shows (i) that artifactuality is not superfluous, though it is indeed puzzling (when displaying otherwise untouched driftwood in accord with the developed sensibilities of a society can count as the creation of an art-work); and (ii) it is not the case (contrary to Glickman's claims) that a natural object can *be* a work of art or that a work can be created though *nothing* be made.

We may summarize the ontological peculiarities of the type/token distinction in the following way: (i) types and tokens are individuated as particulars; (ii) types and tokens are not separable and cannot exist separately from one another; (iii) types are instantiated by tokens and 'token' is an ellipsis for 'token-of-a-type'; (iv) types and tokens may be generated and destroyed in the sense that actual tokens of a novel type may be generated, the actual tokens of a given type may be destroyed, and whatever contingencies may be necessary to the generation of actual tokens may be destroyed or disabled; (v) types are actual abstract particulars in the sense only that a set of actual entities may be individuated as tokens of a particular type; (vi) it is incoherent to speak of comparing the properties of actual token- and type-particulars as opposed to comparing the properties of actual particular tokens-of-a-type; (vii) reference to types as particulars serves exclusively to facilitate reference to actual and possible tokens-of-a-type. These distinctions are sufficient to mark the type/token concept as different from the kind/instance concept and the set/member concept.

Here, a second ontological oddity must be conceded. The driftwood that is made by no one is not the (unique) token that is made of the "beach art" creation; and the artifact, the bottlerack, that Duchamp did not make is not identical with the (probably but not necessarily unique) token that Duchamp did make of the creation called *Bottlerack.* What Duchamp made was a token of *Bottlerack;* and what the manufacturer of bottleracks made was a particular bottlerack that served as the material out of which Duchamp created *Bottlerack* by making a (probably unique) instance of *Bottlerack.* For, consider that Duchamp made something when he created *Bottlerack* but he did not make a bottlerack; also, that no one made the driftwood though someone (on the thesis) made a particular composition of art using the driftwood. If the bottlerack were said to be identical with Duchamp's *Bottlerack* (the token or the type), we should be contradicting ourselves; the same would be true of the driftwood case. Hence, in spite of appearances, there must be an ontological difference between tokens of artwork-types and such physical objects as bottleracks and driftwood that can serve as the materials out of which they are made.

My own suggestion is that (token) works of art are *embodied* in physical objects, not identical with them. I should argue, though this is not the place for it, that persons, similarly, are embodied in physical bodies but not identical with them.[8] The idea is that not only can one particular instantiate another particular in a certain way (tokens of types) but one particular can embody or be embodied in another particular with which it is (necessarily) not identical. The important point is that identity cannot work in the anomalous cases here considered (nor in the usual cases of art) and that what would otherwise be related by way of identity are, obviously, particulars. Furthermore, the embodiment relationship does not invite dualism though it does a require a distinction among kinds of things and among the kinds of properties of things of such kinds. For example, a particular printing of Dürer's *Melancholia I* has the property of being a particular token of *Melancholia I* (the artwork type), but the physical paper and physical print do not, on any familiar view, have the property of being a token of a type. Only objects having such intentional properties as that of "being created" or, as with words, having meaning or the like can have the property of being a token of a type.[9]

What is meant in saying that one particular is embodied in another is: (i) that the two particulars are not identical; (ii) that the existence of the embodied particular presupposes the existence of the embodying particular; (iii) that the embodied particular possess some of the properties of the embodying particular; (iv) that the embodied particular possesses properties that the embodying particular does not possess; (v) that the embodied particular possesses properties of a kind that the embodying particular cannot possess; (vi) that the individuation of the embodied particular presupposes the individuation of the embodying particular. The 'is' of embodiment, then, like the 'is' of identity and the 'is' of composition[10] is a logically distinctive use. On a theory, for instance a theory about the nature of a work of art, a particular physical object will be taken to embody a particular object of another kind in such a way that a certain systematic relationship will hold between them. Thus, for instance, a sculptor will be said to make a particular sculpture by cutting a block of marble: Michelangelo's *Pietà* will exhibit certain of the physical properties of the marble and certain representational and purposive properties as well; it will also have the property of being a unique token of the creation *Pietà*. The reason for theorizing thus is, quite simply, that works of art are the products of culturally informed labor and that physical objects are not. So seen, they must possess properties that physical objects, *qua* physical objects, do not and cannot possess. Hence, an identity thesis leads to palpable contradictions. Furthermore, the conception of embodiment promises to facilitate a nonreductive account of the relationship between physical nature and human culture, without dualistic assumptions. What this suggests is that the so-called mind/body problem is essentially a special form of a more general culture/nature problem. But that is another story.

A work of art, then, is a particular. It cannot be a universal because it is created and can be destroyed; also, because it possesses physical and perceptual properties. But it is a peculiar sort of particular, unlike physical bodies, because (i) it can instantiate another particular; and (ii) it can be embodied in another particular. The suggestion here is that all and only culturally emergent or culturally produced entities exhibit these traits. So the ontological characteristics assigned are no more than the most generic characteristics of art: its distinctive nature remains unanalyzed. Nevertheless, we can discern an important difference between these two properties, as far as art is concerned. For, the first property, that of being able to instantiate another particular, has only to do with individuating works of art and whatever may, contingently, depend upon that; while the second property has to do with the ontologically dependent nature of actual works of art. This is the reason we may speak of type artworks as particulars. They are heuristically introduced for purposes of individuation, though they cannot exist except in the sense in which particular tokens of particular type artworks exist. So we can never properly *compare* the properties of a token work and a type work.[11] What we may compare are alternative tokens of the same type—different printings of the same etching or different performances of the same sonata. In short, every work of art is a token-of-a-type; there are no tokens or types *tout court*. Again, this is not to say that there are no types or that an artist cannot create a new kind of painting. It is only to say that so speaking is an ellipsis for saying that a certain set of particulars are tokens of a type and that the artist is credited with so working with the properties of things, instantiated by the members of that set, that they are construed as tokens of a particular type.

So the dependencies of the two ontological traits mentioned are quite different. There are no types that are separable from tokens because there are no tokens except tokens-of-a-type. The very process for individuating tokens entails individuating types, that is, entails individuating different sets of particulars as the alternative tokens of this or that type. There is nothing left over to discuss. What may mislead is this: the concept of different tokens of the same type is intended, in the arts, to accommodate the fact that the aesthetically often decisive differences among tokens of the same type (alternative performances of a sonata, for instance) need not matter as far as the individuation of the (type) work is concerned.[12] But particular works of art cannot exist except as embodied in physical objects. This is simply another way of saying that works of art are culturally emergent entities; that is, that works of art exhibit properties that physical objects cannot exhibit, but do so in a way that does not depend on the presence of any substance other than what may be ascribed to purely physical objects. Broadly speaking, those properties are what may be characterized as functional or intentional properties and include design, expressiveness, symbolism, representation, meaning, style, and the like. Without prejudice to the nature of either art or persons, this way of viewing art suggests a very convenient linkup with the functional theory of mental traits.[13] Be that as it may, a reasonable theory of art could hold that when physical materials are worked in accord with a certain artistic craft then there emerges, culturally, an object embodied in the former that possesses a certain orderly array of functional properties of the kind just mentioned. Any object so produced may be treated as an artifact. Hence, works of art exist as fully as physical objects but the condition on which they do so depends on the independent existence of some physical object itself. Works of art, then, are culturally emergent entities, tokens-of-a-type that exist embodied in physical objects.

## Notes

1. Jack Glickman, "Creativity in the Arts," in Lars Aagaard-Mogensen, ed., *Culture and Art* (Nyborg and Atlantic Highlands, N.J.: F. Løkkes Forlag and Humanities Press, 1976), p. 140.

2. *Loc. cit.*

3. Difficulties of this sort undermine the recent thesis of Nicholas Wolterstorff's, namely, that works of art are in fact kinds. Cf. Nicholas Wolterstorff, "Toward an Ontology of Art Works," *Nous* IX (1975), 115–142. Also, Joseph Margolis, *Art and Philosophy* (Atlantic Highlands, N.J.: Humanities Press, 1978), ch. 5.

4. Cf. Nelson Goodman, *The Structure of Appearance* (Indianapolis: Bobbs-Merrill, 2nd ed., 1966).

5. The subtleties of the type/token distinction are discussed at length in Margolis, *loc. cit.*

6. *Op. cit.,* p. 144.

7. *Ibid.,* p. 143.

8. A fuller account of the concept of embodiment with respect to art is given in *Art and Philosophy,* ch. 1. I have tried to apply the notion to all cultural

entities—that is, persons, works of art, artifacts, words and sentences, machines, institutionalized actions, and the like—in *Persons and Minds* (Dordrecht: D. Reidel, 1977). Cf. also "On the Ontology of Persons," *New Scholasticism* X (1976), 73–84.

9. This is very close in spirit to Peirce's original distinction between types and tokens. Cf. *Collected Papers of Charles Sanders Peirce,* ed. Charles Hartshorne and Paul Weiss (Cambridge: Harvard University Press, 1939), vol. 4, par. 537.

10. Cf. David Wiggins, *Identity and Spatio-Temporal Continuity* (Oxford: Basil Blackwell, 1967).

11. This is one of the signal weaknesses of Wolterstorff's account, *loc. cit.,* as well as of Richard Wollheim's account; cf. *Art and Its Objects* (New York: Harper, 1968).

12. This counts against Nelson Goodman's strictures on the individuation of artworks. Cf. *Languages of Art* (Indianapolis: Bobbs-Merrill, 1968) and Joseph Margolis, "Numerical Identity and Reference in the Arts," *British Journal of Aesthetics* X (1970), 138–146.

13. Cf. for instance Hilary Putnam, "Minds and Machines," in Sidney Hook, ed., *Dimensions of Mind* (Englewood Cliffs, N.J.: Prentice-Hall, 1960), and Jerry Fodor, *Psychological Explanation* (New York: Random House, 1968).

# 14.                     Art and Authenticity
## NELSON GOODMAN

*... the most tantalizing question of all: If a fake is so expert that even
after the most thorough and trustworthy examination its authenticity is
still open to doubt, is it or is it not as satisfactory at work of art as if it
were unequivocally genuine?* Aline B. Saarinen*

## 1 The Perfect Fake

Forgeries of works of art present a nasty practical problem to the collector,
the curator, and the art historian, who must often expend taxing amounts
of time and energy in determining whether or not particular objects are
genuine. But the theoretical problem raised is even more acute. The
hardheaded question why there is any aesthetic difference between a
deceptive forgery and an original work challenges a basic premise on which
the very functions of collector, museum, and art historian depend. A
philosopher of art caught without an answer to this question is at least as
badly off as a curator of paintings caught taking a Van Meegeren for a
Vermeer.

The question is most strikingly illustrated by the case of a given work
and a forgery or copy or reproduction of it. Suppose we have before us,
on the left, Rembrandt's original painting *Lucretia* and, on the right, a
superlative imitation of it. We know from a fully documented history that
the painting on the left is the original; and we know from X-ray
photographs and microscopic examination and chemical analysis that the
painting on the right is a recent fake. Although there are many differences

*New York Times Book Review,* July 30, 1961, p. 14.
From Nelson Goodman, *Languages of Art* (Indianapolis: Hackett Publishing Co., 1976), pp.
99–123. Reprinted with permission of the author.

between the two—e.g., in authorship, age, physical and chemical characteristics, and market value—we cannot see any difference between them; and if they are moved while we sleep, we cannot then tell which is which. by merely looking at them. Now we are pressed with the question whether there can be any aesthetic difference between the two pictures; and the questioner's tone often intimates that the answer is plainly *no,* that the only differences here are aesthetically irrelevant.

We must begin by inquiring whether the distinction between what can and what cannot be seen in the pictures by 'merely looking at them' is entirely clear. We are looking at the pictures, but presumably not 'merely looking' at them, when we examine them under a microscope or fluoroscope. Does merely looking, then, mean looking without the use of any instrument? This seems a little unfair to the man who needs glasses to tell a painting from a hippopotamus. But if glasses are permitted at all, how strong may they be, and can we consistently exclude the magnifying glass and the microscope? Again, if incandescent light is permitted, can violet-ray light be ruled out? And even with incandescent light, must it be of medium intensity and from a normal angle, or is a strong raking light permitted? All these cases might be covered by saying that 'merely looking' is looking at the pictures without any use of instruments other than those customarily used in looking at things in general. This will cause trouble when we turn, say, to certain miniature illuminations or Assyrian cylinder seals that we can hardly distinguish from the crudest copies without using a strong glass. Furthermore, even in our case of the two pictures, subtle differences of drawing or painting discoverable only with a magnifying glass may still, quite obviously, be aesthetic differences between the pictures. If a powerful microscope is used instead, this is no longer the case; but just how much magnification is permitted? To specify what is meant by merely looking at the pictures is thus far from easy; but for the sake of argument,[1] let us suppose that all these difficulties have been resolved and the notion of 'merely looking' made clear enough.

Then we must ask who is assumed to be doing the looking. Our questioner does not, I take it, mean to suggest that there is no aesthetic difference between two pictures if at least one person, say a cross-eyed wrestler, can see no difference. The more pertinent question is whether there can be any aesthetic difference if nobody, not even the most skilled expert, can ever tell the pictures apart by merely looking at them. *But notice now that no one can ever ascertain by merely looking at the pictures that no one ever has been or will be able to tell them apart by merely looking at them.* In other words, the question in its present form concedes that no one can ascertain by merely looking at the pictures that there is no aesthetic difference between them. This seems repugnant to our questioner's whole motivation. For if merely looking can never establish that two pictures are aesthetically the same, something that is beyond the reach of any given looking is admitted as constituting an aesthetic difference. And in that case, the reason for not admitting documents and the results of scientific tests becomes very obscure.

The real issue may be more accurately formulated as the question whether there is any aesthetic difference between the two pictures *for me* (or for *x*) if I (or *x*) cannot tell them apart by merely looking at them. But this is not quite right either. For I can never ascertain merely by looking at the pictures that even I shall never be able to see any difference between them. And to concede that something beyond any given looking at the pictures by me may constitute an aesthetic difference between them *for me* is, again, quite at odds with the tacit conviction or suspicion that activates the questioner.

Thus the critical question amounts finally to this: is there any aesthetic difference between the two pictures for *x* at *t,* where *t* is a suitable period of time, if *x* cannot tell them apart by merely looking at them at *t?* Or in other words, can anything that *x* does not discern by merely looking at the pictures at *t* constitute an aesthetic difference between them for *x* at *t?*

## 2 The Answer

In setting out to answer this question, we must bear clearly in mind that what one can distinguish at any given moment by merely looking depends not only upon native visual acuity but upon practice and training.[2] Americans look pretty much alike to a Chinese who has never looked at many of them. Twins may be indistinguishable to all but their closest relatives and acquaintances. Moreover, only through looking at them when someone has named them for us can we learn to tell Joe from Jim upon merely looking at them. Looking at people or things attentively, with the knowledge of certain presently invisible respects in which they differ, increases our ability to discriminate between them—and between other things or other people—upon merely looking at them. Thus pictures that look just alike to the newsboy come to look quite unlike to him by the time he has become a museum director.

Although I see no difference now between the two pictures in question, I may learn to see a difference between them. I cannot determine now by merely looking at them, or in any other way, that I *shall* be able to learn. But the information that they are very different, that the one is the original and the other the forgery, argues against any inference to the conclusion that I *shall not* be able to learn. And the fact that I may later be able to make a perceptual distinction between the pictures that I cannot make now constitutes an aesthetic difference between them that is important to me now.

Furthermore, to look at the pictures now with the knowledge that the left one is the original and the other the forgery may help develop the ability to tell which is which later by merely looking at them. Thus, with information not derived from the present or any past looking at the pictures, the present looking may have a quite different bearing upon future lookings from what it would otherwise have. The way the pictures in fact differ constitutes an aesthetic difference between them for me now because my knowledge of the way they differ bears upon the role of the present looking in training my perceptions to discriminate between these pictures, and between others.

But that is not all. My knowledge of the difference between the two pictures, just because it affects the relationship of the present to future lookings, informs the very character of my present looking. This knowledge instructs me to look at the two pictures differently now, even if what I see is the same. Beyond testifying that I may learn to see a difference, it also indicates to some extent the kind of scrutiny to be applied now, the comparisons and contrasts to be made in imagination, and the relevant associations to be brought to bear. It thereby guides the selection, from my past experience, of items and aspects for use in my present looking. Thus not only later but right now, the unperceived difference between the two pictures is a consideration pertinent to my visual experience with them.

In short, although I cannot tell the pictures apart merely by looking at them now, the fact that the left-hand one is the original and the right-hand one a forgery constitutes an aesthetic difference between them for me now because knowledge of this fact (1) stands as evidence that there may be a difference between them that I can learn to perceive, (2) assigns the present looking a role as training toward such a perceptual discrimination, and (3) makes consequent demands that modify and differentiate my present experience in looking at the two pictures.[3]

Nothing depends here upon my ever actually perceiving or being able to perceive a difference between the two pictures. What informs the nature and use of my present visual experience is not the fact or the assurance that such a perceptual discrimination is within my reach, but evidence that it may be; and such evidence is provided by the known factual differences between the pictures. Thus the pictures differ aesthetically for me now even if no one will ever be able to tell them apart merely by looking at them.

But suppose it could be *proved* that no one ever will be able to see any difference? This is about as reasonable as asking whether, if it can be proved that the market value and yield of a given U.S. bond and one of a certain nearly bankrupt company will always be the same, there is any financial difference between the two bonds. For what sort of proof could be given? One might suppose that if nobody—not even the most skilled expert—has ever been able to see any difference between the pictures, then the conclusion that I shall never be able to is quite safe; but, as in the case of the Van Meegeren forgeries[4] (of which, more later), distinctions not visible to the expert up to a given time may later become manifest even to the observant layman. Or one might think of some delicate scanning device that compares the color of two pictures at every point and registers the slightest discrepancy. What, though, is meant here by "at every point"? At no mathematical point, of course, is there any color at all; and even some physical particles are too small to have color. The scanning device must thus cover at each instant a region big enough to have color but at least as small as any perceptible region. Just how to manage this is puzzling since "perceptible" in the present context means "discernible by merely looking," and thus the line between perceptible and nonperceptible regions seems to depend on the arbitrary line between a magnifying glass and a microscope. If some such line is drawn, we can never be sure that the delicacy of our instruments is superior to the maximal attainable acuity of unaided perception. Indeed, some experimental psychologists are inclined to conclude that every measurable difference in light can sometimes be detected by the naked eye.[5] And there is a further difficulty. Our scanning device will examine color—that is, reflected light. Since reflected light depends partly upon incident light, illumination of every quality, of every intensity, and from every direction must be tried. And for each case, especially since the paintings do not have a plane surface, a complete scanning must be made from every angle. But of course we cannot cover every variation, or even determine a single absolute correspondence, in even one respect. Thus the search for a proof that I shall never be able to see any difference between the two pictures is futile for more than technological reasons.

Yet suppose we are nevertheless pressed with the question whether, if proof *were* given, there would then be any aesthetic difference for me between the pictures. And suppose we answer this farfetched question in the negative. This will still give our questioner no comfort. For the net result would be that if no difference between the pictures can in fact be perceived, then the existence of an aesthetic difference between them will rest entirely upon what is or is not proved by means other than merely looking at them. This hardly supports the contention that there can be no aesthetic differences without a perceptual difference.

Returning from the realm of the ultra-hypothetical, we may be faced with the protest that the vast aesthetic difference thought to obtain between the Rembrandt and the forgery cannot be accounted for in terms of the search for, or even the discovery of, perceptual differences so slight that they can be made out, if at all, only after much experience and long practice. This objection can be dismissed at once; for minute perceptual differences can bear enormous weight. The clues that tell me whether I have caught the eye of someone across the room are almost indiscernible. The actual differences in sound that distinguish a fine from a mediocre performance can be picked out only by the well-trained ear. Extremely subtle changes can alter the whole design, feeling, or expression of a painting. Indeed, the slightest perceptual differences sometimes matter the most aesthetically; gross physical damage to a fresco may be less consequential than slight but smug retouching.

All I have attempted to show, of course, is that the two pictures can differ aesthetically, not that the original is better than the forgery. In our example, the original probably is much the better picture, since Rembrandt paintings are in general much better than copies by unknown painters. But a copy of a Lastman by Rembrandt may well be better than the original. We are not called upon here to make such particular comparative judgments or to formulate canons of aesthetic evaluation. We have fully met the demands of our problem by showing that the fact that we cannot tell our two pictures apart merely by looking at them does not imply that they are aesthetically the same—and thus does not force us to conclude that the forgery is as good as the original.

The example we have been using throughout illustrates a special case of a more general question concerning the aesthetic significance of authenticity. Quite aside from the occurrence of forged duplication, does it matter whether an original work is the product of one or another artist or school or period? Suppose that I can easily tell two pictures apart but cannot tell who painted either except by using some devices like X-ray photography. Does the fact that the picture is or is not by Rembrandt make any aesthetic difference? What is involved here is the discrimination not of one picture from another but of the class of Rembrandt paintings from the class of other paintings. My chance of learning to make this discrimination correctly—of discovering projectible characteristics that differentiate Rembrandts in general from non-Rembrandts—depends heavily upon the set of examples available as a basis. Thus the fact that the given picture belongs to the one class or the other is important for me to know in learning how to tell Rembrandt paintings from others. In other words, my present (or future) inability to determine the authorship of the given picture without use of scientific apparatus does not imply that the authorship makes no aesthetic difference to me; for knowledge of the authorship, no matter how obtained, can contribute materially toward developing my ability to determine without such apparatus whether or not any picture, including this one on another occasion, is by Rembrandt.

Incidentally, one rather striking puzzle is readily solved in these terms. When Van Meegeren sold his pictures as Vermeers, he deceived most of the best-qualified experts; and only by his confession was the fraud revealed.[9] Nowadays even the fairly knowing layman is astonished that any competent judge could have taken a Van Meegeren for a Vermeer, so obvious are the differences. What has happened? The general level of aesthetic sensibility has hardly risen so fast that the layman of today sees more acutely than the expert of twenty years ago. Rather, the better information now at hand makes the discrimination easier. Presented with a single unfamiliar picture at a time, the expert had to decide whether it was enough like known Vermeers to be by the same artist. And every time a Van Meegeren was added to the corpus of pictures accepted as Vermeers, the criteria for acceptance were modified thereby; and the mistaking of further Van Meegerens for Vermeers became inevitable. Now, however, not only have the Van Meegerens been subtracted from the precedent-class for Vermeer, but also a precedent-class for Van Meegeren has been established. With these two precedent-classes before us, the characteristic differences become so conspicuous that telling other Van Meegerens from Vermeers offers little difficulty. Yesterday's expert might well have avoided his errors if he had had a few known Van Meegerens handy for comparison. And today's layman who so cleverly spots a Van Meegeren may well be caught taking some quite inferior school-piece for a Vermeer.

In answering the questions raised above, I have not attempted the formidable task of defining "aesthetic" in general,[7] but have simply argued that since the exercise, training, and development of our powers of discriminating among works of art are plainly aesthetic activities, the aesthetic properties of a picture include not only those found by looking at it but also those that determine how it is to be looked at. This rather obvious fact would hardly have needed underlining but for the prevalence of the time-honored Tingle-Immersion theory,[8] which tells us that the proper behavior on encountering a work of art is to strip ourselves of all the vestments of knowledge and experience (since they might blunt the immediacy of our enjoyment), then submerge ourselves completely and gauge the aesthetic potency of the work by the intensity and duration of the resulting tingle. The theory is absurd on the face of it and useless for dealing with any of the important problems of aesthetics; but it has become part of the fabric of our common nonsense.

### 3 The Unfakable

A second problem concerning authenticity is raised by the rather curious fact that in music, unlike painting, there is no such thing as a forgery of a known work. There are, indeed, compositions falsely purporting to be by Haydn as there are paintings falsely purporting to be by Rembrandt; but of the *London Symphony,* unlike the *Lucretia,* there can be no forgeries. Haydn's manuscript is no more genuine an instance of the score than is a printed copy off the press this morning, and last night's performance no less genuine than the premiere. Copies of the score may vary in accuracy, but all accurate copies, even if forgeries of Haydn's manuscript, are equally genuine instances of the score. Performances may vary in correctness and quality and even in 'authenticity' of a more esoteric kind; but all correct performances are equally genuine instances of the work.[9] In contrast, even the most exact copies of the Rembrandt painting are simply imitations or forgeries, not new instances, of the work. Why this difference between the two arts?

Let us speak of a work of art as *autographic* if and only if the distinction between original and forgery of it is significant; or better, if and only if even the most exact duplication of it does not thereby count as genuine.[10] If a work of art is autographic, we may also call that art autographic. Thus painting is autographic, music nonautographic, or *allographic*. These terms are introduced purely for convenience; nothing is implied concerning the relative individuality of expression demanded by or attainable in these arts. Now the problem before us is to account for the fact that some arts but not others are autographic.

One notable difference between painting and music is that the composer's work is done when he has written the score, even though the performances are the end products, while the painter has to finish the picture. No matter how many studies or revisions are made in either case, painting is in this sense a one-stage and music a two-stage art. Is an art autographic, then, if and only if it is one-stage? Counterexamples come readily to mind. In the first place, literature is not autographic though it is one-stage. There is no such thing as a forgery of Gray's *Elegy.* Any accurate copy of the text of a poem or novel is as much the original work as any other. Yet what the writer produces is ultimate; the text is not merely a means to oral readings as a score is a means to performances in music. An unrecited poem is not so forlorn as an unsung song; and most literary works are never read aloud at all. We might try to make literature into a two-stage art by considering the silent readings to be the end products, or the instances of a work; but then the lookings at a picture and the listenings to a performance would qualify equally as end products or instances, so that painting as well as literature would be two-stage and music three-stage. In the second place, printmaking is two-stage and yet autographic. The etcher, for example, makes a plate from which impressions are than taken on paper. These prints are the end products; and although they may differ appreciably from one another, all are instances of the original work. But even the most exact copy produced otherwise than by printing from that plate counts not as an original but as an imitation or forgery.

So far, our results are negative: not all one-stage arts are autographic and not all autographic arts are one-stage. Furthermore, the example of printmaking refutes the unwary assumption that in every autographic art a particular work exists only as a unique object. The line between an autographic and an allographic art does not coincide with that between a singular and a multiple art. About the only positive conclusion we can draw here is that the autographic arts are those that are singular in the earliest stage; etching is singular in its first stage—the plate is unique—and painting in its only stage. But this hardly helps; for the problem of explaining why some arts are singular is much like the problem of explaining why they are autographic.

## 4 The Reason

Why, then, can I no more make a forgery of Haydn's symphony or of Gray's poem that I can make an original of Rembrandt's painting or of his etching *Tobit Blind?* Let us suppose that there are various handwritten copies and many editions of a given literary work. Differences between them in style and size of script or type, in color of ink, in kind of paper, in number and layout of pages, in condition, etc., do not matter. All that matters is what may be called *sameness of spelling:* exact correspondence as sequences of letters, spaces, and punctuation marks. Any sequence—even a forgery of the author's manuscript or of a given edition—that so corresponds to a correct copy is itself correct, and nothing is more the original work than is such a correct copy. And since whatever is not an original of the work must fail to meet such an explicit standard of correctness, there can be no deceptive imitation, no forgery, of that work. To verify the spelling or to spell correctly is all that is required to identify an instance of the work or to produce a new instance. In effect, the fact that a literary work is in a definite notation, consisting of certain signs or characters that are to be combined by concatenation, provides the means for distinguishing the properties constitutive of the work from all contingent properties—that is, for fixing the required features and the limits of permissible variation in each. Merely by determining that the copy before us is spelled correctly we can determine that it meets all requirements for the work in question. In painting, on the contrary, with no such alphabet of characters, none of the pictorial properties—none of the properties the picture has as such—is distinguished as constitutive; no such feature can be dismissed as contingent, and no deviation as insignificant. The only way of ascertaining that the *Lucretia* before us is genuine is thus to establish the historical fact that it is the actual object made by Rembrandt. Accordingly, physical identification of the product of the artist's hand, and consequently the conception of forgery of a particular work, assume a significance in painting that they do not have in literature.[11]

What has been said of literary texts obviously applies also to musical scores. The alphabet is different; and the characters in a score, rather than being strung one after the other as in a text, are disposed in a more complex array. Nevertheless, we have a limited set of characters and of positions for them; and correct spelling, in only a slightly expanded sense, is still the sole requirement for a genuine instance of a work. Any false copy is wrongly spelled—has somewhere in place of the right character either another character or an illegible mark that is not a character of the notation in question at all.

But what of performances of music? Music is not autographic in this second stage either, yet a performance by no means consists of characters from an alphabet. Rather, the constitutive properties demanded of a performance of the symphony are those *prescribed in* the score; and performances that comply with the score may differ appreciably in such musical features as tempo, timbre, phrasing, and expressiveness. To determine compliance requires, indeed, something more than merely knowing the alphabet; it requires the ability to correlate appropriate sounds with the visible signs in the score—to recognize, so to speak, correct pronunciation though without necessarily understanding what is pronounced. The competence required to identify or produce sounds called for by a score increases with the complexity of the composition, but there is nevertheless a theoretically decisive test for compliance; and a performance, whatever its interpretative fidelity and independent merit, has or has not all the constitutive properties of a given work, and is or is not strictly a performance of that work, according as it does or does not pass this test. No historical information concerning the production of the performance can affect the result. Hence deception as to the facts of production is irrelevant, and the notion of a performance that is a forgery of the work is quite empty.

Yet there are forgeries of performances as there are of manuscripts and editions. What makes a performance an instance of a given work is not the same as what makes a performance a premiere, or played by a certain musician or upon a Stradivarius violin. Whether a performance has these latter properties is a matter of historical fact; and a performance falsely purporting to have any such property counts as a forgery, not of the musical composition but of a given performance or class of performances.

The comparison between printmaking and music is especially telling. We have already noted that etching, for example, is like music in having two stages and in being multiple in its second stage; but that whereas music is autographic in neither stage, printmaking is autographic in both. Now the situation with respect to the etched plate is clearly the same as with respect to a painting: assurance of genuineness can come only from identification of the actual object produced by the artist. But since the several prints from this plate are all genuine instances of the work, however much they differ in color and amount of ink, quality of impression, kind of paper, etc., one might expect here a full parallel between prints and musical performances. Yet there can be prints that are forgeries of the *Tobit Blind* but not performances that are forgeries of the *London Symphony*. The differences is that in the absence of a notation, not only is there no test of correctness of spelling for a plate but there is no test of compliance with a plate for a print. Comparison of a print with a plate, as of two plates, is no more conclusive than is comparison of two pictures. Minute discrepancies may always go unnoticed; and there is no basis for ruling out any of them as inessential. The only way of ascertaining whether a print is genuine is by finding out whether it was taken from a certain plate.[12] A print falsely purporting to have been so produced is in the full sense a forgery of the work.

Here, as earlier, we must be careful not to confuse genuineness with aesthetic merit. That the distinction between original and forgery is aesthetically important does not, we have seen, imply that the original is superior to the forgery. An original painting may be less rewarding than an inspired copy; a damaged original may have lost most of its former merit; an impression from a badly worn plate may be aesthetically much further removed from an early impression than is a good photographic reproduction. Likewise, an incorrect performance, though therefore not strictly an instance of a given quartet at all, may nevertheless—either because the changes improve what the composer wrote or because of sensitive interpretation—be better than a correct performance.[13] Again, several correct performances of about equal merit may exhibit very different specific aesthetic qualities—power, delicacy, tautness, stodginess, incoherence, etc. Thus even where the constitutive properties of a work are clearly distinguished by means of a notation, they cannot be identified with the aesthetic properties.

Among other arts, sculpture is autographic; cast sculpture is comparable to printmaking while carved sculpture is comparable to painting. Architecture and the drama, on the other hand, are more nearly comparable to music. Any building that conforms to the plans and specifications, any performance of the text of a play in accordance with the stage directions, is as original an instance of the work as any other. But architecture seems to differ from music in that testing for compliance of a building with the specifications requires not that these be pronounced, or transcribed into sound, but that their application be understood. This is true also for the stage directions, as contrasted with the dialogue, of a play. Does this make architecture and the drama less purely allographic arts? Again, an architect's plans seem a good deal like a painter's sketches; and painting is an autographic art. On what grounds can we say that in the one case but not the other a veritable notation is involved? Such questions cannot be answered until we have carried through some rather painstaking analysis.

Since an art seems to be allographic just insofar as it is amenable to notation, the case of the dance is especially interesting. Here we have an art without a traditional notation; and an art where the ways, and even the possibility, of developing an adequate notation are still matters of controversy. Is the search for a notation reasonable in the case of the dance but not in the case of painting? Or, more generally, why is the use of notation appropriate in some arts but not in others? Very briefly and roughly, the answer may be somewhat as follows. Initially, perhaps, all arts are autographic. Where the works are transitory, as in singing and reciting, or require many persons for their production, as in architecture and symphonic music, a notation may be devised in order to transcend the limitations of time and the individual. This involves establishing a distinction between the constitutive and the contingent properties of a work (and in the case of literature, texts have even supplanted oral performances as the primary aesthetic objects). Of course, the notation does not dictate the distinction arbitrarily, but must follow generally—even though it may amend—lines antecedently drawn by the informal classification of performances into works and by practical decisions as to what is prescribed and what is optional. Amenability to notation depends upon a precedent practice that develops only if works of the art in question are commonly either ephemeral or not producible by one person. The dance, like the drama and symphonic and choral music, qualifies on both scores, while painting qualifies on neither.

The general answer to our somewhat slippery second problem of authenticity can be summarized in a few words. A forgery of a work of art is an object falsely purporting to have the history of production requisite for the (or an) original of the work. Where there is a theoretically decisive test for determining that an object has all the constitutive properties of the work in question without determining how or by whom the object was produced, there is no requisite history of production and hence no forgery of any given work. Such a test is provided by a suitable notational system with an articulate set of characters and of relative positions for them. For texts, scores, and perhaps plans, the test is correctness of spelling in this notation; for buildings and performances, the test is compliance with what is correctly spelled. Authority for a notation must be found in an antecedent classification of objects or events into works that cuts across, or admits of a legitimate projection that cuts across, classification by history of production; but definitive identification of works, fully freed from history of production, is achieved only when a notation is established. The allographic art has won its emancipation not by proclamation but by notation.

## 5 A Task

The two problems of authenticity I have been discussing are rather special and peripheral questions of aesthetics. Answers to them do not amount to an aesthetic theory or even the beginning of one. But failure to answer them can well be the end of one; and their exploration points the way to more basic problems and principles in the general theory of symbols.

Many matters touched upon here need much more careful study. So far, I have only vaguely described, rather than defined, the relations of compliance and of sameness of spelling. I have not examined the features that distinguish notations or notational languages from other languages and from nonlanguages. And I have not discussed the subtle differences between a score, a script, and a sketch. What is wanted now is a fundamental and thoroughgoing inquiry into the nature and function of notation in the arts. . .

## Notes

1. And only for the sake of argument—only in order not to obscure the central issue. All talk of mere looking in what follows is to be understood as occurring within the scope of this temporary concession, not as indicating any acceptance of the notion on my part.

2. Germans learning English often cannot, without repeated effort and concentrated attention, hear any difference at all between the vowel sounds in "cup" and "cop." Like effort may sometimes be needed by the native speaker of a language to discern differences in color, etc., that are not marked by his elementary vocabulary. Whether language affects actual sensory discrimination has long been debated among psychologists, anthropologists, and linguists; see the survey of experimentation and controversy in Segall, Campbell, and Hershkovits, *The Influence of Culture on Visual Perception* (Indianapolis and New York, The Bobbs-Merrill Co., Inc., 1966), pp. 34–48. The issue is unlikely to be resolved without greater clarity in the use of "sensory," "perceptual," and "cognitive," and more care in distinguishing between what a person can do at a given time and what he can learn to do.

3. In saying that a difference *between the pictures* that is thus relevant to my present experience in looking at them constitutes an aesthetic difference between them, I am of course not saying that everything (e.g., drunkenness, snow blindness, twilight) that may cause my experiences of them to differ constitutes such an aesthetic difference. Not every difference in or arising from how the pictures happen to be looked at counts; only differences in or arising from how they are to be looked at. Concerning the aesthetic, more will be said later in this section and in VI, 3–6.

4. For a detailed and fully illustrated account, see P. B. Coremans, *Van Meegeren's Faked Vermeers and De Hooghs,* trans. A. Hardy and C. Hutt (Amsterdam, J. M. Meulenhoff, 1949). The story is outlined in Sepp Schüller, *Forgers, Dealers, Experts,* trans. J. Cleugh (New York, G. P. Putnam's Sons, 1960), pp. 95–105.

5. Not surprisingly, since a single quantum of light may excite a retinal receptor. See M. H. Pirenne and F.H.C. Marriott, "The Quantum Theory of Light and the Psycho-Physiology of Vision," in *Psychology,* ed. S. Koch (New York and London, McGraw-Hill Co., Inc., 1959), vol. 1, p. 290; also Theodore C. Ruch, "Vision," in *Medical Psychology and Biophysics* (Philadelphia, W. B. Saunders Co., 1960), p. 426.

6. That the forgeries purported to have been painted during a period from which no Vermeers were known made detection more difficult but does not essentially alter the case. Some art historians, on the defensive for their profession, claim that the most perceptive critics suspected the forgeries very early; but actually some of the foremost recognized authorities were completely taken in and for some time even refused to believe Van Meegeren's confession. The reader has a more recent example now before him in the revelation that the famous bronze horse, long exhibited in the Metropolitan Museum and proclaimed as a masterpiece of classical Greek sculpture, is a modern forgery. An official of the museum noticed a seam that apparently neither he nor anyone else had ever seen before, and scientific testing followed. No expert has come forward to claim earlier doubts on aesthetic grounds.

7. I shall come to that question much later, in Chapter VI.

8. Attributed to Immanuel Tingle and Joseph Immersion (ca. 1800).

9. There may indeed be forgeries of performances. Such forgeries are performances that purport to be by a certain musician, etc; but these, if in accordance with the score, are nevertheless genuine instances of the work. And what concerns me here is a distinction among the arts that depends upon whether there can be forgeries of works, not upon whether there can be forgeries of instances of works. See further what is said in Section 4 below concerning forgeries of editions of literary works and of musical performances.

10. This is to be taken as a preliminary version of a difference we must seek to formulate more precisely. Much of what follows in this chapter has likewise the character of an exploratory introduction to matters calling for fuller and more detailed inquiry in later chapters.

11. Such identification does not guarantee that the object possesses the pictorial properties it had originally. Rather, reliance on physical or historical identification is transcended only where we have means of ascertaining that the requisite properties are present.

12. To be original a print must be from a certain plate but need not be printed by the artist. Furthermore, in the case of a woodcut, the artist sometimes only draws upon the

block, leaving the cutting to someone else—Holbein's blocks, for example, were usually cut by Lützelberger. Authenticity in an autographic art always depends upon the object's having the requisite, sometimes rather complicated, history of production; but that history does not always include ultimate execution by the original artist.

13. Of course, I am not saying that a correct(ly spelled) performance is correct in any of a number of other usual senses. Nevertheless, the composer or musician is likely to protest indignantly at refusal to accept a performance with a few wrong notes as an instance of a work; and he surely has ordinary usage on his side. But ordinary usage here points the way to disaster for theory (see V,2).

# Bibliography to Part Three

The idealist theory of art, associated chiefly with the work of R. G. Collingwood and Benedetto Croce, is most clearly represented in:
  R. G. Collingwood, *Principles of Art* (Oxford, 1935);
  W. B. Gallie, "The Function of Philosophical Aesthetics," *Mind* LVII (1948), 302-321;
  John Hospers, "The Croce-Collingwood Theory of Art," *Philosophy* XXXI (1956), 291-308.

The phenomenological account, which resists both the idealist and materialist alternatives, appears most forcefully in:
  Roman Ingarden, "Aesthetic Experience and Aesthetic Object," *Philosophy and Phenomenological Research* XXI (1961);
  Roman Ingarden, in Part One.
  Roman Ingarden, *The Cognition of the Literary Work,* trans. Ruth Crowley and Kenneth R. Olson (Evanston, 1973);
See also, however:
  Mikel Dufrenne, *The Phenomenology of Aesthetic Experience,* trans. Edward S. Casey *et al.* (Evanston, 1973), for critical adjustments in the theory;
and:
  Henri Focillon, *Life of Forms in Art,* trans. Charles Beecher Hogan (New York, 1948);
  Susanne Langer, *Feeling and Form* (New York, 1953);
  J. P. Sartre, *Imagination: A Psychological Critique,* trans. Forrest Williams (Ann Arbor, 1962).

On the type/token distinction and the treatment of works of art as universals, see:
  Jay E. Bachrach, "Type and Token and the Identification of the Work of Art," *Philosophy and Phenomenological Research* XXXI (1971), 415-420;
  A. Harrison, "Works of Art and Other Cultural Objects, *Proceedings of the Aristotelian Society* LXVII (1968), 105-128;
  Richard Rudner, "The Ontological Status of the Esthetic Object," *Philosophy and Phenomenological Research* X (1949-50), 380-389;

Charles L. Stevenson, "On the Reasons That Can Be Given for the Interpretation of a Poem," in Joseph Margolis (ed.), *Philosophy Looks at the Arts* (New York, 1962, 1st ed.);

Jeanne Wacker, "Particular Works of Art," *Mind* LIX (1960), 223–233.

These issues are closely linked to the cultural nature of art; hence, to the attempt to define or characterize art in terms of institutions or the contrast with "real things." On the latter issue, see particularly:

Gregory Battcock, *The New Art* (New York, 1966);

Timothy Binkley, "Deciding about Art," in Lars Aagaard-Mogensen (ed.), *Culture and Art* (Nyborg and Atlantic Highlands, 1976);

Arthur C. Danto, "Artworks and Real Things," *Theoria* XXXIX (1973), 1–17;

Hal Foster (ed.), *The Anti-Aesthetic; Essays on Post-Modern Culture* (Port Townsend, 1983).

Lucy Lippard, *Six Years: The Dematerialization of the Art Object from 1966 to 1972* (New York, 1973);

Ursula Meyer, *Conceptual Art* (New York, 1972).

See, also, Bibliography to Part Two.

# Part Four

# Representation in Art

The contemporary discussion of representational art is largely, though not entirely, associated with the appearance of Ernst Gombrich's *Art and Illusion* (1960). There, Gombrich insists that there is no innocent eye. Particularly in the visual arts, the temptation arises to construe representation in terms of given visual resemblances, to dwell on visual illusions, and to omit therefore the enormously complex background of beliefs, theories, assumptions, and the like against which one "sees" visual objects as we do. But the attempt to develop a general account of representation ranging over all the arts and even beyond the arts suggests the inadequacy—though not necessarily the irrelevance—of considerations of sensory similarity and perceptual illusion. Gombrich (1963) in fact links representation and (visual) illusion too closely. And if he may be taken to fix one pole of the current discussion of representation—emphasizing conditions of perception, Nelson Goodman (to some extent, in response to Gombrich's own claims) may be taken to fix the opposite pole—emphasizing rather the logical conditions of representation and, correspondingly, the conceptual and non-conceptual conditions of our appreciation of representation. In Goodman's hands (1976, 2nd ed.), the development leads to a larger view about the very nature of art (see Part Three) and adumbrates an even more comprehensive theory about the characteristic activities of man.

Goodman definitely shows that resemblance cannot in any independently operative way be said to be a necessary condition of representation (typically in painting), let alone a necessary and sufficient condition. He takes denotation to be "the core of representation" and to be "independent of resemblance." On the other hand, Gombrich's emphasis had been on illusion, and illusion suggests a disposition of some sort to construe certain visual displays in terms of resemblances—to some extent in spite of one's background beliefs or, at any rate, of variable and transient beliefs.

Objections to the innocent eye need not entail that there are no favored resemblances, given the larger functioning of perception in survival, to which the human eye is prone; these may be due, on different theories, to the convergent features of all human cultures or to underlying biological regularities. In effect, the admission is the reverse side of Gombrich's thesis. Goodman will have none of this, however, for he believes that there are no favored relations at all of such a kind. The issue has enormous importance because Goodman is committed to an utterly uncompromising form of nominalism; the possibility of biologically grounded resemblances suggests a basis for the admission of universals—or, at any rate, a fuller reconciliation with realism. It is, however, in exploring representation as a classificatory procedure, involving one-term or two-term predicates, that Goodman excels.

Gombrich's question has very much focused attention on the general discussion of both representation and pictorial resemblance. We may gather an initial impression of the salient puzzles by noting, first, the themes of two specimen papers (previously included in the second edition of this anthology), one by Richard Wollheim, the other by Patrick Maynard.

Wollheim (1965) pursues Gombrich's issue, partly in sympathy with Gombrich's distinctions, partly in opposition. He favors the view, to some extent convergent with both Gombrich's and Goodman's (though he does not discuss Goodman), that representation has an intentional aspect. But he also wishes, against Gombrich, to distinguish sharply between representation and illusion: the first concerns the way in which certain elements function intentionally without affecting our perceptual beliefs (or without regard to that); the second, as in *trompe l'oeil*, may even override our beliefs. Maynard (1972) also pursues Gombrich's distinction but more in terms of explicating our sense of realism, fidelity, perceptual convincingness, without falling afoul of Goodman's criticism of Gombrich and yet without conceding a purely relativistic view of representational realism. So Maynard, too, avoids construing representation in terms of illusion; but he attempts to develop a conception of pictorial realism that is not illusionistic and is not merely controlled by representational conventions. In this regard, returning to the psychology—even the biology—of perception, he is inclined to resist Goodman's polar extreme at the same time that he avoids Gombrich's fatal linkage. But apart from quarrels about details, the admission of representational properties requires a counterpart admission of the complexity of the nature of aesthetic experience (see Part One) and of the nature of artworks (see Parts Two and Three).

More recent papers have pressed more boldly (though also more argumentatively) in terms both of the extreme possibilities posed by the

usual debates and of new options that a wider perspective invites regarding
the complexities of human culture. Marx Wartofsky (1979) embraces the
radical thesis that human vision itself is an "artifact" produced by such
other artifacts as pictures. This, of course, challenges, as Wartofsky himself
sees, the very undertaking of a theory of natural vision. The problem
concerns the relationship between the biology of vision and the cultural
grooming of visual perception. There is, first of all, the theoretical issue
of whether there are definable biological limits on the cultural variability
of perception; and second, whether there are any visual phenomena that
Wartofsky's thesis cannot accommodate. It may well be that the ecological
optics of J. J. Gibson (1966, 1979) is too naive to accommodate the
interpretive dimension of perceptual occasions indissolubly linked with
culturally induced habits and expectations: certainly, Gibson—whose theory
is centrally implicated in the debate between Gombrich and Goodman—fails to make suitable sense of two-dimensional paintings within his
ecological account. But Gibson does show, nevertheless, that a strong case
can be mounted for biologically constrained (informational) invariances
within the range of normal perception—at the human as well as at the
animal level. In fact, if the argument holds at the animal level, it is difficult
to see how it can be denied at the human. On the other hand, some
commentators—Alan and Judith Tormey (1979), for instance—specifically
challenging Goodman's thesis, which in effect Wartofsky favors, have
demonstrated, as in reporting the "X-ray" art of the Australian aborigines
and others and the surprisingly analogous practices of Western artists, that
objects are often represented in ways meant to preserve realist information
about the way things are believed to be rather than merely to preserve the
way they "appear" (in however many culturally divergent ways); and that,
consequently, the spontaneous recognition of such representations is somehow grounded in deeper biological regularities than Wartofsky (also,
Goodman) fails to acknowledge.

Peter Kivy (1984) offers a plausible account of the possibilities of
representation—even of a sort of pictorial representation—in the most recalcitrant context of all, that of music. He rejects mimesis, and explores the
prospect of defending pictorial resemblance by according expressiveness a
place in musical representation. Here, Kivy's concern centers on the
viability of such a theory, not on a full-scale account of representation as
such; he considers representational possibilities, then, both in terms of the
expression of arousable emotions and of the expressiveness of what is itself
expressive of emotion. This leads him to what he regards as the "optimal
form" of musical representation. But he warns against construing representation exclusively in terms of expression.

Joseph Margolis (1986) attempts to place the very question of representational function within the ontologically larger question of the intentionality or aboutness of art works—that is, insisting that representation is a restricted and conceptually dependent distinction that arises only within a larger intentional space; and that that "space" is, precisely, identifiable only by distinguishing the cultural and natural worlds. By means of this strategy, he is able to contrast the representationality of a painting, say, from representations in paintings—hence, to address the question of pictorial resemblance in terms that simply disallow a disjunction between natural and "artifactual" perception among humans. In this way, once again, the necessity of bridging the differences between Anglo-American and Continental theories of art may be made more convincing.

# 15.  Reality Remade
## NELSON GOODMAN

> Art is not a copy of the real world.
> One of the damn things is enough.*

## 1 Denotation

Whether a picture ought to be a representation or not is a question much less crucial than might appear from current bitter battles among artists, critics, and propagandists. Nevertheless, the nature of representation wants early study in any philosophical examination of the ways symbols function in and out of the arts. That representation is frequent in some arts, such as painting, and infrequent in others, such as music, threatens trouble for a unified aesthetics; and confusion over how pictorial representation as a mode of signification is allied to and distinguished from verbal description on the one hand and, say, facial expression on the other is fatal to any general theory of symbols.

The most naive view of representation might perhaps be put somewhat like this: "*A* represents *B* if and only if *A* appreciably resembles *B*," or "*A* represents *B* to the extent that *A* resembles *B*." Vestiges of this view, with assorted refinements, persist in most writing on representation. Yet more error could hardly be compressed into so short a formula.

Some of the faults are obvious enough. An object resembles itself to the maximum degree but rarely represents itself; resemblance, unlike representation, is reflexive. Again, unlike representation, resemblance is symmetric:

---

*Reported as occurring in an essay on Virginia Woolf. I have been unable to locate the source.

From Nelson Goodman, *Languages of Art* (Indianapolis: Hackett Publishing Co., 1976), Chapter I. Reprinted with permission of the author.

*B* is as much like *A* as *A* is like *B*, but while a painting may represent the Duke of Wellington, the Duke doesn't represent the painting. Furthermore, in many cases neither one of a pair of very like objects represents the other: none of the automobiles off an assembly line is a picture of any of the rest; and a man is not normally a representation of another man, even his twin brother. Plainly, resemblance in any degree is no sufficient condition for representation.[1]

Just what correction to make in the formula is not so obvious. We may attempt less, and prefix the condition "If *A* is a picture, . . ." Of course, if we then construe "picture" as "representation," we resign a large part of the question: namely, what constitutes a representation. But even if we construe "picture" broadly enough to cover all paintings, the formula is wide of the mark in other ways. A Constable painting of Marlborough Castle is more like any other picture than it is like the Castle, yet it represents the Castle and not another picture—not even the closest copy. To add the requirement that *B* must not be a picture would be desperate and futile; for a picture may represent another, and indeed each of the once popular paintings of art galleries represents many others.

The plain fact is that a picture, to represent an object,[2] must be a symbol for it, stand for it, refer to it; and that no degree of resemblance is sufficient to establish the requisite relationship of reference. Nor is resemblance *necessary* for reference; almost anything may stand for almost anything else. A picture that represents—like a passage that describes—an object refers to and, more particularly, *denotes*[3] it. Denotation is the core of representation and is independent of resemblance.

If the relation between a picture and what it represents is thus assimilated to the relation between a predicate and what it applies to, we must examine the characteristics of representation as a special kind of denotation. What does pictorial denotation have in common with, and how does it differ from, verbal or diagrammatic denotation? One not implausible answer is that resemblance, while no sufficient condition for representation, is just the feature that distinguishes representation from denotation of other kinds. Is it perhaps the case that if *A* denotes *B*, then *A* represents *B* just to the extent that *A* resembles *B*? I think even this watered-down and innocuous-looking version of our initial formula betrays a grave misconception of the nature of representation.

## 2 Imitation

"To make a faithful picture, come as close as possible to copying the object just as it is." This simple-minded injunction baffles me; for the object before me is a man, a swarm of atoms, a complex of cells, a fiddler, a friend, a fool, and much more. If none of these constitute the object as it is, what else might? If all are ways the object is, then none is *the* way the object is.[4] I cannot copy all these at once; and the more nearly I succeeded, the less would the result be a realistic picture.

What I am to copy then, it seems, is one such aspect, one of the ways the object is or looks. But not, of course, any one of these at random—not, for example, the Duke of Wellington as he looks to a drunk through a raindrop. Rather, we may suppose, the way the object looks to the normal eye, at proper range, from a favorable angle, in good light, without instrumentation, unprejudiced by affections or animosities or interests, and unembellished by thought or interpretation. In short, the object is to be copied as seen under aseptic conditions by the free and innocent eye.

The catch here, as Ernst Gombrich insists, is that there is no innocent eye.[5] The eye comes always ancient to its work, obsessed by its own past and by old and new insinuations of the ear, nose, tongue, fingers, heart, and brain. It functions not as an instrument self-powered and alone, but as a dutiful member of a complex and capricious organism. Not only how but what it sees is regulated by need and prejudice.[6] It selects, rejects, organizes, discriminates, associates, classifies, analyzes, constructs. It does not so much mirror as take and make; and what it takes and makes it sees not bare, as items without attributes, but as things, as food, as people, as enemies, as stars, as weapons. Nothing is seen nakedly or naked.

The myths of the innocent eye and of the absolute given are unholy accomplices. Both derive from and foster the idea of knowing as a processing of raw material received from the senses, and of this raw material as being discoverable either through purification rites or by methodical disinterpretation. But reception and interpretation are not separable operations; they are thoroughly interdependent. The Kantian dictum echoes here: the innocent eye is blind and the virgin mind empty. Moreover, what has been received and what has been done to it cannot be distinguished within the finished product. Content cannot be extracted by peeling off layers of comment.[7]

All the same, an artist may often do well to strive for innocence of eye. The effort sometimes rescues him from the tired patterns of everyday seeing, and results in fresh insight. The opposite effort, to give fullest rein to a personal reading, can be equally tonic—and for the same reason. But the most neutral eye and the most biased are merely sophisticated in different ways. The most ascetic vision and the most prodigal, like the sober portrait and the vitriolic caricature, differ not in how *much* but only in *how* they interpret.

The copy theory of representation, then, is stopped at the start by inability to specify what is to be copied. Not an object the way it is, nor all the ways it is, nor the way it looks to the mindless eye. Moreover, something is wrong with the very notion of copying any of the ways an object is, any aspect of it. For an aspect is not just the object-from-a-given-distance-and-angle-and-in-a-given-light; it is the object as we look upon or conceive it, a version or construal of the object. In representing an object, we do not copy such a construal or interpretation—we *achieve* it.[8]

In other words, nothing is ever represented either shorn of or in the fullness of its properties. A picture never merely represents *x*, but rather represents *x as* a man or represents *x to be* a mountain, or represents *the fact that x is* a melon. What could be meant by copying a fact would be hard to grasp even if there were any such things as facts; to ask me to copy *x* as a soandso is a little like asking me to sell something as a gift; and to speak of copying something to be a man is sheer nonsense. We shall presently have to look further into all this; but we hardly need look further to see how little is representation a matter of imitation.

The case for the relativity of vision and of representation has been so conclusively stated elsewhere that I am relieved of the need to argue it at any length here. Gombrich, in particular, has amassed overwhelming evidence to show how the way we see and depict depends upon and varies with experience, practice, interests, and attitudes. But on one matter Gombrich and others sometimes seem to me to take a position at odds with such relativity; and I must therefore discuss briefly the question of the conventionality of perspective.

## 3 Perspective

An artist may choose his means of rendering motion, intensity of light, quality of atmosphere, vibrancy of color, but if he wants to represent space correctly, he must—almost anyone will tell him—obey the laws of perspective. The adoption of perspective during the Renaissance is widely accepted as a long stride forward in realistic depiction. The laws of perspective are supposed to provide absolute standards of fidelity that override differences in style of seeing and picturing. Gombrich derides "the idea that perspective is merely a convention and does not represent the world as it looks," and he declares "One cannot insist enough that the art of perspective aims at a correct equation: It wants the image to appear like the object and the object like the image."[9] And James J. Gibson writes: ". . . it does not seem reasonable to assert that the use of perspective in paintings is merely a convention, to be used or discarded by the painter as he chooses. . . . When the artist transcribes what he sees upon a two-dimensional surface, he uses perspective geometry, of necessity."[10]

Obviously the laws of the behavior of light are no more conventional than any other scientific laws. Now suppose we have a motionless, monochromatic object, reflecting light of medium intensity only. The argument runs:[11]—A picture drawn in correct perspective will, under specified conditions, deliver to the eye a bundle of light rays matching that delivered by the object itself. This matching is a purely objective matter, measurable by instruments. And such matching constitutes fidelity of representation; for since light rays are all that the eye can receive from either picture or object, identity in pattern of light rays must constitute identity of appearance. Of course, the rays yielded by the picture under the specified conditions match not only those yielded by the object in question from a given distance and angle but also those yielded by any of a multitude of other objects from other distances and angles.[12] Identity in pattern of light rays, like resemblance of other kinds, is clearly no sufficient condition for representation. The claim is rather that such identity is a criterion of fidelity, of correct pictorial representation, where denotation is otherwise established.

If at first glance the argument as stated seems simple and persuasive, it becomes less so when we consider the conditions of observation that are prescribed. The picture must be viewed through a peephole, face on, from a certain distance, with one eye closed and the other motionless. The object also must be observed through a peephole, from a given (but not usually the same) angle and distance, and with a single unmoving eye. Otherwise, the light rays will not match.

Under these remarkable conditions, do we not have ultimately faithful representation? Hardly. Under these conditions, what we are looking at tends to disappear rather promptly. Experiment has shown that the eye cannot see normally without moving relative to what it sees;[13] apparently, scanning is necessary for normal vision. The fixed eye is almost as blind as the innocent one. What can the matching of light rays delivered under conditions that make normal vision impossible have to do with fidelity of representation? To measure fidelity in terms of rays directed at a closed eye would be no more absurd. But this objection need not be stressed; perhaps enough eye motion could be allowed for scanning but not for seeing around the object.[14] The basic trouble is that the specified conditions of observation are grossly abnormal. What can be the grounds for taking the matching of light rays delivered under such extraordinary conditions as a measure of fidelity? Under no more artificial conditions, such as the interposition of suitably contrived lenses, a picture far out of perspective could also be made to yield the same pattern of light rays as the object. That with clever enough stage-managing we can wring out of a picture drawn in perspective light rays that match those we can wring out of the object represented is an odd and futile argument for the fidelity of perspective.

Furthermore, the conditions of observation in question are in most cases not the same for picture and object. Both are to be viewed through a peephole with one transfixed eye; but the picture is to be viewed face on at a distance of six feet while the cathedral represented has to be looked at from, say, an angle of 45° to its facade and at a distance of two hundred feet. Now not only the light rays received but also the attendant conditions determine what and how we see; as psychologists are fond of saying, there is more to vision than meets the eye. Just as a red light says "stop" on the highway and "port" at sea, so the same stimulus gives rise to different visual experience under different circumstances. Even where both the light rays and the momentary external conditions are the same, the preceding train of visual experience, together with information gathered from all sources, can make a vast difference in what is seen. If not even the former conditions are the same, duplication of light rays is no more likely to result in identical perception than is duplication of the conditions if the light rays differ.

Pictures are normally viewed framed against a background by a person free to walk about and to move his eyes. To paint a picture that will under these conditions deliver the same light rays as the object, viewed under any conditions, would be pointless even if it were possible. Rather, the artist's task in representing an object before him is to decide what light rays, under gallery conditions, will succeed in rendering what he sees. This is not a matter of copying but of conveying. It is more a matter of 'catching a likeness' than of duplicating—in the sense that a likeness lost in a photograph may be caught in a caricature. Translation of a sort, compensating for differences in circumstances, is involved. How this is best carried out depends upon countless and variable factors, not least among them the particular habits of seeing and representing that are ingrained in the viewers. Pictures in perspective, like any others, have to be read; and the ability to read has to be acquired. The eye accustomed solely to Oriental painting does not immediately understand a picture in perspective. Yet with practice one can accommodate smoothly to distorting spectacles or to pictures drawn in warped or even reversed perspective.[15] And even we who are most inured to perspective rendering do not always accept it as faithful representation: the photograph of a man with his feet thrust forward looks distorted, and Pike's Peak dwindles dismally in a snapshot. As the saying goes, there is nothing like a camera to make a molehill out of a mountain.

So far, I have been playing along with the idea that pictorial perspective obeys laws of geometrical optics, and that a picture drawn according to the standard pictorial rules will, under the very abnormal conditions outlined above, deliver a bundle of light rays matching that delivered by the scene portrayed. Only this assumption gives any plausibility at all to the argument from perspective; but the assumption is plainly false. By the pictorial rules, railroad tracks running outward from the eye are drawn converging, but telephone poles (or the edges of a facade) running upward from the eye are drawn parallel. By the 'laws of geometry' the poles should also be drawn converging. But so drawn, they look as wrong as railroad tracks drawn parallel. Thus we have cameras with tilting backs and elevating lens-boards to 'correct distortion'—that is, to make vertical parallels come out parallel in our photographs; we do not likewise try to make the railroad tracks come out parallel. The rules of pictorial perspective no more follow from the laws of optics than would rules calling for drawing the tracks parallel and the poles converging. In diametric contradiction to what Gibson says, the artist who wants to produce a spatial representation that the present-day Western eye will accept as faithful must defy the 'laws of geometry.'

If all this seems quite evident, and neatly clinched by Klee,[16] there is nevertheless impressive weight of authority on the other side,[17] relying on the argument that all parallels in the plane of the facade project geometrically as parallels onto the parallel plane of the picture. The source of unending debate over perspective seems to lie in confusion concerning the pertinent conditions of observation. In Figure 1, an observer is on ground level with eye at $a$; at $b,c$ is the facade of a tower atop a building; at $d,e$ is a picture of the tower facade, drawn in standard perspective and to a scale such that at the indicated distances picture and facade subtend equal angles from $a$. The normal line of vision to the tower is the line $a,f$; looking much higher or lower will leave part of the tower facade out of sight or blurred. Likewise, the normal line of vision to the picture is $a,g$. Now although picture and facade are parallel, the line $a,g$ is perpendicular to the picture, so that vertical parallels in the picture will be projected to the eye as parallel, while the line $a,f$ is at an angle to the facade so that vertical parallels there will be projected to the eye as converging upward. We might try to make picture and facade deliver matching bundles of light rays to the eye by either (1) moving the picture upward to the position $h,i$, or (2) tilting it to the position $j,k$, or (3) looking at the picture from $a$ but at the tower from $m$, some stories up. In the first two cases, since the picture must be also nearer the eye to subtend the same angle, the scale will be wrong for lateral (left-wing) dimensions. What is more important, none of these three conditions of observation is anywhere near normal. We do not usually hang pictures far above eye level, or tilt them drastically bottom toward us, or elevate ourselves at will to look squarely at towers.[18] With eye and picture in normal position, the bundle of light rays delivered to the eye by the picture drawn in standard perspective is very different from the bundle delivered by the facade.

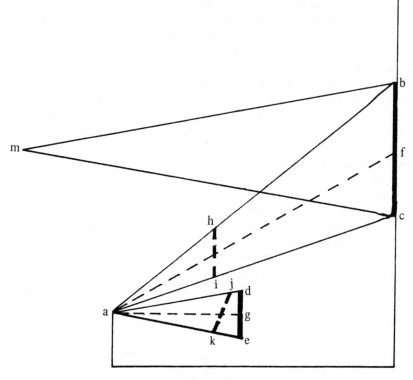

*Figure 1*

This argument by itself is conclusive, but my case does not rest upon it. The more fundamental arguments advanced earlier would apply with full force even had the choice of official rules of perspective been less whimsical and called for drawing as convergent all parallels receding in any direction. Briefly, the behavior of light sanctions neither our usual nor any other way of rendering space; and perspective provides no absolute or independent standard of fidelity.

### 4 Sculpture

The troubles with the copy theory are sometimes attributed solely to the impossibility of depicting reality-in-the-round on a flat surface. But imitation is no better gauge of realism in sculpture than in painting. What is to be portrayed in a bronze bust is a mobile, many-faceted, and fluctuating person, encountered in ever-changing light and against miscellaneous backgrounds. Duplicating the form of the head at a given instant is unlikely to yield a notably faithful representation. The very fixation of such a momentary phase embalms the person much as a photograph taken at too short an exposure freezes a fountain or stops a racehorse. To portray faithfully is to convey a person known and distilled from a variety of experiences. This elusive conceit is nothing that one can meaningfully try to duplicate or imitate in a static bronze on a pedestal in a museum. The sculptor undertakes, rather, a subtle and intricate problem of translation.

Even where the object represented is something simpler and more stable than a person, duplication seldom coincides with realistic representation. If in a tympanum over a tall Gothic portal, Eve's apple were the same size as a Winesap, it would not look big enough to tempt Adam. The distant or colossal sculpture has also to be *shaped* very differently from what it depicts in order to be realistic, in order to 'look right.' And the ways of making it 'look right' are not reducible to fixed and universal rules; for how an object looks depends not only upon its orientation, distance, and lighting, but upon all we know of it and upon our training, habits, and concerns.

One need hardly go further to see that the basic case against imitation as a test of realism is conclusive for sculpture as well as for painting.

## 5 Fictions

So far, I have been considering only the representation of a particular person or group or thing or scene; but a picture, like a predicate, may denote severally the members of a given class. A picture accompanying a definition in a dictionary is often such a representation, not denoting uniquely some one eagle, say, or collectively the class of eagles, but distributively eagles in general.

Other representations have neither unique nor multiple denotation. What, for example, do pictures of Pickwick or of a unicorn represent? They do not represent anything; they are representations with null denotation. Yet how can we say that a picture represents Pickwick, or a unicorn, and also say that it does not represent anything? Since there is no Pickwick and no unicorn, what a picture of Pickwick and a picture of a unicorn represent is the same. Yet surely to be a picture of Pickwick and to be a picture of a unicorn are not at all the same.

The simple fact is that much as most pieces of furniture are readily sorted out as desks, chairs, tables, etc., so most pictures are readily sorted out as pictures of Pickwick, of Pegasus, of a unicorn, etc., without reference to anything represented. What tends to mislead us is that such locutions as "picture of" and "represents" have the appearance of mannerly two-place predicates and can sometimes be so interpreted. But "picture of Pickwick" and "represents a unicorn" are better considered unbreakable one-place predicates, or class-terms, like "desk" and "table." We cannot reach inside any of these and quantify over parts of them. From the fact that *P* is a picture of or represents a unicorn we cannot infer that there is something that *P* is a picture of or represents. Furthermore, a picture of Pickwick is a picture of a man, even though there is no man it represents. Saying that a picture represents a soandso is thus highly ambiguous as between saying what the picture denotes and saying what kind of picture it is. Some confusion can be avoided if in the latter case we speak rather of a 'Pickwick-representing-picture' or a 'unicorn-representing-picture' or a 'man-representing-picture' or, for short, of a 'Pickwick-picture' or 'unicorn-picture' or 'man-picture.' Obviously a picture cannot, barring equivocation, both represent Pickwick and represent nothing. But a picture may be of a certain kind—be a Pickwick-picture or a man-picture—without representing anything.[19]

The difference between a man-picture and a picture of a man has a close parallel in the difference between a man-description (or man-term) and a description of (or term for) a man. "Pickwick," "the Duke of Wellington," "the man who conquered Napoleon," "a man," "a fat man," "the man with three heads," are all man-descriptions, but not all describe a man. Some denote a particular man, some denote each of many men, and some denote nothing.[20] And although "Pickwick" and "the three-headed man" and "Pegasus" all have the same null extension, the second differs from the first in being, for example, a many-headed-man-description, while the last differs from the other two in being a winged-horse-description.

The way pictures and descriptions are thus classified into kinds, like most habitual ways of classifying, is far from sharp or stable, and resists codification. Borderlines shift and blur, new categories are always coming into prominence, and the canons of the classification are less clear than the practice. But this is only to say that we may have some trouble in telling whether certain pictures (in common parlance) 'represent a unicorn,' or in setting forth rules for deciding in every case whether a picture is a man-picture. Exact and general conditions under which something is a soandso-picture or a soandso-description would indeed be hard to formulate. We can cite examples: Van Gogh's *Postman* is a man-picture; and in English, "a man" is a man-description. And we may note, for instance, that to be a soandso-picture is to be a soandso-picture as a whole, so that a picture containing or contained in a man-picture need not itself be a man-picture. But to attempt much more is to become engulfed in a notorious philosophical morass; and the frustrating, if fascinating, problems involved are no part of our present task. All that directly matters here, I repeat, is that pictures are indeed sorted with varying degrees of ease into man-pictures, unicorn-pictures, Pickwick-pictures, winged-horse-pictures, etc., just as pieces of furniture are sorted into desks, tables, chairs, etc. And this fact is unaffected by the difficulty, in either case, of framing definitions for the several classes or eliciting a general principle of classification.

The possible objection that we must first understand what a man or a unicorn is in order to know how to apply "man-picture" or "unicorn-picture" seems to me quite perverted. We can learn to apply "corncob pipe" or "staghorn" without first understanding, or knowing how to apply, "corn" or "cob" or "corncob" or "pipe" or "stag" or "horn" as separate terms. And we can learn, on the basis of samples, to apply "unicorn-picture" not only without ever having seen any unicorns but without ever having seen or heard the word "unicorn" before. Indeed, largely by learning what are unicorn-pictures and unicorn-descriptions do we come to understand the word "unicorn"; and our ability to recognize a staghorn may help us to recognize a stag when we see one. We may begin to understand a term by learning how to apply either the term itself or some larger term containing it. Acquiring any of these skills may aid in acquiring, but does not imply possessing, any of the others. Understanding a term is not a precondition, and may often be a result, of learning how to apply the term and its compounds.[21]

Earlier I said that denotation is a necessary condition for representation, and then encountered representations without denotation. But the explanation is now clear. A picture must denote a man to represent him, but need not denote anything to be a man-representation. Incidentally, the copy theory of representation takes a further beating here; for where a representation does not represent anything there can be no question of resemblance to what it represents.

Use of such examples as Pickwick-pictures and unicorn-pictures may suggest that representations with null denotation are comparatively rare. Qute the contrary; the world of pictures teems with anonymous fictional persons, places, and things. The man in Rembrandt's *Landscape with a Huntsman* is presumably no actual person; he is just the man in Rembrandt's etching. In other words, the etching represents no man but is simply a man-picture, and more particularly a the-man-in-Rembrandt's-*Landscape-with-a-Huntsman*-picture. And even if an actual man be depicted here, his identity matters as little as the artist's blood-type. Furthermore, the information needed to determine what if anything is denoted by a picture is not always accessible. We may, for example, be unable to tell whether a given representation is multiple, like an eagle-picture in the dictionary, or fictive, like a Pickwick-picture. But where we cannot determine whether a picture denotes anything or not, we can only proceed as if it did not—that is, confine ourselves to considering what kind of picture it is. Thus cases of indeterminate denotation are treated in the same way as cases of null denotation.

But not only where the denotation is null or indeterminate does the classification of a picture need to be considered. For the denotation of a picture no more determines its kind than the kind of picture determines the denotation. Not every man-picture represents a man, and conversely not every picture that represents a man is a man-picture. And in the difference between being and not being a man-picture lies the difference, among pictures that represent a man, between those that do and those that do not represent him as a man.

## 6 Representation-as

The locution "represents . . . as" has two quite different uses. To say that a picture represents the Duke of Wellington as an infant, or as an adult, or as the victor at Waterloo is often merely to say that the picture represents the Duke at a given time or period—that it represents a certain (long or short, continuous or broken) temporal part or 'time-slice' of him. Here "as . . ." combines with the *noun* "the Duke of Wellington" to form a description of one portion of the whole extended individual.[22] Such a description can always be replaced by another like "the infant Duke of Wellington" or "the Duke of Wellington upon the occasion of his victory at Waterloo." Thus these cases raise no difficulty; all that is being said is that the picture represents the object so described.

The second use is illustrated when we say that a given picture represents Winston Churchill as an infant, where the picture does not represent the infant Churchill but rather represents the adult Churchill as an infant. Here, as well as when we say that other pictures represent the adult Churchill as an adult, the "as . . ." combines with and modifies the *verb*; and we have genuine cases of *representation-as*. Such representation-as wants now to be distinguished from and related to representation.

A picture that represents a man denotes him; a picture that represents a fictional man is a man-picture; and a picture that represents a man as a man is a man-picture denoting him. Thus while the first case concerns only what the picture denotes, and the second only what kind of picture it is, the third concerns both the denotation and the classification.

More accurate formulation takes some care. What a picture is said to represent may be denoted by the picture as a whole or by a part of it.

Likewise, a picture may be a soandso-picture as a whole or merely through containing a soandso-picture.[23] Consider an ordinary portrait of the Duke and Duchess of Wellington. The picture (as a whole) denotes the couple, and (in part) denotes the Duke. Furthermore, it is (as a whole) a two-person-picture, and (in part) a man-picture. The picture represents the Duke and Duchess as two persons, and represents the Duke as a man. But although it represents the Duke, and is a two-person-picture, it obviously does not represent the Duke as two persons; and although it represents two persons and is a man-picture, it does not represent the two as a man. For the picture neither is nor contains any picture that as a whole both represents the Duke and is a two-man-picture, or that as a whole both represents two persons and is a man-picture.

In general, then, an object $k$ is represented as a soandso by a picture $p$ if and only if $p$ is or contains a picture that as a whole both represents $k$ and is a soandso-picture.[24] Many of the modifiers that have had to be included here may, however, be omitted as understood in what follows; for example, "is or contains a picture that as a whole both represents Churchill and is an adult-picture" may be shortened to "is an adult-picture representing Churchill."

Everyday usage is often careless about the distinction between representation and representation-as. Cases have already been cited where in saying that a picture represents a soandso we mean not that it denotes a soandso but that it is a soandso-picture. In other cases, we may mean both. If I tell you I have a picture of a certain black horse, and then I produce a snapshot in which he has come out a light speck in the distance, you can hardly convict me of lying; but you may well feel that I misled you. You understandably took me to mean a picture of the black horse as such; and you therefore expected the picture not only to denote the horse in question but to be a black-horse-picture. Not inconceivably, saying a picture represents the black horse might on other occasions mean that it represents the horse as black (i.e., that it is a black-thing-picture representing the horse) or that it represents the black thing in question as a horse (i.e., that it is a horse-picture representing the black thing).

The ambiguities of ordinary use do not end there. To say that the adult Churchill is represented as an infant (or as an adult) is to say that the picture in question is an infant-picture (or an adult-picture). But to say that Pickwick is represented as a clown (or as Don Quixote) cannot mean that the picture is a clown-picture (or Don-Quixote-picture) representing Pickwick; for there is no Pickwick. Rather, what is being said is that the picture belongs to a certain rather narrow class of pictures that may be described as Pickwick-as-clown-pictures (or Pickwick-as-Don-Quixote-pictures).

Distinctions obscured in much informal discourse thus need to be carefully marked for our purposes here. Being a matter of monadic classification, representation-as differs drastically from dyadic denotative representation. If a picture represents $k$ as a (or the) soandso, then it denotes $k$ and is a soandso-picture. If $k$ is identical with $h$, the picture also denotes and represents $h$. And if $k$ is a suchandsuch, the picture also represents a (or the) suchandsuch, but not necessarily *as* a (or the) suchandsuch. To represent the first Duke of Wellington is to represent Arthur Wellesley and also to represent a soldier, but not necessarily to represent him *as* a soldier; for some pictures of him are civilian-pictures.

Representations, then, are pictures that function in somewhat the same way as descriptions.[25] Just as objects are classified by means of, or under, various verbal labels, so also are objects classified by or under various pictorial labels. And the labels themselves, verbal or pictorial, are in turn classified under labels, verbal or nonverbal. Objects are classified under "desk," "table," etc., and also under pictures representing them. Descriptions are classified under "desk-description," "centaur-description," "Cicero-name," etc.; and pictures under "desk-picture," "Pickwick-picture," etc. The labeling of labels does not depend upon what they are labels for. Some, like "unicorn," apply to nothing; and as we have noted, not all pictures of soldiers are soldier-pictures. Thus with a picture as with any other label, there are always two questions: what it represents (or describes) and the sort of representation (or description) it is. The first question asks what objects, if any, it applies to as a label; and the second asks about which among certain labels apply to it. In representing, a picture at once picks out a class of objects and belongs to a certain class or classes of pictures.[26]

## 7 Invention

If representing is a matter of classifying objects rather than of imitating them, of characterizing rather than of copying, it is not a matter of passive reporting. The object does not sit as a docile model with its attributes neatly separated and thrust out for us to admire and portray. It is one of countless objects, and may be grouped with any selection of them; and for every such grouping there is an attribute of the object. To admit all classifications on equal footing amounts to making no classification at all. Classification involves preferment; and application of a label (pictorial, verbal, etc.) as often *effects* as it records a classification. The 'natural' kinds are simply those we are in the habit of picking out for and by labeling. Moreover, the object itself is not ready-made but results from a way of taking the world. The making of a picture commonly participates in making what is to be pictured. The object and its aspects depend upon organization; and labels of all sorts are tools of organization.

Representation and description thus involve and are often involved in organization. A label associates together such objects as it applies to, and is associated with the other labels of a kind or kinds. Less directly, it associates its referents with these other labels and with their referents, and so on. Not all these associations have equal force; their strength varies with their directness, with the specificity of the classifications in question, and with the firmness of foothold these classifications and labelings have secured. But in all these ways a representation or description, by virtue of how it classifies and is classified, may make or mark connections, analyze objects, and organize the world.

Representation or description is apt, effective, illuminating, subtle, intriguing, to the extent that the artist or writer grasps fresh and significant relationships and devises means for making them manifest. Discourse or depiction that marks off familiar units and sorts them into standard sets under well-worn labels may sometimes be serviceable even if humdrum. The marking off of new elements or classes, or of familiar ones by labels of new kinds or by new combinations of old labels, may provide new insight. Gombrich stresses Constable's metaphor: "Painting is a science . . . of which pictures are but the experiments."[27] In representation, the artist must make use of old habits when he wants to elicit novel objects and connections. If his picture is recognized as almost but not quite referring to the commonplace furniture of the everyday world, or if it calls for and yet resists assignment to a usual kind of picture, it may bring out neglected likenesses and differences, force unaccustomed associations, and in some measure remake our world. And if the point of the picture is not only successfully made but is also well taken, if the realignments it directly and indirectly effects are interesting and important, the picture—like a crucial experiment—makes a genuine contribution to knowledge. To a complaint that his portrait of Gertrude Stein did not look like her, Picasso is said to have answered, "No matter; it will."

In sum, effective representation and description require invention. They are creative. They inform each other; and they form, relate, and distinguish objects. That nature imitates art is too timid a dictum. Nature is a product of art and discourse.

## 8 Realism

This leaves unanswered the minor question what constitutes realism of representation. Surely not, in view of the foregoing, any sort of resemblance to reality. Yet we do in fact compare representations with respect to their realism or naturalism or fidelity. If resemblance is not the criterion, what is?

One popular answer is that the test of fidelity is deception, that a picture is realistic just to the extent that it is a successful illusion, leading the viewer to suppose that it is, or has the characteristics of, what it represents. The proposed measure of realism, in other words, is the probability of confusing the representation with the represented. This is some improvement over the copy theory; for what counts here is not how closely the picture duplicates an object but how far the picture and object, under conditions of observation appropriate to each, give rise to the same responses and expectations. Furthermore, the theory is not immediately confounded by the fact that fictive representations differ in degree of realism; for even though there are no centaurs, a realistic picture might deceive me into taking it for a centaur.

Yet there are difficulties. What deceives depends upon what is observed, and what is observed varies with interests and habits. If the probability of confusion is 1, we no longer have representation—we have identity. Moreover, the probability seldom rises noticeably above zero for even the most guileful *trompe-l'oeil* painting seen under ordinary gallery conditions. For seeing a picture as a picture precludes mistaking it for anything else; and the appropriate conditions of observation (e.g., framed, against a uniform background, etc.) are calculated to defeat deception. Deception enlists such mischief as a suggestive setting, or a peephole that occludes frame and background. And deception under such nonstandard conditions is no test of realism; for with enough staging, even the most unrealistic picture can deceive. Deception counts less as a measure of realism than as evidence of magicianship, and is highly atypical mishap. In looking at the most realistic picture, I seldom suppose that I can literally reach into the distance, slice the tomato, or beat the drum. Rather, I recognize the images as signs for the objects and characteristics represented—signs that work instantly and unequivocally without being confused with what they denote. Of course, sometimes where deception does occur—say, by a painted window in a mural—we may indeed call the picture realistic; but such cases provide no basis for the usual ordering of pictures in general as more or less realistic.

Thoughts along these lines have led to the suggestion that the most realistic picture is the one that provides the greatest amount of pertinent information. But this hypothesis can be quickly and completely refuted. Consider a realistic picture, painted in ordinary perspective and normal color, and a second picture just like the first except that the perspective is reversed and each color is replaced by its complementary. The second picture, appropriately interpreted, yields exactly the same information as the first. And any number of other drastic but information-preserving transformations are possible. Obviously, realistic and unrealistic pictures may be equally informative; informational yield is no test of realism.

So far, we have not needed to distinguish between fidelity and realism. The criteria considered earlier have been as unsatisfactory for the one as for the other. But we can no longer equate them. The two pictures just described are equally correct, equally faithful to what they represent, provide the same and hence equally true information; yet they are not equally realistic or literal. For a picture to be faithful is simply for the object represented to have the properties that the picture in effect ascribes to it. But such fidelity or correctness or truth is not a sufficient condition for literalism or realism.

The alert absolutist will argue that for the second picture but not the first we need a key. Rather, the difference is that for the first the key is ready at hand. For proper reading of the second picture, we have to discover rules of interpretation and apply them deliberately. Reading of the first is by virtually automatic habit; practice has rendered the symbols so transparent that we are not aware of any effort, of any alternatives, or of making any interpretation at all.[28] Just here, I think, lies the touchstone of realism: not in quantity of information but in how easily it issues. And this depends upon how stereotyped the mode of representation is, upon how commonplace the labels and their uses have become.

Realism is relative, determined by the system of representation standard for a given culture or person at a given time. Newer or older or alien systems are accounted artificial or unskilled. For a Fifth-Dynasty Egyptian the straightforward way of representing something is not the same as for an eighteenth-century Japanese; and neither way is the same as for an early twentieth-century Englishman. Each would to some extent have to learn how to read a picture in either of the other styles. This relativity is obscured by our tendency to omit specifying a frame of reference when it is our own. "Realism" thus often comes to be used as the name for a particular style or system of representation. Just as on this planet we usually think of objects as fixed if they are at a constant position in relation to the earth, so in this period and place we usually think of paintings as literal or realistic if they are in a traditional[29] European style of representation. But such egocentric ellipsis must not tempt us to infer that these objects (or any others) are absolutely fixed, or that such pictures (or any others) are absolutely realistic.

Shifts in standard can occur rather rapidly. The very effectiveness that may attend judicious departure from a traditional system of representation sometimes inclines us at least temporarily to install the newer mode as standard. We then speak of an artist's having achieved a new degree of realism, or having found new means for the realistic rendering of (say) light or motion. What happens here is something like the 'discovery' that not the earth but the sun is 'really fixed.' Advantages of a new frame of reference, partly because of their novelty, encourage its enthronement on some occasions in place of the customary frame. Nevertheless, whether an object is 'really fixed' or a picture is realistic depends at any time entirely upon what frame or mode is then standard. Realism is a matter not of any constant or absolute relationship between a picture and its object but of a relationship between the system of representation employed in the picture and the standard system. Most of the time, of course, the traditional system is taken as standard; and the literal or realistic or naturalistic system of representation is simply the customary one.

Realistic representation, in brief, depends not upon imitation or illusion or information but upon inculcation. Almost any picture may represent almost anything; that is, given picture and object there is usually a system of representation, a plan of correlation, under which the picture represents the object.[30] How correct the picture is under that system depends upon how accurate is the information about the object that is obtained by reading the picture according to that system. But how literal or realistic the picture is depends upon how standard the system is. If representation is a matter of choice and correctness a matter of information, realism is a matter of habit.

Our addiction, in the face of overwhelming counterevidence, to thinking of resemblance as the measure of realism is easily understood in these terms. Representational customs, which govern realism, also tend to generate resemblance. That a picture looks like nature often means only that it looks the way nature is usually painted. Again, what will deceive me into supposing that an object of a given kind is before me depends upon what I have noticed about such objects, and this in turn is affected by the way I am used to seeing them depicted. Resemblance and deceptiveness, far from being constant and independent sources and criteria of representational practice are in some degree products of it.[31]

### 9 Depiction and Description

Throughout, I have stressed the analogy between pictorial representation and verbal description because it seems to me both corrective and suggestive. Reference to an object is a necessary condition for depiction or description of it, but no degree of resemblance is a necessary or sufficient condition for either. Both depiction and description participate in the formation and characterization of the world; and they interact with each other and with perception and knowledge. They are ways of classifying by means of labels having singular or multiple or null reference. The labels, pictorial or verbal, are themselves classified into kinds; and the interpretation of fictive labels, and of depiction-*as* and description-*as*, is in terms of such kinds. Application and classification of a label are relative to a system;[32] and there are countless alternative systems of representation and description. Such systems are the products of stipulation and habituation in varying proportions. The choice among systems is free; but given a system, the question whether a newly encountered object is a desk or a unicorn-picture or is represented by a certain painting is a question of the propriety, under that system, of projecting the predicate "desk" or the predicate "unicorn-picture" or the painting over the thing in question, and the decision both is guided by and guides usage for that system.[33]

The temptation is to call a system of depiction a language; but here I stop short. The question what distinguishes representational from linguistic systems needs close examination. One might suppose that the criterion of realism can be made to serve here, too; that symbols grade from the most realistic depictions through less and less realistic ones to descriptions. This is surely not the case; the measure of realism is habituation, but descriptions do not become depictions by habituation. The most commonplace nouns of English have not become pictures.

To say that depiction is by pictures while description is by passages is not only to beg a good part of the question but also to overlook the fact that denotation by a picture does not always constitute depiction; for example, if pictures in a commandeered museum are used by a briefing officer to stand for enemy emplacements, the pictures do not thereby represent these emplacements. To represent, a picture must function as a pictorial symbol; that is, function in a system such that what is denoted depends solely upon the pictorial properties of the symbol. The pictorial properties might be roughly delimited by a loose recursive specification.[34] An elementary pictorial characterization states what color a picture has at a given place on its face. Other pictorial characterizations in effect combine many such elementary ones by conjunction, alternation, quantification, etc. Thus a pictorial characterization may name the colors at several places, or state that the color at one place lies within a certain range, or state that the colors at two places are complementary, and so on. Briefly, a pictorial characterization says more or less completely and more or less specifically what colors the picture has at what places. And the properties correctly ascribed to a picture by pictorial characterization are its pictorial properties.

All this, though, is much too special. The formula can easily be broadened a little but resists generalization. Sculptures with denotation dependent upon such sculptural properties as shape do represent, but words with denotation dependent upon such verbal properties as spelling do not. We have not yet captured the crucial difference between pictorial and verbal properties, between nonlinguistic and linguistic symbols or systems, that makes the difference between representation in general and description.

What we have done so far is to subsume representation with description under denotation. Representation is thus disengaged from perverted ideas of it as an idiosyncratic physical process like mirroring, and is recognized as a symbolic relationship that is relative and variable. Furthermore, representation is thus contrasted with nondenotative modes of reference.

## Notes

1. What I am considering here is pictorial representation, or depiction, and the comparable representation that may occur in other arts. Natural objects may represent in the same way: witness the man in the moon and the sheep-dog in the clouds. Some writers use "representation" as the general term for all varieties of what I call symbolization or reference, and use "symbolic" for the verbal and other nonpictorial signs I call nonrepresentational. "Represent" and its derivatives have many other uses, and while I shall mention some of these later, others do not concern us here at all. Among the latter, for example, are the uses according to which an ambassador represents a nation and makes representations to a foreign government.

2. I use "object" indifferently for anything a picture represents, whether an apple or a battle. A quirk of language makes a represented object a subject.

3. Not until the next chapter will denotation be distinguished from other varieties of reference.

4. In "The Way the World Is," *Review of Metaphysics* XIV (1960), 48–56, I have argued that the world is as many ways as it can be truly described, seen, pictured, etc., and that there is no such thing as *the* way the world is. Ryle takes a somewhat similar position (*Dilemmas* [Cambridge, England: Cambridge University Press, 1954], pp. 75–77) in comparing the relation between a table as a perceived solid object and the table as a swarm of atoms with the relation between a college library according to the catalogue and according to the accountant. Some have proposed that the way the world is could be arrived at by conjoining all the several ways. This overlooks the fact that conjunction itself is peculiar to certain systems; for example, we cannot conjoin a paragraph and a picture. And any attempted combination of all the ways would be itself only one—and a peculiarly indigestible one—of the ways the world is. But what is *the world* that is in so many ways? To speak of ways the world is, or ways of describing or picturing the world, is to speak of world-descriptions or world-pictures, and does not imply there is a unique thing—or indeed anything—that is described or pictured. Of course, none of this implies, either, that nothing is described or pictured. See further section 5 and note 19 below.

5. In *Art and Illusion* (New York: Pantheon Books, 1960), pp. 297–298 and elsewhere. On the general matter of the relativity of vision, see also such works as R. L. Gregory, *Eye and Brain* (New York: McGraw-Hill Book Co., 1966), and Marshall H. Segall, Donald Campbell, and Melville J. Herskovits, *The Influence of Culture on Visual Perception* (Indianapolis and New York: The Bobbs-Merrill Co., Inc., 1966).

6. For samples of psychological investigation of this point, see Jerome S. Bruner's "On Perceptual Readiness," *Psychological Review* LXIV (1957), 123–152, and other articles there cited; also William P. Brown, "Conceptions of Perceptual Defense," *British Journal of Psychology Monograph Supplement* XXXV (Cambridge, England: Cambridge University Press, 1961).

7. On the emptiness of the notion of epistemological primacy and the futility of the search for the absolute given, see my *Structure of Appearance* (2nd ed.; Indianapolis and New York: The Bobbs-Merrill Co., Inc., 1966—hereinafter referred to as *SA*), pp. 132–145, and "Sense and Certainty," *Philosophical Review* LXI (1952), 160–167.

8. And this is no less true when the instrument we use is a camera rather than a pen or brush. The choice and handling of the instrument participate in the construal. A photographer's work, like a painter's, can evince a personal style. Concerning the 'corrections' provided for in some cameras, see section 3 below.

9. *Art and Illusion*, pp. 254 and 257.

10. From "Pictures, Perspective, and Perception," *Daedalus* (Winter 1960), p. 227. Gibson does not appear to have explicitly retracted these statements, though his interesting recent book, *The Senses Considered as Perceptual Systems* (Boston: Houghton Mifflin Co., 1966), deals at length with related problems.

11. Substantially this argument has, of course, been advanced by many other writers. For an interesting discussion see D. Gioseffi, *Prospettiva Artificialis* (Trieste: Università degli studi di Trieste, Istituto di Storia dell'Arte Antica e Moderna, 1957), and a long review of the same by M. H. Pirenne in *The Art Bulletin* XLI (1959), 213–217. I am indebted to Professor Meyer Schapiro for this reference.

12. Cf. Gombrich's discussion of 'gates' in *Art and Illusion*, pp. 250–251.

13. See L. A. Riggs, F. Ratliff, J. C. Cornsweet, and T. Cornsweet, "The Disappearance of Steadily Fixated Visual Objects," *Journal of the Optical Society of America* XLIII (1953), 495–501. More recently, the drastic and rapid changes in perception that occur during fixation have been investigated in detail by R. M. Pritchard, W. Heron, and D. I. Hebb in "Visual Perception Approached by the Method of Stabilized Images," *Canadian Journal of Psychology* XIV (1960), 67–77. According to this article, the image tends to regenerate, sometimes transformed into meaningful units not initially present.

14. But note that owing to the protuberance of the cornea, the eye when rotated, even with the head fixed, can often see slightly around the sides of an object.

15. Adaptation to spectacles of various kinds has been the subject of extensive experimentation. See, for example, J. E. Hochberg, "Effects of Gestalt Revolution: The Cornell Symposium on Perception," *Psychological Review* LXIV (1959), 74–75; J. G. Taylor, *The Behavioral Basis of Perception* (New Haven: Yale University Press, 1962), pp. 166–185; and Irvin Rock, *The Nature of Perceptual Adaptation* (New York: Basic Books, Inc., 1966). Anyone can readily verify for himself how easy it is to learn to read pictures drawn in reversed or otherwise transformed perspective. Reversed perspective often occurs in Oriental, Byzantine, and mediaeval art; sometimes standard and reversed perspective are even used in different parts of one picture—see, for example, Leonid Ouspensky and Vladimir

Lossky, *The Meaning of Icons* (Boston: Boston Book and Art Shop, 1952), p. 42 (note 1), p. 200. Concerning the fact that one has to learn to read pictures in standard perspective, Melville J. Herskovits writes in *Man and His Works* (New York: Alfred A. Knopf, 1948), p. 381: "More than one ethnographer has reported the experience of showing a clear photograph of a house, a person, a familiar landscape to people living in a culture innocent of any knowledge of photography, and to have the picture held at all possible angles, or turned over for an inspection of its blank back, as the native tried to interpret this meaningless arrangement of varying shades of grey on a piece of paper. For even the clearest photograph is only an interpretation of what the camera sees."

16. [Ed.—Goodman included a] frontispiece to this chapter. As Klee remarks, the drawing looks quite normal if taken as representing a floor but awry as representing a facade, even though in the two cases parallels in the object represented recede equally from the eye.

17. Indeed, this is the orthodox position, taken not only by Pirenne, Gibson, and Gombrich, but by most writers on the subject. Some exceptions, besides Klee, are Erwin Panofsky, "Die Perspektive als 'Symbolische Form,'" *Vorträge der Bibliothek Warburg* (1924–1925), pp. 258ff; Rudolf Arnheim, *Art and Visual Perception* (Berkeley: University of California Press, 1954), e.g., pp. 92ff, and elsewhere; and in an earlier day, one Arthur Parsey, who was taken to task for his heterodox views by Augustus de Morgan in *Budget of Paradoxes* (London, 1872), pp. 176–177. I am indebted to Mr. P. T. Geach for this last reference. Interesting discussions of perspective will be found in *The Birth and Rebirth of Pictorial Space*, by John White (New York: Thomas Yoseloff, 1958), chs. 8 and 13.

18. The optimal way of seeing the tower facade may be by looking straight at it from *m*; but then the optimal way of seeing the railroad tracks would be by looking down on them from directly above the midpoint of their length.

19. The substance of this and the following two paragraphs is contained in my paper, "On Likeness of Meaning," *Analysis* I (1949), 1–7, and discussed further in the sequel, "On Some Differences about Meaning," *Analysis* XIII (1953), 90–96. See also the parallel treatment of the problem of statements 'about fictive entities' in "About," *Mind* LXX (1961), especially pp. 18–22. In a series of papers from 1939 on (many of them reworked and republished in *From a Logical Point of View* [Cambridge, Mass.: Harvard University Press, 1953]), W. V. Quine had sharpened the distinction between syncategorematic and other expressions, and had shown that careful observance of this distinction could dispel many philosophical problems.

I use the device of hyphenation (e.g., in "man-picture") as an aid in technical discourse only, not as a reform of everyday usage, where the context normally prevents confusion and where the impetus to fallacious existential inference is less compulsive, if not less consequential, than in philosophy. In what follows, "man-picture" will always be an abbreviation for the longer and more usual "picture representing a man," taken as an unbreakable one-place predicate that need not apply to all or only to pictures that represent an actual man. The same general principle will govern use of all compounds of the form "——picture." Thus, for example, I shall not use "Churchill-picture" as an abbreviation for "picture painted by Churchill" or for "picture belonging to Churchill." Note, furthermore, that a square-picture is not necessarily a square picture but a square-representing-picture.

20. Strictly, we should speak here of utterances and inscriptions; for different instances of the same term may differ in denotation. Indeed, classifying replicas together to constitute terms is only one, and a far from simple, way of classifying utterances and inscriptions into kinds. See further *SA*, pp. 359–363, and also chapter IV [of *Languages of Art*].

21. To know how to apply all compounds of a term would entail knowing how to apply at least some compounds of all other terms in the language. We normally say we understand a term when we know reasonably well how to apply it and enough of its more usual compounds. If for a given "———picture" compound we are in doubt about how to apply it in a rather high percentage of cases, this is also true of the correlative "represents as a ———" predicate. Of course, understanding a term is not exclusively a matter of knowing what inferences can be drawn from and to statements containing the term.

22. I am indebted to Mr. H. P. Grice and Mr. J. O. Urmson for comments leading to clarification of this point. Sometimes, the portion in question may be marked off along other than temporal lines. On the notion of a temporal part, see *SA*, pp. 127–129.

23. The contained picture may, nevertheless, denote given objects and be a soandso-picture *as a result* of its incorporation in the context of the containing picture, just as "triangle" through occurrence in "triangle and drums" may denote given musical instruments and be a musical-instrument-description.

24. This covers cases where *k* is represented as a soandso by either a whole picture or part of it. As remarked in the latter part of note 19 above, there are restrictions upon the admissible replacements for "soandso" in this definitional schema; an old or square picture or one belonging to Churchill does not thereby represent him as old or square or self-possessed.

25. The reader will already have noticed that "description" in the present text is not confined to what are called definite descriptions in logic but covers all predicates from proper names through purple passages, whether with singular, multiple, or null denotation.

26. The picture does not denote the class picked out, but denotes the no or one or several members of that class. A picture of course belongs to countless classes, but only certain of these (e.g., the class of square-pictures, the class of Churchill-pictures) and not others (e.g., the class of square pictures, the class of pictures belonging to Churchill) have to do with what the picture represents-as.

27. From Constable's fourth lecture at the Royal Institution in 1836; see C. R. Leslie, *Memoirs of the Life of John Constable*, ed. Jonathan Mayne (London: Phaidon Press, 1951), p. 323.

28. Cf. Descartes, *Meditations on the First Philosophy*, trans. E. S. Haldane and G. R. T. Ross (New York: Dover Publications, Inc., 1955), I, 155; also Berkeley, "Essay Towards a New Theory of Vision," in *Works on Vision*, ed. C. M. Turbayne (New York: The Bobbs-Merrill Co., Inc., 1963), p. 42.

29. Or conventional; but "conventional" is a dangerously ambiguous term: witness the contrast between "very conventional" (as "very ordinary") and "highly conventional" or "highly conventionalized" (as "very artificial").

30. Indeed, there are usually many such systems. A picture that under one

(unfamiliar) system is a correct but highly unrealistic representation of an object may under another (the standard) system be a realistic but very incorrect representation of the same object. Only if accurate information is yielded under the standard system will the picture represent the object both correctly and literally.

31. Neither here nor elsewhere have I argued that there is no constant relation of resemblance; judgments of similarity in selected and familiar respects are, even though rough and fallible, as objective and categorical as any that are made in describing the world. But judgments of complex overall resemblance are another matter. In the first place, they depend upon the aspects or factors in terms of which the objects in question are compared; and this depends heavily on conceptual and perceptual habit. In the second place, even with these factors determined, similarities along the several axes are not immediately commensurate, and the degree of total resemblance will depend upon how the several factors are weighted. Normally, for example, nearness in geographical location has little to do with our judgment of resemblance among buildings but much to do with our judgment of resemblance among building lots. The assessment of total resemblance is subject to influences galore, and our representational customs are not least among these. In sum, I have sought to show that insofar as resemblance is a constant and objective relation, resemblance between a picture and what it represents does not coincide with realism: and that insofar as resemblance does coincide with realism, the criteria of resemblance vary with changes in representational practice.

32. [Ed.— ... ] a symbol system (not necessarily formal) embraces both the symbols and their interpretation, and a language is a symbol system of a particular kind. A formal system is couched in a language and has stated primitives and routes of derivation.

33. On the interaction between specific judgment and general policy, see my *Fact, Fiction, and Forecast* (2nd ed.: Indianapolis and New York; The Bobbs-Merrill Co., Inc., 1965—hereinafter referred to as *FFF*), pp. 63–64. The propriety of projecting a predicate might be said to depend upon what similarities there are among the objects in question; but with equal truth, similarities among the objects might be said to depend upon what predicates are projected (cf. note 31 above, and *FFF*, pp. 82, 96–99, 119–120). Concerning the relationship between the 'language theory' of pictures outlined above and the much discussed 'picture theory' of language, see "The Way the World Is" (cited in note 4 above), pp. 55–56.

34. The specification that follows has many shortcomings, among them the absence of provision for the often three-dimensional nature of picture surfaces. But while a rough distinction between pictorial and other properties is useful here [Ed.— ...], nothing very vital rests on its precise formulation.

# 16.    Picturing and Representing
## MARX W. WARTOFSKY

The thesis I want to present in this chapter, although stated very baldly, is: human vision is a cultural and historical product of the creative activity of making pictures. To put it somewhat differently, *human* vision is an artifact, produced by means of other artifacts—for example, by pictures; as such, it is a historically variable mode of perception, which changes with changes in our modes of representation. What follows from this thesis, if it is true, are two radical conclusions—one, methodological, the other, epistemological.

The methodologically radical conclusion is that all theoretical attempts to construct a theory of vision, which presuppose that seeing is an essential, unchanging structure of process; or that the human eye is describable in some generic physiological way, are, if not fundamentally mistaken, then essentially incomplete. For the plasticity of the visual system, if I am right, is such that it requires a historical account of its development and not simply a biological account of its evolution, whether phylogenetically or ontogenetically.

The radical epistemological conclusion is that there is no intrinsically veridical, or "correct," mode of representation, that is, there is no criterion of veridicality that is not itself a product of the social and historical choices of norms of visual representation. There is, therefore, no canon of truth in perception that can be established by reduction to the physiology of vision, or to optics, or to some species-specific biological, or even ecological, account. That is not to say that we do not inherit the mammalian eye, nor is it to say that human vision is not based in an evolved, adaptive

From Marx. W. Wartofsky, "Picturing and Representing," in Calvin F. Nodine and Dennis F. Fisher (eds.), *Perception and Pictoral Representation* (New York: Praeger Publishers, 1979). Reprinted with permission of the author and Praeger Publishers.

structure which develops with the speciation of Homo sapiens. However, truth in perception, as I will argue, is bound to canons of the veridicality of representation; these, in turn, have a history and are rooted in our social practice and in our own activities of picturing and representing. Thus, it is we who *create* the very norms of veridicality by our pictorial practice. Such norms are not arbitrary, though they are conventional; they are not biological but historical.

The larger theoretical enterprise of which the thesis that I propose is a part may be characterized as a historical epistemology. I will present one specific aspect of such a historical theory of vision, which I have begun to develop elsewhere (Wartofsky 1972, 1976). At issue is the question of how representation is possible in the specific mode of representation that we call *picturing*—and, more specifically, in that subcategory of pictures which we call *paintings*.

My argument may be summarized in five points. First, the act of representing something pictorially is a creative act. That is to say, it does not depend on some antecedent notion that something (a picture) "looks like" or "resembles" or "represents" something else (for example, a scene, an object, a person, and so forth), but rather that it is *we* who create the similarity which counts as representational. Similarity is not given, but achieved; made, not discovered. It is invented and created.

Second, the perceptual system—and the visual system in particular—is biologically evolved to take certain things in the visual world as being *like* or *resembling* others, by virtue of the forms of life activity of a given species, that is, the means by which its individual members preserve themselves in existence and reproduce the species life. These canons of resemblance, similarity, or identity are mapped into the neural and neuromuscular structure of the species; they may be said to be coded into its genetic structure by natural selection. The human species, however, has a radically alternative mode of mapping its forms of life activity into structure, and this is by means of canons of visual representation, that is, embodied rules for taking one thing as a representation of something else. Pictures—or rather styles of pictorial representation—exemplify canons of representation, by means of which we come to *see* the visual world as *like* the picture.

Third, the rules of linear perspective in painting and drawing are *not* "correct" representations of the way things "look" but rather proposals to see things the way they are represented pictorially. When they come to look the way they are pictured, it is because we have adopted the rule of picturing as a rule of seeing the world—that is, we *see* by way of our picturing.

Fourth, the alleged paradox of pictures—namely, that the three-dimensional world is represented in a two-dimensional image of the world—is not a paradox; it is dissolved when we recognize that in taking a picture as a representation of the world, we come to take the world as a two-dimensional picture, which is, in *this* respect, like what pictures or represents it. When we are fooled, then the picture is no longer, properly speaking, a picture. However, we are rarely fooled. The argument is this: We say that representational pictures (for example, paintings) "look" three dimensional, that is, they "look like" the three-dimensional objects or scenes which they represent. However, we take the world to "look" three dimensional only by contrast to the two-dimensionality of pictures. The visual concept of "three dimensionality" is thus a constructive concept, which depends upon reference to, or a relation to, the two dimensionality of pictures. We would have no distinctive notion of the three dimensionality of the visual world except for the distinction we come to draw between it and two-dimensional representations of it. In short, the making of two-dimensional representations, or pictures, is what generates the contrastive visual concept of three dimensionality. I would suggest that the geometry which defines the plane projection of a solid is likewise dependent on the more primitive notion of a picture, that is, a representation or configuration in the two-dimensional plane.

Fifth, and finally, modes of picturing change, with changes in form of our social, technological, and intellectual praxis; representation has a history, and thus, in coming to adopt different modes of representation, we literally change our visual world. Human vision is an artifact created and changed by the modes of picturing. Different modes of picturing have different theories. We have *adopted* the theory of linear perspective as our theory of veridical representation. It is not incorrect. But neither is it correct. Veridicality is not a given feature of a mode of picturing. It is defined by the theory of pictorial representation that we come to adopt.

So much for the summary of my argument. Now to the question posed for this volume: "What is a painting?" The question needs to be specified more concretely in order to be answered. It has many answers, depending on what it is that is being asked. A merely ostensive definition—"that's a painting" (pointing at one)—will not do, but it does hide a deeper answer. Namely, paintings are the sorts of things that are *taken* to be paintings. Thus revised, the question becomes, "What is it we take to be a painting?"

I plan to deal with only one aspect of this question here, namely, that of pictorial representation, which is *one* of the things paintings do (or are taken to do). In order to deal with this question, however, there is a more general characterization I want to give to paintings, apart from, but related to their representational capacities, that is, paintings are artifacts, made things, the products of intentional human activity, and insofar as they are representational, they are intended as representations—that is, they are artifacts whose purpose it is to represent something.

The question then becomes, "How do the kinds of artifacts called *pictures* represent?" What is *made* in such a way as to come to represent something else? More specifically, in the case of painting, how do arrangements of lines, areas, colors, and gradients of dark and light on a two-dimensional plane surface come to represent three-dimensional objects, scenes, and persons?

There are several possible answers to this question. I will examine three, but first, I would like to frame my approach so that the context of my considerations will be clear. There are several general points to be made. First, if (as is clear and undisputed) representation has a history and if (as is yet unclear and in dispute) this history is a crucial factor in the historical and cultural evolution of the human visual system, then the history of art becomes an essential component of the theory of vision: alternative modes of representation, the history of styles in painting, the theoretical analysis and reconstruction of the visual concepts of space, objects, and relations, which are characteristic of a given style or period, the phenomenological reconstruction of the modes of intentionality that identify an art-historical epoch, or a school all become essential components of any theory of vision, as crucial as the study of the psychology or physiology of vision and inseparable from these latter inquiries.

Second, since modes of representation are not simply or abstractly visual matters but involve also the larger social, technological, political, scientific, and even ideological contexts of human cognitive practice, a theory of vision is embedded in this larger framework of human social activity. Our seeing is a mode of our activity; just as vision cannot be conceived of simply as an activity of the eye, taken out of its context as part of the mammalian brain, and of the whole organism, so, too, it cannot be conceived of simply as the activity of the visual system, taken out of the context of the form of life in which this system operates, in which it develops, and which it is capable of transforming. To put this another way: it is neither the eye nor the visual system that sees. Rather, it is *we* who see, by means of the eye or the visual system. Similarly, it is not feet that walk. Rather, it is *we* using our feet. I could not walk without feet or see without eyes, but the *I* that sees, walks, talks, paints, argues, and gives papers at symposia is a social being, an individuated member of a life-form which is essentially historical and social. No mode of the life activity of such an individual can be adequately characterized, therefore, by abstractive reduction to the particular organs or apparatus by means of which this life activity proceeds. In this regard, the approach I am proposing is analogous to James Gibson's ecological approach to vision, but it differs sharply from his in that the ecology I am suggesting here is not a natural or biologically defined one but a cultural, or sociohistorical, "ecology." In short, vision, or seeing, is not merely the after-product, the epiphenomenon, of a given apparatus in a given environment or simply the operation of an organ. It is a creative activity that can be transformed and which, in turn, can itself transform a given form of life.

Third, and finally, if vision is a historically variable mode of cognitive practice that changes with alterations in our modes of representation, then the evolution of our visual system, as a cultural artifact, is, in contrast with its evolution as a biological system, no longer Darwinian but Lamarckian. That is to say, in the cultural evolution of *this* artifact, that is, of vision, there is transmission of acquired characteristics from one generation to the next. The mode of transmission is, therefore, no longer genetic but becomes social or cultural. The visual culture of a society or of an age is not inherited by the operation of genetic transmission or by means of the biochemical structures or codes that have been selected out, preserved, and developed by natural selection but rather by means of social structures—in particular, visual artifacts and modes of picturing. To put it simply, the artifact is to cultural evolution what the gene is to biological evolution. Cultural evolution, in contrast with biological evolution, is Larmarckian and not Darwinian. Such a thesis makes it possible to account for the plasticity and also the rapidity of cultural evolution; further, it is directly opposed to the current theoretical approaches to human cognition, as well as to human sociality, which find it necessary to focus on the alleged biological or genetic constraints on, or determinants of, modes of human activity.

To summarize this introductory discussion: (1) we see by way of our picturing—changes in our modes of cognition, in general, and in our modes of vision, in particular, are concomitant with changes in our modes of social practice, in general, and with our modes of pictorial representation, in particular; (2) the human visual system is therefore not simply the biological structure of our species evolution but an artifact produced by our own creative activity of picturing and seeing; thus, its plasticity cannot be defined reductively in biological, that is, physiological or genetic, terms.

Against this larger framework, let me now turn to the specific question, "How is representation possible?" The title of this chapter, "Picturing and Representing," is intended to correct a certain initial tendency to hypostatize: "Pictures and representations" suggests, I think, that we *begin* with certain entities already understood. I want to put in question what it is we understand by such entities and to emphasize that pictures picture and representations represent by virtue of the fact that they are the products of an activity that *intends* them as picturing and representing. That is, for something to *be* a picture, it needs to be *made* as a picture and *taken* as a picture; for something to *be* a representation, it has to be *intended* to represent, and this intention has to be understood in taking it *as* a representation. Nothing, then, is a picture or a representation in itself apart from being made as one or taken as one. There are no entities, then, which may "objectively" be characterized in this way. Instead, things of a certain sort are constituted as pictures and representations by makers and viewers. There is a radical consequence to this view as well: if nothing is intrinsically a picture or a representation, then we cannot ascribe a set of intrinsic properties to something that would identify it as a picture. In effect, *anything* can *be* a picture or a representation if it is made to be one or is taken as one. Let me make clear that I propose this in the strongest way, without qualification, that is, it is not the case that certain things are taken to be pictures or representations *because* they exhibit certain visual properties but, rather, that they come to exhibit certain visual properties *because* they are taken to be pictures or representations.

Now, this flies in the face of common sense—or seems to, for, in fact, not everything *is* taken to be a picture or a representation; in fact, a very narrow range of things is so taken at any given time or in any given culture. However, this narrow range itself *is* variable: some things *not* taken or made as pictures in one context are pictures in another. Moreover, insofar as pictures represent, it would appear that the relation of representing is based on some relation between some properties of the picture and some properties of what it is taken to represent, usually, a relation of resembling, or similarity, or likeness. The pictorial representation is said to be a representation by virtue of being a *likeness;* therefore, a successful representation shares properties with its reference.

My first claim, against this common view, is not original but is shared with Goodman (1976), upon whose more systematic and elaborrated argument on thie point I will rely. It is that representation requires no relation of resemblance, or likeness, but is rather constituted as an act of reference. My second claim, however, goes beyond this, though it is in the same spirit. It is that likeness, resemblance, or similarity is itself not *given* in our visual perception; it is not a primitive, irreducible relation, as Mill took it to be (in Nagel 1950), but is itself an *achieved* relation, that is, one which is constructed and, therefore, construable (compare Manns 1971). Things come to be similar, to resemble each other, be likenesses by virtue of being *made* as similar, or alike, or being taken as resembling each other. Thus, even in the relation of representation in which it is alleged that the representation is *like* what it represents, I am arguing that it is so by virtue of our taking it to be so, in a given respect. It is we who *create* similarity, resemblance, or likeness in those forms of pictorial representation that are said to be based on it. We do so, I would argue, by producing artifacts that are specifically intended to be like other things, to represent them, in this way. The classic story here, of course, is about Picasso's portrait of Gertrude Stein. When told that it did not look like her, he answered: "It will."

On the basis of one interpretation, this may be no more than to say that in making a representation, we imitate what it is that is being represented, that is, we construct something that is similar to what it is to represent—in effect, we make a copy. In this case, then, there should be no surprise that there is resemblance, likeness, or similarity, for is not the representation made expressly to be like what it represents? But this interpretation—the common one—begs precisely the question that it sets out to answer. For in order to make something that is similar to, or resembles, something else, we have to establish *what* the feature is which is being "copied" in this sense, *and* that something else in fact resembles it. Imitating, copying, or reproducing the features of a given object, scene, or relation requires therefore just that creative act of *achieving* the likeness, of establishing that something resembles something else, which is presupposed as a *given* in the standard view. In a second interpretation, one thing may be said to re-present another, not in being like it, or resembling it, in some common properties—for example, same shape, or color, or same relation among parts—but, rather, in causally effecting the same response. Therefore, the representation comes to represent by virtue of bringing about the same physiological response or visual experience as the thing or scene represented, though it does so by means that are dissimilar. So, for example, in this view, paintings of landscapes or figures are pictorial artifacts and, thus, two-dimensional arrays: they are not themselves "like," in this sense, the three-dimensional objects or spaces that they represent. Yet, they are arranged in such a way as to deliver the "same" or a similar light flux to the retina, and thus initiate similar visual responses.

This view, perhaps the most popular psychological theory of representation, retains semblance in the phenomenal experience, or in the response, though it gives up identity or even similarity in the stimulus. In this sense, it presupposes that similarity in the response is passive—a matter of equivalent causal or antecedent conditions, whose equivalence is judged by the sameness of the response.

The faults with this view are many. But let me simply point to one experimental fact: the recognition of pictures as representations of x ranges over pictures that are obviously *not* similar to each other in any respect one could define as "causally equivalent." Gibson would evade this point by arguing that for all their dissimilarity, such a range of alternative pictorial representations are all alike in transmitting the same higher-order visual *invariances* criteria for object or scene recognition, though through the range of transformations. But such *invariances*, in Gibson's ecological optics, are taken to be objective features of the ambient light, and the organism—in this case, the human one, or, perhaps, the higher vertebrate in general—has so evolved its visual system as to be able to pick up these invariances directly—that is, without processing lower-order variations. The net is woven, so to speak, in order to catch fish of only a certain size (or a higher order) and to let all the smaller ones (or those of a lower order) slip through unnoticed.

This interpretation begs the question in a different way from the first, for it *presupposes* as *invariant* just those features that representations represent—for example, so-called real shape or real size in the case of perceptual constancies—and, thus, does not explain how representation is possible; in fact, it theoretically constructs an explication of *one* kind of representation—namely, that which is constructed in accordance with the rules of linear perspective—that it takes to be canonical. It is no surprise then—in fact, it is inevitable, because circular—that in Gibson's view, what we see is what there is, and representations succeed because they re-present what we see.

If I deny that we have direct access to the way things really *are*, at least as the real objects in our ecological space or the space of our species' life activity, then how else is representation possible? What links representation to *representandum*: how do we have access to the properties of the visual world so that we know how to represent them successfully?

To take a step further, I would propose that we do not come to have visual concepts of the properties of the visual world *except* by such a process of creating representations of it. Nature comes to imitate art precisely because what we make of nature as an object of vision is constituted, in large part, by how we choose to represent it.

Before proceeding with the argument, it may be useful to make explicit some distinctions that have thus far been merely suggested. I have stated that human vision is itself an artifact, produced by other artifacts, namely, pictures. I call something an artifact if it is a product of human activity, in the sense that it comes into being as the result of intentional human making and is made or constructed with an end-in-view or for a use or purpose. This use or purpose defines the artifact as what it is, so that an artifact is what it is made *for*: it is, in short, a teleological entity. It may be odd to talk of vision or seeing in this way, but in fact, it is we who have shaped our vision to certain uses—who have adopted, adapted, and replaced different visual modes in our pursuit of different interests and ends. We have, in effect, learned to read the visual world in different ways, depending on our interests and needs.

One objection to such a view is, obviously, that the physiology of the visual system, though it may be understood as a biological adaptation to a form of life, is not itself the product of our own deliberate design nor is it subject to our intentional manipulation. We cannot be said to "change" our visual physiology as our interests or purposes change, for the structure is a genetically determined one and its evolution to the present species-form is the product of natural and not cultural selection. Within the confines of gross physiology, this is, I believe, evidently true. The adaptive variation of the visual system, in the course of species evolution, is the work of natural selection. But even here, we may characterize this species evolution as the mapping into the organism's genetic makeup of those features of its life-world and life activity that are requisite for its species-survival. The story is different, however, for the development of vision beyond the species level that is, for the differentiation of visual perceptions which proceed with cultural evolution or with historical changes in the human forms of life. One may go so far as to claim (with Penfield 1966) that the physiological ontogenesis of the neural system in general (and for the visual cortex in particular) is a differentiated one, which maps into the individual's neural structure the specific modes of experience and activity that characterize the life history of that individual. But one need not go so far to see that the visual system as a *way of seeing* is subject to the variability of modes of visual re-presentation.

What then *are* pictures and representations, and specifically, what is a painting? Let me make a distinction between pictures and representations. Pictures are visual artifacts, that is to say, pictures are made to be seen. Many other artifacts, are of course, also visible, but by visual artifact, I mean something expressly made for the purpose of being seen. Pictures, on the other hand, do not exhaust the class of visual artifacts. One may include, here, any marks, signs, objects, or expressions that are expressly made to be seen or any entities which come to be taken principally as objects of vision. So, for example, physiognomic expression, hand signs, sculpted objects, signs or markings of warning, direction, ownership, kinship, and so forth, may be taken as visual artifacts in this sense, that is, that they are intended to be seen and to communicate a meaning visually. Thus, modes of dress, scarification, gestures, and facial expressions are all such artifacts. Pictures, as a special class of such artifacts, I will take to be as those that are made upon a plane surface (thus, not gestures or sculptures for example) and which depend on line or color as their visual means. Not all pictures are representations, though all pictures may be said to have meaning. Moreover, natural objects or scenes may be *taken* pictorially, though they are not made things. Thus, we may see a tree, a sunset, or a cloud *as* a picture when we take it principally as a visual artifact, that is, as a meaningful form or shape seen as if it were on a plane surface. The force of this particular qualification will be seen later, since I will argue that it is by means of our activity of picturing that we come to be able to *see* the world *as* a picture and that the standard theory of vision which underlies constancy theory, in perception, and which proposes linear perspective as the correct representation of the visual world is based on an interpretation of the three-dimensional visual world as a two-dimensional picture.

Pictures, then, are visual artifacts made to be seen—and when understood in this way, seen as pictures. The ubiquitousness of the pictorial in human life leads us to forget that picture making and picture seeing are learned activities of the species. I would go further and suggest that picturing, both in making and seeing, is a fundamental form of the life activity of the human species and, in this sense, I am proposing that it is this activity that shapes human vision and develops it beyond the biological inheritance of the mammalian eye.

If all pictures are not representations, all pictures may be taken to be representations. Visual representations, briefly, are visual artifacts expressly made or understood as referring to something beyond themselves. Thus, there are nonvisual representations that are not pictures, for example, vocal reference in speech or gestural ostension; so, too, there are visual modes of reference that are not pictorial. Representation is symbolic. That is, one thing stands for another, under an interpretation given in a symbol system of which the representation is a part.

There is much more to be said about these distinctions, and Goodman's pioneering work (1976) goes a long way in developing this analysis. I will not pursue it here. But in summary, for the purposes of this chapter, I will distinguish pictures from representations, insofar as there are pictures that do not represent and representations that are not pictorial. More generally still, I will hold that *all* artifacts are putative representations, insofar as the very use, or understanding, or recognition and identification of an artifact as what it is requires that we take it as a representation of the mode of activity involved in its use or in its production. The artifact "represents," literally, in being taken as an imitation of an action, that is, the embodiment of the intentionality involved in its production, reproduction, or use. Thus, for example, a tool or a weapon, such as an ax or a spear, is not only something made to be used for a certain end but is also itself a representation of the action involved in its use and in its production or reproduction. An ax therefore, as a visual artifact, represents the activity of chopping and a spear, the activity of throwing in order to kill in the hunt. Moreover, the artifact also represents the mode of activity involved in its production or reproduction: it is a prototype of its replicas and a model of its own process of production.

What, then, marks off pictorial representations from the wider class of artifacts as putative representations? Again, the emphasis is on intentions, that is, what is intended in the making and taking of such visual artifacts. A spear is made for hunting and also represents the mode of action of the hunt. A spear-picture, on the other hand, is not made for hunting but is made expressly as a representation of a spear. It is principally made as a visual artifact, not a hunting artifact; its very intentionality is distinct in this sense; its purpose is different. Moreover, the representation is detached from use or from production: it functions independently of the activities or contexts of what it represents. Such a relatively autonomous act of representing is made possible by the picture, for it is in the express creation of something as a visual artifact, as something made to be seen, that the separation from other contexts of use becomes possible. It is not that representational pictures have no use but that their intended use is different. The use-value of a picture (representational or not) is in its being seen, whatever other purposes such visual presentation may have, for example, didactic, formal, expressive, informative, and so forth. The use-value of a representational picture is in its visual representation of its referent. It is in this sense that I argued earlier that something is a representation insofar as it is made to be, or taken to be, a representation. The features that come to be called representational will then depend on what is taken to serve this function. Anything can; but not everything, in fact, is chosen to do so. What is chosen to function as representational is a complex question, *not* to be resolved by appeal to physiological (or ecological) optics. Rather, it demands comparative study of what in fact has been taken as representational or what, in various alternative canons, continues to be taken as representational.

Pictures that represent, then, are artifacts which guide or shape our vision of the world, leading us to take *this* as like *that*, to pick out features of the seen world that are referred to by the representations we make, where the act of reference is itself a creative act and not merely a matching of pregiven similarities or identities. One may say, then, that representational pictures are *heuristic* and *didactic* artifacts. They teach us to see: they guide our vision in such a way that the seen world becomes the world scene.

*References*

Gibson, J., "The Ecological Approach to the Visual Perception of Pictures." *Leonardo* 11 (1978): 227–235.

Goodman, N. *Languages of Art.* 2d ed. Indianapolis, Ind.: Hackett, 1976.

Manns, J. W. "Representation, Relativism, and Resemblance." *The British Journal of Aesthetics* 11 (1971): 281–287.

Nagel, E., ed. *John Stewart Mill's Philosophy of Scientific Method.* New York: Hafner, 1950.

Penfield, W. "Comments and Discussion." In *Brain and Conscious Experience*, edited by J. C. Eccles, p. 248. New York: Springer-Verlag, 1966.

Wartofsky, M. "Pictures, Representations and the Understanding." In *Logic and Art—Essays in Honor of Nelson Goodman*, edited by R. Rudner and I. Scheffler, pp. 150–262. Indianapolis and New York: Bobbs-Merrill, 1972.

———. "Perception, Representation and the Forms of Action: Towards an Historical Epistemology." In *Ajatus* (Yearbook of the Philosophical Society of Finland), vol. 36, *Aesthesis: Essays on the Philosophy of Perception* (1976), pp. 19–43.

# 17.    Representation as Expression
## PETER KIVY

*1*

Honegger's *Pacific 231* has forced itself upon our attention frequently . . . as perhaps the paradigm of musical illustration: the most musically success-ful sound picture in the literature. For this reason . . . what Honegger said about his work is so altogether surprising. "I have not attempted the imitation of the sound of an engine in *Pacific 231*, but the expression of a visual impression and physical pleasure in a musical construction," he is quoted as remarking in an interview.[1] It is surprising, of course, because if *any* musical composition succeeds as an easily recognizable imitation of sound in music, it is Honegger's. If he did not intend this remarkable imitation of an engine, we must assume what is almost beyond belief: that the resemblance is purely fortuitous, a lucky (or unlucky) accident.

Why should Honegger have said such an extraordinary thing? That he was so self-deluded as not to have known what he was in fact doing, compositionally, seems as much beyond belief as that the remarkable picture of sound *in* sound was unintended. Yet so strong was his desire not to be taken for an imitator of sounds that he was impelled to say about his work what could not possibly have been true.

It is tempting to think that Honegger, like me, is really rejecting the concept of *imitation* rather than denying that his composition is a picture of sounds that, in fact, sounds remarkably like what it pictures. Or perhaps what Honegger really intended to convey, by hyperbole, is that *Pacific 231* is not *merely* an imitation or illustration of sounds, but an expressive

From Peter Kivy, *Sound and Semblance: Reflections on Musical Representation*, Chapter VII. Copyright © 1984 by Princeton University Press. Reprinted with permission of Princeton University Press. Some examples have been deleted; those that remain have not been renumbered.

musical composition in its own right, with some of the same *musical* values to be found in all serious symphonic writing. (It surely is no accident, in this regard, that he gave it the subtitle, *Mouvement Symphonique.*) All this may have a grain of truth in it. The piece is a fine example of symphonic writing, with many lyrical and expressive passages. It is not merely a sound picture, like, say, Mossolov's *The Iron Foundry.* But Honegger, after all, said what he said; and perhaps it would be more fruitful (not to say more honest) to try to understand what exactly he did say, and why he said it, rather than to try to say not what he said but what he *meant* (or what he *meant* to *say*). For what he said is not, by any means, unique in the history of music. The prejudice against musical illustration, and in favor of musical expression—they almost invariably come in each other's company—is deep-seated in composers, and of long standing in the profession. It behooves us to take this seriously, and to fathom its import.

*2*

How far back in time the argument between illustration and expression can be pushed I do not know, but it is clear that the Renaissance madrigal composers were devoted—their critics might have said addicted—to musical representation. And these so-called "madrigalisms" in which they indulged, along with certain criticisms their efforts elicited from the theorists preparing the way for monody, opera, and the musical Baroque, constitute a clear enough example of the tension between the concepts of musical representation and musical expression to provide us with a reasonable starting point, if not a true historical beginning.

Musicologists would surely agree that one of the most important of such theorists working in the seam between Renaissance and Baroque was Vincenzo Galilei (father of Galileo). He laid the theoretical foundations for the development of monody and opera, and, in the process, made illuminating remarks of a critical nature on Renaissance music in general, and musical representation in particular. The latter are of some interest to us here, and I will quote them at some length. Gallei writes:

> [Composers] will say that they are imitating the words when among the conceptions of these there are any meaning "to flee" or "to fly"; these they will declaim with the greatest rapidity and the least grace imaginable. In connection with the words meaning "to disappear," "to swoon," "to die," or actually "to be extinct" they have made the parts break off so abruptly, that instead of inducing the passion corresponding to any of these, they have aroused laughter and at other times

contempt in the listeners, who felt they were being ridiculed. Then
with words meaning "alone," "two," or "together" they have caused
one lone part, or two, or all parts together to sing with unheard-of
elegance. . . . And then, as sometimes happens, the conceptions they
have had in hand have made mention of the rolling of the drum, or
of the sound of the trumpet or any other such instrument, they have
sought to represent its sound in their music, without minding at all
that they were pronouncing these words in some unheard-of-man-
ner. . . . At another time, finding the line:

> He descended into hell, into the
> lap of Pluto,

they have made one part of the composition descend in such a way
that the singer has sounded more like someone groaning to frighten
children and terrify them than like anyone singing sense. In the
opposite way, finding this one:

> This one aspires to the stars,

in declaiming it they have ascended to a height that no one shrieking
from excessive pain, internal or external, has ever reached.[2]

What strikes the reader straightaway about Vincenzo Galilei's difficulty
with representational music is not that he thinks representation in music
to be impossible; rather, that it always seems to him to be a violation of
musical good taste in one way or another. Thus, when composers represent
"fleeing" or "flying" with running passages, they must be executed "with
the greatest rapidity and the least grace imaginable." When they represent
the sounds of instruments (in vocal music, of course) they represent them
"without minding at all that they were pronouncing these words in some
unheard-of manner." When they represent ascent or descent with an ascending or descending line, they either take the voice so low that "the singer
has sounded more like someone groaning to frighten children," or take it
so high that the singer seems to be "shrieking from excessive pain."

But why, one wonders, need this necessarily be the case? Can't good
taste and representation be served at the same time, even if it was not by
the composers whom Galilei takes to task? Why must running passages
be written so that they have to be taken too fast when they represent
flight? Why can't the trumpet's sound be represented with proper declama-
tion? And surely there is no need to take an ascending or descending line
beyond the acceptable range of the voice, in representing ascent and
descent. The thing can be done in moderation, one would think, and the
idea still come across. There must, one suspects, be something deeper here

than this, for Galilei is not just saying that composers in his time have been doing representation badly. He is making a stronger claim, presumably: that, in principle, if it is done it *must* be done badly. Where, though, is the argument for that?

A hint is dropped, I think, in the passage just quoted, where Galilei says: "In connection with the words meaning 'to disappear,' 'to swoon,' 'to die,' or actually 'to be extinct' they have made the parts break off so abruptly, that *instead of inducing the passion corresponding to any of these* [my italics] they have aroused laughter and at other times contempt in the listeners. . . ." Two points are worth noting here. First, Galilei is suggesting that there is something altogether appropriate in *arousing emotions* in listeners, as there is something inherently inappropriate in *representing* anything, even when music is capable of so doing: that is to say, arousing emotions is peculiarly musical, part of the special genius of the art, whereas representation is not, but, rather, something alien to it, even where possible. Second, he suggests that there is something the composer can do entirely consonant with the emotive character of music, in lieu of representation, namely, arouse in the listener the emotion (or emotions) corresponding to the things he might wish to represent: in this case, one assumes, the emotions we tend to associate with disappearing, swooning, dying, or being dead (whatever these might be).

*3*

The development of such hints as Galilei's into a doctrine of musical representation by way of musical expression awaited the advent, in the eighteenth century, of what Paul Oskar Kristeller has aptly called "The Modern System of the Arts."[3] When music, literature, and the visual arts had been gathered up into one class of objects—or, perhaps, as this was in process—theories were naturally required to explain (a) what it was about these seemingly disparate activities of writing, painting, sculpting, composing, that made them all of a piece, all of the same genus; and (b) what, nevertheless, distinguished them from one another. The prominent view, of course, was that the fine arts or beaux-arts, the arts of the beautiful, were, as Aristotle and Plato had long ago conjectured, the arts of imitation. That being the case, how was music, first of all, to be considered one of the fine arts at all, since so little of it seemed to be imitative in any obvious sense of that word, cuckoo calls aside? And, second, what was it about *musical* imitation, if there really were such a species of the thing, that distinguished it from painterly imitation, say, or literary representation? What was the peculiarly *musical* genius of musical imitation?

The problem, and its most pervasive solution for the Enlightenment, is best displayed in one of the more influential aesthetic treatises of the time, Batteux's *Les beaux arts reduits à un même principe* (1747). The very title of Batteux's work poses the problem in admirably succinct terms: How to reduce the arts of the beautiful, the fine arts, to a single principle. That principle, of course, was the imitation of la belle nature, according to Batteux. But how reduce music to the imitation of nature, while still retaining what was thought, since ancient times, to be the peculiarly *musical* in it: that is to say, its *emotive* "content"? The answer was clearly dictated by the "même principe." If emotive content was music's "difference," and the imitation of nature its "genus," then its whole nature must be the imitation of the emotions. Thus, for Batteux, "the principal object of music and dance [is] the imitation of the sentiments or passions."[4]

But what could it mean to "imitate" a sentiment or passion? Whatever might plausibly be described as an imitation of a passion or sentiment (if anything can), it would not seem to be music. What *can* be imitated or represented by music, Batteux (quite correctly, I believe) concluded, are the tones of voice with which our passions and sentiments are expressed.[5] And because music can "imitate" passionate human speech, it has the emotive import of that speech: it has, Batteux insists, "a meaning, a sense" (une signification, un sens).[6] Usually, that meaning or sense was cashed in, in the eighteenth century, in terms of the propensity of music to arouse in the listener the emotions which it was described as possessing: its significance or sense was a dispositional property, gained through the imitation of the "natural language" of passionate speech.

The arousal theory of musical expression was not, as I have argued elsewhere, the only one in the running.[7] But it surely was the most common one; and, more important for our purposes, the one that became, in the eighteenth century (unfortunately, I think), most intimately connected with the theory of musical representation as musical expression. Thus it became common for Enlightenment writers to recommend to the composer that he not try, as the Baroque composers had done, to "paint" or "imitate" things in his music, but, rather, that he try to make music that would arouse in the listener the emotion that would be felt if that object were actually present and perceived. Johann Adam Hiller, for example, in his essay "On the Imitation of Nature in Music," suggests that if music is to represent, say, a ghost or spirit, it must not "attempt to portray the quivering or drifting around of the spirit; it attempts only to portray it fearfully."[8] Or again, Jean-Jacques Rousseau says of the composer: "He will not directly represent things, but excite in the soul the same movement [that is, emotion] which we feel in seeing them."[9]

It is important to realize fully just how influential this doctrine of representation as expression has been, not only among critics, theorists, and philosophers, but among composers as well; and, it should be added, not just as an understandable reaction in the sixteenth and eighteenth centuries against real or imagined "literalism" in musical representation, but an attractive, one might almost say mesmerizing, alternative to musical representation in which one can have one's musical cake and eat it too, under the assumption that musical representation is at least unmusical and in bad taste, and, perhaps, even impossible. Without multiplying examples beyond endurance, let me simply call the reader's attention to some of the better known and more striking instances of the view in the past one hundred fifty years. There is, to begin with, the obvious and important case of Beethoven's Sixth Symphony, obvious because Beethoven himself apparently embraced the theory of musical representation as musical expression, explicitly if not always in practice (as we shall see); important because he not only expressed his belief in the theory, but gave us a masterpiece to exemplify it. A barren theory we can perhaps afford to ignore; but a theory fecund enough, in the hands of a genius, to produce the *Pastoral*, we ignore at our peril.

The clearest statement of what Beethoven intended in the *Pastoral* is to be found in the following sketchbook notations: "Every kind of painting loses by being carried too far in instrumental music. *Sinfonia pastorella* . . . it is [a record of] sentiments rather than a painting in sounds." And again: "*Pastoral* Symphony not a painting, but an expression of those sentiments evoked in men by their enjoyment of the country, a work in which some emotions of country life are described" (1807–1808).[10] Beethoven, of course, is not one with whom we tend to associate tone painting and program music: he is our paradigm of the "pure" instrumental composer, so it comes as no real surprise to us that in his one "programmatic" symphony he disavows musical illustrationism. More surprising is the fact that Berlioz, whose name is almost synonymous with the musical program and musical representation, apparently made a similar disavowal in regard to what we take to be his quintessential programmatic effort, *Symphonie fantastique*. Thus Edward T. Cone takes Berlioz as intending "not to describe scenes and incidents, but to depict his hero's reactions to them,"[11] and adds: "Berlioz makes this clear in a footnote to one of the early editions of the program, where he firmly rejects, for example, the 'notion of painting *mountains'* in favor of the attempt to express 'the *emotion* aroused in the soul . . . by the sight of these imposing masses.'"[12] Moreover, it is clear, I think, from the vigor with which Cone goes on to persuade us of Berlioz' espousal of musical representation as musical expression that it is Cone's view as well, and that he is somewhat relieved to find Berlioz, the arch-illustrator, really on the side of the angels after all. He concludes:

Berlioz's position, then, seems to be that an instrumental composition is the communication of an experience, transformed into abstract sound. A program can tell us something about the subject of that experience and the specific circumstances giving rise to it. But the experience the music records is not the event described by the program; it is the reaction of the subject to that event.[13]

Quite in line with this interpretation of musical representation as musical expression, although considerably less subtle, is J.W.N. Sullivan's, in his popular biography of Beethoven. Sullivan writes that what he calls the peculiar character of program music

does not consist in any correspondences that may exist between auditory and other physical perceptions, but in the analogy between the musical emotions communicated and the emotions aroused by the external situation that forms the programme of the composition. If it be said, for instance, that Debussy's L'Après-midi d'un Faune makes the impression of "a vegetable world alive in quivering hot sunshine . . . the life of trees, streams and lakes, the play of light upon water and on clouds, the murmur of plants drinking, and feeding in the sunlight," it is not because musical sounds can evoke images of heat and light and vegetables, but because a man in such surroundings may typically experience emotions analogous to those communicated by the music. Programme music, in the strict sense, may be defined as music that communicates musical experiences analogous to extramusical experiences that may be associated with some definite external situation. It does not, any more than any other music, depict any part of the external world.[14]

Enough examples have been adduced, I think, to make the point that the theory of musical representation as musical expression of some kind has been ubiquitous in the history of Western art music from the Renaissance to the present. What must now be determined is how much truth (if any) there is in the theory and (antecedently) how that theory can best be understood.

## 4

In order to evaluate the theory of musical representation as musical expression we must first become somewhat clearer about what the theory is, and, in particular, how the word "expression" is to be construed.

We saw that the theory, as it emerged in the Enlightenment, generally construed the emotive content of music to be its disposition to arouse emotions in the listener. On such a theory, then, expression is to be understood as arousal, and "the music is $\phi$" (where "$\phi$" names an emotion or mood) as "the music arouses $\phi$ in the listener." But it is by no means clear that emotive expression, or depiction, or evocation was so construed by all of those since the eighteenth century who have believed that musical representation is really a matter of musical expression, or depiction, or evocation. Beethoven, to begin with, says that he intends the *Pastoral* to be an "*expression* of those sentiments evoked in men by their enjoyment of the country," and again, "a work in which some emotions of country life are *described*." Nowhere does he tell us (so far as I know) how we are to construe "express" and "describe" in this regard; nor is there any suggestion that he thought the *Pastoral* was to *arouse* the emotions of country life in the listener. Certainly "describe" would be an odd word to choose if arousal were intended, and although "express" would at least be consistent with "arouse," at least as it was used in the Enlightenment (which was, essentially, as a term of art), it would scarcely by synonymous with it in is presystematic use.

Nor does Berlioz, as interpreted by Cone, commit himself to saying that music arouses the emotions which its objects of representation would arouse if perceived. He too uses the noncommital "express"; and Cone himself, neither in his account of Berlioz nor in the representation of his own views, commits himself to construing musical expression as emotive stimulation.

Sullivan, indeed, is committed to a theory of musical expression as emotive arousal, derived, no doubt, from Tolstoy, whose views Sullivan's closely resemble. "Music as an expressive act," Sullivan tells us, "evokes states of consciousness in the hearer which are analogous to states that may be produced by extra-musical means. It is usual to describe these states as 'emotions.'" And again: "The most valuable states or 'emotions' that music arouses are those that spring from the richest and deepest spiritual context."[15] Among the four post-Enlightenment examples, then, of the theory of musical representation as musical expression—Beethoven's Berlioz', Sullivan's, Cone's—only Sullivan's forces us to construe expression as arousal; the others leave it an open question, and even seem recalcitrant to such an interpretation where words like "describe" are used.

There are, I think, fairly persuasive reasons for not (under ordinary circumstances at least) construing "the music is $\phi$" as "the music *arouses* $\phi$" (where "$\phi$" names an emotion or mood). I have presented some of them elsewhere, as have others; and there would be nothing to gain by rehearsing such arguments at any great length here.[16] It will suffice to point out the following. (a) Emotions are generally aroused by a combination of experiences (for example, falling in love) and beliefs (for example, believing that your lover is unfaithful) that music cannot provide. (b) Emotions characteristically make themselves evident in certain observable ways (for example, behavioral expression and physiological symptom) which listeners do not display (that is, they do not get red in the face and shake their fists when listening to the angry contortions of Beethoven's *Grosse Fuge*). (c) People generally try to avoid, if they can, experiencing such unpleasant emotions as sadness and anguish, whereas they by no means avoid sad and anguished music per se, suggesting that such music is not sad or anguished in virtue of arousing these emotions in listeners. (d) The only clear case of music arousing full-blooded *nonmusical* emotions—that is, by association with personal experiences—is a case quite irrelevant to our emotive characterizations of music qua art work; for although the first chorus of Handel's *Judas Maccabaeus* (for example) always fills me with cheerful feelings of nostalgia, because I performed in it during a particularly happy period of my life, which it invariably recalls to me, it remains a wonderfully mournful and melancholy piece. And so I would describe it to anyone, in spite of my personal associations, private to me, and no part of the music as a public object.

It would seem, then, that if we are to have any hope of formulating an at least initially plausible theory of musical representation as musical expression, we cannot, for the foregoing reasons, construe musical expression as emotive arousal. How then is it to be construed? Again, I must refer the reader elsewhere for my fully elaborated views on this question.[17] Briefly, I would suggest, as others have done, that the operative word in this regard be "expressive" rather than "expression" or "express" (although the words do to a certain extent overlap).[18] Weeping willows and the faces of Saint Bernards are *expressive* of sadness, but they need not make us sad. Nor are they, properly speaking, *expressions* of sadness. For to truly say that someone is *expressing* sadness, he or she would have to be actually experiencing that emotion—that is to say, he or she would have to *be sad*; but weeping willows cannot experience emotions, and Saint Bernards' faces are expressive of sadness whether or not the creatures are sad or happy (or stuffed). We recognize the emotive properties of music, I suggest, in very much the same way we recognize the sadness of the weeping willow or the Saint Bernard's face, as properties of the object rather than as dispositions to arouse emotions in us, or as expressions of vegetable souls, depressed canines, or composers. The emotions, then, are "in" the music, not in us; but in no very mysterious sense (for symphonies no more have souls than do weeping willows). Just as many creatures and insentient objects possess expressive properties, so too does our music. But I cannot go into the details of this possession here, nor need the reader accept my version of them, just as long as he or she is willing to accept, at least as a working hypothesis, the claim that in *many* (I do not even say *all*) of the central cases, music is φ (where "φ" is the name of an emotion or mood) in the way that the weeping willow or the Saint Bernard's face is sad: as *expressive* of the emotion or mood.

We can now formulate the thesis that musical representation is musical expression in a version that does not, at least, fail immediately for irrelevant reasons. We need not, that is to say, understand the musical representation of a mountain as involving the impossible task of making me feel the way I would feel if I saw the mountain: music can only do that by sheerest accident. What music can do, perhaps, is be expressive of the emotions one might feel in contemplating a mountain, or (more important) be expressive of the same emotions that the mountain might be expressive of (since mountains, I presume, like weeping willows, or the faces of Saint Bernards, can, and often do possess expressive properties). The theory of musical representation as musical expression, then, in its optimal form, is the theory of musical representation as musical *expressiveness:* that music represents things by being expressive either of the emotions that those things might arouse in us if we were experiencing them face to face, or by being expressive of the emotions those things are expressive of, or both. It is this version of the theory of musical representation as musical expression that I wish now to examine critically.

5

It appears to me that anyone who has followed the argument . . . must believe, as I do, that the theory of musical representation as *solely* musical expressiveness is wholly false. Too many examples have been adduced that are clearly sound pictures and representations of various kinds, and not so in virtue of being expressive either of the emotions their objects might arouse, or of what the objects themselves might be expressive of, for the theory of musical representation as musical expressiveness pure and simple, to stand in unqualified form. Can it stand in any form at all? I think that it can, in a fairly obvious version, which perhaps can best be gleaned from looking not at what composers say, but at what they do. Consider, for a moment, some of the illustrative effects Beethoven achieves in the *Pastoral:* in particular, in the second and fourth movements, entitled, respectively, *Szene am Bach* (Scene by a Brook) and *Gewitter, Sturm* (Thunderstorm).

The *Szene am Bach* is one hundred thirty-six measures long (in $\frac{6}{8}$ time); and of these one hundred thirty-six measures, at least one hundred three contain a running sixteenth-note figure, the following being a fairly representative example (Example 24).

EXAMPLE 24
Beethoven, Sixth Symphony, Op. 68
Second Movement

That the movement is called *Szene am Bach*, and that it is permeated by
this "flowing" figure is not, needless to say, an accident. It is, of course,
the traditional representation of running water that we have already seen
in Mendelssohn's setting of "The waters gather, they rush along," and
Schubert's representation of the brook in *Die Schöne Müllerin*. It "flows"
through the entire movement, sometimes in the foreground, sometimes the
background—but its presence is always felt.

Nor is this the only purely illustrative music in the movement; for it is
in the *Szene am Bach* that we hear the . . . cuckoo, nightingale, and quail.
And well before the entrance of these three characters—they appear only
in the coda—we have heard the unmistakable representation of less carefully
painted (and unnamed) warblers in the strings (Example 25).

More obvious still is the musical thunderstorm which comprises the
fourth movement. The noise is all there, in the most naively pictorial way,
with grumbling double basses and rolling tympani. Nor does Beethoven
omit the lightning, which cuts jaggedly across the musical texture, in the
first violins and violas (Example 26).

Thus, no matter what Beethoven says about the *Pastoral*, there are

EXAMPLE 25

plenty of musical representations and pictures in it. But what *does* he say, after all? Only that it is not *so much* a pictorial work as an expressive one. And that is the truth, I suppose. There are certainly more expressive features in the *Pastoral* than there are purely illustrative ones. That, perhaps, is all Beethoven was saying, except, of course, for the implicit and implied prescription for listening: "Don't concentrate too much on the

EXAMPLE 26
Beethoven, Sixth Symphony, Op. 68, Fourth Movement

illustrative features, or look for them where they do not exist, just because my symphony is called 'Pastoral' and has movements with descriptive titles. If you do, you may miss the far more numerous expressive features that I intended you to hear, and with which I achieve most of my illustrative and musical effects."

In what way, then, can expressiveness contribute to musical illustration? For that, clearly, is what I am suggesting takes place in the *Pastoral* (and elsewhere, of course), and what I am certain Beethoven must have been

EXAMPLE 27
Mendelssohn, Overture, Op. 26 *(The Hebrides* or *Fingal's Cave)*

quite well aware of. The illustrative and expressive features of a well-wrought musical composition cannot, after all, be wholly unrelated.

The answer, I think, is more or less obvious. The objects of musical illustrations, as well as the musical illustrations themselves, can possess expressive properties; if one can represent, say, the brightness of the sun, as Haydn does, by giving a bright quality to his music, one can represent it too (or, rather, help to represent it) by giving the music whatever *expressive* properties the sun might possess: in Haydn's case, joy, for one. Brooks, as opposed to rivers, are gay and lively, as well as flowing. Beethoven has represented his brook, in the *Pastoral*, by making his music flow, with the help of the "flowing" sixteenth-note figure that permeates the second movement. He has also represented it—its liveliness and gaiety, that is—by making his music lively and gay, and since thunderstorms are somber, brooding, ominous, as well as noisy, Beethoven has made the fourth movement—*Gewitter, Sturm*—not only noisy, but somber, brooding, and ominous as well.

Another example, perhaps, will drive the point home. Mendelssohn titles his familiar overture, Opus 26, *Fingal's Cave* or *The Hebrides*. As a musical seascape (of which there are many examples), it is unsurpassed, and seldom equalled. It begins with the unmistakably seething ebb and flow of a heavy sea, represented by the persistent repetition of a musical figure obviously designed to give the impression of a periodic wave motion or swell. The motive "ripples" and "heaves," and is both melodically and harmonically constructed to allow for its reiteration on various scale degrees, and in various keys, for the purpose of representing the lapping or breaking of waves on the rocky coast (Example 27).

But what makes this a representation of the Scottish seas and not, perhaps, the sea at Brighton or Coney Island on a sunny day in July? These musical waves *could* break anywhere, were it not, of course, for their expressive quality—dark, brooding, melancholy, like the expressive quality of the Hebrides' seas themselves. It is, thus, by a union of illustrative and expressive features that Mendelssohn achieves his musical seascape. And it is, perhaps, somewhat misleading to distinguish illustrative and expressive features in such contexts as these (or, rather, it should be made plain that they are all illustrative but not all expressive, the expressive being a subclass); for on our construal of the expressive, these features of music are as illustrative as those we have been calling illustrative, being all illustrative by being all properties that are shared, one way or another, by music and by its objects of representation.

But there are, we said, two kinds of expressive features that might figure in the theory of musical illustration as musical expression: the features already discussed, that music and the objects of its representations might share: the gaiety of the brook, the brooding quality of the Hebrides' seas; and the emotions that such objects might arouse in the spectator: the terror a thunderstorm might evoke in a child, or the awe and wonder of the Alps. What role, if any, might these latter features play in musical illustration?

Often, it is clear, the two kinds will tend to coincide: that is to say, the gloom of a dark, densely wooded forest is *also* the emotion it would tend to evoke in the spectator. The gaiety of a brook is *also* the gaiety it might make me feel. Indeed, we sometimes say "*X* is $\phi$" (where "$\phi$" names an emotion or mood) when we mean not that *X* is expressive of $\phi$ but that *X* is evocative of $\phi$ (as in "sad news" or "glad tidings"). Now in cases where the emotion aroused is also the emotion of the object is expressive of, composers tend not to distinguish carefully between them (they are, after all, composers, not philosophers), and even if they were so to distinguish them, it would be all one with their compositions. Whether Beethoven, say, intended to make his music expressive of the gaiety of the brook, or the gaiety of the spectator, which the brook might arouse, the music, in either case, was made expressive of gaiety. And whether

Beethoven intended it or not, the gaiety of *Szene am Bach* contributes to the representation of the brook. If it was also supposed to be expressive of the gaiety the brook might arouse in a spectator (Beethoven, perhaps), it achieved this at the same stroke.

Sometimes, however, an emotion that an object, scene, or event might tend to arouse in a spectator will not be an emotion that the object, scene, or event is expressive of. In such a case, would making music meant to illustrate the object, scene, or event expressive of that emotion, contribute in any way to the illustration? The answer to this question seems to depend very much on how widely one might want to construe "contribute" or "illustration" or both. My own instinct (and that is all it is) is to construe them widely, simply because illustrations, representations, and pictures come in such an enormous variety, and what contributes to them is so much a matter of the enormous freedom and flexibility of intellect, imagination, and communication. Certainly, in the *direct* way in which an expressive property of an object can (by being made an expressive property of a musical representation) contribute to that representation, dispositional properties of objects (which is, of course, what we are talking about) cannot so contribute when they are made expressive properties of musical illustrations. The resurrection of the dead, which the faithful await (in the *Credo* of the mass) is a joyous occasion more in the dispositional than expressive sense of the word. It will *cause* joy in the spectator or participant. This is the joy that musical settings of the text are almost invariably expressive of. Does this expressive property contribute to the representation of the event? (The musical settings are, with equal frequency, replete with rising musical figures to represent the raising of the dead.) Not in any direct sense. On the other hand, one would find it singularly odd, jarring, even inappropriate to come upon a setting of "et expecto resurrectionem mortuorum" expressive not of joy but of some opposite emotion like grief or melancholy. One would look for an explanation: some point being made, or some musical exigency being served. And if emotive appropriateness is thought of as contributing to the musical representation, then I suppose both kinds of emotive properties of objects—the expressive and the dispositional—contribute to musical illustration when made expressive properties of it. This, then, is the grain of truth in the otherwise false thesis that musical illustration is really musical expression (or expressiveness) tout court.

6

What has emerged, then, not very surprisingly, from this examination of the "musical illustration as musical expression" thesis is simply that the thesis is overstated. Clearly, both directly and indirectly—as common expressive property and dispositional property of objects, but expressive property of musical illustrations—expressiveness *contributes* to musical illustration: indeed, in the former case, is a species of it. However, that all musical illustration comes in the end to musical expressiveness of one kind or another is plainly false: too many nonexpressive pictorial and representational techniques have been adduced in the preceding pages for that thesis to stand unchallenged and unmodified.

But it would be ending this chapter on a false note, I think, to simply conclude that the thesis is false as it stands and true as amended. For perhaps it was never meant to be taken for truth at all. It has been enunciated, more often than not, not as a revelation of musical reality but as a passionate statement of musical policy. It is, in other words, more normative or prescriptive than neutrally descriptive: a call to musical reform or revolution. The "illustrationism" of the madrigalists was rejected as unmusical by Galilei, as was the "illustrationism" of the Baroque composers by the preclassical defenders of sentiment and the "natural." Far from being denounced as impossible, such musical pictures and representations were all too possible according to their critics, their possibility proved, as Aristotle would say, by their very palpable actuality, cluttering, as they did, the music of those whose styles were being rejected by another generation.

How music is to be composed—whether it should or should not be pictorial or representational—these are matters, of course, for composers, not philosophers to decide. For Beethoven to have turned his back on a good deal of the "tone painting" of the Baroque (as Haydn, by the way, did not, in the *Creation* and *Seasons*) was, doubtless, a wise stylistic choice on the composer's part, and one that only Beethoven himself could have made. This, needless to say, does not make any more plausible the charge that Bach's illustrationism—the product of perhaps the greatest musical intellect the West has seen—is "unmusical." If Bach is unmusical, then Shakespeare is not a poet, and all things [are] possible. *Unmusical* for Beethoven's style, no doubt; but supremely, sublimely musical for Bach's and Handel's.

But such normative questions are not to the present purpose. It suffices for me to have shown that expressiveness is part of musical representation, but not the whole. There I must let the matter . . . rest.

*Notes*

1. Quoted in the pocket edition of the score (Paris: Editions Salabert, n.d.). My translation.

2. Vincenzo Galilei, *Dialogo della musica antica e della moderna* (1581), trans. Oliver Strunk, *Source Readings in Music History*, ed. Strunk, p. 317.

3. Paul Oskar Kristeller, "The Modern System of the Arts," *Journal of the History of Ideas* 12 (1951) and 13 (1952).

4. Charles Batteux, *Les beaux arts reduits à un même principe* (Paris, 1747). My translation.

5. *Ibid.,* p. 270.

6. *Ibid.,* p. 277.

7. See, for example, my "What Mattheson said," *The Music Review* 34 (1973); and Peter Kivy, *The Corded Shell* (Princeton: Princeton University Press, 1980), chapters 3 and 5.

8. Hiller, "Nature in Music," p. 536. My translation.

9. Jean-Jacques Rousseau, *A Dictionary of Music*, trans. William Waring (London, n.d.), p. 199 (in the article "Imitation").

10. *Beethoven: Letters, Journals and Conversations*, p. 53.

11. Edward T. Cone, *The Composer's Voice* (Berkeley and Los Angeles: University of California Press, 1974), p. 83.

12. *Ibid.,* pp. 83–84n.

13. *Ibid.,* p. 84.

14. J. W. N. Sullivan, *Beethoven: His Spiritual Development* (New York: Vintage Books, 1960), p. 38.

15. *Ibid.,* pp. 34–35.

16. For my own view of the matter, see *The Corded Shell*, pp. 22–23, 29–33, et passim.

17. *Ibid.,* especially Chapters 5–8.

18. Alan Tormey, *The Concept of Expression: A Study in Philosophical Psychology and Aesthetics* (Princeton: Princeton University Press, 1971), chapters 4 and 5.

# 18.　Puzzles of Pictorial Representation
## *JOSEPH MARGOLIS*

If cultures are real, if they are the actual milieux in which humans live
and flourish and make and do the things they do, then there is no
convincing sense in which art and nature can be opposed as the unreal
and the real or as instantiating different orders of reality inferior or
superior one to the other. Jean-Paul Sartre is perhaps the contemporary
theorist of the arts who has confused this question with the more profound
one of distinguishing, within one world, the mark of the cultural and the
mark of the natural.[1] Sartre had supposed the difference to rest with that
between the perceptible and the imperceptible; whereas one might better
claim that, for instance, the *visible* may be construed in a variety of ways
theoretically, but in none can it be convincingly affirmed that what we
report as perceptually accessible is ever free of the nonsensory, formative
complexities of our cultural habits of perceptual discrimination.

There is, among animals, no reporting of sensory experience. Among
humans, there is no reporting of what is naturally and sensorily perceived—neutrally with regard to cultural inference or interpretation; although there are theories enough about how to sort the two. There is,
therefore, no reportable comparison between sub- or de-cultural and
culturated perception.[2] Hence, for instance, the glib disputes about the
natural or conventional status of linear perspective and so-called naturalistic painting—popularized most recently by the disagreement between E. H.
Gombrich and Nelson Goodman—are simply badly mismanaged. Realism
at the present time, of every sort that aspires to afford a common ground
for the cognitive achievements of science and the cognizable constructions
of art, is indissolubly linked to that form of idealism at least that rejects
the sheer transparency of the actual world.[3] Once that indissoluble linkage
is admitted, and once the cultural is put on an ontological par with the
physical and the natural, the entire theory of art—in particular the theory

of representational art, of the intentionality of art, of the vexed question of naturalistic painting—cannot fail to be profoundly affected. We have, then, by the obvious expedient of retreating from immediate quarrels to the less disputable commonplaces of our age, moved to outflank certain troublesome and unproductive speculations about the world of art. But we have as yet only promised an economy.

Of course, even at this point an advantage suggests itself. If for instance we allow ourselves the easy concession of construing Brunelleschi's great dome of the Santa Maria del Fiore as an ineliminable artwork, then we see at once that art *is*, first, whether it *represents* anything at all; that it cannot represent anything if it is not real; that it need not represent anything despite being real; and that it may yet have properties that, whether or not including in any instance the representational, are such as to raise serious doubts about their being characterizable as merely or solely physical or natural. One may perhaps dare to say that we are considering the same generic puzzle in considering the relationship between sound and language, stones and cathedrals, nature and culture, movement and action, time and history, perceptual ecology and perspectival drawing, *Homo sapiens* and persons. This suggests the sense in which, opposing Sartre's extravagance, reformulating the dispute between Gombrich and Goodman, and linking these two matters together as versions of the same question, we signify that an issue like that of how to understand natural perspective bears decisively on much more than, casually reviewed, it may seem to do.

What often misleads the unwary theorist, to put the issue in its crudest form, is simply that if language is, generally or *en bloc*, "about" the world, then it both *represents* the world and is either not *real* in the sense in which the world is real (and language is "about" *it* but not *of* it) or exhibits some order of reality other than that of the real world. Both conclusions are untrue; both arguments are *non sequiturs*; and both sets of disorders may be quite readily drawn from Sartre's characterization of art. Sartre's motive seems to have been to elevate art by treating it as "unreal," that is, as superior to the (merely) perceivable world. Others, for instance in accord with the theme of the unity of science program, have meant thereby to eliminate language—and culture—from seriously complicating the theory of science.[4] But if, by an admittedly boldly chosen term of art, we say that the cultural is the Intentional—not yet venturing an analysis, but stipulating by the use of the capital "I" some complex order of significative property that indissolubly links, on the one hand, whatever belongs collectively to the prevailing practices of human societies as well as to the conscious and deliberate intentions of individual persons and, on the other hand, what belongs narrowly to the semantic and further functional use of language that services the paradigmatic activity of man (speech) and that serves as the precondition of every other nonlinguistic activity that man exhibits (painting, for instance)—then, clearly, the representational is itself a special instance of the Intentional or a distinction that presupposes the other. Brunelleschi's dome is Intentional, culturally significant, in a way that clearly invites a suitable specification; but there is no reason to suppose that it must be assignably representational in addition to its being, perhaps, expressive of or endowed with the gathering spirit of Brunelleschi's own perception of the Florentine world; and even if it were representational in some particular regard—as, rather conventionally, it has been said of the drive to achieve, or represent in a literal way, the divinely infinite in the Gothic vault—the one could not reasonably replace the other.

The same is true of painting, though it is intuitively less obvious, since the two-dimensional naturally invites a collapsing of the notions of what *is*, as an artwork, and of what, in being such, is *significant*. But even in language, though as in uttering a statement, what is thereby said represents some state of affairs in the world, uttering statements in actual conversation is an Intentional activity (in our invented sense), a form of uttering that cannot be exhausted by the representational function of the other. Furthermore, the representational function presupposes and instantiates the other, is a restricted distinction within the other's full scope, and may even be absent without diminishing in any way the presence of the other. It is not at all clear, for instance, that the poems of Sappho *represent* anything at all, though they appear to be the significant utterances of the poet herself: as opposed, say, to its being true (or at least reasonable to hold) that the lines of Shakespeare's *Richard III* represent (in some complex way) the movement of the life of a historical king. The global theory of mimesis, therefore, is distinctly unsound.[5] In any case, the actuality of art is neither diminished nor enhanced by its Intentionality or "aboutness"; and its aboutness is never exhausted by or merely equivalent to the contingency of its being representational.

All this is put at serious risk in saying—which we do insouciantly enough—that art and language are "about" the world. The assumption here is that one knows straightforwardly what that means. But there is reason to doubt that we do. "Aboutness" may be taken as a near-synonym for our term of art, "Intentionality" (with capital "I"). But if so, then aboutness is, in the logical sense, not transitive and, in the grammatical sense, not necessarily relational *and*, in the global sense fitted to the world of culture, not necessarily or invariably representational.[6] Vermeer's *Lady Reading a Letter at an Open Window*, for instance, undoubtedly "about" the seventeenth-century Dutch world already so altered from Rembrandt's, and understandably offered as a specimen of representational painting, does not in any obvious sense *denote that world*, the actual Dutch world (reference to which facilitates our "understanding" the painting in question, that is, our recognizing it in some suitably detailed way as an actual cultural artifact of the Dutch world). It is true that there is *represented in it* a young woman, a casement, a letter, a table, a carpet, a drapery, a chair. These, thus represented, need not be taken to denote anything, the would-be denotata being perhaps not parts of the actual world. But what is represented *in* the painting is represented only on the sufferance of the larger "aboutness" or Intentionality of the painting as a real artifact possessing the peculiar significative or cultural properties that it does possess. One of Kandinsky's familiar *Improvisations* represents nothing, neither denotatively nor non-denotatively, though it discloses an artifactually visible "world," is significant in that sense, is "about" that world, is Intentionally so structured. There is, in this respect, no difference between the Vermeer and the Kandinsky.

There is one trivial, overinflated maneuver that ensures the representational nature of all painting and (if necessary) all art. That is the thesis that art is inherently self-referential, that is, that an artwork must be taken as exemplifying (as by expression) the properties it possesses. Cloth samples do something like this, it is true. But only by an extravagance—for instance, to save a semiotic theory of art—could one say that every painting or every artwork refers to the (or the salient) properties it merely possesses (whatever we suppose the complexity of such properties to be);[7] or to say, apparently more cautiously, that insofar at least as an artwork possesses "expressive" properties (which, perhaps, both the Vermeer and the Kandinsky may be said to do, in being "about" the visual "worlds" they respectively disclose), they represent what, reflexively, they refer to.[8] If of course, as is often the case, what is represented in a painting need not exist in the real world, then in order to hold that a painting refers to what it thus represents, one must (on the standard view) also hold that it makes reference in a most distinctive way—magically, by way of metaphor, fictively, or the like; or that, in making reference in the ordinary way, the properties it possesses, that serve such reference, it possesses magically, metaphorically, fictively, or the like.

There are "objects" represented in the Vermeer; there are none in the Kandinsky. But both are "expressive" in the generous sense conceded, the sense (in the grammatical use) of being intransitively "about" the artifactual, visible "world," by which aboutness each uniquely controls our access to that world. For perceiving *them* pertinently *is* perceiving their visible "worlds." If this is so, then, in a very firm sense, whatever other senses we may assign the term "representation," *no* painting is primarily a representation, in that it does not substitute or stand in or is imagined to stand in for another thing but discloses—uniquely, to those rightly trained in the pertinent cultural skills and practices—a visible "world" not otherwise thus accessible.[9]

This is the essential point of speaking of aboutness or Intentionality, the point of the systematic difference between the cultural and the natural. It is not, as Sartre supposes, that the first is perceivable and the second, not; it is rather that the *perception* of the second is complicated by *nonsensory* structures of aboutness or significance or Intentionality *and that so also is the perception of the natural*, even though *its* objects do not as such exhibit aboutness.[10] Furthermore, if we insist that every imagined or "intended world" or every significant message or communication accessed (repeatedly accessible) through the exchanged utterances of culturally apt agents—merely *presented* or thus accessible—are also thereby *represented by*, or themselves *represent through*, such utterances (via brush strokes and dance steps, say, as well as *via* speech acts), we risk trivializing the use of the notion of representation.[11]

Of course, in spite of all this (or better, because of it), paintings may be representations and often are. The general rationale is already—prophetically—captured in Roger Bacon's *Opus majus*, in which Bacon promotes a strict knowledge of science and geometry as a way of understanding how God's grace orders the created world: "It is impossible," Bacon says, "for the spiritual sense to be known without a knowledge of the literal sense." Hence, as he goes on: "Since . . . artificial works, like the ark of Noah, and the temple of Solomon and of Ezechiel and of Esdra and other things of this kind almost without number are placed in Scripture, it is not possible for the literal sense to be known, unless a man have these works depicted in his sense, but more so when they are pictured in their physical forms; and thus have the sacred writers and sages of old employed pictures and various figures, that the literal truth might be evident to the eye, and as a consequence the spiritual truth also. For in Aaron's vestments were described the world and the great deeds of the fathers."[12] But whether particular paintings are actually emblematic in this sense, in representing pictorially what may be propositionally extracted as a lesson—an issue that has been notably disputed with regard to the interpretation of Dutch painting[13]—is a contingent question at best, hardly one that would decide whether, in failing the emblematic criterion, a would-be painting was not an artwork at all or did not exhibit the required aboutness. The important thing about the emblematic interpretation of (Dutch) painting is that it offers a coherent possibility even if it is a mistaken one.[14] The thesis holds, as Svetlana Alpers summarizes the matter (in order to reject it), that "Dutch art . . . only appears realistic . . . is [rather] a realized abstraction."[15] (The most familiar emblematic device is that of illustrated proverbs, but the claim is surely more far-reach-ing.) Nevertheless, the representation of meaningful scenes is not the emblematic representation of meanings. Right or wrong, however, the thesis points to the importance of distinguishing between the aboutness of paintings and the further possibility of their specifically representational function. The emblematic possibilities of Breughel's *Proverbs* may not bear at all on the representational possibilities of Breughel's *Seasons*; and the representational possibilities of van Eyck's Arnolfini and his bride may not capture at all the ulterior function of the painting as a documentary utterance.

Samuel Edgerton, addressing the direct consequence of views like Bacon's on the emerging worldiness of the Renaissance some centuries later, remarks that, as far as he can determine, in the Brancacci Chapel of the Santa Maria della Carmine, two frescoes, Masaccio's *Tribute Money* and Masolino's *Raising of Tabitha and Healing of the Cripple*, "are the first in the entire history of art to illustrate the scientific-artistic principle of [what Edgerton terms] horizon line isocephaly."[16] Edgerton does not say that, in employing Brunelleschi's rules for the use of perspective, these artists were representing those rules or their use of perspective itself or, emblematically, the grace of God through perceptual geometry. (Neither isocephaly nor the vanishing point principle is actually explicit in Brunelleschi's handbook.) And even if we supposed that, given the occasion, there was some application of Bacon's instruction, such an application must already be fading into a new perspectival practice regarding aboutness.

Aboutness is a monadically complex rather than simple or atomic feature of predicable structure: what is identified, in understanding pertinent utterances (in speech or painting, for instance), is relationally identified *within* and only within the scope of that monadic structure. That is, it is Intentionally emergent. Thus we speak of the meaning *of* a statement or *of* what a painting represents. But the seeming detachment of meanings and representations from those culturally freighted utterances that control access *to* them (again, relationally characterized) is of course misleading. There are no independent meanings or representations that human speakers and artists somehow collect or select or contingently link their efforts to: that is the way of Platonism.[17] The only escape from Platonism—if we mean to escape, in the present context—is to treat aboutness monadically: that way, the reality or fictionality of the world thus subtended becomes an independent, contingent, entirely debatable issue; otherwise, the "world" represented (for instance, as in Rembrandt's using Hendrickje as a model for "rendering" Bathsheba) *requires* that Bathsheba exist (and "be as the painting shows her to be") even though "Hendrickje need not exist."[18] No, representation partakes of aboutness essentially; hence, it, too, is monadic, *both* in the sense appropriate to an entire painting's being a representation and in the sense of there being various things represented in it. Hence, too, the logically (not necessarily epistemically) *further* question of whether what, identified *within* the scope of the monadic structure (by a heuristic use of a relational idiom), occurs or exists independently of the aboutness or representational structure must be conceded to be a legitimate question; but is is, logically, an independent and contingent matter. Monadic representation, therefore, is an equivocal notion: it signifies either the instantiation of the generic Intentionality or aboutness of a painting or the fictional or merely imagined status of what is thus represented judged with respect to the actual world; both monadic representation (in the second sense) and dyadic representation (as in portraiture) signify logically complex findings *relating* paintings and the actual world.

Two considerations suggest themselves, therefore: first, representation, in the sense of an entire painting's being representational rather than in the sense of details within a painting's being representations, may well be uncertain, indeterminate, and not even always important to establish; second, the representationality of a painting is an ulterior function of its very Intentionality or aboutness. That is certainly the point that Bacon captures so clearly. What we may add is that such representationality may be either propositional (as in the emblematic sense) or non-propositional or both. Perhaps Jan Steen's *"Easy Come, Easy Go"* may fairly illustrate the first; and Rembrandt's *Bathsheba*, the second. But surely, in either sense, that by which what is represented is represented (by forms drawn from considering Hendrickje to represent Bathsheba, or by the image of the Steen interior to represent the proverb) are not themselves thus or thereby represented or are not themselves represented in the same sense in which Bathsheba and the proverb are represented.

A felicitous distinction for holding the difference in place is afforded by the old notion of *natura naturans* and *natura naturata*: in the space of human culture, possibly less quarrelsomely than in the context of nature, cultural phenomena must be bodied forth (rendered) first in order to function in whatever distinctive way they do. Aboutness or Intentionality serves in this *dual* way, but the first is presupposed by the functioning of the second. Painting, for instance, is "about" in the monadic sense in which what is emergently complex within its intransitively uttered structure is thus located only on the condition of its having been first suitably uttered: Sappho's uttering her poems first raises the question of what *they*, the poems, thus rendered or uttered, represent; the strokes drawn by Rembrandt studying or conjuring up Hendrikje in order to represent Bathsheba do not represent those strokes or Hendrikje in the sense required (despite the naturalness of the ordinary idiom); and the assumed parity between the image and the associated proverb in the Steen interior merely shows the double function of the image—in the sense of aboutness or representational utter*ing* and in the sense of aboutness or what is represent*ed*.

What we now see is that the representationality *of* a painting is a functionally specialized, optional, and dependent (further) role of a painting's essential aboutness; also, that representations *in* a painting presuppose such aboutness in virtue of which they function as the details they do—that is, that only thus do natural marks become significant marks or embody culturally significant forms. But such emergence or transformation does not entail a change from the perceivable to the interpreted and therefore not perceivable; furthermore, it must be emphasized, the very recognition of the representational (in the second sense) depends upon and is impossible without a grasp or tacit mastery of the perceptual practices of a particular contingent culture. We are speaking here of the conceptual structure of paintings, not of the order or range of what may be discovered in them. It is entirely possible that, failing to understand what is being represented in a painting may decisively impoverish what we can perceive of the world it discloses. Thus, not knowing what in the iconographical sense is to be understood to be represented in a given painting may well impoverish our perception of it—for example, as in not grasping the documentary function of Jan van Eyck's *Giovanni Arnolfini and His Wife*, according to the well-known interpretation,[19] or for that matter, the nonconformity of Flemish perspective of van Eyck's period with the perspective rules of Brunelleschi's Florence;[20] or, for that matter, as in Michel Foucault's bold speculation about Velázquez's *Las Meninas*, to the effect that "Perhaps there exists, in this painting by Velázquez, the representation as it were, of Classical representation, and the definition of the space it opens up to us"—so that "representation, freed finally from the relation that was impeding it [the relation of resemblance to actual figures], can offer itself as representation in its pure form."[21]

It is quite usual to speak of representation as either relational or non-relational, dyadic or monadic, as depending on whether what is represented exists or not. But if representation may be *of* the propositional, then both the monadic/dyadic distinction and the notorious question of resemblance cannot fail to be distinctly local issues. Monadic representation, "representation-as," cannot resemble what does not exist, is fictional, or merely imagined (though it may represent aptly what it actually represents, for instance in accord with a descriptive text);[22] but the representation of a maxim, for instance, does not even raise the question of resemblance (as opposed to aptness) and is not suitably captured conceptually by the notion of the pictorial representation of what is itself sensorily visible—whether monadically or dyadically. On the other hand, pictorial or visual resemblance obtains independently of representation, although it is true and important to bear in mind that *visual resemblance may be enhanced by the governing function of representation*—even where it is not determinately particular. One may remember, for instance, having spotted on occasion Matisse women in the New York subway or Modigliani women at fashionable restaurants. And Picasso's famous remark to Gertrude Stein on the occasion of his having painted her in her prime is less a prophecy of how she would age (though the possibility has point) than it is an insight into the influence of the practice of painting and of perceiving paintings on the subsequent perception of our *world*. What, we may ask, then becomes of the famous question of the natural resemblance between painting and object or of what is alleged to be the merely conventional nature of similarity?

The question has two foci: the first, largely neglected; the second, largely ill-presented. They are, nevertheless, closely linked and, together, they enable us to collect in a coherent and compendious way most of, if not all, the proliferating issues regarding representation. The first is the famous problem of universals. We shall not, of course, attempt to solve it here.[23] But it bears particularly on the troubling questions of naturalistic painting and natural perspective—both of which affect rather special, if notorious, puzzles about representation. The reason, familiarly, concerns the question of resemblance or perceived similarity.[24] There are two arguments to press: one to the effect that resemblance is a cognitively pertinent concern (usually, as in painting, perceptual); the other to the effect that resemblances, like any other putatively cognizable features of the world, are not cognitively transparent. The one directly bears on the fortunes of nominalism; the other draws directly on the overwhelming contemporary consensus that, cognitively, realism and idealism are indissolubly linked.

The point about nominalism is marvellously elementary: it is impossible to account for the spontaneous *extension* of perceptual and linguistic practice—as in the use of natural languages and cultural habit—by any strictly nominalistic theory. The reason is simply that nominalism has no way of accounting for the spontaneous application of distinctions first introduced by way of a finite number of exemplars. Every account of how general terms are extended to apply to new cases or of whether newly encountered objects, representations of objects, and the like resemble or fail to resemble whatever we have already collected in an initial repertory of classified items requires a reasonably regular and reliable ability to extend such general distinctions to new cases so that the society possessing those distinctions will also spontaneously support their extension (variably, divergently, transiently) without first arriving at an explicit consensus case by case. There you have the defeat of nominalism—in any *epistemically* pertinent application. Resemblances must have a basis *both* in the biology of the human species (though not necessarily hardwired or nativist) *and* in the diverging cultural practices that exploit that biology in relatively more determinate ways. We may think of the biological as a relatively stable template that cultures progressively build novel but cognate distinctions upon and more and more determinately specify or alter.[25]

This consideration fixes the essential difficulty of Nelson Goodman's insistence, for example, against Gombrich, when Goodman (*rightly*) holds (effectively, in agreement with Gombrich) that "Dyadic likeness between particulars will not serve to define those classes of particulars that have a common quality throughout."[26] Both Goodman and Gombrich undoubtedly reject "the myths of the innocent eye and of the absolute given" as, as Goodman puts it, "unholy accomplices."[27] But Goodman, adhering to his well-known nominalism, will not and cannot concede an effective biological or cultural basis for spontaneously recognizing resemblances—in the sense of extension already introduced. As Goodman puts it: "Realism is a matter not of any *constant* or absolute relationship between a picture and its object but of a relationship between the system of representation employed in the picture and the standard system. . . . Realistic representation, in brief, depends not upon imitation or illusion or information but upon *inculcation*."[28] The trouble is that Goodman does not resolve or even address the essential fact that *even the use of a system of representation (or "inculcation"), in the extending sense given, defeats the strict nominalist:* for what is the basis for the *successful* extended use of any such system? Gombrich understands Goodman's point, here, to be that "there is no such thing as resemblance to nature."[29] He is right in a way but not precisely enough. For Goodman goes on to say, "That a picture looks like nature *often* means only that it looks the way nature is *usually* painted" and "Resemblance and deceptiveness, far from being *constant* and *independent* sources and criteria of representational practice are *in some degree* products of it."[30] In this qualification by way of the vague, Goodman betrays himself, because he cannot quite insist on the point Gombrich assigns him and he cannot quite concede that his own careful formulation (at the very moment we allow it) actually entails the rejection of nominalism and mere conventionalism and entails as well the admission of some habituated basis for extending the use of systematic distinctions. There is, in fact, no other way to see the matter.

Gombrich's point, which concedes (in fact, always insisted on) the need to learn the representational conventions of a society (rejecting the innocent eye), really opposes "extreme [that is, mere] conventionalism"— pressing the basically biological thesis that "Recognizing an image is certainly a complex process and draws on many human faculties, both inborn and acquired. But without a natural starting point we could never have acquired that skill."[31] The double issue, then, is: (1) the inadequacy of nominalism or extreme conventionalism to accommodate the natural extension of *any* general distinctions, even those that have a strongly conventional nature (possibly radically divergent, plural orientations): and (2) the inextricably symbiotic complexity of human perception, that will not yield to any compositional factoring of the natural and the conventional but insists nevertheless on the effective dependence of the conventional (however specified) *upon* the biologically natural, even if subsequently culturally skewed. In fact, (2) is also a determinate version of what we have already suggested regarding the realist/idealist distinction.

The second, usually ill-presented focus regarding resemblance in representational contexts or regarding the representational use of resemblance asks whether resemblance is or is not conventional. One way of reading the question invites us to answer whether there are determinate similarities in the real world independent of human cognition, that cognition detects *as such*. The answer to that reading is flatly no: both Goodman and Gombrich are agreed on that. This is (at least) part of the point of Goodman's denying "any constant or absolute relationship between a picture and its object" and any "constant and independent sources and criteria of representational practice" (that is, aptness of representation). And this is also part of the point of Gombrich's rejection of the "innocent eye."

But Goodman rejects as well the strong salience or, more boldly, the unique "success" of the evolution of linear perspective in two-dimensional representation; and Gombrich insists on it.[32] So perspective signifies in its own terms as well as metonymically (for other forms of possible resemblance) the need for a second reading. On that second reading, for Goodman, there is no empirically likely basis for testing—perhaps not even a logically formulable, pertinent option for testing—whether particular modes of representation are rightly favored over others, species-wide, because of "natural" resemblances between pictures and what they picture; and, for Gombrich, there *is* empirical evidence confirming just that. Goodman challenged the thesis both in Gombrich's and J. J. Gibson's version (Gombrich readily following Gibson).[33] Gombrich concedes the point: "Nelson Goodman is certainly right when he protests that the behavior of light does not tell us how we see things."[34] But Gombrich moves on more promisingly to theorize about the way in which ecologically *shifting* perception (in Gibson's sense) leads us to draw pictures *into* the phenomenal world itself—hence, that there is a fair sense in which although "the world does not look like a picture . . . a picture can look like the world."[35]

The problem of natural perspective remains (and perhaps must remain) incompletely resolved—certainly if we mean (as Gombrich seems to mean) to answer whether it is uniquely successful thus. But if we answer only in terms of salience, in terms of characteristic tendencies among diverging (or potentially diverging) alternatives, then it is difficult to deny that Gombrich is more right than Goodman. In fact, as we have already noted, Goodman's own view entails (and must entail) the concession—which he does not acknowledge explicitly. In saying that, we take note, well after the fact, of how the second reading of our question should go. It goes this way: Are there determinate similarities that humans appear to favor in the real world they perceive and between the world and their pictorial representations of the world? This is the important form of the second question—helped by our answer to the problem of universals and compatible with the rejection of cognitive transparency.

Once we grasp this, both the history of linear perspective and the theoretical quarrels about pictorial representation fall into place. As Gombrich firmly and correctly remarks, natural perspective and the rendering of physiognomic likeness are guided by the phenomenal appearance of the world—not by the geometry of light. But of course the phenomenal appearance of the world is also elastic and is itself shaped or guided (variably) by the network of perceptual and non-perceptual practices of different cultures. The important point is that the alternative options are all biologically grounded, that is, that the cultural variants must themselves be biologically grounded in order to be viable—as in the resolution of the problem of perceptual universals. So there is no need to share Gombrich's inclination to favor the unique validity of what Gombrich calls the "evolution of perspective representation."[36] But resisting that option does not drive us to Goodman's option.

The opposition between the "conventional" and the "natural" only makes sense if one denies the realist/idealist symbiosis *and* if one ignores the cognitive problem regarding universals. Within that complex, there is room for both elements—though *not* determinately or disjunctively; and within that complex, it is entirely possible, empirically, to demonstrate that *some* forms of representation *are* more "natural" than others: either more likely to be closer to original biological dispositions or behaviorally more apt within the space of a particular culture (or even more apt in terms of recognizability within the perceptual practices of an alien culture). But what this shows is the simple fact that the success of spontaneous recognition cannot (*contra* Goodman) be merely an artifact of "representational systems [or] pictorial purpose alone."[37]

Beyond this, what we must take note of is the further fact that pictorial realism—that is, the use of representational forms that phenomenally resemble the world—*depends on key saliences only* and is able to tolerate considerable fuzziness regarding the "rules" of representation. Thus, for example, in the phenomenon of horizon line isocephaly (as in the Masaccio and Masolino frescoes), the use of isocephaly together with fixing the vanishing point on the isocephalic line itself permits us to tolerate small variations in the legibility of the compared sizes of particular figures: we are often aided more by occlusion and intended spatial relationships than by strict scale. It is, furthermore, rather amusing to consider what we could make of Velázquez's *Las Meninas* construed in Foucault's way—but also by intruding a sense of wicked trickery with regard to isocephaly. Then, the use of the dwarf and midget at the right of the painting, more or less in the same isocephalic line as the Infanta, raises odd questions about the relative size of the figures represented—a matter complicated by the kneeling of one maid on the Infanta's right and the apparent breach of isocephaly by the tall maid on her left, as well as by the "witty" uncertainty of the size of the dog. A cognate isocephalic puzzle then appears in the line that links Velázquez himself, the mirror image of Philip and Maria Ana, the court officer in the doorway, and the other two adults at the right of the painting; for now the illusion is obviously an illusion, since the distance of the mirrored image baffles the isocephalic order if not first correctly interpreted. In fact a number of Velázquez's paintings seem to query the bearing of creatures of anomalous size, also the bearing of the imputed size of representations lined up with actual creatures and represented "materialistically" as well within one and the same visual image. Velázquez's own training in painting, through Pacheco, renders his interest in the problem entirely reasonable.[38] These considerations favor construing Velázquez's painting as a representation of represent*ing* by painting (Foucault's point) rather than (or merely than) as a representation of *a* represented scene, a would-be painting (as recently suggested by John Searle).[39] Thus, it also confirms the usefulness of the distinction between aboutness and representation.

But we must not lose sight of the point that the biological grounding of natural perspective does not entail the unique validity of any particular perspectival canon. *If*, as Gombrich, following Gibson, had originally supposed, linear perspective and visual resemblance depend primarily or essentially on the geometry of light, then a uniquely correct canon might have been possible. But *if*, as Gombrich concedes to Goodman—and, in conceding that, surpasses Goodman's conventionalism—these phenomena depend on the regularities of phenomenal perception (where phenomenal perception may well be confined by a painting's frame and the practice within which it is normally perceived), then there is room for alternative, incompatible modes of perspectival rendering equally or comparably "correct." Thus, van Eyck's perspective precedes Brunelleschi's. But if, as Panofsky observes, the Arnolfini has a number of distinct vanishing points, it hardly follows that the Arnolfini is not perspectivally correct. One might for instance argue that ecological perception, even of paintings, is or may be more favorable to alternative vanishing points than to a fixed point.[40]

The puzzle about perspectival realism begins of course with Brunelleschi's famous mirror experiment, which may be reasonably reconstructed.[41] The Brunelleschi experiment depends on the surprise that follows when, standing in an appropriately fixed place inside the middle door of the Santa Maria del Fiore, one peeps through a small hole located in the back of Brunelleschi's own painting (now lost) of the Santo Giovanni (the Florentine Baptistery) at the represented spot corresponding to one's actual place (one's eye), one first sees what purports to be a perspectivally accurate picture of the Baptistery reflected in a mirror and then, when the mirror is removed, one sees the Baptistery itself, which seems not to have been altered or to be different from the painting in any essential particular. Brunelleschi's experiment, even admitting the limitations of fixed-point perception, certainly confirms the "naturalness" of the perspective he introduced; and certainly, the fixed point of the peephole should not be confused with the representationally fixed point or vanishing point of Masaccio's and Masolino's frescoes—influenced by Brunelleschi. *Their* work clearly shows the import of Brunelleschi's discovery *for* a moving or ecological perspective represented *at* a pictorially fixed point. It goes without saying that pictorial representation rarely tries to capture the difference between focal and peripheral vision *at a fixed point.*[42] Nevertheless, regarding Brunelleschi-like possibilities involving a moderately restricted ecological perspective in an ambient world, one can find a stunning confirmation in René Magritte's devilishly clever *Les Promenades d'Euclide.* Magritte's device helps to clarify the sense of natural similarity, without yielding to the extremes of conventionalism or transparency; and, perhaps by allusion, helps even to reinforce the sense in which Velázquez's painting could well be a witty commentary of some sort on Brunelleschi's original experiment rather than a merely realistic representation. In any case, it helps as well to remind us of our distinction between aboutness and representation.

All in all, then, representation is an optional instantiation of Intentionality or aboutness—which is itself monadic, in the essential sense that whatever is culturally emergent with respect to what enables us to construe physical marks as, or as embodying,[43] significant marks, emerges only within the space of such aboutness. The monadic or dyadic standing of representations thus "naturated" is a mixed and logically dependent consideration raised regarding paintings and the actual world. Within the scope of representation, pictorial resemblance must still share, with visual resemblance perceived in nature, some biological disposition. But since the cultural and the natural cannot be disjunctively sorted, since realist and idealist elements in perception are not merely compositionally linked, since cognitive transparency is everywhere denied, since resemblance is phenomenally perceived, resemblance may be said to be natural in being spontaneous—but cannot be shown among diverging cultures to entail a unique or uniquely favored canon for all. To say that much, however, is hardly to deny the validity of a moderate grading and ranking of natural resemblance—capable of accommodating nonconverging practices of perspective and representation.

There is another, extremely large way of viewing representation, which we can only barely broach here. To mention it, however, is to ensure the congruent power of the distinctions already introduced. The theory that language literally represents an independent world, as in veridical science, presupposes some version of the correspondence theory of truth—the "adequation" of word and world complete with operative criteria. That thesis is viable only on the strength of accepting the cognitive transparency of reality, in however sanguine or attenuated a degree. But the entire thrust of contemporary science and philosophy opposes such transparency—which is hardly the same as opposing the legitimate realism of science. It may not be wide of the mark to suggest that, within Western philosophy, the rejection of the thesis of transparency is most characteristically focused in (if not actually induced by) Wittgenstein's replacement of the conceptual model of his own *Tractatus* and Nietzsche's earlier and more radical repudiation of the structural match of language and world.[44] A propositional model best suits a representational theory of language: truth, then, is easily construed in terms of picturing or resemblance—its analogue, in experience, is systematized in Cartesian and Lockeian versions of representationalism; and fictional or imaginative uses of language (or painting) are merely construed as parasitic uses of representational devices naturally first suited for veridical science (or, say, "uniquely successful" linear perspective).

The rise of the speech-act theory of language grows jointly out of a grasp of intentional complexities regarding truth and reference that a purely propositionalized model (Bertrand Russell's, for example) could not satisfactorily accommodate,[45] and an appreciation that deeds and work are actually executed by the "mere" activity of speaking.[46] When these themes are themselves integrated with a full-bodied adherence to the rejection of cognitive transparency and to the two themes with which we began this account—namely, the inextricability of realist and idealist elements in the achievements of science and the equal reality of the languaged world of culture and the world of what we call physical nature (accessible only through the other)—then we are led to treat discourse *about* nature as discourse that: first, "natures" (in a culturally pertinent but irreducible way) the world that language thereby discloses or is monadically "about"; and, secondly, constitutes our actual engagement with that world thus "natured," including of course our occasional efforts to represent what we find in it or can imagine on the strength of our familiarity with it. The independent world is thus "second-natured" in being rendered linguistically intelligible, just as we ourselves, as persons, are the "second-natured" realizations of *Homo sapiens*. Neither achievement is possible without the disposing power of physical and biological nature. The two are really symbiotically one. Furthermore, the "first" natures of physical nature and *Homo sapiens* are themselves extrapolated by human persons exploring their languaged world. This final sketch, therefore, suggests the important sense in which the resolution of the puzzles of pictorial representation effectively requires a full-scale theory of the relationship between nature and culture.

But the sense in which language makes a languaged world accessible to linguistically apt humans, relative to which the natural world—as it is independent of being thus captured—is posited always and only from within a languaged world, affords the global model within which all the puzzles of representation and aboutness may be perspicuously placed. Perhaps it helps, in closing, therefore, to remark that the surprising identity of artwork and object, as in a Jasper Johns painting of a target (that *is* a target), or the ease of wrongly identifying a Robert Morris earthwork as a mere stretch of earth (which it is *not*), or the peculiar shock of viewing a Duane Hanson hyperlifelike sculpture (the *Museum Guard*, for example, which we cannot at first discern as a sculpture), is an instance (all are instances) of how an artwork can present a familiar world without any representational function at all. Yet each does what it does only within the invention of a cultural world and the conditions of "aboutness" internal to it, on which alone what each is "about" becomes accessible.

*Notes*

1. Jean-Paul Sartre, *Imagination: A Psychological Critique*, trans. Forrest Williams (Ann Arbor: University of Michigan Press, 1962).

2. Arthur Danto, who sees the difficulty of Sartre's theory, nevertheless follows Sartre in theorizing about the perception of paintings: all his very good puzzle cases regarding the "indistinguishability" of paintings and non-paintings and sets of

different paintings are fatally infected with this mistake. See for instance, Arthur C. Danto, *The Transformation of the Commonplace* (Cambridge: Harvard University Press, 1981), particularly chs. 1 and 2. Thus, Danto remarks, characteristically, "That there should exist indiscernible artworks—indiscernible at least with respect to anything the eye or ear can determine—has been evident." (p. 33). See also, Arthur C. Danto, "The Artworld," *Journal of Philosophy* LXI (1964); but also, *Jean-Paul Sartre* (New York: Viking, 1975), pp. 29–31.

3. For a sense of what is at stake here, see Joseph Margolis, "A Sense of *Rapprochement* between Analytic and Continental Philosophy," *History of Philosophy Quarterly* II (1985); and "Scientific Realism as a Transcendental Issue," *Manuscrito,* VII (1984).

4. One of the most influential, brief developments of this theme appears in Wilfrid Sellars, "Philosophy and the Scientific Image of Man," in *Science, Perception and Reality* (London: Routledge and Kegan Paul, 1963).

5. This goes against the subtle revival of mimesis in Monroe C. Beardsley, *The Possibility of Criticism* (Detroit: Wayne State University Press, 1970).

6. There is some convergence here but also much disagreement with Danto's use of "aboutness"; cf. for instance, *The Transformation of the Commonplace*, pp. 84–85.

7. The theory is Nelson Goodman's, in *Languages of Art* (Indianapolis: Bobbs-Merrill, 1968), particularly ch. 2.

8. Cf. Goodman, *op. cit.*, p. 95.

9. Compare Danto, *The Transfiguration of the Commonplace*, pp. 18–19, 71–78.

10. This is the fatal flaw not only of Sartre's theory but of Danto's as well; for following Sartre to this extent, Danto rightly emphasizes "the difference between a plain mark and a meaningful one" but he construes it also to be the difference "between a thing and a rule for its interpretation," *Jean-Paul Sartre*, p. 30. No, the difference concerns rather a difference in theories of perception matched to an admitted difference between natural and cultural things. The confusion subverts Danto's well-known examples of what are said to be *perceptually* "indistinguishable"—but are only *sensorily* indistinguishable.

11. Cf. Danto, *The Transformation of the Commonplace*, pp. 18–19.

12. Robert Belle Burke, *The Opus Majus of Roger Bacon* (Philadelphia: University of Pennsylvania, 1962), vol. 1, pp. 232–233.

13. See Svetlana Alpers, *The Art of Describing* (Chicago: University of Chicago Press, 1983), Appendix: and Peter C. Sutton (org.), *Masters of Seventeenth-Century Dutch Genre Painting* (Philadelphia: Philadelphia Museum of Art, distributed by University of Pennsylvania Press, 1984), "Masters of Dutch Genre Painting."

14. The principal advocate seems to be a certain E. de Jongh, whom Alpers identifies.

15. Alpers, *op. cit.*, p. 229.

16. Samuel Y. Edgerton, Jr., *The Renaissance Rediscovery of Linear Perspective* (New York: Harper and Row, 1976), p. 87.

17. The most elaborate recent version of this sort of theory has been developed by Nicholas Wolterstorff, *Works and Worlds of Art* (Oxford: Clarendon, 1980).

18. *Ibid.*, pp. 262–263.

19. This is Goodman's characteristic emphasis, of course, *op. cit.*, pp. 27–31. Danto follows him to this extent, *The Transformation of the Commonplace*, ch. 3. See also the special number, "Representation," *Social Research* LI (1984).

20. Erwin Panofsky, *Early Netherlandish Painting* (Cambridge: Harvard University Press, 1964), vol. 1, p. 7. Panofsky observes that the Arnolfini "has four central vanishing points instead of one"; see also p. 202.

21. Michel Foucault, *The Order of Things* (in trans.) (New York: Random House, 1970), p. 16.

22. The point is disputed, unconvincingly, by David Novitz, "Black Horse Pictures: Exposing the Picturing Relation," *Journal of Aesthetics and Art Criticism* XXXIV (1975).

23. See further, Joseph Margolis, "Berkeley and Others on the Problem of Universals," in Colin Turbayne (ed.), *Berkeley: Critical and Interpretive Essays* (Minneapolis: University of Minnesota Press, 1982).

24. It is worth remarking that, commenting on Magritte's paintings, which would otherwise be easily treated as merely representational (however fanciful), Foucault introduces the pointedly perceptive distinction between *"resemblance"* and *"similitude"* (that is, in the French). Magritte himself seems to have been willing to follow Foucault in this. Things do not (both hold) have *resemblances: resemblances* are imposed by reference to artifactually introduced categorial systems serving representational functions; but things have *similitudes*, that is, the capacity to invite a kind of "horizontal" slippage, as, as in Magritte's paintings, when a leaf takes the shape of a tree and a ship at sea, the form of the sea. See Michel Foucault, *This Is Not a Pipe*, trans. James Harkness (Berkeley: University of California Press, 1982).

25. See Elinor Rosch, "On the Internal Structure of Perceptual and Semantic Categories," in T. M. Moore (ed.), *Cognitive Development and the Acquisition of Language* (New York: Academic Press, 1973); "Classification of Real-world Objects: Origins and Representations in Cognition," in S. Ehrlich and E. Tulving (eds.), *La Memoire sémantique* (Paris: Bulletin de psychologie, 1976).

26. Nelson Goodman, "Seven Strictures of Similarity," in Lawrence Foster and J. W. Swanson (eds.). *Experience & Theory* (Amherst: University of Massachusetts Press, 1970), p. 25.

27. Nelson Goodman, *Languages of Art*, p. 8; cf. E. H. Gombrich, *Art and Illusion*, 2nd ed. (New York: Pantheon, 1961), *passim*.

28. *Languages of Art*, p. 38; italics added.

29. E. H. Gombrich, *The Image and the Eye* (Ithaca: Cornell University Press, 1982), p. 279.

30. *Languages of Art*, p. 39; italics added.

31. *The Image and the Eye*, pp. 280, 287. The entire essay, "Image and Code: Scope and Limits of Conventionalism in Pictorial Representation" repays attention. See also E. H. Gombrich, "The 'What' and the 'How': Perspective Representation and the Phenomenal World," in Richard Rudner and Israel Scheffler (eds.), *Logic and Art: Essays in Honor of Nelson Goodman* (Indianapolis: Bobbs-Merrill, 1972); also, Marx W. Wartofsky, "Pictures, Representation, and the Understanding," in the same volume.

32. *Languages of Art*, pp. 10–19; "The 'What' and the 'How': Perspective Representation and the Phenomenal World," particularly p. 148.

33. See James J. Gibson, *The Senses Considered as Perceptual Systems* (Boston: Houghton Mifflin, 1966).

34. "The 'What' and the 'How,'" p. 132.

35. *Ibid.*, pp. 138, 141.

36. *Ibid.*, p. 148.

37. Alan Tormey and Judith Farr Tormey, "Seeing, Believing, and Picturing," in Calvin F. Nodine and Dennis R. Fisher (eds.), *Perception and Pictorial Representation* (New York: Praeger, 1979), p. 294.

38. Francisco Pacheco, Velázquez's father-in-law, shows a distinct interest in Alberti, for instance. See his *Arte de la Pintura*, 2 vols., ed. F. J. Sanchez Canton (Madrid: Instituto de Valencia de Don Juan, 1956).

39. This way of reading Velázquez's painting goes somewhat contrary to the one interestingly proposed by Searle. See John R. Searle, "*Las Meninas* and the Paradoxes of Pictorial Representation," *Critical Inquiry* VI (1980). There are serious but irrelevant difficulties in Searle's interpretation. But what is important, here, is that Searle concedes no variability or tolerance *if* "classical representation" is invoked—a point quite alien to Foucault's reading. Thus it is that he takes too literally the notion that the representation must obtain from *one determinate point of view*. Gombrich had already observed (favoring Gibson) that realistic representation had to accommodate an ecologically shifting point of view. But if we also add that the point of view needs only to be *salient*, not in any sense strictly correct phenomenally (whether fixed or moving) to ensure realism, then we need not insist on Searle's preference for a fixed point of view. Not finding this readily confirmed and insisting on "classical representation," Searle opts instead for the point of view's being that "of the model and not . . . that of the artist" (p. 483)—that is, the point of view of Philip and Ana ("offstage"). The difference between Searle's and Foucault's interpretation is a double one; for one thing, Searle believes *Las Meninas* to be a representation of *a* representation (cf. p. 488), whereas Foucault takes it to be a representation of (the entire mode or illusion of classical) representation, that is, the act of rendering or uttering representations; for a second, Searle believes the representation to be naturalistic when seen from the point of view of the subjects, Philip and Ana, whereas Foucault takes it that, *qua* naturalistic, the painting merges the points of view of the painter, the subject, and the viewer. Joel Snyder (whose recent piece on *Las Meninas* appeared after completing this essay) has conclusively shown the untenability of Searle's and Foucault's second claim; in his own voice, he suggests another reading that is not entirely out of sympathy with Foucault's first claim, one in fact that is congenial with, though quite different from, the one here suggested. Velázquez's witty use of the paintings in the neighborhood of the mirror then makes novel sense—somewhat in the same way that Matisse often exploits in his "confusing" paintings and parts of paintings with parts of natural scenes. See Joel Snyder, "*Las Meninas* and the Mirror of the Prince," *Critical Inquiry* XI (1985).

40. Panofsky, *loc. cit.*

41. The full account is conveniently provided in Edgerton, *loc. cit.*; also, in John White, *The Birth and Rebirth of Pictorial Space*, 2nd ed. (Boston: Boston Book and Art shop, 1967), ch. 8. The accounts are drawn from Antonio Manetti's *Life of Brunelleschi*, evidently written some decades later.

42. This is perhaps the fatal difficulty of Searle's argument—which is not to say that that is the fatal difficulty of his interpretation of Velázquez's painting.

43. On the use of "embodying," see Joseph Margolis, *Art and Philosophy* (Atlantic Highlands, N.J.: Humanities Press, 1978), chs. 2 and 3.

44. Friedrich Nietzsche, "On Truth and Lies in a Nonmoral Sense," in Daniel Breazeale (trans. and ed.), *Philosophy and Truth: Selections from Nietzsche's Notebooks of the Early 1870's* (Atlantic Highlands, N.J.: Humanities Press, 1979).

45. The essential discussion, here, is that of P. F. Strawson, "On Referring," *Mind* LIX (1950).

46. The classic source is of course J. L. Austin, *How To Do Things with Words* (Oxford: Clarendon, 1962).

# Bibliography to Part Four

The problem of representation has been focused, in recent years, by the appearance of E. H. Gombrich's views about pictorial representation and Nelson Goodman's general theory of representation and the referential functions of art. Particularly relevant are:

E. H. Gombrich, *Art and Illusion* (London, 1962, 2nd ed.), chapters 7–9;

E. H. Gombrich, "Meditations on a Hobby Horse," in *Meditations on a Hobby Horse and Other Essays on the Theory of Art* (London, 1963).

Gombrich was himself influenced by J. J. Gibson's theories of the ecological nature of perception, which form an essential part of the literature regarding perceptual realism:

James J. Gibson, *The Senses Considered as Perceptual Systems* (Boston, 1966);

James J. Gibson, *The Ecological Approach to Visual Perception* (Boston, 1979);

James J. Gibson, "The Information Available in Pictures," *Leonardo* IV (1971), 27–35.

See further, on the perception of pictures and pictorial resemblance:

Samuel Y. Edgerton, Jr., *The Renaissance Rediscovery of Linear Perspective* (New York, 1975);

Margaret A. Hagen (ed.), *The Perception of Pictures,* 2 vols. (New York, 1980);

Calvin F. Nodine and Dennis F. Fisher (eds.), *Perception and Pictorial Representation* (New York, 1979).

Among the livelier discussions bearing on the issue of representation, the following may be mentioned:

Max Black, "How Do Pictures Represent?" in E. H. Gombrich, Julian Hochberg and Max Black, *Art, Perception and Reality* (Baltimore, 1972);

Arthur C. Danto, "Works of Art and Mere Representations," *The Transfiguration of the Commonplace* (Cambridge, 1981);

B. Falk, "Portraits and Persons," *Proceedings of the Aristotelian Society* LXXI (1974–1975), 181–200;

E. H. Gombrich, "The 'What' and the 'How': Perspective Representation and the Phenomenal World," in Richard Rudner and Israel Scheffler (eds.), *Logic & Art* (Indianapolis, 1972);

Göran Hermerén, *Representation and Meaning in the Visual Arts* (Lund, 1969);

Julian Hochberg, "The Representation of Things and People," in E. H. Gombrich, Julian Hochberg and Max Black, *Art, Perception and Reality* (Baltimore, 1972);

Patrick Maynard, "Depiction, Vision, and Convention," *American Philosophical Quarterly* IX (1972), 243–250;

David Novitz, *Pictures and Their Use in Communications* ('s Gravenhage, The Netherlands, 1977);

Risto Pitkänen, *On the Analysis of Pictorial Representation, Acta Philosophica Fennica,* vol. 31, no. 4 (Amsterdam, 1980);

Jenefer Robinson, "Some Remarks on Goodman's Language Theory of Pictures," *British Journal of Aesthetics* XIX (1979);

L. R. Rogers, "Representation and Schemata," *British Journal of Aesthetics* V (1965), 159–178;

Richard Rudner, "On Seeing What We Shall See," in Richard Rudner and Israel Scheffler (eds.), *Logic & Art* (Indianapolis, 1972);

Roger Squires, "Depicting," *Philosophy* XLIV (1969), 193–204;

Robert H. Thouless, "Phenomenal Regression to the Real Object," *British Journal of Psychology* XXI (1930–1931), 339–359; XXII (1931–1932), 1–30;

Kendall L. Walton, "Pictures and Make-Believe," *Philosophical Review* LXXXII (1973), 283–319;

Marx W. Wartofsky, "Pictures, Representation, and the Understanding," in Richard Rudner and Israel Scheffler (eds.), *Logic & Art* (Indianapolis, 1972);

Richard Wollheim, *On Art and the Mind* (London, 1973).

Representation in music was, formerly, the center of the controversy. Discussion often focused on:

Eduard Hanslick, *The Beautiful in Music,* trans. Gustav Cohen (Indianapolis, 1957).

See also:

V. A. Howard, "On Musical Expression," *British Journal of Aesthetics* XI (1970), 268–280;

Leonard B. Meyer, *Emotion and Meaning in Music* (Chicago, 1956);

Leonard B. Meyer, *Music, The Arts and Ideas* (Chicago, 1967).

See also, Bibliography to Part Five.

# Part Five

## The Intentional Fallacy and Expressive Qualities

Representational art raises the general question of the relevance of an artist's intention in the appreciation of art (see Part One). It is of course possible to construe representation, as Goodman does, in logical or functional terms. But it may be reasonably argued that, whatever the puzzles generated, the question is ultimately one of intentional considerations—though not necessarily psychological ones.

It is characteristic of empiricist tendencies, as of extensionalist tendencies, which obtain in somewhat different mixes in Beardsley and Goodman, that problems of intentionality (or even of artists' intentions—a more restricted issue) are either dismissed, muted, made marginal, or otherwise assigned a very limited role in the philosophy of art. The Continental emphasis, however, on intentionality, stemming originally from the work of Franz Brentano and Edmund Husserl, and the rise of strongly historicized theories of artworks, texts, and interpretation, stemming chiefly from the work of Martin Heidegger and the hermeneutic tradition—notably, the work of Hans-Georg Gadamer—challenge in a fundamental way the dominant tendencies of Anglo-American aesthetics.

The issue of the Intentional Fallacy, therefore, is a special, rather heavily debated, version of more general puzzles regarding what may be critically eligible or relevant (that is, short of true or false, or correct or incorrect) in describing and interpreting works of art and performing particular works. Characteristically, we ask whether, say, James Joyce intended *Finnegans Wake* to be construed this way or that, or whether Stanislavski's production of *The Cherry Orchard* accords with Chekhov's intentions. The questions are quite familiar. But one may puzzle over the critical eligibility of these very questions. Is it "aesthetically" relevant to inquire regarding the artist's intention? As soon as the question is put in this form, we see that the issue depends on the ease with which we may decide what the aesthetic point of view in criticism is (see Part One). Are we faced with a finding or a ruling? If a finding, how are we to judge conflicting opinions here? If a ruling, what is the force of the term 'fallacy'? We notice that critics, in their practice, sometimes appeal to the artist's intention. What then is the logical status of a judgment that such appeals are inadmissible? And how may the artist's intention be determined: through autobiographical materials? through psychoanalysis? through cultural conventions? through the properties of the work of art itself? And will the answer be quite general for all the arts? For example, will adjustments be advisable when we possess a composer's musical notation?

The issue of the Fallacy is tangentially related to that of the artist's expression, since one variant of the view that the artist expresses himself is to hold that to understand a work one must, or at least on occasion one may have to, know the artist's intention. Sometimes the relationship is reversed and one insists that the merit of a work is to be judged solely or chiefly on whether the artist's intention has been fulfilled—either, on internal grounds, in the work actually produced or, as in the performing arts, in accord with a notation. More directly, the issue of the Fallacy presupposes some fairly clean-cut conception of what "the work of art" is (see Parts Two and Three). Otherwise, we should have difficulty determining the relevance or irrelevance of critical comments—whether intentionally oriented, psychoanalytically oriented, or oriented in terms of cultural history or in accord with frankly partisan convictions (e.g., Marxist, Roman Catholic). So the issue of the Fallacy spreads inevitably to that of the general relationship of critical interpretations to the work of art. If we ask ourselves how we define the boundaries of a poem, what are the implications of a changing tradition of dramatic and musical performance, we are at once placed at the center of the difficulties. If a psychoanalytically oriented interpretation of *Hamlet* be eligible, why not one that accords with Shakespeare's autobiographical remains? And if we may at times restrict dramatic and musical performances in terms of period style, why not in terms of the artist's intention? May we perhaps judge with equal ease, in the context of appreciation, that some particular performance is both ingenious and not in accord with the artist's original conception? And what are the differences, with regard to appreciation itself, between two such remarks as these? What in fact is properly meant by 'the artist's intention'?

All these questions have been focused memorably by the appearance of Wimsatt and Beardsley's essay (1954). The essay has attracted considerable attention and a very large part of the professionally relevant literature since its appearance is explicitly concerned to defend or criticize its views. A number of questions may be usefully sorted, here. For one thing,

Wimsatt and Beardsley construe 'intentional' not only in psychological terms but also in terms of an artist's conscious plan. In effect, what they are concerned about is what, broadly speaking, is central to so-called autobiographical considerations. Many who have criticized them are inclined to think that the "intentional" aspects of a work—even aspects bearing on the artist's "plan"—may be discerned in the work itself. Now, it is not clear whether Wimsatt and Beardsley would be entirely opposed to reference to such features—presumably not—though it is also not clear whether so-called intentionalists have ever meant to rely on biographical considerations somehow not manifest or confirmed at all in some actual work. Again, along these lines, it is not entirely obvious how, as in the performing arts, reference to the artist's plan—mediated by a notation, possibly by biographical information—can be altogether avoided. Granting this, counterpart moves seem possible in the other arts.

Sometimes, Wimsatt and Beardsley understand the Fallacy to be what might be termed (if it were a fallacy) the Romantic Fallacy, that an artist is, at the moment of creation, expressing himself or his age. But this invites us to consider that *some* of the features of given works of art may well be expressive in either of these two senses, as well as to concede that to construe them thus need not rest on independent evidence of a plan in the artist's mind. Criticism of the one thesis seems not to be tantamount to criticism of the other. Again, they do not sort out with complete success puzzles connected with the problem of allusiveness and meaning. If, for example, as both Wimsatt and Beardsley on separate occasions have maintained, meanings depend on usage and usage includes the author's usage (even if idiosyncratic), then it is difficult to see how to free the objective specification of meaning altogether from intentional factors, however they may be attenuated. This bears in an important way on Wimsatt and Beardsley's would-be distinction between "internal and external evidence" and, more generally, on the theory of the nature of a work of art (see Part Three). More recently, Beardsley in particular—as with a number of theorists of literature—has been attracted to a speech-act model. But such a model is incapable of being developed along non-intentionalistic lines. And the intentional factors involved cannot be freed altogether from contextual and psychological considerations.

In general, a speech-act model of meaning is inherently intentionalistic; although, contrary to standard speech-act theory (for instance, John Searle's, 1969), it need hardly be confined to the conscious intentions of speaking or writing agents; and meanings, complicated by speech-act considerations, can certainly not be confined in any merely psychological or solely individualistic sense. The very notions of language, meaning, tradition, practice, style, history, and the like are inherently societal "possessions." The irony is that the early Continental emphasis on intentionality—explicitly, in Brentano and Husserl; implicitly, in the pioneer hermeneutic work of Friedrich Schleiermacher (1977) and his followers, for instance, E. D. Hirsch, Jr. (1967)—is also strongly inclined (with whatever adjustments) to confine the notion initially to contexts of individual psychology, rational egos, or the like.

Among the most vigorous and detailed criticisms of Wimsatt and Beardsley's position is a paper by Frank Cioffi (1963-1964), which stresses, among other things, that the relation of intention to interpretation is unpredictable and variable (hence cannot be ruled out as a general policy), and that art (Cioffi confined himself to the literary arts) is such that our appreciation of it is affected by the artist's relation to his own work. These appear to be quite sensible observations, though their force against Wimsatt and Beardsley depends in part on how we construe the latter's distinction between internal and external evidence—which is not entirely explicit.

More recently, Guy Sircello (1972) has identified a range of attributes properly ascribed to works of art that may reasonably be expressed as well in terms of the artist's intentions. These are interesting because they spring to mind in the most natural way, cannot properly be ascribed to particular works without attention to something like a plan in the artist's mind or psychological intention or intentional state, and because their possession by works of art confirms distinctive aspects of the nature of artworks as such (see Parts One and Two). They may be characterized as expressive properties, though this is not to say that all expressive qualities are properly formulable in terms of the artist's intentional states. The conflation of the two themes is the central feature of the Romantic theory of art: Wimsatt and Beardsley are right in supposing that it cannot be an adequate theory of art; the question is whether they rightly claim that it has no application at all. The principal feature of Sircello's account, however, is that, although these properties may be ascribed to works of art, they cannot be detected by attention to the work of art itself—in any sense in which it is frequently claimed that works of art are directly perceivable (see Part One). Alternatively put, it is not clear *what* we mean to say, given these complications, in saying that a given artwork is perceivable or somehow perceivable without regard to the intentional, historical, cultural, and related ("imperceptible") preconditions on which "it"—the artwork, not merely a physical object—becomes perceivable. This, for instance, may well be the right way to unpack Danto's notion of the "is" of artistic identification, although, ironically, that notion is not called into play when Danto (1981) develops his well-known account of numerically different but perceptually indistinguishable paintings (a series of red *canvases*). The large problem of intentionality, then, actually colors the theory of *perceptual* discrimination itself—hence, the theory of aesthetic qualities. This has been largely ignored in the more-or-less empiricist-minded theories favored in the Anglo-American tradition, even when the very thesis of empiricism is being criticized as too narrow.

On the other hand, Alan Tormey (1971) argues persuasively that expressive qualities need not, and cannot all, be dependent on the actual intentional states of artists. He provides, therefore, for a set of predicates (e.g., *tenderness, sadness, anguish, nostalgia*) which designate expressive properties in works of art because when applied to human persons they designate intentional states.

The question remains whether works of art actually have such properties or whether they may validly be attributed to them for some other reason. There is a strong tendency to hold that such attributions are, somehow, metaphorical. Both Goodman and Beardsley have been inclined to construe them thus. But the justifiability of that view depends ultimately on the theory of the ontology of art (see Part Three), because to hold that a work of art could not literally possess an expressive property, or to hold that the expressive property it does possess must depend on a metaphoric application of a predicate that rightly designates only what may be literally ascribed to human beings, favors certain theories of the nature of artworks over others (see Goodman, Part Three).

The problem of intentionality, then, cannot be confined to the narrowly psychological (as in Beardsley's view) and cannot be disjoined from the complexities of societal history. That is the principal contribution, to the philosophy of art, of the work of the continuing Continental traditions of phenomenology and hermeneutics. But, as already noted, until fairly recently the principal themes of both these traditions have—taking terms somewhat informally—been inclined to favor the mental life of individuals and the timeless fixing of historical change. In the hermeneutic tradition, E. D. Hirsch (1967) is at once the direct descendant of Schleiermacher's romantic conception of intention and the Continentally oriented opponent of Beardsley's New Critical rejection of authors' intentions. But, in serving in that role, Hirsch is also the most prominent American opponent of the post-Heideggerian version of hermeneutics—that is, the strongly historicized alternative that denies that textual interpretation can be confined to the recovery of an original author's intention and must instead be construed in terms of a certain appropriately disciplined consensus formed and reformed within the very flux of cultural life. The latter is almost the invention of Hans-Georg Gadamer (represented in Part Six).

Here, Hirsch states very fairly Gadamer's version of the hermeneutic position and his own fundamental objections to it. It is clear, however, that Hirsch counts both on *not* radically historicizing the human cognition of historical change and on the relatively sedimented fixity of the actual artifacts of different historical eras. Both of these commitments are of course opposed by Gadamer. In this regard, Hirsch is obliged to develop a peculiarly ambivalent theory of period styles: on the one hand, it must be rather strictly construed in order to widen the romantic conception sufficiently and in a sufficiently disciplined way, so as to go beyond explicit or conscious intention; on the other, it must not be so rigidly formulated that the hermeneut is bound to advocate an essentialism with respect to human history or to deny the open texture of a developing style. The puzzle thus produced is a version of that of the so-called hermeneutic circle. But it is useful to note that, in the Anglo-American tradition, notably in Goodman's theory (1978), the characterization of style is usually not reconciled with a strongly historicized (as opposed to a historically periodized) conception meant to come to terms with the challenge of the hermeneutic circle. For, construed in the hermeneutic sense, style could not be satisfactorily captured by a notation—in the manner said to hold of the allographic arts.

# 19. The Intentional Fallacy

### W. K. WIMSATT, JR. AND
### MONROE C. BEARDSLEY

> He owns with toil he wrote the following scenes;
> But, if they're naught, ne'er spare him for his pains:
> Damn him the more; have no commiseration
> For dullness on mature deliberation.
>
> William Congreve
> Prologue to *The Way of the World*

*I*

The claim of the author's "intention" upon the critic's judgment has been challenged in a number of recent discussions, notably in the debate entitled *The Personal Heresy*, between Professors Lewis and Tillyard. But it seems doubtful if this claim and most of its romantic corollaries are as yet subject to any widespread questioning. The present writers, in a short article entitled "Intention" for a *Dictionary*[1] of literary criticism, raised the issue but were unable to pursue its implications at any length. We argued that the design or intention of the author is neither available nor desirable as a standard for judging the success of a work of literary art, and it seems to us that this is a principle which goes deep into some differences in the history of critical attitudes. It is a principle which accepted or rejected points to the polar opposites of classical "imitation" and romantic expression. It entails many specific truths about inspiration, authenticity, biography, literary history, and scholarship, and about some trends of contemporary poetry, especially its allusiveness. There is hardly a problem of

From W. K. Wimsatt, *The Verbal Icon* (Lexington: University of Kentucky Press, 1954), Chapter I. Reprinted with permission of the authors and the University of Kentucky Press.

literary criticism in which the critic's approach will not be qualified by his view of "intention."

"Intention," as we shall use the term, corresponds to *what he intended* in a formula which more or less explicitly has had wide acceptance. "In order to judge the poet's performance, we must know *what he intended*." Intention is design or plan in the author's mind. Intention has obvious affinities for the author's attitude toward his work, the way he felt, what made him write.

We begin our discussion with a series of propositions summarized and abstracted to a degree where they seem to us axiomatic.

1. A poem does not come into existence by accident. The words of a poem, as Professor Stoll has remarked, come out of a head, not out of a hat. Yet to insist on the designing intellect as a *cause* of a poem is not to grant the design or intention as a *standard* by which the critic is to judge the worth of the poet's performance.

2. One must ask how a critic expects to get an answer to the question about intention. How is he to find out what the poet tried to do? If the poet succeeded in doing it, then the poem itself shows what he was trying to do. And if the poet did not succeed, then the poem is not adequate evidence, and the critic must go outside the poem—for evidence of an intention that did not become effective in the poem. "Only one *caveat* must be borne in mind," says an eminent intentionalist[2] in a moment when his theory repudiates itself; "the poet's aim must be judged at the moment of the creative act, that is to say, by the art of the poem itself."

3. Judging a poem is like judging a pudding or a machine. One demands that it work. It is only because an artifact works that we infer the intention of an artificer. "A poem should not mean but be." A poem can *be* only through its *meaning*—since its medium is words—yet it *is*, simply *is*, in the sense that we have no excuse for inquiring what part is intended or meant. Poetry is a feat of style by which a complex of meaning is handled all at once. Poetry succeeds because all or most of what is said or implied is relevant; what is irrelevant has been excluded, like lumps from pudding and "bugs" from machinery. In this respect poetry differs from practical messages, which are successful if and only if we correctly infer the intention. They are more abstract than poetry.

4. The meaning of a poem may certainly be a personal one, in the sense that a poem expresses a personality or state of soul rather than a physical object like an apple. But even a short lyric poem is dramatic, the response of a speaker (no matter how abstractly conceived) to a situation (no matter how universalized). We ought to impute the thoughts and attitudes of the poem immediately to the dramatic *speaker*, and if to the author at all, only by an act of biographical inference.

5. There is a sense in which an author, by revision, may better achieve his original intention. But it is a very abstract sense. He intended to write a better work, or a better work of a certain kind, and now has done it. But it follows that his former concrete intention was not his intention. "He's the man we were in search of, that's true," says Hardy's rustic constable, "and yet he's not the man we were in search of. For the man we were in search of was not the man we wanted."

"Is not a critic," asks Professor Stoll, "a judge, who does not explore his own consciousness, but determines the author's meaning or intention, as if the poem were a will, a contract, or the constitution? The poem is not the critic's own." He has accurately diagnosed two forms of irresponsibility, one of which he prefers. Our view is yet different. The poem is not the critic's own but the author's (it is detached from the author at birth and goes about the world beyond his power to intend about it or control it). The poem belongs to the public. It is embodied in language, the peculiar possession of the public, and it is about the human being, an object of public knowledge. What is said about the poem is subject to the same scrutiny as any statement in linguistics or in the general science of psychology.

A critic of our *Dictionary* article, Ananda K. Coomaraswamy, has argued[3] that there are two kinds of inquiry about a work of art: (1) whether the artist achieved his intentions; (2) whether the work of art "ought ever to have been undertaken at all" and so "whether it is worth preserving." Number (2), Coomaraswamy maintains, is not "criticism of any work of art *qua* work of art," but is rather moral criticism; number (1) is artistic criticism. But we maintain that (2) need not be moral criticism: that there is another way of deciding whether works of art are worth preserving and whether, in a sense, they "ought" to have been undertaken, and this is the way of objective criticism of works of art as such, the way which enables us to distinguish between a skillful murder and a skillful poem. A skillful murder is an example which Coomaraswamy uses, and in his system the difference between the murder and the poem is simply a "moral" one, not an "artistic" one, since each if carried out according to plan is "artistically" successful. We maintain that (2) is an inquiry of more worth than (1), and since (2) and not (1) is capable of distinguishing poetry from murder, the name "artistic criticism" is properly given to (2).

## II

It is not so much a historical statement as a definition to say that the intentional fallacy is a romantic one. When a rhetorician of the first century

A.D. writes: "Sublimity is the echo of a great soul," or when he tells us that "Homer enters into the sublime actions of his heroes" and "shares the full inspiration of the combat," we shall not be surprised to find this rhetorician considered as a distant harbinger of romanticism and greeted in the warmest terms by Saintsbury. One may wish to argue whether Longinus should be called romantic, but there can hardly be a doubt that in one important way he is.

Goethe's three questions for "constructive criticism" are "What did the author set out do do? Was his plan reasonable and sensible, and how far did he succeed in carrying it out?" If one leaves out the middle question, one has in effect the system of Croce—the culmination and crowning philosophic expression of romanticism. The beautiful is the successful intuition-expression, and the ugly is the unsuccessful; the intuition or private part of art is *the* aesthetic fact, and the medium or public part is not the subject of aesthetic at all.

> The Madonna of Cimabue is still in the Church of Santa Maria Novella; but does she speak to the visitor of to-day as to the Florentines of the thirteenth century?
> *Historical interpretation* labors . . . to reintegrate in us the psychological conditions which have changed in the course of history. It . . . enables us to see a work of art (a physical object) as its *author saw* it in the moment of production.[4]

The first italics are Croce's, the second ours. The upshot of Croce's system is an ambiguous emphasis on history. With such passages as a point of departure a critic may write a nice analysis of the meaning or "spirit" of a play by Shakespeare or Corneille—a process that involves close historical study but remains aesthetic criticism—or he may, with equal plausibility, produce an essay in sociology, biography, or other kinds of nonaesthetic history.

*III*

> I went to the poets; tragic, dithyrambic, and all sorts. . . . I took them some of the most elaborate passages in their own writings, and asked what was the meaning of them. . . . Will you believe me? . . . there is hardly a person present who would not have talked better about their poetry than they did themselves. Then I knew that not by wisdom do poets write poetry, but by a sort of genius and inspiration.

That reiterated mistrust of the pets which we hear from Socrates may have been part of a rigorously ascetic view in which we hardly wish to participate, yet Plato's Socrates saw a truth about the poetic mind which the world no longer commonly sees—so much criticism, and that the most inspirational and most affectionately remembered, has proceeded from the poets themselves.

Certainly the poets have had something to say that the critic and professor could not say; their message has been more exciting: that poetry should come as naturally as leaves to a tree, that poetry is the lava of the imagination, or that it is emotion recollected in tranquility. But it is necessary that we realize the character and authority of such testimony. There is only a fine shade of difference between such expressions and a kind of earnest advice that authors often give. Thus Edward Young, Carlyle, Walter Pater:

> I know two golden rules from *ethics*, which are no less golden in *Composition*, than in life. 1. *Know thyself*; 2dly, *Reverence thyself*.

> This is the grand secret for finding readers and retaining them: let him who would move and convince others, be first moved and convinced himself. Horace's rule, *Si vis me flere*, is applicable in a wider sense than the literal one. To every poet, to every writer, we might say: Be true, if you would be believed.

> Truth! there can be no merit, no craft at all, without that. And further, all beauty is in the long run only *fineness* of truth, or what we call expression, the finer accommodation of speech to that vision within.

And Housman's little handbook to the poetic mind yields this illustration:

> Having drunk a pint of beer at luncheon—beer is a sedative to the brain, and my afternoons are the least intellectual portion of my life—I would go out for a walk of two or three hours. As I went along, thinking of nothing in particular, only looking at things around me and following the progress of the seasons, there would flow into my mind, with sudden and unaccountable emotion, sometimes a line or two of verse, sometimes a whole stanza at once.

This is the logical terminus of the series already quoted. Here is a confession of how poems were written which would do as a definition of poetry just as well as "emotion recollected in tranquility"—and which the young poet might equally well take to heart as a practical rule. Drink a pint of beer, relax, go walking, think on nothing in particular, look at things, surrender yourself to yourself, search for the truth in your own soul, listen to the sound of your own inside voice, discover and express the *vraie vérité*.

It is probably true that all this is excellent advice for poets. The young imagination fired by Wordsworth and Carlyle is probably closer to the verge of producing a poem than the mind of the student who has been sobered by Aristotle or Richards. The art of inspiring poets, or at least of inciting something like poetry in young persons, has probably gone further in our day than ever before. Books of creative writing such as those issued from the Lincoln School are interesting evidence of what a child can do.[5] All this, however, would appear to belong to an art separate from criticism—to a psychological discipline, a system of self-development, a yoga, which the young poet perhaps does well to notice, but which is something different from the public art of evaluating poems.

Coleridge and Arnold were better critics than most poets have been, and if the critical tendency dried up the poetry in Arnold and perhaps in Coleridge, it is not inconsistent with our argument, which is that judgment of poems is different from the art of producing them. Coleridge has given us the classic "anodyne" story, and tells what he can about the genesis of a poem which he calls a "psychological curiosity," but his definitions of poetry and of the poetic quality "imagination" are to be found elsewhere and in quite other terms.

It would be convenient if the passwords of the intentional school, "sincerity," "fidelity," "spontaneity," "authenticity," "genuineness," "originality," could be equated with terms such as "integrity," "relevance," "unity," "function," "maturity," "subtlety," "adequacy," and other more precise terms of evaluation—in short, if "expression" always meant aesthetic achievement. But this is not so.

"Aesthetic" art, says Professor Curt Ducasse, an ingenious theorist of expression, is the conscious objectification of feelings, in which an intrinsic part is the critical moment. The artist corrects the objectification when it is not adequate. but this may mean that the earlier attempt was not successful in objectifying the self, or "it may also mean that it was a successful objectification of a self which, when it confronted us clearly, we disowned and repudiated in favor of another."[6] What is the standard by which we disown or accept the self? Professor Ducasse does not say. Whatever it may be, however, this standard is an element in the definition of art which will not reduce to terms of objectivication. The evaluation of the work of art remains public; the work is measured against something outside the author.

## IV

There is criticism of poetry and there is author psychology, which when applied to the present or future takes the form of inspirational promotion;

but author psychology can be historical too, and then we have literary biography, a legitimate and attractive study in itself, one approach, as Professor Tillyard would argue, to personality, the poem being only a parallel approach. Certainly it need not be with a derogatory purpose that one points out personal studies, as distinct from poetic studies, in the realm of literary scholarship. Yet there is danger of confusing personal and poetic studies; and there is the fault of writing the personal as if it were poetic.

There is a difference between internal and external evidence for the meaning of a poem. And the paradox is only verbal and superficial that what is (1) internal is also public: it is discovered through the semantics and syntax of a poem, through our habitual knowledge of the language, through grammars, dictionaries, and all the literature which is the source of dictionaries, in general through all that makes a language and culture; while what is (2) external is private or idiosyncratic; not a part of the work as a linguistic fact: it consists of revelations (in journals, for example, or letters or reported conversations) about how or why the poet wrote the poem—to what lady, while sitting on what lawn, or at the death of what friend or brother. There is (3) an intermediate kind of evidence about the character of the author or about private or semiprivate meanings attached to words or topics by the author or by a coterie of which he is a member. The meaning of words is the history of words, and the biography of an author, his use of a word, and the associations which the word had for *him*, are part of the word's history and meaning.[7] But the three types of evidence, especially (2) and (3), shade into one another so subtly that it is not always easy to draw a line between examples, and hence arises the difficulty for criticism. The use of biographical evidence need not involve intentionalism, because while it may be evidence of what the author intended, it may also be evidence of the meaning of his words and the dramatic character of his utterance. On the other hand, it may not be all this. And a critic who is concerned with evidence of type (1) and moderately with that of type (3) will in the long run produce a different sort of comment from that of the critic who is concerned with (2) and with (3) where it shades into (2).

The whole glittering parade of Professor Lowes's *Road to Xanadu*, for instance, runs along the border between types (2) and (3) or boldly traverses the romantic region of (2). "'Kubla Khan,'" says Professor Lowes, "is the fabric of a vision, but every image that rose up in its weaving had passed that way before. And it would seem that there is nothing haphazard or fortuitous in their return." This is not quite clear—not even when Professor Lowes explains that there were clusters of associations, like hooked atoms, which were drawn into complex relation with other clusters in the deep well of Coleridge's memory, and which then coalesced and issued forth as poems. If there was nothing "haphazard or fortuitous" in the way the images returned to the surface, that may mean (1) that Coleridge could not produce what he did not have, that he was limited in his creation by what he had read or otherwise experienced, or (2) that having received certain clusters of associations, he was bound to return them in just the way he did, and that the value of the poem may be described in terms of the experiences on which he had to draw. The latter pair of propositions (a sort of Hartleyan associationism which Coleridge himself repudiated in the *Biographia*) may not be assented to. There were certainly other combinations, other poems, worse or better, that might have been written by men who had read Bartram and Purchas and Bruce and Milton. And this will be true no matter how many times we are able to add to the brilliant complex of Coleridge's reading. In certain flourishes (such as the sentence we have quoted) and in chapter headings like "The Shaping Spirit," "The Magical Synthesis," "Imagination Creatrix," it may be that Professor Lowes pretends to say more about the actual poems than he does. There is a certain deceptive variation in these fancy chapter titles; one expects to pass on to a new stage in the argument, and one finds—more and more sources, more and more about "the streamy nature of association."[8]

"Wohin der Weg?" quotes Professor Lowes for the motto of his book. "Kein Weg! Ins Unbretretene." Precisely because the way is *unbetreten*, we should say, it leads away from the poem. Bartram's *Travels* contains a good deal of the history of certain words and of certain romantic Floridian conceptions that appear in "Kubla Khan." And a good deal of that history has passed and was then passing into the very stuff of our language. Perhaps a person who has read Bartram appreciates the poem more than one who has not. Or, by looking up the vocabulary of "Kubla Khan" in the *Oxford English Dictionary*, or by reading some of the other books there quoted, a person may know the poem better. But it would seem to pertain little to the poem to know that *Coleridge* had read Bartram. There is a gross body of life, of sensory and mental experience, which lies behind and in some sense causes every poem, but can never be and need not be known in the verbal and hence intellectual composition which is the poem. For all the objects of our manifold experience, for every unity, there is an action of the mind which cuts off roots, melts away context—or indeed we should never have objects or ideas or anything to talk about.

It is probable that there is nothing in Professor Lowes's vast book which could detract from anyone's appreciation of either *The Ancient Mariner* or "Kubla Khan." We next present a case where preoccupation with evidence of type (3) has gone so far as to distort a critic's view of a poem (yet a case not so obvious as those that abound in our critical journals).

In a well-known poem by John Donne appears this quatrain:

> Moving of th'earth brings harmes and feares,
>     Men reckon what it did and meant,
> But trepidation of the spheares,
>     Though greater farre, is innocent.

A recent critic in an elaborate treatment of Donne's learning has written of this quatrain as follows:

> He touches the emotional pulse of the situation by a skillful allusion to the new and the old astronomy. . . . Of the new astronomy, the "moving of the earth" is the most radical principle; of the old, the "trepidation of the spheares" is the motion of the greatest complexity. . . . The poet must exhort his love to quietness and calm upon his departure; and for this purpose the figure based upon the latter motion (trepidation), long absorbed into the traditional astronomy, fittingly suggests the tension of the moment without arousing the "harmes and feares" implicit in the figure of the moving earth.[9]

The argument is plausible and rests on a well substantiated thesis that Donne was deeply interested in the new astronomy and its repercussions in the theological realm. In various works Donne shows his familiarity with Kepler's *De Stella Nova*, with Galileo's *Siderius Nuncius*, with William Gilbert's *De Magnete*, and with Clavius's commentary on the *De Sphaera* of Sacrobosco. He refers to the new science in his Sermon at Paul's Cross and in a letter to Sir Henry Goodyer. In *The First Anniversary* he says the "new philosophy calls all in doubt." In the *Elegy* on *Prince Henry* he says that the "least moving of the center" makes "the world to shake."

It is difficult to answer argument like this, and impossible to answer it with evidence of like nature. There is no reason why Donne might not have written a stanza in which the two kinds of celestial motion stood for two sorts of emotion at parting. And if we become full of astronomical ideas and see Donne only against the background of the new science, we may believe that he did. But the text itself remains to be dealt with, the analyzable vehicle of a complicated metaphor. And one may observe: (1) that the movement of the earth according to the Copernician theory is a celestial motion, smooth and regular, and while it might cause religious or philosophic fears, it could not be associated with the crudity and earthiness of the kind of commotion which the speaker in the poem wishes to discourage; (2) that there is another moving of the earth, an earthquake, which has just these qualities and is to be associated with the tear-floods and sigh-tempests of the second stanza of the poem; (3) that "trepidation" is an appropriate opposite of earthquake, because each is a shaking or vibratory motion; and "trepidation of the spheares" is "greater farre" than an earthquake, but not much greater (if two such motions can be compared as to greatness) than the annual motion of the earth; (4) that reckoning what it "did and meant" shows that the event has passed, like an earthquake, not like the incessant celestial movement of the earth. Perhaps a knowledge of Donne's interest in the new science may add another shade of meaning, an overtone to the stanza in question, though to say even this runs against the words. To make the geocentric and heliocentric antithesis the core of the metaphor is to disregard the English language, to prefer private evidence to public, external to internal.

## V

If the distinction between kinds of evidence has implications for the historical critic, it has them no less for the contemporary poet and his critic. Or, since every rule for a poet is but another side of a judgment by a critic, and since the past is the realm of the scholar and critic, and the future and present that of the poet and the critical leaders of taste, we may say that the problems arising in literary scholarship from the intentional fallacy are matched by others which arise in the world of progressive experiment.

The question of "allusiveness," for example, as acutely posed by the poetry of Eliot, is certainly one where a false judgment is likely to involve the intentional fallacy. The frequency and depth of literary allusion in the poetry of Eliot and others has driven so many in pursuit of full meanings to the *Golden Bough* and the Elizabethan drama that it has become a kind of commonplace to suppose that we do not know what a poet means unless we have traced him in his reading—a supposition redolent with intentional implications. The stand taken by F. O. Matthiessen is a sound one and partially forestalls the difficulty.

> If one reads these lines with an attentive ear and is sensitive to their sudden shifts in movement, the contrast between the actual Thames and the idealized vision of it during an age before it flowed through a megalopolis is sharply conveyed by that movement itself, whether or not one recognizes the refrain to be from Spenser.

Eliot's allusions work when we know them—and to a great extent when we do not know them—through their suggestive power.

But sometimes we find allusions supported by notes, and it is a nice question whether the notes function more as guides to send us where we may be educated, or more as indications in themselves about the character of the allusions. "Nearly everything of importance . . . that is apposite to an appreciation of 'The Waste Land,'" writes Matthiessen of Miss Weston's book, "has been incorporated into the structure of the poem itself, or into Eliot's Notes." And with such an admission it may begin to appear that it would not much matter if Eliot invented his sources (as Sir Walter Scott invented chapter epigraphs from "old plays" and "anonymous" authors, or as Coleridge wrote marginal glosses for *The Ancient Mariner*). Allusions to Dante, Webster, Marvell, or Baudelaire doubtless gain something because these writers existed, but it is doubtful whether the same can be said for an allusion to an obscure Elizabethan:

> The sound of horns and motors, which shall bring Sweeney to Mrs. Porter in the spring.

"Cf. Day, *Parliament of Bees*": says Eliot,

> When of a sudden, listening, you shall hear,
> A noise of horns and hunting, which shall bring
> Actaeon to Diana in the spring,
> Where all shall see her naked skin.

The irony is completed by the quotation itself; had Eliot, as is quite conceivable, composed these lines to furnish his own background, there would be no loss of validity. The conviction may grow as one reads Eliot's next note: "I do not know the origin of the ballad from which these lines are taken: it was reported to me from Sydney, Australia." The important word in this note—on Mrs. Porter and her daughter who washed their feet in soda water—is "ballad." And if one should feel from the lines themselves their "ballad" quality, there would be little need for the note. Ultimately, the inquiry must focus on the integrity of such notes as parts of the poem, for where they constitute special information about the meaning of phrases in the poem, they ought to be subject to the same scrutiny as any of the other words in which it is written. Matthiessen believes the notes were the price Eliot "had to pay in order to avoid what he would have considered muffling the energy of his poem by extended connecting links in the text itself." But it may be questioned whether the notes and the need for them are not equally muffling. F. W. Bateson has plausibly argued that Tennyson's "The Sailor Boy" would be better if half the stanzas were omitted, and the best versions of ballads like "Sir Patrick Spens" owe their power to the very audacity with which the minstrel has taken for granted the story upon which he comments. What then if a poet finds he cannot take so much for granted in a more recondite context and rather than write informatively, supplies notes? It can be said in favor of this plan that at least the notes do not pretend to be dramatic, as they would if written in verse. On the other hand, the notes may look like unassimilated material lying loose beside the poem, necessary for the meaning of the verbal symbol, but not integrated, so that the symbol stands incomplete.

We mean to suggest by the above analysis that whereas notes tend to seem to justify themselves as external indexes to the author's *intention*, yet they ought to be judged like any other parts of a composition (verbal arrangement special to a particular context), and when so judged their reality as parts of the poem, or their imaginative integration with the rest of the poem, may come into question. Matthiessen, for instance, sees that Eliot's titles for poems and his epigraphs are informative apparatus, like the notes. But while he is worried by some of the notes and thinks that Eliot "appears to be mocking himself for writing the note at the same time that he wants to convey something by it," Matthiessen believes that the "device" of epigraphs "is not at all open to the objection of not being sufficiently structural." "The *intention*," he says, "is to enable the poet to secure a condensed expression in the poem itself." "In each case the epigraph *is designed* to form an integral part of the effect of the poem." And Eliot himself, in his notes, has justified his poetic practice in terms of intention.

> The Hanged Man, a member of the traditional pack, fits my purpose in two ways: because he is associated in my mind with the Hanged God of Frazer, and because I associate him with the hooded figure in the passage of the disciples to Emmaus in Part V. . . . The man with Three Staves (an authentic member of the Tarot pack) I associate, quite arbitrarily, with the Fisher King himself.

And perhaps he is to be taken more seriously here, when off guard in a note, than when in his Norton Lectures he comments on the difficulty of saying what a poem means and adds playfully that he thinks of prefixing to a second edition of *Ash Wednesday* some lines from *Don Juan*:

> I don't pretend that I quite understand
> My own meaning when I would be *very* fine;
> But the fact is that I have nothing planned
> Unless it were to be a moment merry.

If Eliot and other contemporary poets have any characteristic fault, it may be in *planning* too much.

Allusiveness in poetry is one of several critical issues by which we have illustrated the more abstract issue of intentionalism, but it may be for today the most important illustration. As a poetic practice allusiveness would appear to be in some recent poems an extreme corollary of the romantic intentionalist assumption, and as a critical issue it challenges and brings to light in a special way the basic premise of intentionalism. The following instance from the poetry of Eliot may serve to epitomize the practical implications of what we have been saying. In Eliot's "Love Song of J. Alfred Prufrock," toward the end, occurs the line: "I have heard the mermaids singing, each to each," and this bears a certain resemblance to a line in a Song by John Donne, "Teach me to heare Mermaides singing," so that for the reader acquainted to a certain degree with Donne's poetry, the critical question arises: Is Eliot's line an allusion to Donne's? Is Prufrock thinking about Donne? Is Eliot thinking about Donne? We suggest that there are two radically different ways of looking for an answer to this question. There is (1) the way of poetic analysis and exegesis, which inquires whether it makes any sense if Eliot-Prufrock *is* thinking about Donne. In an earlier part of the poem, when Prufrock asks, "Would it have been worth while, . . . To have squeezed the universe into a ball," his words take half their sadness and irony from certain energetic and passionate lines of Marvell's "To His Coy Mistress." But the exegetical inquirer may wonder whether mermaids considered as "strange sights" (to hear them is in Donne's poem analogous to getting with child a mandrake root) have much to do with Prufrock's mermaids, which seem to be symbols of romance and dynamism, and which incidentally have literary authentication, if they need it, in a line of a sonnet by Gérard de Nerval. This method of inquiry may lead to the conclusion that the given resemblance between Eliot and Donne is without significance and is better not thought of, or the method may have the disadvantage of providing no certain conclusion. Nevertheless, we submit that this is the true and objective way of criticism, as contrasted to what the very uncertainty of exegesis might tempt a second kind of critic to undertake: (2) the way of biographical or genetic inquiry, in which, taking advantage of the fact that Eliot is still alive, and in the spirit of a man who would settle a bet, the critic writes to Eliot and asks him what he meant, or if he had Donne in mind. We shall not here weigh the probabilities—whether Eliot would answer that he meant nothing at all, had nothing at all in mind—a sufficiently good answer to such a question—or in an unguarded moment might furnish a clear and, within its limit, irrefutable answer. Our point is that such an answer to such an inquiry would have nothing to do with the poem "Prufrock"; it would not be a critical inquiry. Critical inquiries, unlike bets, are not settled in this way. Critical inquiries are not settled by consulting the oracle.

*Notes*

1. *Dictionary of World Literature*, Joseph T. Shipley, ed. (New York, 1942), 326–329.
2. J. E. Spingarn, "The New Criticism," in *Criticism in America* (New York, 1924), pp. 24–25.
3. Ananda K. Coomaraswamy, "Intention," in *American Bookman* I (1944), 41–48.
4. It is true that Croce himself in his *Ariosto, Shakespeare and Corneille* (London, 1920), ch. 7, "The Practical Personality and the Poetical Personality," and in his *Defence of Poetry* (Oxford, 1934), p. 24, and elsewhere, early and late, has delivered telling attacks on emotive geneticism, but the main drive of the *Aesthetic* is surely toward a kind of cognitive intentionalism.
5. See Hughes Mearns, *Creative Youth* (Garden City, 1925), esp. pp. 27–29. The technique of inspiring poems has apparently been outdone more recently by the study of inspiration in successful poets and other artists. See, for instance, Rosamond E. M. Harding, *An Anatomy of Inspiration* (Cambridge, 1940); Julius Portnoy, *A Psychology of Art Creation* (Philadelphia, 1942); Rudolf Arnheim and others, *Poets at Work* (New York, 1947); Phyllis Bartlett, *Poems in Process* (New York, 1951); Brewer Ghiselin, ed., *The Creative Process: A Symposium* (Berkeley and Los Angeles, 1952).
6. Curt Ducasse, *The Philosophy of Art* (New York, 1929), p. 116.
7. And the history of words *after* a poem is written may contribute meanings which if relevant to the original pattern should not be ruled out by a scruple about intention.
8. Chs. 8, "The Pattern," and 16, "The Known and Familiar Landscape," will be found of most help to the student of the poem.
9. Charles M. Coffin, *John Donne and the New Philosophy* (New York, 1927), 97–98.

# 20.  Intention and Interpretation in Criticism
## *FRANK CIOFFI*

If we adapt Wittgenstein's characterization of philosophy: "putting into order our notions as to what can be said about the world," we have a programme for aesthetics: "putting into order our notions as to what can be said about works of art."

One of the tasks of such a programme would be to elucidate the relation in which biographical data about an author, particularly of the kind loosely known as knowledge of his intentions, stand to those issues we call matters of interpretation. *I.e.*, the relation between questions like these:

Whether it is Goethe who is referred to in the first line of the first canto of *In Memoriam*.

Whether it is the poet who is speaking in the concluding lines of *Ode on a Grecian Urn*.

Whether Pope is 'screaming with malignant fury' in his character of Sporus.

Whether Hamlet in his famous soliloquy is contemplating suicide or assassination.

Whether Milton's Satan in his speech in Book IV beginning 'League with thee I seek' may be wholly or partly sincere.

Whether the governess who tells the story in James's *Turn of the Screw* is a neurotic case of sex-repression and the ghosts not real ghosts but hallucinations.

Whether Wordsworth's Ode: *Intimations of Immortality* is 'a conscious farewell to his art, a dirge sung over his departing powers' or is a 'dedication to new powers'; and whether the 'timely utterance' referred to in that poem is *My Heart Leaps Up* or *Resolution and Independence*.

From *Proceedings of the Aristotelian Society*, n.s., LXIV (1963–1964), 85–106. Copyright © 1964 by The Aristotelian Society. Reprinted with permission of the Editor of The Aristotelian Society.

Whether we are meant to reflect that Othello becomes jealous very quickly on very little provocation.

Whether the Moses of Michelangelo is about to hurl the tablets of the law to the ground or has just overcome an impulse to do so.

Whether Shakespeare's Sonnet 73 contains an allusion to despoilt and abandoned monasteries.

Whether the image which floats before Yeats's mind in *Among School Children*, 'hollow of cheek,' is of an old woman or of one beautiful in a *quattrocento* way.

Whether the metaphors in Othello's soliloquy which begins 'Steep me in poverty to the very lips' are deliberately inappropriate so as to suggest the disorder of Othello's mind.

Whether Ford Maddox Ford's novel *Parade's End* is a trilogy or a tetralogy.

Whether on reading the line 'in spite of that we call this Friday good' from *East Coker* we are to think of Robinson Crusoe's friend.

Whether Gertrude's marriage to Claudius was incestuous.

Whether Othello was black or brown.

Whether Pippit in Eliot's *A Cooking Egg* is young or old, of the same social status as the speaker or not, and whether the connotations of the expression 'penny-world' in that poem are sordid or tender.

Whether in *The Mystery of Edwin Drood* Dickens has deepened his analysis of Victorian society to include Imperialism; and whether John Jasper in that novel is a member of the Indian sect of Thugs.

Whether we should identify with Strether in *The Ambassadors* and whether the Ververs in *The Golden Bowl* are unqualifiedly admirable.

And statements like these:

That Eliot associates the Hanged Man, a member of the traditional tarot pack, with the Hanged God of Frazer and with the hooded figure in the passage of the disciples to Emmaus.

That Hopkins said: The Sonnet on Purcell means this: 1–4 I hope Purcell is not damned for being a protestant because I love his genius, *etc., etc.* 'Low lays him' means 'lays him low,' 'listed is enlisted' *etc., etc.*

That Wordsworth wrote *Resolution and Independence* while engaged on the first part of the Immortality Ode.

That Henry James in 1895 had his faith in himself shaken by the failure of his plays.

That Donne's *Valediction: Forbidding Mourning* was addressed to his wife.

That James was conversant enough with English ways to know that no headmaster would have expelled a boy belonging to a county family without grave reasons.

That A. E. Housman vehemently repudiated the view that his poem *1887* contained a gibe at the Queen.

That Swift was philanthropic and well-loved by his friends.

That Maude Gonne was an old woman when Yeats wrote *Among School Children*.

That Keats in his letters uses the word 'beauty' to mean something much more subtle than is ordinarily meant by it.

That Eliot meant the lines 'to Carthage then I came, burning, burning, burning . . .' to evoke the presence of St. Augustine and the Buddha, of Western and Eastern Asceticism.

That Abraham Cowley had had very little to do with women.

That ruined monasteries were a not uncommon sight in 1685.

That Henry James meant his later novels to illustrate his father's metaphysical system.

That Conrad in *The Arrow of Gold* has an unrealistic and sentimentalized portrait of a woman.

That Wordsworth nowhere in his work uses the word 'glory' to refer to his creative powers.

That Eliot told someone that Richards in his account of *A Cooking Egg* was 'barking up the wrong tree.'

That Tennyson shortly before his death told an American gentleman that he was referring to Goethe when he wrote 'of him who sings to one clear harp in divers tones.'

That there were no industrial mills when Blake wrote "Jerusalem."

That in the book of *Genesis* Moses shattered the tablets of the law.

That Dickens wrote a letter at the time of the Sepoy mutiny advocating the extermination of the Indian people.

In this paper I have assembled and invented examples of arguments which use biographical claims to resolve questions of interpretation and confronted them with a meta-critical dogma to the effect that there exists an operation variously known as analyzing or explicating or appealing to the text and that criticism should confine itself to this, in particular eschewing biographical enquiries.

By now any of you who are at all interested in this topic must have had the phrase 'the intentional fallacy' occur to you. This phrase owes its currency to a widely anthologized and often-alluded-to paper of that title by two Americans, Wimsatt and Beardsley. I want now to try to bring what they say in it into relation with the issue I have raised.

*I*

The first statement of their thesis runs: "The design or intention of the author is neither available nor desirable as a standard for judging the success of a literary work of art." These words don't really mean what they say. They don't mean that an artist may have intended to create a masterpiece but for all that have failed to do so; for the authors go on to say of their thesis that it entails "many specific truths about inspiration, authenticity, biography, literary history and scholarship," etc., and none of these specific truths follows from the truism that knowledge of an artist's intentions cannot provide us with criteria for judging of his success. The charitable conviction that they mean more than this is borne out by a later statement of the thesis; this time to the effect that it is a thesis about the *meaning* of a work of art that they are concerned to advance: that certain ways of establishing this meaning are legitimate whereas others are not. So, presumably, what they intended to say is: "the design or intention of an author is neither available nor desirable as a standard for judging the meaning of a literary work of art." But no argument can profitably be conducted in these terms. For if a discrepancy should come to light between a reader's interpretation of a work and the interpretation of the author or his contemporaries, no way of determining which of these could be properly described as *the* meaning of the work could be produced.

What an author meant, by a poem, say, what his contemporaries took him to mean, what the common reader makes of it and what makes the best poem of it are usually concomitant and allow us to speak of *the* meaning without equivocation. If when confronted by instances in which this concomitance breaks down we appeal to only one of the ordinarily coincident features as if we had a settled convention behind us, the question becomes intractable. If the question is expressed instead as "How should this poem be read?" it at least becomes clearer what the issues are. So the thesis becomes, "The design or intention of an author is neither available nor desirable as a standard for judging how a work of literature should be read." But does any criticism of literature consist of the provision of standards by which you may judge how the work should be read? One of the pieces of criticism which the authors have provided in their paper as an illustration of how it should be done concerns Eliot's *The Love Song of J. Alfred Prufrock.* They say that when Prufrock asks, "would it have been worth while . . . to have squeezed the universe into a ball," "his words take half their sadness and irony from certain energetic and passionate lines of Marvell's *To His Coy Mistress.*" This may be true and it may be helpful but nothing in it answers to the description of providing a standard by which the work may be read. What they have done or have tried to do is to produce in the reader a more adequate response to Eliot's lines by reminding him of Marvell's. If we bring their thesis in line with their practice it becomes: "The design or intention of the author is neither available nor desirable as a means of influencing a reader's response to a literary work." But since they give as an example of what they consider as irrelevant to criticism the fact that Coleridge read Purchas, Bartram, Milton and Bruce and this is not a fact about either his design or his intention it is obvious that they mean something rather wider than this, something which the expression 'biographical data' would be a closer approximation to. This gives us "biographical data about an author, particularly concerning his artistic intentions, is not desirable [I omit available as probably being just a sign of nervousness] as a means of influencing a reader's response to a literary work."

What any general thesis about the relevance of intention to interpretation overlooks is the heterogeneity of the contexts in which questions of interpretation arise. This heterogeneity makes it impossible to give a general answer to the question of what the relevance of intention to interpretation is. There are cases in which we have an interpretation which satisfies us but which we feel depends on certain facts being the case. It may involve an allusion and we may wish to be reassured that the author was in a position to make the allusion. In this case biographical facts act as a kind of sieve which exclude certain possibilities. Then there is the case where we are puzzled, perhaps by an allusion we don't understand, perhaps by syntax, and reference to the author's intention, though it does not guarantee a favorable response, may at least relieve this perplexity and make one possible. There are cases in which we suspect irony but the text is equivocal, and cases where we aren't sure what view the author wishes us to take of the situation he places before us. Then there are the most interesting cases, those in which the text seems unmistakably to call for a certain interpretation and this is found satisfying, but in which we learn with surprise that it has been explicitly repudiated by the author. Even within the same kind of context the author's intention will vary in relevance depending on the kind of question involved; whether it concerns the meaning of a word or the tone of a passage, the view to be taken of a character or a situation or the general moral of an entire work.

Why did Wimsatt and Beardsley think they had a general answer to the question of deciding what the response to a work of literature should be? This is what they say:

There is a difference between internal and external evidence for the meaning of a poem. And the paradox is only verbal and superficial that what is (1) internal is also public. It is discovered through the semantics and syntax of a poem, through our habitual knowledge of the language, through grammars, dictionaries and all the literature which is a source of dictionaries, in general through all that makes a language and culture; while what is (2) external is private or idiosyncratic; not a part of the work as a linguistic fact; it consists of revelations (in journals, for example, or letters, or reported conversations) about how or why the poet wrote the poem—to what lady, while sitting on what lawn, or at the death of what friend or brother. There

is (3) an intermediate kind of evidence about the character of the
author or about private or semi-private meanings attached to words
or topics by an author or by a coterie of which he is a member. The
meanings of words is the history of words, and the biography of an
author, his use of a word, and the associations which the word had
for him are part of the word's history and meaning. But the three
types of evidence, especially (2) and (3), shade into one another so
subtly that it is not always easy to draw a line between examples, and
hence arises the difficulty for criticism.

It is not clear from this account what the authors mean to exclude as
illicit sources of interpretive data. Once the author's character and the
private associations a word may have for him are admitted among these,
along with all that makes a language and a culture, what is there left to
commit fallacies with? Were it not that their illustrations give a much
clearer impression of their attitude than their attempts at explicit formulation of it do, and show it to be much more restrictive, they could be
suspected of advancing one of those enchanted theses which possess the
magical power of transforming themselves into truisms at the touch of a
counterexample. They say of a line in Eliot's *The Love Song of J. Alfred
Prufrock:* "I have heard the mermaids singing each to each" that it bears
some resemblance to a line of Donne's: "Teach me to heare Mermaids
singing" so that the question arises whether Eliot's line contains an allusion
to Donne's. They go on to say that there are two radically different ways
of answering this question. The way of poetic exegesis and the way of
biographical enquiry, and the latter would not be a critical enquiry and
would have nothing to do with the poem. The method of poetic exegesis
consists of asking whether it would make any sense if Donne's mermaids
were being alluded to. The biographical approach would be to ask Eliot
what he thought at the time he wrote it, whether he had Donne's mermaids
in mind. The answer to this question would be critically irrelevant. It is
not surprising that their example bears them out since it was hand-chosen,
as it were. To expose its tendentiousness we need only take an example
in which it was felt that a literary allusion would enhance the value of the
lines. Let us take their own example of Marvell's *To His Coy Mistress*,
familiarity with which they maintain enhances the value of certain lines of
Eliot's. If we take the case of someone not familiar with Marvell's *To His
Coy Mistress*, then the biographical claim that Eliot alludes to it in
Prufrock would enhance its value for them. If on the other hand they
merely applied the test of poetic exegesis and incorporated the allusion to
Marvell's *To His Coy Mistress* into the poem without knowing whether
Eliot was alluding to it, it is doubtful whether their appreciation would

survive the discovery that he was not. If a critical remark is one which has the power to modify our apprehension of a work, then biographical remarks can be critical. They can serve the eliminative function of showing that certain interpretations of a work are based on mistaken beliefs about the author's state of knowledge.

## II

We can illustrate this eliminative function of biographical data by taking the very case on which Wimsatt and Beardsley based their arguments as to its irrelevance. They quote a quatrain from John Donne's *A Valediction: Forbidding Mourning:*

> Moving of the earth brings harmes and fears,
> Men reckon what it did and meant,
> But trepidation of the spheares,
> Though greater farre, is innocent.

They then go on to criticize an interpretation of this quatrain which basing itself on the biographical fact that Donne was intensely interested in the new astronomy and its theological repercussions sees in the phrase 'Moving of the earth' an allusion to the recently discovered rotation of the earth round the sun. Wimsatt and Beardsley show the unlikelihood of this, not by disputing the well-authenticated facts concerning Donne's interest in astronomy, which would be to use a biographical method, but through an analysis of the text. They maintain that whereas the fear which is produced by the rotation of the earth is a metaphysical, intellectual one, the fear which Donne is attempting to discourage is of the emotional kind which an earthquake is more likely to produce and that this accords better with the 'tear-floods' and 'sigh-tempests' of the poem's second stanza than the earth's rotation. Let us concede that the authors have made it very plausible that Donne was alluding not to the heliocentric theory of the earth's rotation but to earthquakes. The gratuitousness of the conclusion which they draw from this becomes apparent if we ask the following question: have they established that Donne was not referring to the rotation of the earth as conclusively as the fact that Donne was ignorant of the heliocentric theory that would establish it? Wouldn't this external fact outweigh all their internal ones?

At this point someone who finds my question unrhetorical is thinking to himself 'dark satanic mills.' It is true that the knowledge that the poem that prefaces Blake's *Milton* is not an expression of the Fabian sentiments it has been traditionally taken as has not caused the traditional interpretation to be abandoned. I suggest that what we have in this case is something in the nature of a spontaneous adaptation of Blake's poem. It is unlike what we ordinarily consider an adaptation in not being conscious (initially at any rate) and not involving any physical change in the work adapted. Does the fact that this was possible in the case of Blake's lyric reflect adversely on it as poem? Does the fact that the melody of *God Save the Queen* could be fitted with new words and become the national anthem of a republican nation reflect on it? The combination of resolution and exaltation which characterize Blake's poem carries over into its adaptation; it functions like a melody. We should see cases like that of "Jerusalem" as continuous with more obvious cases of adaptation. When Pistol tells *French* audiences that his "*rendezvous* is quite cut off," his Doll lies dying of Maladie of *Naples*. Does anything follow as to the relevance or irrelevance of an author's intentions? Then neither does it in the case of *Jerusalem*. It would only follow if the discovery that a work was an adaptation made no difference. There is one sort of literature in which adaptation is a matter of indifference: jokes. Wilkes becomes Disraeli and Disraeli becomes Birkenhead. The two Jews become two Irishmen or two Chinese. But then, we speak of the author of a poem but not of the author of a joke. I am saying: we don't stand in the same relation to Blake's lyric after changing our conviction as to what he meant to convey as we did before. If the case were one in which the discrepancy between the author's interpretation and the reader's were one as to the very emotions expressed and not just the accompanying imagery our attitude would be very different. Frank Harris read A. E. Housman's poem *1887* as an anti-imperialist gibe and the expression 'God Save the Queen' which recurs in it as a sarcastic jeer until Housman revealed otherwise. Thereafter he naturally found it difficult to do so in spite of his conviction both as to the superiority of his interpretation and its greater consonance with Housman's general outlook. ("How was I to know that someone steeped in a savage disgust of life could take pleasure in outcheapening Kipling at his cheapest?")

The following examples should make it clear how inept Wimsatt's and Beardsley's characterization of the role of biographical data in critical discourse is. An example which seems to support their account is Leavis' reaction to John Middleton Murry's attempt to give the word 'beauty' in the concluding couplet of Keat's *Ode on a Grecian Urn* a less limiting sense based on the use Keats made of the word in his letters. "To show from the letters that 'beauty' became for Keats a very subtle and embracing concept and that in his use the term takes on meanings that it could not possibly have for the uninitiated is gratuitous and irrelevant. However, his use of the word may have developed as he matured, 'beauty' is the term he used and in calling what seemed to him the supreme thing in life 'beauty' he expresses a given bent—the bent everywhere manifest in the quality of his verse, in its loveliness . . . and that beauty in the *Ode on a Grecian Urn* expresses this bent is plain, that it should as the essence of the poem, and there is nothing in the poem to suggest otherwise."

This may sound as if a general principle akin to Wimsatt's and Beardsley's is being employed, but that this is not so Leavis's practice elsewhere shows. For example, "Hopkins' *Henry Purcell* is a curious special case, there can be few readers who have not found it strangely expressive and few who could have elucidated it without extraneous help. It is not independent of the explanatory note by Hopkins that Bridges prints. Yet when one approaches it with the note fresh in mind, the intended meaning seems to be sufficiently in the poem to allay at any rate the dissatisfaction caused by baffled understanding." We must not be misled by the expression "a curious special case." Leavis's dealings with *The Waste Land* make it clear that the only question which arises in connection with notes or other extraneous aids to understanding is not one of their legitimacy but of their efficacy. For example, Leavis says of *The Waste Land* that it "sometimes depends on external support in ways that can hardly be justified . . . for instance, the end of the third section 'The Fire Sermon.' . . . No amount of reading of the *Confessions* or *Buddhism in Translation* will give these few words power to evoke the kind of presence that seems necessary to the poem." Of another passage he writes: "it leaves too much to Miss Weston; repeated recourse to *Ritual and Romance* will not invest it with the virtues it would assume." On the other hand, of Eliot's note on *Tiresias*, Leavis remarks, "if Mr. Eliot's readers have a right to a grievance, it is that he has not given this note more salience." 'Power to evoke,' 'Invest with Virtues,' these are not the idioms in which the probative value of statements is weighed.

Wimsatt and Beardsley are aware of the problem posed them by Eliot's notes to *The Waste Land* and make the suggestion that the notes should be considered as part of the poem. They thus become internal evidence, and may be consulted with a good conscience. Does it follow that since the effectiveness of certain lines in *Prufrock* depends on familiarity with Marvell's *Coy Mistress*, Marvell's poem should be considered part of Eliot's, or does this not follow because whereas we are expected to be familiar with Marvell's poem, familiarity with the contents of Eliot's notes is not expected of us? Then is this what the distinction between external and internal evidence comes to; the difference between what we can and can't be expected to know? and how is it decided what we can be expected to know? Leavis has said of Quinton Anderson's book on Henry James, "thanks to the light shed by Mr. Anderson, we can see in the peculiar impressiveness of Mrs. Lowder of the *Wings of the Dove* a triumph of morality art." Is Mr. Anderson's book also to be considered part of James's *Wings of the Dove* then?

No amount of tinkering can save Wimsatt and Beardsley's distinction between internal and external evidence. It isn't just that it's made in the wrong place, but that it is misconceived from the start. A reader's response to a work will vary with what he knows; one of the things which he knows and with which his responses will vary is what the author had in mind, or what he intended. The distinction between what different people know of an author before reading his work or what the same person knows on successive occasions can't be a logical one. When is a remark a critical remark about the poem and when a biographical one about the author? The difficulty in obeying the injunction to ignore the biographical facts and cultivate the critical ones is that you can't know which is which until after you have read the work in the light of them.

The assumption which stultifies their exposition is the conception of critical argument as the production and evaluation of evidence. They say that there are two kinds of evidence: that provided by poetic exegesis and that provided by biographical enquiry. But the examples they give of poetic exegesis seem not to be evidence but conclusions or judgments. For example, that the lines from *Prufrock* take half their sadness and irony from lines in a poem of Marvell's, or that the mermaids in *Prufrock* derive no benefit from a reminiscence of the mermaids in Donne. We could construe these statements as evidence, only by taking them as biographical statements about Wimsatt and Beardsley, but so taken they would stand in the same relation to critical judgment as biographical statements about Eliot. If a critical remark fails to confirm or consolidate or transform a reader's interpretation of a work it will then become for him just evidence of something or other, perhaps the critic's obtuseness. Biographical remarks are no more prone to this fate than any others.

*III*

In the sixth stanza of Yeats's *Among School Children* there occur the lines:

> Plato thought nature but a spume that plays
> Upon a ghostly paradigm of things;
> Solider Aristotle played the taws
> Upon the bottom of a king of kings.

Many editions give the first word of the third line 'solider' as 'soldier.' This is due to a compositor's error, a transposition of two letters which went unnoticed because by a fluke instead of producing gibberish, it produced the English word 'soldier.'

The American critic Delmore Schwartz was thus led to advance his well-known interpretation to the effect that the expression 'soldier Aristotle' alludes to a legend that Aristotle accompanied Alexander on his military expedition to India. Since there is obviously a contrast intended between the unworldliness of Plato and the down-to-earthness of Aristotle, Schwartz's military interpretation accords well with the rest of the poem. But in spite of this, now that we know of the error wouldn't we insist on the restoration of the lines as Yeats wrote them and regard the view that there is a military allusion in the lines as a mistake? It might be objected that this is not to the point because the case here is one of a discrepancy between what the author *wrote* and what we made of it and not between what he *meant* and what we made of it.

But can this distinction be upheld? Can't we imagine cases where the words were homophones? In such a case the only distinction between what an author wrote and a mistaken reading would be what he meant. In fact, we needn't imagine such a case. Hopkins's note on his poem *Henry Purcell* provides us with one: "One thing disquiets me: I *meant* 'fair fall' to mean 'fair (fortune be) fall': it has since struck me that perhaps 'fair' is an adjective proper and in the predicate and can only be used in cases like 'fair fall the day,' that is 'may the day fall, turn out fair.' My lines will yield a sense that way indeed, but I never meant it so." Is the possible meaning mentioned but rejected by Hopkins any more tenable than 'soldier Aristotle'?

There is thus no doubt that there are cases in which knowledge of an author's avowed intention in respect of his work exercises a coercive influence on our apprehension of it. The question now arises: When doesn't it? My answer is, "When the issue is of a complexity comparable to that which would cause us to discount his avowed intention in respect of something not a work of literature." To put it another way, we tend to think that there are cases where we override the author's intention and persist in an interpretation which he has rejected, but what we are really doing could less misleadingly be described as favoring one criterion of intention as against another. If we establish the existence of a discrepancy between the interpretation we give to a work of art, and that of the author, we haven't shown that the work has a meaning independent of what the author intends because what the author intends will now be the interpretation given to the work by us and his own statement as to its meaning an aberration. The notion of the author's intention is logically tied to the interpretation we give to his work. It's not just that our language works this way; but that our minds do. Confronted with a choice between saying that an effect so complex could have come about by accident and that the author was mistaken we would opt for the latter. The work will be considered more conclusive evidence of his intention than his own statements. The color flows back.

Edmund Wilson's dealings with Henry James's *The Turn of the Screw* bring this out clearly. *The Turn of the Screw* was generally considered a superior ghost story until Wilson popularized the view that the ghosts were figments of the narrator's imagination and the work a study in thwarted Anglo-Saxon spinsterdom. He thought he had discovered that the text was skillfully ambiguous so as never unequivocally to imply the ghosts' objective existence. He was able to interpret some passages in James's preface to the book to similar effect. The publication of James's notebooks some years later, however, made it clear that James's conscious intention was to produce a ghost story. At the same time Wilson came to admit that the text itself was not completely reconcilable with his thesis that the ghosts were hallucinatory. Nevertheless, Wilson continued to insist that it was not a straightforward ghost story, but a study in the neurotic effects of repressed sexuality. His arguments for this provide an excellent example of what I have called the color flowing back. Instead of simply enjoying a gratuitous effect for its own sake, Wilson convinces himself on the basis of certain biographical facts about James that at the time the book was written, his faith in himself had been shaken and that "in *The Turn of the Screw*, not merely is the governess self-deceived, but that James is self-deceived about her. The doubt that some readers feel as to the soundness of the governess' story are the reflection of doubts communicated unconsciously by James himself."

The real interest of this kind of example is that it brings out quite clearly what otherwise is not so apparent; that there is an implicit biographical reference in our response to literature. It is, if you like, part of our concept of literature. It is only when it is missing that we notice that it was always there.

I want now to deal with some notorious ostensible counterexamples. This is the fifth stanza of Yeats's *Among School Children:*

> What young mother a shape upon her lap
> Honey of generation had betrayed,
> And that must sleep, shriek, struggle to escape
> As recollection or the drug decide,
> Would think her son, did she but see that shape
> With sixty or more winters on its head
> Compensation for the pang of his birth,
> Or the uncertainty of his setting forth?

There is an accompanying note to this poem which indicates that the phrase "honey of generation" is taken from an essay of Porphyry's and that Yeats has arbitrarily used it to refer to "the drug that destroys the recollection of pre-natal freedom." It is then, the shape upon the mother's lap, the child, which has been betrayed by being born. John Wain has put forward a reading according to which it is the mother who has been betrayed, and "honey of generation" is an allusion to the sexual pleasure which accompanies conception, and the desire for which has betrayed her. Doesn't this example show the irrelevance of intention? Not necessarily. It could be interpreted as a case where we take the poem as better evidence of what the poet intended than his own explicit remarks on the subject. To persist in an interpretation in spite of an author's explicit disavowal of it is not necessarily to show an indifference to the author's intention. For we may feel that he was mistaken as to what his intention was. A case which comes to mind is Goldsmith's withdrawal of the gloss he offered on the word "slow" in the first line of his poem, *The Traveller*, "Remote un-friended, melancholy, *slow*." Goldsmith said it meant "tardiness of locomotion" until contradicted by Johnson. "No sir. You do not mean tardiness of locomotion. You mean that sluggishness of mind that comes upon a man in solitude."

Though it might be true, as Wimsatt and Beardsley say, that critical enquiries are not settled like bets, neither may questions of intention. I can't resort here to the argument I used in the case of Donne's *Valediction* and ask you to imagine what your attitude to Wain's interpretation would be if you were convinced that Yeats was ignorant of the fact on which it is based, since this fact, that sexual pleasure is an incentive to procreation, is not such as can be overlooked. Nevertheless, I want to maintain that we don't, if we accept Wain's interpretation, think it an accident that it should be possible to read the text as he does, but we feel that the ambiguity which makes it possible was the result of a connection in Yeats's mind between the expression "honey of generation" and sexual pleasure. (In fact, this can be demonstrated.)

In order to convince you that an implicit biographical influence is at work even in Wain's interpretation, I want you to imagine the case altered in some important respects. Imagine that the reading according to which it is the mother who is betrayed, was also that of Yeats, and that there was no footnote referring to Porphyry's essay, of which Yeats was completely ignorant, but that a reader familiar with it and sharing its views on prenatal existence, insisted on taking the expression "honey of generation" as an allusion to the drug which destroys the recollection of prenatal freedom and, therefore, to the infant and not the mother as betrayed. Wouldn't our attitude to this interpretation be quite different from our attitude to Wain's? Wouldn't we feel it perverse? And since it can't be the text which makes it perverse but only the facts about Yeats as we have imagined them, doesn't our implicit biographical or intentionalistic approach to literature emerge quite clearly here? Of course, there are cases where the pleasure we take in literature doesn't depend on this implicit biographical reference. Literature, as Wittgenstein probably said, is a motley. Nursery rhymes come to mind as the most notable example. But in general we do make such a reference. Eliot's attitude toward a line of Cyril Tourneur's illustrates this reluctance to take pleasure in what is accidental and unintended. The line is: "The poor benefit of a bewildering minute," which is given as "The poor benefit of a bewitching minute" in the texts both of Churton Collins and of Nicoll who mention no alternative reading. Eliot comments: "*it is a pity* if they be right for 'bewildering' is much the richer word here." It has been argued that if the folio text of *Henry V* was right and Theobald's lovely guess wrong so that Shakespeare made the dying Falstaff allude to a painting rather than babble of green fields most of us would persist in reading the traditional and incorrect version. We probably would but it would worry us; and if "a babbled of green fields" wasn't even Theobald's guess but a transcriber's or printer's unthinking error, it would worry us even more. The suspicion that a poetic effect is an artifact is fatal to the enjoyment which literature characteristically offers. If the faces on Mount Rushmore were the effect of the action of wind and rain, our relation to them would be very different.

*IV*

In the course of their criticism of the interpretation of Donne's poem which saw in it an allusion to the rotation of the earth round the sun Wimsatt and Beardsley remark, "But the text itself remains to be dealt with . . ."!

Where understanding fails, says Goethe, there immediately comes a word to take its place. In the case the word is "text." Let us appeal to the text. But what is the text? These critics talk of the text of a poem as if it had an outline as neat and definite as the page on which it is printed. If you remind yourself of how questions about what is 'in the text' are settled you will see that they involve a great deal which is not 'in the text'. Though there are many occasions on which we can make the distinction in an immediately intelligible and nontendentious way, where an interpretative issue has already arisen, the use of a distinction between internal, licit considerations, and external, illicit ones is just a form of question-begging.

What are we to say of attempts to support an interpretation by citing other works of the author? For example, Leavis on Conrad's *Heart of*

*Darkness*; "If any reader of that tale felt that the irony permitted a doubt regarding Conrad's attitude towards the Intended, the presentment of Rita (in *The Arrow of Gold*) should settle it." Isn't this illicit? Isn't the common authorship of several works a biographical fact?

What of the use of previous drafts of a work for critical purposes? Leavis in commenting on Hopkins's *Spelt from Sybil's Leaves* is able to enforce his point that "Hopkins' positives waver and change places and he is left in terrible doubt by showing that in a previous draft of the poem the word-order in the phrase 'black, white; right, wrong' was conventionally symmetrical 'black, white; wrong, right'." The only doubt which might arise is connection with Leavis's point is whether the word order may have been altered to avoid a rhyme, but this is equally intentionalistic.

Marius Bewley supports his interpretation of James's *The Turn of the Screw* by pointing out that when James collected his stories for the definitive edition he put it in the same volume as one called *The Liar*.

Even if the anti-intentionalist thesis were qualified to accommodate all these there would still be a fundamental objection to it.

You must all have had the experience while reading of having the words suddenly undergo a radical transformation as you realized you had missed the end of a quotation, say, and mistaken the speaker. The more familiar the speakers the greater the transformation when you realized your mistake. Doesn't this illustrate the importance of implicit biographical assumptions in interpreting what we read? Here's an illustration: In Rudyard Kipling's *Loot* occur the lines:

> An' if you treat a nigger to a dose of cleanin'-rod
> 'E's like to show you everything he owns.

Hugh Kingsmill has quoted these lines as an example of Kipling's brutality, and even Kipling's biographer Edward Shanks is embarrassed by them. Edmund Wilson, on the other hand, in his well-known essay on Kipling, says this about them: "Kipling was interested in the soldier for his own sake, and made some effort to present his life as it seemed to the soldier himself. The poem called *Loot*, for example, which appears to celebrate a reprehensible practice is in reality perfectly legitimate because it simply describes one of the features of the soldier's experience in India. There is no moral one way or the other." T. S. Eliot takes a similar line in his introduction to his selection of Kipling's verse.

How is this issue to be decided? By an appeal to the text? Isn't it rather our sense of Kipling which will determine the side we come down on? A sense built up not only from the other tales but from his autobiography and other sources as well? Don't these throw a 'field of force' round the work? If it had been written by someone else wouldn't this make a difference to our apprehension of it? Isn't this like the case described by Wittgenstein in the *Philosophical Investigations*? "I see a picture which represents a smiling face. What do I do if I take the smile now as a kind one, now as a malicious one? Don't I often imagine it with a spatial and temporal context which is one either of kindness or of malice? Thus I might supply the picture with the fancy that the smiler was smiling down at a child at play, or again on the suffering of an enemy."

The difference of opinion between F. R. Leavis and Marius Bewley over James's *What Maisie Knew* is an excellent illustration of an interpretation depending on 'the fiction I surround it with'. Unfortunately it is too long to quote, but the gist of it is that Bewley finds the atmosphere of the book one of horror and its theme the meaning and significance of evil, whereas Leavis can detect no horror and sees it as an extraordinarily high-spirited comedy reminiscent of the early part of David Copperfield. Bewley in attempting to locate the source of their difference says that it has its "origin in areas not readily open to literary-critical persuasion" and "that the way one senses the presence of evil and horror in the novel may be due to one's conception of them outside the novel."

There is one aspect of our response to a work of literature to which biographical data seem to have particular relevance and that is our conviction as to an author's sincerity. It is certain that there are cases where biographical considerations are genuinely relevant and equally certain that there are cases where they are intrusions which we feel we ought not to allow to condition our response. But it is difficult to know where the line should be drawn. I suppose that we would all consider Beethoven's inability to get on with Scott's *Kenilworth* because "This man writes for money" as eccentric, though the decline in Trollope's reputation which followed his revelation as to his methods of composition and his businesslike attitude toward his writing in his autobiography, show it is not rare. Perhaps these responses should be considered more as moral gestures, like refusing to hear Gieseking perform, rather than as aesthetic responses.

A good example of a response which is genuinely critical but which we would all consider misplaced is Johnson's criticism of Abraham Cowley's *The Mistress*: "But the basis of all excellence is truth: he that professes love ought to feel its power. Petrarch was a real lover and Laura doubtless deserved his tenderness. Of Cowley we are told by Barnes, who had means enough of information, that whatever he may talk of his own inflammability, and the variety of characters by which his heart was divided, he in reality was in love but once, and then never had resolution to tell his passion!

"This consideration cannot but abate in some measure the reader's esteem for the work. . . ."

Another, perhaps slightly less conclusive example is provided by Johnson's remarks on Cowley's poem on the death of Hervey ". . . but when he wishes to make us weep he forgets to weep himself, and diverts his sorrow by imagining how his crown of bays, if he had it would *crackle* in the *fire*. It is the odd fate of this thought to be the worse for being true. The bay leaf crackles remarkably as it burns, as therefore this property was not assigned to it by chance, the mind must be thought sufficiently at ease that could attend to such minuteness of physiology." It might be argued that Johnson has indicated a source of dissatisfaction *in* the poem, the bay leaves image. But it is what this enabled him to infer about something *outside* the poem concerning Cowley which abated his esteem. If he could have been convinced that Cowley was ignorant of the propensity of bay leaves to crackle remarkably and the felicity of his image therefore fortuitous, Johnson would presumably have liked the poem better. But it would be a mistake to think Johnson simply absurd here. Suppose that the poem in question were Bishop King's *Exequy* and the biographical fact that he was never married and therefore never bereaved. Some of us would decide it didn't matter, some that it did and some would oscillate. This is an example of the more general dilemma which arises when an empirical concomitance on which we habitually depend and so regular that it has influenced the build of our concepts, disintegrates. Van Meegeren's *Disciples at Emmaus*, the poems of Ern Malley, Macpherson's *Ossian*, Chatterton's *Rowley*, all point the same moral.

D. W. Harding raised a related issue in a vivid form some years ago. He wrote: "We think of it (a work of art) as being a human product, as implicitly sanctioning and developing interests and ideals and attitudes of our own. That being so it does become disconcerting to find that for the author it satisfied certain impulses which we ourselves are glad not to possess, or which if we do possess we think better left unsatisfied. The same thing goes on in social intercourse of a simpler kind than literature. We enjoy the *bon mot* with which our friend disposes of a charlatan, but if we know that he is incidentally working off irrelevant spite against either the charlatan or the world in general the flavour of the remark is spoilt. The *bon mot* is as good as ever regarded as something impersonal, but as a human product it no longer gives us pure satisfaction—an element of distaste or regret comes in and makes our state of mind more complex. Many people find this more complex attitude extremely difficult to maintain . . . especially because in most actual cases the neurotic flaw can be detected in the work itself." But once in possession of biographical data it is difficult to be sure what is "in the work itself." Leavis has suggested it is a pity much is known of Pope's life since the expression of spite, envy, venom, and malice so often found in his work is a consequence of the distorting effect of this knowledge.

What I have called "putting a field of force round a work," surrounding it with a web of associations, may be effective even when it doesn't deserve to be. But this kind of suggestibility is a risk all critical remarks run and not merely biographical ones. Would anyone have found the last few lines of Bishop King's *Exequy* productive of an effect of terror if Eliot had not said so? And would Eliot himself if he had not first come across them in Poe's *The Assignation*? It is the fact that we can speak of criticism which is effective but mistaken which makes the analogy with argument so tempting for there too we speak of conclusions seeming to follow but not following; so it seems that we can have specious criticism in the same sense in which we have specious argument. But this is an illusion. You don't show that a response to a work of literature is inadequate or inappropriate in the way that you show that the conclusion of an argument has been wrongly drawn.

Wittgenstein has some remarks in Part Two of the *Investigations*, which shed light on the nature of the intractability which characterizes so much critical argument and makes its prevalence less surprising. His remarks though concerned with the question of the genuineness of an expression of feeling have a more general application. He contrasts our judgments about sincerity with those about color. "I am sure, *sure* that he is pretending: but some third person is not. Can I always convince him? And if not, is there some error in his reasoning or observations?" Though there are those whose judgment is better in such matters and rules for determining this, these do not form a system and only experienced people can apply them. There are consequences which distinguish correct from incorrect judgment, but these are of a diffuse kind and like the rules incapable of general formulation. ". . . only in scattered cases can one arrive at a correct and fruitful judgment." It is not surprising, then, that "the game often ends with one person relishing what another does not."

## Conclusion

What I have been saying is this: a conviction that a poet stands in a certain relation to his words conditions our response to them. That this should be so seems to me part of the physiognomy of literature (as Wittgenstein might have put it). We are not ordinarily aware of this as these convictions tend to be held in solution in 'the work itself.' It is only in exceptional circumstance that we crystallize them out as explicit beliefs and become aware of the role they play. Why should anyone wish to deny this? Because it is then only a step to the production of phantasy-theses like Wimsatt's and Beardsley's, "What is said about a poem is subject to the same scrutiny as any statement in linguistics or in the general science of psychology."

This in its turn has its source in the determination to tidy up the activity of reading and to reduce what it involves to a neat logically homogenous set of considerations such as guarantee a readily communicable rationale. The idea of a work of literature as 'a linguistic fact' or an 'integrated symbol' is comparable to the notions of 'a concept' in philosophy or 'behavior' in psychology in being the manifestation of an irresistible demand for discrete, coherent, and enduring objects of investigation. But, "Literature is a motley."

# 21.     Expressive Properties of Art

## GUY SIRCELLO

Romantic ideas about mind and its relation to art did not receive their clearest expression until the twentieth century. Then philosophers like Croce, Collingwood, Cassirer, Dewey, and Langer tried to spell out exactly how it is that art can be expressive. But to many other twentieth-century philosophers, especially to those working in the various "analytical" styles whose intellectual ancestry was anything but Romantic, those philosophical discussions of expression in art were puzzling. This puzzlement can best be seen in the work of Monroe Beardsley and O. K. Bouwsma, philosophers who represent two distinct strains in recent analytical philosophy.

I think it is fair to understand the puzzlement of both Beardsley and Bouwsma in the following way. We understand relatively well what it is for a *person* to express such things as feelings, emotions, attitudes, moods, etc. But if we say that sonatas, poems, or paintings also express those sorts of things either we are saying something patently false or we are saying someting true in an uninformative, misleading, and therefore pointless way. For to say of works of art that they express those sorts of things seems to imply that they are very much like persons. Therefore, unless we believe that philosophers who think of art as expression believe the unbelievable, that is, that art has feelings, attitudes, and moods and can express them, we must believe that such philosophers are trying, however inadequately, to come to grips with genuine truths about art.

Furthermore, there is such an obvious disparity between the nature of art and the thesis that art can express the same sorts of things that people do that we cannot understand that thesis as simply a clumsy and inept way of stating some truths about art. We must understand it, rather, as a kind of *theoretical* statement, that is, as a deliberately contrived and elaborated way of construing some simple facts about art. Both Beardsley and Bouwsma thus speak of the "Expression *Theory*" of art.

What are the facts which the Expression Theory is meant to interpret? Although Beardsley and Bouwsma differ slightly in the way they put the point, they agree that works of art have "anthropomorphic" properties. That is, we may often properly characterize works of art as, for example, gay, sad, witty, pompous, austere, aloof, impersonal, sentimental, etc. A "theory" of art as expression, therefore, can say no more than that artworks have properties designated by the same words which designate feelings, emotions, attitudes, moods, and personal characteristics of human beings.

The nature of these properties has not been probed very deeply by analytical critics of the Expression Theory. Beardsley calls them "qualities." Bouwsma prefers to call them "characters," pointing out their affinity with the "characters" of a number of things like sounds, words, numerals, and faces. In case this suggestion is unhelpful, Bouwsma further invites us to conceive the relation of the "character" to the art work in terms of the relation of redness to the apple in a red apple. At this point he is exactly in line with Beardsley, who mentions a red rose instead of a red apple.[1]

The Bouwsma-Beardsley position on the question of expression in art is currently rather widely accepted. Indeed, John Hospers, writing in the *Encyclopedia of Philosophy* has, in effect, canonized the view.[2] Accordingly, I shall refer to it henceforth as the Canonical Position. Now despite the fact that it has illuminated the concept of expression in art, the Canonical Position is false in some respects and inadequate in others. In this chapter ... I shall argue (1) that attributions of "characters," or "anthropomorphic qualities," to works of art come in a number of different varieties, (2) that the simple thing-property relation is not an adequate model for understanding any of those varieties, (3) that there are far better reasons for calling art "expressive" than are allowed by the Canonical interpretation of Expression Theory, (4) that the presence of "anthropomorphic qualities" in works of art is not the only fact about art which makes it expressive, and (5) that the features of art which make it expressive have precise parallels in nonartistic areas of culture such as philosophy, historiography, and science.

The Canonical Position has two incorrect presuppositions. The first is that works of art are very much like such natural objects as roses and apples as well as, I suppose, such natural quasi- and non-objects as hills, brooks, winds, and skies. The second is that the anthropomorphic predicates of art are not essentially different from simple color terms like "red" and "yellow." No one has seriously argued, as far as I know, that any art work is *just* like some natural "object." Everyone admits that there are basic differences between art and nature, most of them related to the fact that art is made by human beings and natural things are not. What the first presupposition of the Canonical Position amounts to, therefore, is that as far as the anthropomorphic predicates are concerned works of art are not different from natural objects.[3]

It is fairly easy to show that this presupposition is false by the following strategy. Anthropomorphic predicates are applied to natural things in virtue of certain nonanthropomorphic properties of those things. Of course these properties vary, depending on the particular predicate as well as on the thing to which it applied. Hills, for example, may be austere in virtue of their color, their vegetation (or lack of it), or their contours; an ocean may be angry in virtue of its sound and the force and size of its waves; a tree may be sad in virtue of the droop and shape of its branches. With respect to a number of art works to which anthropomorphic predicates are applied, I shall inquire what it is about those works in virtue of which the predicates are applicable. This strategy will yield categorial features of art which do not belong to natural things.

(1) Like most of Raphael's Madonna paintings, the one called *La Belle Jardinière* can be described as calm and serene. It is fairly clear what there is about this painting which makes it calm and serene: the regular composition based on an equilateral triangle, the gentle and loving expressions on the faces of the Mother, the Child, and the infant John the Baptist, the placid landscape, the delicate trees, the soft blue of the sky, the gentle ripples in the Mother's garments blown by a slight breeze, and, finally, the equanimity and quiet with which the artist views his subject and records the details of the scene.

(2) We might reasonably describe Hans Hofmann's *The Golden Wall* as an aggressive abstract painting. But in this painting there is no representational content in the usual sense and therefore nothing aggressive is depicted. What is aggressive is the color scheme, which is predominantly red and yellow. Blue and green are also used as contrasting colors, but even these colors, especially the blue, are made to look aggressive because of their intensity. Furthermore, by the way they are juxtaposed, the patches of color are made to appear as though they were rushing out toward the observer and even as though they were competing with one another in this rush toward the observer.

(3) We might say of Poussin's *The Rape of the Sabine Women* (either version, but especially the one in the Metropolitan Museum of Art in New York City) that it is calm and aloof. Yet it is quite clear that the depicted

scene is *not* calm and that no one in it, with the possible exception of Romulus, who is directing the attack, is aloof. It is rather, as we say, that Poussin calmly observes the scene and paints it in an aloof, detached way.

(4) Breughel's painting called *Wedding Dance in the Open Air* can be aptly if superficially described as gay and happy. In this case however it is surely the occasion and the activities of the depicted peasants which are happy. Perhaps the prominent red used throughout the painting can be called "gay." The faces of the peasants however are neither happy nor gay. They are bland, stupid, and even brutal. It is this fact which makes the painting ironic rather than gay or happy. Yet there is certainly nothing about a peasant wedding, the dull peasants, or their heavy dance which is ironic. The irony lies in the fact that the painter "views," "observes," or depicts the happy scene ironically.

(5) John Milton's "L'Allegro" is not only "about" high spirits, but it is surely a high-spirited, i.e., gay and joyful, poem. The gaiety and joy are evident in several ways. First, the scenes and images are gay and joyful: Zephir playing with Aurora, maids and youths dancing and dallying, the poet himself living a life of "unreproved" pleasure with Mirth. Second, the diction and rhythms are lighthearted: "Haste thee nymphs and bring with thee / Jest and youthful Jollity, / Quips and Cranks, and wanton Wiles, / Nods, and Becks and Wreathed Smiles."

(6) Another sort of example entirely is William Wordsworth's sentimental poem "We Are Seven." This poem is quite obviously not *about* sentimentality. It purports simply to record the conversation between the poet and a child. Neither the child nor the poet (that is, the "character" in the poem), moreover, is sentimental. The child matter-of-factly reports her firm conviction there are still seven members of her family despite the fact that two of them are dead. The poet is trying, in a rather obtuse and hard-headed sort of way, to get her to admit that there are only five. But the little girl is made to win the point by having the last word in the poem. She is thus made to seem "right" even though no explicit authorization is given to her point of view. By presenting the little girl's case so sympathetically, Wordsworth (the poet who wrote the poem, not the "character" in the poem) treats the attitude of the little girl, as well as the death of her siblings, sentimentally.

(7) The case of "The Dungeon" by Coleridge is different again. At least the first half of this poem is angry. But it is not about anger or angry persons. It is a diatribe in verse (and certainly not a poor poem on that account) against the cruelty, injustice, and wasteful ineffectiveness of prisons.

(8) T. S. Elliot's "The Lovesong of J. Alfred Prufrock" can, with considerable justice, be called a compassionate poem. In this case it is quite

clear that the compassion exists in the way in which the character Prufrock
is portrayed as a gentle and sensitive, if weak, victim of ugly and sordid
surroundings.

(9) Suppose that we say that the second movement of Beethoven's
"Eroica" symphony is sad with a dignified and noble sadness characteristic
of Beethoven. In this case the sadness is in the slowness of the tempo, and
the special quality of the sadness comes from the stateliness of the march
rhythm, from the use of "heavy" instruments like horns and tympani and
from the sheer length of the movement.

(10) A somewhat different case is presented by Mozart's music for
Papageno, which is gay, carefree, light-headed and lighthearted like
Papageno himself. What differentiates this case from (9), of course, is that
the Mozart music is intended to suit a certain kind of character, whereas
the Beethoven has no clear and explicit "representational" content. Despite
this difference, however, the "anthropomorphic qualities" of the Mozart
music are, like those of the Beethoven, audible in properties of the sound:
in the simple harmonies, tripping rhythms, and lilting melodies of
Papageno songs.

(11) A slightly different case from either (9) or (10) is that presented by
the first movement of Vivaldi's "Spring" Concerto. The first lilting, happy
theme represents the joyful advent of spring. This is followed by the gentle
music of the winds and waters of spring. Next, this pleasantness is
interrupted by the angry music representing a thunder shower, after which
the happy, gentle music returns. In this music the "programmatic" content
is clear and explicit because we know the poetry from which Vivaldi
composed the music.

(12) Quite different from the three cases immediately preceding is the
witty Grandfather theme from Prokoviev's *Peter and the Wolf.*
Grandfather's music, played by a bassoon, is large, lumbering, and pompous like Grandfather himself. But what makes it witty is that it portrays
a dignified old man as just a bit ridiculous. through the music Prokoviev
pokes gentle fun at the old man, fun which is well-motivated by the story
itself. For in the end Peter turns out to be more than equal to the danger
which Grandfather has ordered him to avoid.

(13) Finally, there is music like the utterly impersonal and detached
music of John Cage, exemplified in *Variations II* played by David Tudor
on (with) the piano. But where can we locate the "qualities" of impersonality and detachment in Cage's music? They do not seem to be
"properties" of the sounds and sound-sequences in the way that gaiety is
a property of Papageno's music or sadness is a property of Beethoven's.
Indeed, we feel that these "anthropomorphic qualities" of Cage's music
depend on the very fact that the sounds themselves are completely lacking

in "human" properties. They are as characterless as any of a thousand random noises we hear every day. In fact, *Variations II* does have the apparent randomness and disorganization of mere noise. But we would not be inclined to call *any* random sequences of noises "impersonal" and "detached," even if they sounded very much like the sounds of *Variations II*. The predicates "impersonal" and "detached" are not applied to Cage's music simply in virtue of some features of its sounds. These "qualities" of *Variations II* arise rather from the fact that the composer presents what sounds like mere noise as music. Cage offers this "noise" for us to attend to and concentrate upon. Moreover, he offers it to us without "comment," and with no intention that it evoke, represent, or suggest anything beyond itself. That is to say, Cage offers these noiselike sounds in a totally uninvolved, detached, impersonal way, seeking in no way to touch our emotional life.

From the preceding examples we can see that there are some respects in which anthropomorphic predicates are applied to works of art in virtue of features of those works which they share or could share with some natural things. In the Raphael it is the composition of the painting which accounts in part for the "calm" of the painting. but "composition" here refers simply to the configuration of lines and shapes, which sorts of features can of course be shared by natural objects. Similarly, the aggressiveness of Hofmann's painting is due to its colors and their arrangement. In the Beethoven and Mozart examples the anthropomorphic qualities are traceable to features of sound which can be present in natural phenomena. The ocean crashing on the shore, a twig tapping against a windowpane, the gurgle of a stream—all of these can have "tempi," "rhythms," and even "tone color." Natural "melodies" are present in the rustle of trees and the howl of winds as well as in the songs of birds. Even the anthropomorphic qualities of verbal art can be like properties of natural things. For, as the example of "L'Allegro" shows, such qualities can be attributed to poetry at least partly in virtue of the tempo and rhythm of its verses.

Some of the above examples of anthropomorphic qualities applied to art, however, show that such qualities sometimes belong to works of art in virtue of what those works represent, describe, depict, or portray. Thus the calm and serenity of the Raphael is due in part to the countryside, the sky, the garments, and the faces depicted; the gaiety of the Breughel comes from the gaiety of the depicted scene, and the high spirits of Milton's poem are due to the gay, happy scenes and images described and presented. In cases of this sort, neither paintings nor poems are comparable to natural things with respect to the way they bear their anthropomorphic qualities. And the situation is similar with respect to all other forms of representational art, whether prose fiction, drama, ballet, opera, or sculpture. Only architecture and music are generally incapable of bearing anthropomorphic qualities in this way. This is true, moreover, even for music with a sort of representational content such as the Mozart music mentioned in (10) above. For it is not due to the fact that Mozart's songs are written for a gay, lighthearted character that they are properly described as gay and lighthearted. It is rather that the songs suit Papageno precisely in virtue of the gaiety and lightheartedness of their "sound" and are thereby capable of portraying him musically.

There is a second way in which anthropomorphic predicates may be applied to artworks which is unlike the ways in which such predicates apply to natural things. In the discussion of (1) through (13) above we discovered the following:

(*a*) *La Belle Jardinière* is calm and serene partly because Raphael *views* his subject calmly and quietly.

(*b*) *The Rape of the Sabine Women* is aloof and detached because Poussin calmly *observes* the violent scene and *paints* it in an aloof, detached way.

(*c*) *Wedding Dance in the Open Air* is an ironic painting because Breughel *treats* the gaiety of the wedding scene ironically.

(*d*) "We Are Seven" is a sentimental poem because Wordsworth *treats* his subject matter sentimentally.

(*e*) "The Dungeon" is an angry poem because in it the poet angrily *inveighs* aginst the institution of imprisonment.

(*f*) "The Lovesong of J. Alfred Prufrock" is a compassionate poem because the poet compassionately *portrays* the plight of his "hero."

(*g*) Prokoviev's Grandfather theme is witty because the composer wittily *comments* on the character in his ballet.

(*h*) Cage's *Variations II* is impersonal because the composer *presents* his noiselike sounds in an impersonal, uninvolved way.

I have italicized the verbs in the above in order to point up the fact that the respective anthropomorphic predicate is applied to the work of art in virtue of what the artist *does* in that work. In order to have a convenient way of referring to this class of anthropomorphic predicates, I shall henceforth refer to what verbs of the sort italicized above designate as "artistic acts." I do not intend this bit of nomenclature to have any metaphysical import. That is, I do not mean that the viewings, observings, paintings, presentings, portrayings, and treatings covered by the term "artistic acts" all belong to a category properly called "acts." Nor do I mean that all activities properly called "artistic" are covered by my term "artistic act." As shall come out later, many artistic activities are neither identical with, constituents of, nor constituted by "artistic acts." Further-more, I do not want to suggest that "artistic acts" have anything more in common than what I have already pointed out and what I shall go on to specify. To do a complete metaphysics of artistic acts might be an interesting philosophical job but one which would distract me from my main purpose [here].

What the preceding discussion has shown is that the view of art presup-posed by the Canonical Position ignores complexities in works of art which are essential in understanding how they can bear anthropomorphic predicates. Even more significant is the discovery that anthropomorphic predicates apply to art works in virtue of "artistic acts" in these works. For, as I shall argue presently at length, it is precisely this feature of artworks which enables them to be *expressions* and which thereby shows that the Canonical Position has missed a great deal of truth in classical Expression Theory.

As far as I know, no adherent of the Canonical Position, with one exception to be noted below, has recognized the existence of what I call "artistic acts," much less seen their relevance to expression in art. But it is not difficult to anticipate the first defensive move a proponent of the Canonical Position would likely make against the threat posed by "artistic acts." It would go somewhat as follows. What the "discovery" of "artistic acts" shows is merely that not all applications of anthropomorphic predi-cates to art works attribute qualities to those works. They merely *seem* to do so because of their grammatical form. But in fact statements of this sort say nothing at all about the art work; they describe the artist. After all, "artistic acts" are acts of the artists, and they cannot possibly be acts of (i.e., performed by) the art works themselves.

However superficially plausible this objection is, it can be shown to have little force. First, the objection presupposes a false dichotomy: a statement must be descriptive either of a work of art *or* of its artist. On the contrary, there seems to be no reason why when we talk in the above examples of the painting's aloofness, the poem's sentimentality, etc., we cannot be talking *both* about the painting or poem and about how Poussin painted or how Wordsworth treated his subject. And it is in fact the case that we are talking about both. The best proof of this is that the *grounds* for the truth of the descriptions of artistic acts in (*a*) through (*g*) above can come from the art work in question. One knows by looking at Poussin's painting that he has painted the scene in an aloof, detached way. The cold light, the statuesque poses, the painstaking linearity, are all visible in the work. Similarly, we recognize by reading Wordsworth's poem that he treats his subject sentimentally. That is just what it is to give the child, who believes that the dead are present among the living, the advantage over the matter-of-fact adult. We can also recognize the impersonality of *Variations II* by listening to its neutral, noiselike sounds. A test for statements describing art in anthropomorphic terms is always and quite naturally a scrutiny of the art, even when the terms are applied in virtue of "artistic acts."

Moreover, it is not as if this sort of attention to the work of art were merely a second-best way of testing such statements. One does not look, listen, or read in order to *infer* something about the aloof way Poussin painted, the compassionate way Eliot portrayed his hero, etc. We must not imagine that had we actually been with the artist at work, we could *really*, i.e., immediately and indubitably, have seen his aloofness, compassion, sentimentality, etc. How absurd to think that when Poussin's way of painting is described as aloof, what is meant is that Poussin arched his eyebrows slightly, maintained an impassive expression on his face, and moved his arms slowly and deliberately while he painted the picture. Or that because Eliot portrays Prufrock compassionately, he penned the manuscript of his poem with tears in his eyes. Not only would such facts not be needed to support statements about Poussin's aloofness or Eliot's compassion, but they are totally irrelevant to such statements. For even if we knew the way Poussin looked and moved when he was painting the Sabine picture or the way Eliot's face looked when he penned "Prufrock," we could not infer that the painting and poem were, respectively, aloof and compassionate in the ways we are discussing.

The foregoing considerations do not mean that the "artistic acts" in question are not truly acts of the artists, that is, are not truly something which the artists have done. Nor do they imply that these artistic acts are phantom acts, airy nothings existing mysteriously in works of art and disembodied from any agents.[4] They simply mean that these acts are not identifiable or describable independently of the works "in" which they are done. Probably nothing makes this point clearer than the fact that descriptions of artistic acts of this sort can be known to be true even when little or nothing is known about the author, much less what he looked like and what his behavior was like at the precise time that he was making his art. It can be truly said, for example, that Homer describes with some sentimentality the meeting of the returned Odysseus and aged dog Argos. And yet it would be absurd to say that the truth of that statement waits upon some detailed knowledge about Homer, even the existence of whom is a matter of considerable dispute.

Artistic acts are peculiar in that descriptions of them are at once and necessarily descriptions of art works. They are in this way distinguishable from other sorts of acts of artists which contribute to the production of works of art, e.g., looking at the canvas, chiseling marble, penning words, applying paint, revising a manuscript, thinking to oneself, etc. But artistic acts, for all their peculiarity, are not entirely alone in the universe; there are other sorts of things which people do which are analogous to artistic acts in significant ways. Note the following: A person may scowl angrily, and thereby have an angry scowl on his face; he may smile sadly and thereby have a sad smile on his face; he may gesture impatiently and thus make an impatient gesture; he may shout defiantly and produce thereby a defiant shout; he may pout sullenly and a sullen pout will appear on his face; his eyes may gleam happily and there will be a happy gleam in his eyes; he may tug at his forelock shyly or give a shy tug at his forelock. What is interesting about these clauses is that they show how an anthropomorphic term can be applied either adverbially to "acts" or adjectivally to "things" without a difference in the sense of the term or of the sentences in which it is used. This sort of shift in the grammatical category of a term is clearly analogous to what is possible with respect to those anthropomorphic predicates applied to works of art in virtue of their artistic acts. Thus one may, without change of meaning, say either that Eliot's "Prufrock" is a compassionate poem or that Eliot portrays Prufrock compassionately in his poem; that Poussin paints his violent scene in an aloof detached way or that the Sabine picture is an aloof, detached painting.[5]

This grammatical shift is possible in both sorts of cases because of the inseparability of the "act" and the "thing." One does not *infer* from a smile on a person's face that he is smiling any more than one *infers* that Eliot portrayed Prufrock compassionately from his compassionate poem, and for analogous reasons. The "acts" of smiling, pouting, shouting, tugging are not even describable without also and at once describing the smile, pout, shout, or tug. Smiling, after all, is not an act which produces or results in a smile so that something could interfere to prevent the smiling from bringing off the smile. "Smiling" and "smile," we are inclined to say, are simply two grammatically different ways of referring to the same "thing."[6]

Now the parallel I want to point out is not between smile-smiling, pout-pouting, tug-tugging, on the one hand, and poem-portraying, picture-(act of) painting, music-presenting, on the other. For clearly Poussin's Sabine painting is more than (is not simply identical with) Poussin's aloof way of painting the violent scene; Eliot's poem is more than his compassionate way of portraying its title character; Cage's music is more than his impersonal presentation of noiselike sounds. When we have described these artistic acts we have not by any means completely described the respective art works. The analogy rather is between smile-smiling and portrayal-portraying, presentation-presenting, treatment-treating, view-

viewing, etc. Therefore, when we designate artistic acts by a noun term, those acts seem to be "parts" or "moments" of the works of art to which they pertain. We may then more properly understand the way in which an anthropomorphic adjective applies to an art work in virtue of such a "part" in something like the way in which a person's whole face is called sad in virtue merely of his sad smile or his sad gaze, or in which a person's behavior is generally angry in virtue (merely) of his quick movements and angry tone of voice. In these cases, too, it is not as if the terms "sad" and "angry" *completely* described the face or the behavior or even all parts and aspects of the face and behavior even though they can *generally* characterize the face and the behavior.

The foregoing comparison points out that not only is it the case that anthropomorphic predicates do not always apply to art works the way predicates, anthropomorphic or not, apply to natural objects, but that sometimes anthropomorphic predicates apply to works of art rather like the way that they apply to verbal, gestural, and facial *expressions.* For sad smiles are characteristic expressions of sadness in a person; angry scowls, of anger; shy tugs at forelocks, of diffidence; sullen pouts, of petulance. And this is an all-important point which the Canonical Position has missed in its interpretation of the Expression Theory of Art. Had proponents of the Canonical Position pursued their inquiry into anthropomorphic predicates further, they would have been forced to question whether such predicates apply to art in the way they apply to objects or in the way they apply to common human expressions.

Instead of pursuing this line of questioning, however, they were misled by the noun-adjective form of their favorite example—sad music—into their object-quality interpretation of Expression Theory, an interpretation which of course makes that "theory" seem very far removed indeed from the "facts" which were alleged to have motivated it. Small wonder that Beardsley's final judgment on Expression Theory is that it "renders itself obsolete" after it has reminded us that anthropomorphic predicates may reasonably be applied to art works. Even O. K. Bouwsma, who of all the proponents of the Canonical Position comes closest to the point I am maintaining, was not able to see quite where his comparison between sad music and sad faces leads. For instead of making a transition from sad faces to sad *expressions* on faces, he takes the (rather longer) way from sad faces to red apples.

There is more to the comparison between artistic acts and facial, vocal, and gestural expression than the formal or grammatical similarities just noted. Even more important are the parallels between the "significance" of things like sad smiles and angry scowls and the "significance" of aloofness or irony in paintings, sentimentality or compassion in poems, and impersonality or wittiness in music. For there are parallels between what facial, gestural, and vocal expressions, on the one hand, and artistic acts, on the other, can tell us about the persons responsible for them. In order to draw out these parallels explicitly I shall use the cases of an angry scowl and a compassionate portrayal in the mode of Eliot's "Prufrock."

First, it is obvious that an angry scowl on a person's face might well mean that the person is angry. It might be more than simply an expression of anger; it might be an expression of *his* anger. Now it should need very little argument to show that a compassionate poem like "Prufrock" might be an expression of the poet's own compassion. He might be a person with a generally sympathetic and pitying attitude toward modern man and his situation. In that case, a poem like "Prufrock," at least a poem with "Prufrock's" kind of compassion, is precisely what one could expect from the poet, just as one could expect an angry man to scowl angrily. But just as we cannot reasonably expect that *every* time a person is angry he scowls angrily, we cannot expect that every man who is a poet and who has compassion toward his fellows will produce poetry with the compassion of "Prufrock." If a man can keep his anger from showing in his face, a poet can, with whatever greater difficulties and whatever more interesting implications for himself and his poetry, keep his compassion from showing in his poetry.

Moreover, just as there is no necessity that a man's anger show in his face, there is no necessity that an angry scowl betoken anger in the scowler. There is a looseness of connection between anger and angry expressions which is matched by a looseness between compassion and compassionate poems. One reason that a man might have an angry scowl on his face is that he is *affecting* anger, for any of a number of reasons. Now although the range of reasons for affecting compassion in his poetry might be different from the range of reasons for affecting anger in his face, it is nevertheless possible that a corpus of poetry with "Prufrock's" sort of compassion might betoken nothing more than an affectation of compassion. This might be the case if, for example, the poet is extremely "hard" and sarcastic but thinks of these traits as defects. He might then quite deliberately write "compassionate" poetry in order to mask his true self and present himself to the world as the man he believes he should be.

On the other hand, both angry scowls and compassionate poetry might be the result simply of a desire to imitate. Children especially will often imitate expressions on people's faces, but even adults sometimes have occasion to imitate such expressions, e.g., in relating an anecdote. A poet might write poems with Eliot's sort of compassion in them in imitation of Eliot's early attitude. This imitation might be executed by a clever teacher in order to show more vividly than by merely pointing them out the means

Eliot used to convey his special sympathy in "Prufrock." Or Eliot might be imitated because his techniques and style, together with the attitudes they imply, have become fashionable among serious poets or because these attitudes strike a responsive chord among serious poets. The latter sorts of imitation are rather like the imitations which a child might make of a person whom he regards as a model. It is not unusual for a girl who admires a female teacher, say, to practice smiling in that teacher's kind, gentle way or for a very young boy at play to "get angry" in the same way he has seen his father get angry.

A poet might write poems with the compassion of "Prufrock," not because he is either affecting or imitating the attitude of that poem, but because he is *practicing* writing poetry in different styles and different "moods." This may be just something like a technical exercise for him, or it may be part of a search for a characteristic attitude or stance which seems to be truly "his own." He thus "tries on" a number of different poetic "masks," so to speak, to see how they fit him. In a similar way, an adolescent girl grimacing before her mirror might "try on" various facial expressions to see how they "look on her" and to discover which is her "best," or perhaps her most characteristic, face: innocent, sullen, sultry, haughty, or even angry.

Finally, an angry scowl on a face might be there when the person is portraying an angry person on the stage. There is a similar sort of situation in which compassionate poetry might be written not as betokening a characteristic of the poem's real author but as betokening the traits of a *character* in a play or novel who is *represented* as having written the poem. No actual examples of such a character come immediately to mind; but we surely have no trouble imagining a master of stylistic imitation writing a novelized account of modern literature in which he exhibits examples of the "Prufrock"-like poetry of an Eliot-like figure.

What I have argued so far is not that all art is expression, nor even that all art works with artistic acts anthropomorphically qualified are expression. My argument shows only that artistic acts in works of art are remarkably like common facial, vocal, and gestural expressions. It also demonstrates that precisely in virtue of their artistic acts and of the similarity they bear to common kinds of expressions, works of art may serve as expressions of those feelings, emotions, attitudes, moods, and/or personal characteristics of their creators which are designated by the anthropomorphic predicates applicable to the art works themselves. And it thereby demonstrates that one presupposition of the Canonical Position is clearly wrong: namely, that art works, insofar as they allow of anthropomorphic predicates, are essentially like natural things untouched by man.

But the second presupposition of the Canonical Position, to wit, that anthropomorphic predicates of art are like simple color words, is also false. It is false with respect to all the three ways, distinguished earlier, that anthropomorphic predicates can be applied to works of art. And it is *a fortiori* false with respect to those predicates which are applied to art in two or three ways at once, as most of them are. The falsity of the presupposition can be brought out in an interesting way by showing how the three ways of applying anthropomorphic predicates to art bear a certain resemblance to color attributions which are rather unlike simply calling a (clearly) red rose red or an (indubitably) green hill green.

Suppose that a sign painter is painting a sign in three colors: yellow, red, and blue. Since the sign is large, he is required to move his equipment several times during the job. Suppose that he employs an assistant to attend to this business. Now we can imagine that the painter will have occasion to give directions to his assistant. He might say, "Bring me the red bucket, but leave the blue and yellow ones there, since I'll need them on that side later." Now if we suppose that the color of all the paint containers is black, when the painter calls for the "red bucket," he must mean "the bucket of red paint," and would surely be so understood by his assistant. In the context the phrase "red bucket" only *appears* to have the same grammatical form as "red rose." I suggest that to the extent that a painting or other representational work of art is called "gay" or "sad" solely in virtue of its subject matter or parts thereof, the latter terms function *more* like "red" in "red bucket" than in "red rose."

It is a common opinion that "sad" in "sad smile" and "gay" in "gay laughter" function metaphorically.[7] There may well be a use of "metaphor" such that the opinion is true. Whether there is such a use will not be determined until there exists a thorough philosophical study of metaphor; and I do not intend to offer one here. But even if it turns out to be true that such uses of anthropomorphic words are metaphorical, it cannot be very useful simply to say it. For such uses *appear* not to be metaphorical at all. After all, it is not as if calling a smile sad were representing the smile as, as it were, feeling sad, acting sad, weeping, and dragging its feet. To see a smile's sadness is not to discern the tenuous and subtle "likeness" between the smile and a sad person. It is much more straightforward to think that a smile is sad because it is a smile *characteristic* of a sad person who smiles; that laughter is gay because such laughter is *characteristic* laughter of persons who are gay. In this respect "sad smile" is rather like "six-year-old behavior" or "Slavic cheekbones." These phrases do not indirectly point to unexpected similarities between a sort of behavior and six-year-old children or between cheekbones and persons. They designate, respectively, behavior which is *characteristic* of six-year-old children and cheekbones *characteristic* of Slavs. And there is no inclination at all to call these phrases "metaphorical."

Yet to say that a sad smile is a smile characteristic of sad people is not to deny what the Canonical Position affirms, namely, that "sad" designates a "property" or "character" of the smile. Surely there is something about the smile which marks it as sad: its droopiness, its weakness, its wanness. But the term "sad" still has a different import from "droopy," "weak," or "wan" when applied to smiles, even though all the latter terms are also characteristic smiles of sad persons. The difference is that the term "sad" *explicitly* relates the character of the smile to sadness of persons. A comparable sort of color term might be "cherry red." "Cherry red" is like the term "bright red with bluish undertones" in that they both designate roughly the same shade of red, which is characteristic of cherries. But the former term is unlike the latter in that it *explicitly* relates the color to cherries.

It might seem that the Canonical Position would be correct in its interpretation of anthropomorphic terms as they apply to those features of works of art which they can share with natural things. For the term "sad" applied to the second movement of the "Eroica" and to a weeping willow must surely denote some properties of the music and of the tree. And they do: drooping branches in the tree; slow rhythm and "heavy" sound in the Beethoven. But "sad" differs from "drooping," "slow," and "heavy" as in the preceding case; it immediately relates the properties of the sounds and the branches to properties of other things which are sad. In these cases "sad" does function metaphorically, harboring, as it were, a comparison within itself. To find an analogy among color words, this use of "sad" is like "reddish." Like "reddish," which quite self-consciously does not denote true redness, "sad" in "sad tree" does not denote true sadness but only a kind of likeness of it. This use of "sad" is also arguably analogous to the use of "red" in "His face turned red with shame." But whether "sad tree" and "sad rhythm" are closer to "reddish clay" or to "red face" is, if determinable at all, unimportant for my print. For "reddish clay" and "red face" are equally unlike "red rose" and "red apple" when the latter refer to a full-blown American Beauty and a ripe Washington Delicious.

In this section I have argued that anthropomorphic terms, when applied to art, are *more* like "red" in "red bucket (of paint)," "cherry red" in "cherry red silk," or "reddish" in "reddish clay" than like "red" in "red rose." But, in truth, anthropomorphic predicates of art are not *very* much like any of these. The reason is that what all anthropomorphic predicates ultimately relate to are human emotions, feelings, attitudes, moods, and personal traits, none of which are very much at all like colors. But there is point in drawing out the comparison between anthropomorphic predicates and color-terms more complicated than "red" in "red rose." The point is that "red" as applied to bucket, "cherry red," and "reddish" are all in some way relational terms in ways that "red" said of a rose is not. "Red bucket" means "bucket *of* red paint"; "cherry red" means "the red *characteristic of* cherries"; and "reddish" means "of a color *rather like* red." Had proponents of the Canonical Position troubled to refine their comparison between anthropomorphic predicates and color predicates, they might have been forced to recognize the relational aspects of the former. Eventually they might have been led to see that anthropomorphic terms finally relate to various forms of the "inner lives" of human beings. And *that* is where Expression Theory begins. The Canonical model of the red rose (or apple) ultimately fails to help us understand how anthropomorphic predicates apply to art because such predicates are not very much like simple quality-words and what they apply to are not very much like natural objects.

In spite of all the above arguments, the Canonical Position is not left utterly defenseless. Although it is the notion of "artistic acts" which is most threatening to the Canonical Position, proponents of that position have been almost totally unaware of this threat. Not totally unaware, however. There is a brief passage in Monroe Beardsley's book *Aesthetics: Problems in the Philosophy of Criticism* in which he mentions an artist's "treatment" and "handling," two examples of what I have called "artistic acts." Beardsley does not relate them, however, to the analysis of anthropomorphic terms. He discusses them under the rubric "misleading idioms," and he suggests that all talk about art concerning "handling" and "treatment" not only can be but should be translated into talk which makes no mention of these sorts of acts.[8]

These are meager clues, but from them it is possible to excogitate an objection to my notion of "artistic arts" which a defender of the Canonical Position might raise. We should first note a remark which Beardsley makes elsewhere in his book when he is concluding his interpretation of Expression Theory. He states that all remarks about the expressiveness of an art work can be "translated" into statements about the anthropomorphic qualities either of the subject matter or of the "design," i.e., roughly the properties which the work could share with natural things.[9] A defense against the notion of "artistic acts" might thus run as follows: Any statement which describes an artistic act anthropomorphically can be "translated" into a statement which describes features of the work of art other than its artistic acts. So stated, however, the defense is ambiguous; it has two plausible and interesting interpretations. First, it might mean that any anthropomorphic description of an artistic act in a work can be replaced, without loss of meaning, by a description of the subject matter and/or design of the work in terms of the same anthropomorphic predicate. Or it might mean that there are descriptions, of whatever sort, of the subject matter and/or design of a work which, given any true anthropomorphic description of an artistic act in that work, entail that description.

The first interpretation of the objection is easily shown to be false. All that is required is that some examples of art be adduced in which anthropomorphic predicates are applicable with some plausibility to an "artistic act" but which are in no other way plausibly attributable to the work. Let us look again at the works of Poussin, Eliot, and Prokoviev discussed earlier in this chapter.

In the Poussin painting of the rape of the Sabines there is nothing about the violent subject matter which could be called "aloof." Certainly the attackers and the attacked are not aloof. Romulus, the general in charge, is a relatively *calm* surveyor of the melee, but he cannot be called aloof, partly because we cannot see him well enough to tell what his attitude is. "Aloof" does not apply with regard to the formal elements of the Poussin painting either. It is difficult even to imagine what "aloof" lines, masses, colors, or an "aloof" arrangement thereof might be. The light in the painting is rather cold, and that feature does indeed contribute to the aloofness of the work. "Cold light" is not, however, the same as "aloof light," which does not even appear to be a sensible combination of words.

A similar analysis is possible with respect to Eliot's "Prufrock." If we consider the "material" elements of the poem—its rhythm, meter, sound qualities, etc.—we realize that "compassionate" simply cannot apply to those features meaningfully. Moreover, there is nothing about the subject matter of "Prufrock" which is compassionate. Certainly Prufrock himself is not compassionate; he is simply confused, a victim of his own fears and anxieties, and of the meanness and triviality of his routinized life and soulless companions.

Finally, the wittiness of Prokoviev's Grandfather theme cannot be supposed to be a "property" of the music the way its comic qualities are. The music is amusing, or comic, because the wheeziness of the bassoon is funny and because the melody imitates the "structure" of a funny movement (one *must* move in an amusing way to that melody). Moreover, although Grandfather himself is funny, he is definitely not witty. What is comical, amusing, or funny is not always witty. To be witty is generally to make, say, or do something comical, amusing, or funny "on purpose." That is why Prokoviev's musical *portrayal* of a comical grandfather is witty. Similar analyses of the Breughel painting, the Wordsworth poem, and the Cage music mentioned previously could obviously be carried out. But the point, I take it, is already sufficiently well made.

The second interpretation of the hypothetical attack on the importance of artistic acts borrows any initial plausibility it possesses from the fact that anthropomorphic descriptions of artistic acts can be "explained" or "justified" in terms which neither mention artistic acts nor use any of the terms which describe them. For example, one might point out the irony in the Breughel painting discussed above by noting the combination of the gay scene and the dull faces of its participants. Or one might justify the "aloofness" he sees in the Poussin by remarking on the cold light, clear lines, and statuesque poses in a scene of violence and turmoil. And in discussing the impersonality of *Variations II* it is necessary to mention that the Cage work sounds like accidentally produced noise, which is senseless and emotionally neutral, but that this noiselike sound is to all *other* appearances music, i.e., it is scored, it is performed on a musical instrument, it is even reproduced on recordings. From these facts about the way in which anthropomorphic descriptions are justified, it might seem plausible that the statements which figure in the justification *entail* the original description. But such is not the case, as the following will show.

It has been suggested that the reason that Breughel's peasant faces are dull and stupid-looking is that the painter was simply unable to paint faces which were happy. Whether the suggestion is true or well supported by the evidence is not an issue here. What is important is that were there any reason for believing Breughel to have been incompetent in that way, then there might be (not necessarily "would be") that much less reason for believing that there is irony in Breughel's *Wedding Dance*. That is because Breughel's incompetence and Breughel's irony *can* in this case function as mutually exclusive ways of accounting for a "discrepancy" in the picture. Of course, there are ways of admitting both the incompetence and the irony. It is possible to suppose, for example, that Breughel used his particular incompetence in making an ironic "statement" about peasant existence. Such a supposition would imply that Breughel was aware of his limitation and made use of it in his work. However, were it *known* that the *only* reason for the discrepancy in the painting was Breughel's incompetence, the "irony" would disappear. It makes no difference, incidentally, that such a thing could probably *never* be known. I am making a logical point regarding the way an attribution of a certain sort to an "artistic act" relates to other aspects of a painting like the Breughel. In short, certain facts about the painting's subject matter do indeed "ground" the attribution but by no means logically entail that attribution. And that is so for the good reason that the same facts about the subject matter are consistent with a supposition about Breughel which might be incompatible with the description of the painting as ironic.

A similar point can be illustrated in Poussin's Sabine painting. In that work there is a discrepancy between the violent scene, on the one hand, and the "still," clear figures, on the other. Two persons might agree about the character of the figures and the character of the depicted scene, however, and yet disagree whether these facts entail that Poussin painted the rape of the Sabines in an aloof, reserved way. One viewer might think simply that the work is incoherent, that Poussin's coldly classical means are not suited to the end he had in mind, namely, to depict the violence of the event. In this quite reasonable view, the discrepancy makes the painting "fall apart" rather than "add up" to an aloof and reserved point of view. Here then are two incompatible descriptions of a work which are equally well grounded on facts which allegedly "entail" one of the descriptions. I am mindful that it might be objected that there are other features of the Sabine painting than the ones mentioned which preclude the judgment of "incoherence" and necessitate the judgment of "aloofness." The best I can say is that there seem to me to be no such additional features contributing to the "aloofness" of the painting and that the burden of proof is upon those who disagree.[10]

Finally, let us suppose that a devoted listener of traditional Western music scoffs at the description of Cage's *Variations II* as "impersonal music." He insists that it is nothing but what it sounds like—meaningless noise. He charges that Cage is a fraud whose "music" is a gigantic hoax, a put-on, and that Cage is laughing up his sleeve at those who take him seriously, perform his "scores," record the performances, and listen gravely to his nonsense. He has, the traditional listener says, read some of Cage's "ideological" material relating to his "music" but he has noted how laden with irony it is. To him that shows that Cage is not to be taken seriously because he does not take himself seriously. Now such a doubter does not disagree with the description of *Variations II* which is used to justify calling it "impersonal." The disagreement concerns rather the way we are to assess John Cage. Are we to judge him to be a responsible and serious, albeit radically innovative, composer of music or not? It is only when Cage's seriousness is assumed that the term "impersonality" applies to his music. Otherwise, the aforementioned justification for calling it impersonal is equally justification for calling it nonsense.

What the above three cases demonstrate is that a true anthropomorphic description of an artistic act might presuppose conditions having nothing necessarily to do with the way the formal elements and/or subject matter are describable. The conditions mentioned are (1) the competence of the artist, (2) the coherence of the work, (3) the seriousness of the artist. But there are surely other examples which would bring light to other conditions of this sort. With sufficient ingenuity one could likely discover and/or construct examples of art in which anthropomorphic descriptions of artistic acts would or would not be applicable depending upon how one assessed the artist with respect to, say, his maturity, his sanity, his self-consciousness, his sensitivity, or his intelligence.

Now it is probably too rigid to regard "competence," "coherence," "seriousness," "maturity," "sanity," and the rest as denoting necessary *conditions* for the legitimate description of all artistic arts. It is probably not true that the artist *must* be serious, competent, sane, etc., and that the work *must* be coherent in order for any anthropomorphic description (of an artistic act) to apply to any work. What these terms should be taken as denoting are "parameters" according to which an artist or a work can be measured in whatever respect is relevant in a particular case. To do so would be to admit that there is probably not a single set of particular conditions of these sorts presupposed in *all* descriptions of artistic acts. Naming these parameters simply points out the *sorts* of considerations which *might* be relevant in particular descriptions of artistic acts, leaving it an open question which of these parameters are relevant, and to what degree, in particular cases.

In any event, what the recognition of such parameters means is that any attempt to save the Canonical Position by "eliminating" descriptions of artistic acts in favor of "logically equivalent" descriptions of formal elements and/or represented subject matter is doomed to fail. For the description of artistic acts in anthropomorphic terms does presuppose something about the artist which cannot be known *simply* by attending to his art. A similar point holds with respect to common expressions. The look of a sullen pout on a person's face does not mean that the person is pouting sullenly if we discover that the look results from the natural lay of his face. And thus it is that no description simply of the configuration of the person's face can *entail* the statement that the person is pouting sullenly.

But it is equally true that the assertion that a person is pouting sullenly is incompatible with the claim that the person's face has the same configuration as it does when he is not pouting sullenly. The sullen pout *must* make a difference visible on the face. Analogously, for an anthropomorphic predicate of an artistic act to be applicable to a work of art there *must* be *some* features of the material elements and/or the subject of the work which *justify* the attribution of the term, even though they do not *entail* that attribution. One thing, however, is never presupposed or implied when an anthropomorphic predicate is truly applied to a work, namely, that the predicate is truly applicable to the *artist*. In this, too, works of art are like expression.

*Notes*

1. Cf. Monroe Beardsley, *Aesthetics: Problems in the Philosophy of Criticism* (New York: Harcourt, Brace, 1958), pp. 321–332; and O. K. Bouwsma, "The Expression Theory of Art," in *Philosophical Analysis*, ed. Max Black (Ithaca: Cornell University Press, 1950), pp. 75–101.

2. *The Encyclopedia of Philosophy*, ed. Paul Edwards (New York: Macmillan and The Free Press, 1967), I, 47.

3. I hope it is clear that throughout this discussion the emphasis is on "natural," not on "object." But I will, for convenience, use the terms "object" and "thing" to cover non-objects and non-things as well.

4. Nor are they "virtual," i.e., unreal, acts, as I have maintained in another place. Cf. my "Perceptual Acts and Pictorial Art: A Defense of Expression Theory," *Journal of Philosophy* LXII (1965), 669–677. Giving these acts a separate and unusual metaphysical status not only complicates the universe needlessly, it is unfaithful to the commonsense facts of the situation. There are no good reasons to deny what our ways of talking implicitly affirm, namely, that "artistic acts," perceptual and otherwise, are "acts" of the artist.

5. Of course it is true that sometimes when anthropomorphic terms are predicated of artworks, they apply to subject matters and to "material" aspects of the work such as lines, colors, sounds, masses, etc., as well as to "artistic acts." My point above is only that anthropomorphic adjectives may be applied to a work only in virtue of an artistic act, in which case it is, without change of meaning, immediately applicable in adverbial form to that act.

6. It is no objection to this assertion that in virtue of the natural lay of their faces some people have perpetual "smiles," "smirks," "pouts," etc., on their faces even when they do not smile, smirk, or pout. Of course, a "smile" of this sort is different from a smile; that is what the scare quotes signify. But even though a person with such a "smile" on his face is not thereby smiling, he is, significantly, "smiling."

7. Nelson Goodman's recent theory of expression seems to depend rather heavily on the opinion that such uses of anthropomorphic predicates are metaphorical. As far as I can tell, however, Goodman merely asserts and does not argue for this opinion. Nor does he offer anything more than the briefest sketch of a theory of metaphor, which could be used to support his assertion. See his *Languages of Art: An Approach to a Theory of Symbols* (Indianapolis: Bobbs-Merrill, 1968), pp. 50–51, 80–95.

8. Beardsley, *Aesthetics*, pp. 80 ff.

9. *Ibid.*, p. 332.

10. These statements commit me to the position that a positive judgment about the Poussin cannot be deduced from any descriptions of the painting of the sort which "ground" its aloofness. For arguments in favor of this general position see my "Subjectivity and Justification in Aesthetic Judgments," *Journal of Aesthetics and Art Criticism* XXVII (1968), 3–12.

# 22.    Art and Expression: A Critique
## ALAN TORMEY

### 1

If the analysis developed [earlier] is correct in its general outlines, it should be possible to derive from it a number of implications bearing on the adequacy of attempts to understand art as a form of expression.

The history of the philosophy of art could, without excessive distortion, be written as a study of the significance of a handful of concepts. The successive displacement of 'imitation' by 'representation,' and of 'representation' by 'expression,' for example, marks one of the more revealing developments in the literature of aesthetics; and it would be only a slight exaggeration to claim that from the close of the eighteenth century to the present, 'expression; and its cognates have dominated both aesthetic theorizing and the critical appraisal of the arts. One purpose of this chapter will be to explore the claim that works of art or the activities of the artist can best be understood as a form of expression.

### 2

Let us first consider some of the contentions of philosophers who have advanced expression theories of art. It has generally been recognized that some distinction must be made at the outset between the process and the product of art: we must distinguish between the artist's activity in constructing a work of art and the outcome of that activity, the work itself. It matters, that is, whether 'expression' is predicated of the process, the product, or both. Many, including Dewey, Reid, Ducasse, Santayana, and

From "Art and Expression: A Critique," in Alan Tormey, *The Concept of Expression: A Study in Philosophical Psychology and Aesthetics*, pp. 97–106 and 122–124. Copyright 1971 by Princeton University Press. Reprinted with permission of Princeton University Press.

Collingwood,[1] have been explicit about this distinction, and have advocated predicating 'expression' of both process and product. These writers are committed to maintaining that there is a noncontingent and specifiable relation between the artist's activity and the work of art. More precisely, they are committed to the position that the artist, in creating the work, is expressing something,[2] which is then to be found "embodied," "infused," or "objectified" in the work itself. For such theorists, the "central problem of the aesthetic attitude" is "how a feeling can be got into an object"[3] or, alternately, how the artist in expressing his feelings embodies them in the art work.

Common to all theories of this type are two assumptions: (1) that an artist, in creating a work of art, is invariably engaged in expressing something; and (2) that the expressive qualities of the artwork are the direct consequence of this act of expression. I shall argue that there is no reason to accept these assumptions; but first we must consider a logically prior contention which is almost universally accepted by Expression theorists. This contention is that aesthetic, or artistic expression is something quite different from the symptomatic behavioral display of inner states.[4] Vincent Tomas summarizes this view in these words:

> Behavior which is merely symptomatic of a feeling, such as blushing when one is embarrassed or swearing when one is angry, is not artistic expression of feeling. Collingwood says it is just a "betrayal" of feeling. Dewey says it is "just a boiling over" of a feeling, and Ducasse says it is "a merely impulsive blowing off of emotional steam." As Hospers says, "A person may give vent to grief without expressing grief." Unlike merely giving vent to or betraying a feeling, artistic expression consists in the deliberate creation of something which "embodies" or "objectifies" the feeling.[5]

The corollary is that "embodying" or "objectifying" a feeling is equivalent to (artistically) expressing it. It is important to notice that these distinctions have been made in the interest of sustaining some favored version of the Expression theory; and since the appropriation of 'expression' for this purpose involves a significant departure from ordinary usage, we may reasonably demand some justification for this procedure.

On this point Dewey is the most thorough and articulate, and I shall confine my criticism to his version of the argument. Dewey writes that:

> Not all outgoing activity is of the nature of expression. At one extreme, there are storms of passion that break through barriers and that sweep away whatever intervenes between a person and something

he would destroy. There is activity, but not, from the standpoint of the one acting, expression. An onlooker may say, "What a magnificent expression of rage!" But the enraged being is only raging, quite a different matter from *expressing* rage. Or, again, some spectator may say, "How that man is expressing his own dominant character in what he is doing or saying." But the last thing the man in question is thinking of is to express his character; he is only giving way to a fit of passion.[6]

Dewey is concerned to protect us from the "error" which has invaded aesthetic theory "that the mere giving way to an impulsion, native or habitual, constitutes expression."[7] He adds that "emotional discharge is a necessary but not a sufficient condition of expression" on the grounds that: "While there is no expression, unless there is urge from within outwards, the welling up must be clarified and ordered by taking into itself the values of prior experiences before it can be an act of expression."[8] There can be no expression without inner agitation then, but the mere discharging of inner impulsions is insufficient to constitute an expression. "To express is to stay by, to carry forward in development, to work out to completion",[9] and, "Where there is . . . no shaping of materials in the interest of embodying excitement, there is no expression."[10]

Dewey offers these remarks as *evidence* for the adequacy of the Expression theory, whereas they follow in fact only if one has already assumed its truth. They are thinly disguised stipulations and not, as Dewey would have it, independently discoverable truths *about* expression. The circularity of this procedure can best be seen in his refusal to admit anything as an expression which does not result in the production of an object or state of affairs that embodies some aesthetically valuable quality.[11] But there are more serious objections. Dewey clearly wants to confine 'expression' to activities which are intentionally or voluntarily undertaken. (It must be an expression "from the standpoint of the one acting"; the involuntary venting of rage is ruled out with the comment that "the last thing the man in question is thinking of is to express his character; he is only giving way to a fit of passion.") But there is an existing distinction, and one which we would normally employ here, between voluntary and involuntary expression.[12] Dewey offers us no reason for abandoning this in favor of his stipulative restriction, other than an implicit appeal to the very theory which requires the sacrifice, and we are entitled to a more compelling argument before adopting this way of speaking.[13]

One reason for Dewey's insistence on this restriction is obvious. Many activities and behavioral patterns that are called 'expressions' are irrelevant to the production of aesthetically interesting objects. Most Expression theorists agree that the artist is engaged in doing something quite different from the man who merely vents his rage or airs his opinions—that he is doing something which bears little resemblance to commonly recognized varieties of expressive behavior. But the fact that the artist *is* doing something so apparently different ought to suggest not that he alone is expressing while others are not, but that the aesthetically relevant activity of the artist may not be an expression at all. Rather than being shown in creative activity the real meaning of 'expression,' we are offered a stipulation which would undermine most of the paradigmatic examples of expressive behavior in the interests of promoting a debatable theory.

The upshot of this is that, if "aesthetic expression" as a process is not to be understood in relation to pre-analytic notions of expressive behavior, then it must be understood in relation to something else—the something else here being the aesthetic qualities of the created product, the work of art.

In turning to the expressive qualities of the object, we are not leaving behind the act of expression, for even if we center attention on the properties of the work itself ("the object that is expressive, that says something to us"[14]) Dewey reminds us that "isolation of the act of expressing from the expressiveness possessed by the object leads to the notion that expression is merely a process of discharging personal emotion";[15] and that, "Expression as personal act and as objective result are *organically connected* with each other [italics added]."[16] But it is just here that Expression theories fail to convince, for the nature of this supposed connection is far from obvious, and no adequate analysis has yet been offered by anyone committed to this view. The argument for such a connection is usually established somewhat in the following way: aesthetic objects, including works of art, are said to possess certain perceptible physiognomic or "expressive" qualities such as 'sadness,' 'gaiety,' 'longing'; and where these are qualities of intentionally structured objects it is reasonable to assume that their presence is the intended consequence of the productive activity of the artist. But the Expression theorist is not content with this; he will go on to assert that, since the aesthetically relevant qualities of the object are *expressive* qualities, the productive activity must have been an act of expression and, moreover, an act of expressing just those feeling states whose analogues are predicated of the object. The situation can be represented more schematically in the following way:

(*E-T*) If art object *O* has expressive quality *Q*, then there was a prior activity *C* of the artist *A* such that in doing *C*, *A* expressed his *F* for *X* by imparting *Q* to *O* (where *F* is a feeling state and *Q* is the qualitative analogue of *F*).

The *E-T* represents a core-theory which I believe to be shared, e.g., by Dewey, Ducasse, Collingwood, Carritt, Gotshalk, Santayana, Tolstoy, and Véron, whatever their further differences might be.[17] I shall argue that the *E-T* contains an error traceable to the tendency to treat all the cognate forms of 'expression' as terms whose logical behavior is similar. The particular mistake here arises from assuming that the existence of *expressive qualities* in a work of art implies a prior act of *expression*.

Now, to say that an object has a particular expressive quality is to say something, first of all, about the object. (Even those who argue that 'the music is sad' can be translated as 'the music makes me feel sad' or 'has a disposition to make me, or others, feel sad' will agree that their accounts are only plausible on the assumption that the object has *some* properties which are at least causally relevant to the induced feeling.) But the Expression theorist is committed to the further assumption of a *necessary* link between the qualities of the art work and certain states of the artist. Critics of this theory have been quick to observe that this would commit us to treating all art works as autobiographical revelations. Moreover, it would entail that descriptions of the expressive qualities of an art work were falsifiable in a peculiar way. If it turned out that Mahler had experienced *no* state of mind remotely resembling despair or resignation during the period of the composition of *Das Lied von der Erde*, the Expression theorist would be obliged to conclude that we were mistaken in saying that the final movement (*Der Abschied*) of that work was expressive of despair or resignation; and this seems hardly plausible, since it implies that statements ostensibly about the music itself are in fact statements about the composer.[18] If works of art *were* expressions, in the way that behavior and language are expressions of states of a person, that is precisely what we would say. Normal imputations of expression *are* falsifiable, and the assertion that a person's behavior constitutes an expression of something is defeated when it can be shown that the imputed inference is unwarranted.[19] But statements about the expressive qualities of an art work remain, irresolutely, statements *about* the work, and any revision or rejection of such statements can be supported only by referring to the work itself. 'That's a sad piece of music' is countered not by objections such as, 'No, he wasn't' or 'He was just pretending' (referring to the composer), but by remarking 'You haven't listened carefully' or 'You must listen again; there are almost no minor progressions and the tempo is *allegro moderato*.'

Descriptions attributing expressive qualities to works of art then are not subject to falsification through the discovery of any truths about the inner life of the artist. An Expression theorist could of course grasp the other horn, arguing that the presence of quality $Q$ in $O$ is *sufficient* evidence of the occurrence of state $S$ in $A$, such that $A$ felt $F$ for $X$. But in ruling out the possibility of independent and conflicting evidence of the artist's feeling states, the Expression theorist secures his position by the simple expedient of making it analytically true; and no one, to my knowledge, has wished to claim that the *E-T* is an empty, though indisputable truth.

That a theory of art-as-expression which entails these difficulties should have been embraced so widely is due in part to a misunderstanding of the logic of 'expression' and 'expressive.' I would argue that statements attributing expressive (or physiognomic) properties to works of art should be construed as statements about the works themselves;[20] and that the presence of expressive properties does not entail the occurrence of a prior *act* of expression. Misunderstanding of this latter point has contributed greatly to the uncritical acceptance of the *E-T*.

## 3

'Expressive,' despite its grammatical relation to 'expression,' does not always play the logical role that one might expect. There are occasions on which the substitution of one term for the other is semantically harmless. 'His gesture was an expression of impatience' may in some contexts be replaced without noticeable alteration in meaning by 'His gesture was expressive of impatience.' But there are other contexts in which 'expression' and 'expressive' are significantly disparate. The remark that 'Livia has a very expressive face' does not entail that Livia is especially adept at expressing her inner states, nor does it entail that she is blessed with an unusually large repertoire of moods and feelings which she displays in a continuous kaleidoscope of facial configurations.

To make this clear I shall need to appeal to another distinction, developed in an earlier chapter,[21] between the two syntactic forms, '$\phi$ expression' (*A*) and 'expression of $\phi$' (*B*). That distinction was intended to establish that instances of *B* are inference-warranting while instances of *A* are descriptive, and that *A* and *B* are logically independent in the sense that that no statement containing an instance of *A* (or *B*) entails another statement containing an instance of *B* (or *A*). (A cruel expression in a human face does not automatically entitle us to infer that cruelty is being expressed.)

Now, the assertion that a person has an expressive face is not equivalent to the assertion that he is expressing, or is disposed to express, his inner states through a set of facial configurations; or rather the equivalence is not guaranteed. The difficulty is that 'expressive' is systematically ambiguous. It *may* be an alternate reading of 'is an expression of . . .' or it may be understood as a one-place predicate with no inferential overtones. Which of these meanings it has in a particular instance will depend upon what substitutions we are willing to make and what further questions we are prepared to admit. If, for example, the question 'expressive of what?' is blocked, we can conclude that 'expressive' is not functioning here in a variant of syntactic form *B*. '*X* is expressive' does not *entail* that there is an inner state *S* such that *S* is being expressed, any more than the appearance of a cruel expression in a face entails that cruelty is being expressed.

The statement that '*X* is expres*sive*' then may be logically complete, and to say of a person's gesture or face that it is *expressive* is not invariably to legitimize the question 'expressive of what?' In such cases we may say that 'expressive' is used intransitively. Still, we would not call a face (intransitively) expressive unless it displayed considerable mobility. A face that perpetually wore the *same* expression would not be expressive, and appreciation of this point should contribute to an understanding of the intransitive (*I*) sense of 'expressive.' A face is expressive (*I*) when it displays a wide range of expressions (*A*). Thus the successive appearance of sad, peevish, sneering, and puzzled expressions on the face of a child may lead us to say that he has an expressive face without committing us to a set of implications about the inner state of the child.

The meaning of 'expressive' (*I*) is not exhausted, however, through correlation with indefinitely extended sets of expressions (*A*) for which there are established names. To this extent, 'expressive' (*I*) is dispositional. It refers to the disposition of a face (or a body) to assume a variety of plastic configurations regardless of whether any momentary aspect of the face is describable as an expression (*A*) or not; and since it is clear that we have neither names nor definite descriptions for many of the geometrical patterns the human face and body can assume, the domain of 'expressive' (*I*) is both wider and less precise than 'expression' (*A*). It may refer at times simply to the capacity or disposition of a person to move or use his body in varied and perceptually interesting ways.[22] But whatever the correct analysis of 'expressive' (*I*), the fact remains that its use imposes no inferential commitments, and we may use it, just as we use 'expression' (*A*) to refer to certain qualities of persons and objects without implying the existence of some correlated *act* of expression.

*4*

It may be objected that all this, at best, discloses some interesting features of the use of 'expression' and 'expressive' in ordinary language which, from the standpoint of the Expression theorist, are entirely irrelevant. On the contrary, I believe these distinctions are crucial for an understanding of the very art form to which Expression theorists have made most frequent appeal. The point I want to develop here is that the language used by composers and performers of music is at variance with the conception of musical activity derivable from the *E-T*. This is not merely an instance of the naïveté of artists in contrast with the ability of philosophers to provide reflective analyses of a complex enterprise. It is rather that 'expressive' has a particular and quasi-technical meaning *within* the language used by musicians—a meaning which is logically similar to the intransitive sense of 'expressive,' which is clearly distinguishable from 'expression' (*B*), and whose use does not therefore commit us to any version of the *E-T*.

There are numerous passages in the music of the Romantic period (and later) which are marked *expressivo* ("expressively" or "with expression"). Now this is a particular instruction for the performance of the indicated passage or phrase, and as such it can be compared with the instructions *agitato, grazioso, dolce, leggiero, secco, stürmisch, schwer,* and *pesante.* All these are indications to the performer that the passage is to be played in a certain manner, and to play *espressivo* is merely to play in one manner rather than another. It is not to play well rather than badly, or to play with, rather than without some particular feeling, nor is it to succeed rather than fail to communicate the composer's intentions, feelings, or ideas. All these misconceptions are the result of a category mistake. One does not play *agitato* or *pesante* and *espressivo*; the choice must come from among alternatives all of which are logically similar members of a single category.[23] Moreover, to play *espressivo* is not to be engaged in expressing anything, any more than to play *leggiero* is to express lightness. (Nor, similarly does the composition of an expressive work entail that the *composer* be expressing anything.) Failure to realize this has led some adherents of the Expression theory into associating an expressive musical performance with some presumed *act* of expression on the part of the performer, the composer, or both, and thence with some particular feeling state which is attributable to them.[24]

It would follow from the *E-T* that we might always be mistaken in thinking that a performer had played a phrase expressively, since the correctness of this belief would depend on the truth of some psychological statement about the performer's inner states. But *espressivo* (expressively) is an adverbial characterization of a *manner* of performance, and the suggestion that follows from the *E-T*, that an expressive performance *must* be linked noncontingently to some particular inner state of the performer, is untenable.

It might be objected at this point that both the Expression theorist and I have misconceived the role of 'expressive,' for in critical usage 'expressive' may characterize entire performances or personal styles of performance (one might argue that Oistrakh's performance of the Sibelius *Violin Concerto* was more expressive than Heifetz's, or that generally, *A*'s playing was more expressive than *B*'s). 'Expressive' is still intransitive in this role, but it resists reduction to specific occurrences of passages played *espressivo*.[25] And it is this usage which may lead to the suggestion that 'expressive' has a primarily *evaluative* function in critical discourse. 'Expressive' does not, on this view, license inferences nor label particular or even general features of the object to be assessed, rather it does the assessing. Thus, calling a performance expressive would be to approve, applaud, or commend, not to detect, notice, or describe.

But there are two related and, I think, decisive objections to this suggestion. For even where 'expressive' is used to characterize a style or an entire performance and cannot be explicated by reference to particular occurrences of *espressivo* passages, the possibility remains that the expressiveness may be misplaced. There are omnipresent opportunities for misplaced expressiveness in musical performances, and we should find something peculiarly offensive in an expressive performance of Stravinsky's *L'Histoire du Soldat* or Bartok's *Allegro Barbaro*. Appropriate and effective performances of such works require the absence, or perhaps even the deliberate suppression of expressiveness. Similarly, austere performances of austere works are not *bad* performances; and to call performances of such works expressive may well be to condemn them. If 'expressive' were primarily an evaluative device, the notion of misplaced expressiveness would be self-contradictory, or at best paradoxical. Similar remarks apply to works as well as performances, and describing a particular work as nonexpressive is not equivalent to condemning it, nor is it prima facie evidence of its lack of artistic worth.

The second error results from failure to notice the first. Whether 'expressive' may be correctly *used* to praise a performance is a function of whether an expressive performance is appropriate to the work being performed. Where it *is* appropriate, and the performance commensurately expressive, *calling* it so may also serve to commend it. But this does no more to show that 'expressive' is an essentially evaluative predicate of our critical language than commending figs for their sweetness shows that 'sweet' is an essentially evaluative predicate of our culinary language. That we prefer expressive to nonexpressive performances of Rachmaninoff and Chopin implies that we regard expressiveness as required for an appropriate reading of the Romantic architecture of their works; it does not imply that 'expressive' is an aesthetic variant of 'good.'

We shall gain a better view of the issue, I think, if we consider how we might teach someone to play expressively or, conversely, how we might teach someone to recognize an expressive performance. If a student asks: 'What must I do to play this passage expressively?' we cannot give him a rule to follow such as: 'You must always play such passages in *this* way.' Of course we can give him a rule of sorts—'To play expressively you must vary the dynamics of the phrase; you must stress some notes more than others, and you must not play with rhythmic rigidity'—but we cannot give him a precise rule specifying *which* notes to stress or where and how to vary the dynamics. There are no paradigmatic examples of expressive playing from which a universal rule could be extracted and applied to other phrases. No phrase can be played expressively without *some* deviation from literal note values, without *some* modulations in the dynamic level, but the choice of where and how is not rule-governed.[26] The student who merely follows our second-order rule and plays the passage with rhythmic freedom and some dynamic modulation may produce a grotesquely unmusical and inexpressive result.

The problem is analogous to teaching someone to recognize an expressively played passage. There are no rules that will help here either. (If someone had no idea what to listen for, we might say: 'It happens when the pianist closes his eyes' or 'Watch for him to sway from the waist' and so on.) It may be thought that the difficulty here is much the same as that of showing the face in the cloud to someone whose aspect-blindness allows him to perceive only the cloud. There is an analogous kind of expression-deafness, but the analogy is only partial, and it is apt to mislead. Expression-deafness is closer to aspect-blindness than to color-blindness. There is no way to *teach* a color-blind person to see the normal range of colors, but we may succeed in getting someone to see the face in the cloud or the 'aspects' of the duck-rabbit figure; and we may succeed, analogously, in teaching someone to recognize an expressive performance. But the analogy cannot be stretched to a perfect fit. Recognition of the expressiveness in Grumiaux's performance of the Debussy *Sonata for Violin and Piano* presupposes that we are able to discriminate among a number of qualities that are predicable of musical performances. To hear a performance as expressive is also to hear that it is *not* dry, strained, heavy, agitated, or hollow. The identification presupposes, in other words, that we are conversant with a highly complex set of predicates and with their logical relations to one another. Recognition of the duck in the duck-rabbit figure, on the other hand, seems not to presuppose any comparably complex discriminatory abilities. Ducks and duck-like shapes may be recognizable even to those whose acquaintance with the zoological world is limited to ducks. But talk of expressive performances or works can occur meaningfully only within a developed language of musical criticism, and it implies an ability to discriminate and select from among a number of logically similar predicates.

There is no possibility that someone should learn to use 'expressive' correctly and yet be unable correctly to apply any other aesthetic predicate, as one might learn to use 'duck' correctly without at the same time being able to correctly apply other zoological predicates. (Seeing the figure as a duck is more closely analogous to hearing the sounds as music than to hearing the music as expressive.)

Aesthetic predicates are not learned independently of one another in some discursive or ostensive fashion. They acquire significance for us only in relation to one another as we become reflective and articulate participants in the art world.[27]

Despite the popularity of aspect and "seeing-as" models in recent discussions of aesthetic perception, considerations such as this seriously impair the attempt to explain our perception of aesthetic qualities by analogy with the perception of aspects, or as instances of "seeing-as."[28] Aspect perception has been a useful model in freeing us from the temptation to think of aesthetic objects as ontologically peculiar and distinct from, say, the material objects we hang on our walls; but it is misleading when it suggests that seeing, or hearing, an art work as *expressive* (or garish, or sentimental) is no different from spotting the face in the cloud or the duck in the figure.

5

The Expression theorist of course may object that he is not concerned so much with the language of musicians or critics as with the possibility of giving a theoretical description of the art which would enable us to grasp certain aesthetically relevant features of the processes of creating, performing, and attending to musical compositions. We must, I think, admit that there is a sense in which it would be correct to say that a piece of music may be an expression (*B*). . . . But this admission concedes nothing to the *E-T*, for the only sense in which 'expression' (*B*) is admissible here is inconsistent with the *E-T*.

The admission amounts to this: Aside from certain occurrences of nonverbal behavior and linguistic utterances there is a class of things we may call indirect or secondary expressions. The manner of a woman's dress, the way she wears her hair, or the arrangement of her room may "express" some aspect of her character. My handwriting, my preferences in literature, my style at poker, and my choice of friends may likewise reveal something of my inner states and dispositions. It is legitimate to speak of these as expressions (*B*) where they satisfy the conditions of being evidential or inference-warranting, and lead, correctly, to the attribution of an intentional state.[29] It is clear that this is often the case, that we do make such inferences, and that the conditions for expression are satisfied here as well as in cases of direct or primary expression in language and behavior.

And if my style of playing poker expresses my temerity or my avarice, why should not my style of painting landscapes express something of me as well? Or my style of playing the flute? The conditions of a warranted inference to an intentional state may be as well met by art as by action; and there are impressive examples in the literature of psychoanalysis of the use of art works to unlock the psychic labyrinths of the artist.[30] It is this sense in which I concede that an art work may be an expression of something: it may contribute material leading to a correct inference to an intentional state of the artist. But I contend that this does nothing to support the *E-T*, and further, that it does nothing to distinguish art from any other product of human activity.

We should recall that the *E-T* entails that the (successful) artist, by his creative activity, imparts a quality to the work which is *descriptively analogous* to the feeling state expressed by him (sadness-'sadness') and ought therefore to be recognizable as the embodiment of his feeling without assistance from extra-perceptual sources of knowledge. But, far from being clear that this is always the case with successful works of art, it would seem in some instances to be impossible. It will be best to illustrate this point with an example. Carl Nielsen completed his Sixth Symphony during the years 1924–25, and it was during this period of the composer's life that "he was harassed by ill health and depression, puzzled by the notoriety enjoyed by what seemed to him to be musical nihilism, and upset over the seeming failure of his own work to take hold beyond the borders of his native land. . . . It is not unreasonable to suppose that this is the source of some of the exasperation that manifests itself particularly in the second and final movements of the Sixth Symphony."[31] (The second movement is referred to later as "a bitter commentary on the musical modernism of the 1920's.")

Now the second movement of the Nielsen symphony is marked *Humoresque*, and the prevailing impression left by the music itself is that of lighthearted buffoonery. It may not be unreasonable, as the program notes suggest, to conclude that Nielson was venting exasperation, bitterness, or disappointment here, but it is difficult to see how such an inference could have been suggested by attending to the qualities of the music alone. The music does not *sound* exasperated or disappointed, nor can I see how any piece of music *could* have these as perceptible qualities. The movement sounds humorous, and there is an obvious reference to Prokofiev's *Peter and the Wolf*; but the suggestion that Nielsen was manifesting exasperation or commenting bitterly on musical modernism in this piece can have arisen only with the acquisition of some extra-musical information about the composer's life. If the critic *now* wants to maintain that the Sixth Symphony is an expression of Nielsen's bitterness and disappointment, we may agree that this is at least a plausible inference given the truth of the biographical data. But we must also point out that this has little to do with the aesthetically relevant expressive qualities of the music itself. This is something of a paradox for the *E-T*. In order for the Nielsen symphony to be an expression of the composer's bitterness and disappointment (i.e., to be a secondary expression) it must have certain perceptible qualities which, together with the biographical data, will yield an inference. But the qualities of the music here are not, and *cannot* be analogues of the intentional state of the composer. The music is humorous, the composer is disappointed. And he cannot inject his bitterness and disappointment into the music in the way that is required by the *E-T*. There is no sense in which the *music* is disappointed. Even if we suppose it to be true that Nielsen was disappointed, exasperated, or bitter, and that the critic's inferences are correct, there is nothing in this to establish the presence of a noncontingent relation between the perceptible qualities of the music and any particular state of mind of the composer. Such linkages are contingent, and dependent in every case on the possession of some extra-musical knowledge of the composer's life. In itself, humor in a piece of music no more guarantees the presence of bitterness than it invariably betrays a carefree state of mind. Paralleling the distinction between syntactic forms *A* and *B*, the expressive qualities of a work of art are logically independent of the psychological states of the artist, and humor (or sadness) in a madrigal is neither necessary nor sufficient for amusement (or despair) in a Monteverdi.

Thus, even where we speak of a piece of music as an expression (*B*) of some state of mind, this use fails to meet the requirements of the *E-T*. There is no direct, noncontingent relation between qualities of the work and states of the artist as the *E-T* supposes (*F* and *Q* are not related in the required way). The relation is contingent and mediated by extra-musical considerations, including in some instances appeal to psychological theories. Secondly, it is often *impossible* to impart a feeling quality to a work which will perceptually reflect the artist's feeling state (e.g., disappointment). And, finally, the presence of an expressive quality in a work of art is never sufficient to guarantee the presence of an analogous feeling state in the artist. What the music "expresses" is logically independent of what, if anything, the composer expresses.[32]

It follows from this that statements of the form, 'The music expresses $\phi$,' or 'The music is expressive of $\phi$' must, if we are to understand them as making relevant remarks about the music and not as making elliptical remarks about the composer, be interpreted as intensionally equivalent to syntactic form *A*; that is, they are to be understood as propositions containing 'expression' or 'expressive' as syntactic parts of a one-place predicate denoting some perceptible quality, aspect, or *gestalt* of the work itself. Moreover, 'The *music* expresses $\phi$' cannot be interpreted as an instance of the use of 'expression' (*B*) since it would make no sense to ask for the *intentional object* of the music. The sadness of the music is not sadness *over* or *about* anything.[33] I am not claiming that everyone who uses these constructions does in fact understand them to have this meaning, but I am contending that this is the only interpretation which is both coherent and which preserves the aesthetic relevance of such assertions.

## 6

To recapitulate, neither playing expressively nor composing "expressive" music entails that one *be* expressing anything.[34] They require only that the product of the relevant activity have certain phenomenal properties that can be characterized as noninferentially expressive. And once we have shed the tendency to look behind the expressive qualities in an art object for some correlated act of expression we shall be closer to a correct understanding of the relation of the artist to his work; or rather, we shall be relieved at least of a persistent misunderstanding of the relation. Musicians, and artists generally, do not "express" themselves in their work in any sense that is intelligible, consistent, and aesthetically relevant. This is not to say that there is no relation between the artist's activity and the resultant expressive qualities of the work, but rather to argue that it must be something other than that envisaged by the *E-T*. It would be less misleading, if a little archaic, to say simply that the relation is one of making or creating. The artist is not expressing something which is then infused into the work by alchemical transformation; he is making an expressive object. What he does to accomplish this remains, of course, as complex and mystifying as before, and I have nothing to add to the numerous attempts to explain the "creative process" except to argue that, whatever it may be, it is not identical with some act or process of expression.

One aspiration of aesthetics has always been to demonstrate that the creation of art works is a unique and exalted form of human activity. Even those like Dewey who have been determined to narrow the gap between art and ordinary experience reflect the urge to find something extraordinary in art. To conclude that the traditional concept of art-as-expression fails to realize this aim is not to abandon the conviction that there is something singular in the creative process; it is only to abandon a theory which fails to do justice to that conviction, and to reveal the need to give it more trenchant and persuasive formulation.

The theory that art is an or *the* expression of the human spirit is either trivial or false; for the sense in which art is an expression of a state of mind or character of the artist does not establish a relevant distinction between art and any other form of human activity, and the attempt to utilize the concept of expression to distinguish artistic or creative activity from more mundane affairs leads only to incoherence and absurdity. If there is a residue of truth in the *E-T*, it is that works of art often have expressive qualities. But so do natural objects, and there is nothing in this to compel us to the conclusion entailed by the *E-T*. The only way that we can interpret the notion of art-as-expression which is both coherent and aesthetically relevant is to construe statements referring to works of art and containing some cognate form of 'expression' as references to certain properties of the works themselves . . . .

## Notes

1. [Ed.—note omitted.]
2. There is a range of values for the variable here; 'feeling,' 'attitude,' 'idea,' 'mood,' and 'outlook' have all been suggested at some time, but 'feeling' is the favored substitution.
3. Bernard Bosanquet, *Three Lectures on Aesthetic* (London: Macmillan, 1915), p. 74.
4. [Ed.—note omitted.]
5. "The Concept of Expression in Art," *Philosophy Looks at the Arts* [Ed.—first edition], ed. Joseph Margolis (New York: Scribner's, 1962), p. 31. The quotations are taken from Collingwood, *The Principles of Art*; Dewey, *Art as Experience*; Ducasse, *Art, the Critics, and You*; and Hospers, *Meaning and Truth in the Arts*.
6. *Art as Experience*, p. 61.
7. *Loc. cit.*
8. *Loc. cit.*
9. *Ibid.*, p. 62.
10. *Loc. cit.*
11. Chs. 4 and 5 of *Art as Experience*.
12. [Ed.—note omitted.]
13. Dewey makes more of this than most Expression theorists, but even those, like Ducasse, who admit the use of 'expression' to describe involuntary revelations of inner states, have argued the *aesthetic* expression is something quite distinct, and not to be confused with the former.
14. Dewey, *Art as Experience*, p. 82.
15. *Loc. cit.*
16. *Loc. cit.*
17. Harold Osborne has summarized the Expression theory in a somewhat different manner: "The underlying theory is, in its baldest form, that the artist lives through a certain experience; he then makes an artifact which in some way embodies that experience; and through appreciative contemplation of this artifact other men are able to duplicate in their own minds the experience of the artist. What is conveyed to them is . . . an experience of their own as similar as possible to the artist's experience in all its aspects." (*Aesthetics and Criticism* [London:

Routledge and Kegan Paul, 1955], p. 143). My formulation is constructed to call attention to the Expression theorist's view of the relation between the activity of the artist and the expressive qualities of the work.

18. If it is objected that the composer is expressing some *remembered* or unconscious feelings of this sort, we can strengthen the example by supposing it to be false that the composer had ever experienced, consciously or otherwise, the feeling corresponding to the feeling-quality attributed to the music. The logical point remains untouched in any case.

19. [Ed.—note omitted.]

20. [Ed.—note omitted.]

21. [Ed.—note omitted.]

22. Notice, e.g., that we can refer to the movements of a Thai dancer performing a *Lakon* as expressive even though we may have no idea what the movements "mean" and no precise language in which to describe them.

23. Many of the commonly encountered instructions for performance are incompatible, though of course this is not true of all. *Leggiero* and *animoso* are clearly compatible, and the opening bars of Debussy's *Prélude à L'Après-Midi D'Un Faune'* are marked *doux et espressif*; but the indication '*secco, expressivo*' would be contradictory, and contradictory in the same way that incompatible imperatives are contradictory—the performer could not simultaneously carry out both instructions.

24. When the difficulty of naming particular feeling states becomes apparent, the Expression theorist may resort to the sui generis category of "aesthetic emotions."

25. There is a strong analogy between the intransitively expressive performance and the intransitively expressive face.

26. See Frank Sibley, "Aesthetic Ceoncepts," *Philosophical Review* LXVIII (1959), 421–450, for a cogent discussion of the general question of rule-governed and sufficient conditions in aesthetic discourse.

27. See also Arthur C. Danto, "The Artworld," *Journal of Philosophy* LXI (1964), 571–584.

28. See, e.g., B. R. Tilghman, "Aesthetic Perception and the Problem of the 'Aesthetic Object,'" *Mind* LXXV (1966), 351–368; Virgil C. Aldrich, *Philosophy of Art* (Englewood Cliffs: Prentice-Hall, 1963). A recent illustration of some of the limitations of aspect-perception models in aesthetics may be found in Peter Kivy, "Aesthetic Aspects and Aesthetic Qualities," *Journal of Philosophy* LXV (1968), 85–93. The *locus classicus* for discussions of the problem is Wittgenstein, *Philosophical Investigations*, part 2.

29. [Ed.—note omitted.]

30. Freud's study of Leonardo is perhaps the best known of such attempts; but Jung has made more consistent use of art works in his routine analytic practice. Cf. particularly *Symbols of Transformation*, tr. R. F. C. Hull, Bollingen Series XX:5 (New York: Pantheon, 1956).

31. Quoted from the notes to *Music of the North*, Vol. 8: Carl Nielsen, Symphony No. 6, "Sinfonia Semplice," Mercury Classics Recordings, MG 10137.

32. Many of these points may be extended beyond music, though I am not

concerned to argue here for the applicability of all of these remarks to the other arts. Freud's analysis of Leonardo, for example, makes use of certain features of the paintings (the similarity of facial expression in the *Gioconda* and the *Madonna and Child with Saint Anne*; the incompleteness of many of the canvases, etc.); yet none of Freud's analytic inferences are based on qualities of the paintings alone. They are rooted in his interpretation of the available biographical material. I would suggest, though I cannot pursue it here, that inferences from works of art *alone*— whether from music, fiction, or architecture—to the character of the artist are generally suspect.

33. Much has been made of the difference between "real" feelings and "aesthetic" feelings; between, for instance, life-sadness and music-sadness, and I would suggest that at least the promise of an explanation lies in the fact that intentional objects are present in the former and absent from the latter.

34. There is a trivial sense in which these activities may always be an expression of something—an expression of the desire to get the phrase right, for instance—but such expressions are irrelevant to the *E-T* for reasons given above.

# 23.    Gadamer's Theory of Interpretation

## E. D. HIRSCH, JR.

Under the somewhat ironic title *Wahrheit und Methode* (Tübingen, 1960), Hans-Georg Gadamer has published the most substantial treatise on hermeneutic theory that has come from Germany in this century. In scope, length, and learning it bears comparison with Boeckh's *Encyclopädie* (Leipzig, 1877), and it is precisely in such a comparison that the deliberate irony of Professor Gadamer's title appears, for this is a polemic against that nineteenth-century preoccupation with objective truth and correct method of which Boeckh's work was representative and its full title symptomatic—*Encyclopädie und Methodologie der philologischen Wissenschaften*. Against this preoccupation Gadamer protests that there can be no *Methodologie* of textual interpretation because interpretation is not, after all, a *Wissenschaft* whose aim is objective and permanent knowledge. Truth cannot reside, as Boeckh thought, in the genuine re-cognition of an author's meaning (*"das Erkennen des Erkannten"*), for this unrealizable ideal naïvely disregards the fact that every putative re-cognition of a text is really a new and different cognition in which the interpreter's own historicity is the specifica differentia. The historicity of understanding (*"die Geschichtlichkeit des Verstehens"*) is what the nineteenth century overlooked. No method can transcend the interpreter's own historicity, and no truth can transcend this central truth.

What is new in Gadamer's theory is not this central thesis, which is widely held and probably has more adherents than critics, but his mode of presentation.[1] He introduces new concepts and gives old words new meanings. *Vorurteil*, for example, is not to be avoided but welcomed; interpretation does not require the neutralization of one's personal horizon

From E. D. Hirsch, Jr., *Validity in Interpretation* (New Haven, Conn.: Yale University Press, 1967), Appendix II. Reprinted with permission of the author and Yale University Press.

but involves a process of *Horizontverschmelzung;* the history of interpretation is a history of application—a *Wirkungsgeschichte.* In addition to these concepts, Gadamer presents a detailed criticism of earlier hermeneutic theories, a series of extremely valuable excursuses into the history of ideas, and an illuminating theory of art as *Spiel.* Quite apart from its theoretical argument, *Wahrheit und Methode* is a book of substance that has begun to radiate an influence far beyond Germany. In America, James M. Robinson has observed that "in the present situation Dilthey and increasingly Heidegger are being superseded by the Heidelberg philosopher Hans-Georg Gadamer, a former pupil of Heidegger and Bultmann, whose *magnum opus* grounds the humanities in a hermeneutic oriented not to psychologism or existentialism, but rather to language and its subject matter."[2]

Gadamer's book extends and codifies the main hermeneutical concepts of Bultmann, Heidegger, and their adherents and can be considered a summa of what Robinson calls "The New Hermeneutic." *Wahrheit und Methode* has been welcomed by Robinson and other theologians and by continental literary critics as a philosophical justification for "vital and relevant" interpretations that are unencumbered by a concern for the author's original intention. On this point "The New Hermeneutic" reveals its affinities with "The New Criticism" and the newer "Myth Criticism." All three have impugned the author's prerogative to be the determiner of textual meaning. Gadamer, however, grounds his anti-intentionalism partially in aesthetics (like the New Critics) and not at all in the collective unconscious (like the Myth Critics), but primarily in the radical historicism of Martin Heidegger.

Gadamer owes much of the vocabulary and context of his exposition to Heidegger. "Distance in time could only be thought of in its hermeneutical productiveness after Heidegger had lent an existential sense to the idea of understanding" (p. 281).[3] But despite the modesty with which Gadamer dedicates his work to "the new aspect of the hermeneutical problem disclosed by Heidegger's existential analysis of human being" (p. 245), the theory he puts forward belongs in many of its features to a skepticism regarding historical knowledge that long predated *Sein und Zeit.* Still, Gadamer does owe to Heidegger the positive embracing of historically distorted knowledge as something "real" and "phenomenal" in contrast to academic pseudo-knowledge which is "abstract" and "constructed." For "in view of the historicity of our being, the rehabilitation of (a text's) original conditions is a futile undertaking. What is rehabilitated from an alien past is not the original. In its continued alienation it has a merely secondary existence" (p. 159).

That is the flavor of Gadamer's attack on the philological tradition in

Germany and its "naïve" aspirations to objectivity. From the start it had been a dead and spiritless enterprise that lacked validity, vitality, and *humane Bedeutung*. However, the new hermeneutics Gadamer offers to replace the tradition of Schleiermacher, Humboldt, Droysen, Boeckh, Steinthal, Dilthey, and Simmel may be more destructive in its implications than he had reckoned. In any case, his theory contains inner conflicts and inconsistencies which not one of the above masters would have allowed to pass into print.

## Tradition and the Indeterminacy of Meaning

Although the nature of textual meaning is a crucial subject for hermeneutic theory, Gadamer does not devote a substantial discussion to it. His primary concern is to attack the premise that textual meaning is the same as the author's meaning. To suppose that a text means what its author meant is to Gadamer pure romantic *Psychologismus*, for a text's meaning does not lie in mental processes, which are in any case inaccessible, but in the subject matter or thing meant, the *Sache*, which, while independent of author and reader, is shared by both. Thus, the motto to the central section of Gadamer's book is Luther's dictum, *"Qui non intellegit res, non potest ex verbis sensum elicere."* The *res*, not the author, is the determiner of meaning.

Luther's point as I understand it is firmly valid. It is impossible to elicit the sense of the word "railroad" unless one knows what a railroad is. However, Luther carefully distinguishes, as Gadamer does not, between *res* and *sensus*. Indeed, Gadamer identifies meaning and subject matter—as though meaning were an autonomous entity quite independent of consciousness—which is a repudiation not simply of psychologism but of consciousness itself. It will not do to invoke Husserl as an ally on this point (p. 211), since Husserl's repudiation of psychologism consisted in distinguishing between mental acts, meanings, and things, not in abolishing the former two. Husserl describes meaning as distinct from, yet dependent on, mental acts, and for him the author alone is the determiner of a text's meaning.[4] While Gadamer is right to reject the loose identification of mental processes and meanings in Schleiermacher and Dilthey, his exposition appears to imply that textual meaning can somehow exist independently of individual consciousness.

He finds sanction for this supposed independence in the nature of written language: "It seems to us to be the distinguishing feature and dignity of literary art that in it language is not speech. That is to say, while remaining independent of all relation of speaking, or being addressed, or being persuaded, it still possesses meaning and form" (p. 177).

Accordingly, a written text is not to be considered as recorded speech, but as an independent piece of language. "Actually the condition of being written down is central to the hermeneutic phenomenon because the detachment of a written text from the writer or author as well as from any particular addressee or reader gives it an existence of its own" (p. 369). The text, being independent of any particular human consciousness, takes on the autonomous being of language itself. As Heidegger inimitably put the case:

> Der Mensch spricht nur, indem er der Sprache entspricht.
> Die Sprache spricht.
> Ihr Sprechen spricht für uns im Gesprochenen.[5]

But the matter can be put another way. If the language of a text is not speech but rather language speaking its own meaning, then whatever that language says to us is its meaning. It means whatever we take it to mean. Reduced to its intelligible significance, the doctrine of the autonomy of a written text is the doctrine of the indeterminacy of textual meaning.

The implications of that doctrine are not altogether shirked by Gadamer. "The meaning of a text goes beyond its author not just sometimes but always. Understanding is not a reproductive but always a productive activity" (p. 280). Furthermore, "the winning of the true sense contained in a text or artistic work never comes to an end. It is an infinite process" (p. 282). Thus *the* meaning of the text is a never-exhausted array of possible meanings lying in wait for a never-ending array of interpreters. But if this is so, it follows that no single interpretation could ever correspond to the meaning of the text, for no actual interpretation could ever be the same as an array of possible meanings. By no magical road could an actual interpretation or even an infinite series of them ever be made identical with a locus of possibilities. Quite clearly, to view the text as an autonomous piece of language and interpretation as an infinite process is really to deny that the text has *any* determinate meaning, for a determinate entity is what it is and not another thing, but an inexhaustible array of possibilities is an hypostatization that is nothing in particular at all.

Though he has not clearly defined the issue, Gadamer may have wished to avoid this disconcerting consequence by conceiving of a text's meaning as changing in time, yet determinate at any given point in time. This concept of a historically changing meaning preserves the infinite productiveness of interpretation without relinquishing the idea of a determinate meaning, for it is only when a text does mean something and not just anything that interpretation is a plausible enterprise. But here a problem arises. Suppose, as it often happens, two readers disagree about the meaning of a text at exactly the same moment of time. What principle would they have for determining who is more nearly right? They could not measure their interpretations against what the text had meant in the past, since it no longer means what it meant before. Apparently there is no way of determining what a text means at a given moment. So again, under this hypothesis, the meaning is indeterminate, since we cannot distinguish even in principle, much less in practice, between what it means and what it does not mean.

It is, perhaps, to avoid this nihilistic conclusion that Gadamer introduces the concept of tradition: "The substance of literature is not the dead persistence of an alien being that exists simultaneously with the experienced reality of a later time. Literature is rather a function of spiritual conservation and tradition, and therefore carries into every present its hidden history" (p. 154). I take this to mean that the changing substance of a text is determined by the widespread cultural effects and manifestations it has passed through, and that this wider significance is commonly understood and accepted within any present culture. "In truth, the important thing is to recognize distance in time as a positive and productive possibility of understanding. It is not a yawning abyss, but is filled out through the continuity of its coming hither and by that tradition in whose light shines everything that comes down to us" (p. 281).

The idea of tradition is essential to Gadamer because it points to a principle for resolving disagreements between contemporary readers. The reader who follows the path of tradition is right, and the reader who leaves this path is wrong. The determinate meaning of a text at a given point in time is what a present culture would generally take that meaning to be. The principle seems analogous to legal pragmatism in which a law means what the judges take it to mean, but in law there is a hierarchy of judges, and a papal-like authority accrues to the highest judge. Gadamer's concept of tradition lacks this hierarchical structure and therefore cannot in fact save the day. For the concept of tradition with respect to a text is no more or less than the history of how a text has been interpreted. Every new interpretation by its existence belongs to and alters the tradition. Consequently, tradition cannot really function as a stable, normative concept, since it is in fact a changing, descriptive concept. (It is a notable characteristic of theories which reject the prerogative of the author that they attempt illicitly to convert neutral, descriptive concepts into normative ones.) The futility of performing this legerdemain appears when we observe that the original problem has not disappeared but has cropped up again in another form. For the problem of determining the true character of a changing tradition is the same as the problem of determining the true character of a changing meaning. Without a genuinely stable norm we cannot even in principle make a valid choice between two differing interpretations, and we are left with the consequence that a text means nothing in particular at all.

## Repetition and the Problem of Norms

As the foregoing makes clear, the problem of norms is crucial. If we cannot enunciate a principle for distinguishing between an interpretation that is valid and one that is not, there is little point in writing books about texts or about hermeneutic theory. Gadamer himself, when he argues against the most extreme form of non-normative theory, faces squarely up to this:

> If a work is not complete in itself how can we have a standard against which to measure the validity of our perception and understanding? A fragment arbitrarily broken off from a continuing process cannot contain a compelling norm. And from this it follows that all must be left to the perceiver to make what he can out of what lies before him. One way of understanding the form is as legitimate as another. There is no criterion of validity. Nor does the poet himself possess one (even the aesthetic of "genius" confirms that), rather, each encounter with the work ranks as a new creation. This seems to me an untenable hermeneutic nihilism (p. 90).

What is the compelling norm that vanquishes this nihilism? Gadamer's most precise statements are those which declare what the norm is not: "Norm concepts like the meaning of the author or the understanding of the original reader represent in truth mere empty blanks that are filled up by understanding from occasion to occasion" (p. 373). In that case what is left? There is left the assertion that a text, despite the fact that its meaning changes, nevertheless does represent a stable and repeatable meaning. Gadamer rightly perceives that without this there can be no norm and no valid interpretation, although his acceptance of the exigency is grudging:

> The meaning of a written sign is in principle identifiable and repeatable. Only that which is identical in each repetition is that which was really laid down in the written sign. Yet it is at once clear that here "repetition" cannot be taken in a strict sense. It does not mean a referring back to some primal original in which something was said or written. The understanding of a written text is not repetition of something past, but participation in a present meaning (p. 370).

This seems to say that the meaning of the text is self-identical and repeatable and, in the next breath, that the repetition is not really a repetition and the identity not really an identity. This kind of reasoning stands as eloquent testimony to the difficulties and self-contradictions that confront Gadamer's theory as soon as one asks the simple question: What constitutes a valid interpretation? Gadamer's most sustained attempt to solve this problem is now to be examined.

### Explication and the Fusion of Horizons

If an interpreter cannot overcome the distorting perspective of his own historicity, no matter how hard he tries, then it follows that "one understands differently when one understands at all" (p. 280). An apparent confirmation of this doctrine has been observed by all teachers who read student examinations. Experience has taught them that the student who expresses an idea in his own words has probably understood the idea, while the one who merely repeats the lecturer's words probably has not. We seem to be led to the skeptical and psychologistic conclusion that each man, being different, has to understand differently in order to understand at all.

But is this a correct inference from the phenomenon? The example of the lecturer and his students really points in the opposite direction. The indication that a student has understood the lecturer is not merely that he has expressed himself in different words, for he would also plausibly do that if he had misunderstood the speaker. The sign that he has understood the lecturer's meaning is that he has expressed a similar or equivalent meaning even though his words are different. If the meaning had not been translated into a new idiom with some success we would have no grounds for inferring that the student had understood. That which he has understood is, after all, a meaning, not an expression, and this is precisely why the lecturer may begin to feel uneasy when he finds merely his own expression repeated.

It follows that the proper form of Gadamer's dictum is that one tends to *express* a meaning differently when one understands at all. It is literally nonsense to state that one understands only when one does not understand. However, Gadamer attempts to salvage this apparent contradiction by equating understanding with explication: "In the last analysis, understanding and explication are the same" (p. 366). This remarkable assertion is defended by the following argument: "Through explication the text is to be brought to speech. But no text and no book can speak when it does not speak a language that reaches others. And so explication must find the right language if it would really make the text speak" (p. 375). A past text cannot be understood until it has been explicated in the idiom of the present day. Thus, the speaking of the mute text can occur only in and through a modern commentary. Since the being understood or speaking of the text is effected by an explication, it follows that explication and understanding are "in the last analysis" the same.

With this highly insubstantial argument Gadamer has set out to topple one of the firmest distinctions in the history of hermeneutic theory, that between the *subtilitas intelligendi* and the *subtilitas explicandi*—the art of understanding a text and the art of making it understood by others. Attempting to efface this distinction results only in logical embarrassment before the simplest questions, such as, "What does the explicator understand before he makes his explication?" Gadamer's difficulty in coping with this basic question is quite apparent when he comes to describe the process of interpretation. He cannot say that the interpreter understands the original sense of the text, since that would be to disregard the historicity of understanding. He cannot say, on the other hand, that the interpreter understands his own subsequent explication, since that would be patently absurd.

His solution is to opt for a compromise: "The real meaning of a text as it addresses itself to an interpreter . . . is always *codetermined* by the historical situation of the interpreter" (p. 280, my italics). Thus, what an interpreter understands is neither wholly the result of his own perspective nor wholly that of the original perspective. It is rather the product of a fusion between these two, which Gadamer calls a *Horizontverschmelzung*. "In the process of understanding there always occurs a true fusion of perspectives in which the projection of the historical perspective really brings about a sublation of the same" (p. 290). Thus, the perspective and idiom of the interpreter are always partly constitutive of his understanding.

Once again Gadamer's attempted solution turns out, on analysis, to exemplify the very difficulty it was designed to solve. How can an interpreter fuse two perspectives—his own and that of the text—unless he has somehow appropriated the original perspective and amalgamated it with his own? How can a fusion take place unless the things to be fused are made actual, which is to say, unless the original sense of the text has been understood? Indeed, the fundamental question which Gadamer has not managed to answer is simply this: how can it be affirmed that the original sense of a text is beyond our reach and, at the same time, that valid interpretation is possible?

Gadamer is much more conciliatory to the ideal of valid interpretation than his assumptions warrant. If he were true to his assumption of radical historicity, that which he calls a fusion of historical perspectives could not be affirmed at all. If the interpreter is really bound by his own historicity, he cannot break out of it into some halfway house where past and present are merged. At best he can only gather up the leftover, unspeaking inscriptions from the past and wring from them, or impose on them, some meaning in terms of his own historical perspective. For once it is admitted that the interpreter can adopt a fused perspective different from his own contemporary one, then it is admitted in principle that he *can* break out of his own perspective. If that is possible, the primary assumption of the theory is shattered.

## The Historicity of Understanding

I have examined the three principal concepts by which Gadamer has tried to salvage the idea of valid interpretation from the ruins of his-toricity—tradition, quasi-repetition, and horizon-fusion. All three ideas have this interesting common feature: they each constitute an attempt to fuse together the past and the present while still acknowledging their incompatible separateness. This inner contradiction has been the focus of my attack on Gadamer's theory. On the other hand, I recognize the validity of Gadamer's insistence that a vital, contemporary understanding of the past is the only understanding worth having and his rightness in insisting on the differentness in the cultural givens and shared attitudes between a past age and the present one. What is wanted is to preserve these truths without committing contradictions and abolishing logically necessary distinctions.

The fundamental distinction overlooked by Gadamer is that between the meaning of a text and the significance of that meaning to a present situation. It will not do to say in one breath that a written text has a self-identical and repeatable meaning and in the next that the meaning of a text changes. Instead of reproducing this paradox in a concept like quasi-repetition, Gadamer should have tried to resolve it by observing that the word "meaning" has been given two distinct senses. There is a difference between the meaning of a text (which does not change) and the meaning of a text to us today (which changes). The meaning of a text is that which the author meant by his use of particular linguistic symbols. Being linguistic, this meaning is communal, that is, self-identical and reproducible in more than one consciousness. Being reproducible, it is the same whenever and wherever it is understood by another. However, each time this meaning is construed, its meaning to the construer (its sig-nificance) is different. Since his situation is different, so is the character of his relationship to the construed meaning. It is precisely because the meaning of the text is always the same that its relationship to a different situation is a different relationship. This is surely what Gadamer wishes to call attention to by his insistence on vitality and change. It is what he means or should have meant by the concept of *Horizontverschmelzung*. He could have avoided self-contradiction by perceiving that this melting or fusing always involves two processes that are separate and distinct no matter how entangled they may be in a given instance of understanding. One process is the interpreter's construing and understanding of textual meaning. This act of construing is prior to everything else. But the interpreter also finds a way to relate this construed meaning to himself and, in the case of written criticism, to recast it in his own idiom. This recasting *could* be called a fusion of horizons, but it would be more accurate to call it a perception of the relevance assumed by the text when its meaning is related to a present situation.

This resolution of Gadamer's contradictions does, of course, disregard the historicity of understanding, since it assumes that an interpreter can construe the original meaning of a past text. Gadamer found himself in contradictions precisely because he disallowed this possibility. Now, by what right do I return to a pre-Heideggerian naïveté and allow it? First, I would point out that my account by no means abandons the concept of historicity—assuming that the word is taken to represent a fundamental differentness between past and present cultures. What I deny is not the fact of difference but the asserted impossibility of sameness in the construing of textual meaning.

On what grounds is this impossibility asserted by Gadamer? He does not argue the case but assumes that it has been established by Heidegger. Heidegger, on Gadamer's interpretation, denies that past meanings can be reproduced in the present because the past is ontologically alien to the present. The being of a past meaning cannot become the being of a present meaning, for being is temporal and differences in time are consequently differences in being. If this is the argument on which Gadamer wishes to found his doctrine of historicity, he should acknowledge that it is ultimately an argument against written communication in general and not just against communication between historical eras. For it is merely arbitrary, on this argument, to hold that a meaning fifty years old is ontologically alien while one three years or three minutes old is not. It is true that Heidegger introduces the concept of *Mitsein* which corresponds to the idea of cultural eras, but this does not solve the problem. The ontical character of time does not in itself require the arbitrary slicing up of time into homogeneous periods.

But the doctrine of radical historicity might, after all, be true. It states that all present acts of understanding fail to re-cognize past meanings. This seems to be a statement like "All swans are white," that is, a statement which could be falsified. However, it is really not that kind of empirical statement at all, since there is no way of being certain in *any* act of understanding (much less in all such acts) that the author's meaning has or has not been reproduced. The doctrine of radical historicity is ultimately a dogma, an idea of reason, an act of faith. So, of course, is the contrary doctrine: *not* all acts of understanding fail to re-cognize past meanings. While neither dogma could be falsified, one may very well be more probable than the other.

The less skeptical position is more probable primarily because it coheres with the rest of experience while the radically historicistic position does not. If we believe from experience that linguistic communication through texts past or present has *ever* occurred, then the dogma of radical historicity is rendered improbable. The historicist dogma is not really a dogma about the ontological nature of time, since it does not deny the possibility of written communication between persons living in the "same" period, inhabiting the "same" milieu, and speaking the "same" language. However, this sameness is an illicit abstraction which conceals the fact that each moment is a different period, a different milieu, and even a different language. If the historicist wishes to emphasize the possibility of communication within a given period, he had better not insist that time itself is the decisive differentiating factor that distinguishes one "period" from another.

If time is not the decisive differentiating factor, the following consequence ensues. To say that men of different eras cannot understand each other is really to say that men who exist in significantly different situations and have different perspectives on life cannot understand each other. If it is right to think that all men exist in situations that are significantly different from one another and that all have different perspectives, then the historicist dogma reduces to simple psychologism: men in general, being different from one another, cannot understand the meanings of one another. The saving concepts of *Mitsein* and *Tradition* are mirages. Even though there are always shared elements in a culture which constitute its very substance, *all* men in a culture do not share the same general perspective on life, the same assumptions; they do not always speak the same idiom. It is a naïve abstraction to consider any period in the past or the present as having this kind of homogeneity.

Indeed, the great insight of historicism, as Meinecke has shown, is not that various cultural eras are uniform in themselves and different from one another, but that men are significantly different from one another. Differences of culture are manifestations of this root possibility of differences among men. The Heideggerian version of the historicist insight renders itself meaningless if it denies the ontological status of individuality and uniqueness among men who live in the same culture. Indeed, the concept of a homogeneous present culture is empirically false and cannot suffice to bridge the gap between persons of the same period. That is the real ontological gap—the one that subsists between persons, not the one that subsists between historical eras. If the former can be bridged, as Gadamer and Heidegger admit, then so can the latter, for the historicity of understanding is, in its fundamental significance, merely an instance of the multiplicity of persons.

## Prejudice and Pre-Understanding

The firmest conception and most powerful weapon in Gadamer's attack on the objectivity of interpretation is not the doctrine of historicity but the doctrine of prejudice (*Vorurteil*). This concept is Gadamer's version of a hermeneutic principle that was first clearly perceived by Schleiermacher, then fully elaborated by Dilthey and Husserl, and finally given an existential turn by Heidegger. It will be my purpose in this final section to turn my critique of Gadamer's book to good account by showing how the concept of *Vorurteil* has a significance far more positive than that given it in *Wahrheit und Methode*. I shall suggest, though by necessity briefly, the methodological importance of the doctrine for conducting all forms of textual interpretation.

The doctrine of prejudgment is briefly as follows. The meaning of a text (or anything else) is a complex of submeanings or parts which hang together. (Whenever the parts do not cohere, we confront meaninglessness or chaos, not meaning.) Thus the complex of parts is not a merely mechanical collocation, but relational unity in which the relations of the parts to one another and to the whole constitute an essential aspect of their character as parts. That is, the meaning of a part as a part is determined by its relationship to the whole. Thus, the nature of a partial meaning is dependent on the nature of the whole meaning to which it belongs. From the standpoint of knowledge, therefore, we cannot perceive the meaning of a part until after we have grasped the meaning of the whole, since, only then can we understand the function of the part within the whole. No matter how much we may emphasize the quasi-independence of certain parts or the priority of our encounter with parts before any sense of the whole arises, still we *cannot* understand a part as such until we have a sense of the whole. Dilthey called this apparent paradox the hermeneutic circle and observed that it was not vicious because a genuine dialectic always occurs between our idea of the whole and our perception of the parts that constitute it. Once the dialectic has begun, neither side is totally determined by the other.

The doctrine of pre-understanding is logical or phenomenological rather than empirical, and it would no doubt be very difficult to devise an empirical test for it. Nevertheless, we might take as an example a sentence like "He words me Gyrles" (*Antony and Cleopatra,* Act V). How do we know (if we do know) that "words" is a verb unless we have already dimly grasped the sentence as a whole? We might say something about normal syntax and the grammatical exigencies of "he," "me," and the terminal "s," but that is possible only because we have submerged the normal function of "words."[6] It is conceivable to misread the sentence: "He says 'Gyrles' to me" or "He, that is Gyrles, words me," and such misreadings would imply different preliminary guesses about the nature of the whole. Though it is right to argue that some words of a sentence are always less variable and dependent than others, these are still, at best, simply clues or possibilities that do not become determinate until they fall into place within the whole—no matter how vaguely that whole may be perceived. In fact, this preliminary perception is always vague since it is by necessity, without parts, unarticulated. It is an adumbration, a pre-apprehension rather than an articulated understanding. A close analogy is the dim adumbration of an answer that we must always project in order to ask a question in the first place.

Gadamer's argument for the necessity of *Vorurteil* in interpretation is accomplished by transforming the concept of pre-apprehension into the word "prejudice," for if our understanding of a text is always governed by a pre-understanding, it follows that this preliminary adumbration must come from ourselves since it does not and cannot come from the as yet indeterminate text. What we supply by way of pre-understanding must therefore be constituted by our own expectations, attitudes, and predispositions—in short, from our own prejudices. This is by no means a troublesome conclusion in Gadamer's view. The fact that our interpretations are always governed by our prejudices is really the best guarantee that texts will have significance for us. Instead of trying to overcome our prejudices—an attempt which cannot succeed and can result only in artificial, alien constructions—we should welcome them as the best means of preserving the vitality of our inheritance and our tradition.[7]

The argument is powerful, but clearly its validity depends on the truth of its major premise that pre-apprehensions are identical with or composed of prejudices. If that is so, then the principle tenet of all perspectivistic, psychologistic, and historicistic theories must be true. In fact, however, the substitution of "predisposition" or "prejudice" for "pre-understanding" hides an illicit and false equation. The word "predisposition" or "prejudice" connotes the idea of a preferred or habitual stance, making the equation imply that an interpreter cannot alter his habitual attitudes even if he wants to. But this is false, since interpreters have been known to alter their view of a text's meaning, rare as this occurrence may be. If, on the other hand, prejudice is taken to mean not just the interpreter's habitual attitudes, but the whole array of attitudes that he can adopt, then certainly a pre-apprehension must be a prejudice; however, this becomes an empty tautology since any stance I adopt must ipso facto be possible for me, and the word "prejudice" loses its desired connotations. One could, of course, reply that an interpreter's possible stances are limited by his historicity even though he may to some extent alter his habitual ones, but this again is an assertion that has nothing to do with the logical necessity of pre-understanding. It is merely a repetition of the historicist dogma that we cannot re-cognize past meanings. The notion of *Vorurteil* adds nothing to this previously assumed dogma except to give it a misleading flavor of logical rigor.

The doctrine of pre-understanding is in fact altogether neutral with respect to historicity and prejudice. Ultimately it is no more or less than the doctrine of the logical priority of the hypothesis. The preliminary grasp of a text that we must have before we can understand it is the hermeneutical version of the hypothesis we must have about data before we can make sense of them. (The claim that hypotheses are induced from or generated out of data has lost favor, not least because it fails to explain how differing hypotheses can be generated from the same data.) Pre-understanding is not, of course, a neat and simple model for the hypothetico-deductive process, since the data it explains are constituted to a large extent by the hypothesis itself. That is to say, the contours of the words in a sentence are determined very substantially by our pre-apprehension of the form and meaning of the sentence, whereas in a perfect model the data would act as they chose regardless of our hypothesis about them. This highly constitutive character of hermeneutic hypotheses explains why they tend to be self-confirming and why it is hard to convince anyone to change his interpretation of a text.

However, as Dilthey saw, the hermeneutic hypothesis is not completely self-confirming since it has to compete with rival hypotheses about the same text and is continuously measured against those components of the text which are least dependent on the hypothesis. Thus, one further indication that preliminary hermeneutic hypotheses (pre-apprehensions) are not the same as prejudices is that hypotheses in general cannot be reduced to habitual attitudes or modes of thought. If that were true, new hypotheses could not appear. In fact, nobody knows just how hypotheses arise. Certainly to equate them with predispositions is to reduce all new ideas about data to old prejudices—a strange destiny for a notion like the special theory of relativity, for example.[8]

Since a pre-understanding is a vague hypothesis that is constitutive of understanding, and since understanding is therefore partly dependent on pre-understanding, the problem of achieving a valid pre-apprehension of the text is a crucial problem in interpretation. What is a valid pre-apprehension? Bluntly stated, it is a correct preliminary grasp of the author's meaning. But how unsatisfactory this answer is! There is no way of knowing in advance just what the author may be getting at, and there are so many possible preliminary guesses that the chance of hitting on the right one is extremely slim—so slim, apparently, that a deep skepticism regarding the likelihood of valid interpretation seems warranted.

However, the probability appears less slim, as indeed it is, if we formulate the problem more accurately. To speak individualistically simply in terms of an inaccessible authorial intention is to misrepresent the problem. Our chances of making a correct preliminary guess about the nature of someone's verbal meaning are enormously increased by the limitations imposed on that meaning through cultural norms and conventions. A single linguistic sign can represent an identical meaning for two persons because its possible meanings have been limited by convention. By the same token, the larger linguistic configurations which an interpreter confronts also have this conventional and normative character. This is what makes correct pre-apprehension reasonably likely to occur, for not just words, but sentences, and not just sentences, but utterances as long as *War and Peace* are partly governed by the norms and conventions deposited by previous usages.[9] That is to say, all communicable speech acts, written or spoken, belong to a limited number of genres. Now, a genre is a kind and shape of utterance those norms and conventions have been partly fixed through past usage. Every communicable utterance belongs to a genre so defined, and in communicated speech there can be no such thing as a radically new genre, for so-called new genres are always, by linguistic and social necessity, extensions and variations of existing norms and conventions. The most primitive and fundamental genres are the sentences—the smallest units of communicable speech—but every larger utterance also possesses with varying degrees of rigidity the normative and conventional character of single-sentence utterances.

This is what gives the interpreter's pre-understanding a good chance of being correct, for the author's meaning has a shape and scope that is governed by conventions which the interpreter can share as soon as he is familiar with those conventions.[10] In the process of interpretation, therefore, a preliminary guess or pre-apprehension with respect to a text is really a guess about the genre to which the text belongs, and the most appropriate form of the question, "What is the nature of a valid pre-apprehension?" is the question, "To what genre does this text belong?" Indeed, this is the most important question an interpreter could ask about a text, since its answer implies the way the text should be understood with respect to its shape and emphasis as well as the scope and direction of its meanings.

Schleiermacher, whose aphorisms on interpretation are among the most profound contributions to hermeneutics, deserves credit for first laying bare the fundamental importance of genre. "Uniqueness in speech," he said, "shows itself as a deviation from the characteristics that determine the genre," for in every case of understanding, "the whole is apprehended as genre—*Das Ganze wird ursprünglich verstanden als Gattung*."[11] In this insight Schleiermacher laid the foundation for that ideal discipline which impelled his thinking on hermeneutics—a truly general theory of interpretation. For the concept of genre cuts through all particular varieties of biblical, poetical, historical, and legal interpretation of texts because the notion of genre in itself determines an intrinsic mode of proceeding. To be concerned with the precise genre of a text is to give every text its due and to avoid the external imposition of merely mechanical methods and canons of interpretation.

Finally, the concept of genre calls attention to the necessity of self-critical thinking in interpretation, for there can be no apodictic certainty that our preliminary guess regarding a text's genre is correct. Yet that guess governs and constitutes what we subsequently say about the text. Thus our self-confirming pre-understanding needs to be tested against all the relevant data we can find, for our idea of genre is ultimately a hypothesis like any other, and the best hypothesis is the one that best explains all the relevant data. This identity of genre, pre-understanding, and hypothesis suggests that the much-advertised cleavage between thinking in the sciences and the humanities does not exist. The hypothetico-deductive process is fundamental in both of them, as it is in all thinking that aspires to knowledge.

*Notes*

1. One very important critic has been Emilio Betti whose *Teoria generale della interpretazione* is by far the most significant recent treatise in the tradition of Schleiermacher and Dilthey. In a later booklet, *Die Hermeneutik als allgemeine Methodik der Geisteswissenschaften* (Tübingen, 1962), he takes sharp issue with Gadamer, Bultmann, and their followers.

2. See "Hermeneutic Since Barth," in *The New Hermeneutic*, eds. J. M. Robinson and J. B. Cobb, Jr. (New York, 1964), p. 69.

3. The page references throughout are to Gadamer, *Wahrheit und Methode*. The translations are mine.

4. See *Logische Untersuchungen*, pp. 91–97.

5. Heidegger, *Unterwegs zur Sprache*.

6. These grammatical exigencies are, in any case, components of pre-understanding.

7. Such arguments invariably use the monolithic "we" and "our" and so assume the existence of a nonexistent unanimity and homogeneity.

8. The best discussion of hypotheses in interpretation is to be found in R. S. Crane, *The Languages of Criticism and the Structure of Poetry* (Toronto, 1953), pp. 176–180. Crane implicitly connects the concepts of genre and hypothesis (see pp. 146, 167).

9. Saussure makes an elegant and helpful distinction between "actualities" and "virtualities" in language, the former being usages which have already been realized, and the latter extensions of meaning made possible by the former. Every time a virtuality is actualized, new virtualities are thereby created. See Saussure, *Cours de linguistique générale*.

10. This is not circular, since the probable conventions under which a text was written may be discovered by studying other texts and other authors within his culture.

11. *Hermeneutik*, pp. 46, 47.

# Bibliography to Part Five

Most current discussions of the artist's intentions and their bearing on the content of a work of art are still focused on William Wimsatt and Monroe Beardsley's original paper. Among the earlier papers of interest are:

Henry Aiken, "The Aesthetic Relevance of Artists' Intentions," *Journal of Philosophy* LII (1955), 742–753;

Leslie Fiedler, "Archetype and Signature: A Study of the Relationship Between Biography and Poetry," *Sewanee Review* LX (1952), 253–273;

Isabel Hungerland, "The Concept of Intention in Art Criticism," *Journal of Philosophy* LII (1955), 733–742;

Richard Kuhns, "Criticism and the Problem of Intention," *Journal of Philosophy* LVII (1960), 5–23;

Erwin Panofsky, "The History of Art as a Humanistic Discipline," in T. M. Greene (ed.), *The Meaning of the Humanities* (Princeton, 1940);

Theodore Redpath, "Some Problems of Modern Aesthetics," in C. A. Mace (ed.), *British Philosophy in the Mid-Century* (London, 1957);

Eliseo Vivas, "Mr. Wimsatt on the Theory of Literature," *Comparative Literature* VII (1955), 344–361.

The most prominent survey of the general question of intention, outside the narrow domain of aesthetics, is provided in:

G.E.M. Anscombe, *Intention* (Oxford, 1957).

The literature on intentions has mushroomed since that time, and more recent discussions reflect the newer currents in this larger topic. Among the more interesting recent discussions of the problem of intention in the criticism of the arts are:

Sidney Gendin, "The Artist's Intentions," *Journal of Aesthetics and Art Criticism* XXIII (1964), 193–196;

*Genre* I (July, 1968): Symposium on E. D. Hirsch's views;

Göran Hermerén, "Intention and Interpretation in Literary Criticism," *New Literary History* VII (1975–76), 57–82;

J. Kemp, "The Work of Art and the Artist's Intentions," *British Journal of Aesthetics* IV (1964), 150–151;

Berel Lang, "The Intentional Fallacy Revisited," *British Journal of Aesthetics* XIV (1974), 306–314;

Colin Lyas, "Personal Qualities and the Intentional Fallacy," in *Royal Institute of Philosophy Lectures (1971–1972)*, vol. 6 (London, 1973);

Joseph Margolis, *Art and Philosophy* (Atlantic Highlands, 1980); ch. 8;

David Newton-de Molina (ed.), *On Literary Intention* (Edinburgh, 1976);

Stein H. Olsen, "Authorial Intention," *British Journal of Aesthetics* XIII (1973);

Richard E. Palmer, *Hermeneutics: Interpretation Theory in Schleiermacher, Dilthey, Heidegger, and Gadamer* (Evanston, 1969);

Anthony Savile, "The Place of Intention in the Concept of Art," *Proceedings of the Aristotelian Society* LXIX (1968–1969), 101–124;

William Wimsatt, Jr., "Genesis: A Fallacy Revisited," in P. Demetz *et al.* (eds.), *The Discipline of Criticism* (New Haven, 1968).

The Continental sources must include at least:

Franz Brentano, *Psychology from an Empirical Standpoint,* ed. Oskar Kraus; English Edition ed. Linda L. McAlister (London, 1973);

E. D. Hirsch, Jr., *Validity in Interpretation* (New Haven, 1967);

E. D. Hirsch, Jr., *The Aims of Interpretation* (Chicago, 1976);

Edmund Husserl, *Logical Investigations,* 2 vols., trans. J. N. Findlay (London, 1970);

Edmund Husserl, *Ideas: General Introduction to Pure Phenomenology,* trans. W. R. Boyce Gibson (New York, 1931);

F.D.E. Schleiermacher, *Hermeneutics: The Handwritten Manuscripts,* ed. Heinz Kimmerle, trans. James Duke and Jack Forstman (Missoula, Montana, 1977).

The problem of intention, particularly with respect to literary works but also in general for art as such, has been complicated by recent appeals to the speech-act model of language and the counterpart theory of art as utterance. The speech-act model itself is closely associated with the following:

J. L. Austin, *How To Do Things with Words* (Oxford, 1962);

H. P. Grice, "Meaning," *Philosophical Review* LXVI (1957), 377–388;

John R. Searle, *Speech Acts* (Cambridge, 1969).

Its best-known application, in philosophical aesthetics, to literature is to be found in:

Monroe C. Beardsley, *The Possibility of Criticism* (Detroit, 1970), though this entails a kind of intentionalism.

Other recent efforts to apply the notion to literature include:

Richard Ohmann, "Speech Acts and the Definition of Literature," *Philosophy and Rhetoric* IV (1971), 1–19;

Richard Ohmann, "Speech, Literature and the Space Between," *New Literary History* V (1974), 37–63;

Mary Louise Pratt, *Toward A Speech Act Theory of Literary Discourse* (Bloomington, 1977).

See also:

Umberto Eco, *A Theory of Semiotics* (Bloomington, 1976), for a somewhat confused generalization of the communicative model entailed.

The most sustained current discussions of expression and expressive qualities may be found in:
Guy Sircello, *Mind & Art* (Princeton, 1972);
Alan Tormey, *The Concept of Expression* (Princeton, 1971).


Other earlier, well-known discussions of expression include:
Rudolf Arnheim, "The Gestalt Theory of Expression," *Philosophical Review* LVI (1949), 156–171;
Rudolf Arnheim, "The Priority of Expression," *Journal of Aesthetics and Art Criticism* VIII (1949), 106–109;
Otto Baensch, "Art and Feeling," in Susanne K. Langer (ed.), *Reflections on Art* (Baltimore, 1958);
John Benson, "Emotion and Expression," *Philosophical Review* LXXVI (1967), 335–357;
O. K. Bouwsma, "The Expression Theory of Art," reprinted in William Elton (ed.), *Aesthetics and Language* (Oxford, 1954);
Karl Britton, "Feelings and their Expression," *Philosophy* XXXII (1957), 97–111;
John Hospers, "The Concept of Artistic Expression," reprinted (revised) in Morris Weitz (ed.), *Problems in Aesthetics* (New York, 1959);
Susanne K. Langer, *Feeling and Form* (New York, 1953), chapter 3;
Susanne K. Langer, *Problems of Art* (New York, 1957);
Douglas Morgan, "The Concept of Expression in Art," in *Science, Language, and Human Rights* (Philadelphia, 1952);
Vincent Tomas, "The Concept of Expression in Art," in *Science, Language, and Human Rights* (Philadelphia, 1952);


Other more recent statements include:
John Hospers (ed.), *Artistic Expression* (New York, 1971);
George F. Todd, "Expression without Feeling," *Journal of Aesthetics and Art Criticism* XXX (1972);
Richard Wollheim, "On Expression and Expressionism," *Revue Internationale de Philosophie* XVIII (1964), 270–289;
Richard Wollheim, "Expression," in *Royal Institute of Philosophy Lectures* (1966–67), vol. 1.


On expression in music, see:
Donald Callen, "Transfiguring the Emotions in Music," in Joseph Margolis (ed.), *The Worlds of Art and the World* (Amsterdam, 1984), pp. 69–91;
Peter Kivy, *The Corded Shell; Reflections on Musical Expression* (Princeton, 1980);
Peter Kivy, *Sound and Semblance; Reflections on Musical Representation* (Princeton, 1984);
Paul Thom, "The Corded Shell Strikes Back," in Margolis, *The Worlds of Art and the World*, pp. 92–108.


See, also, Bibliography to Part Four.

The classic target of most earlier discussions of expression is found in:
Benedetto Croce, *Aesthetic,* trans. Douglas Ainslie, 2nd ed. (London, 1922). Also of interest in this regard are:
R. G. Collingwood, *The Principles of Art* (Oxford, 1938), chapters 6–7, 9; Alan Donagan, "The Croce-Collingwood Theory of Art," *Philosophy* XXXIII (1958), 162–167.
John Hospers, "The Croce-Collingwood Theory of Art," *Philosophy* XXXI (1956), 3–20.
Milton Nahm, "The Philosophy of Aesthetic Expression; The Crocean Hypothesis," *Journal of Aesthetics and Art Criticism* XIII (1955), 458–468.

On the question of style, see the lively discussion in:
Berel Lang (ed.), *The Concept of Style* (Philadelphia, 1979);
also,
Nelson Goodman, *Ways of Worldmaking* (Indianapolis, 1978), II.

# Part Six
# The Objectivity of Criticism
# and Interpretation

The most strategic question to raise about a theory of criticism is, What is the author's theory of the nature of a work of art? Alternative views of the fundamental nature of art force us to adopt alternative views about the objectivity and possible truth of particular critical claims and judgments; and insistence that interpretive and evaluative judgments can or cannot be straightforwardly true or false draws in its wake a suitably congruent conception of what it is to be a work of art. Thus, theorists who construe works of art as, or on the model of, standard physical objects are inclined to construe interpretive judgments as hardly more than a difficult species of description; and those who treat works of art as rather complex entities of a cultural sort will be more hospitable to the view that the work of interpretation may not be restricted to discovering or "unearthing" properties somehow merely hidden in an artwork. Correspondingly, those theorists who claim that works of art are, in some sense, fully perceptually accessible may, if they think that works of art have inherent value, actually hold that evaluative judgments are equally true or false; and those who believe that values cannot inhere in objects like discriminable properties or who believe that appraisals of value depend on considerations going well beyond perceivable qualities will be disposed to concede the joint defensibility of competing evaluations—if any can be objectively defended at all.

Objectivity in criticism begins to appear, therefore, as a complex and controversial matter. On the simplest view, objective judgments are true because they conform in the appropriate way to the actual properties that works of art possess. On a more generous view, judgments are objectively true because, although they ascribe properties or values that cannot all be supposed to inhere independently in artworks themselves, they conform to what are taken to be the correct canons for such ascriptions. On a more extreme view, critical judgments can be defended on the basis of canons of relevance or of certain minimal constraints of objectivity—for instance, as exhibiting congruence with what are admitted to be the objectively describable properties of particular works—but not in a way that would exclude all otherwise incompatible judgments. Here, we are obliged to retreat from the severe and exclusive alternatives of truth and falsity to such weaker values as plausibility or reasonableness; but, if we wish, we may still speak of objectivity, the objectivity with which, say, plausible interpretations or reasonable appraisals may be made.

Obviously, what is at stake is the rejection or acceptance of some form of relativism in interpretation, evaluation, and appreciation. Some hold that relativism is basically incoherent, since it would require that a given judgment must be both true and false. But this is a mistake if, as suggested, we may temper our conception of objectivity by retreating from a model of truth and falsity to a weaker set of values such as plausibility. If, reflecting on the practice of criticism, we are persuaded that greater conceptual flexibility must be admitted than the simpler version of objectivity would allow, we must be prepared to make corresponding adjustments both in our theory of critical judgments and in our theory of the nature of art. Or if, theorizing about art itself, we are led to the view that we cannot in principle preclude the validity of otherwise incompatible claims or the legitimacy of alternative ways of responding to particular works, then we must be prepared to make adjustments both in our theory of the function of criticism and of the logic of judgments.

The extreme alternatives with respect to the entire range of criticism—adhering still to some conception of objectivity—are dialectically represented in the theories of Monroe Beardsley (1970) and Joseph Margolis (1976). Throughout his career, focused principally in his influential book *Aesthetics: Problems in the Philosophy of Criticism* (1958), Beardsley has been identified with the most uncompromising version of objectivity in judgment. This has for example entailed a strenuous rejection of the authority or relevance of an author's or artist's intention (see Part Five), on the grounds that the work of art is a self-contained object accessible in some perceptually fair sense to the objective appreciation of competent agents (see Parts One and Three). Beardsley has pursued this theme in great detail through all its ramifications in the domain of aesthetics. He has, therefore, provided us with a fully fashioned theory of art and criticism committed to the seemingly neutral thesis that the central judgments of aesthetic concern—the description, interpretation, evaluation of art—are simply true or false. Margolis has attempted to construct an alternative account of comparable range (*Art and Philosophy* [1978]): he assigns a metaphysical complexity to art, in virtue of which the kind of objectivity Beardsley would sustain cannot be defended; and he construes the actual work of critics and of the appreciative efforts of amateurs of art as requiring and supporting the defensibility of claims and judgments that would be contradictory on the model of truth and falsity.

The issues at stake may be summarized in the following way. The theory of objective judgment of any kind must be matched with a theory of the nature of the domain with respect to which exemplary objectivity obtains. On the most conventional philosophical view—now under considerable fire in both the Anglo-American and Continental traditions—objectivity entails either the full applicability of the bipolar truth values, true and false, to all bona fide judgments or that condition plus the even more strenuous condition that all pertinent domains are cognitively transparent to a correctly disciplined inquiry. These are certainly close to Beardsley's assumptions. Nevertheless, it is theoretically quite possible to retreat from both those conditions, distributively, without necessarily giving up a viable conception of objectivity. One may, for instance, complicate the notion of transparency in progressively strenuous ways—moving through Kantian, through Hegelian, through Marxist, through Husserlian, through Heideggerian, through hermeneutic, through deconstructive, challenges without at all abandoning minimal notions of discipline fitted, however carefully, to the recognizable work of habituated inquiries. Correspondingly, one may, on a characterization of a given domain—for instance, regarding the structure, boundaries, properties, integrity, fixity of literary texts—theorize that only truth-like values weaker than the bipolar values *would* be objectively supported by a responsible inquiry. Here, objectivity comes to favor questions of ontological and epistemological relevance and of whatever rigor may be ascribed to the practices of inquiry thereupon preferred. Viewed against such a backdrop, relativism is simply the reasoned retreat—distributively—to truth-values weaker than the bipolar pair—*not* the defense of contradictory claims (Pythagoreanism, on some views) or the defense of radically compartmentalized inquiries incommensurable with others seemingly addressed to the same or very closely related claims (radical incommensurabilism).

Still, the posting of critical judgments by persons of some authority and the responses of others of some sensibility suggest a further complication: appreciation does not appear to be compelled by arguments however fairly managed. Sometimes, the issue has been pursued in terms of an emotivist theory of values, so that no reasons—taken simply as reasons rather than as influencing causes—could lead one to a certain judgment. Sometimes, the issue is more convincingly viewed in terms of the difference between value judgments or verdicts and appreciative responses. Arnold Isenberg, in a relatively early paper (1949), had pursued the latter distinction in an influential way. The issue in fact lends itself to several divergent theses—that are not quite clearly sorted by Isenberg himself: one stresses that the logic of critical arguments cannot be taken to govern the critically informed responses of an aesthetically engaged agent; another stresses that when he makes a critical judgment or verdict about a work of art, an informed agent is actually responding for quite particular reasons, in a context in which there are no pertinent arguments of a logically compelling form. The second thesis is, in fact, closer to Isenberg's view, though the first provides a viable alternative. One might also insist on a difference between arguments leading to entailed conclusions and arguments, as in appreciative and verdictive settings, that favor certain conclusions, not by strict entailment and not by any usual inductive canon. Claims similar to Isenberg's, somewhat more generalized regarding the propriety of viewing appreciation in terms of judgments that would take truth-values, may be found also in Roger Scruton (1974) and Alan Tormey (1973). Part at least of the motivation for such views may be offset by invoking relativism—but not all. The question these theorists must face is, *what* discipline can be assigned the pertinent judgments? what supporting reasons or grounds? what weight to argument? For when these considerations are pressed, it is difficult to see how to avoid the normal concerns of objectivity.

Actually, value judgments are ubiquitous in aesthetics. In a sense, one thinks of the analysis of these as the aesthetician's most distinctive concern. The discussion of recent years still shows the marked influence of Immanuel Kant's neat and exclusive division of moral and aesthetic judgments (see Part One) and of G. E. Moore's exposure of the so-called Naturalistic Fallacy. Nevertheless, to some extent, the Kantian emphasis loses its force as it becomes clear that moral judgments may well be appreciative and not, as such, concerned to direct anyone's conduct and that aesthetic judgments (as in the criticism of a work in progress) may well be intended to direct another's efforts and, in doing so, come to construe these efforts as the solving of a practical problem. Also, the force of Moore's criticism declines as philosophers attempt (as they do) to treat evaluation in terms of certain distinctive uses to which sentences are put rather than in terms of the qualities that may be found in things. Isenberg's analysis has a somewhat Kantian-like quality in the sense that the logical distinction of critical judgments is to be marked out, but it goes substantially beyond Kant's observations in the sense both that the relevant considerations cannot be squared with a Kantian scheme of things and that something of the actual reasoning that lies behind a critical judgment is developed. If one were to look for a related thesis elsewhere in the literature of aesthetics, perhaps the most useful comparison that might recommend itself would be to Frank Sibley's well-known paper (see Part

One). There is also a certain Moorian quality to Isenberg's account, except that the particular features of a work that the critic sorts out are not, apparently, actual bits of goodness or beauty spotted so to say, but rather features that, for a given critic, enlist his preference or an expression of his (informed) taste. Comparison with Santayana suggests itself. Complications regarding validity obviously abound.

Value-laden remarks range themselves in an extensive spectrum. There are comments that merely express our taste; there are comments that express our appreciation; there are comments that appraise and rank and grade works of art; there are commendations and recommendations that we make. We may expect, therefore, that there will be no simple, comprehensive theory of evaluation that will hold for the variety of remarks we are to account for.

We may, however, simplify certain of the principal distinctions in the following way. Let us admit that, sometimes, remarks that assign some value to a work of art are merely expressions of one's own particular taste, that is, of one's own likes or dislikes. These are, surely, idiosyncratic, at best matters of fact, and call for no justification (though taste may itself be evaluated). Let us admit, further, that some remarks are appreciative, that is, assign some value to a work of art for relevant reasons. One's taste will not be mentioned here: the reasons one supplies to another will not include mention of one's own likes and dislikes (though these will be expected to be in accord with the remarks made). Another may confirm that the reasons given do mention features that can be noticed in the work and that reasons of the sort given are pertinent to appreciation. But since taste is involved, no one else is bound to appreciate the work for the same reasons and in the same way. Hence, one may be called on to defend or make plausible and clear his own appreciative attitude toward a given work, but he cannot be called on to show that his appreciation is true or correct; his appreciative remarks cannot be disputed beyond a measure of plausibility, except in the uninteresting sense that he may have contradicted himself or made an error regarding some quality of the work in question. Finally, we may admit that works of art may be evaluated, that is, judged to have this or that sort of merit on grounds that do not concern one's own likes and dislikes (whatever they may be). And these judgments may be open to full dispute, though not necessarily to bipolar values.

To concede these possibilities, however, is to concede the need that Isenberg's account imposes on us to pursue the distinctions he himself alludes to. And to concede that is to return us to the dialectical alternatives posed by Beardsley's and Margolis's claims. I. C. Jarvie (1967) has, for one, vigorously pressed the need for distinguishing response and judgment in criticism. In doing so, he has attended in an exploratory way to the difficulty of locating the objectivity of criticism, to the realistic sense in which argument appears to break down in the context of aesthetic dispute, to the need for avoiding subjectivism. His useful suggestion is that the objectivity of criticism lies in the nature of institutions rather than in formulable rules. But he tends somewhat to assimilate relativism to subjectivism and he does not say precisely how appeal to institutions can preclude a form of relativism.

Within the Continental tradition, the challenge to simplistic theories of objectivity comes mainly from two directions: one, emphasis on a strongly historicized view of the interpretation of texts and artworks *and* of the meaningful integrity of texts and artworks themselves (hermeneutics); the other, emphasis on the questionable and question-begging presumption of the fixable identity and unity, in any given interval of attention, of anything that could be regarded as a text or artwork (deconstruction and post-structuralism). The first theme is most effectively developed by Hans-Georg Gadamer (1975); the second, by Roland Barthes (1979). Developments of both sorts are profoundly influenced by the intersection of the remarkably different interests of Husserl's phenomenology and Nietzsche's perspectivism—particularly as those come together in Heidegger's speculations.

Gadamer is certainly the leading figure of contemporary hermeneutics. Generally speaking, he insists, with Wilhelm Dilthey, on the radical distinction of the human world and the human studies; but, unlike Dilthey and opposed to Dilthey's own attempt to construct a novel, Kantian-like critique and method for the human sciences, as well as opposed to any pretensions favoring the unity of science program, Gadamer pretty well dismisses questions of method and refuses to feature (without utterly disallowing) questions of truth. This, of course, is why Hirsch (see Part Five) is so much opposed to Gadamer's version of hermeneutics. Gadamer's master theme is that of the "fusion of horizons." His idea (thus far in accord with Heidegger) is that human existence is inherently historicized. Since that is so, our history is continuous with the history in which the artists of the past have formed the very culture in which we live. To live responsively in one's own time is to absorb the "prejudices" of that time (another Heideggerian theme—also, in a way, a Husserlian theme); to respond to the texts of the past is to respond to the way in which they still "speak" to our (new) prejudices. The authentic process in which the implied dialogue obtains is the fusion of the horizons of some putative past vision and whatever is the present vision. But Gadamer resists what he takes to be the subversive, relativistic import of Heidegger's theme. In fact, he insists that there is one inclusive tradition (presumably of the Western world) that moves and collects and changes conservatively within the flux of historical time. It is for this reason, perhaps, that he emphasizes more the authenticity of responding to texts than the objectivity with which interpretive judgments are assessed. But essential to his position is the denial of the fixity of textual meaning, of its reduction to authorial intent, and of its discernibility by way of applying professional canons of any sort; and these themes are increasingly shared by a variety of philosophical approaches not themselves committed to a narrowly hermeneutic approach.

Barthes's essay is, by now, a rather famous piece of purple. But it remains peculiarly canny and perceptive, and it affords what may well be the briefest introduction to the more florid forms of French post-structuralist thought—sympathetic at once with Jacques Derrida's deconstruction and with Michel Foucault's version of Nietzschean perspectivism. Barthes himself had practiced as a fairly conventional structuralist of the Saussurean stripe. But in *S/Z* (1974), he completely subverts the literal program of the structuralists, showing instead—very much in accord with the spirit of "From Work to Text"—how it may simply be used to transform a "writerly" text into a "readerly" text (see, also, *The Pleasure of the Text*, 1975). The point of Barthes's essay (and later work), and the point of what has come to be called the "erotics of reading," is to reject utterly the pretensions of *system* of every sort: say, with respect to interpretation as well as with respect to fixing the boundaries of what is to be interpreted. The "text" becomes in a sense a viable way of focusing the entire sprawling materials of our culture. But, Barthes insists, the Text is inherently "plural," incapable of being finally or reliably captured by any formalizable approach—or even of being incrementally analyzed by any persistent program. Extreme as it may be, Barthes's theme, then, cannot fail to remind us of the more cautious themes of Gadamer's work—and of the salient lines of criticism now dominating the whole of Western philosophy.

# 24.    The Testability of an Interpretation
### MONROE C. BEARDSLEY

Surely there are many literary works of which it can be said that they are understood better by some readers than by others. It is that fact that makes interpretation possible and (sometimes) desirable.

For if A understands *Sordello* better than B does, he may be able to help B understand what he understands but B does not. No doubt there are many ways in which A might do this. One is by reading the poem aloud in a manner that reflects his understanding of it. Another is by telling B what the work means; and any such statement, or set of statements, used to report discovered meaning in a literary text I shall call a "literary interpretation" or (for brevity in the present context) "interpretation."

Common usage among critics and literary theorists seems to sanction this broad definition of the term, and I resign myself to it here, though I hold out hope for distinguishing "interpretation" in a narrower sense from two other operations of literary exegesis.[1] I would prefer to reserve the term "interpretation" for exposing what I call the "themes" and "theses" of a literary work; the term "explication" for exposing the marginal or implicit meanings of words, phrases, and sentences (metaphors, for instance); and the term "elucidation" for exposing implied features of the world of the work (inferred motivations and character traits, for instance). On this occasion I shall conform to general practice by considering all three critical operations as acts of interpretation, and the sentences produced by these operations as interpretation-statements. Explication is evidently the most basic; since we can hardly be sure we know what is going on in a poem, much less what it symbolizes or says about the world, until we understand the interrelationships of meaning at the level of verbal texture.

From Monroe C. Beardsley, *The Possibility of Criticism* (Detroit: Wayne State University Press, 1970). Reprinted with permission of the author and Wayne State University Press.

## 1

One of the main and recurrent themes [here favored] might be called the vindication of critical rationality. Put less pretentiously, my thesis (or one of them) is that the processes of criticism, when they are performed well, have much reasonableness in them. The deliberations the critic goes through in his characteristic commerce with literary texts are rational deliberations, in important part; and the conclusions he reaches through them are (or can be) reasonable conclusions, in that reasons can be given to support their claims to truth.

Even if these generalizations have an appearance of acceptability when cast in abstract form, they may well become dubitable when applied to particular sorts of critical statement. That is what we have to find out. It must be acknowledged that the issues are complex and debatable.

For one thing, some critical theorists have recently emphasized the element of creativity in interpretation. By comparing literary interpretation with the performing artist's interpretation of score or script (which is a vital cooperation with the composer or dramatist in perfecting an actual aesthetic object), they have suggested that the literary interpreter, too, has a certain leeway, and does not merely "report" on "discovered meaning," as I said earlier, but puts something of his own into the work; so that different critics may produce different but equally legitimate interpretations, like two sopranos or two ingenues working from the same notations. I find myself rather severe with this line of thought. There is plenty of room for creativity in literary interpretation, if that means thinking of new ways of reading the work, if it means exercising sensitivity and imagination. But the moment the critic begins to use the work as an occasion for promoting his own ideas, he has abandoned the task of interpretation. Yet can we really draw a line here? That is the question.

The literary interpreter can be likened to practitioners of many other trades—not only to the singer and dancer but to the coal miner, the hunter, the pilgrim, and the rapist. Each of these similitudes casts light on aspects of his work, but none is perfectly just. For his results, unlike theirs, issue in the form of statements. He claims to supply information we lack. And such a claim, when it could be challenged, calls for the support of reasons. The critic cannot avoid, in some way, *arguing*.[2]

Nevertheless, the view persists—and even grows—that there is something peculiar about interpretation-statements that gives them a distinct logical status and makes them undeserving of the adjectives that we apply to ordinary claims to provide information. Consider, for example, Stuart Hampshire's remark in a symposium on interpretation a few years ago:

> If correctness is taken to imply finality, then I see no reason to accept this as the right epithet of praise for a critical interpretation. Some

interpretations are impossible, absurd, unplausible, farfetched, strained, inappropriate, and the object does not permit many of the interpretations that have been suggested. But the epithet of praise is more likely to be "illuminating," "plausible," even "original," also "interesting." "True interpretation" is an unusual form of words in the context of criticism. "Correct interpretation" does sometimes occur in these contexts; but it isn't standard and even less is it universal.[3]

That interpretations may be original and interesting, I would not wish to deny, though I would consider such praise faint enough to qualify as ironic condemnation. (If all you can say of my interpretation of a poem is that it is "interesting," I somehow do not feel I have convinced you.) It may be that we are not usually given to saying things like "Your interpretation is true," though "Your interpretation is false" strikes me as a little more familiar. Certainly interpretations are "right" or "wrong," and there are *mis*interpretations. Moreover, the statements that are given as interpretations ("This poem has such-and-such a meaning") can be called true or false without embarrassment at the idiom. Indeed, if they could not be true or false, I do not see how they could be illuminating or plausible. Hampshire objects to the phrase "correct interpretation" because it implies some rule of procedure to which the interpretative act conforms. I agree that the implication is there; I think it belongs there.

Hampshire's conditional at the beginning of the quotation "If correctness is taken to imply finality" brings out another reason why he thinks that interpretations are not true or false, strictly speaking: "it is typical of works of art that they should normally be susceptible of some interpretation and not susceptible of just one interpretation."[4] It is typical of the practice of criticism, especially in our own time (when the incentives to come up with novel interpretations, and the rewards of doing so, are great), that works of art are subjected to constant reinterpretation. But Hampshire's implication is that there can be no way of choosing among multiple interpretations, and no ground for regarding any particular one as most acceptable or exclusively acceptable. I do not agree. However, this question has been discussed more extensively by Joseph Margolis, to whose views I now turn.[5]

Margolis says that an interpretation can be "reasonable," but not "simply true or false."[6] I find this position puzzling. For I do not see how an interpretation could be reasonable unless reasons can be given to show its superiority to some alternatives; and I do not see how the reasons could count unless they are reasons for thinking it true. But Margolis's main thesis is that

> The philosophically most interesting feature of critical interpretation is its tolerance of alternative and seemingly contrary hypotheses. . . . Given the goal of interpretation, we do not understand that an admissible account necessarily precludes all others incompatible with it.[7]

Margolis points me out as one of those who has espoused the old-fashioned view that if two proposed interpretations of an aesthetic object are logically incompatible, then at least one of them must be rejected. It is, he says, a mistake to think that "there is some ideal object of criticism toward which all relevant experiences of a given work converge. . . . If we simply examine the practice of critics, I think we shall find no warrant at all for the claim."

My own examination of the practice of critics has led me to question this sweeping statement. I find the critic Samuel Hynes, for example, contrasting the opinions of Clark Emery and Hugh Kenner on the *Cantos* and adding: "Obviously they cannot both be right; if the passage describes an earthly paradise, then it cannot be a perversion of nature."[8] I find E. D. Hirsch remarking: "No doubt Coleridge understood *Hamlet* rather differently from Professor Kittredge. The fact is reflected in their disparate interpretations. . . . Both of them would have agreed that at least one of them must be wrong."[9] I find Frank Kermode commenting in a similar vein on the line between "liberty" and "license" in interpretation.[10]

We do not discover, according to Margolis's view, that interpretations are true or false, but only that they are "plausible"—and though two incompatible statements cannot both be true, they can both be plausible. But plausibility is at least an appearance of truth based upon some relevant evidence, and any statement that is plausible must be *in principle* capable of being shown to be true or false. Margolis does not deal with any of the sorts of real-life dispute over interpretation that exercise critics most—for example, Wordsworth's Lucy poem, discussed [earlier in Beardley's text]. It seems that when he is talking about interpretations, he has in mind a Freudian or Marxist or Christian "interpretation." This is bringing to bear upon the work an "admissible myth,"[11] or looking at the work through the eyes of some such grand system. If that is the kind of thing that is in question, then I have no quarrel with his principle of tolerance. The story of "Jack and the Beanstalk," for example, can no doubt be taken as Freudian symbolism, as a Marxist fable, or as Christian allegory. I emphasize the phrase "can be taken as." It is true that "readings" such as these need not exclude each other. But the reason is surely that they do not bring out of the work something that lies momentarily hidden in it; they are rather ways of *using* the work to illustrate a preexistent system of thought. Though they are sometimes called "interpretations" (since this word is extremely obliging), they merit a distinct label, like *superimpositions*.

The issue between Margolis and myself, then, can be stated in this way: he holds that all interpretations have what he calls a "logical weakness," i.e., they tolerate each other even when they are incompatible. In contradiction to this view, I hold that there are a great many interpretations that obey what might be called the principle of "the Intolerability of Incompatibles," i.e., if two of them are logically incompatible, they cannot both be true. Indeed, I hold that *all* the literary interpretations that deserve the name obey this principle. But of course I do not wish to deny that there are cases of ambiguity where *no* interpretation can be established over its rivals; nor do I wish to deny that there are many cases where we cannot be sure that we have the correct interpretation.

## 2

Interpretations come in various sizes as well as shapes: some apply to individual words, phrases, or sentences, and thus concern what I call "local meanings" of the text; others purport to say what is meant by the work as a whole or some large part of it, and I shall call the meanings they claim to establish "regional meanings." The regional meanings (when they call for interpretation) evidently depend on the local ones. Consider once again the Lucy poem, and the question whether there is a hint of pantheism in its second stanza.

The poem is not explicitly pantheistic like, for example, the "Lines Composed a Few Miles above Tintern Abbey":

> And I have felt
> A presence that disturbs me with the joy
> Of elevated thoughts; a sense sublime
> Of something far more deeply interfused,
> Whose dwelling is the light of setting suns,
> And the round ocean and the living air,
> And the blue sky, and in the mind of man:
> A motion and a spirit, that impels
> All thinking things, all objects of all thought,
> And rolls through all things.

(It is interesting to note how "rolls" and "things" are used in this passage.) If there is pantheism in "A Slumber Did My Spirit Seal," it must be brought into the poem indirectly, either by the connotations of the words or by the suggestions (that is, the non-logical implications) of the syntax. Let us examine one problem of each type.

First, what I call "*suggestion.*" The words "rocks" and "stones" and "trees" are placed in parallel syntactical situations, and this suggests, quite definitely, that the objects they denote are similar in some important respect. But a suggestion that two different things are similar can go in either direction, and we have to decide between them. Melvin Rader, in his recent book on Wordsworth's philosophy, says that Wordsworth (taking him as the speaker in this poem) "evidently felt that Lucy in her grave was wholly assimilated to inorganic things."[12] But is this evident? She is assimilated to rocks and stones and trees—but trees are certainly not inorganic things. Rader seems to take the parallelism as suggesting that the trees (and a fortiori the dead Lucy) are like rocks and stones, blind passive victims of external mechanical forces. But one could take the comparison the other way and come out with the opposite interpretation: by putting the word "trees" at the end, the speaker gives it emphasis; therefore, he is really suggesting that rocks and stones (and a fortiori the dead Lucy) are like trees in having an inner life of their own.

Thus we can bring the issue to a fairly sharp decision point. If the speaker is suggesting that Lucy and trees are like rocks and stones, we have a hint of mechanistic materialism. If he is suggesting that rocks and stones and Lucy are like trees, then we have a hint of pantheism (or at least animism).

Consider next a connotation problem. The speaker says that the dead Lucy has no force, no motion, and no sense-awareness—but then he says that she does have a motion, after all, since she lies near the surface of the earth and thus participates fully in its rotation. She is "rolled round in earth's diurnal course." The question is, How much can we legitimately find in the meaning of "rolled" here? Now the available repertoire of connotations for the word "rolled" is certainly quite rich. We can open up some of them by thinking of kinds of motion that we would strictly describe as "rolling"—that of the billiard ball, the snowball on the hill, the hoop propelled by a child. By exploring these familiar contexts for the term in its literal standard uses, we remind ourselves of the various forms of motion that can be classified as rolling. And by contrasting these forms of motion, we inventory the potential connotations of the term. There are steady boring motions, ungainly decelerating motions (the wagon rolling to a stop), scary accelerating motions (the car rolling downhill), etc. But what about the present context? Here what must strike us forcibly is the way the other words in this line qualify and specify the motion that Lucy has: it is a regular motion, with a constant rate; it is a comparatively slow and gentle motion, since one revolution takes twenty-four hours; it is an orderly motion, since it follows a simple circular path.

In none of these respects is it terrifying or demeaning; if anything, it is comforting and elevating. If we accept these connotations, the poem contains a hint of pantheism, or at least animism.

If these little exercises in close reading have a point, then, interpreting this poem is not a matter of willfully superimposing some precast intellectual scheme upon it. There really is something in the poem that we are trying to dig out, though it is elusive. And if we do come up with a decision, the interpretation-statement in which we express it will be subject to that fine principle of the Intolerability of Incompatibles. (If the poem is pantheistic, it is *not* non-pantheistic.)

In this discussion, I have strewn a number of ifs in my wake, and now is the time to convert them into categorical assertions. I have been giving a very simple model of a process if interpretation, showing how, if we can decide on the local meanings (connotations and suggestions), we can support the regional interpretations (such as that a poem is pantheistic). My defense of literary interpretation, then, has to go back to the basic premises and to the basic problem, which is the problem of meaning itself.

The issue we must now confront is precisely whether we ought to call these connotations and suggestions meanings at all—strictly speaking. It will no doubt be agreed that the word "rolled" does have a meaning, which the dictionary will supply: it applies to rotary motions of macroscopic objects, let us say, but not to other sorts of motion. To talk this way is indeed to talk about the meaning of a word, and such talk can be tested by empirical (that is, lexicographical) inquiry. But when it comes to the connotations of the word, are we on the same safe ground? When we say, for example, that the word can hint at a fearsome sort of motion or a gentle motion, at monotonous repetition or at steadiness and order—where do we get these ideas? The dictionary does not report them, and we are not obliged to take them into account when we ordinarily use the word in speaking of wheels, balls, hoops, etc.

Perhaps these connotations should not be considered part of meaning, strictly speaking, at all, but rather as psychological associations that individual readers may or may not be inclined to have when they read the word. In that case, no one could be told that he has to have these associations, or ought to have them, or that he has failed to understand the poem if he does not have them. The interpreter, according to that view, could only report his own associations, which might or might not chance to correspond with others'; and if another interpreter reported opposed associations, all we could ask is that he be equally sincere. Such reports would no longer be incompatible; nor would they give information about the meaning of the poem.

A consistent defender of this skeptical view of interpretation will no doubt extend his position to cover suggestions as well. Suppose one critic reports that Wordsworth's line about rocks and stones and trees suggests to him that the first two are as alive as the third, and another reports that it suggests to him that the third is as dead as the first two. Again both reports may be sincere, and therefore incorrigible, confessions of psychological response. But, according to the skeptic, the critics are not talking about anything that can be called the meaning of the poem; and so again their interpretations cannot be regarded as testable or as interpersonally valid.

If connotations and suggestions are not a part of meaning but something psychological and personal, then the alleged regional meanings that depend on them must be equally subjective and relative. It follows that the statement that Wordsworth's poem is pantheistic has the same status as the statements I have called "superimpositions." The interpreter is simply showing one way of taking the poem, and he cannot exclude others.

The question is, then, Are the connotations and the suggestions in poetry really part of the poem's meaning? To answer this question, we shall have to consider the nature of meaning.

*3*

I propose to bring to bear upon our present problem a most interesting and persuasive account of meaning that has been worked out by William Alston and the late J. L. Austin, following out Ludwig Wittgenstein's original insights into language.[13] This account begins with the concept of a certain sort of verbal action, one that essentially requires the use of units of language, namely sentences or (in special cases) utterances that are understood to be substitutes for sentences. It has not so far been possible to give a satisfactory general characterization of these linguistic acts; the most helpful clue to recognizing them is that suggested by Austin. He distinguished between the acts that we perform *in* using sentences (these he called "illocutionary acts") and acts that we perform *by* using sentences (these he called "perlocutionary acts"). In using language, we may assert, argue, ask, order, promise, beg, appraise, implore, advise, consent, etc. *By means of* such acts, we may achieve certain effects upon other people: we may convince, inspire, enroll, please, enrage, inform, deceive, etc. In general, these results can also be obtained in other ways than be using language, but when they are obtained by means of language, then the language-user is performing a perlocutionary act. An illocutionary act may be intended to produce effects: for example, you argue to convince, you command to influence conduct. But whether or not you succeed in convincing, you have still argued, if you have used certain sentences in certain ways; and a command that is not obeyed is still a command.

The basic Wittgensteinian insight was that using language is a form of activity that is guided by rules—it was for this reason that he frequently used the analogy of playing games, and spoke of "language-games." Alston's proposal is that the difference between one type of illocutionary act and another is a matter of the rules that we tacitly submit ourselves to in choosing the appropriate form of expression. For example, suppose I want to tell someone to do something. I can say, "I command you to do it" or "I advise you to do it" (there are numerous alternatives, of course). The difference lies in what I implicitly "represent" to be the case in using these expressions.[14] When I command I claim to be in a position of authority over the person I am speaking to; but I can advise without claiming authority.

Now I can, of course, command or advise without saying "I command" or "I advise." I may choose a form of words that, by some convention, represents the speaker as being, or as not being, in a position of authority—as certain forms of written discourse constitute military orders, or the prescription blank purports to be the issuance of a physician. If I simply say, "Send in your resignation," and this utterance by itself would be, under the circumstances, ambiguous, I can provide a context that makes it a command or a piece of advice. Suppose I say to someone, "Send in your resignation." He might ask whether I have any authority over him; and if I admit that I have none, then I am admitting that I was not commanding. Or, to put the matter another way, if I should say to him, "I know I have no authority over you, but I command you to send in your resignation," I would be talking a kind of nonsense.

By exploring the conditions that are represented as holding in performing a particular sort of illocutionary act, we can characterize each type of act and distinguish one type from another. Some of these sets of conditions are complicated and subtle, and require much careful analysis. For example, when I promise someone to do something, what are the represented conditions? Some of them can easily be stated:

In promising Y to do A, X represents
(1) that A is an action by X,
(2) that A is within X's power,
(3) that A is a future action,
(4) that Y wants X to do A,
(5) that X intends to do A.

There are others. Notice again that the act of promising does not depend on its results; even if X does not keep his word, he has still made the promise. But other elements of the illocutionary act are essential to its nature: X cannot promise (strictly speaking) that someone else will do something (he can promise that he will make the other person do it, though); X cannot promise today to do something yesterday. Such promises are void. It is true that in one sense X can promise to do something he knows he cannot do, or does not intend to do (then his promise is insincere), but to promise seriously is to make a commitment to sincerity.

We are to think of these conditions as so many rules that are tacitly recognized by the speech community in which these illocutionary acts are performed. When a sentence in a particular language can be used to perform a certain illocutionary act—when, that is, its use is understood as involving the speaker's representing certain conditions to hold—then it may be said to have a certain "illocutionary-act potential." This illocutionary-act potential of a sentence is what Alston identifies as its *meaning*. And further he proposes to say that when two sentences have the same illocutionary-act potential, then they have the same meaning.

It seems clear that we can speak of the meanings of sentences in this way, but ordinarily it is more common to speak of the meanings of words. Alston explains this notion ingeniously by pointing out that the words that appear in sentences make their distinctive contribution to the meanings of those sentences.

> Thus it would seem plausible to think of two words as having the same meaning if and only if they make the same contribution to the illocutionary-act potentials of the sentences in which they occur; and whether or not they do can be tested by determining whether replacing one with the other would bring about any change in the illocutionary-act potentials of the sentences in which the replacements are carried out.[15]

Thus the meaning of a particular word or phrase is *its* (indirect) illocutionary-act potential. Not that a word or phrase can (normally) be used to perform an illocutionary act, but that it contributes in a distinctive way to the illocutionary-act potentials of sentences. The meaning of "milk" is its capacity to play a role in acts of describing milk, buying milk, explaining how to milk a cow, etc. And to say that a word has several meanings is to say that its total (indirect) illocutionary-act potential includes the capacity to make various distinct contributions to the illocutionary-act potentials of sentences in which it may occur.

All this is, of course, a mere sketch. Numerous complications are required for a fully developed theory of meaning. And there may be difficulties. But let us assume for the present that the theory is basically right—that when we are concerned with meaning, we are concerned with illocutionary-act potential. Then we must see whether this account offers help in resolving the issue stated earlier, whether the connotations of words and the suggestions of sentences are part of their meaning.

Consider suggestion first. Compare:

(1) He took the pill and became ill.
(2) He became ill and took the pill.

Now I hope it will be agreed that there is something that can be said by both these sentences; there is an illocutionary-act potential that they share. Moreover, each suggests something that the other does not: (1) suggests that the illness came after, and as a consequence of, the pill-taking; (2) suggests that the pill-taking came after, and as a remedy for, the illness. Is this difference in suggestion a difference in illocutionary-act potential—and therefore a difference in meaning? It seems to me that it is.

Now it is not clear just how illocutionary acts are to be divided and counted, or when we have one rather than two. But if we say that there is one illocutionary act performed in both (1) and (2), since in both cases the speaker represents that two actions were performed by a single person, then we must say that there is another illocutionary act performed in (1) and still another performed in (2)—for in (1) the speaker represents a certain temporal and causal order and in (2) its reverse. There is no doubt a further difference between what is stated and what is suggested by each sentence, but I think this is a difference in the force or intensity of the illocutionary act.

The notion that illocutionary acts can be performed with various degrees of force may be surprising, but it is not, I think, paradoxical. Take, for example, acts of engaging to do something. We can imagine a whole spectrum of these acts, ranging from the most solemn covenants, signed in blood, through promises and contracts, down to the most half-hearted, casual sort of commitment in which you can hardly be sure that a commitment has been made at all (as when someone says, in a tone carrying absolutely no conviction, that he reckons he will help you paint the house). Assertion can be made firmly and decidedly, or it can trail off into a mere insinuation or hesitant suggestion. Now when we have a sentence that is used to state one thing and to suggest another thing, there is a great difference in the force of the two simultaneous illocutionary acts. One is the primary illocutionary act; the other is secondary. This relationship is reversed in the case of irony, where the suggested ironic meaning is in fact put forth more intensely than the stated meaning. It might be said that the less intense the illocutionary act, the less responsibility the speaker assumes for its requisite conditions. But the main point I am concerned with here is that what is suggested by a sentence has a claim to be considered part of the illocutionary-act potential of the sentence.

Alston does not discuss suggestion, but he does discuss connotations (which he calls "associations"), and his conclusion is that they are not a part of meaning. He offers as his example some lines of Keats and a paraphrase of them:

> Keats: "O, for a draught of vintage! that hath been
> Cooled a long age in the deep-delvèd earth!"
> Alston: "O, for a drink of wine that has been reduced in temperature
> over a long period in ground with deep furrows in it!"[16]

Alston concedes that the word "earth" has many special associations that are lacking in the word "ground," but he says,

> I cannot see that in saying "It came from the earth" I am taking responsibility for any conditions over and above those for which I am taking responsibility in saying "It came out of the ground."[17]

And so, by his account of meaning, Alston concludes that the difference between "ground" and "earth" is not a difference of meaning.

Now there are two questions here that ought to be kept separate. First, do "earth" and "ground" differ in meaning? Second, do they have different meanings in this context?

As to the first question, if the meaning of each word is its total illocutionary-act potential, then there is no doubt that the words have different meanings. For there are many illocutionary acts performable with the help of one that will clearly fail if the other is substituted. I can not conceive that Paul Tillich could have called his deity "the earth of being"; and we will not get the right picture if we substitute "earth" in the description of a house having a good deal of ground around it. On the other hand, "ground" will not do for "earth" in the phrase "earth-mother" (Alston's example) or in the phrase "salt of the earth."

The second question is whether earth and ground have different meanings, or only different associations, in the particular context of Alston's examples. Let us formulate part of the texts as imperatives:

(1) Bring me a draft of vintage that hath been cooled in the earth.
(2) Bring me a drink of wine that has been reduced in temperature in the ground.

I do not deny that both can be used to perform the same illocutionary act of ordering wine from the waiter. As far as that particular act is concerned, one will do as well as the other—provided the waiter is literate enough to understand all the words. If there is a difference of meaning embedded in the connotations of the different words, it will have to be because there is also a difference in *other* illocutionary acts simultaneously performed with these sentences.

To make clear the kind of difference I have in mind, I will introduce another example in which connotations are not involved. Compare:

(1)  Bring me my slippers.
(2)  Bring me my favorite slippers, which are such a comfort to me.

There is a particular illocutionary act which both of these sentences can be used to perform, under identical circumstances; and the nature of this act can be analyzed in terms of the represented conditions; for example, that there is one and only one pair of slippers singled out by the context; that the speaker does not already have them on; that the speaker wants them; that the hearer is in a position to bring them; etc. But obviously they do not have the same meaning, for the second one purveys information totally lacking from the first. A second illocutionary act is added in the second case: the act of praising the slippers on the ground that they comfort the speaker. The second case is a compound illocutionary act, though the syntax makes the ordering primary, the praising secondary.

This difference between the two slipper orders is like the difference between the two wine orders. I have to concede that the latter difference is somewhat more subtle. Keats's speaker does not use a set formula, like "Vintage is the most!" or "When you're out of vintage, you're out of wine." He relies on the connotations of "draft," "vintage," "cooled," and "earth." But he says something (though in a sense parenthetically) about the delicious flavor of the wine he wants, about the care required for its production, and about the satisfaction that drinking it is expected to give. He represents something to be the case. To ask for "vintage" is to ask for an old wine, but it is not to ask for any old wine. In short, the wine is praised in Keats's lines, but not in Alston's: a secondary illocutionary act is performed, as well as the primary one.[18]

*4*

The possibility of criticism depends not only on the existence of a text, an object susceptible of independent study, but also on the availability of a kind of method or principled procedure, by which proposed interpretations can be tested and can be shown to succeed or fail as attempts to make textual meanings explicit. I have not tried to set forth a whole interpretive procedure, and I have ignored many problems that must be tackled in working out and defending such a procedure. I have concentrated on one problem, which, though by no means the whole story, is (in my view) very basic: what sort of evidence can be appealed to in testing an interpretation? I have tried to answer this question, to show that public semantic facts, the connotations and suggestions in poems, are the stubborn data with which the interpreter must come to terms, even in his most elaborate, imaginative, and daring proposals.

Without such data to rely on, the interpretive process is in danger of degenerating into idle fancy or arbitrary invention. It is well known that when we come to a poem with an idea in mind of what it may be about to add up to, what we find in it will be much affected by our mental set. If we can pick and choose among the potential meanings of the work and arrange them to suit our mood, we can often spin out remarkable "readings." There is plenty of evidence to show what the ingenuity of critics can do when no semantic holds are barred. But I am arguing that there are some features of the poem's meaning that are antecedent to, and independent of, the entertaining of an interpretive hypothesis; and this makes it possible to check such hypotheses against reality, instead of letting them become self-confirming through circular reasoning.

If we make the distinction between regional interpretations of the work as a whole, or some large segment of it, and the more localized facts that support them, then we can formulate the interpretation problem as that of connecting macro-meanings with micro-meanings. In order to accept a proposed macro-meaning, we must be able to see it as emerging from the micro-meanings, as growing out of them and yet as making a whole that is more than the sum of the parts. Thus interpreting a poem is not like arranging a sack of children's blocks in a deliberately selected and imposed order. Nor is it like decoding a message bit by bit with the help of an appropriate code book. It is more like putting a jigsaw puzzle together, or tracing out contours on a badly stained old parchment map. But it can be done better or worse; and the results can be judged by reason.

In trying to resolve the problem I originally set for myself, I seem to have done something else. I have unexpectedly turned up a new answer to an old question. And though the answer may at first appear odd, it will, I think, prove more attractive on reflection. What is a poem? A poem is an imitation of a compound illocutionary act.

We have seen that even a single sentence may be used in performing two or more illocutionary acts, of rather different types, together. The speaker in a lyric poem may plead, threaten, cajole, deplore, reminisce, and pronounce a curse in sequence or almost simultaneously. Even in the Lucy poem, small as it is, the speaker compares two life-situations, praises Lucy, and expresses a mixture of resignation and regret. But the whole poem can be thought of as a single act, made up of several: the compound illocutionary act of its fictional speaker. Richard Wilbur has shown very clearly[19] how the shape of Robert Burns's poem "O My Luve's Like a Red, Red Rose" is defined by a series of illocutionary acts, such as praising, assuring, bidding farewell, promising, but with a rising curve of emotion in a single "thought or mood, which is developed to full intensity."[20]

It is surprising, and even unsettling, to find oneself reviving the term "imitation" after all its years of enforced retirement from most aesthetic circles. One of the problems in applying this concept to poems has been the difficulty of saying what it is that is imitated. The doctrine of illocutionary acts gives us a solution of this problem. The so-called "poetic use of language" is not a real use, but a make-believe use. A poem can, of course, be used in performing an illocutionary act—it may, for example, be enclosed in a box of candy or accompanied by a letter endorsing its sentiments. But the writing of a poem, as such, is not an illocutionary act; it is the creation of a fictional character performing a fictional illocutionary act.

But will this description really apply to all poems? The most serious counterexamples are didactic poems of various sorts—for example, *De rerum natura*.[21] Surely, it might be said, Lucretius in this poem is not merely imitating a series of illocutionary acts, but actually performing them, for he means to marshal actual facts and arguments, to preserve the memory of his master Epicurus, and to bring to mankind final liberation from the fear of death.

One way of meeting this objection would be to restrict the original generalization to lyric poems, setting aside the *Essay on Man, Paradise Lost,* and *English Bards and Scotch Reviewers.* I choose the bolder alternative of holding that even didactic poems are not to be taken as the verbal residues of real illocutionary acts. What makes them didactic is not, I think, that they are arguments rather than "expressions of emotion" (whatever that may be), but that they *imitate* arguments rather than pleadings, laments, or cries of joy.

Part of my reason for this view has been well stated by Paul Fussell, Jr.:

> Meter, one of the primary correlatives of meaning in a poem, can "mean" in at least three ways. First, all meter, by distinguishing rhythmic from ordinary statement, objectifies that statement and impels it in the direction of a significant formality and even ritualism. The ritual "frame" in which meter encloses experience is like the artificial border of a painting: like a picture frame, meter reminds the apprehender unremittingly that he is not experiencing the real object

of the "imitation" (in the Aristotelian sense) but is experiencing instead that object transmuted into symbolic form.[22]

It does not matter how sincerely the poet believes his doctrines, or how fondly he hopes to persuade others. If he goes about making speeches, writing letters, and distributing textbooks, then he is indeed arguing. But if he embodies his doctrines in a discourse that flaunts its poetic form (in sound and in meaning) and directs attention to itself as an object of rewarding scrutiny, then—so to speak—the illocutionary fuse is drawn. His utterance relinquishes its illocutionary force for aesthetic status, and takes on the character of being an appearance or a show of living language use. Of course, those of us who are interested in the history of philosophy can *read* Lucretius as a philosopher—can extract what he says about atoms and the void—and place these passages in other contexts where they can function as real arguments and can be judged as such. And because of this, there is perhaps no great harm in referring to these passages as arguments, even as they stand in *De rerum natura*—just as we speak of characters in a novel as disputing, even though we are aware that since the characters are nonexistent people, no real disputing is taking place.

To characterize poems in the way I have proposed is to give a genus, not the differentia. Not all imitations of illocutionary acts are poems: for example, to mimic what someone has said, to tell a joke, to say something for the purpose of testing a public address system. What makes a discourse a literary work (roughly speaking) is its exploitation to a high degree of the illocutionary-act potential of its verbal ingredients—or, in more usual terminology, its richness and complexity of meaning. And what makes a literary work a poem is the degree to which it condenses that complexity of meaning into compact, intense utterance.

It may seem that we have taken a very long way around to this final and familiar formula: that poems are distinguished by their complexity of meaning. But this commonplace ought to take on added significance from the route by which we reached it. For we see that the poem's complexity is not accidental or adventitious but a natural development of what it essentially is: the complex imitation of a compound illocutionary act.

*Notes*

1. See my *Aesthetics,* pp. 129–130, 242–247, 401–403.
2. I say this notwithstanding the dogmatic denial of it by Frank Cioffi in "Intention and Interpretation in Criticism": "You don't show that a response to a work of literature is inadequate or inappropriate in the way that you show that the conclusion of an argument has been wrongly drawn." But it seems to me the literary

interpreter is not concerned with the adequacy of our "response" to the work but only with the adequacy of our *understanding* of the work. It is true that a proposed interpretation often does not need to be argued, because we can see at once how it fits. But if we are hesitant about accepting it, we can always ask for a display of reasons—i.e., an argument.

3. Hampshire, in Sidney Hook, ed., *Art and Philosophy*, p. 108.

4. Hampshire.

5. See Margolis, *The Language of Art and Art Criticism* (Wayne State University Press, 1965), part 3; and also his comments in Hook, ed., *Art and Philosophy*, pp. 265–268.

6. *Language of Art*, p. 76.

7. *Ibid.*, pp. 91–92.

8. Hynes, "Whitman, Pound, and the Prose Tradition," in *The Presence of Walt Whitman*, English Institute Papers (Columbia University Press, 1962), pp. 129–130.

9. Hirsch, *Validity in Interpretation* (Yale University Press, 1967), p. 137.

10. *The New York Review of Books*, September 24, 1964, apropos of Jan Kott's *Shakespeare*.

11. Margolis, *Language of Art*, p. 93.

12. *Wordsworth: A Philosophical Approach* (Oxford: Clarendon Press, 1967), p. 172.

13. See William Alston, *Philosophy of Language* (Englewood Cliffs, N.J.: Prentice-Hall, 1964); J. L. Austin, *How to Do Things with Words* (Harvard University Press, 1962).

14. Alston speaks of "taking responsibility" for certain conditions in performing a particular illocutionary act; I prefer the term "represent," which has been suggested and used by Elizabeth Beardsley; see "A Plea for Deserts," *American Philosophical Quarterly* 6 (January 1969): 33–42.

15. Alston, p. 37.

16. *Ibid.*, p. 45.

17. *Ibid.*, p. 46.

18. Another way of analyzing the difference would perhaps be more congenial to Alston's view, though I think it would be oversimplified: we could say that in asking for "vintage . . . cooled in the earth" rather than "wine . . . reduced in temperature in the ground," he represents that what he desires is wine of high quality, and if this condition is taken to concern the attitude of the speaker, it would be assigned by Alston to the "emotive meaning" of the term (see Alston, pp. 47–48).

19. See "Explaining the Obvious," in "Speaking of Books" column of *The New York Times Book Review*, March 17, 1968.

20. One interesting use that can be made of this concept of a poem is to bring out the basic differences, sometimes called "rhetorical," between different kinds of poetry. English Augustan poetry, for example, gets its character largely from the preponderance of certain closely related kinds of pretended illocutionary act: asserting, denying, judging, contrasting, arguing, etc.; see William K. Wimsatt, "The Augustan Mode in English Poetry," *ELH: A Journal of English Literary History* 20 (March 1953): 1–14.

21. I want to thank Joseph Margolis for bringing this counterexample and counterargument to my attention.

22. *Poetic Meter and Poetic Form* (New York: Random House, 1965), p. 14. A closely similar view has been well defended by Seymour Chatman: "Meter, then, is the sign of a certain kind of discourse. . . . It is one of the 'variety of well-understood conventions by which the fictional use of language is signalled'" (*A Theory of Meter* [The Hague: Mouton, 1965], p. 221).

## 25. Robust Relativism

### JOSEPH MARGOLIS

There seems to be a simple way to refute relativism. Construe it as a conservative thesis: that, for some set of judgments, it is not the case that no judgments can in principle be valid (skepticism) or that judgments can be validly defended on one principle only (what Richard Henson has recently termed "universalism").[1] Assign truth-values, then, to judgments on relativistic grounds and assume that, in relevantly significant disputes, the correct assignment of incompatible truth-values depends on the use of competing (relativistic) "principles." There is no need to attempt to individuate such principles. The point of the exercise is that, on the hypothesis, relativism leads to contradiction, since judgments would then be able to be validly shown to be both true and false.

The argument is impeccable but indecisive—for an elementary reason. Grant only that a putatively relativistic set of judgments lacks truth-values (true and false) but takes values of other sorts or takes "truth-values" other than true and false. For example, if judgments are said to be probable (on the evidence) rather than true, then it is quite possible that judgments otherwise incompatible—as true or false—are equiprobable (on the evidence).[2] This is not to say that considerations of probability entail relativism; but it is also not to deny that they could be construed relativistically. In any case, the refutation of relativism fails so far forth if there is a set of judgments that relativism claims for its own, to which not truth and falsity but values that, interpreted on the model of truth-assignments, would lead to contradiction do not therefore thus do so. It is of course also possible to hold that judgments are relativized in the sense that every validating "principle" is said to subtend its own sector of judgments and that no two

From *The Journal of Aesthetics and Art Criticism*, XXXV (1976), 37–46. Reprinted with permission of the author and the *Journal*.

principles have intersecting sectors.[3] But, although this is a possible strategy, it is quite uninteresting, since what we want to consider are the prospects of a *robust* relativism, that is, a relativism that admits some range of *competing* claims, claims for which there are at least minimal grounds justifying the joint application of competing principles—hence, that admits not only incompatible judgments relative to any particular principle but also what may be called "incongruent" judgments, judgments that construed in terms of truth and falsity would be incompatible *and* that involve the use of predicates jointly accessible to competing principles. The weaker form of relativism is uninteresting whether truth itself is thought to be relativized to a particular language[4] or whether a restricted range of judgments is thought to be defensible only in terms of some particular convention or "implicit agreement."[5]

Still, the distinction between the two sorts of relativism suggests some necessary constraints that a viable and robust relativism would entail: (1) the rejection of skepticism and universalism for a given set of judgments; (2) the provision that such a set of judgments takes values other than truth and falsity and includes incongruent judgments; (3) the rejection of cognitivism (entailed by [(2)], in any case—that is, the rejection of the view that, for the properties ascribed in the judgments in question, we possess a matching cognitive faculty [perception for instance] the normal exercise of which enables us to make veridical discriminations of their presence or absence);[6] (4) the admission of the joint relevance of competing principles in validating the ascriptions or appraisals in question (entailed by [(2)], in any case—that is, the admission of some theory explaining such tolerance).[7] On reflection, these four conditions appear to be sufficient as well as necessary for the provision of a robust relativism. They are, in any case, jointly compatible and, together, they undercut what may fairly be taken to be the least specialized attack on relativism that could be mounted. I shall take a theory to be relativistic, therefore, if it meets our four conditions—which, on the analysis sketched, is equivalent to the first two. It is important and useful to note that no constraints at all are placed on the kinds of judgment that may be construed relativistically, for instance, as between judgments that are and are not value judgments.

Having said this much, let me proceed, first, polemically, to provide grounds for thinking that, in the context of aesthetics or of the aesthetic appreciation of the arts, there are at least three distinct ranges of judgment that may be strongly defended as tolerating or even requiring a relativistic construction; and secondly, more affirmatively but very briefly, to sketch a theory in virtue of which those findings may be sustained. In the first portion of the argument, then, I shall try to show that, for each of the three domains to be marked out, well-known arguments (at least implicitly) opposed to a relativistic construction are inherently indecisive. In the second portion of the argument, then, I shall try to say what it is about the nature of art and judgment that sustains a relativistic thesis. It should be said at once, however, that it is no part of my thesis that *all* judgments (taken collectively) may be defensibly construed as behaving relativistically—which of course would involve construing truth relativistically. That would be tantamount to retreating to a radical version of the weaker sense of relativism; and, in any case, I am persuaded that such a view is incoherent. So it may be insisted that a further condition (5) should be appended, namely, that relativistic sets of judgments presuppose some range of non-relativistic judgments, or that relativistic judgments are dependent on there being some viable range of non-relativistic judgments. But I take (5) to be entailed by (1). In any case, the provision precludes the possible embarrassment of conceding that we may wish to hold it *true* that relativistic judgments ("incongruent" in the sense supplied) do have the values (other than true and false) that they are said to have. It may also be claimed that genuinely relativistic theories should be distinguished sharply from theories that merely admit that the validity of any range of judgments is relative to the supporting evidence or supporting considerations on which that is said to depend. So a further condition (6) may be required, namely, that a set of judgments is relativistic if their validation is determined by considerations bearing on the individual sensibilities of anyone who relevantly judges. (This may in fact be the fair sense of the relativistic interpretation of Protagoras' dictum.) But, the thesis to which (6) is contrasted is itself tautological; and, also, (6) appears to be entailed by (2). Still, (6) is essential, since it is surely with regard to varying personal sensibilities that we anticipate the relevant specimens to arise; and (6) precludes mere expressions of differing preference, since the expression of a preference is not as such a judgment.

Turn, now, to our specimens.

Frank Sibley, in a well-known series of papers, has argued that a particularly important set of aesthetic properties are not in any positive way "condition-governed" and that their discrimination requires the exercise of taste or perceptiveness. As he puts it,

> We say that a novel has a great number of characters and deals with life in a manufacturing town; that a painting uses pale colors, predominantly blues and greens, and has kneeling figures in the foreground; that the theme in a fugue is inverted at such a point and that there is a stretto in the close; that the action of a play takes place in the span of one day and that there is a reconciliation scene in the

fifth act. Such remarks may be made by, and such features pointed out to, anyone with normal eyes, ears, and intelligence. On the other hand, we also say that a poem is tightly-knit or deeply moving; that a picture lacks balance, or has a certain serenity and repose, or that the grouping of the figures sets up an exciting tension; or that the characters in a novel never really come to life, or that a certain episode strikes a false note. It would be neutral enough to say that the making of such judgments as these requires the exercise of taste, perceptiveness, or sensitivity, of aesthetic discrimination or appreciation; one would *not* say this of my first group. Accordingly, when a word or expression is such that taste or perceptiveness is required in order to apply it, I shall call it an *aesthetic* term or expression, and I shall, correspondingly, speak of *aesthetic* concepts or *taste* concepts.[8]

About these, Sibley claims, "there are no non-aesthetic features which serve in *any* circumstances as logically *sufficient* condition's for applying aesthetic terms. Aesthetic or taste concepts are not in *this* respect condition-governed at all."[9] Of course, Sibley clearly means to hold that the discrimination involved is, in some sense, perceptual or perception-like—informed by taste or perceptiveness—*and* that the capacity in question is not to be understood in terms of any form of intuitionism.[10]

It is, admittedly, not clear whether Sibley can escape intuitionism; and it is entirely reasonable to claim that *some* of the concepts that Sibley regards as aesthetic *are* condition-governed and that some that he regards as nonaesthetic (and that are also condition-governed) *are*, on a perfectly reasonable usage, actually aesthetic or aesthetically important—for instance, the discrimination of the fugal form and its complications and the discrimination of musical unity.[11] The central question remains, what of those uses of aesthetic terms that are not condition-governed, in Sibley's sense? Can these be reasonably construed as objectively discerned *in* the work in question? Here, Sibley himself concedes the possibility that ascriptions of the sort he has in mind ("graceful," "dainty," "moving," "plaintive," "balanced," "lacking in unity," and the like—what he sometimes calls "tertiary or *Gestalt* properties, among others") may merely be "*apt* rather than *true*."[12] Sibley himself opts for the objectivity of such qualities on the basis of considerations that quite clearly fail to exclude a decisive alternative. He notices that simple qualities like color admit of "ultimate proof" (that is, proof that they are present) only in the way in which that proof is "tied to an overlap of agreement in sorting, distinguishing and much else which links people present and past; . . . where different sets of people agree amongst themselves thus (e.g., groups of similarly color-blind people), it is reference to the set with the most detailed discrimination that we treat as conclusive."[13]

His argument continues in the following way:

> When I say the only ultimate test or proof, I mean that, since colors are simple properties in the sense that no other visible feature makes something the color it is, one cannot appeal to other features of an object in virtue of possessing which, by some rule of meaning, it can be said to be red or blue, as one can with such properties as triangular, etc. With colors there is no such intermediate appeal; only directly an appeal to agreement. But *if* there are aesthetic properties—the supposition under investigation—they will, despite dissimilarities, be like colors in this respect. For though, unlike colors, they will be dependent on other properties of things, they cannot, since they are not entailed by the properties responsible for them, be ascribed by virtue of the presence of other properties and some rule of meaning. Hence a proof will again make no intermediate appeal to other properties of the thing, but directly to agreement.[14]

Sibley adds that "this agreement is not easy to describe. Not *any* agreement will do; the fact that some of us, here and now, make identical discriminations need not settle the color of things."[15] This shows reasonably clearly that Sibley thinks that the "perception" of aesthetic or tertiary qualities is not dissimilar in an essential regard from the perception of colors: the agreement involved is an agreement about perceived (though dependent) qualities. And so, in effect, Sibley subscribes to some form of cognitivism (if not intuitionism); he must reject our condition (3)—hence, relativism. But that's just it. What Sibley needs is a *theory* of perception and perceptual qualities that would justify construing the qualities in question as perceptual qualities and not merely as qualities such that, in a sense that conforms to the enormous variability of such judgments, it would be *apt* but not *true* to say that this poem or sculpture "has" it. In an earlier paper, Sibley says quite explicitly that "aesthetics deals with a kind of perception," and appeals to the case of the color-blind man to clarify the nature of defective aesthetic perception.[16] On the other hand, in spite of his insistence that "some aesthetic judgments may be characterized as right, wrong, true, false, undeniable," he actually favors the alternative theory at times, conceding that, even for his own cases, "for some range of judgments we prefer terms like 'reasonable,' 'admissible,' 'understandable' or 'eccentric' to 'right' and 'wrong.'"[17]

Sibley also has considerable difficulty in explaining how to select the aesthetic "elite" whose discrimination is relatively reliable simply because he fails to supply a theory of the requisite perception in terms of which to account for and to correct the discrimination of any would-be aesthetic percipient. But the absence of such a theory places his advocacy of cognitivism in doubt, since, for *any* claim that putatively relies on the exercise of a cognitive faculty (perceptual, for instance), a theoretical basis must be provided for distinguishing between what actually *is* the case and what only *seems* to be so.[18] This condition must be satisfied whether the properties in question are said to be simple or complex. Sibley's admission, however, of what it may be *apt* but not true to say is incompatible with his particular claims of aesthetic objectivity, since judgments of what may be apt but not true to say cannot preclude incongruence (in the sense supplied). His concession, in short, precludes the application of the requisite "is"/"seems" contrast, where the concession has force; and where he would deny its force, he lacks the requisite theory. Hence, Sibley's position is subject to a complex dilemma: either (*a*) his aesthetic concepts are condition-governed (since dependent) and thus enter inferentially into judgments that are straightforwardly true or false; or else (*b*) they are not condition-governed (though dependent) and, since they enter into judgments that are straightforwardly true or false, Sibley is committed to some sort of intuitionism; or else (*c*) they are not condition-governed (though dependent) and enter into judgments that can be apt or inapt or the like but not true or false.

It is, I think, fair to say that the concepts Sibley is chiefly concerned with ("graceful," "moving," "balanced," "unified," and the like) have a definite use in judgments that depend on the individual sensibilities of different persons. He himself concedes the point, which is tantamount to conceding a relativistic thesis. Some of his opponents (Peter Kivy, for instance)[19] wish to show that these concepts are used in an ordinary condition-governed way, but they have not shown (and it is difficult to imagine how they could possibly show) that such concepts are never, or are not even characteristically, used in a way that is either not condition-governed (in Sibley's sense) or if condition-governed not governed in such a way as to lead to judgments that are straightforwardly true or false. Let it suffice, then, that judgments that Sibley says involve taste or perceptiveness or sensibility—ranging over much of what is typically noted in appreciative discourse, without directly involving (but not necessarily excluding) evaluative distinctions[20]—may be construed, and may even need to be construed, relativistically.

The other two quarrels I wish to pick are drawn from Monroe Beardsley's relatively recent book, *The Possibility of Criticism*.[21] Again, I mean to argue in each case primarily on the basis of internal evidence.

In speaking about a critic's judgments (he confines himself here to

judgments of literature), Beardsley has the following straightforward view
to present:

> What is the point of making a literary judgment and arguing for it?
> My answer to this question—which I shall defend here—is simple and
> old-fashioned. It is to inform someone how good a literary work is.
> But philosophers are rightly suspicious of this so-called "informing,"
> if it merely evokes verbal agreement but brings no further satisfaction
> to the hearer. . . . [Still] there is a proximate end in judging—namely,
> to provide information about value.[22]

Judgments of course call for supporting reasons. Beardsley claims that the
reasons a critic supplies in order to justify his judgment conform to the
"'ordinary' sense" of reasons; that is, they "have a bearing on the *truth* of
the judgments." He adds that "the relevance of such reasons presupposes
that the judgments can be true or false"; but he concedes in the very same
context, noting that this runs contrary to his own view about criticism,
that "there might be reasons for making a certain judgment that are not
reasons for saying it is true, if it should be the case that judgments cannot
be true or false."[23] So Beardsley in effect concedes our condition (2) or at
least an essential part of it. He even concludes as a result: "So our first
question is whether in fact critical judgments have a truth-value—i.e., are
either true or false"[24]—which, under the circumstances, we must understand
to mean, whether all relevant judgments are true or false.

But he never does show that they are. He does mention P. H. Nowell-
Smith's account purporting to show that even so-called verdictives (in
J. L. Austin's sense), estimates for instance, though not usually said to be
true or false, nevertheless "surely involve a claim to truth, which may be
allowed or disallowed."[25] But he considers no other possibilities. His
principal effort is actually directed against an argument of Michael
Scriven's, which purports to show that critical reasoning is impossible, in
the sense that justifying or explaining reasons is impossible to supply in
the way required to support ascriptions of truth.[26] Scriven's argument, as
Beardsley summarizes it, holds that "it must be possible for us to know
that the reason is true, and also to know that it *is* a reason for the
conclusion, *before* knowing that the conclusion is true" (the so-called
"independence requirement").[27] Beardsley seems to take it that the refutation of Scriven's thesis entails his own favored view—that critical judgments
(in particular, estimates, as he puts it, of "the greatest amount of artistic
goodness that [e.g.,] the poem allows of actualizing in any one encounter
with it") have truth-value. "This," he says, "I am convinced, is what the
critic estimates."[28] Again, his argument against Scriven runs as follows:

But *if*, as I claim, these judgments are estimates, then some reasons *must* be used by the critics in arriving at them, and *therefore* there must be some basic features of literary works that are always merits or defects.[29]

But this begs the question with which Beardsley originally began. For, *if* justification or explanatory reasons may be provided for utterances (judgments) that lack truth-value, then it cannot be shown that if judgments include estimates and if estimates call for supporting reasons, then all judgments have truth-value. Some estimates may and some may not, in the sense given; and some critical judgments may not behave in the way Beardsley claims estimates do. Also, it is difficult to see how, unless by some sort of cognitivism or the weaker version of relativism, judgments of the kind mentioned above ("concerning the greatest amount of artistic goodness," etc.) could possibly be said to be straightforwardly true or false. In fact, what Scriven's argument tends to show, as a by-benefit, is that a significant range of critical value judgments, though they call for supporting reasons, rest on considerations that actually preclude the ascription of the value *true*; for, as Scriven says, agreement about how some valuational condition must be satisfied often (Scriven apparently thinks, always) "does not exceed the degree of our initial agreement about the merit of the work of art."[30] I take this to accord with what I have elsewhere termed "appreciative judgments," that is, judgments that call for pertinent justifying or explanatory reasons but that, depending as they do on personal taste, cannot be binding on another, cannot be simply true, cannot be said to support the relevant distinction between a work's actually having the value in question or only appearing to.[31] With respect to such judgments, I claim, we may say only that it is reasonable, extreme, eccentric, etc., *to say* that a work has this or that degree of merit rather *than* that it demonstrably *has* it. Hence, even such judgments conform to whatever semantic constraints obtain on the use of the predicates in question. There are, therefore, judgments (including some that Beardsley himself considers) that would support the relativistic view, and that might even require it—the view, that is, that justifying reasons may be admitted where particular judgments cannot take the value "true" (and do not, in Nowell-Smith's sense, involve a claim to truth).

The third quarrel concerns the nature of the interpretation, as opposed to the description, of a work of art; and here, I am simply responding to Beardsley's criticism of my own earlier statements on the matter.[32] The issue directly concerns what may be definitely found *in* a work and what lies *outside* it. Beardsley opposes what I and others emphasize as "the element of creativity in interpretation." He says, "I find myself rather severe with this line of thought," that is, the suggestion "that the literary interpreter, too [like the performing artist] has a certain leeway, and does not merely 'report' on 'discovered meaning,'... but puts something of his own into the work; so that different critics may produce different but equally legitimate interpretations, like two sopranos or two ingenues working from the same notations."[33]

But there are difficulties in his account. For one thing, though he subscribes to what he terms "the Principle of Independence" (that is, "that literary works exist as individuals and can be distinguished from other things"), he claims that what he terms "the Principle of Autonomy" is a postulate "that is logically complementary to the first" (that is, "that literary works are self-sufficient entities, whose properties are decisive in checking interpretations and judgments.[34]) But I would maintain—and have tried to demonstrate elsewhere[35]—that problems about the numerical identity of a work of art can be managed without any commitment respecting the demarcation between description and interpretation, the demarcation between what is in a work and what is not. Only if one held, in addition to a theory about individuating works of art, a compelling theory about the nature and properties of works of art, could one hope to sustain the so-called Principle of Autonomy—by actually providing criteria for determining putatively internal properties to be or actually not to be internal. Beardsley offers no such theory, as far as I know. But then, it follows, as a second consideration, that he may well have misdescribed the "latitudinarian" view of interpretation; interpretations (in the sense he rejects) may not be simple "superimpositions," as he says, that is, "interpretations" that are merely "ways of *using* the work to illustrate a pre-existent system of thought [say, in taking the story of 'Jack and the Beanstalk' as Freudian symbolism or as a Marxist fable]";[36] they may actually be needed precisely because there is no sharp demarcation line between what is internal and what is external to a work of art *and* because what is uncertain *in this respect may be important in terms of aesthetic appreciation.* Thirdly, the admission of so-called superimpositions would itself be a telling concession if (as is in fact the case) Beardsley has not yet provided the requisite theory in virtue of which superimpositions and "genuine" interpretations can be logically demarcated. Fourthly, the implied admission that there *is* a certain latitude that holds in music and the other performing arts raises (unresolved) questions both about whether there is a clear sense, for all the arts, of the tenability of the Principles of Independence and Autonomy and about what may be the formulable (and relevant) differences between literature and the performing arts. Fifthly, Beardsley himself concedes, in a context in which he opposes an extreme view ingeniously supported by Frank Cioffi,[37] that

> Some things are definitely said in the poem and cannot be overlooked; others are suggested, as we find on careful reading; others are gently hinted, and whatever methods of literary interpretation we use, we can never establish them decisively as "in" or "out." Therefore whatever comes from without, but yet can be taken as an interesting extension of what is surely in, may be admissible. It merely makes a larger whole. But this concession will not justify extensive borrowings from biography.[38]

I cannot see how this concession, generously advanced though it may be, can fail to undermine Beardsley's Principle of Autonomy. Even the question of biographical reference and of intentional interpretation surely becomes moot—which is not to say of course that critical interpretation lacks rigor altogether.

A sixth consideration concerns the nature of language itself, since Beardsley here restricts himself to literary interpretation. First of all, he rests his case on the strength of the thesis that the interpretation of "textual meaning" (as opposed to "authorial meaning"—in the sense proposed by E. D. Hirsch)[39] is "the proper task of the literary interpreter" and that such meaning "lies momentarily hidden" in, say, some poem, "really is something in the poem that we are trying to dig out, though it is elusive."[40] But even apart from his confidence about determining textual meaning, Beardsley seems entirely prepared to concede that meanings may accrue to a literary text because of the historical conditions under which a living language is used. In his effort to contrast textual and authorial meaning, for instance, he says that "the meaning of a text can change after its author has died. . . . The *OED* furnishes abundant evidence that individual words and idioms acquire new meanings and lose old meanings as time passes; these changes can in turn produce changes of meaning in sentences in which the words appear." He offers a curious instance from the work of Mark Akenside, acknowledges that a certain eighteenth-century phrase "has . . . acquired a new meaning," and even speaks of "today's textual meaning of the line" (in question).[41]

But *if* he allows changing textual meanings, he *cannot* preclude the possibility of incompatible and non-converging literary interpretations in rendering a coherent account, unless he also maintains that there is an executive rule (unformulated) for determining which textual meaning (changing through diachronic changes in language itself) to prefer; after all, large portions of an entire text may be subject to similar changes and may therefore support plural interpretations. But secondly, in this regard, the very theory of linguistic meaning to which he subscribes—William Alston's theory of "illocutionary act potentials" (regardless of its own defensibility)[42]—depends precisely on speakers' intentions; consequently, once again, Beardsley cannot, on his own principles, preclude the prospect of defending non-converging ("creative") literary interpretations. Finally, with regard to literature (*and* certainly with regard to the other arts), the critic's interpretation is *not* restricted, as Beardsley claims, merely to ferreting out textual meanings; it is often concerned (as even the admission of diachronic changes in meaning confirm) with plausible ways in which what may be called the artistic design (the internal coherent order of the work) may be construed.[43] In fact, the case that Beardsley puts before us (introduced by Hirsch) of Cleanth Brooks's and F. W. Bateson's incompatible interpretations of Wordsworth's *A Slumber Did My Spirit Seal* bears this point out convincingly.[44] Unfortunately, neither interpretation, however plausible, is entirely unproblematic. Bateson's pantheistic interpretation cannot be supported on the basis solely of the so-called textual meaning of the lines *No motion has she now, no force, / She neither hears nor sees; / Rolled round in earth's diurnal course, / With rocks, and stones, and trees.* And Brooks's interpretation (which, rightly understood, emphasizes the lover's shock—almost in a clinical sense—reacting to Lucy's death and consequent inertness) is somewhat careless about textual meanings but not in a way that vitiates his interpretation. The upshot is that Wordsworth's Lucy poem, contrary to Beardsley's claim, does appear to support two different interpretations of the poem's larger meaning or design (that is, roughly the picture of the imaginative world disclosed in the poem), *without even entailing different interpretations of the poem's textual meaning.* There seems to be no way to preclude the possibility.

There is then no reason to deny that interpretation sometimes serves to convey a sense of virtuosity in fathoming what is hidden (but describable) in a work of art. But there is no reason to insist that interpretation functions only thus. Beardsley discounts incompatible interpretations in accord with what he calls "the principle of 'the Intolerability of Incompatibles,' i.e., if two [interpretations] are logically incompatible, they cannot both be true [and they implicitly claim to be true]." "Indeed," Beardsley says, "I hold that *all* of the literary interpretations that deserve the name obey the principle."[45] He does not deny that there are "interpretations" that could not be jointly true and yet may be said to be plausible; but these are not true interpretations, are merely what he calls "superimpositions." And he fails to notice that falsity may be opposed to both truth and plausibility.[46] Also, he has not provided either an explicit theory of the nature of a work of art or the requisite criteria for determining what is internal and what external to the work of art itself; consequently, he cannot in principle preclude plural and incompatible interpretations of a literary work just as he cannot in principle distinguish between superimpositions and interpretations that specify what is "momentarily hidden" in a piece of literature. Hence, he cannot preclude a relativistic conception of interpretation—which may well be not merely tolerated but required.

I have now, I hope, shown (polemically) that a relativistic conception of aesthetic appreciation, of critical judgments (of value), and of literary interpretations is viable, not unreasonable, and possibly even required by the ways in which we attend to works of art. I shall have to be extremely brief about my reasons for thinking that a relativistic account is actually required for these and related distinctions. The argument centers on two considerations. First of all, works of art are what I should call culturally emergent entities.[47] I wish to avoid here theorizing in too detailed a way about the nature of art, since our issue does not require it and since controversial details may easily deflect us from our purpose. But the most familiar properties of art, its artifactuality, its internal purposiveness, its being assignable meanings (in various senses), forms, designs, styles, symbolic and representational functions, and the like all call for a sensitivity to cultural distinctions that cannot in any obvious way be directly accessible (unless by postulating some ad hoc intuitionism) to any cognitive faculty resembling sensory perception. But culturally freighted phenomena are notoriously open to intensional quarrels, that is, to identification under alternative descriptions; and there is no obvious way in which to show that plural, non-converging, and otherwise incompatible characterizations of cultural items can be sorted as correct or incorrect in such a way that a relativistic account would be precluded. The proliferation of intensional divergences is as close to the heart of the cultural as anything we might otherwise suggest. One has only to think of ideologies, ideals, schools of thought, traditions as well as the deep informality of the so-called rules of language and of artistic creation. This suggests why it is that the appreciation, the interpretation, and the evaluation of art should behave in accord with relativistic expectations. In particular, the relativistic theory of interpretation is sometimes resisted because one wishes to avoid the somewhat unfortunate habit of speaking of art's being inherently incomplete or defective and awaiting the interpretive critic's contribution in order actually to *finish* the work. What is initially defective or incomplete, of course, is our understanding, not the work; but the nature of the defect is such that, for conceptual reasons, we cannot be certain that what is supplied by way of interpretation is really in principle descriptively available in the work itself—on the basis of any familiar perceptual or perception-like model, which after all offers us the best prospect of the requisite control. One can expect, therefore, a certain conceptual congruence between the theory of art and the latitude tolerated in the practice of critical interpretation.

The second consideration concerns the nature of values themselves. I should hold (controversially, I admit) that persons like works of art are culturally emergent entities—not natural creatures like the members of *Homo sapiens*: chiefly, because the mastery of language is essential to being a person.[48] If this were granted, then the possibility of defending *any* form of cognitivism (moral, aesthetic, or any other) with respect to the values appropriate to persons or to their characteristic work is radically undermined. Consequently, the prospects of avoiding a relativistic account of values (and of value judgments), even were it possible to avoid such an account of the presumably descriptive and interpretive levels of our appreciative concern with art, is nearly nil. But noticeably with respect to values, if cognitivism is defeated,[49] then we can either retreat to the robust or weaker form of relativism or else, even further but with inevitable dissatisfaction, to a skepticism about values.

There appear to be no other promising strategies.[50]

## Notes

1. In an untitled and as yet unpublished book on ethical relativism.

2. Cf. C. G. Hempel, "Inductive Inconsistencies," in *Aspects of Scientific Explanation* (New York, 1965). Cf. also G. H. von Wright, "Remarks on the Epistemology of Subjective Probability," in Ernest Nagel *et al.*, eds., *Logic, Methodology and Philosophy of Science* (Stanford University Press, 1962).

3. This is, roughly, the theme of conventionalism in values.

4. Cf. Alfred Tarski, "The Semantic Conception of Truth," *Philosophy and Phenomenological Research* IV (1944), 341–376; cf. also W. V. Quine, *Word and Object* (Cambridge, 1960), pp. 23–24; and Donald Davidson, "Truth and Meaning," *Synthese* III (1967), 304–322. The requirements of the coherence of interlinguistic communication entail the inadequacy of such a conception: even if ascriptions of "truth" are relativized, we require a conception of truth that is not language-relative even if what is true can only be formulated in a way that is subject to the local features of particular languages.

5. The thesis has been defended most recently by Gilbert Harman, "Moral Relativism Defended," *Philosophical Review* LXXXIV (1975), 3–22. Harman's thesis is relativistic not merely in the trivial sense that supporting reasons are relative to considerations of some sort but because "the source of the reasons" (for doing something—Harman's concern here is with moral relativism) is one's "sincere intention to observe a certain agreement," ibid., 10.

6. The argument is indifferent to the kind of property considered, though moral properties have traditionally been the principal object of concern. Cf. Joseph Margolis, "Moral Cognitivism," *Ethics* LXXXV (1975), 136–141.

7. It is possible that one might argue that (2) signifies only that, were the relevant judgments interpreted so as to take truth and falsity as truth-values, we

should be commited to a single arena of dispute; that the admission of other values does not entail the relevance of competing validating principles. But the intention here is to formulate constraints for the robust, not the weaker, version of relativism. Hence, provision must be made—even if separately, via (4)—for the joint relevance of competing principles.

8. Frank Sibley, "Aesthetic Concepts," *Philosophical Review* LXVIII (1959), 421–450; reprinted (with extensive minor revisions) in Joseph Margolis, *Philosophy Looks at the Arts* (New York, 1962).

9. *Loc. cit.*

10. Cf. Frank Sibley, "Objectivity and Aesthetics," *Proceedings of the Aristotelian Society*, Supplementary XLII (1968), 31–54.

11. Cf. Peter Kivy, *Speaking of Art* (The Hague, 1973), chs. 1–3; also Joseph Margolis, *The Language of Art and Art Criticism* (Detroit, 1965), ch. 8.

12. "Objectivity and Aesthetics."

13. *Loc. cit.*

14. *Loc. cit.*

15. *Loc. cit.*

16. Cf. Frank Sibley, "Critical Judgments of Aesthetic Value," *Philosophical Review* LXXIV (1965), 135–159.

17. "Objectivity and Aesthetics."

18. Cf. Isabel Hungerland, "The Logic of Aesthetic Concepts" (Presidential Address of the Pacific Division of the American Philosophical Association, 1962), *Proceedings and Addresses of the American Philosophical Association* XXXVI, 43–66. Hungerland's statement is, however, too extreme in that it fails to provide for condition-governed concepts.

19. *Loc. cit.*

20. Cf. Kivy, *op. cit.*, p. 17.

21. Detroit, 1970.

22. *Ibid.,* pp. 63–64.

23. *Ibid.,* p. 71.

24. *Ibid.*

25. *Ibid.*

26. Cf. Michael Scriven, "The Objectivity of Aesthetic Evaluation," *The Monist* L (1969), 159–187.

27. Beardsley, *op. cit.*, pp. 77f.

28. *Ibid.,* p. 75.

29. *Ibid.,* p. 82.

30. Scriven, *op. cit.*, p. 179.

31. Cf. Joseph Margolis, *The Language of Art and Art Criticism* (Detroit, 1965), ch. 10; and *Values and Conduct* (Oxford, 1971), ch. 1.

32. *The Language of Art and Art Criticism*, chs. 5–6.

33. Beardsley, *op. cit.*, pp. 39–40.

34. *Ibid.,* p. 16.

35. *The Language of Art and Art Criticism*, ch. 4.

36. Beardsley, *op. cit.*, pp. 43–44.

37. Cf. Frank Cioffi, "Intention and Interpretation in Criticism," *Proceedings*

of the Aristotelian Society LXIV (1963–1964), 85–103. Cf. also, Stuart Hampshire, "Types of Interpretation," in Sidney Hook, ed., Art and Philosophy.

38. Beardsley, op. cit., p. 36.

39. Cf. E. D. Hirsch, Validity in Interpretation (New Haven, 1967); also Joseph Margolis, review of above, in Shakespeare Studies II (1970), 407–414.

40. Beardsley, op. cit., pp. 32, 44, 47.

41. Ibid., pp. 19–20.

42. Cf. William Alston, Philosophy of Language (Englewood Cliffs, 1964); and Joseph Margolis, "Meaning, Speakers' Intentions, and Speech Acts," Review of Metaphysics XIX (1973), 1007–1022.

43. Cf. The Language of Art and Art Criticism, ch. 3.

44. Cf. Cleanth Brooks, "Irony as a Principle of Structure," in M. D. Zabel, ed., Literary Opinion in America (New York, 1951); and F. W. Bateson, English Poetry: A Critical Introduction (London, 1950).

45. Beardsley, op. cit., p. 44.

46. Ibid., pp. 42–44.

47. Cf. Joseph Margolis, "Works of Art as Physically Embodied and Culturally Emergent Entities," British Journal of Aesthetics XIV (1974), 187–196.

48. Cf. "Works of Art as Physically Embodied and Culturally Emergent Entities"; also Joseph Margolis, "Mastering a Natural Language: Rationalists vs. Empiricists," Diogenes no. 84 (1973), pp. 41–57.

49. Cf. "Moral Cognitivism"; also Values and Conduct.

50. I had seen, in manuscript, Professor Annette Barnes's paper, "Half an Hour Before Breakfast," criticizing my theory of the logic of interpretive judgments (JAAC, Spring, 1976). I have taken no account of her charges here, both because the paper had not been published at the time this essay was completed (it was in fact completed before I saw her paper) and because I had attempted to answer her in detail, by letter. Suffice it to say that her charges go wrong in a number of ways: (i) I do not maintain that contradictory accounts of anything can be defended as true, either separately or jointly; only that what would, on a model of truth and falsity, be contradictory, may be jointly defended as plausible or reasonable or the like; (ii) Barnes offers a set of alternative versions of a tolerance principle for admitting diverging interpretations, that she wrongly takes to be exhaustive and therefore, to capture my own view in a multiple dilemma: not exhaustive both because several of her alternatives involve self-contradictory features (which I explicitly avoid) and because no provision is made for truth-values other than "true" and "false"; (iii) Barnes make no provision for what I term the asymmetry of truth and falsity: that, for instance, the "false" is opposed both to the "true" and the "plausible" and the considerations of plausibility do not entail the relevance of considerations of truth; (iv) my argument regarding the logic of interpretation is only applied to those entities that we call works of art; it does not presuppose any theory of the nature of a work of art, though it is compatible with an independent theory that I also support; (v) on my view, it follows that, if interpretation behaves as I claim it does, the properties ascribed to a work of art by way of interpretive criticism cannot be said to be in the work in the sense in which description would require; some of the paradoxes that Barnes attributes to my position simply fail to take account of this important point.

# 26.                    Hermeneutical Experience
## *H.-G. GADAMER*

My revival of the expression 'hermeneutics', with its long tradition, has apparently led to some misunderstandings.[1] I did not intend to produce an art or technique of understanding, in the manner of the earlier hermeneutics. I did not wish to elaborate a system of rules to describe, let alone direct, the methodical procedure of the human sciences. Nor was it my aim to investigate the theoretical foundation of work in these fields in order to put my findings to practical ends. If there is any practical consequence of the present investigation, it certainly has nothing to do with an unscientific 'commitment'; instead, it is concerned with the 'scientific' integrity of acknowledging the commitment involved in all understanding. My real concern was and is philosophic: not what we do or what we ought to do, but what happens to us over and above our wanting and doing.

Hence the methods of the human sciences are not at issue here. My starting point is that the historic human sciences, as they emerged from German romanticism and became imbued with the spirit of modern science, maintained a humanistic heritage which distinguishes them from all other kinds of modern research and brings them close to other, quite different, extra-scientific experiences, and especially those proper to art. In Germany (which has always been prerevolutionary) the tradition of aesthetic humanism remained vitally influential in the development of the modern conception of science. In other countries more political consciousness may have entered into 'the humanities', lettres: in short, everything formerly known as the humaniora.

This does not prevent the methods of modern natural science from having an application to the social world. Possibly the growing rationaliza-

From Hans-Georg Gadamer, *Truth and Method* (New York, 1975), pp. xvi–xxvi, 333–341. Reprinted by permission of Sheed and Ward, Ltd.

tion of society and the scientific techniques of its administration are more characteristic of our age than the vast progress of modern science. The methodical spirit of science permeates everywhere. Therefore I did not remotely intend to deny the necessity of methodical work within the human sciences (Geisteswissenschaften). Nor did I propose to revive the ancient dispute on method between the natural and the human sciences. It is hardly a question of a contrast of methods. To this extent, Windelband and Rickert's question concerning the limits of concept-formation in the natural sciences seems to me misconceived. The difference that confronts us is not in the method, but in the objectives of knowledge. The question I have asked seeks to discover and bring into consciousness something that methodological dispute serves only to conceal and neglect, something that does not so much confine or limit modern science as precede it and make it possible. This does not make its own immanent law of advance any less decisive. It would be vain to appeal to the human desire for knowledge and the human capacity for achievement to be more considerate in their treatment of the natural and social orders of our world. Moral preaching in the guise of science seems rather absurd, as does the presumption of a philosopher who deduces from principles the way in which 'science' must change in order to become philosophically legitimate.

Therefore it seems quite erroneous in this connection to invoke the famous Kantian distinction between quaestio juris and quaestio facti. Kant certainly did not wish to lay down for modern science what it must do in order to stand honorably before the judgment seat of reason. He asked a philosophic question: What are the conditions of our knowledge, by virtue of which modern science is possible, and how far does it extend? Thus the following investigation also asks a philosophic question. But it does not ask it only of the so-called human sciences (among which precedence would then be accorded to certain traditional disciplines). It does not ask if only of science and its modes of experience, but of all human experience of the world and human living. It asks (to put it in Kantian terms): How is understanding possible? This is a question which precedes any action of understanding on the part of subjectivity, including the methodical activity of the 'understanding sciences' (verstehende Geisteswissenschaften) and their norms and rules. Heidegger's temporal analytics of human existence (Dasein) has, I think, shown convincingly that understanding is not just one of the various possible behaviors of the subject, but the mode of being of There-being itself. This is the sense in which the term 'hermeneutics' has been used here. It denotes the basic being-in-motion of There-being which constitutes its finiteness and historicity, and hence includes the whole of its experience of the world. Not caprice, or even an elaboration of a single aspect, but the nature of the thing itself makes the movement of understanding comprehensive and universal.

I cannot agree with those who maintain that the limits of the hermeneutical aspect are revealed in confrontation with extra-historical modes of being, such as the mathematical or aesthetic.[2] Admittedly it is true that, say, the aesthetic quality of a work of art depends on structural laws and a level of embodied form and shape which ultimately transcend all the limitations of its historical origin or cultural context. I shall not discuss how far, in relation to a work of art, the 'sense of quality' represents an independent possibility of knowledge, or whether, like all taste, it is not only formally developed, but also shaped and fashioned.[3] At any rate, taste is necessarily formed by something that does not indicate for what that taste is formed. To that extent, it may always include particular, preferred types of content and exclude others. But in any case it is true that everyone who experiences a work of art gathers this experience wholly within himself: namely, into the totality of his self-understanding, within which it means something to him. I go so far as to assert that the achievement of understanding, which in this way embraces the experience of the work of art, surpasses all historicism in the sphere of aesthetic experience. Of course there appears to be an obvious distinction between the original world structure established by a work of art, and its continued existence in the changed circumstances of the world thereafter.[4] But where exactly does the dividing line lie between the present world and the world that comes to be? How is the original life-significance transformed into the reflected experience that is cultural significance? It seems to me that the concept of aesthetic non-differentiation, which I have coined in this connection, is wholly valid; that here there are no clear divisions, and the movement of understanding cannot be restricted to the reflective pleasure prescribed by aesthetic differentiation. It should be admitted that, say, an ancient image of the gods that was not displayed in a temple as a work of art in order to give aesthetic, reflective pleasure, and is now on show in a museum, contains, in the way it stands before us today, the world of religious experience from which it came; the important consequence is that its world is still part of ours. It is the hermeneutic universe that embraces both.[5]

There are other respects in which the universality of the hermeneutical aspect cannot be arbitrarily restricted or curtailed. No mere artifice of composition persuaded me to begin with the experience of art in order to assure the phenomenon of understanding that breadth which is proper to it. Here the aesthetics of genius has done important preparatory work in showing that the experience of the work of art always fundamentally surpasses any subjective horizon of interpretation, whether that of the artist or that of the recipient. The *mens auctoris* is not admissible as a yardstick for the meaning of a work of art. Even the idea of a work-in-itself, divorced from its constantly renewed reality of being experienced, always has something abstract about it. I think I have already shown why this idea only describes an intention, but does not permit a dogmatic solution. At any rate, the purpose of my investigation is not to offer a general theory of interpretation and a differential account of its methods (which E. Betti has done so well) but to discover what is common to all modes of understanding and to show that understanding is never subjective behavior toward a given 'object', but toward its effective history—the history of its influence; in other words, understanding belongs to the being of that which is understood.

Therefore I do not find convincing the objection that the reproduction of a musical work of art is interpretation in a different sense from, say, the process of understanding when reading a poem or looking at a painting. All reproduction is primarily interpretation and seeks, as such, to be correct. In this sense it, too, is 'understanding'.[6]

I believe that the universality of the hermeneutical viewpoint cannot be restricted even where it is a question of the multitude of historical concerns and interests subsumed under the science of history. Certainly there are many modes of historical writing and research. There is no question of every historical observation being based on a conscious act of reflection on effective-history. The history of the North American Eskimo tribes is certainly quite independent of whether and when these tribes influenced the 'universal history of Europe'. Yet one cannot seriously deny that reflection on effective-history will prove to be important even in relation to this historical task. Whoever reads, in fifty or a hundred years, the history of these tribes as it is written today will not only find it old-fashioned (for in the meantime he will know more or interpret the sources more correctly) he will also be able to see that in the 1960s people read the sources differently because they were moved by different questions, prejudices, and interests. Ultimately historical writing and research would be reduced to nullity if withdrawn from the sphere of the study of effective-history. The very universality of the hermeneutical problem precedes every kind of interest in history, because it is concerned with what is always fundamental to the historical question?[7] And what is historical research without the historical question? In the language that I use, justified by investigation into semantic history, this means: application is an element of understanding itself. If, in this connection, I put the legal historian and the practising lawyer on the same level, I do not deny that the former has exclusively a 'contemplative', and the other a practical, task. Yet application is involved in the activities of both. How could the legal meaning of a law be different for either? It is true that, for example, the judge has the practical task of passing judgment, and many considerations of legal politics may enter in, which the legal historian (with the same law before him) does not consider. But does that make their legal understanding of the law any different? The judge's decision, which has a practical effect on life, aims at being a correct and never an arbitrary application of the law; hence it must rely on a 'correct' interpretation, which necessarily includes the mediation between history and the present in the act of understanding itself.

The legal historian, of course, will also have to evaluate 'historically' a law correctly understood in this way, and this always means that he must assess its historical importance; since he will always be guided by his own historical fore-understanding and prejudices, he may do this 'wrongly'. That means that again there is mediation between the past and the present: that is, application. The course of history, to which the history of research belongs, generally teaches us this. But it obviously does not mean that the historian has done something which he should not have done, and which he should or could have been prevented from doing by some hermeneutical canon. I am not speaking of the errors of legal history, but of accurate findings. The legal historian—like the judge—has his 'methods' of avoiding mistakes, in which I agree entirely with the legal historian.[8] But the hermeneutical interest of the philosopher begins only when error has been successfully avoided. Then both historians and dogmaticians testify to a truth that extends beyond what they know, insofar as their own transient present is discernible in what they do.

From the viewpoint of philosophical hermeneutics, the contrast between historical and dogmatic method has no absolute validity. This raises the question of the extent to which the hermeneutical viewpoint itself enjoys historical or dogmatic validity.[9] If the principle of effective-history is made into a general structural element in understanding, then this thesis undoubtedly includes no historical relativity, but seeks absolute validity—and yet a hermeneutical consciousness exists only under specific historical conditions. Tradition, part of whose nature is the handing-on of traditional material, must have become questionable for an explicit consciousness of the hermeneutic task of appropriating tradition to have been formed. Hence we find in Augustine such a consciousness in regard to the old testament; and, during the Reformation, Protestant hermeneutics developed from an insistence on understanding scripture solely on its own basis (sola scriptura) as against the principle of tradition held by the Roman church. But certainly since the birth of historical consciousness, which involves a fundamental distance between the present and all historical transmission, understanding has been a task requiring methodical direction. My thesis is that the element of effective-history is operative in all understanding of tradition, even where the methodology of the modern historical sciences has been largely adopted, which makes what has grown historically and has been transmitted historically an object to be established like an experimental finding—as if tradition were as alien and, from the human point of view, as unintelligible, as an object of physics.

Hence there is a certain legitimate ambiguity in the concept of the consciousness of history, as I have used it. This ambiguity is that it is used to mean at once the consciousness obtained in the course of history and determined by history, and the very consciousness of this gaining and determining. Obviously the burden of my argument is that this quality of being determined by effective-history still dominates the modern, historical and scientific consciousness and that beyond any possible knowledge of this domination. The effective-historical consciousness is so radically finite that our whole being, achieved in the totality of our destiny, inevitably transcends its knowledge of itself. But that is a fundamental insight which ought not to be limited to any specific historical situation; an insight which, however, in the face of modern historical research and of the methodological ideal of the objectivity of science, meets with particular resistance in the self-understanding of science.

We are certainly entitled to ask the reflective historical question: Why, just now, at this precise moment in history, has this fundamental insight into the element of effective-history in all understanding become possible? My investigations offer an indirect answer to this question. Only after the failure of the naïve historicism of the very century of historicism does it become clear that the contrast between unhistorical-dogmatic and historical, between tradition and historical science, between ancient and modern, is not absolute. The famous querelle des anciens et des modernes ceases to be a real alternative.

Hence what is here asserted, the universality of the hermeneutic aspect and especially what is elicited about language as the form in which understanding is achieved, embraces the 'pre-hermeneutic' consciousness as well as all modes of hermeneutic consciousness. Even the naïve appropriation of tradition is a 'retelling', although it ought not to be described as a 'fusion of horizon'.

And now to the basic question: How far does the aspect of understanding itself and its linguisticity reach? Can it support the general philosophical inference in the proposition, 'Being that can be understood is language'? Surely the universality of language requires the untenable metaphysical conclusion that 'everything' is only language and language event? True, the obvious reference to the ineffable does not necessarily affect the universality of language. The infinity of the dialogue in which understanding is achieved makes any reference to the ineffable itself relative. But is understanding the sole and sufficient access to the reality of history? Obviously there is a danger that the actual reality of the event, especially its absurdity and contingency, will be weakened and seen falsely in terms of sense-experience.

Hence it was my purpose to show that the historicism of Droysen and Dilthey, despite all the opposition of the historical school to Hegel's spiritualism, was seduced by its hermeneutic starting point into reading history as a book: as one, moreover, intelligible from the first letter to the last. Despite all its protest against a philosophy of history in which the necessity of the idea is the nucleus of all events, the historical hermeneutics of Dilthey could not avoid letting history culminate in intellectual history. That was my criticism. Yet surely this danger recurs in regard to the present work? However, the traditional formation of ideas, especially the hermeneutic circle of whole and part, which is the starting point of my attempt to lay the foundations of hermeneutics, does not necessarily require this conclusion. The idea of the whole is itself to be understood only relatively. The totality of meaning that has to be understood in history or tradition is never the meaning of the totality of history. The danger of Docetism seems banished when historical tradition is not conceived as an object of historical knowledge or of philosophical conception, but as an effective moment of one's own being. The finite nature of one's own understanding is the manner in which reality, resistance, the absurd, and the unintelligible assert themselves. If one takes this finiteness seriously, then one must also take the reality of history seriously.

The same problem makes the experience of the 'Thou' so decisive for all self-understanding. The section on experience has a systematic and a key position in my investigations. There the experience of the 'Thou' also throws light on the idea of the effective-historical experience. The experience of the 'Thou' also manifests the paradoxical element that something standing over against me asserts its own rights and requires absolute recognition; and in that very process is 'understood'. But I believe that I have shown correctly that this understanding does not at all understand the 'Thou', but what the 'Thou' truly says to us. One truth I refer to is the truth that becomes visible to me only through the 'Thou', and only by my letting myself be told something by it. It is the same with historical tradition. It would not deserve the interest we take in it if it did not have something to teach us that we could not know by ourselves. It is in this sense that the statement 'being that can be understood is language' is to be read. It does not intend an absolute mastery over being by the one who understands but, on the contrary, that being is not experienced where something can be constructed by us and is to that extent conceived, but that it is experienced where what is happening can merely be understood.

This involves a question of philosophical procedure, which was raised in a number of critical comments on my book. I should like to call it the 'problem of phenomenological immanence'. It is true that my book is phenomenological in its method. This may seem paradoxical inasmuch as Heidegger's criticism of the transcendental question and his thinking of 'reversal' form the basis of my treatment of the universal hermeneutic problem. I consider, however, that the principle of phenomenological demonstration can be applied to this usage of Heidegger's, which at last reveals the hermeneutic problem. I have therefore preserved the term 'hermeneutics', which the early Heidegger used, not in the sense of a methodical art, but as a theory of the real experience that thinking is. Hence I must emphasize that my analyses of play or of language are intended in a purely phenomenological sense.[10] Play is more than the consciousness of the player; and so it is more than a subjective attitude. Language is more than the consciousness of the speaker; so it, too, is more than a subjective attitude. This is what may be described as an experience of the subject and has nothing to do with 'mythology' or 'mystification'.[11]

This fundamental methodical approach has nothing to do with any metaphysical conclusions. In writings published subsequently, especially in my research reports 'Hermeneutik und Historismus' and 'Die phäno-menologische Bewegung' (in the *Philosophische Rundschau*) I have recorded my acceptance of the conclusions of Kant's *Critique of Pure Reason,* and regard statements that proceed by wholly dialectical means from the finite to the infinite, from human experience to what exists in itself, from the temporal to the eternal, as doing no more than set limits, and consider that philosophy can derive no actual knowledge from them. Nevertheless, the tradition of metaphysics and especially of its last great creation, Hegel's speculative dialectic, remains close to us. The task, the 'infinite relation', remains. But the mode of demonstrating it seeks to free itself from the embrace of the synthetic power of the Hegelian dialectic, and even from the 'logic' which developed from the dialectic of Plato, and to take its stand in the movement of that discourse in which word and idea first become what they are.[12]

Hence the demand for a reflexive self-grounding, as made from the viewpoint of the speculatively conducted transcendental philosophy of Fichte, Hegel, and Husserl, is unfulfilled. But is the discourse with the whole of our philosophical tradition, in which we stand, and which, as philosophers, we are, purposeless? Do we need to justify what has always supported us?

This raises a final question which concerns less the method than the contents of the hermeneutic universalism that I have outlined. Does not the universality of understanding involve a one-sidedness in its contents, inasmuch as it lacks a critical principle in relation to tradition and, as it were, espouses a universal optimism? However much it is the nature of tradition to exist only through being appropriated, it still is part of the nature of man to be able to break with tradition, to criticize and dissolve it, and is not what takes place in the work of remaking the real into an instrument of human purpose something far more basic in our relationship to being? To this extent, does not the ontological universality of understanding result in a certain one-sidedness? Understanding certainly does not mean merely the assimilation of traditional opinion or the acknowledgment of what tradition has made sacred. Heidegger, who first described the idea of understanding as the universal determinateness of There-being, means the very projective character of understanding, i.e., the futural character of There-being. I shall not deny, however, that within the universal context of the elements of understanding I have emphasized the element of the assimilation of what is past and handed down. Heidegger also, like many of my critics, would probably feel the lack of an ultimate radicality in the drawing of conclusions. What does the end of metaphysics as a science mean? What does its ending in science mean? When science expands into a total technocracy and thus brings on the 'cosmic night' of the 'forgetfulness of being', the nihilism that Nietzsche prophesied, then may one look at the last fading light of the sun that is set in the evening sky, instead of turning around to look for the first shimmer of its return?

It seems to me, however, that the one-sidedness of hermeneutic universalism has the truth of a corrective. It enlightens the modern attitude of making, producing, and constructing about the necessary conditions to which it is subject. In particular, it limits the position of the philosopher in the modern world. However much he may be called to make radical inferences from everything, the role of prophet, of Cassandra, of preacher, or even of know-all does not suit him.

What man needs is not only a persistent asking of ultimate questions, but the sense of what is feasible, what is possible, what is correct, here and now. The philosopher, of all people, must, I think, be aware of the tension between what he claims to achieve and the reality in which he finds himself.

The hermeneutic consciousness, which must be awakened and kept awake, recognizes that in the age of science the claim of superiority made by philosophic thought has something vague and unreal about it. But it seeks to confront the will of man, which is more than ever intensifying its criticism of what has gone before to the point of becoming a utopian or eschatological consciousness, with something from the truth of remembrance: with what is still and ever again real.

### The Logic of Question and Answer

Thus we come back to the point that the hermeneutic phenomenon also contains within itself the original meaning of conversation and the struc-

ture of question and answer. For a historical text to be made the object
of interpretation means that it asks a question of the interpreter. Thus
interpretation always involves a relation to the question that is asked of
the interpreter. To understand a text means to understand this question.
But this takes place, as we showed, by our achieving the hermeneutical
horizon. We now recognize this as the horizon of the question within
which the sense of the text is determined.

Thus a person who seeks to understand must question what lies behind
what is said. He must understand it as an answer to a question. If we go
back behind what is said, then we inevitably ask questions beyond what
is said. We understand the sense of the text only by acquiring the horizon
of the question that, as such, necessarily includes other possible answers.
Thus the meaning of a sentence is relative to the question to which it is
a reply, i.e., it necessarily goes beyond what is said in it. The logic of the
human sciences is, then, as appears from what we have said, a logic of
the question.

Despite Plato we are not very ready for such a logic. Almost the only
person I find a link with here is R. G. Collingwood. In a brilliant and
cogent critique of the 'realist' Oxford school, he developed the idea of a
logic of question and answer, but unfortunately never developed it systematically.[13] He clearly saw what was missing in naïve hermeneutics
founded on the prevailing philosophical critique. In particular the practice
that Collingwood found in English universities of discussing 'statements',
though perhaps a good training of intelligence, obviously failed to take
account of the historicality that is part of all understanding. Collingwood
argues thus: We can understand a text only when we have understood the
question to which it is an answer. But since this question can be derived
solely from the text and accordingly the appropriateness of the reply is
the methodological presupposition for the reconstruction of the question,
any criticism of this reply from some other quarter is pure mock-fighting.
It is like the understanding of works of art. A work of art can be
understood only if we assume its adequacy as an expression of the artistic
idea. Here also we have to discover the question which it answers, if we
are to understand it as an answer. This is, in fact, an axiom of all
hermeneutics which we describe as the 'fore-conception of completion'.[14]

This is, for Collingwood, the nerve of all historical knowledge. The
historical method requires that the logic of question and answer be applied
to historical tradition. We shall understand historical events only if we
reconstruct the question to which the historical actions of the persons
concerned were the answer. As an example, Collingwood cites the Battle
of Trafalgar and Nelson's plan on which it was based. The example is
intended to show that the course of the battle helps us to understand
Nelson's real plan, because it was successfully carried out. The plan of his

opponent, however, because it failed, cannot be reconstructed from the events. Thus understanding the course of the battle and understanding the plan that Nelson carried out in it are one and the same process.[15]

In fact we cannot avoid the discovery that the logic of question and answer has to reconstruct two different questions that have also two different answers: the question of meaning in the course of a great event and the question of whether this event went according to plan. Clearly, the two questions coincide only when the plan coincides with the course of events. But this is a presupposition that, as men involved in history, we cannot maintain as a methodological principle when concerned with a historical tradition which deals with such men. Tolstoy's celebrated description of the council of war before the battle, in which all the strategic possibilities are calculated and all the plans considered, thoroughly and perceptively, while the general sits there and sleeps, but in the night before the battle goes round all the sentry posts, is obviously a more accurate account of what we call history. Kutusov gets nearer to the reality and the forces that determine it than the strategists of the war council. The conclusion to be drawn from this example is that the interpreter of history always runs the risk of hypostasizing the sequence of events when he sees their significance as that intended by actors and planners.[16]

This is a legitimate undertaking only if Hegel's conditions hold good, i.e., that the philosophy of history is made party to the plans of the world spirit and on the basis of this esoteric knowledge is able to mark out certain individuals as of world-historical importance, there being a real coordination between their particular ideas and the world-historical meaning of events. But it is impossible to derive a hermeneutical principle for the knowledge of history from these cases that are characterized by the coming together of the subjective and objective in history. In regard to historical tradition Hegel's theory has, clearly, only a limited truth. The infinite web of motivations that constitutes history only occasionally and for a short period acquires in a single individual the clarity of what has been planned. Thus what Hegel describes as an outstanding case rests on the general basis of the disproportion that exists between the subjective thoughts of an individual and the meaning of the whole course of history. As a rule we experience the course of events as something that continually changes our plans and expectations. Someone who tries to stick to his plans discovers precisely how powerless his reason is. There are odd occasions when everything happens, as it were, of its own accord, i.e., events seem to be automatically in accord with our plans and wishes. On these occasions we can say that everything is going according to plan. But to apply this experience to the whole of history is to undertake a great extrapolation that entirely contradicts our experience.

The use that Collingwood makes of the logic of question and answer in hermeneutical theory is now made ambiguous by this extrapolation. Our understanding of written tradition as such is not of a kind that we can simply presuppose that the meaning that we discover in it agrees with that which its author intended. Just as the events of history do not in general manifest any agreement with the subjective ideas of the person who stands and acts within history, so the sense of a text in general reaches far beyond what its author originally intended.[17] But the task of understanding is concerned in the first place with the meaning of the text itself.

This is clearly what Collingwood had in mind when he denied that there is any difference between the historical question and the philosophical question to which the text is supposed to be an answer. Nevertheless, we must hold on to the point that the question that we are concerned to reconstruct has to do not with the mental experiences of the author, but simply with the meaning of the text itself. Thus it must be possible, if we have understood the meaning of a sentence, i.e., have reconstructed the question to which it is really the answer, to enquire also about the questioner and his meaning, to which the text is, perhaps, only the imagined answer. Collingwood is wrong when he finds it methodologically unsound to differentiate between the question to which the text is imagined to be an answer and the question to which it really is an answer. He is right only insofar as the understanding of a text does not generally involve such a distinction, if we are concerned with the object of which the text speaks. The reconstruction of the ideas of an author is a quite different task.

We shall have to ask what are the conditions that apply to this different task. For it is undoubtedly true that, compared with the genuine hermeneutical experience that understands the meaning of the text, the reconstruction of what the author really had in mind is a limited undertaking. It is the seduction of historicism to see in this kind of reduction a scientific virtue and regard understanding as a kind of reconstruction which in effect repeats the process of how the text came into being. Hence it follows the ideal familiar to us from our knowledge of nature, where we understand a process only when we are able to reproduce it artificially.

I have shown above[18] how questionable is Vico's statement that this ideal finds its purest fulfillment in history, because it is there that man encounters his own human historical reality. I have asserted, against this, that every historian and literary critic must reckon with the fundamental non-definitiveness of the horizon in which his understanding moves. Historical tradition can be understood only by being considered in its further determinations resulting from the progress of events. Similarly, the literary critic, who is dealing with poetic or philosophical texts, knows that they are inexhaustible. In both cases it is the progress of events that brings out new aspects of meaning in historical material. Through being reactualized in understanding, the texts are drawn into a genuine process in exactly the same way as are the events themselves through their continuance. This is what we described as the effective-historical element within the hermeneutical experience. Every actualization in understanding can be regarded as a historical potentiality of what is understood. It is part of the historical finiteness of our being that we are aware that after us others will understand in a different way. And yet it is a fact equally well established that it remains the same work, the fullness of whose meaning is proved in the changing process of understanding, just as it is the same history whose meaning is constantly being further determined. The hermeneutical reduction to the author's meaning is just as inappropriate as the reduction of historical events to the intentions of their protagonists.

We cannot, however, simply take the reconstruction of the question to which a given text is an answer simply as an achievement of historical method. The first thing is the question that the text presents us with, our response to the word handed down to us, so that its understanding must already include the work of historical self-mediation of present and tradition. Thus the relation of question and answer is, in fact, reversed. The voice that speaks to us from the past—be it text, work, trace—itself poses a question and places our meaning in openness. In order to answer this question, we, of whom the question is asked, must ourselves begin to ask questions. We must attempt to reconstruct the question to which the transmitted text is the answer. But we shall not be able to do this without going beyond the historical horizon it presents us with. The reconstruction of the question to which the text is presumed to be the answer takes place itself within a process of questioning through which we seek the answer to the question that the text asks us. A reconstructed question can never stand within its original horizon: for the historical horizon that is outlined in the reconstruction is not a truly comprehensive one. It is, rather, included within the horizon that embraces us as the questioners who have responded to the word that has been handed down.

Hence it is a hermeneutical necessity always to go beyond mere reconstruction. We cannot avoid thinking about that which was unquestionably accepted, and hence not thought about, by an author, and bringing it into the openness of the question. This is not to open the door to arbitrariness in interpretation, but to reveal what always takes place. The understanding of the word of the tradition always requires that the reconstructed question be set within the openness of its questionableness, i.e., that it merge with the question that tradition is for us. If the 'historical' question emerges by itself, this means that it no longer raises itself as a question. It results from the coming to an end of understanding—a wrong turning at which we get stuck.[19] It is part of real understanding, however, that we regain the concepts of a historical past in such a way that they also include our own comprehension of them. I earlier called this 'the fusing of horizons'. We can say, with Collingwood, that we understand only when we understand the question to which something is the answer, and it is true that what is understood in this way does not remain detached in its meaning from our own meaning. Rather, the reconstruction of the question, from which the meaning of a text is to be understood as an answer, passes into our own questioning. For the text must be understood as an answer to a real question.

The close relation that exists between question and understanding is what gives the hermeneutic experience its true dimension. However much a person seeking understanding may leave open the truth of what is said, however much he may turn away from the immediate meaning of the object and consider, rather, its deeper significance, and take the latter not as true, but merely as meaningful, so that the possibility of its truth remains unsettled, this is the real and basic nature of a question, namely to make things indeterminate. Questions always bring out the undetermined possibilities of a thing. That is why there cannot be an understanding of the questionableness of an object that turns away from real questions, in the same way that there can be the understanding of a meaning that turns away from meaning. To understand the questionableness of something is always to question it. There can be no testing or potential attitude to questioning, for questioning is not the positing, but the testing of possibilities. Here the nature of questioning indicates what is demonstrated by the operation of the Platonic dialogue.[20] A person who thinks must ask himself questions. Even when a person says that at such and such a point a question might arise, that is already a real questioning that simply masks itself, out of either caution or politeness.

This is the reason that all understanding is always more than the mere recreation of someone else's meaning. Asking it opens up possibilities of meaning and thus what is meaningful passes into one's own thinking on the subject. Questions that we do not ourselves ask, such as those that we regard as out of date or pointless, are understood in a curious fashion. We understand how certain questions came to be asked in particular historical circumstances. Understanding such questions means, then, understanding the particular presuppositions whose demise makes the question no longer relevant. An example is perpetual motion. The horizon of meaning of such questions is only apparently still open. They are no longer understood as questions. For what we understand, in such cases, is precisely that there is no question.

To understand a question means to ask it. To understand an opinion is to understand it as the answer to a question.

The logic of question and answer that Collingwood elaborated does away with talk of the permanent problem that underlay the relation of the 'Oxford realists' to the classics of philosophy, and hence with the problem of the history of problems developed by neokantianism. History of problems would be truly history only if it acknowledged the identity of the problem as a pure abstraction and permitted itself a transformation into questioning. There is no such thing, in fact, as a point outside history from which the identity of a problem can be conceived within the vicissitudes of the various attempts to solve it. It is true that all understanding of the texts of philosophy requires the recognition of the knowledge that they contain. Without this we would understand nothing at all. But this does not mean that we in any way step outside the historical conditions in which we find ourselves and in which we understand. The problem that we recognize is not in fact simply the same if it is to be understood in a genuine question. We can regard it as the same only because of our historical shortsightedness. The standpoint that is beyond any standpoint, a standpoint from which we could conceive its true identity, is a pure illusion.

We can understand the reason for this now. The concept of the problem is clearly the formulation of an abstraction, namely the detachment of the content of the question from the question that in fact first reveals it. It refers to the abstract schema to which real and really motivated questions can be reduced and under which they can be subsumed. This kind of 'problem' has fallen out of the motivated context of questioning, from which it receives the clarity of its sense. Hence it is insoluble, like every question that has no clear unambiguous sense, because it is not properly motivated and asked.

This confirms also the origin of the concept of the problem. It does not belong in the sphere of those 'honestly motivated refutations'[21] in which the truth of the object is advanced, but in the sphere of dialectic as a weapon to amaze or make a fool of one's opponent. In Aristotle, the word problema refers to those questions that appear as open alternatives because there is evidence for both views and we think that they cannot be decided by reasons, since the questions involved are too great.[22] Hence problems are not real questions that present themselves and hence acquire the pattern of their answer from the genesis of their meaning, but are alternatives that can only be accepted as themselves and thus can only be treated in a dialectical way. This dialectical sense of the 'problem' has its place in rhetoric, not in philosophy. It is part of the concept that there can be no clear decision on the basis of reasons. That is why Kant sees the rise of the concept of the problem as limited to the dialectic of pure reason. Problems are 'tasks that emerge entirely from its own womb', i.e., products of reason itself, the complete solution of which it cannot hope to achieve.[23] It is interesting that in the nineteenth century, with the collapse of the direct tradition of philosophical questioning and the rise of historicism, the concept of the problem acquires a universal validity—a sign of the fact that the direct relation to the questions of philosophy no longer exists. It is typical of the embarrassment of the philosophical consciousness that when faced with historicism, it took flight into the abstraction of the concept of the problem and saw no problem about the manner in which problems actually 'exist'. The history of problems in neokantianism is a bastard of historicism. The critique of the concept of the problem that is conducted with the means of a logic of question and answer must destroy the illusion that there are problems as there are stars in the sky.[24] Reflection on the hermeneutical experience transforms problems back to questions that arise and that derive their sense from their motivation.

The dialectic of question and answer, that was disclosed in the structure of the hermeneutical experience, now permits us to state in more detail the type of consciousness that effective-historical consciousness is. For the dialectic of question and answer that we demonstrated makes understanding appear as a reciprocal relationship of the same kind as conversation. It is true that a text does not speak to us in the same way as does another person. We, who are attempting to understand, must ourselves make it speak. But we found that this kind of understanding, 'making the text speak', is not an arbitrary procedure that we undertake on our own initiative but that, as a question, it is related to the answer that is expected in the text. The anticipation of an answer itself presumes that the person asking is part of the tradition and regards himself as addressed by it. This is the truth of the effective-historical consciousness. It is the historically experienced consciousness that, by renouncing the chimera of perfect enlightenment, is open to the experience of history. We described its realization as the fusion of the horizons of understanding, which is what mediates between the text and its interpreter.

The guiding idea of the following discussion is that the fusion of the horizons that takes place in understanding is the proper achievement of language. Admittedly, the nature of language is one of the most mysterious questions that exist for man to ponder on. Language is so uncannily near to our thinking and when it functions it is so little an object that it seems to conceal its own being from us. In our analysis of the thinking of the human sciences, however, we came so close to this universal mystery of language that is prior to everything else, that we can entrust ourselves to the object that we are investigating to guide us safely in the quest. In other words we are seeking to approach the mystery of language from the conversation that we ourselves are.

If we seek to examine the hermeneutical phenomenon according to the model of the conversation between two persons, the chief thing that these apparently so different situations have in common—the understanding of a text and the understanding that occurs in conversation—is that both are concerned with an object that is placed before them. Just as one person seeks to reach agreement with his partner concerning an object, so the interpreter understands the object of which the text speaks. This understanding of the object must take place in a linguistic form; not that the understanding is subsequently put into words, but in the way in which the understanding comes about—whether in the case of a text or a conversation with another person who presents us with the object—lies the coming-into-language of the thing itself. Thus we shall first consider the structure of conversation proper, in order to bring out the specific character of that other form of conversation that is the understanding of texts. Whereas up to now we have emphasized the constitutive significance of the question for the hermeneutical phenomenon, in terms of the conversation, we must now demonstrate the linguistic nature of conversation, which is the basis of the question, as an element of hermeneutics.

Our first point is that language, in which something comes to be language, is not a possession at the disposal of one or the other of the interlocutors. Every conversation presupposes a common language, or, it creates a common language. Something is placed in the center, as the Greeks said, which the partners to the dialogue both share, and concerning which they can exchange ideas with one another. Hence agreement concerning the object, which it is the purpose of the conversation to bring about, necessarily means that a common language must first be worked out in the conversation. This is not an external matter of simply adjusting our tools, nor is it even right to say that the partners adapt themselves to one another but, rather, in the successful conversation they both come under the influence of the truth of the object and are thus bound to one another in a new community. To reach an understanding with one's partner in a dialogue is not merely a matter of total self-expression and the successful assertion of one's own point of view, but a transformation into a communion, in which we do not remain what we were.[25]

## Notes

1. E. Betti, *Die Hermeneutik als allgemeine Methodik der Geisteswissenschaften* Tübingen, 1962; F. Wieacker, 'Notizen zur rechtshistorischen Hermeneutik', *Nachr. d. Ak. d. W.* Göttingen, phil.-hist. Kl. 1963, pp. 1–22.
2. O. Becker, 'Die Fragwurdigkeit der Tranzendierung der aesthetischen Dimen-

sion der Kunst (im Hinblick auf den 1 Teil von *Wahrheit und Methode*)', *Phil. Rundsch.* 10, 1962, pp. 225–238.

3. In his *Traktat vom Schonen,* Frankfurt, 1935, Kurt Riezler attempted a transcendental deduction of the 'sense of quality'.

4. See H. Kuhn's recent work: *Vom wesen des Kunstwerkes* (1967).

5. The vindication of allegory, which is pertinent here, began some years ago with Walter Benjamin's major work, *Der Ursprung des deutschen Trauerspiels* (1927).

6. On this point I can invoke Hans Sedlmayr's papers despite their admittedly different emphasis, now collected as *Kunst und Wahrheit* (Rowohlts Deutsche Enzypelopädie, 71) especially pp. 87ff.

7. H. Kuhn, 'Wahrheit und geschichtliches Verstehen', *Histor. Ztschr.* 193/2 1961, pp. 90–121.

8. Betti, Wieacker, *op cit;* Hellebrand, 'Die Zeitbogen', *Arch. F. Rechts u. Sozialphil.* 49, 1963, pp. 57–76.

9. K. O. Apel, *Hegelstudien,* II, Bonn, 1963, pp. 314–322.

10. Wittgenstein's concept of 'language games' seemed quite natural to me when I came across it. Cf 'The Phenomenological Movement', pp. 37f.

11. My postscript to the Reclam edition of Heidegger's essay on the work of art (pp. 108f) and, more recently, the essay in the FAZ of September 26, 1964. See also *Die Sammlung* 1965, no. 1.

12. O. Pöggeler has made an interesting suggestion (*Philos. Literaturanzeiger* 16, pp. 12f), about what Hegel would have said about this, through the mouth of Rosenkranz.

13. Cf. Collingwood's *Autobiography* which, at my suggestion, was published in German translation as *Denken,* p. 30ff, as well as the unpublished dissertation of Joachim Finkeldei, *Grund und Wesen des Fragens,* Heidelberg, 1954. A similar position is adopted by Croce (who influenced Collingwood) in his *Logic,* where he understands every definition as an answer to a question and hence historical. (*Logic as Science of the Pure Concept,* tr. Ainsley, London 1917.)

14. Cf. p. 261f above, and my critique of Guardini in the *Philosophische Rundschau* 2, pp. 82–92, where I said: 'All criticism of literature is always the self-criticism of interpretation'.

15. Collingwood, *An Autobiography,* Galaxy ed, Oxford 1970, p. 70.

16. There are some good observations on this subject in Erich Seeberg's 'Zum Problem der pneumatischen Exegese' in the *Sellin-Festschrift,* p. 127ff.

17. See pp. 161, 263 above [in *Truth and Method*].

18. Pp. 196f and 244f above [in *Truth and Method*].

19. See the account of this wrong turning of the historical in my analysis above [in *Truth and Method*], p. 159ff, of the theologico-political treatise of Spinoza.

20. Cf. p. 325ff above [in *Truth and Method*].

21. Plato, *Ep* VII, 344b.

22. Aristotle, *Topics,* I, II.

23. *Critique of Pure Reason,* A 321ff.

24. Nicolai Hartmann, in his essay, 'Der philosophische Gedanke und seine Geschichte', in the *Abhandlungen der preussischen Akademie der Wissenschaften,*

1936, 5, rightly pointed out that the important thing is to realize once more in our own minds what the great thinkers realized. But when, in order to hold something fixed against the inroads of historicism, he distinguished between the constancy of what the 'real problems are concerned with and the changing nature of the way in which they have to be both asked and answered, he failed to see that neither 'change', nor 'constancy', the antithesis of 'problem' and 'system', nor the criterion of achievements' is in agreement with the character of philosophy as knowledge. When he wrote that 'only when the individual makes his own the enormous intellectual experience of the centuries, and his own experience is based on what he has recognized and what has been well tried, can that knowledge be sure of its own further progress' (p. 18), he interpreted the 'systematic acquaintance with the problems' according to the model of a process of knowledge that does not at all measure up to the complicated reticulation of tradition and history, which we have seen in hermeneutical consciousness.

    25. Cf. my 'Was ist Wahrheit?', *Zeitwende* 28, 1957, pp. 226–237.

# 27.

# From Work to Text
## *ROLAND BARTHES*

Over the past several years, a change has been taking place in our ideas about language and, as a consequence, about the (literary) work, which owes at least, its phenomenal existence to language. This change is obviously linked to current developments in, among other fields, linguistics, anthropology, Marxism, and psychoanalysis (the word "link" is used here in a deliberately neutral fashion: it implies no decision about a determination, be it multiple and dialectical). The change affecting the notion of the work does not necessarily come from the internal renewal of each of these disciplines, but proceeds, rather, from their encounter at the level of an object that traditionally depends on none of them. *Interdisciplinary* activity, valued today as an important aspect of research, cannot be accomplished by simple confrontations between various specialized branches of knowledge. Interdisciplinary work is not a peaceful operation: it begins *effectively* when the solidarity of the old disciplines breaks down—a process made more violent, perhaps, by the jolts of fashion—to the benefit of a new object and a new language, neither of which is in the domain of those branches of knowledge that one calmly sought to confront.

It is precisely this uneasiness with classification that allows for the diagnosis of a certain mutation. The mutation that seems to be taking hold of the idea of the work must not, however, be overestimated: it is part of an epistemological shift [*glissement*] rather than of a real break [*coupure*], a break of the kind which, as has often been remarked, supposedly occurred during the last century, with the appearance of Marxism and

From Roland Barthes, "From Work to Text," from Juosé V. Harari (ed.), in *Textual Strategies: Perspectives in Post-Structuralist Criticism* (Ithaca, N.Y.: Cornell University Press, 1979). Reprinted with permission of Cornell University Press.

Freudianism. No new break seems to have occurred since, and it can be said that, in a way, we have been involved in repetition for the past hundred years. Today history, our history, allows only displacement, variation, going-beyond, and rejection. Just as Einsteinian science requires the inclusion of the *relativity of reference points* in the object studied, so the combined activity of Marxism, Freudianism, and structuralism requires, in the case of literature, the relativization of the *scriptor*'s, the reader's, and the observer's (the critic's) relationships. In opposition to the notion of the *work*—a traditional notion that has long been and still is thought of in what might be called Newtonian fashion—there now arises a need for a new object, one obtained by the displacement or overturning of previous categories. This object is the *Text*. I realize that this word is fashionable and therefore suspect in certain quarters, but that is precisely why I would like to review the principal propositions at the intersection of which the Text is situated today. These propositions are to be understood as enunciations rather than arguments, as mere indications, as it were, approaches that "agree" to remain metaphoric. Here, then, are those propositions: they deal with method, genre, the sign, the plural, filiation, reading (in an active sense), and pleasure.

(1) The Text must not be thought of as a defined object. It would be useless to attempt a material separation of works and texts. One must take particular care not to say that works are classical while texts are avant-garde. Distinguishing them is not a matter of establishing a crude list in the name of modernity and declaring certain literary productions to be "in" and others "out" on the basis of their chronological situation. A very ancient work can contain "some text," while many products of contemporary literature are not texts at all. The difference is as follows: the work is concrete, occupying a portion of book-space (in a library, for example); the Text, on the other hand, is a methodological field.

This opposition recalls the distinction proposed by Lacan between "reality" and the "real": the one is displayed, the other demonstrated. In the same way, the work can be seen in bookstores, in card catalogues, and on course lists, while the text reveals itself, articulates itself according to or against certain rules. While the work is held in the hand, the text is held in language: it exists only as discourse. The Text is not the decomposition of the work; rather it is the work that is the Text's imaginary tail. In other words, *the Text is experienced only in an activity, a production*. It follows that the Text cannot stop, at the end of a library shelf, for example; the constitutive movement of the Text is a *traversal* [*traversée*]: it can cut across a work, several works.

(2) Similarly, the Text does not come to a stop with (good) literature; it cannot be apprehended as part of a hierarchy or even a simple division

of genres. What constitutes the Text is, on the contrary (or precisely), its subversive force with regard to old classifications. How can one classify Georges Bataille? Is this writer a novelist, a poet, an essayist, an economist, a philosopher, a mystic? The answer is so uncertain that manuals of literature generally chose to forget about Bataille; yet Bataille wrote texts—even, perhaps, always one and the same text.

If the Text raises problems of classification, that is because it always implies an experience of limits. Thibaudet used to speak (but in a very restricted sense) about limit-works (such as Chateaubriand's *Life of Rancé*, a work that today indeed seems to be a "text"): the Text is that which goes to the limit of the rules of enunciation (rationality, readability, and so on). The Text tries to situate itself exactly *behind* the limit of *doxa* (is not public opinion—constitutive of our democratic societies and powerfully aided by mass communication—defined by its limits, its energy of exclusion, its *censorship*?). One could literally say that the Text is always *paradoxical*.

(3) Whereas the Text is approached and experienced in relation to the sign, the work closes itself on a signified. Two modes of signification can be attributed to this signified: on the one hand, one can assume that it is obvious, in which case the work becomes the object of a "science of the letter" (philology); on the other hand, one can assume that the signified is secret and ultimate, in which case one must search for it, and the work then depends upon a hermeneutic, an interpretation (Marxist, psychoanalytic, thematic, for example). In brief, the work itself functions as a general sign and thus represents an institutional category of the civilization of the Sign. The Text, on the contrary, practices the infinite deferral of the signified [*le recul infini du signifié*]: the Text is *dilatory;* its field is that of the signifier. The signifier must not be conceived as "the first stage of meaning," its material vestibule, but rather, on the contrary, as its *aftermath* [*après-coup*]. In the same way, the signifier's *infinitude* does not refer back to some idea of the ineffable (of an unnamable signified) but to the idea of *play.* The engendering of the perpetual signifier within the field of the text should not be identified with an organic process of maturation or a hermeneutic process of deepening, but rather with a serial movement of dislocations, overlappings, and variations. The logic that governs the Text is not comprehensive (seeking to define "what the work means") but metonymic; and the activity of associations, contiguities, and cross-references coincides with a liberation of symbolic energy. The work (in the best of cases) is moderately symbolic (its symbolism runs out, comes to a halt), but the Text is *radically* symbolic. *A work whose integrally symbolic nature one conceives, perceives, and receives is a text.*

In this way the Text is restored to language: like language, it is structured but decentered, without closure (here one might note, in reply to the scornful insinuation of "faddishness" which is often directed against structuralism, that the epistemological privilege presently granted to language proceeds precisely from our discovery in language of a paradoxical idea of structure, a system without end or center).

(4) The Text is plural. This does not mean just that it has several meanings, but rather that it achieves plurality of meaning, an *irreducible* plurality. The Text is not coexistence of meanings but passage, traversal; thus it answers not to an interpretation, liberal though it may be, but to an explosion, a dissemination. The Text's plurality does not depend on the ambiguity of its contents, but rather on what could be called the *stereographic plurality* of the signifiers that weave it (etymologically the text is a cloth; *textus,* from which text derives, means "woven").

The reader of the Text could be compared to an idle subject (a subject having relaxed his "imaginary"[1]): this fairly empty subject strolls along the side of a valley at the bottom of which runs a *wadi* (I use *wadi* here to stress a certain feeling of unfamiliarity). What he sees is multiple and irreducible; it emerges from substances and levels that are heterogeneous and disconnected: lights, colors, vegetation, heat, air, bursts of noise, high-pitched bird calls, children's cries from the other side of the valley, paths, gestures, clothing of close and distant inhabitants. All these *occurrences* are partially identifiable: they proceed from known codes, but their combination is unique, founding the stroll in difference that can be repeated only as difference. This is what happens in the case of the Text: it can be itself only in its difference (which does not mean its "individuality"); its reading is semelfactive (which renders all inductive-deductive sciences of texts illusory—there is no "grammar" of the text) and yet completely woven with quotations, references, and echoes. These are cultural languages (and what language is not?), past or present, that traverse the text from one end to the other in a vast stereophony.

Every text, being itself the intertext of another text, belongs to the intertextual, which must not be confused with a text's origins: to search for the "sources of" and "influence upon" a work is to satisfy the myth of filiation. The quotations from which a text is constructed are anonymous, irrecoverable, and yet *already read:* they are quotations without quotation marks. The work does not upset monistic philosophies, for which plurality is evil. Thus, when it is compared with the work, the text might well take as its motto the words of the man possessed by devils: "My name is legion, for we are many" (Mark 5:9).

The plural or demonic texture that divides text from work can carry with it profound modifications in the activity of reading and precisely in the areas where monologism seems to be the law. Some of the "texts" of the Scriptures that have traditionally been recuperated by theological (historical or anagogical) monism may perhaps lend themselves to a diffraction of meaning, while the Marxist interpretation of the work, until now resolutely monistic, may be able to materialize itself even further by pluralizing itself (if, of course, Marxist "institutions" allow this).

(5) The work is caught up in a process of filiation. Three things are postulated here: a *determination* of the work by the outside world (by race, then by history), a *consecution* of works among themselves, and an *allocation* of the work to its author. The author is regarded as the father and the owner of his work; literary research therefore learns to *respect* the manuscript and the author's declared intentions, while society posits the legal nature of the author's relationship with his work (these are the "author's rights," which are actually quite recent; they were not legalized in France until the Revolution).

The Text, on the other hand, is read without the father's signature. The metaphor that describes the Text is also distinct from that describing the work. The latter refers to the image of an *organism* that grows by vital expansion, by "development" (a significantly ambiguous word, both biological and rhetorical). The Text's metaphor is that of the *network*:[2] if the Text expands, it is under the effect of a *combinatorial*, a *systematics*[3] (an image which comes close to modern biology's views on the living being).

Therefore, no vital "respect" is owed to the Text: it can be broken (this is exactly what the Middle Ages did with two authoritative texts, the Scriptures and Aristotle). The Text can be read without its father's guarantee: the restitution of the intertext paradoxically abolishes the concept of filiation. It is not that the author cannot "come back" into the Text, into his text; however, he can only do so as a "guest," so to speak. If the author is a novelist, he inscribes himself in his text as one of his characters, as another figure sewn into the rug; his signature is no longer privileged and paternal, the locus of genuine truth, but rather, ludic. He becomes a "paper author": his life is no longer the origin of his fables, but a fable that runs concurrently with his work. There is a reversal, and it is the work which affects the life, not the life which affects the work: the work of Proust and Genet allows us to read their lives as a text. The word "bio-graphy" reassumes its strong meaning, in accordance with its etymology. At the same time, the enunciation's sincerity, which has been a veritable "cross" of literary morality, becomes a false problem: the *I* that writes the text is never, itself, anything more than a paper *I*.

(6) The work is ordinarily an object of consumption. I intend no demagoguery in referring here to so-called consumer culture, but one must realize that today it is the work's "quality" (this implies, ultimately, an

appreciation in terms of "taste") and not the actual process of reading that can establish differences between books. There is no structural difference between "cultured" reading and casual subway reading. The Text (if only because of its frequent "unreadability") decants the work from its consumption and gathers it up as play, task, production, and activity. This means that the Text requires an attempt to abolish (or at least to lessen) the distance between writing and reading, not by intensifying the reader's projection into the work, but by linking the two together in a single signifying process [*pratique signifiante*].

The distance separating writing from reading is historical: during the era of greatest social division (before the institution of democratic cultures), both reading and writing were class privileges. Rhetoric, the great literary code of those times, taught *writing* (even though speeches and not texts were generally produced). It is significant that the advent of democracy reversed the order: (secondary) school now prides itself on teaching how to *read* (well), and not how to *write*.

In fact, *reading* in the sense of *consuming* is not *playing* with the text. Here "playing" must be understood in all its polysemy. The text itself *plays* (like a door on its hinges, like a device in which there is some "play"); and the reader himself plays twice over: playing the Text as one plays a game, he searches for a practice that will re-produce the Text; but, to keep that practice from being reduced to a passive, inner mimesis (the Text being precisely what resists such a reduction), he also *plays* the Text in the musical sense of the term. The history of music (as practice, not as "art") happens to run quite parallel to the history of the Text. There was a time when "practicing" music lovers were numerous (at least within the confines of a certain class), when "playing" and "listening" constituted an almost undifferentiated activity. Then two roles appeared in succession: first, that of the *interpreter,* to whom the bourgeois public delegated its playing; second, that of the music lover who listened to music without knowing how to play it. Today, post-serial music has disrupted the role of the "interpreter" by requiring him to be, in a certain sense, the coauthor of a score which he completes rather than "interprets."

The Text is largely a score of this new type: it asks the reader for an active collaboration. This is a great innovation, because it compels us to ask "who *executes* the work?" (a question raised by Mallarmé, who wanted the audience to *produce* the book). Today only the critic *executes* the work (in both senses). The reduction of reading to consumption is obviously responsible for the "boredom" that many people feel when confronting the modern ("unreadable") text, or the avant-garde movie or painting: to suffer from boredom means that one cannot produce the text, play it, open it out, *make it go.*

(7) This suggests one final approach to the Text, that of pleasure. I do not know if a hedonistic aesthetic ever existed, but there certainly exists a pleasure associated with the work (at least with certain works). I can enjoy reading and rereading Proust, Flaubert, Balzac, and even—why not?—Alexandre Dumas; but this pleasure, as keen as it may be and even if disengaged from all prejudice, remains partly (unless there has been an exceptional critical effort) a pleasure of consumption. If I can read those authors, I also know that I cannot *rewrite* them (that today, one can no longer write "like that"); that rather depressing knowledge is enough to separate one from the production of those works at the very moment when their remoteness founds one's modernity (for what is "being modern" but the full realization that one cannot begin to write the same works once again?). The Text, on the other hand, is linked to enjoyment [*jouissance*], to pleasure without separation. Order of the signifier, the Text participates in a social utopia of its own: prior to history, the Text achieves, if not the transparency of social relations, at least the transparency of language relations. It is the space in which no one language has a hold over any other, in which all languages circulate freely.

These few propositions, inevitably, do not constitute the articulation of a theory of the Text. This is not just a consequence of the presenter's insufficiencies (besides, I have in many respects only recapitulated what is being developed around me); rather, it proceeds from the fact that a theory of the Text cannot be fully satisfied by a metalinguistic exposition. The destruction of metalanguage, or at least (since it may become necessary to return to it provisionally) the questioning of it, is part of the theory itself. Discourse on the Text should itself be only "text," search, and textual toil, since the Text is that *social* space that leaves no language safe or untouched, that allows no enunciative subject to hold the position of judge, teacher, analyst, confessor, or decoder. The theory of the Text can coincide only with the activity of writing.

## Notes

1. "Qui aurait détendu en lui tout imaginaire." *Imaginary* is not simply the opposite of real. Used in the Lacanian sense, it is the register, the dimension of all images, conscious or unconscious, perceived or imagined.—Ed. [of translation].

2. Barthes uses here the word *reseau*. I have chosen to translate it by "network" (rather than "web," for instance) at the risk of overemphasizing the mechanical implications of the metaphor.—Ed. [of translation].

3. *Systematics* is the science (or method) of classification of living forms.—Ed. [of translation].

# Bibliography to Part Six

Among the earlier discussions of the objective status of criticism are:

Monroe C. Beardsley, *Aesthetics* (New York, 1958), chapters 10–11;

Pepita Haezrahi, "Propositions in Aesthetics," *Proceedings of the Aristotelian Society* LVII (1956–57), 177–206);

Stuart Hampshire, "Logic and Appreciation," reprinted in William Elton (ed.), *Aesthetics and Language* (Oxford, 1954);

Bernard Harrison, "Some Uses of 'Good' in Criticism," *Mind* LXIX (1960), 206–222;

Bernard C. Heyl, "Relativism Again," *Journal of Aesthetics and Art Criticism* V (1946), 54–61;

Isabel C. Hungerland, *Poetic Discourse* (Berkeley, 1958), chapter 3;

Arnold Isenberg, "Perception, Meaning, and the Subject Matter of Art," *Journal of Philosophy* XLI (1944), 561–575;

Arnold Isenberg, "Critical Communication," *Philosophical Review* LVIII (1949), 330–334;

William E. Kennick, "Does Traditional Aesthetics Rest on a Mistake?" *Mind* (1958), 317–334;

Helen Knight, "The Use of 'Good' in Aesthetic Judgments," reprinted in William Elton (ed.), *Aesthetics and Language* (Oxford, 1954);

Margaret Macdonald, "Some Distinctive Features of Arguments Used in Criticism of the Arts," reprinted (revised) in William Elton (ed.), *Aesthetics and Language* (Oxford, 1954);

Harold Osborne, *Aesthetics and Criticism* (London, 1955), chapter 1;

J. A. Passmore, "The Dreariness of Aesthetics," reprinted in William Elton (ed.), *Aesthetics and Language* (Oxford, 1954);

Charles L. Stevenson, "Interpretation and Evaluation in Aesthetics," in Max Black (ed.), *Philosophical Analysis* (Ithaca, 1950);

Charles L. Stevenson, "On the Reasons That Can Be Given for the Interpretation of a Poem," in Joseph Margolis (ed.), *Philosophy Looks at the Arts* (New York, 1962, 1st ed.);

Jerome Stolnitz, "On Objective Relativity in Aesthetics," *Journal of Philosophy* LVII (1960);

Paul Ziff, "Reasons in Art Criticism," in Israel Scheffler (ed.), *Philosophy and Education* (Boston, 1958).


Particularly pertinent to the puzzles of appreciation and evaluation, though not focused on aesthetic issues, are:

P. H. Nowell-Smith, *Ethics* (London, 1954), chapter 12; John Wisdom, "Gods," reprinted in *Philosophy and Psycho-analysis* (Oxford, 1953).


More recent discussions of interest include:

Karl Aschenbrenner, *The Concepts of Criticism* (Dordrecht, 1974);

Monroe C. Beardsley, *The Possibility of Criticism* (Detroit, 1970);

John Casey, *The Language of Criticism* (London, 1966);

Marcia Cavell, "Critical Dialogue," *Journal of Philosophy* LXVII (1970), 339–351;

Stanley Cavell, "Aesthetic Problems of Modern Philosophy," in Max Black (ed.), *Philosophy in America* (Ithaca, 1965);

Donald W. Crawford, "Causes, Reasons, and Aesthetic Objectivity," *American Philosophical Quarterly* VIII (1971), 266–274;

Denis Dutton, "Criticism and Method," *British Journal of Aesthetics* XIII (1973), 232–242;

Denis Dutton, "Plausibility and Aesthetic Interpretation," *Canadian Journal of Philosophy* VII (1977), 327–340;

J. N. Findlay, "The Perspicuous and the Poignant," *British Journal of Aesthetics* I (1967), 3–19;

E. D. Hirsch, Jr., *Validity in Interpretation* (New Haven, 1967);

I. C. Jarvie, "The Objectivity of Criticism of the Arts," *Ratio* IX (1967), 67–83;

Stefan Morawski. "On the Objectivity of Aesthetic Judgment," *British Journal of Aesthetics* VI (1966), 315–328;

Harold Osborne, "Taste and Judgment in the Arts," *Journal of Aesthetic Education* V (1971), 13–28;

A. G. Pleydell-Pearce, "Objectivity and Value in Judgments of Aesthetics," *British Journal of Aesthetics* X (1970), 25–38;

Colin Radford and Sally Minogue, "The Complexity of Criticism: Its Logic and Rhetoric," *Journal of Aesthetics and Art Criticism* XXXIV (1976), 411–429;

Colin Radford and Sally Minogue, *The Nature of Criticism* (Brighton, 1981);

Theodore Redpath, "Some Problems of Modern Aesthetics," in C. A. Mace (ed.), *British Philosophy in the Mid-Century* (London, 1966);

Michael Scriven, "The Objectivity of Aesthetic Evaluation," *The Monist* L (1966), 159–187;

Roger Scruton, *Art and Imagination* (London, 1974), part 1;

F. N. Sibley, "Aesthetic and Non-Aesthetic," *Philosophical Review* LXXIV (1965), 135–159;

F. N. Sibley, "Objectivity and Aesthetics," *Proceedings of the Aristotelian Society,* suppl. vol. 42 (1968), 31–54;

F. N. Sibley, "Particularity, Art and Evaluation," *Proceedings of the Aristotelian Society,* suppl. vol. 48 (1974), 1–21;

Guy Sircello, *A New Theory of Beauty* (Princeton, 1975);

M. A. Slote, "Rationality of Aesthetic Value Judgements," *Journal of Philosophy* LXVIII (1971), 821–839;

F. G. Sparshott, *The Concept of Criticism* (Oxford, 1967);

Alan Tormey, "Critical Judgments," *Theoria* XXXIX (1973), 35–49;

Bruce Vermazen, "Comparing Evaluations of Works of Art," *Journal of Aesthetics and Art Criticism* XXXIV (1975), 7–14.

A systematic account of relativism and its import, not centered, however, on the philosophy of art, may be found in:

Joseph Margolis, *Pragmatism without Foundations; Reconciling Relativism and Realism* (Oxford, 1986).

On the Continental literature ranging chiefly through Heideggerean, hermeneutic, deconstructive, and post-structuralist views, it may perhaps be best to offer some of the better anthologies, for purposes of sampling. The following will of course provide helpful further bibliographies:

Josué V. Harari (ed.), *Textual Strategies* (Ithaca, 1979);

Richard Macksey and Eugenio Donato (eds.), *The Structuralist Controversy* (Baltimore, 1972);

Gary Shapiro and Alan Sica (eds.), *Hermeneutics* (Amherst, 1984);

Hugh J. Silverman and Don Ihde (eds.), *Hermeneutics and Deconstruction* (Albany, 1985);

William V. Spanos (ed.), *Martin Heidegger and the Question of Literature* (Bloomington, 1976);

William V. Spanos et al. (eds.), *The Question of Textuality* (Bloomington, 1982);

Susan R. Suleiman and Inge Crosman (eds.), *The Reader in the Text* (Princeton, 1980);

Jane P. Tompkins (ed.), *Reader-Response Criticism* (Baltimore, 1980);

Robert Young, *Untying the Text* (London, 1981).

Barthes's views may be usefully gathered from:

Roland Barthes, *S/Z,* trans. Richard Miller (New York, 1984);

Roland Barthes, *The Pleasure of the Text,* trans. Richard Miller (New York, 1975).

Gadamer's views are essentially collected in his masterwork:

Hans-Georg Gadamer, *Truth and Method,* from 2nd ed., trans. Garrett Barden and John Cumming (New York, 1975).

Heidegger's principal essays of relevance are collected in:

Martin Heidegger, *Poetry, Language, Thought,* trans. Albert Hofstadter (New York, 1971).

See also the Bibliography to Part Seven.

# Part Seven
# Metaphor

The literary arts have been of philosophical interest chiefly in terms of the puzzles generated by the concepts of fiction and metaphor. Literature, of course, raises an important challenge to conventional views about aesthetic interests and aesthetic qualities (see Part One); its admission strengthens as well the need to provide a sufficiently general account of representation (see Part Four). Also, there is developing at the present time a strong interest in providing an analysis of literary pieces in terms of a speech-act model, now that that notion has become a settled part of the professional equipment of both philosophers and linguisticians. To some extent, speech-act features have always been a consideration in theorizing about fiction and metaphor, though recent discussions are explicitly indebted to the work of J. L. Austin, H. P. Grice, and John Searle and of innumerable others who have built on their original insights.

Philosophically considered, fiction interests us chiefly in the respects in which the sentences of a story may or may not function as do statements of fact. This is not to restrict the sort of sentences that appear in a story but rather to draw attention to the logical peculiarities involved in conceding that what is being told is a story. On the face of it, then, stories are not lies or false statements. The question is, what are the properties of sentences that enter into a story, insofar merely as fiction is concerned?

Whatever the account put forward, complications of at least two distinct sorts will have to be examined. One concerns the fact that stories are based on an experience of the world, sometimes even cast as historical or biographical novels. So one sometimes declares a story to be "true" or "true to life" or some such thing and even considers that the story may refer to the things of the world. The master question here is verisimilitude; and the philosophical puzzle, in a nutshell, is to reconcile the facts about these sorts of stories with the apparently fundamental thesis that fiction, as fiction, cannot be true or false.

A second set of questions arises from the fact that, sometimes, statements of fact or moral maxims and the like may be told in story form, statements and maxims that are, on independent grounds, true or false, accurate or inaccurate, defensible or indefensible. And these questions call for a distinction between the special logical features of sentences insofar as they are used to tell a story and the features of a fictional style of speaking that is bound to some ulterior use of language—a distinction, say, between *Alice in Wonderland* and Aesop's *Fables*. One comes then to consider the differences between a fictional use of sentences and a fictional style that may relate to any use of sentences, such as stating a fact or prescribing a moral rule.

Once a contrast of this sort is admitted, the study of fiction suggests interesting comparisons. What, for instance, are the differences between telling a story and speaking jokingly or ironically? For all these clearly concern ways of waiving or reversing considerations of truth and falsity and the like. These bear, therefore, on the discrimination of a certain favored set of speech acts. What, furthermore, may one say about poetry and drama? Do these concern uses of language like the fictional use of language or are they rather styles of language that may be fitted to any otherwise legitimate use of language, like making statements or judgments or recommendations? Both because of these complexities and because speaking jokingly and speaking ironically (irony of course is actually designated a trope) seem to involve certain distinctive speech acts and certain distinctive uses of words, we are led quite naturally to the topic of metaphor.

The study of metaphor, on the other hand, inevitably invites comment on the general nature of figurative language. It turns out that figures of speech are often merely ornamental, in the sense that their analysis reveals no distinctive logical features that a comprehensive philosophical account of language would wish to accommodate. Metaphor does not seem to be ornamental in this sense. It undoubtedly has important implications for a theory of meaning.

It may be easily supposed that, since one speaks of metaphor as of a particular sort of figure, that all metaphors behave in the same way essentially. This may be disputed at once in at least one important respect. It is a matter of debate whether all metaphors may be paraphrased or not. To hold that metaphors can be correctly and more or less accurately paraphrased is, in effect, to hold that figurative language reduces to literal language, that the metaphoric remainder is merely an ornament, in a philosophically uninteresting sense. On the other hand, to hold that metaphors (at least certain sorts of metaphor) cannot be paraphrased is to suggest that a special account must be given of figurative sense, that metaphor is itself philosophically interesting and would provide specimen expressions whose meaning cannot be determined in those ways appropriate to literal sense. The evidence seems to be that, particularly in poetry, non-paraphrasable metaphors abound. The question is, what is the meaning of such expressions which, if taken literally, may even appear as nonsense, and how do we decide about their meaning?

The important clue lies in the parasitic nature of metaphor. Quite obviously, it trades on the literal meanings of the words it joins together in unexpected ways. We may also notice, incidentally, that the "literal sense" on which it trades has an enormous spread—from standard dictionary meanings to looser suggestions, associations, even private asides. The question is, how does metaphor trade on literal sense? To put the matter this way is to see at once the inadequacy (though not the irrelevance) of any talk of resemblance and similarity. Resemblance is the favorite theme among theories of metaphor, but by itself it fails to touch on the *use* of resemblance and similarity (possibly also the use of lack of resemblance) that distinguishes metaphor proper from literal comparison, analogy, catachresis, simile, possibly even synecdoche and metonymy (see Part Four). Metaphor is particularly troublesome both because there is no question that the invention of metaphors involves taking liberties with the meanings of expressions and because to understand the figurative sense of such inventions requires attention to speakers' intentions and the exploitation of a linguistic tradition that cannot be neatly reduced to explicit rules. The admission of metaphor, therefore, must affect profoundly the adequacy of any theory of language.

In particular, although metaphor is taken to be parasitic on or exploitative of standard usage, there is no viable sense in which the relation between the two is hierarchically ordered in some discernible way: one must posit, in order to explicate a metaphor, *some* usage as standard; but natural languages fail to recognize compartmentalized levels of ordinary speech and usage. Hence, the issue of metaphor can be made to be quite troublesome to any systematic analysis of language, truth, meaning, relationship to the world, or the like. This is in fact the essential inspiration of Friedrich Nietzsche's remarkably influential account of the inherently metaphoric ("lying") nature of human language (1979). Its influence can be traced in Heidegger, Gadamer, Barthes, Derrida, Foucault, Deleuze, de Man (1983) and others. The important thing is that its theme—essentially, the most radicalized rejection of the correspondence theory of truth—begins to affect the distinction between fiction and reality, reference, truth claims, and the determination of meaning. In a way, it is Nietzsche who, perhaps surprisingly, remains one of the principal sources for the rejection of system—that sense in which, in the Continental tradition, has been most strenuously favored by the structuralists and, in both the Anglo-American and Continental traditions, by the unity of science movement. Hence, it is of particular importance in understanding the force of all our specimen essays on metaphor.

One also notices, reverting to the tropes, that the principal tropes—irony, synecdoche, metonymy, and metaphor—undoubtedly will not lend themselves to a single comprehensive analysis. One has only to see that irony directly affects the primary uses of language, such as making a statement or asking a question—speech acts, in short. One sees that it need not otherwise involve any departure from the literal sense of the words it employs; that, on the other hand, metaphor is not at all directly linked with speech acts, that it is more a semantic than a syntactical matter. In this sense, it is more closely related to codes and slang (though it cannot be identified with these) than it is to telling a story, speaking jokingly or ironically, or stating a fact. Also, it may be noted, an inevitable quibble dogs all candidate theories. The distinctions between metaphor, synecdoche, and metonymy are construed in stricter and looser ways by different theorists; in fact, some examples taken to be absolutely telling against a particular account may be found rejected as ineligible by the partisans of another theory. And this calls for caution in gauging the force of all arguments pro and con.

Max Black's discussion of metaphor (1954–1955) is generally conceded to be one of the indispensable papers on the subject. Black isolates a kind of metaphor (the "interaction view") that resists paraphrase. But his reasons for holding that these cannot be paraphrased have to do more with a view of the peculiarities of cognitive discovery than with the semantic function of metaphor as such. Black's account has had considerable influence, therefore, in the development of a theory of scientific theories. There is, also, much in what Black says that bears directly on the semantic function of metaphor that deserves to be further explored. The difficulty with the interaction view is simply that once the putative cognitive discovery is assimilated by a given community, the metaphor must fade (catachresis). But it is simply not true that non-paraphrasable metaphors always involve a new intellectual discovery; nor is it true that the assimilation of whatever might be supposed to have been the cognitive achievement associated with a metaphor entails the decline of that metaphor or its paraphrasability. The full force of Black's view depends on a further account of what we suppose the relationship between language and the world to be. But Black does not pursue the matter in the spirit now dominant in the newer Continental manner (see Black, 1962).

Jacques Derrida's use of the theme we are here calling Nietzschean, which is in fact quite close to the theme of Heidegger's essential subversion of the phenomenology of his own mentor, Edmund Husserl, is quintessentially expressed in Derrida's famous—or infamous—essay, "Differance" (1982). The point of that essay—which in a way undermines at once and for the same reasons both Husserlian phenomenology and Saussurean structuralism (which may be gauged more clearly from Derrida's *Of Grammatology*, 1976)—is to draw attention to the indiscernible and inexpressible surd, *difference* (spelled with an *a*), that must be posited to make the linguistic engine of the correspondence between word and world work. This deliberately negative thesis has, actually, *no* positive application or program or method or rational discipline or the like to afford. It is rather, like the *via negativa* of theology, meant to justify us in affirming that no effort at system can be counted on to capture any legitimizing linkage between language and things. Nevertheless, it is an extraordinary fact that the Derridean thesis has converted an immense army of discussants, in the arts and elsewhere, to what is taken to be *another*—but now more disciplined, stricter—form of inquiry than the entire previous tradition has been able to advance. This is simply a misunderstanding of the original thesis, although it is of course true that Derrida himself has been attracted to the analysis of texts and theories while informed by his own deconstructive orientation. In effect, here, discussing metaphor, Derrida (1982) recovers the notion in what he takes to be the strongest feature of Nietzsche's account. It would not, however, be too forceful a claim to hold that Paul de Man for instance (1983), as well as others of the so-called Yale Critics, shows the way to what has now fashionably come to be called deconstructive criticism. But if what has already been said is fair, deMan's and similar programs are simply too sanguine, and Derrida's cannot really be assigned *any* particular critical program—which is not to say the deconstructive discovery is either pointless or easily set aside.

Paul Ricoeur (1981) is essentially a gifted peacemaker, possibly the most successful at the moment in mediating inventively between Husserl and Heidegger, between phenomenology and hermeneutics, between hermeneutics and Frankfurt Critical theory, between traditional philosophy and deconstruction, between Continental and Anglo-American philosophy. What in effect Ricoeur attempts to show is that the puzzles of metaphor are, in brief, the puzzles of interpreting longer texts; and that, correspondingly, the reasonableness of pursuing the latter bears as well on the former. Ricoeur, therefore, takes account of the possibility of radically undermining all disciplined inquiry, but he turns away from that temptation in order to recover (as far as possible) some semblance of rational method, without either yielding too much in the direction of those excessive and naive forms of confidence that Husserl, Heidegger, Gadamer, Derrida, Foucault, Barthes, and Jürgen Habermas have in various ways decried, or yielding too much in the direction of intellectual anarchy, stalemate, or mere subversion. He is, in this sense, ultimately a hermeneut—but one who is more sanguine about method than Gadamer and clearer about the in-eliminability of truth claims than the more extreme progeny of Nietzsche.

## 28.                                   Metaphor

*MAX BLACK*

Metaphors are no arguments, my pretty maiden.

> *The Fortunes of Nigel*, Book 2, Chapter 2

To draw attention to a philosopher's metaphors is to belittle him—like praising a logician for his beautiful handwriting. Addiction to metaphor is held to be illicit, on the principle that whereof one can speak only metaphorically, thereof one ought not to speak at all. Yet the nature of the offense is unclear. I should like to do something to dispel the mystery that invests the topic; but since philosophers (for all their notorious interest in language) have so neglected the subject, I must get what help I can from the literary critics. They, at least, do not accept the commandments, "Thou shalt not commit metaphor," or assume that metaphor is incompatible with serious thought.

*I*

The questions I should like to see answered concern the "logical grammar" of "metaphor" and words having related meanings. It would be satisfactory to have convincing answers to the questions: "How do we recognize a case of metaphor?" "Are there any criteria for the detection of metaphors?" "Can metaphors be translated into literal expressions?" "Is metaphor properly regarded as a decoration upon 'plain sense'?" "What are the relations between metaphor and simile?" "In what sense, if any, is a metaphor 'creative'?" "What is the point of using a metaphor?" (Or, more briefly, "What do we *mean* by 'metaphor'?" The questions express attempts

From *Proceedings of the Aristotelian Society*, LV (1954–1955), 273–294 (now with a minor correction). Reprinted with permission of the Editor of the Aristotelian Society.

to become clearer about some uses of the word "metaphor"—or, if one prefers the material mode, to analyze the notion of metaphor.)

The list is not a tidy one, and several of the questions overlap in fairly obvious ways. But I hope they will sufficiently illustrate the type of inquiry that is intended.

It would be helpful to be able to start from some agreed list of "clear cases" of metaphor. Since the word "metaphor" has some intelligible uses, however vague or vacillating, it must be possible to construct such a list. Presumably, it should be easier to agree whether any given item should be included than to agree about any proposed analysis of the notion of metaphor.

Perhaps the following list of examples, chosen not altogether at random, might serve:

1. "The chairman ploughed through the discussion."
2. "A smokescreen of witnesses."
3. "An argumentative melody."
4. "Blotting-paper voices" (Henry James).
5. "The poor are the Negroes of Europe" (Chamfort).
6. "Light is but the shadow of God" (Sir Thomas Browne).
7. "Oh dear white children, casual as birds. Playing amid the ruined languages" (Auden).

I hope all these will be accepted as unmistakable *instances* of metaphor, whatever judgments may ultimately be made about the meaning of "metaphor." The examples are offered as clear cases of metaphor, but, with the possible exception of the first, they would be unsuitable as "paradigms." If we wanted to teach the meaning of "metaphor" to a child, we should need simpler examples like "The clouds are crying" or "The branches are fighting with one another." (Is it significant that one hits upon examples of personification?) But I have tried to include some reminders of the possible complexities that even relatively straightforward metaphors may generate.

Consider the first example—"The chairman ploughed through the discussion." An obvious point to begin with is the contrast between the word "ploughed" and the remaining words by which it is accompanied. This would be commonly expressed by saying that "ploughed" has here a metaphorical sense, while the other words have literal senses. Though we point to the whole sentence as an instance (a "clear case") of metaphor, our attention quickly narrows to a single word, whose presence is the proximate reason for the attribution. And similar remarks can be made about the next four examples in the list, the crucial words being, respectively, "smokescreen," "argumentative," "blotting-paper," and "Negroes."

(But the situation is more complicated in the last two examples of the list. In the quotation from Sir Thomas Browne, "Light" must be supposed to have a symbolic sense, and certainly to mean far more than it would in the context of a textbook on optics. Here, the metaphorical sense of the expression "the shadow of God" imposes a meaning richer than usual upon the subject of the sentence. Similar effects can be noticed in the passage from Auden [consider for instance the meaning of "white" in the first line]. I shall have to neglect such complexities in this paper.)

In general, when we speak of a relatively simple metaphor, we are referring to a sentence or another expression, in which *some* words are used metaphorically, while the remainder are used non-metaphorically. An attempt to construct an entire sentence of words that are used metaphorically results in a proverb, an allegory, or a riddle. No preliminary analysis of metaphor will satisfactorily cover even such trite examples as "In the night all cows are black." And cases of symbolism (in the sense in which Kafka's castle is a "symbol") also need separate treatment.


## II

"The chairman ploughed through the discussion." In calling this sentence a case of metaphor, we are implying that at least one word (here, the word "ploughed") is being used metaphorically in the sentence, and that at least one of the remaining words is being used literally. Let us call the word "ploughed" the *focus* of the metaphor, and the remainder of the sentence in which that word occurs the *frame*. (Are *we* now using metaphors—and mixed ones at that? Does it matter?) One notion that needs to be clarified is that of the "metaphorical use" of the focus of a metaphor. Among other things, it would be good to understand how the presence of one frame can result in metaphorical use of the complementary word, while the presence of a different frame for the same word fails to result in metaphor.

If the sentence about the chairman's behavior is translated word for word into any foreign language for which this is possible, we shall of course want to say that the translated sentence is a case of the *very same* metaphor. So, to call a sentence an instance of metaphor is to say something about its *meaning,* not about its orthography, its phonetic pattern, or its grammatical form.[1] (To use a well-known distinction, "metaphor" must be classified as a term belonging to "semantics" and not to "syntax"—or to any *physical* inquiry about language.)

Suppose somebody says, "I like to plough my memories regularly." Shall we say he is using the same metaphor as in the case already discussed, or not? Our answer will depend upon the degree of similarity we are prepared to affirm on comparing the two "frames" (for we have the same "focus" each time). Differences in the two frames will produce *some* differences in the interplay[2] between focus and frame in the two cases. Whether we regard the differences as sufficiently striking to warrant calling the sentences *two* metaphors is a matter for arbitrary decision. "Metaphor" is a loose word, at best, and we must beware of attributing to it stricter rules of usage than are actually found in practice.

So far, I have been treating "metaphor" as a predicate properly applicable to certain expressions, without attention to any occasions on which the expressions are used, or to the thoughts, acts, feelings, and intentions of speakers upon such occasions. And this is surely correct for *some* expressions. We recognize that to call a man a "cesspool" is to use a metaphor, without needing to know who uses the expression, or on what occasions, or with what intention. The rules of our language determine that some expressions must count as metaphors; and a speaker can no more change this than he can legislate that "cow" shall mean the same as "sheep." But we must also recognize that the established rules of language leave wide latitude for individual variation, initiative, and creation. There are indefinitely many contexts (including nearly all the interesting ones) where the meaning of a metaphorical expression has to be reconstructed from the speaker's intentions (and other clues) because the broad rules of standard usage are too general to supply the information needed. When Churchill, in a famous phrase, called Mussolini "that *utensil*," the tone of voice, the verbal setting, the historical background, helped to make clear *what* metaphor was being used. (Yet, even here, it is hard to see how the phrase "that utensil" could ever be applied to a man except as an insult. Here, as elsewhere, the general rules of usage function as limitations upon the speaker's freedom to mean whatever he pleases.) This is an example, though still a simple one, of how recognition and interpretation of a metaphor may require attention to the *particular circumstances* of its utterance.

It is especially noteworthy that there are, in general, no standard rules for the degree of *weight* or *emphasis* to be attached to a particular use of an expression. To know what the user of a metaphor means, we need to know how "seriously" he treats the metaphorical focus. (Would he be just as content to have some rough synonym, or would only *that* word serve? Are we to take the word lightly, attending only to its most obvious implications—or should we dwell upon its less immediate associations?) In speech we can use emphasis and phrasing as clues. But in written or printed discourse, even these rudimentary aids are absent. Yet this somewhat elusive "weight" of a (suspected or detected)[3] metaphor is of great practical importance in exegesis.

To take a philosophical example. Whether the expression "logical form" should be treated in a particular frame as having a metaphorical sense will depend upon the extent to which its user is taken to be conscious of some supposed analogy between arguments and other things (vases, clouds, battles, jokes) that are also said to have "form." Still more will it depend upon whether the writer wishes the analogy to be active in the minds of his readers; and how much his own thought depends upon and is nourished by the supposed analogy. We must not expect the "rules of language" to be of much help in such inquiries. (There is accordingly a sense of "metaphor" that belongs to "pragmatics," rather than to "semantics"—and this sense may be the one most deserving of attention.)

## III

Let us try the simplest possible account that can be given of the meaning of "The chairman ploughed through the discussion," to see how far it will take us. A plausible commentary (for those presumably too literal-minded to understand the original) might run somewhat as follows:

"A speaker who uses the sentence in question is taken to want to say *something* about a chairman and his behavior in some meeting. Instead of saying, plainly or *directly,* that the chairman dealt summarily with objections, or ruthlessly suppressed irrelevance, or something of the sort, the speaker chose to use a word ('ploughed') which, strictly speaking, means something else. But an intelligent hearer can easily guess what the speaker had in mind."[4]

This account treats the metaphorical expression (let us call it "*M*") as a substitute for some other literal expression ("*L*," say) which would have expressed the same meaning, had it been used instead. On this view, the meaning of *M,* in its metaphorical occurrence, is just the *literal* meaning of *L.* The metaphorical use of an expression consists, on this view, of the use of that expression in other than its proper or normal sense, in some context that allows the improper or abnormal sense to be detected and appropriately transformed. (The reasons adduced for so remarkable a performance will be discussed later.)

Any view which holds that a metaphorical expression is used in place of some equivalent *literal* expression, I shall call a *substitution view of* metaphor. (I should like this label to cover also any analysis which views the entire sentence that is the locus of the metaphor as replacing some set of literal sentences.) Until recently, one or another form of a substitution view has been accepted by most writers (usually literary critics or writers of books on rhetoric) who have had anything to say about metaphor.

To take a few examples. Whately defines a metaphor as "a word substituted for another on account of the Resemblance or Analogy between their significations."[5] Nor is the entry in the Oxford Dictionary (to jump to modern times) much different from this: "Metaphor: The figure of speech in which a name or descriptive term is transferred to some object different from, but analogous to, that to which it is properly applicable; an instance of this, a metaphorical expression."[6] So strongly entrenched is the view expressed by these definitions that a recent writer who is explicitly arguing for a different and more sophisticated view of metaphor, nevertheless slips into the old fashion by defining metaphor as "saying one thing and meaning another."[7]

According to a substitution view, the focus of a metaphor, the word or expression having a distinctively metaphorical use within a literal frame, is used to communicate a meaning that might have been expressed literally. The author substitutes *M* for *L;* it is the reader's task to invert the substitution, by using the literal meaning of *M* as a clue to the intended literal meaning of *L*. Understanding a metaphor is like deciphering a code or unraveling a riddle.

If we now ask why, on this view, the writer should set his reader the task of solving a puzzle, we shall be offered two types of answer. The first is that there may, in fact, be no literal equivalent, *L,* available in the language in question. Mathematicians spoke of the "leg" of an angle because there was no brief literal expression for a bounding line; we say "cherry lips," because there is no form of words half as convenient for saying quickly what the lips are like. Metaphor plugs the gaps in the literal vocabulary (or, at least, supplies the want of convenient abbreviations). So viewed, metaphor is a species of *catachresis*, which I shall define as the use of a word in some new sense in order to remedy a gap in the vocabulary. Catachresis is the putting of new senses into old words.[8] But if a catachresis serves a genuine need, the new sense introduced will quickly become part of the *literal* sense. "Orange" may originally have been applied to the color by catachresis; but the word is now applied to the color just as "properly" (and unmetaphorically) as to the fruit. "Osculating" curves don't kiss for long, and quickly revert to a more prosaic mathematical contact. And similarly for other cases. It is the fate of catachresis to disappear when it is successful.

There are, however, many metaphors where the virtues ascribed to catachresis cannot apply, because there is, or there is supposed to be, some readily available and equally compendious literal equivalent. Thus in the somewhat unfortunate example.[9] "Richard is a lion," which modern writers have discussed with boring insistence, the literal meaning is taken to be the same as that of the sentence, "Richard is brave."[10] Here, the metaphor is not supposed to enrich the vocabulary.

When catachresis cannot be invoked, the reasons for substituting an indirect, metaphorical, expression are taken to be stylistic. We are told that the metaphorical expression may (in its literal use) refer to a more concrete object than would its literal equivalent; and this is supposed to give pleasure to the reader (the pleasure of having one's thoughts diverted from Richard to the irrelevant lion). Again, the reader is taken to enjoy problem-solving—or to delight in the author's skill at half-concealing, half-revealing his meaning. Or metaphors provide a shock of "agreeable surprise"—and so on. The principle behind these "explanations" seems to be: When in doubt about some peculiarity of language, attribute its existence to the pleasure it gives a reader. A principle that has the merit of working well in default of any evidence.[11]

Whatever the merits of such speculations about the reader's response, they agree in making metaphor a *decoration*. Except in cases where a metaphor is a catachresis that remedies some temporary imperfection of literal language, the purpose of metaphor is to entertain and divert. Its use, on this view, always constitutes a deviation from the "plain and strictly appropriate style" (Whately).[12] So, if philosophers have something more important to do than give pleasure to their readers, metaphor can have no serious place in philosophical discussion.

*IV*

The view that a metaphorical expression has a meaning that is some transform of its normal literal meaning is a special case of a more general view about "figurative" language. This holds that any figure of speech involving semantic change (and not merely syntactic change, like inversion of normal word order) consists in some transformation of a *literal* meaning. The author provides, not his intended meaning, $m$, but some function thereof, $f(m)$; the reader's task is to apply the inverse function, $f^{-1}$, and so to obtain $f^{-1}(f(m))$, i.e., $m$, the original meaning. When different functions are used, different tropes result. Thus, in irony, the author says the *opposite* of what he means; in hyperbole, he *exaggerates* his meaning; and so on.

What, then, is the characteristic transforming function involved in metaphor? To this the answer has been made: either *analogy* or *similarity*. $M$ is either similar or analogous in meaning to its literal equivalent $L$. Once the reader has detected the ground of the intended analogy or simile (with the help of the frame, or clues drawn from the wider context) he can retrace the author's path and so reach the original meaning (the meaning of $L$).

If a writer holds that a metaphor consists in the *presentation* of the underlying analogy or similarity, he will be taking what I shall call a *comparison view* of metaphor. When Schopenhauer called a geometrical proof a mousetrap, he was, according to such a view, *saying* (though not explicitly): "A geometrical proof is *like* a mousetrap, since both offer a delusive reward, entice their victims by degrees, lead to disagreeable surprise, etc." This is a view of metaphor as a condensed or elliptical *simile*. It will be noticed that a "comparison view" is a special case of a "substitution view." For it holds that the metaphorical statement might be replaced by an equivalent literal *comparison*.

Whately says: "The Simile or Comparison may be considered as differing in form only from a Metaphor; the resemblance being in that case *stated,* which in the Metaphor is implied."[13] Bain says that "The metaphor is a comparison implied in the mere use of a term" and adds, "It is in the circumstance of being confined to a word, or at most to a phrase, that we are to look for the peculiarities of the metaphor—in advantages on the one hand, and its dangers and abuses on the other."[14] This view of the metaphor, as condensed simile or comparison, has been very popular.

The chief difference between a substitution view (of the sort previously considered) and the special form of it that I have called a comparison view may be illustrated by the stock example of "Richard is a lion." On the first view, the sentence means approximately the same as "Richard is brave"; on the second, approximately the same as "Richard is *like* a lion (in being brave)," the added words in brackets being understood but not explicitly stated. In the second translation, as in the first, the metaphorical statement is taken to be standing in place of some *literal* equivalent. But the comparison view provides a more elaborate paraphrase, inasmuch as the original statement is interpreted as being about lions as well as about Richard.[15]

The main objection against a comparison view is that it suffers from a vagueness that borders upon vacuity. We are supposed to be puzzled as to how some expression ($M$), used metaphorically, can function in place of some literal expression ($L$) that is held to be an approximate synonym; and the answer offered is that what $M$ stands for (in its literal use) is *similar* to what $L$ stands for. But how informative is this? There is some temptation to think of similarities as "objectively given," so that a question of the form, "Is $A$ like $B$ in respect of $P$?" has a definite and predetermined answer. If this were so, similes might be governed by rules as strict as those controlling the statements of physics. But likeness always admits of degrees, so that a truly "objective" question would need to take some such form as "Is $A$ more like $B$ than like $C$ in respect of $P$?"—or, perhaps, "Is $A$ closer to $B$ than to $C$ on such and such a scale of degrees of $P$?" Yet, in proportion as we approach such forms, metaphorical statements lose their effectiveness and their point. We need the metaphors in just the cases when there can be no question as yet of the precision of scientific statement. Metaphorical statement is not a substitute for a formal comparison or any other kind of literal statement, but has its own *distinctive* capacities and achievements. Often we say, "*X* is *M*," evoking some imputed connection between *M* and an inputed *L* (or, rather, to an indefinite system, $L_1$, $L_2$, $L_3$ ... ) in cases where, prior to the construction of the metaphor, we would have been hard put to it to find any *literal* resemblance between *M* and *L*. It would be more illuminating in some of these cases to say that the metaphor *creates* the similarity than to say that it formulates some similarity antecedently existing.[16]

## V

I turn now to consider a type of analysis I shall call an *interaction view* of metaphor. This seems to me to be free from the main defects of substitution and comparison views and to offer some important insight into the uses and limitations of metaphor.[17]

Let us begin with the following statement: "In the simplest formulation, when we use a metaphor we have two thoughts of different things active together and supported by a single word, or phrase, whose meaning is a resultant of their interaction."[18]

We may discover what is here intended by applying Richards's remark to our earlier example, "The poor are the Negroes of Europe." The substitution view, at its crudest, tells us that something is being *indirectly* said about the poor of Europe. (But what? That they are an oppressed class, a standing reproach to the community's official ideals, that poverty is inherited and indelible?) The comparison view claims that the epigram *presents* some comparison between the poor and the Negroes. In opposition to both, Richards says that our "thoughts" about European poor and (American) Negroes are "active together" and "interact" to produce a meaning that is a resultant of that interaction.

I think this must mean that in the given context the focal word "Negroes" obtains a *new* meaning, which is *not* quite its meaning in literal uses, nor quite the meaning which any literal substitute would have. The new context (the "frame" of the metaphor, in my terminology) imposes *extension* of meaning upon the focal word. And I take Richards to be saying that for the metaphor to work the reader must remain aware of the extension of meaning—must attend to both the old and the new meanings together.[19]

But how is this extension or change of meaning brought about? At one point, Richards speaks of the "common characteristics" of the two terms (the poor and Negroes) as "the ground of the metaphor," (*op cit.*, p. 117), so that in its metaphorical use a word or expression must connote only a *selection* from the characteristics connoted in its literal uses. This, however, seems a rare lapse into the older and less sophisticated analyses he is trying to supersede.[20] He is on firmer ground when he says that the reader is forced to "connect" the two ideas (p. 125). In this "connection" resides the secret and the mystery of metaphor. To speak of the "interaction" of two thoughts "active together" (or, again, of their "interillumination" or "cooperation") is to *use* a metaphor emphasizing the dynamic aspects of a good reader's response to a non-trivial metaphor. I have no quarrel with the use of metaphors (if they are good ones) in talking about metaphor. But it may be as well to use several, lest we are misled by the adventitious charms of our favorites.

Let us try, for instance, to think of a metaphor as a *filter.* Consider the statement, "Man is a wolf." Here, we may say, are *two* subjects—the *principal subject,* Man (or: men) and the *subsidiary subject,* Wolf (or: wolves). Now the metaphorical sentence in question will not convey its intended meaning to a reader sufficiently ignorant about wolves. What is needed is not so much that the reader shall know the standard dictionary meaning of "wolf"—or be able to use that word in literal senses—as that he shall know what I will call the *system of associated commonplaces.* Imagine some layman required to say, without taking special thought, those things he held to be true about wolves; the set of statements resulting would approximate to what I am here calling the system of commonplaces associated with the word "wolf." I am assuming that in any given culture the responses made by different persons to the test suggested would agree rather closely, and that even the occasional expert, who might have unusual knowledge of the subject, would still know "what the man in the street thinks about the matter." From the expert's standpoint, the system of commonplaces may include half-truths or downright mistakes (as when a whale is classified as a fish); but the important thing for the metaphor's effectiveness is not that the commonplaces shall be true, but that they should be readily and freely evoked. (Because this is so, a metaphor that works in one society may seem preposterous in another. Men who take wolves to be reincarnations of dead humans will give the statement "Man is a wolf" an interpretation different from the one I have been assuming.)

To put the matter in another way: Literal uses of the word "wolf" are governed by syntactical and semantical rules, violation of which produces nonsense or self-contradiction. In addition, I am suggesting, literal uses of the word normally commit the speaker to acceptance of a set of standard beliefs about wolves (current platitudes) that are the common possession of the members of some speech community. To deny any such piece of accepted commonplace (e.g., by saying that wolves are vegetarians—or easily domesticated) is to produce an effect of paradox and provoke a demand for justification. A speaker who says "wolf" is normally taken to be implying in some sense of that word that he is referring to something fierce, carnivorous, treacherous, and so on. The idea of a wolf is part of a system of ideas, not sharply delineated, and yet sufficiently definite to admit of detailed enumeration.

The effect, then, of (metaphorically) calling a man a "wolf" is to evoke the wolf-system of related commonplaces. If the man is a wolf, he preys upon other animals, is fierce, hungry, engaged in constant struggle, a scavenger, and so on. Each of these implied assertions has now to be made to fit the principal subject (the man) either in normal or in abnormal senses. If the metaphor is at all appropriate, this can be done—up to a point at least. A suitable hearer will be led by the wolf-system of implications to construct a corresponding system of implications about the principal subject. But these implications will *not* be those comprised in the commonplaces *normally* implied by literal uses of "man." The new implications must be determined by the patterns of implications associated with literal uses of the word "wolf." Any human traits that can without undue strain be talked about in "wolf-language" will be rendered prominent, and any that cannot will be pushed into the background. The wolf-metaphor suppresses some details, emphasizes others—in short, *organizes* our view of man.

Suppose I look at the night sky through a piece of heavily smoked glass on which certain lines have been left clear. Then I shall see only the stars that can be made to lie on the lines previously prepared upon the screen, and the stars I do see will be seen as organized by the screen's structure. We can think of a metaphor as such a screen, and the system of "associated commonplaces" of the focal word as the network of lines upon the screen. We can say that the principal subject is "seen through" the metaphorical expression—or, if we prefer, that the principal subject is "projected upon" the field of the subsidiary subject. (In the latter analogy, the implication-system of the focal expression must be taken to determine the "law of projection.")

Or take another example. Suppose I am set the task of describing a battle in words drawn as largely as possible from the vocabulary of chess. These latter terms determine a system of implications which will proceed to control my description of the battle. The enforced choice of the chess vocabulary will lead some aspects of the battle to be emphasized, others to be neglected, and all to be organized in a way that would cause much more strain in other modes of description. The chess vocabulary filters and transforms: it not only selects, it brings foward aspects of the battle that might not be seen at all through another medium. (Stars that cannot be seen at all, except through telescopes.)

Nor must we neglect the shifts in attitude that regularly result from the use of metaphorical language. A wolf is (conventionally) a hateful and alarming object; so, to call a man a wolf is to imply that he too is hateful and alarming (and thus to support and reinforce dislogistic attitudes). Again, the vocabulary of chess has its primary uses in a highly artificial setting, where all expression of feeling is formally excluded: to describe a battle as if it were a game of chess is accordingly to exclude, by the choice of language, all the more emotionally disturbing aspects of warfare. (Similar by-products are not rare in philosophical uses of metaphor.)

A fairly obvious objection to the foregoing sketch of the "interaction view" is that it has to hold that some of the "associated commonplaces" themselves suffer metaphorical change of meaning in the process of transfer from the subsidiary to the principal subject. And *these* changes, if they occur, can hardly be explained by the account given. The primary metaphor, it might be said, has been analyzed into a set of subordinate metaphors, so the account given is either circular or leads to an infinite regress.

This might be met by denying that *all* changes of meaning in the "associated commonplaces" must be counted as metaphorical shifts. Many of them are best described as *extensions* of meaning, because they do not involve apprehended connections between two systems of concepts. I have not undertaken to explain how such extensions or shifts occur in general, and I do not think any simple account will fit all cases. (It is easy enough to mutter "analogy" but closer examination soon shows all kinds of "grounds" for shifts of meaning with context—and even no ground at all, sometimes.)

Secondly, I would not deny that a metaphor may involve a number of subordinate metaphors among its implications. But these subordinate metaphors are, I think, usually intended to be taken less "emphatically," i.e., with less stress upon *their* implications. (The implications of a metaphor are like the overtones of a musical chord; to attach too much "weight" to them is like trying to make the overtones sound as loud as the main notes—and just as pointless.) In any case, primary and subordinate metaphors will normally belong to the same field of discourse, so that they mutually reinforce one and the same system of implications. Conversely, where substantially new metaphors appear as the primary metaphor is unravelled, there is serious risk of confusion of thought (cf. the customary prohibition against "mixed metaphors").

But the preceding account of metaphor needs correction, if it is to be reasonably adequate. Reference to "associated commonplaces" will fit the commonest cases where the author simply plays upon the stock of common knowledge (and common misinformation) presumably shared by the reader and himself. But in a poem, or a piece of sustained prose, the writer can establish a novel pattern of implications for the literal uses of the key expressions, prior to using them as vehicles for his metaphors. (An author can do much to suppress unwanted implications of the word "contract," by explicit discussion of its intended meaning, before he proceeds to develop a contract theory of sovereignty. Or a naturalist who really knows wolves may tell us so much about them that *his* description of man as a wolf diverges quite markedly from the stock uses of that figure.) Metaphors can be supported by specially constructed systems of implications, as well as by accepted commonplaces; they can be made to measure and need not be reach-me-downs.

It was a simplification, again, to speak as if the implication-system of the metaphorical expression remains unaltered by the metaphorical statement. The nature of the intended application helps to determine the character of the system to be applied (as though the stars could partly determine the character of the observation-screen by which we looked at them). If to call a man a wolf is to put him in a special light, we must not forget that the metaphor makes the wolf seem more human than he otherwise would.

I hope such complications as these can be accommodated within the outline of an "interaction view" that I have tried to present.

## VI

Since I have been making so much use of example and illustration, it may be as well to state explicitly (and by way of summary) some of the chief respects in which the "interaction" view recommended differs from a "substitution" or a "comparison" view.

In the form in which I have been expounding it, the "interaction view" is committed to the following seven claims:

(1) A metaphorical statement has *two* distinct subjects—a "principal" subject and a "subsidiary" one.[21]

(2) These subjects are often best regarded as *"systems* of things," rather than "things."

(3) The metaphor works by applying to the principal subject a system of "associated implications" characteristic of the subsidiary subject.

(4) These implications usually consist of "commonplaces" about the subsidiary subject, but may, in suitable cases, consist of deviant implications established *ad hoc* by the writer.

(5) The metaphor selects, emphasizes, suppresses, and organizes fea-

tures of the principal subject by *implying* statements about it that normally apply to the subsidiary subject.

(6) This involves shifts in meaning of words belonging to the same family or system as the metaphorical expression; and some of these shifts, though not all, may be metaphorical transfers. (The subordinate metaphors are, however, to be read less "emphatically.")

(7) There is, in general, no simple "ground" for the necessary shifts of meaning—no blanket reason that some metaphors work and others fail.

It will be found, upon consideration, that point (1) is incompatible with the simplest forms of a "substitution view," point (7) is formally incompatible with a "comparison view"; while the remaining points elaborate reasons for regarding "comparison views" as inadequate.

But it is easy to overstate the conflicts between these three views. If we were to insist that only examples satisfying all seven of the claims listed above should be allowed to count as "genuine" metaphors, we should restrict the correct uses of the word "metaphor" to a very small number of cases. This would be to advocate a persuasive definition of "metaphor" that would tend to make all metaphors interestingly complex.[22] And such a deviation from current uses of the word "metaphor" would leave us without a convenient label for the more trivial cases. Now it is in just such trivial cases that "substitution" and "comparison" views sometimes seem nearer the mark than "interaction" views. The point might be met by *classifying* metaphors as instances of substitution, comparison, or interaction. Only the last kind are of importance in philosophy.

For substitution-metaphors and comparison-metaphors can be replaced by literal translations (with possible exception for the case of catachresis)—by sacrificing some of the charm, vivacity, or wit of the original, but with no loss of *cognitive* content. But "interaction-metaphors" are not expendable. Their mode of operation requires the reader to use a system of implications (a system of "commonplaces"—or a special system established for the purpose in hand) as a means for selecting, emphasizing, and organizing relations in a different field. This use of a "subsidiary subject" to foster insight into a "principal subject" is a distinctive *intellectual* operation (though one familiar enough through our experiences of learning anything whatever), demanding simultaneous awareness of both subjects but not reducible to any *comparison* between the two.

Suppose we try to state the cognitive content of an interaction-metaphor in "plain language." Up to a point, we may succeed in stating a number of relevant relations between the two subjects (though in view of the extension of meaning accompanying the shift in the subsidiary subject's implication system, too much must not be expected of the literal paraphrase). But the set of literal statements so obtained will not have the same power to inform and enlighten as the original. For one thing, the implications, previously left for a suitable reader to educe for himself, with a nice feeling for their relative priorities and degrees of importance, are not presented explicitly as though having equal weight. The literal paraphrase inevitably says too much—and with the wrong emphasis. One of the points I most wish to stress is that the loss in such cases is a loss in *cognitive* content; the relevant weakness of the literal paraphrase is not that it may be tiresomely prolix or boringly explicit—or deficient in qualities of style; it fails to be a translation because it fails to give the *insight* that the metaphor did.

But "explication," or elaboration of the metaphor's grounds, if not regarded as an adequate cognitive substitute for the original, may be extremely valuable. A powerful metaphor will no more be harmed by such probing than a musical masterpiece by analysis of its harmonic and melodic structure. No doubt metaphors are dangerous—and perhaps especially so in philosophy. But a prohibition against their use would be a wilful and harmful restriction upon our powers of inquiry.[23]

## Notes

1. *Any* part of speech can be used metaphorically (though the results are meagre and uninteresting in the case of conjunctions); any form of verbal expression may contain a metaphorical focus.

2. Here I am using language appropriate to the "interaction view" of metaphor that is discussed later in this paper.

3. Here, I wish these words to be read with as little "weight" as possible!

4. Notice how this type of paraphrase naturally conveys some implication of *fault* on the part of the metaphor's author. There is a strong suggestion that he ought to have made up his mind as to what he really wanted to say—the metaphor is depicted as a way of glossing over unclarity and vagueness.

5. Richard Whately, *Elements of Rhetoric* (7th revised ed., London, 1846), p. 280.

6. Under "Figure" we find: "Any of the various 'forms' of expression, deviating from the normal arrangement or use of words, which are adopted in order to give beauty, variety, or force to a composition; *e.g.,* Aposiopesis, Hyperbole, Metaphor, etc." If we took this strictly we might be led to say that a transfer of a word not adopted for the sake of introducing "beauty, variety, or force" must necessarily fail to be a case of metaphor. Or will "variety" automatically cover *every* transfer? It will be noticed that the O.E.D.'s definition is no improvement upon Whately's. Where he speaks of a "word" being substituted, the O.E.D. prefers "name or

descriptive term." If this is meant to restrict metaphors to nouns (and adjectives?) it is demonstrably mistaken. But, if not, what *is* "descriptive term" supposed to mean? And why has Whately's reference to "Resemblance or Analogy" been trimmed into a reference to analogy alone?

7. Owen Barfield, "Poetic Diction and Legal Fiction," in *Essays Presented to Charles Williams* (Oxford, 1947), pp. 106–127. The definition of metaphor occurs on p. 111, where metaphor is treated as a special case of what Barfield calls "turning." The whole essay deserves to be read.

8. The O.E.D. defines catachresis as: "Improper use of words; application of a term to a thing which it does not properly denote; abuse or perversion of a trope or metaphor." I wish to exclude the pejorative suggestions. There is nothing perverse or abusive in stretching old words to fit new situations. Catachresis is surely a striking case of the transformation of meaning that is constantly occurring in any living language.

9. Can we imagine anybody saying this nowadays and seriously meaning anything? I find it hard to do so. But in default of an authentic context of use, any analysis is likely to be thin, obvious, and unprofitable.

10. A full discussion of this example, complete with diagrams, will be found in Gustaf Stern's *Meaning and Change of Meaning* (Göteborgs Högskolas Årsskrift vol. 38 [1932], part 1), pp. 300 ff. Stern's account tries to show how the reader is led by the context to *select* from the connotation of "lion" the attribute (bravery) that will fit Richard the man. I take him to be defending a form of the substitution view.

11. Aristotle ascribes the use of metaphor to delight in learning; Cicero traces delight in metaphor to the enjoyment of the author's ingenuity in overpassing the immediate, or in the vivid presentation of the principal subject. For references to these and other traditional views, see E. M. Cope, *An Introduction to Aristotle's Rhetoric* (London, 1867), "Appendix B to book 3, ch. 2: *On Metaphor*."

12. Thus Stern (*op. cit.*) says of all figures of speech that "they are intended to serve the expressive and purposive functions of speech better than the 'plain statement'" (p. 296). A metaphor produces an "enhancement" (*Steigerung*) of the subject, but the factors leading to its use "involve the expressive and effective (purposive) functions of speech, not the symbolic and communicative functions" (p. 290). That is to say, metaphors may evince feelings or predispose others to act and feel in various ways—but they don't typically say anything.

13. Whately, *loc. cit.* He proceeds to draw a distinction between "Resemblance, strictly so called, i.e. *direct* resemblance between the objects themselves in question, (as when we speak of '*table*-land,' or compare great waves to *mountains*)" and "Analogy, which is the resemblance of ratios—a similarity of the relations they bear to certain other objects; as when we speak of the '*light* of reason,' or of 'revelation'; or compare a wounded and captive warrior to a stranded ship."

14. Alexander Bain, *English Composition and Rhetoric* (enlarged ed., London, 1887), p. 159.

15. Comparison views probably derive from Aristotle's brief statement in the *Poetics:* "Metaphor consists in giving a thing a name that belongs to something else; the transference being either from genus to species, or from species to genus,

or from species to species, or on grounds of analogy" (1457*b*). I have no space to give Aristotle's discussion the detailed examination it deserves. An able defence of a view based on Aristotle will be found in S. J. Brown's *The World of Imagery* (London, 1927, especially pp. 67 ff).

16. Much more would need to be said in a thorough examination of the comparison view. It would be revealing, for instance, to consider the contrasting types of case in which a formal comparison is preferred to a metaphor. A comparison is often a prelude to an explicit statement of the grounds of resemblance; whereas we do not expect a metaphor to explain itself. (Cf. the difference between *comparing* a man's face with a wolf mask, by looking for points of resemblance—and seeing the human face *as* vulpine.) But no doubt the line between *some* metaphors and *some* similes is not a sharp one.

17. The best sources are the writings of I. A. Richards, especially chapter 5 ("Metaphor") and chapter 6 ("Command of Metaphor") of his *The Philosophy of Rhetoric* (Oxford, 1936). Chapters 7 and 8 of his *Interpretation in Teaching* (London, 1938) cover much the same ground. W. Bedell Stanford's *Greek Metaphor* (Oxford, 1936) defends what he calls an "integration theory" (see especially pp. 101 ff) with much learning and skill. Unfortunately, both writers have great trouble in making clear the nature of the positions they are defending. Chapter 18 of W. Empson's *The Structure of Complex Words* (London, 1914) is a useful discussion of Richards's views on metaphor.

18. *The Philosophy of Rhetoric*, p. 93. Richards also says that metaphor is "fundamentally a borrowing between and intercourse of *thoughts*, a transaction between contexts" (p. 94). Metaphor, he says, requires two ideas "which cooperate in an inclusive meaning" (p. 119).

19. It is this, perhaps, that leads Richards to say that "talk about the identification or fusion that a metaphor effects is nearly always misleading and pernicious" (*op. cit.* p. 127).

20. Usually, Richards tries to show that similarity between the two terms is at best *part* of the basis for the interaction of meanings in a metaphor.

21. This point has often been made. E.g., "As to metaphorical expression, that is a great excellence in style, when it is used with propriety, for it gives you two ideas for one." (Samuel Johnson, quoted by Richards, *op. cit.*, p. 93). The choice of labels for the "subjects" is troublesome. See the "Note on terminology" appended to this paper.

22. I can sympathize with Empson's contention that "The term ['metaphor'] had better correspond to what the speakers themselves feel to be a rich or suggestive or persuasive use of a word, rather than include uses like the *leg* of a table" (*The Structure of Complex Words*, p. 333). But there is the opposite danger, also, of making metaphors too important by definition, and so narrowing our view of the subject excessively.

23. *A note on terminology:* For metaphors that fit a substitution or comparison view, the factors needing to be distinguished are—(i) some word or expression *E;* (ii) occurring in some verbal "frame" *F;* so that (iii) *F(E)* is the metaphorical statement in question; (iv) the meaning *m'(E)* which *E* has in *F(E);* (v) which is the same as the literal meaning, *m(X)*, of some literal synonym, *X*. A sufficient

technical vocabulary would be "metaphorical expression" (for $E$), "metaphorical statement" (for $F(E)$), "metaphorical meaning" (for $m'$) and "literal meaning" (for $m$).

Where the interaction view is appropriate, the situation is more complicated. We may also need to refer (vi) to the principal subject of $F(E)$, say $P$ (roughly, what the statement is "really" about), (vii) the subsidiary subject, $S$ (what $F(E)$ would be about if read literally); (viii) the relevant system of implications, $I$, connected with $S$; and (ix) the resulting system of attributions, $A$, asserted of $P$. We must accept at least so much complexity if we agree that the meaning of $E$ in its setting $F$ depends upon the transformation of $I$ into $A$ by using language, normally applied to $S$, to apply to $P$ instead.

Richards has suggested using the words "tenor" and "vehicle" for the two *"thoughts"* which, in his view, are "active together" (for "the two *ideas* that metaphor, at its simplest, gives us," *op. cit.*, p. 96, my italics) and urges that we reserve "the word 'metaphor' for the whole double unit" (ibid.). But this picture of two *ideas* working upon each other is an inconvenient fiction. And it is significant that Richards himself soon lapses into speaking of "tenor" and "vehicle" as "things" (e.g., on p. 118). Richards's "vehicle" vacillates in reference between the metaphorical expression *(E)*, the subsidiary subject *(S)*, and the connected implication system *(I)*. It is less clear what his "tenor" means: sometimes it stands for the principal subject *(P)*, sometimes for implications connected with that subject (which I have not symbolized above), sometimes, in spite of Richards's own intentions, for the *resulting* meaning (or as we might say the "full import") of $E$ in its context, $F(E)$.

There is probably no hope of getting an accepted terminology so long as writers upon the subject are so much at variance with one another.

# 29. The End of the Book and the Beginning of Writing

## JACQUES DERRIDA

*Socrates, he who does not write—Nietzsche*[1]

However the topic is considered, the *problem of language* has never been simply one problem among others. But never as much as at present has it invaded, *as such*, the global horizon of the most diverse researches and the most heterogeneous discourses, diverse and heterogeneous in their intention, method, and ideology. The devaluation of the word "language" itself, and how, in the very hold it has upon us, it betrays a loose vocabulary, the temptation of a cheap seduction, the passive yielding to fashion, the consciousness of the avant-garde, in other words—ignorance—are evidences of this effect. This inflation of the sign "language" is the inflation of the sign itself, absolute inflation, inflation itself. Yet, by one of its aspects or shadows, it is itself still a sign: this crisis is also a symptom. It indicates, as if in spite of itself, that a historico-metaphysical epoch *must* finally determine as language the totality of its problematic horizon. It must do so not only because all that desire had wished to wrest from the play of language finds itself recaptured within that play but also because, for the same reason, language itself is menaced in its very life, helpless, adrift in the threat of limitlessness, brought back to its own finitude at the very moment when its limits seem to disappear, when it ceases to be selfassured, contained, and *guaranteed* by the infinite signified which seemed to exceed it.

From "The End of the Book and the Beginning of Writing," in Jacques Derrida, *Of Grammatology* (Baltimore/London: The Johns Hopkins University Press, 1977), pp. 6–26. Reprinted with permission of the author and The Johns Hopkins University Press.

## The Program

By a slow movement whose necessity is hardly perceptible, everything that for at least some twenty centuries tended toward and finally succeeded in being gathered under the name of language is beginning to let itself be transferred to, or at least summarized under, the name of writing. By a hardly perceptible necessity, it seems as though the concept of writing—no longer indicating a particular, derivative, auxiliary form of language in general (whether understood as communication, relation, expression, signification, constitution of meaning or thought, etc.), no longer designating the exterior surface, the insubstantial double of a major signifier, *the signifier of the signifier*—is beginning to go beyond the extension of language. In all senses of the word, writing thus *comprehends* language. Not that the word "writing" has ceased to designate the signifier of the signifier, but it appears, strange as it may seem, that "signifier of the signifier" no longer defines accidental doubling and fallen secondarity. "Signifier of the signifier" describes on the contrary the movement of language: in its origin, to be sure, but one can already suspect that an origin whose structure can be expressed as "signifier of the signifier" conceals and erases itself in its own production. There the signified always already functions as a signifier. The secondarity that it seemed possible to ascribe to writing alone affects all signifieds in general, affects them always already, the moment they *enter the game*. There is not a single signified that escapes, even if recaptured, the play of signifying references that constitute language. The advent of writing is the advent of this play; today such a play is coming into its own, effacing the limit starting from which one had thought to regulate the circulation of signs, drawing along with it all the reassuring signifieds, reducing all the strongholds, all the out-of-bounds shelters that watched over the field of language. This, strictly speaking, amounts to destroying the concept of "sign" and its entire logic. Undoubtedly it is not by chance that this *overwhelming* supervenes at the moment when the extension of the concept of language effaces all its limits. We shall see that this overwhelming and this effacement have the same meaning, are one and the same phenomenon. It is as if the Western concept of language (in terms of what, beyond its plurivocity and beyond the strict and problematic opposition of speech [*parole*] and language [*langue*], attaches it *in general* to phonematic or glossematic production, to language, to voice, to hearing, to sound and breadth, to speech) were revealed today as the guise or disguise of a primary writing:[2] more fundamental than that which, before this conversion, passed for the simple "supplement to the spoken word" (Rousseau). Either writing was never a simple "supplement," or it is urgently necessary to construct a new logic of the "supplement." It is this urgency which will guide us further in reading Rousseau.

These disguises are not historical contingencies that one might admire or regret. Their movement was absolutely necessary, with a necessity which cannot be judged by any other tribunal. The privilege of the *phonè* does not depend upon a choice that could have been avoided. It responds to a moment of *economy* (let us say of the "life" of "history" or of "being as self-relationship"). The system of "hearing (understanding)-oneself-speak" through the phonic substance—which *presents itself* as the nonexterior, nonmundane, therefore nonempirical or noncontingent signifier—has necessarily dominated the history of the world during an entire epoch, and has even produced the idea of the world, the idea of world-origin, that arises from the difference between the worldly and the non-worldly, the outside and the inside, ideality and nonideality, universal and nonuniversal, transcendental and empirical, etc.[3]

With an irregular and essentially precarious success, this movement would apparently have tended, as toward its *telos,* to confine writing to a secondary and instrumental function: translator of a full speech that was fully *present* (present to itself, to its signified, to the other, the very condition of the theme of presence in general), technics in the service of language, *spokesman,* interpreter of an originary speech itself shielded from interpretation.

Technics in the service of language: I am not invoking a general essence of technics which would be already familiar to us and would help us in *understanding* the narrow and historically determined concept of writing as an example. I believe on the contrary that a certain sort of question about the meaning and origin of writing precedes, or at least merges with, a certain type of question about the meaning and origin of technics. That is why the notion of technique can never simply clarify the notion of writing.

It is therefore as if what we call language could have been in its origin and in its end only a moment, an essential but determined mode, a phenomenon, an aspect, a species of writing. And as if it had succeeded in making us forget this, and *in wilfully misleading us,* only in the course of an adventure: as that adventure itself. All in all a short enough adventure. It merges with the history that has associated technics and logocentric metaphysics for nearly three millennia. And it now seems to be approaching what is really its own *exhaustion;* under the circumstances—and this is no more than one example among others—of this death of the civilization of the book, of which so much is said and which manifests itself particularly through a convulsive proliferation of libraries. All appearances to the contrary, this death of the book undoubtedly announces (and in a certain sense always has announced) nothing but a death of speech (of a *so-called* full speech) and a new mutation in the history of writing, in history as writing. Announces it at a distance of a few centuries. It is on that scale that we must reckon it here, being careful not to neglect the quality of a very heterogeneous historical duration: the acceleration is such, and such its qualitative meaning, that one would be equally wrong in making a careful evaluation according to past rhythms. "Death of speech" is of course a metaphor here: before we speak of disappearance, we must think of a new situation for speech, of its subordination within a structure of which it will no longer be the archon.

To affirm in this way that the concept of writing exceeds and comprehends that of language, presupposes of course a certain definition of language and of writing. If we do not attempt to justify it, we shall be giving in to the movement of inflation that we have just mentioned, which has also taken over the word "writing," and that not fortuitously. For some time now, as a matter of fact, here and there, by a gesture and for motives that are profoundly necessary, whose degradation is easier to denounce than it is to disclose their origin, one says "language" for action, movement, thought, reflection, consciousness, unconsciousness, experience, affectivity, etc. Now we tend to say "writing" for all that and more: to designate not only the physical gestures of literal pictographic or ideographic inscription, but also the totality of what makes it possible; and also, beyond the signifying face, the signified face itself. And thus we say "writing" for all that gives rise to an inscription in general, whether it is literal or not and even if what it distributes in space is alien to the order of the voice: cinematography, choreography, of course, but also pictorial, musical, sculptural "writing." One might also speak of athletic writing, and with even greater certainty of military or political writing in view of the techniques that govern those domains today. All this to describe not only the system of notation secondarily connected with these activities but the essence and the content of these activities themselves. It is also in this sense that the contemporary biologist speaks of writing and *pro-gram* in relation to the most elementary process of information within the living cell. And, finally, whether it has essential limits or not, the entire field covered by the cybernetic *program* will be the field of writing. If the theory of cybernetics is by itself to oust all metaphysical concepts—including the concepts of soul, of life, of value, of choice, of memory—which until recently served to separate the machine from man,[4] it must conserve the notion of writing, trace, grammè [written mark], or grapheme, until its own historico-metaphysical character is also exposed. Even before being determined as human (with all the distinctive characteristics that have always been attributed to man and the entire system of significations that they imply) or nonhuman, the *grammè*—or the *grapheme*—would thus name the element. An element without simplicity. An element, whether it is understood as the medium or as the irreducible atom, of the arche-synthesis in general, of what one must forbid oneself to define within the system of oppositions of metaphysics, of what consequently one should not even call *experience* in general, that is to say the origin of *meaning* in general.

This situation has always already been announced. Why is it today in the process of making itself known *as such* and *after the fact?* This question would call forth an interminable analysis. Let us simply choose some points of departure in order to introduce the limited remarks to which I shall confine myself. I have already alluded to *theoretical* mathematics; its writing—whether understood as a sensible *graphie* [manner of writing] (and that already presupposes an identity, therefore an ideality, of its form, which in principle renders absurd the so easily admitted notion of the "sensible signifier"), or understood as the ideal synthesis of signifieds or a trace operative on another level, or whether it is understood, more profoundly, as the *passage* of the one to the other—has never been absolutely linked with a phonetic production. Within cultures practicing so-called phonetic writing, mathematics is not just an enclave. That is mentioned by all historians of writing; they recall at the same time the imperfections of alphabetic writing, which passed for so long as the most convenient and "the most intelligent"[5] writing. This enclave is also the place where the practice of scientific language challenges intrinsically and with increasing profundity the ideal of phonetic writing and all its implicit metaphysics (metaphysics *itself*), particularly, that is, the philosophical idea of the *epistémè;* also of *istoria,* a concept profoundly related to it in spite of the dissociation or opposition which has distinguished one from the other during one phase of their common progress. History and knowledge, *istoria* and *epistémè* have always been determined (and not only etymologically or philosophically) as detours *for the purpose of* the reappropriation of presence.

But beyond theoretical mathematics, the development of the *practical methods* of information retrieval extends the possibilities of the "message" vastly, to the point where it is no longer the "written" translation of a language, the transporting of a signified which could remain spoken in its integrity. It goes hand in hand with an extension of phonography and of all the means of conserving the spoken language, of making it function without the presence of the speaking subject. This development, coupled with that of anthropology and of the history of writing, teaches us that phonetic writing, the medium of the great metaphysical, scientific, technical, and economic adventure of the West, is limited in space and time and limits itself even as it is in the process of imposing its laws upon the cultural areas that had escaped it. But this nonfortuitous conjunction of cybernetics and the "human sciences" of writing leads to a more profound reversal.

## The Signifier and Truth

The "rationality"—but perhaps that word should be abandoned for reasons that will appear at the end of this sentence—which governs a writing thus enlarged and radicalized, no longer issues from a logos. Further, it inaugurates the destruction, not the demolition but the de-sedimentation, the de-construction, of all the significations that have their source in that of the logos. Particularly the signification of *truth*. All the metaphysical determinations of truth, and even the one beyond metaphysical ontotheology that Heidegger reminds us of, are more or less immediately inseparable from the instance of the logos, or of a reason thought within the lineage of the logos, in whatever sense it is understood: in the pre-Socratic or the philosophical sense, in the sense of God's infinite understanding or in the anthropological sense, in the pre-Hegelian or the post-Hegelian sense. Within this logos, the original and essential link to the *phonè* has never been broken. It would be easy to demonstrate this and I shall attempt such a demonstration later. As has been more or less implicitly determined, the essence of the *phonè* would be immediately proximate to that which within "thought" as logos relates to "meaning," produces it, receives it, speaks it, "composes" it. If, for Aristotle, for example, "spoken words (ta en tē phonē) are the symbols of mental experience (pathēmata tes psychēs) and written words are the symbols of spoken words" (*De interpretatione*, 1, 16a 3) it is because the voice, producer of *the first symbols,* has a relationship of essential and immediate proximity with the mind. Producer of the first signifier, it is not just a simple signifier among others. It signifies "mental experiences" which themselves reflect or mirror things by natural resemblance. Between being and mind, things and feelings, there would be a relationship of translation or natural signification; between mind and logos, a relationship of conventional symbolization. And the *first* convention, which would relate immediately to the order of natural and universal signification, would be produced as spoken language. Written language would establish the conventions, interlinking other conventions with them.

> Just as all men have not the same writing so all men have not the same speech sounds, but mental experiences, of which these are the *primary symbols (semeīa prótos),* are the same for all, as also are

those things of which our experiences are the images (*De interpretatione*, 1, 16a. Italics added).

The feelings of the mind, expressing things naturally, constitute a sort of universal language which can then efface itself. It is the stage of transparence. Aristotle can sometimes omit it without risk.[6] In every case, the voice is closest to the signified, whether it is determined strictly as sense (thought or lived) or more loosely as thing. All signifiers, and first and foremost the written signifier, are derivative with regard to what would wed the voice indissolubly to the mind or to the thought of the signified sense, indeed to the thing itself (whether it is done in the Aristotelian manner that we have just indicated or in the manner of medieval theology, determining the *res* as a thing created from its *eidos*, from its sense thought in the logos or in the infinite understanding of God). The written signifier is always technical and representative. It has no constitutive meaning. This derivation is the very origin of the notion of the "signifier." The notion of the sign always implies within itself the distinction between signifier and signified, even if, as Saussure argues, they are distinguished simply as the two faces of one and the same leaf. This notion remains therefore within the heritage of that logocentrism which is also a phonocentrism: absolute proximity of voice and being, of voice and the meaning of being, of voice and the ideality of meaning. Hegel demonstrates very clearly the strange privilege of sound in idealization, the production of the concept and the self-presence of the subject.

This ideal motion, in which through the sound what is as it were the simple subjectivity [*Subjektivität*], the soul of the material thing expresses itself, the ear receives also in a theoretical [*theoretisch*] way, just as the eye shape and colour, thus allowing the interiority of the object to become interiority itself [*läßt dadurch das Innere der Gegenstände für das Innere selbst werden*] (*Esthétique*, III. I tr. fr. p. 16).[7] . . . The ear, on the contrary, perceives [*vernimmt*] the result of that interior vibration of material substance without placing itself in a practical relation toward the objects, a result by means of which it is no longer the material form [*Gestalt*] in its repose, but the first, more ideal activity of the soul itself which is manifested [*zum Vorschein kommt*] (p. 296).†

What is said of sound in general is a fortiori valid for the *phonè* by which, by virtue of hearing (understanding)-oneself-speak—an indissociable system—the subject affects itself and is related to itself in the element of ideality.

We already have a foreboding that phonocentrism merges with the historical determination of the meaning of being in general as *presence,* with all the subdeterminations which depend on this general form and which organize within it their system and their historical sequence (presence of the thing to the sight as *eidos,* presence as substance/essence/existence [*ousia*], temporal presence as point [*stigmè*] of the now or of the moment [*nun*], the self-presence of the cogito, consciousness, subjectivity, the co-presence of the other and of the self, intersubjectivity as the intentional phenomenon of the ego, and so forth). Logocentrism would thus support the determination of the being of the entity as presence. To the extent that such a logocentrism is not totally absent from Heidegger's thought, perhaps it still holds that thought within the epoch of onto-theology, within the philosophy of presence, that is to say within philosophy *itself.* This would perhaps mean that one does not leave the epoch whose closure one can outline. The movements of belonging or not belonging to the epoch are too subtle, the illusions in that regard are too easy, for us to make a definite judgment.

The epoch of the logos thus debases writing considered as mediation of mediation and as a fall into the exteriority of meaning. To this epoch belongs the difference between signified and signifier, or at least the strange separation of their "parallelism," and the exteriority, however extenuated of the one to the other. This appurtenance is organized and hierarchized in a history. The difference between signified and signifier belongs in a profound and implicit way to the totality of the great epoch covered by the history of metaphysics, and in a more explicit and more systematically articulated way to the narrower epoch of Christian creationism and infinitism when these appropriate the resources of Greek conceptuality. This appurtenance is essential and irreducible; one cannot retain the convenience or the "scientific truth" of the Stoic and later medieval opposition between *signans* and *signatum* without also bringing with it all its metaphysicotheological roots. To these roots adheres not only the distinction between the sensible and the intelligible—already a great deal—with all that it controls, namely, metaphysics in its totality. And this distinction is generally accepted as self-evident by the most careful linguists and semiologists, even by those who believe that the scientificity of their work begins where metaphysics ends. Thus, for example:

> As modern structural thought has clearly realized, language is a system of signs and linguistics is part and parcel of the science of signs, or *semiotics* (Saussure's *sémiologie*). The mediaeval definition of sign—"*aliquid stat pro aliquo*"—has been resurrected and put forward as still valid and productive. Thus the constitutive mark of any

sign in general and of any linguistic sign in particular is its twofold character: every linguistic unit is bipartite and involves both aspects—one sensible and the other intelligible, or in other words, both the *signans* "signifier" (Saussure's *signifiant*) and the *signatum* "signified" (*signifié*). These two constituents of a linguistic sign (and of sign in general) necessarily suppose and require each other.[8]

But to these metaphysico-theological roots many other hidden sediments cling. The semiological or, more specifically, linguistic "science" cannot therefore hold on to the difference between signifier and signified—the very idea of the sign—without the difference between sensible and intelligible, certainly, but also not without retaining, more profoundly and more implicitly, and by the same token the reference to a signified able to "take place" in its intelligibility, before its "fall," before any expulsion into the exteriority of the sensible here below. As the face of pure intelligibility, it refers to an absolute logos to which it is immediately united. This absolute logos was an infinite creative subjectivity in medieval theology: the intelligible face of the sign remains turned toward the word and the face of God.

Of course, it is not a question of "rejecting" these notions; they are necessary and, at least at present, nothing is conceivable for us without them. It is a question at first of demonstrating the systematic and historical solidarity of the concepts and gestures of thought that one often believes can be innocently separated. The sign and divinity have the same place and time of birth. The age of the sign is essentially theological. Perhaps it will never *end*. Its historical *closure* is, however, outlined.

Since these concepts are indispensable for unsettling the heritage to which they belong, we should be even less prone to renounce them. Within the closure, by an oblique and always perilous movement, constantly risking falling back within what is being deconstructed, it is necessary to surround the critical concepts with a careful and thorough discourse—to mark the conditions, the medium, and the limits of their effectiveness and to designate rigorously their intimate relationship to the machine whose deconstruction they permit; and, in the same process, designate the crevice through which the yet unnameable glimmer beyond the closure can be glimpsed. The concept of the sign is here exemplary. We have just marked its metaphysical appurtenance. We know, however, that the thematics of the sign have been for about a century the agonized labor of a tradition that professed to withdraw meaning, truth, presence, being, etc., from the movement of signification. Treating as suspect, as I just have, the difference between signified and signifier, or the idea of the sign in general, I must state explicitly that it is not a question of doing so in terms of the instance of the present truth, anterior, exterior or superior to the sign, or in terms of the place of the effaced difference. Quite the contrary. We are disturbed by that which, in the concept of the sign—which has never existed or functioned outside the history of (the) philosophy (of presence)—remains systematically and genealogically determined by that history. It is there that the concept and above all the work of deconstruction, its "style," remain by nature exposed to misunderstanding and nonrecognition.

The exteriority of the signifier is the exteriority of writing in general, and I shall try to show later that there is no linguistic sign before writing. Without that exteriority, the very idea of the sign falls into decay. Since our entire world and language would collapse with it, and since its evidence and its value keep, to a certain point of derivation, an indestructible solidity, it would be silly to conclude from its placement within an epoch that it is necessary to "move on to something else," to dispose of the sign, of the term and the notion. For a proper understanding of the gesture that we are sketching here, one must understand the expressions "epoch," "closure of an epoch," "historical genealogy" in a new way; and must first remove them from all relativism.

Thus, within this epoch, reading and writing, the production or interpretation of signs, the text in general as fabric of signs, allow themselves to be confined within secondariness. They are preceded by a truth, or a meaning already constituted by and within the element of the logos. Even when the thing, the "referent," is not immediately related to the logos of a creator God where it began by being the spoken/thought sense, the signified has at any rate an immediate relationship with the logos in general (finite or infinite), and a mediated one with the signifier, that is to say with the exteriority of writing. When it seems to go otherwise, it is because a metaphoric mediation has insinuated itself into the relationship and has simulated immediacy; the writing of truth in the soul, opposed by *Phaedrus* (278a) to bad writing (writing in the "literal" [*propre*] and ordinary sense, "sensible" writing, "in space"), the book of Nature and God's writing, especially in the Middle Ages; all that functions as *metaphor* in these discourses confirms the privilege of the logos and founds the "literal" meaning then given to writing: a sign signifying a signifier itself signifying an eternal verity, eternally thought and spoken in the proximity of a present logos. The paradox to which attention must be paid is this: natural and universal writing, intelligible and nontemporal writing, is thus named by metaphor. A writing that is sensible, finite, and so on, is designated as writing in the literal sense; it is thus thought on the side of culture, technique, and artifice; a human procedure, the ruse of a being accidentally incarnated or of a finite creature. Of course, this metaphor remains enigmatic and refers to a "literal" meaning of writing as the first metaphor. This "literal" meaning is yet unthought by the adherents of this discourse. It is not, therefore, a matter of inverting the literal meaning and the figurative meaning but of determining the "literal" meaning of writing as metaphoricity itself.

In "The Symbolism of the Book," that excellent chapter of *European Literature and the Latin Middle Ages,* E. R. Curtius describes with great wealth of examples the evolution that led from the *Phaedrus* to Calderon, until it seemed to be "precisely the reverse" (tr. fr. p. 372)[9] by the "newly attained position of the book" (p. 374) [p. 306]. But it seems that this modification, however important in fact it might be, conceals a fundamental continuity. As was the case with the Platonic writing of the truth in the soul, in the Middle Ages too it is a writing understood in the metaphoric sense, that is to say a *natural,* eternal, and universal writing, the system of signified truth, which is recognized in its dignity. As in the *Phaedrus,* a certain fallen writing continues to be opposed to it. There remains to be written a history of this metaphor, a metaphor that systematically contrasts divine or natural writing and the human and laborious, finite and artificial inscription. It remains to articulate rigorously the stages of that history, as marked by the quotations below, and to follow the theme of God's book (nature or law, indeed natural law) through all its modifications.

Rabbi Eliezer said: "If all the seas were of ink, and all ponds planted with reeds, if the sky and the earth were parchments and if all human beings practised the art of writing—they would not exhaust the Torah I have learned, just as the Torah itself would not be diminished any more than is the sea by the water removed by a paint brush dipped in it."[10]

Galileo: "It [the book of Nature] is written in a mathematical language."[11]

Descartes: ". . . to read in the great book of Nature . . ."[12]

Demea, in the name of natural religion, in the *Dialogues,* . . . of Hume: "And this volume of nature contains a great and inexplicable riddle, more than any intelligible discourse or reasoning."[13]

Bonnet: "It would seem more philosophical to me to presume that our earth is a book that God has given to intelligences far superior to ours to read, and where they study in depth the infinitely multiplied and varied characters of His adorable wisdom."

G. H. von Schubert: "This language made of images and hieroglyphs, which supreme Wisdom uses in all its revelations to humanity—which is found in the inferior [*nieder*] language of poetry—and which, in the most inferior and imperfect way [*auf der allerniedrigsten und unvollkom-*

*mensten*], is more like the metaphorical expression of the dream than the prose of wakefulness, . . . we may wonder if this language is not the true and wakeful language of the superior regions. If, when we consider ourselves awakened, we are not plunged in a millennial slumber, or at least in the echo of its dreams, where we only perceive a few isolated and obscure words of God's language, as a sleeper perceives the conversation of the people around him."§

Jaspers: "The world is the manuscript of an other, inaccessible to a universal reading, which only existence deciphers."‖

Above all, the profound differences distinguishing all these treatments of the same metaphor must not be ignored. In the history of this treatment, the most decisive separation appears at the moment when, at the same time as the science of nature, the determination of absolute presence is constituted as self-presence, as subjectivity. It is the moment of the great rationalisms of the seventeenth century. From then on, the condemnation of fallen and finite writing will take another form, within which we still live: it is non-self-presence that will be denounced. Thus the exemplariness of the "Rousseauist" moment, which we shall deal with later, begins to be explained. Rousseau repeats the Platonic gesture by referring to another model of presence: self-presence in the senses, in the sensible cogito, which simultaneously carries in itself the inscription of divine law. On the one hand, *representative,* fallen, secondary, instituted writing, writing in the literal and strict sense, is condemned in *The Essay on the Origin of Languages* (it "enervates" speech; to "judge genius" from books is like "painting a man's portrait from his corpse," etc.). Writing in the common sense is the dead letter, it is the carrier of death. It exhausts life. On the other hand, on the other face of the same proposition, writing in the metaphoric sense, natural, divine, and living writing, is venerated; it is equal in dignity to the origin of value, to the voice of conscience as divine law, to the heart, to sentiment, and so forth.

> The Bible is the most sublime of all books, . . . but it is after all a book. . . . It is not at all in a few sparse pages that one should look for God's law, but in the human heart where His hand deigned to write (*Lettre à Vernes*).[14]
>
> If the natural law had been written only in the human reason, it would be little capable of directing most of our actions. But is is also engraved in the heart of man in effaceable characters. . . . There it cries to him (*L'état de guerre.*)[15]

Natural writing is immediately united to the voice and to breath. Its nature is not grammatological but pneumatological. It is hieratic, very close to the interior holy voice of the *Profession of Faith,* to the voice one hears upon retreating into oneself: full and truthful presence of the divine voice to our inner sense: "The more I retreat into myself, the more I consult myself, the more plainly do I read these words written in my soul: be just and you will be happy.... I do not derive these rules from the principles of the higher philosophy, I find them in the depths of my heart written by nature in characters which nothing can efface."[16]

There is much to say about the fact that the native unity of the voice and writing is *prescriptive.* Arche-speech is writing because it is a law. A natural law. The beginning word is understood, in the intimacy of self-presence, as the voice of the other and as commandment.

There is therefore a good and a bad writing: the good and natural is the divine inscription in the heart and the soul; the perverse and artful is technique, exiled in the exteriority of the body. A modification well within the Platonic diagram: writing of the soul and of the body, writing of the interior and of the exterior, writing of conscience and of the passions, as there is a voice of the soul and a voice of the body. "Conscience is the voice of the soul, the passions are the voice of the body" [p. 249]. One must constantly go back toward the "voice of nature," the "holy voice of nature," that merges with the divine inscription and prescription; one must encounter oneself within it, enter into a dialogue within its signs, speak and respond to oneself in its pages.

> It was as if nature had spread out all her magnificence in front of our eyes to offer its text for our consideration.... I have therefore closed all the books. Only one is open to all eyes. It is the book of Nature. In this great and sublime book I learn to serve and adore its author.

The good writing has therefore always been *comprehended.* Comprehended as that which had to be comprehended: within a nature or a natural law, created or not, but first thought within an eternal presence. Comprehended, therefore, within a totality, and enveloped in a volume or a book. The idea of the book is the idea of a totality, finite or infinite, of the signifier; this totality of the signifier cannot be a totality, unless a totality constituted by the signified preexists it, supervises its inscriptions and its signs, and is independent of it in its ideality. The idea of the book, which always refers to a natural totality, is profoundly alien to the sense of writing. It is the encyclopedic protection of theology and of logocentrism against the disruption of writing, against its aphoristic energy, and, as I shall specify later, against difference in general. If I distinguish the text from the book, I shall say that the destruction of the book, as it is now under way in all domains, denudes the surface of the text. That necessary violence responds to a violence that was no less necessary.

## The Written Being/
## The Being Written

The reassuring evidence within which Western tradition had to organize itself and must continue to live would therefore be as follows: the order of the signified is never contemporary, is at best the subtly discrepant inverse or parallel—discrepant by the time of a breath—from the order of the signifier. And the sign must be the unity of a heterogeneity, since the signified (sense or thing, noeme or reality) is not in itself a signifier, a *trace:* in any case is not constituted in its sense by its relationship with a possible trace. The formal essence of the signified is *presence,* and the privilege of its proximity to the logos as *phonè* is the privilege of presence. This is the inevitable response as soon as one asks: "what is the sign?," that is to say, when one submits the sign to the question of essence, to the "ti esti." The "formal essence" of the sign can only be determined in terms of presence. One cannot get around that response, except by challenging the very form of the question and beginning to think that the sign is that ill-named thing, the only one, that escapes the instituting question of philosophy: "what is . . .?"[17]

Radicalizing the concepts of *interpretation, perspective, evaluation, difference,* and all the "empiricist" or nonphilosophical motifs that have constantly tormented philosophy throughout the history of the West, and besides, have had nothing but the inevitable weakness of being produced in the field of philosophy, Nietzsche, far from remaining *simply* (with Hegel and as Heidegger wished) *within* metaphysics, contributed a great deal to the liberation of the signifier from its dependence or derivation with respect to the logos and the related concept of truth or the primary signified, in whatever sense that is understood. Reading, and therefore writing, the text were for Nietzsche "originary"[18] operations (I put that word within quotation marks for reasons to appear later) with regard to a sense that they do not first have to transcribe or discover, which would not therefore be a truth signified in the original element and presence of the logos, as *topos noetos,* divine understanding, or the structure of a priori necessity. To save Nietzsche from a reading of the Heideggerian type, it seems that we must above all not attempt to restore or make explicit a less naive "ontology," composed of profound ontological intuitions acceding to some originary truth, an entire fundamentality hidden under the appearance of an empiricist or metaphysical text. The virulence of Nietzschean thought could not be more completely misunderstood. On the contrary, one must *accentuate* the "naiveté" of a breakthrough which cannot attempt a step outside of metaphysics, which cannot *criticize* metaphysics radically without still utilizing in a certain way, in a certain type or a certain style of *text,* propositions that, read within the philosophic corpus, that is to say according to Nietzsche ill-read or unread, have always been and will always be "naivetés," incoherent signs of an absolute appurtenance. Therefore, rather than protect Nietzsche from the Heideggerian reading, we should perhaps offer him up to it completely, underwriting that interpretation without reserve; in a *certain way* and up to the point where, the content of the Nietzschean discourse being almost lost for the question of being, its form regains its absolute strangeness, where his text finally invokes a different type of reading, more faithful to his type of writing: Nietzsche has *written what* he has written. He has written that writing—and first of all his own—is not originarily subordinate to the logos and to truth. And that this subordination has *come into being* during an epoch whose meaning we must deconstruct. Now in this direction (but only in this direction, for read otherwise, the Nietzschean demolition remains dogmatic and, like all reversals, a captive of that metaphysical edifice which it professes to overthrow. On that point and in that *order of reading,* the conclusions of Heidegger and Fink are irrefutable), Heideggerian thought would reinstate rather than destroy the instance of the logos and of the truth of being as "primum signatum:" the "transcendental" signified ("transcendental" in a certain sense, as in the Middle Ages the transcendental—*ens, unum, verum, bonum*—was said to be the "primum cognitum") implied by all categories or all determined significations, by all lexicons and all syntax, and therefore by all linguistic signifiers, though not to be identified simply with any one of those signifiers, allowing itself to be precomprehended through each of them, remaining irreducible to all the epochal determinations that it nonetheless makes possible, thus opening the history of the logos, yet itself being only through the logos; that is, *being nothing* before the logos and outside of it. The logos *of* being, "Thought obeying the Voice of Being,"[19] is the first and the last resource of the sign, of the difference between *signans* and *signatum.* There has to be a transcendental signified for the difference between signifier and signified to be somewhere absolute and irreducible. It is not by chance that the thought of being, as the thought of this transcendental signified, is manifested above all in the voice: in a language of words [*mots*]. The voice is *heard* (understood)—that undoubtedly is what is called conscience—closest to the self as the absolute effacement of the signifier: pure auto-affection that necessarily has the form of time and which does not borrow from outside of itself, in the world or in "reality," any accessory signifier, any substance of expression foreign to its own spontaneity. It is the unique experience of the signified producing itself spontaneously, from within the self, and nevertheless, as signified concept, in the element of ideality or universality. The unworldly character of this substance of expression is constitutive of this ideality. This experience of the effacement of the signifier in the voice is not merely one illusion among many—since it is the condition of the very idea of truth—but I shall elsewhere show in what it does delude itself. This illusion is the history of truth and it cannot be dissipated so quickly. Within the closure of this experience, the word [*mot*] is lived as the elementary and undecomposable unity of the signified and the voice, of the concept and a transparent substance of expression. This experience is considered in its greatest purity—and at the same time in the condition of its possibility—as the experience of "being." The word "being," or at any rate the words designating the sense of being in different languages, is, with some others, an "originary word" ("*Urwort*"),[20] the transcendental word assuring the possibility of being-word to all other words. As such, it is precomprehended in all language and—this is the opening of *Being and Time*—only this precomprehension would permit the opening of the question of the sense of being in general, beyond all regional ontologies and all metaphysics: a question that broaches philosophy (for example, in the *Sophist*) and lets itself be taken over by philosophy, a question that Heidegger repeats by submitting the history of metaphysics to it. Heidegger reminds us constantly that the sense of being is neither the word "being" nor the concept of being. But as that sense is nothing outside of language and the language of words, it is tied, if not to a particular word or to a particular system of language (concesso non dato), at least to the possibility of the word in general. And to the possibility of its irreducible simplicity. One could thus think that it remains only to choose between two possibilities. (1) Does a modern linguistics, a science of signification breaking the unity of the word and breaking with its alleged irreducibility, still have anything to do with "language?" Heidegger would probably doubt it. (2) Conversely, is not all that is profoundly meditated as the thought or the question of being enclosed within an old linguistics of the word which one practices here unknowingly? Unknowingly because such a linguistics, whether spontaneous or systematic, has always had to share the presuppositions of metaphysics. The two operate on the same grounds.

It goes without saying that the alternatives cannot be so simple.

On the one hand, if modern linguistics remains completely enclosed within a classical conceptuality, if especially it naively uses the word *being* and all that it presupposes, that which, within this linguistics, deconstructs the unity of the word in general can no longer, according to the model of the Heideggerian question, as it functions powerfully from the very opening of *Being and Time,* be circumscribed as ontic science or regional ontology. In as much as the question of being unites indissolubly with the precomprehension of the *word being,* without being reduced to it, the linguistics that works for the deconstruction of the constituted unity of that word has only, in fact or in principle, to have the question of being posed in order to define its field and the order of its dependence.

Not only is its field no longer simply ontic, but the limits of ontology that correspond to it no longer have anything regional about them. And can what I say here of linguistics, or at least of a certain work that may be undertaken within it and thanks to it, not be said of all research *in as much as and to the strict extent that* it would finally deconstitute the founding concept-words of ontology, of being in its privilege? Outside of linguistics, it is in psychoanalytic research that this breakthrough seems at present to have the greatest likelihood of being expanded.

Within the strictly limited space of this breakthrough, these "sciences" are no longer *dominated* by the questions of a transcendental phenomenology or a fundamental ontology. One may perhaps say, following the order of questions inaugurated by *Being and Time* and radicalizing the questions of Husserlian phenomenology, that this breakthrough does not belong to science itself, that what thus seems to be produced within an ontic field or within a regional ontology, does not belong to them by rights and leads back to the question of being itself.

Because it is indeed the *question* of being that Heidegger asks metaphysics. And with it the question of truth, of sense, of the logos. The incessant meditation upon that question does not restore confidence. On the contrary, it dislodges the confidence at its own depth, which, being a matter of the meaning of being, is more difficult than is often believed. In examining the state just before all determinations of being, destroying the securities of onto-theology, such a meditation contributes, quite as much as the most contemporary linguistics, to the dislocation of the unity of the sense of being, that is, in the last instance, the unity of the word.

It is thus that, after evoking the "voice of being," Heidegger recalls that it is silent, mute, insonorous, wordless, originarily *a-phonic (die Gewahr der lautlosen Stimme verborgener Quellen . . .).* The voice of the sources is not heard. A rupture between the originary meaning of being and the word, between meaning and the voice, between "the voice of being" and the *"phonè,"* between "the call of being," and articulated sound; such a rupture, which at once confirms a fundamental metaphor, and renders it suspect by accentuating its metaphoric discrepancy, translates the ambiguity of the Heideggerian situation with respect to the metaphysics of presence and logocentrism. It is at once contained within it and transgresses it. But it is impossible to separate the two. The very movement of transgression sometimes holds it back short of the limit. In opposition to what we suggested above, it must be remembered that, for Heidegger, the sense of being is never simply and rigorously a "signified." It is not by chance that that word is not used; that means that being escapes the movement of the sign, a proposition that can equally well be understood as a repetition of the classical tradition and as a caution with respect to a technical or metaphysical theory of signification. On the other hand, the sense of being is literally neither "primary," nor "fundamental," nor "transcendental," whether understood in the scholastic, Kantian, or Husserlian sense. The restoration of being as "transcending" the categories of the entity, the opening of the fundamental ontology, are nothing but necessary yet provisional moments. From *The Introduction to Metaphysics* onward, Heidegger renounces the project of and the word ontology.[21] The necessary, originary, and irreducible dissimulation of the meaning of being, its occultation within the very blossoming forth of presence, that retreat without which there would be no history of being which was completely *history* and history of *being,* Heidegger's insistence on noting that being is produced as history only through the logos, and is nothing outside of it, the difference between being and the entity—all this clearly indicates that fundamentally nothing escapes the movement of the signifier and that, in the last instance, the difference between signified and signifier *is nothing.* This proposition of transgression, not yet integrated into a careful discourse, runs the risk of formulating regression itself. One must therefore *go by way of* the question of being as it is directed by Heidegger and by him alone, at and beyond onto-theology, in order to reach the rigorous thought of that strange nondifference and in order to determine it correctly. Heidegger occasionally reminds us that "being," as it is fixed in its general syntactic and lexicological forms within linguistics and Western philosophy, is not a primary and absolutely irreducible signified, that it is still rooted in a system of languages and an historically determined "significance," although strangely privileged as the virtue of disclosure and dissimulation; particularly when he invites us to meditate on the "privilege" of the "third person singular of the present indicative" and the "infinitive." Western metaphysics, as the limitation of the sense of being within the field of presence, is produced as the domination of a linguistic form.[22] To question the origin of that domination does not amount to hypostatizing a transcendental signified, but to a questioning of what constitutes our history and what produced transcendentality itself. Heidegger brings it up also when in *Zur Seinsfrage,* for the same reason, he lets the word "being" be read only if it is crossed out (*kreuzweise Durchstreichung*). That mark of deletion is not, however, a "merely negative symbol" (p. 31) [p. 83]. That deletion is the final writing of an epoch. Under its strokes the presence of a transcendental signified is effaced while still remaining legible. Is effaced while still remaining legible, is destroyed while making visible the very idea of the sign. In as much as it de-limits onto-theology, the metaphysics of presence and logocentrism, this last writing is also the first writing.

To come to recognize, not within but on the horizon of the Heideggerian paths, and yet in them, that the sense of being is not a transcendental or trans-epochal signified (even if it was always dissimulated within the epoch) but already, in a truly *unheard of* sense, a determined signifying trace, is to affirm that within the decisive concept of ontico-ontological difference, *all is not to be thought at one go;* entity and being, ontic and ontological, "ontico-ontological," are, in an original style, *derivative* with regard to difference; and with respect to what I shall later call *differance,* an economic concept designating the production of differing/deferring. The ontico-ontological difference and its ground (*Grund*) in the "transcendence of Dasein" (*Vom Wesen des Grundes* [Frankfurt am Main, 1955], p. 16 [p. 29]) are not absolutely originary. Differance by itself would be more "originary," but one would no longer be able to call it "origin" or "ground," those notions belonging essentially to the history of onto-theology, to the system functioning as the effacing of difference. It can, however, be thought of in the closest proximity to itself only on one condition: that one begins by determining it as the ontico-ontological difference before erasing that determination. The necessity of passing through that erased determination, the necessity of that *trick of writing* is irreducible. An unemphatic and difficult thought that, through much unperceived mediation, must carry the entire burden of our question, a question that I shall provisionally call *historial [historiale].* It is with its help that I shall later be able to attempt to relate differance and writing.

The hesitation of these thoughts (here Nietzsche's and Heidegger's) is not an "incoherence": it is a trembling proper to all post-Hegelian attempts and to this passage between two epochs. The movements of deconstruction do not destroy structures from the outside. They are not possible and effective, nor can they take accurate aim, except by inhabiting those structures. Inhabiting them *in a certain way,* because one always inhabits, and all the more when one does not suspect it. Operating necessarily from the inside, borrowing all the strategic and economic resources of subversion from the old structure, borrowing them structurally, that is to say without being able to isolate their elements and atoms, the enterprise of deconstruction always in a certain way falls prey to its own work. This is what the person who has begun the same work in another area of the same habitation does not fail to point out with zeal. No exercise is more widespread today and one should be able to formalize its rules.

Hegel was already caught up in this game. *On the one hand,* he undoubtedly *summed up* the entire philosophy of the logos. He determined ontology as absolute logic; he assembled all the delimitations of philosophy as presence; he assigned to presence the eschatology of parousia, of the selfproximity of infinite subjectivity. And for the same reason he had to debase or subordinate writing. When he criticizes the Leibnizian characteristic, the formalism of the understanding, and mathematical symbolism, he makes the same gesture: denouncing the being-outside-of-itself of the logos in the sensible or the intellectual abstraction. Writing is that forgetting of the self, that exteriorization, the contrary of the interiorizing memory, of the *Erinnerung* that opens the history of the spirit. It is this that the *Phaedrus* said: writing is at once mnemotechnique and the power of forgetting. Naturally, the Hegelian critique of writing stops at the alphabet. As phonetic writing, the alphabet is at the same time more servile, more contemptible, more secondary ("alphabetic writing expresses *sounds* which are themselves signs. It consists therefore of the signs of signs ['*aus Zeichen der Zeichen*,'" *Enzyklopädie,* § 459])[23] but it is also the best writing, the mind's writing; its effacement before the voice, that in it which respects the ideal interiority of phonic signifiers, all that by which it sublimates space and sight, all that makes of it the writing of history, the writing, that is, of the infinite spirit relating to itself in its discourse and its culture:

> It follows that to learn to read and write an alphabetic writing should be regarded as a means to infinite culture (*unendliches Bildungsmittel*) that is not enough appreciated; because thus the mind, distancing itself from the concrete sense-perceptible, directs its attention on the more formal moment, the sonorous word and its abstract elements, and contributes essentially to the founding and purifying of the ground of interiority within the subject.

In that sense it is the *Aufhebung* of other writings, particularly of hieroglyphic script and of the Leibnizian characteristic that had been criticized previously through one and the same gesture. (*Aufhebung* is, more or less implicitly, the dominant concept of nearly all histories of writing, even today. It is *the* concept of history and of teleology.) In fact, Hegel continues: "Acquired habit later also suppresses the specificity of alphabetic writing, which consists in seeming to be, in the interest of sight, a detour [*Umweg*] through hearing to arrive at representations, and makes it into a hieroglyphic script for us, such that in using it, we do not need to have present to our consciousness the mediation of sounds."

It is on this condition that Hegel subscribes to the Leibnizian praise of nonphonetic writing. It can be produced by deaf mutes, Leibniz had said. Hegel:

Beside the fact that, by the practice which transforms this alphabetic script into hieroglyphics, the aptitude for abstraction acquired through such an exercise *is conserved* [italics added], the reading of hieroglyphs is for itself a deaf reading and a mute writing (*ein taubes Lesen und ein stummes Schreiben*). What is audible or temporal, visible or spatial, has each its proper basis and in the first place they are of equal value; but in alphabetic script there is only *one* basis and that following a specific relation, namely, that the visible language is related only as a sign to the audible language; intelligence expresses itself immediately and unconditionally through speech (ibid.).

What writing itself, in its nonphonetic moment, betrays, is life. It menaces at once the breath, the spirit, and history as the spirit's relationship with itself. It is their end, their finitude, their paralysis. Cutting breath short, sterilizing or immobilizing spiritual creation in the repetition of the letter, in the commentary or the *exegesis,* confined in a narrow space, reserved for a minority, it is the principle of death and of difference in the becoming of being. It is to speech what China is to Europe: "It is only to the exegeticism[24] of Chinese spiritual culture that their hieroglyphic writing is suited. This type of writing is, besides, the part reserved for a very small section of a people, the section that possesses the exclusive domain of spiritual culture. . . . A hieroglyphic script would require a philosophy as exegetical as Chinese culture generally is" (ibid.).

If the nonphonetic moment menaces the history and the life of the spirit as self-presence in the breath, it is because it menaces substantiality, that other metaphysical name of presence and of *ousia.* First in the form of the substantive. Nonphonetic writing breaks the noun apart. It describes relations and not apellations. The noun and the word, those unities of breath and concept, are effaced within pure writing. In that regard, Leibniz is as disturbing as the Chinese in Europe: "This situation, the analytic notation of representations in hieroglyphic script, which seduced Leibniz to the point of wrongly preferring this script to the alphabetic, rather contradicts the fundamental exigency of language in general, namely the noun. . . . All difference [*Abweichung*] in analysis would produce another formation of the written substantive."

The horizon of absolute knowledge is the effacement of writing in the logos, the retrieval of the trace in parousia, the reappropriation of difference, the accomplishment of what I have elsewhere called[25] the *metaphysics of the proper* [*le propre*—self-possession, propriety, property, cleanliness].

Yet, all that Hegel thought within this horizon, all, that is, except eschatology, may be reread as a meditation on writing. Hegel is *also* the thinker of irreducible difference. He rehabilitated thought as the *memory productive* of signs. And he reintroduced, as I shall try to show elsewhere, the essential necessity of the written trace in a philosophical—that is to say Socratic—discourse that had always believed it possible to do without it; the last philosopher of the book and the first thinker of writing.

## Notes

1. "Aus dem Gedankenkreise der Geburt der Tragödie," I. 3. *Nietzsche Werke* (Leipzig, 1903), vol. 9, part 2, i, p. 66.

2. To speak of a primary writing here does not amount to affirming a chronological priority of fact. That debate is well-known; is writing, as affirmed, for example, by Metchaninov and Marr, then Loukotka, "anterior to phonetic language?" (A conclusion assumed by the first edition of the Great Soviet Encyclopedia, later contradicted by Stalin. On this debate, cf. V. Istrine, "Langue et écriture," *Linguistique,* op cit., pp. 35, 60. This debate also forms around the theses advanced by P. van Ginneken. On the discussion of these propositions, cf. James Février, *Histoire de l'écriture* [Payot, 1948–59], pp. 5 f.). I shall try to show below why the terms and premises of such a debate are suspicious.

3. I shall deal with this problem more directly in *La voix et le phénomène* (Paris, 1967) [*Speech and Phenomena,* op. cit.].

4. Wiener, for example, while abandoning "semantics," and the opposition, judged by him as too crude and too general, between animate and inanimate etc., nevertheless continues to use expressions like "organs of sense," "motor organs," etc. to qualify the parts of the machine.

5. Cf., e.g., *EP* [*L'Ecriture et la Psychologie des Peuples* (Proceedings of a Colloquium, 1963)], pp. 126, 148, 355, etc. From another point of view, cf. Roman Jakobson, *Essais de linguistique générale* (tr. fr. [Nicolas Ruwet, Paris, 1963], p. 116) [Jakobson and Morris Halle, *Fundamentals of Language* (the Hague, 1956), p. 16].

6. This is shown by Pierre Aubenque (*Le problème de l'être chez Aristotle* (Paris, 1966], pp. 106 f.). In the course of a provocative analysis, to which I am here indebted, Aubenque remarks: "In other texts, to be sure, Aristotle designates as symbol the relationship between language and things: 'It is not possible to bring the things themselves to the discussion, but, instead of things, we can use their names as symbols.' The intermediary constituted by the mental experience is here suppressed or at least neglected, but this suppression is legitimate, since, mental experiences behaving like things, things can be substituted for them immediately. On the other hand, one cannot by any means substitute names for things" (pp. 107–08).

7. Georg Wilhelm Friedrich Hegel, *Werke,* Suhrkamp edition (Frankfurt am Main, 1970), vol. 14, p. 256; translated as *The Philosophy of Fine Art* by F. P.

Osmaston (London, 1920), vol. 3, pp. 15–16.

†Hegel, p. 134; Osmaston, p. 341.

8. Roman Jakobson, *Essais de linguistique générale*, tr. fr., p. 162 ["The Phonemic and Grammatical Aspects of Language in their Interrelations," *Proceedings of the Sixth International Congress of Linguistics* (Paris, 1949), p. 6]. On this problem, on the tradition of the concept of the sign, and on the originality of Saussure's contribution within this continuity, cf. Ortigues, op. cit., pp. 54 f.

9. Ernst Robert Curtius, "Das Buch als Symbol," *Europäische Literatur und lateinische Mittelalter* (Bern, 1948), p. 307. French translation by Jean Bréjoux (Paris, 1956) translated as *European Literature and the Latin Middle Ages*, by Willard R. Trask, Harper Torchbooks edition (New York, 1963), pp. 305, 306.

10. Cited by Emmanuel Levinas, in *Difficile liberté* [Paris, 1963], p. 44.

11. Quoted in Curtius, *op. cit.* (German), p. 326, (English), p. 324; Galileo's word is "philosophy" rather than "nature."

12. *Ibid.* (German) p. 324, (English) p. 322.

13. David Hume, *Dialogues Concerning Natural Religion*, ed. Norman Kemp Smith (Oxford, 1935), p. 193.

§Gotthilf Heinrich von Schubert, *Die Symbolik des Traumes* (Leipzig, 1862), pp. 23–24.

‖ Quoted in Paul Ricoeur, *Gabriel Marcel et Karl Jaspers* (Paris, 1947), p. 45.

14. *Correspondance complète de Jean Jacques Rousseau*, ed. R. A. Leigh (Geneva, 1967), vol. V, pp. 65–66. The original reads "l'évangile" rather than "la Bible."

15. Rousseau, *Oeuvres complètes*, Pléiade edition, vol. III, p. 602.

16. [Derrida's reference is *Emile*, Pléiade edition, vol. 4, pp. 589, 594. My reference is *Emile*, tr. Barbara Foxley (London, 1911), pp. 245, 249. Subsequent references to this translation are placed within brackets.—Trans.]

17. I attempt to develop this theme elsewhere (*Speech and Phenomena*).

18. This does not by simple inversion, mean that the signifier is fundamental or primary. The "primacy" or "priority" of the signifier would be an expression untenable and absurd to formulate illogically within the very logic that it would legitimately destroy. The signifier will never by rights precede the signified, in which case it would no longer be a signifier and the "signifying" signifier would no longer have a possible signified. The thought that is announced in this impossible formula without being successfully contained therein should therefore be stated in another way; it will clearly be impossible to do so without putting the very idea of the sign into suspicion, the "sign-of" which will always remain attached to what is here put in question. At the limit therefore, that thought would destroy the entire conceptuality organized around the concept of the sign (signifier and signified, expression and content, and so on).

19. Postface to *Was ist Metaphysik?* [Frankfurt am Main, 1960], p. 46. The insistence of the voice also dominates the analysis of *Gewissen* [conscience] in *Sein und Zeit* (pp. 267 f.) [pp. 312 f.].

20. Cf. *Das Wesen der Sprache* ["The Nature of Language"], and *Das Wort* ["Words"], in *Unterwegs zur Sprache* [Pfüllingen], 1959 [*On the Way to Language*, tr. Peter D. Hertz (New York, 1971)].

21. [Martin Heidegger, *Einführung in die Metaphysik* (Tübingen, 1953) translated as *An Introduction to Metaphysics* by Ralph Manheim (New Haven, 1959).] Tr. French, Gilbert Kahn [Paris, 1967], p. 50.

22. *Introduction à la métaphysique,* tr. fr. p. 103 [*Einführung* p. 70; *Introduction.* p. 92]. "All this points in the direction of what we encountered when we characterized the Greek experience and interpretation of being. If we retain the usual interpretation of being, the word 'being' takes its meaning from the unity and determinateness of the horizon which guided our understanding. In short: we understand the verbal substantive 'Sein' through the infinitive, which in turn is related to the 'is' and its diversity that we have described. The definite and particular verb form 'is,' the *third person singular of the present indicative,* has here a pre-eminent rank. We understand 'being' not in regard to the 'thou art,' 'you are,' 'I am,' or 'they would be,' though all of these, just as much as 'is,' represent verbal inflections of 'to be.'... And involuntarily, almost as though nothing else were possible, we explain the infinitive 'to be' to ourselves through the 'is.'

"Accordingly, 'being' has the meaning indicated above, recalling the Greek view of the essence of being, hence a determinateness which has not just dropped on us accidentally from somewhere but has dominated our historical being-there since antiquity. At one stroke our search for the definition of the meaning of the word 'being' becomes explicitly what it is, namely a reflection on the source of our hidden history." I should, of course, cite the entire analysis that concludes with these words.

23. *Enzyklopädie der philosophischen Wissenschaften in Grundrisse,* Suhrkamp edition (Frankfurt am Main, 1970), pp. 273-76.

24. *dem Statarischen,* an old German word that one has hitherto been tempted to translate as "immobile" or "static" (see [Jean] Gibelin, [tr. *Lecons sur la philosophie de la religion* (Paris, 1959),]pp. 255-57.

25. "La parole soufflée," *ED.*

# 30. Metaphor and the Central Problem of Hermeneutics

## PAUL RICOEUR

It will be assumed here that the central problem of hermeneutics is that of interpretation. Not interpretation in any sense of the word, but interpretation determined in two ways: the first concerning its field of application, the second its epistemological specificity. As regards the first point, I shall say that there is a problem of interpretation because there are texts, written texts, the autonomy of which creates specific difficulties. By 'autonomy' I understand the independence of the text with respect to the intention of the author, the situation of the work, and the original reader. The relevant problems are resolved in oral discourse by the kind of exchange or intercourse which we call dialogue or conversation. With written texts, discourse must speak by itself. Let us say, therefore, that there are problems of interpretation because the writing-reading relation is not a particular case of the speaking-hearing relation which we experience in the dialogical situation. Such is the most general feature of interpretation as regards its field of application.

Second, the concept of interpretation seems, at the epistemological level, to be opposed to the concept of explanation. Taken together, these concepts form a contrasting pair which has given rise to a great many disputes since the time of Schleiermacher and Dilthey. According to the tradition to which the latter authors belong, interpretation has certain subjective connotations, such as the implication of the reader in the processes of understanding and the reciprocity between interpretation of the text and self-interpretation. This reciprocity is known by the name of

From Metaphor and the Central Problem of Hermeneutics," in Paul Ricoeur, *Hermeneutics and the Human Sciences: Essays on Language, Action and Interpretation*, edited and translated by John B. Thompson (Cambridge: Cambridge University Press, 1981), pp. 165–181. Reprinted with permission of Cambridge University Press and the Editor.

the hermeneutical circle, it entails a sharp opposition to the sort of objectivity and non-implication which is supposed to characterize the scientific explanation of things. Later I shall say to what extent we may be able to amend, indeed to reconstruct on a new basis, the opposition between interpretation and explanation. Whatever the outcome of the subsequent discussion may be, this schematic description of the concept of interpretation suffices for a provisional circumscription of the central problem of hermeneutics: the status of written texts *versus* spoken language, the status of interpretation *versus* explanation.

Now for the metaphor! The aim of this essay is to link up the problems raised in hermeneutics by the interpretation of texts and the problems raised in rhetoric, semantics, stylistics—or whatever the discipline concerned may be—by metaphor.

## *I The Text and Metaphor as Discourse*

Our first task will be to find a common ground for the theory of the text and the theory of metaphor. This common ground has already received a name—discourse; it has yet to be given a status.

One thing is striking: the two sorts of entities that we are considering are of different lengths. In this respect, they can be compared to the sentence, which is the basic unit of discourse. A text can undoubtedly be reduced to a single sentence, as in proverbs or aphorisms; but texts have a maximum length which can extend from a paragraph to a chapter, a book, a collection of 'selected works' or even the corpus of the 'complete works' of an author. Let us use the term 'work' to describe the closed sequence of discourse which can be considered as a text. Whereas texts can be identified on the basis of their maximal length, metaphors can be identified on the basis of their minimal length, that of the word. Even if the rest of this discussion seeks to show that there is no metaphor—in the sense of a word taken metaphorically—in the absence of certain contexts, and consequently even if we are constrained by what follows to replace the notion of metaphor by that of the metaphorical statement which implies at least the length of the sentence, nevertheless the 'metaphorical twist' (to speak like Monroe Beardsley) is something which happens to the word. The change of meaning, which requires the full contribution of the context, affects the word. We can describe the word as having a 'metaphorical use' or a 'non-literal meaning'; the word is always the bearer of the 'emergent meaning' which specific contexts confer upon it. In this sense, Aristotle's definition of metaphor as the transposition of an unusual name (or word) is not invalidated by a theory emphasizing the contextual action which creates the shift of meaning in the word. The word remains the 'focus', even if the focus requires the 'frame' of the sentence, to use the vocabulary of Max Black.

This first, altogether formal remark concerning the difference in length between the text and the metaphor, or better between the *work* and the *word,* is going to help us to elaborate our initial problem in a more precise way: to what extent can we treat the metaphor as a *work in miniature?* The answer to this question will then help us to pose the second: to what extent can the hermeneutical problems raised by the interpretation of texts be considered as a large-scale extension of the problems condensed in the explanation of a local metaphor in a given text?

Is a metaphor a work in miniature? Can a work, say, a poem, be considered as a sustained or extended metaphor? The answer to this first question requires a prior elaboration of the general properties of discourse, if it is true that text and metaphor, work and word, fall within the same category of discourse. I shall not elaborate in detail the concept of discourse, restricting my analysis to the features which are necessary for the comparison between text and metaphor. It is remarkable that all these features present themselves in the form of paradoxes, that is, apparent contradictions.

To begin with, all discourse is produced as an event; as such, it is the counterpart of language understood as code or system. Discourse *qua* event has a fleeting existence: it appears and disappears. But at the same time—and herein lies the paradox—it can be identified and reidentified as the same. This "sameness' is what we call, in a broad sense, its meaning. All discourse, we shall say, is realized as event but understood as meaning. Soon we shall see in what sense the metaphor concentrates this double character of event and meaning.

The second pair of contrasting features stems from the fact that meaning is supported by a specific structure, that of the proposition, which envelops an internal opposition between a pole of singular identification (this man, this table, Monsieur Dupont, Paris) and a pole of general predication (humanity as a class, brightness as a property, equality as a relation, running as an action). Metaphor, we shall also see, rests upon this 'attribution' of characteristics to the 'principal subject' of a sentence.

The third pair of opposing features is the polarity, which discourse primarily in sentential form implies, between sense and reference. That is, discourse implies the possibility of distinguishing between *what* is said by the sentence as a whole and by the words which compose it on the one hand, and *that about which* something is said on the other. To speak is to say something about something. This polarity will play a decisive role in the second and third parts of this essay, where I shall try to connect the problem of explanation to the dimension of 'sense' or the immanent pattern of discourse, and the problems of interpretation to the dimension of 'reference', understood as the power of discourse to apply itself to an extralinguistic reality about which it says what it says.

Fourth, discourse as an act can be considered from the viewpoint of the 'contents' of the propositional act (it predicates a certain characteristic of a certain subject), or from the viewpoint of what Austin called the 'force' of the complete act of discourse (the *speech-act* in his terminology). What is said of the subject is one thing; what I 'do' *in* saying it is another: I can make a mere description, or give an order, or formulate a wish, or give a warning, etc. Hence the polarity between the locutionary act (the act *of* saying) and the illocutionary act (what I do *in* saying). This polarity may seem less useful than the preceding ones, at least at the structural level of the metaphorical statement. Nevertheless, it will play a decisive role when we have to place the metaphor back in the concrete setting of, for example, a poem, an essay, or a work of fiction.

Before developing the dichotomy of sense and reference as the basis of the opposition between explanation and interpretation, let us introduce a final polarity which will play a decisive role in hermeneutical theory. Discourse has not merely one sort of reference but two: it is related to an extralinguistic reality, to the world or a world; and it refers equally to its own speaker, by means of specific procedures which function only in the sentence and hence in discourse—personal pronouns, verbal tenses, demonstratives, etc. In this way, language has both a reference to reality and a self-reference. It is the same entity—the sentence—which supports this double reference: intentional and reflexive, turned toward the thing and toward the self. In fact, we should speak of a triple reference, for discourse refers as much to the one to whom it is addressed as to its own speaker. The structure of personal pronouns similarly designates, as Benveniste taught, the triple reference: 'it' designates the reference to the thing, 'you' the reference to the one to whom the discourse is addressed, and 'I' the reference to the one who speaks. As we shall see later, this connection between the two and even the three directions of reference will provide us with the key to the hermeneutical circle and the basis of our reinterpretation of this circle.

I shall list the basic polarities of discourse in the following condensed fashion: event and meaning, singular identification and general predication, propositional act and illocutionary act, sense and reference, reference to reality and reference to interlocutors. In what sense can we now say that the text and metaphor both rest upon the sort of entity which we have just called discourse?

It is easy to show that all texts are discourses, since they stem from the smallest unit of discourse, the sentence. A text is at least a series of sentences. We shall see that it must be something more in order to be a work; but it is at least a set of sentences, and consequently a discourse. The connection between metaphor and discourse requires a special justification, precisely because the definition of metaphor as a transposition affecting names or words seems to place it in a category of entities smaller than the sentence. But the semantics of the word demonstrates very clearly that words acquire an actual meaning only in a sentence and that lexical entities—the words of the dictionary—have merely potential meanings in virtue of their potential uses in typical contexts. In this respect, the theory of polysemy is a good preparation for the theory of metaphor. At the lexical level, words (if indeed they can already be called that) have more than one meaning; it is only by a specific contextual action of sifting that they realize, in a given sentence, a part of their potential semantics and acquire what we call a determinate meaning. The contextual action which enables univocal discourse to be produced with polysemic words is the model for that other contextual action whereby we draw genuinely novel metaphorical effects from words whose meaning is already codified in the vocabulary. We are thus prepared to allow that even if the meaningful effect which we call metaphor is inscribed in the word, nevertheless the origin of this effect lies in a contextual action which places the semantic fields of several words in interaction.

As regards the metaphor itself, semantics shows with the same force that the metaphorical meaning of a word is nothing which can be found in the dictionary. In this sense, we can continue to oppose metaphorical meaning to literal meaning, if by the latter we understand *any* of the meanings that can be found among the partial meanings codified by the vocabulary. By literal meaning, therefore, we do not understand the supposedly original, fundamental, primitive, or proper meaning of a word on the lexical plane; rather, literal meaning is the totality of the semantic field, the set of possible contextual uses which constitutes the polysemy of a word. So even if metaphorical meaning is something more and other than the actualization of one of the possible meanings of a polysemic word (and all the words in natural languages are polysemic), nevertheless this metaphorical use must be solely contextual, that is, a meaning which emerges as a unique and fleeting result of a certain contextual action. We are thus led to oppose contextual changes of meaning to the lexical changes which concern the diachronic aspect of language as code or system. Metaphor is one such contextual change of meaning.

In this respect, I am partially in agreement with the modern theory of metaphor, as elaborated in English by I. A. Richards, Max Black, Monroe Beardsley, Douglas Berggren, etc.[1] More precisely, I agree with these authors on the fundamental point: a word receives a metaphorical meaning in specific contexts, within which it is opposed to other words taken literally. The shift in meaning results primarily from a clash between literal meanings, which excludes the literal use of the word in question and provides clues for finding a new meaning capable of according with the context of the sentence and rendering the sentence meaningful therein. Consequently, I retain the following points from this recent history of the problem of metaphor: the replacement of the rhetorical theory of substitution by a properly semantic theory of the interaction between semantic fields; the decisive role of semantic clash leading to logical absurdity; the issuance of a particle of meaning which renders the sentence as a whole meaningful. We shall now see how this properly semantic theory—or the interaction theory—satisifies the principal characteristics which we have recognized in discourse.

To begin with, let us return to the contrast between event and meaning. In the metaphorical statement (we shall speak of metaphor as a sentence and no longer as a word), contextual action creates a new meaning which is indeed an event, since it exists only in this particular context; but at the same time, it can be repeated and hence identified as the same. Thus the innovation of an 'emergent meaning' (Beardsley) may be regarded as a linguistic creation; but if it is adopted by an influential part of the language community, it may become an everyday meaning and add to the polysemy of lexical entities, contributing thereby to the history of language as code or system. At this final stage, when the meaningful effect that we call metaphor has rejoined the change of meaning which augments polysemy, the metaphor is no longer living but dead. Only authentic, living metaphors are at the same time 'event' *and* 'meaning'.

Contextual action similarly requires our second polarity, that between singular identification and general predication. A metaphor is said of a 'principal subject'; as 'modifier' of this subject, it works like a kind of 'attribution'. All the theories to which I have referred above rest upon this predicative structure, whether they oppose 'vehicle' to 'tenor' (Richards), 'frame' to 'focus' (Max Black), or 'modifier' to 'principal subject' (Beardsley).

To show that metaphor requires the polarity between sense and reference, we shall need a whole section of this essay; the same thing must be said of the polarity between reference to reality and reference to self. Later it will become clear why, at this stage, I am not in a position to say more about these polarities. We shall require the mediation of the theory of the text in order to discern the oppositions which do not appear so clearly within the narrow limits of a simple metaphorical statement.

Having thus delimited the field of comparison, we are ready to reply to the second question: to what extent can the explanation and interpretation of texts on the one hand, and the explanation and interpretation of metaphors on the other, be regarded as similar processes which are merely applied to two different strategic levels of discourse, the level of the work and that of the word?

## II From Metaphor to the Text: Explanation

I propose to explore a working hypothesis which, to begin with, I shall simply state. From one point of view, the understanding of metaphor can serve as a guide to the understanding of longer texts, such as a literary work. This point of view is that of explanation; it concerns only that aspect of meaning which we have called the 'sense', that is, the immanent pattern of discourse. From another point of view, the understanding of a work taken as a whole gives the key to metaphor. This other point of view is that of interpretation proper; it develops the aspect of meaning which we have called 'reference', that is, the intentional orientation toward a world and the reflexive orientation toward a self. So if we apply explanation to 'sense', as the immanent pattern of the work, then we can reserve interpretation for the sort of inquiry concerned with the *power of a work* to project a world of its own and to set in motion the hermeneutical circle, which encompasses in its spiral both the apprehension of projected worlds and the advance of self-understanding in the presence of these new worlds. Our working hypothesis thus invites us to proceed from metaphor to text at the level of 'sense' and the explanation of 'sense', then from text to metaphor at the level of the reference of a work to a world and to a self, that is, at the level of interpretation proper.

What aspects of the explanation of metaphor can serve as a paradigm for the explanation of a text? These aspects are features of the explanatory process which could not appear so long as trivial examples of metaphor were considered, such as man is a wolf, a fox, a lion (if we read the best authors on metaphor, we observe interesting variations within the bestiary which provides them with examples!). With these examples, we elude the major difficulty, that of *identifying a meaning* which is *new*. The only way of achieving this identification is to construct a meaning which alone enables us to make sense of the sentence as a whole. For what do trivial metaphors rest upon? Max Black and Monroe Beardsley note that the meaning of a word does not depend merely on the semantic and syntactic rules which govern its literal use, but also on other rules (which are nevertheless rules) to which the members of a language community are 'committed' and which determine what Black calls the 'system of associated commonplaces' and Beardsley the 'potential range of connotations'. In the statement, 'man is a wolf' (the example favored by Black!), the principal subject is qualified by one of the features of animal life which belongs to 'the lupine system of associated commonplaces'. The system of implications operates like a filter or screen; it does not merely select, but also accentuates new aspects of the principal subject.

What are we to think of this explanation in relation to our description of metaphor as a new meaning appearing in a new context? As I said above, I entirely agree with the 'interaction view' implied by this explanation; metaphor is more than a simple substitution whereby one word would replace a literal word, which an exhaustive paraphrase could restore to the same place. The algebraic sum of these two operations—substitution by the speaker and restoration by the author or reader—is equal to zero. No new meaning emerges and we learn nothing. As Black says, '"interaction-metaphors" are not expendable. . . . This use of a "subsidiary subject" to foster insight into a "principal subject" is a distinctive intellectual operation.' Hence interaction metaphors cannot be translated into direct language without 'a loss in cognitive content'.[2]

Although this account describes very well the meaningful effect of metaphor, we must ask whether, by simply adding the 'system of associated commonplaces' and cultural rules to the semantic polysemy of the word and semantic rules, this account does justice to the power of metaphor 'to inform and enlighten'. Is not the 'system of associated commonplaces' something dead or at least something already established? Of course, this system must intervene in some way or another, in order that contextual action may be regulated and that the construction of new meaning may obey some prescription. Black's theory reserves the possibility that 'metaphors can be supported by specially constructed systems of implications, as well as by accepted commonplaces'.[3] The problem is precisely that of these 'specially constructed systems of implications'. We must therefore pursue our investigation into the process of interaction itself, if we are to explain the case of new metaphors in new contexts.

Beardsley's theory of metaphor leads us a stage further in this direction. If, following him, we emphasize the role of logical absurdity or the clash between literal meanings within the same context, then we are ready to recognize the genuinely creative character of metaphorical meaning: 'In poetry, the principal tactic for obtaining this result is logical absurdity.'[4] Logical absurdity creates a situation in which we have the choice of either preserving the literal meaning of the subject and the modifier and hence concluding that the entire sentence is absurd, or attributing a new meaning to the modifier so that the sentence as a whole makes sense. We are now faced not only with 'self-contradictory' attribution, but with a 'meaningful self-contradictory' attribution. If I say 'man is a fox' (the fox has chased away the wolf!), I must slide from a literal to a metaphorical attribution if I want to save the sentence. But from where do we draw this new meaning?

As long as we ask this type of question—'from where do we draw . . . ?'—we return to the same type of ineffectual answer. The 'potential range of connotations' says nothing more than the 'system of associated commonplaces'. Of course, we expand the notion of meaning by including 'secondary meanings', as connotations, within the perimeter of full meaning; but we continue to bind the creative process of metaphor to a noncreative aspect of language.

Is it sufficient to supplement this 'potential range of connotations', as Beardsley does in the 'revised verbal-opposition theory',[5] with the properties which do not yet belong to the range of connotations of my language? At first sight, this supplementation ameliorates the theory; as Beardsley forcefully says, 'metaphor transforms a *property* (actual or attributed) into a *sense*'.[6] This change is important, since it must now be said that metaphors do not merely actualize a potential connotation, but establish it 'as a staple one'; and further, 'some of [the object's] relevant properties can be given a new status as elements of verbal meaning'.[7]

However, to speak of properties of *things* (or *objects*), which are supposed not yet to have been signified, is to admit that the new, emergent meaning is not drawn from anywhere, at least not from anywhere in language (the property is an implication of things, not of words). To say that a metaphor is not drawn from anywhere is to recognize it for what it is: namely, a momentary creation of language, a semantic innovation which does not have a status in the language as something already established, whether as a designation or as a connotation.

It may be asked how we can speak of a semantic innovation, a semantic event, as a meaning capable of being identified and reidentified (that was the first criterion of discourse stated above). Only one answer remains possible: it is necessary to take the viewpoint of the hearer or the reader and to treat the novelty of the emergent meaning as the counterpart, on the author's side, of a construction on the side of the reader. Thus the process of explanation is the only access to the process of creation.

If we do not take this path, we do not really free ourselves from the theory of substitution; instead of substituting a literal meaning restored by paraphrase for the metaphorical expression, we substitute the system of connotations and commonplaces. This task must remain a preparatory one, enabling literary criticism to be reconnected to psychology and sociology. The decisive moment of explanation is the construction of a network of interactions which constitutes the context as actual and unique. In so doing, we direct our attention toward the semantic event which is produced at the point of intersection between several semantic fields. This construction is the means by which all the words taken together make sense. Then and only then, the 'metaphorical twist' is both an event and a meaning, a meaningful event and an emergent meaning in language.

Such is the fundamental feature of explanation which makes metaphor a paradigm for the explanation of a literary work. We construct the meaning of a text in a manner similar to the way in which we make sense of all the terms of a metaphorical statement.

Why must we 'construct' the meaning of a text? First, because it is written: in the asymmetrical relation between the text and the reader, one of the partners speaks for both. Bringing a text to language is always something other than hearing someone and listening to his speech. Reading resembles instead the performance of a musical piece regulated by the written notations of the score. For the text is an autonomous space of meaning which is no longer animated by the intention of its author; the autonomy of the text, deprived of this essential support, hands writing over to the sole interpretation of the reader.

A second reason is that the text is not only something written but is a work, that is, a singular totality. As a totality, the literary work cannot be reduced to a sequence of sentences which are individually intelligible; rather, it is an architecture of themes and purposes which can be constructed in several ways. The relation of part to whole is ineluctably circular. The presupposition of a certain whole precedes the discernment of a determinate arrangement of parts; and it is by constructing the details that we build up the whole. Moreover, as the notion of singular totality suggests, a text is a kind of individual, like an animal or a work of art. Its singularity can be regained, therefore, only by progressively rectifying generic concepts which concern the class of texts, the literary genre, and the various structures which intersect in this singular text. In short, understanding a work involves the sort of judgment which Kant explored in the third *Critique*.

What, then, can we say about this construction and this judgment? Here understanding a text, at the level of its articulation of sense, is strictly homologous to understanding a metaphorical statement. In both cases, it is a question of 'making sense', of producing the best overall intelligibility from an apparently discordant diversity. In both cases, the construction takes the form of a wager or guess. As Hirsch says in *Validity in Interpretation,* there are no rules for making good guesses, but there are methods for validating our guesses.[8] This dialectic between guessing and validating is the realization at the textual level of the micro-dialectic at work in the resolution of the local enigmas of a text. In both cases, the procedures of validation have more affinity with a logic of probability than with a logic of empirical verification—more affinity, let us say, with a logic of uncertainty and qualitative probability. Validation, in this sense, is the concern of an argumentative discipline akin to the juridical procedures of legal interpretation.

We can now summarize the corresponding features which underlie the analogy between the explanation of metaphorical statements and that of a literary work as a whole. In both cases, the construction rests upon 'clues' contained in the text itself. A clue serves as a guide for a specific construction, in that it contains at once a permission and a prohibition; it excludes unsuitable constructions and allows those which give more meaning to the same words. Second, in both cases, one construction can be said to be more probable than another, but not more truthful. The more probable is that which, on the one hand, takes account of the greatest number of facts furnished by the text, including its potential connotations, and on the other hand, offers a qualitatively better convergence between the features which it takes into account. A mediocre explanation can be called narrow or forced.

Here I agree with Beardsley when he says that a good explanation satisfies two principles: the principle of congruence and that of plenitude. Until now, we have in fact spoken about the principle of congruence. The principle of plenitude will provide us with a transition to the third part of the essay. This principle may be stated as follows: 'All the connotations which are suitable must be attributed; the poem means all that it can mean.' This principle leads us further than a mere concern with 'sense'; it already says something about reference, since it takes as a measure of plenitude the requirements stemming from an experience which demands to be said and to be equalled by the semantic density of the text. I shall say that the principle of plenitude is the corollary, at the level of meaning, of a principle of full expression which draws our investigation in a quite different direction.

A quotation from Humboldt will lead us to the threshold of this new field of investigation: 'Language as discourse (*Rede*) lies on the boundary between the expressible and the inexpressible. Its aim and its goal is to push back still further this boundary.' Interpretation, in its proper sense, similarly lies on this frontier.

### III From the Text to Metaphor: Interpretation

At the level of interpretation proper, understanding the text provides the key to understanding metaphor. Why? Because certain features of discourse begin to play an explicit role only when discourse takes the form of a literary *work*. These features are the very ones which we have placed under the heading of reference and self-reference. It will be recalled that

I opposed reference to sense, saying that sense is the 'what' and reference the 'about what' of discourse. Of course, these two features can be recognized in the smallest units of language as discourse, namely in sentences. The sentence is about a situation which it expresses, and it refers back to its speaker by means of the specific procedures that we have enumerated. But reference and self-reference do not give rise to perplexing problems so long as discourse has not become a text and has not taken the form of a work. What are these problems?

Let us begin once again from the difference between written and spoken languages. In spoken language, that to which a dialogue ultimately refers is the situation common to the interlocutors, that is, the aspects of reality which can be shown or pointed to; we then say that the reference is 'ostensive'. In written language, the reference is no longer ostensive; poems, essays, works of fiction, speak of things, events, states of affairs, and characters which are evoked but which are not there. And yet literary texts are about something. About what? I do not hesitate to say: about a world, which is the world of the work. Far from saying that the text is without a world, I shall say that only now does man have a world and not merely a situation, a *Welt* and not merely an *Umwelt*. In the same way that the text frees its meaning from the tutelage of mental intention, so too it frees its reference from the limits of, ostensive reference. For us, the world is the totality of references opened up by texts. Thus we speak of the 'world' of Greece, not to indicate what the situations were for those who experienced them, but to designate the non-situational references which outlast the effacement of the first and which then offer themselves possible modes of being, as possible symbolic dimensions of our being-in-the-world.

The nature of reference in the context of literary works has an important consequence for the concept of interpretation. It implies that the meaning of a text lies not behind the text but in front of it. The meaning is not something hidden but something disclosed. What gives rise to understanding is that which points toward a possible world, by means of the non-ostensive references of the text. Texts speak of possible worlds and of possible ways of orientating oneself in these worlds. In this way, disclosure plays the equivalent role for written texts as ostensive reference plays in spoken language. Interpretation thus becomes the apprehension of the proposed worlds which are opened up by the non-ostensive references of the text.

This concept of interpretation expresses a decisive shift of emphasis with respect to the Romantic tradition of hermeneutics. In that tradition, the emphasis was placed on the ability of the hearer or reader to transfer himself into the spiritual life of a speaker or writer. The emphasis, from now on, is less on the other as a spiritual entity than on the world which the work unfolds. To understand is to follow the dynamic of the work, its movement from what it says to that about which it speaks. Beyond my situation as reader, beyond the situation of the author, I offer myself to the possible mode of being-in-the-world which the text opens up and discloses to me. That is what Gadamer calls the 'fusion of horizons' (*Horizontverschmelzung*) in historical knowledge.

The shift of emphasis from understanding the other to understanding the world of his work entails a corresponding shift in the conception of the 'hermeneutical circle'. For the thinkers of Romanticism, the latter term meant that the understanding of a text cannot be an objective procedure, in the sense of scientific objectivity, but that it necessarily implies a pre-understanding, expressing the way in which the reader already understands himself and his work. Hence a sort of circularity is produced between understanding the text and self-understanding. Such is, in condensed terms, the principle of the hermeneutical circle. It is easy to see how thinkers trained in the tradition of logical empiricism could only reject, as utterly scandalous, the mere idea of a hermeneutical circle and consider it to be an outrageous violation of all the canons of verifiability.

For my part, I do not wish to conceal the fact that the hermeneutical circle remains an unavoidable structure of interpretation. An interpretation is not authentic unless it culminates in some form of appropriation (*Aneignung*), if by that term we understand the process by which one makes one's own (*eigen*) what was initially other or alien (*fremd*). But I believe that the hermeneutical circle is not correctly understood when it is presented, first, as a circle between two subjectivities, that of the reader and that of the author; and second, as the projection of the subjectivity of the reader into the reading itself.

Let us correct each of these assumptions in turn. What we make our own, what we appropriate for ourselves, is not an alien experience or a distant intention, but the horizon of a world toward which a work directs itself. The appropriation of the reference is no longer modelled on the fusion of consciousnesses, on empathy or sympathy. The emergence of the sense and the reference of a text in language is the coming to language of a world and not the recognition of another person. The second correction of the Romantic concept of interpretation results from the first. If appropriation is the counterpart of disclosure, then the role of subjectivity must not be described in terms of projection. I should prefer to say that the reader understands himself in front of the text, in front of the world of the work. To understand oneself in front of a text is quite the contrary of projecting oneself and one's own beliefs and prejudices; it is to let the work and its world enlarge the horizon of the understanding which I have of myself. [. . .] Thus the hermeneutical circle is not repudiated but displaced from a subjectivistic level to an ontological plane. The circle is between my mode of being—beyond the knowledge which I may have of it— and the mode opened up and disclosed by the text as the world of the work.

Such is the model of interpretation which I now propose to transfer from texts, as long sequences of discourse, to the metaphor, understood as 'a poem in miniature' (Beardsley). Of course, the metaphor is too short a discourse to unfold this dialectic between the disclosure of a world and the disclosure of oneself in front of that world. Nevertheless, this dialectic points to some features of metaphor which the modern theories cited so far do not seem to take into consideration, but which were not absent from the classical theory of metaphor.

Let us return to the theory of metaphor in Aristotle's *Poetics*. Metaphor is only one of the 'parts' (*mere*) of what Aristotle calls 'diction' (*lexis*). As such, it belongs to a group of discursive procedures—using unusual words, coining new words, abbreviating or extending words—which all depart from the common (*kurion*) use of words. Now what constitutes the unity of *lexis?* Only its function in poetry. *Lexis,* in turn, is one of the 'parts' (*mere*) of tragedy, taken as the paradigm of the poetic work. In the context of the *Poetics,* tragedy represents the level of the literary work as a whole. Tragedy, in the form of a poem, has sense and reference. In Aristotle's language, the 'sense' of tragedy is secured by what he calls the 'fable' (*mythos*). We can understand the latter as the sense of tragedy because Aristotle constantly emphasizes its structural characteristics. The *mythos* must have unity and coherence; it must make of the represented actions something 'whole and complete'. The *mythos* is thus the principal 'part' of tragedy, its 'essence'. All the other parts of tragedy—the 'characters', the 'thoughts', the 'delivery', the 'production'—are linked to the myth as means or conditions, or as the performance of tragedy *qua* myth. We must draw the consequence that it is only in relation to the *mythos* of tragedy that its *lexis,* and hence metaphor, make sense. There is no local meaning of metaphor outside the regional meaning secured by the *mythos* of tragedy.

If metaphor is linked to the 'sense' of tragedy by means of its *mythos,* it is also linked to the 'reference' of tragedy in virtue of its general aim, which Aristotle calls *mimesis.*

Why do poets write tragedies, elaborate fables, use 'unusual' words such as metaphors? Because tragedy itself is connected to a more fundamental human project, that of *imitating* human actions in a *poetic* way. With these two keywords—*mimesis* and *poiesis*—we reach the level which I have called the referential world of the work. Indeed we may say that the Aristotelian concept of *mimesis* already encompasses all the paradoxes of reference. On the one hand, it expresses a world of human actions which is already there; tragedy is destined to express human reality, to express the tragedy of life. But on the other hand, *mimesis* does not mean the duplication of reality; *mimesis* is not a copy: *mimesis* is *poiesis,* that is, construction, creation. Aristotle gives at least two indications of this creative dimension of *mimesis*. First, the fable is an original, coherent construction which attests to the creative genius of the artist. Second, tragedy is an imitation of human actions which makes them appear better, higher, more noble than they are in reality. Could we not say that *mimesis* is the Greek term for what we have called the non-ostensive reference of the literary work, or in other words, the Greek term for the disclosure of a world?

If this is right, we are now in a position to say something about the *power* of metaphor. I speak now of power and no longer of structure or even of process. The power of metaphor stems from its connection, internal to the poetic work, with three features: first, with the other procedures of the *lexis;* second, with the *fable,* which is the essence of the work, its immanent sense; and third, with the intentionality of the work as a whole, that is, with its intention to represent human actions as higher than they are in reality—and therein lies the *mimesis.* In this sense, the power of the metaphor arises from the power of the poem as a totality.

Let us apply these remarks, borrowed from Aristotle's *Poetics,* to our own description of metaphor. Could we say that the feature of metaphor which we have placed above all others—its nascent or emergent character—is linked to the function of poetry as the creative imitation of reality? Why should we invent new meanings, meanings which exist only in the instant of discourse, if it were not to serve the *poiesis* in the *mimesis?* If it is true that the poem creates a world, then it requires a language which preserves and expresses its creative power in specific contexts. By taking the *poiesis* of the poem together with metaphor as emergent meaning, we shall give sense to both at the same time, to poetry and to metaphor.

Thus the theory of interpretation paves the way for an ultimate approximation to the power of the metaphor. The priority given to the interpretation of the text in this final stage of the analysis does not mean that the relation between the two is not reciprocal. The explanation of metaphor, as a local event in the text, contributes to the interpretation of the work as a whole. We could even say that if the interpretation of local metaphors is illuminated by the interpretation of the text as a whole and by the clarification of the kind of world which the work projects, then in turn the interpretation of the poem as a whole is controlled by the explanation of the metaphor as a local phenomenon of the text.

As an example of this reciprocal relation between the regional and local aspects of the text, I shall venture to mention a possible connection, implicit in Aristotle's *Poetics,* between what he says about *mimesis* on the one hand and metaphor on the other. *Mimesis,* as we have seen, makes human actions appear higher than they are in reality; and the function of metaphor is to transpose the meanings of ordinary language by way of unusual uses. Is there not a mutual and profound affinity between the project of making human actions appear better than they are and the special procedure of metaphor which raises language above itself?

Let us express this relation in more general terms. Why should we draw new meanings from our language if we have nothing new to say, no new world to project? The creations of language would be devoid of sense unless they served the general project of letting new worlds emerge by means of poetry . . .

Allow me to conclude in a way which would be consistent with a theory of interpretation which places the emphasis on 'opening up a world'. Our conclusion should also 'open up' some new perspectives, but on what? Perhaps on the old problem of the imagination which I have carefully put aside. Are we not ready to recognize in the power of imagination, no longer the faculty of deriving 'images' from our sensory experience, but the capacity for letting new worlds shape our understanding of ourselves? This power would not be conveyed by images, but by the emergent meanings in our language. Imagination would thus be treated as a dimension of language. In this way, a new link would appear between imagination and metaphor. We shall, for the time being, refrain from entering this half-open door.

## Notes

1. On this subject, see: I. A. Richards, *The Philosophy of Rhetoric* (New York: Oxford University Press, 1936); Max Black, *Models and Metaphors* (Ithaca: Cornell University Press, 1962); Monroe Beardsley, *Aesthetics* (New York: Harcourt, Brace and World, 1958), and 'The Metaphorical Twist', *Philosophy and Phenomenological Research* 20 (1962), pp. 293–307; Douglas Berggren, 'The Use and Abuse of Metaphor, I and II', *Review of Metaphysics* 16 (1962), pp. 237–258, and 16 (1963), pp. 450–472.

2. *Models and Metaphors,* p. 46.

3. *Ibid.,* p. 43; see condition 4 in his summary, p. 44.

4. *Aesthetics,* p. 138.

5. Cf. 'The Metaphorical Twist'.

6. *Ibid.,* p. 302.

7. *Ibid.*

8. Cf. Eric D. Hirsch, Jr., *Validity in Interpretation* (New Haven: Yale University Press, 1967), chapter 5.

# Bibliography to Part Seven

The topic of fiction, which had been represented in the second edition of this anthology, remains so intimately linked with the fortunes of metaphor, as remarked in the introductory notes to Part Seven, that we shall include, here, references to fiction in the narrow sense. But that convergence is generally not perceived in the standard Anglo-American accounts of fiction. Very much the same may be said, however, of the Anglo-American discussion of metaphor. Of the earlier literature on fiction, two quite interesting symposia have appeared in the *Proceedings of the Aristotelian Society:*
  "Imaginary Objects," suppl. vol. 12 (1933), including contributions by R. B. Braithewaite, Gilbert Ryle, and G. E. Moore;
  "The Language of Fiction," suppl. vol. 27 (1954), including the paper by Margaret Macdonald printed here and a contribution by Michael Scriven.
The first of these symposia contains what are very nearly the only contributions of Moore and Ryle to aesthetics. A convenient resumé of the principal issues may be found in:
  Monroe C. Beardsley, *Aesthetics* (New York, 1958), chapters 3, 8–9.

Among discussions of the same period may be noted:
  R. K. Elliott, "Poetry and Truth," *Analysis* XXVII (1967), 77–85;
  T. M. Greene, *The Arts and the Art of Criticism* (Princeton, 1940), chapter 23;
  Sidney Hook (ed.), *Art and Philosophy* (New York, 1966), pt. 3;
  John Hospers, *Meaning and Truth in the Arts* (Chapel Hill, 1946), chapters 5–8;
  John Hospers, "Literature and Human Nature," *Journal of Aesthetics and Art Criticism* XVII (1958), 45–57;
  John Hospers, "Implied Truths in Literature," *Journal of Aesthetics and Art Criticism* XIX (1960); 37–46;
  Isabel Hungerland, "Contextual Implication," *Inquiry* IV (1960), 211–258;
  Arnold Isenberg, "The Esthetic Function of Language," *Journal of Philosophy* XLVI (1949), 5–20;
  Peter Mew, "Facts in Fiction," *Journal of Aesthetics and Art Criticism* XXXI (1973), 329–337;
  I. A. Richards, *Science and Poetry* (London, revised 1935);

Morris Weitz, *Philosophy of the Arts* (Cambridge, 1950), chapter 8;

Morris Weitz, "Truth in Literature," *Revue Internationale de Philosophie* IX (1955), 116–129;

Morris Weitz, *Hamlet and the Philosophy of Literary Criticism* (Chicago, 1964);


More recent accounts of fiction have focused on the problem of reference to nonexistent entities. Pertinent accounts may be found in:

Charles Crittenden, "Fictional Existence," *American Philosophical Quarterly* III (1966), 317–321;

Richard M. Gale, "The Fictive Use of Language," *Philosophy* XLVI (1971), 324–340;

Joseph Margolis, *Art and Philosophy* (Atlantic Highlands, 1978), chapter 12;

Thomas G. Pavel, "'Possible Worlds' in Literary Semantics," *Journal of Aesthetics and Art Criticism* XXXIV (1975), 165–176;

Nicholas Wolterstorff, "Worlds of Works of Art," *Journal of Aesthetics and Art Criticism* XXXV (1976), 121–132;

John Woods, *The Logic of Fiction* (The Hague, 1974).


Among the earlier discussions of metaphor of interest are the following:

Owen Barfield, "Poetic Diction and Legal Fiction," in *Essays Presented to Charles Williams* (Oxford, 1947);

Monroe C. Beardsley, *Aesthetics* (New York, 1958), chapter 3;

Cleanth Brooks, "The Heresy of Paraphrase," in *The Well Wrought Urn* (New York, 1947);

Scott Buchanan, *Poetry and Mathematics* (New York, 1929);

William Empson, *The Structure of Complex Words* (New York, 1951);

Martin Foss, *Symbol and Metaphor in Human Experience* (Princeton, 1951);

Paul Henle, "Metaphor," in Paul Henle (ed.), *Language, Thought and Culture* (Ann Arbor, 1958);

Isabel Hungerland, *Poetic Discourse* (Berkeley, 1958), chapter 4;

I. A. Richards, *The Philosophy of Rhetoric* (London, 1936), chapters 5 and 6;

Gustaf Stern, "Meaning and Change of Meaning," in *Götesborgs Högskolas Årsskrift* Vol. XXXVIII, 1932: 1 (Göteborg, 1931), chapter 9;

Andrew Ushenko, "Metaphor," *Thought* XXX (1955), 421–435;

Philip Wheelwright, *The Burning Fountain* (Bloomington, 1954).


More recent discussions include:

Monroe C. Beardsley, "The Metaphorical Twist," *Philosophy and Phenomenological Research* XXII (1962);

Monroe C. Beardsley, "Metaphor," *Encyclopedia of Philosophy*, vol. 5 (New York, 1967);

Timothy Binkley, "On the Truth and Probity of Metaphor," *Journal of Aesthetics and Art Criticism* XXXIII (1974), 171–180;

Stanley Cavell, "Aesthetic Problems of Modern Philosophy," in Max Black (ed.), *Philosophy in America* (Ithaca, 1965);

Ted Cohen, "Figurative Speech and Figurative Acts," *Journal of Philosophy* LXII (1975), 669–684;

Ted Cohen, "Notes on Metaphor," *Journal of Aesthetics and Art Criticism* XXXIV (1976), 249–259;

Mary Hesse, *Models and Analogies in Science* (London, 1963);

Joseph Margolis, *Art and Philosophy* (Atlantic Highlands, 1978), chapter 13;

Colin M. Turbayne, *The Myth of Metaphor* (Columbia, 1970, rev.).

There are many new anthologies on metaphor. One convenient one is:

Mark Johnson (ed.), *Philosophical Perspectives on Metaphor* (Minneapolis, 1981). This provides a good annotated bibliography. It does not, however, pursue the Nietzschean tradition, though Nietzsche is mentioned briefly. On Nietzsche, one must include:

Friedrich Nietzsche, "On Truth and Lie in a Nonmoral Sense," in *Philosophy and Truth; Selections from Nietzsche's Notebooks of the early 1870's,* trans. and ed. Daniel Breazeale (Atlantic Highlands, 1979).

For a sense of the direct influence of Nietzsche (or Nietzsche through Derrida), see

Paul deMan, *Blindness and Insight,* 2nd ed. rev. (Minneapolis, 1983);

Paul deMan, *Allegories of Reading* (New Haven, 1979);

Jonathan Arac *et al.* (eds.), *The Yale Critics: Deconstruction in America* (Minneapolis, 1983).

Jacques Derrida, *Margins of Philosophy,* trans. Alan Bass (Chicago, 1982);

Jacques Derrida, *Of Grammatology,* trans. Gayatri Chakravorty Spivak (Baltimore, 1976);

Further on Ricoeur on metaphor:

Paul Ricoeur, *The Rule of Metaphor; Multi-disciplinary Studies of Meaning in Language,* trans. Robert Czerny *et al.* (Toronto, 1977).

For a sample of the recent development of deconstructive criticism, see:

Harold Bloom *et al., Deconstruction and Criticism* (New York, 1979);

Jonathan Culler, On *Deconstruction; Theory and Criticism after Structuralism* (Ithaca, 1982);

Vincent B. Leitch, *Deconstructive Criticism* (New York, 1983);

Christopher Norris, *Deconstruction: Theory and Practice* (London, 1982)

Christopher Norris, *The Deconstructive Turn* (London, 1983);

Christopher Norris, *Contest of Faculties* (London, 1985);

Michael Ryan, *Marxism and Deconstruction* (Baltimore, 1982);

Henry Staten, *Wittgenstein and Derrida* (Lincoln, 1984).

# Notes on the Contributors

**Roland Barthes.** Late of L'Ecole Pratique des Hautes Etudes. Author, *Writing Degree Zero* (1967), *Elements of Semiology* (1967), *S/Z* (1974), *The Pleasure of the Text* (1975), *Image Music Text* (1977).

**Monroe C. Beardsley.** Late Professor of Philosophy, Temple University. Author, *Aesthetics from Classical Greece to the Present* (1965), *Aesthetics* (1968), *The Possibility of Criticism* (1970). Co-editor, *Aesthetic Inquiry: Essays on Art Criticism and the Philosophy of Art* (1967).

**Timothy Binkley.** Chairman of Humanities, School of Visual Arts (New York City). Author, *Wittgenstein's Language* (1973) and articles in aesthetics.

**Max Black.** Susan Linn Sage Professor of Philosophy, Cornell University. Author, *The Nature of Mathematics* (1933), *Language and Philosophy* (1949), *Models and Metaphors* (1962), *Margins of Precision* (1970). Editor, *Philosophical Analysis* (1950), *Philosophy in America* (1965). Editor, *Philosophical Review, Contemporary Philosophy Series*. Director, The Society for the Humanities, Cornell University.

**Frank Cioffi.** Professor of Philosophy, University of Essex. Co-editor, *Explanation in the Behavioural Sciences* (1970).

**Ted Cohen.** Professor of Philosophy, University of Chicago. Author of numerous papers in aesthetics. Co-editor, *Essays in Kant's Aesthetics* (1982).

**Arthur Danto.** Johnsonian Professor of Philosophy, Columbia University. Author, *Analytical Philosophy of History* (1965), *Analytical Philosophy of Knowledge* (1968), *Mysticism and Morality* (1972), *Analytical Philosophy of Action* (1973), *Jean-Paul Sartre* (1975), *The Transfiguration of the Commonplace* (1981). Co-editor, *Journal of Philosophy*. Art Critic, *The Nation*.

**Jacques Derrida.** Author, *Positions* (1972), *Speech and Phenomena* (1973),

*Writing and Difference* (1978), *Of Grammatology* (1976), *Dissemination* (1981), *Margins of Philosophy* (1982).

**George Dickie.** Professor of Philosophy, University of Illinois at Chicago Circle. Author, *Art and the Aesthetic* (1974), *The Art Circle* (1984). Co-editor, *Aesthetics: A Critical Anthology* (1977).

**Hans-Georg Gadamer.** Professor Emeritus, University of Heidelberg; Distinguished Visiting Professor, Boston College. Author, *Truth and Method* (1975), *Philosophical Hermeneutics* (1976), *Hegel's Dialectic* (1976), *Kleine Schriften,* 4 vols. (1972–1979), *Dialogue and Dialectic* (1980), *Reason in the Age of Science* (1981).

**Jack Glickman.** Assistant Professor of Philosophy, College at Brockport, State University of New York. Editor, *Moral Philosophy* (1976), and author of articles in aesthetics.

**Nelson Goodman.** Professor of Philosophy, Harvard University. Author, *Problems and Projects* (1972), *Languages of Art* (2nd ed., 1976), *The Structure of Appearance* (3rd ed., 1977), *Fact, Fiction, and Forecast* (3rd ed., 1977), *Ways of Worldmaking* (1978), *Of Mind and Other Matters* (1984).

**E. D. Hirsch, Jr.** Kenan Professor of English, University of Virginia. Author, *Validity in Interpretation* (1967), *The Aims of Interpretation* (1976), *The Philosophy of Composition* (1977).

**Roman Ingarden.** Late Professor of Philosophy, Jagellonian University, Cracow. Author, *The Literary Work of Art* (1973), *The Cognition of the Literary Work of Art* (1973).

**Peter Kivy.** Professor of Philosophy, Rutgers University. Author, *The Cordea Shell* (1980), *Sound and Semblance* (1984).

**Joseph Margolis.** Professor of Philosophy, Temple University. Author, *The Language of Art and Art Criticism* (1965), *Psychotherapy and Morality* (1966), *Values and Conduct* (1971), *Knowledge and Existence* (1973), *Negativities: The Limits of Life* (1975), *Persons and Minds* (1977), *Art and Philosophy* (1980), *Culture and Cultural Entities* (1984), *Philosophy of Psychology* (1984), *Pragmatism without Foundations* (1986).

**Paul Ricoeur.** Dean, Faculty of Letters and Human Sciences, University of Pars X—Nanterre; John Nuveen Professor Emeritus, Divinity School, Professor of Philosophy, and member of Committee on Social Thought, University of Chicago. Author, *History and Truth* (1965), *Husserl: An Analysis of His Phenomenology* (1967), *Freud and Philosophy: An Essay on Interpretation* (1970), *The Conflict of Interpretations* (1974), *Interpretation Theory* (1976), *The Rule of Metaphor* (1977), *Hermeneutics and the Human Sciences* (1981), *Time and Narrative,* 2 vols. (1984–1985).

**F. N. Sibley.** Professor and Head, Department of Philosophy, University of Lancaster. Editor, *Perception* (1971), and author of numerous articles in aesthetics.

**Guy Sircello.** Professor of Philosophy, University of California at Irvine. Author, *Mind & Art* (1972), *A New Theory of Beauty* (1975).

**Alan Tormey.** Professor of Philosophy, University of Maryland, Baltimore County. Author, *The Concept of Expression* (1971).

**Kendall Walton.** Associate Professor of Philosophy, University of Michigan. Author of articles in aesthetics.

**Marx Wartofsky.** Professor of Philosophy, City University of New York. Editor, *Philosophical Forum*. Co-editor, Boston Studies in the Philosophy of Science. Author, *Feuerbach* (1977), *Conceptual Foundations of Scientific Thought* (1986).

**Morris Weitz.** Late Professor of Philosophy, Brandeis University. Author, *Philosophy of the Arts* (1950), *Philosophy in Literature* (1963), *Hamlet and the Philosophy of Literary Criticism* (1964), *The Opening Mind* (1977). Editor, *Problems in Aesthetics* (1959) and revised, *Twentieth-Century Philosophy* (1966).

**William K. Wimsatt, Jr.** Late Professor of English, Yale University Author, *Philosophic Words* (1948), *The Verbal Icon* (1954), Co-author, *Literary Criticism* (1957).

**Richard Wollheim.** Professor of Philosophy, Columbia University. Author, *F. H. Bradley* (1959), *Art and Its Objects* (1968, 1980), *Sigmund Freud* (1971), *On Art and the Mind* (1973), *The Thread of Life* (1984). Editor, *Freud: A Collection of Critical Essays* (1974).

**Nicholas Wolterstorff.** Professor of Philosophy, Calvin College. Author, *On Universals* (1970), *Reason Within the Bounds of Religion* (1976).

# Index

References to complete selections are given in italics.